THE  GUIDE

TO

CLASSICAL
MUSIC

THE *Virgin* GUIDE TO

CLASSICAL
MUSIC

Jeremy J. Beadle

First published in Great Britain in 1993 by
Virgin Books
an imprint of Virgin Publishing Ltd
338 Ladbroke Grove
London W10 5AH

A catalogue record for this title is available from the British Library

ISBN 0 86369 658 9

Text design by Roger Kohn

Typeset by TW Typesetting, Plymouth, Devon
Printed and bound in Great Britain by Mackays of Chatham Ltd, Chatham, Kent.

CONTENTS

Introduction   vii

Acknowledgements   viii

   I   Early music   2
  II The Symphony   26
 III The Concerto   90
 IV Opera   134
  V Chamber & solo instrumental music   212
 VI Choral & other non-operatic vocal music   248
VII Non-Symphonic Orchestral music   272

Your ideal starter kit in 100 CD purchases   287

Glossary   295

Index   299

To my mother and Father
Irene Taylor Beadle (1921–1987)
Peter Digby Beadle (1920–1992)

INTRODUCTION

This *Guide* is aimed at everyone who's found that he or she likes classical music, but who gets slightly baffled by the way that people talk and write about it.

The book aims to do three things. First, it tries to tell the story of music, starting from around a thousand years ago. After bringing the story up to about 1600 (where we usually start applying the label 'Baroque'), I have chosen to describe the development of each of the main forms of classical music, as the book's second intention is to describe how these different forms work and how they have developed. (When each major composer first crops up, there's a general piece about him or her. At the end of it, you'll find a >> symbol, which leads you to the pages where I talk about their other work.)

The third aim of the book is to provide a reasonably full discussion of the major (and some lesser but interesting) recordings of each work discussed, offering fairly forthright opinions on each and not flinching from recommendations.

Obviously, all opinions expressed here are my own. I don't expect every reader to agree with everything I say; after all, critics are only subjective human beings like everyone else. My own prejudices will become evident fairly quickly, but I've tried not to let them colour my view to the point of distortion.

A word about the discography: for each recording discussed fully I have provided the catalogue number; the number of CDs in the set; the price range in which the disc is sold; the recording mode; and the year of recording, where available.

Price ranges can be variable, but generally 'Full price' means between £12 and £14.50 per CD (some record companies have lower 'Full prices' than others, and major chain-stores tend to charge a bit more than smaller, specialist shops); 'Mid-price' means between about £7.50 and £10; 'Bargain price' between £4.50 and £6.50 (a Naxos 'Bargain price' is cheaper than a Deutsche Grammophon 'Bargain price').

Recording modes describe how the recording was: a) recorded in the first place; b) mixed and/or edited; c) finally transcribed. D stands for Digital, A for Analogue. It goes without saying that every CD has a final D.

Most discs made nowadays carry details of their recording dates; but where older discs haven't offered this information, I've substituted the year of release of the original format. Where this information wasn't available, however, I have had to leave a blank. And finally, those recordings of genuine excellence are indicated thus: ✪.

ACKNOWLEDGEMENTS

There are a few people I'd like to thank: Anthony Sellors, for his support and encouragement and for pointing me in interesting directions at moments of weariness; Ríona MacNamara at Virgin Publishing, for her patient, speedy editing; my sister, Jocelynne Beadle Bell, for being there at moments of stress. But, sadly, the two people to whom I owe the greatest debt of gratitude aren't around to receive my thanks: my mother and father, who allowed me to form an interest in music and helped me to develop it as far as I wanted, never complaining about the strange noises I was making on the piano or clarinet, rarely objecting to the volume I chose to play records at. I couldn't have asked for more loyal, supportive parents – and this book is a meagre way of thanking them.

JEREMY J. BEADLE
June 1993

THE *Virgin* GUIDE TO
CLASSICAL MUSIC

I

Early music

INTRODUCTION

In many ways, early music is the worst possible point at which to start a book like this. And probably, even as recently as 20 or 30 years ago, I wouldn't have devoted more than a few paragraphs to discussing it. In fact, 20 or 30 years ago there weren't that many recordings of early music around, and the whole field belonged to a few enthusiasts. All that has changed rather radically, and some of the best-known performers on the classical music scene devote themselves entirely to early music, while some record labels are completely given over to it.

WHAT DO WE MEAN BY EARLY MUSIC?

Early music is a terribly nebulous and inexact term, and can be used, in one sentence, to refer to a piece of plainchant or a single-line melody from the ninth or tenth centuries, and then in the next sentence to a fiendishly complex piece of polyphonic vocal harmony from the late fifteenth or early sixteenth century. In contexts such as record shops or the annual awards given by the doyen of classical music magazines, *The Gramophone,* the words 'early music' mean anything from the dawn of time up to about 1600, when (or whenabouts) the 'Baroque' is deemed to have begun, although the musical sounds and practices normally associated with the Renaissance held on longer in some parts of Europe, mainly in countries at the edge like England and Portugal.

- The aim of this section of the book is
- to provide a narrative of how music
- developed from relatively simple
- one-line plainsong to the extraordinary
- complex harmonics involving 12, 13,
- 19, or – in Thomas Tallis's motet
- *Spem in alium,* one of the most
- justifiably celebrated pieces from the
- sixteenth century – 40 different vocal
- lines.

PLAINCHANT

- Rather than offering any speculation
- about what kind of music the Ancient
- Greeks might have had (such
- speculation was so rife in the
- Renaissance that they invented a
- whole musical system based around
- theories for which there was no solid
- evidence), or discussing the internal
- evidence of musical practice in biblical
- times, the most sensible place to start
- seems to be with one of the great

Hildegard of Bingen
1098–1179

Hildegard was born in 1098 in a small village called Bermersheim in Germany (as it now is). At the age of 8 she was placed in a small community of nuns attached to a monastery in Bingen (about 25 miles from Mainz).

In 1141 she became Abbess of the community and had a religious vision in which fiery tongues of creativity descended from Heaven and settled on her; after this there was no stopping her. She wrote books about natural history, about medicine, the earliest known morality play, a book of visions; and for the rest of her life she put together a collection of music and poetry called *Symphonia armonie celestium revelationum* (Symphony of the harmony of celestial revelations).

She was also an important political figure, and corresponded with just about every pope, monarch, archbishop and abbess on the continent of Europe at the time.

---

composers of single-line melody, Hildegard of Bingen. Something of a twelfth-century superstar, Hildegard is probably the only composer ever to come close to being canonised. The rediscovery of her music over the last couple of decades is typical of the growth of interest in early music in that time; look her up in reference books of the 1960s and earlier and you won't find a single mention of her! Now Hildegard is even famous in the pop world, as the appropriation of one of her melodies by the group The Beloved in their hit 'The Sun Rising' led to a legal battle over recording copyright.

Hildegard's music is first and foremost a mode of religious expression and represents the ultimate consummation of the whole concept and purpose of plainchant (also called plainsong, of which the best-known version is probably Gregorian Chant). Plainchant is the setting of religious and liturgical texts (the various bits of the services like the Mass, Vespers, Matins, Benediction and so on) to a single melodic line. The purpose behind the music wasn't to give singers an opportunity to show off, but to intensify and heighten the religious experience: to provide, if you like, a way of concentrating the attention upon the spiritual meaning of the words being sung.

DISCOGRAPHY
The disc that started the Hildegard revival is *A Feather on the Breath of God* by Gothic Voices, ~~directed by Christopher Page~~. It deservedly won one of the annual awards given by the magazine *The Gramophone*. Christopher Page's ensemble Gothic Voices is one of *the* major early music outfits, and on this disc the line-up comprises some of the best and most intelligent performers of the pre-Classical repertoire. This disc offers eight pieces by Hildegard, all sung with the right kind of expression (designed to show up the music rather than the singers to best advantage) and with intelligent use of instrumental accompaniment. Its only possible disadvantage is that at 43 minutes it's a bit short for a full-priced disc; but its merits outweigh that

drawback (this is a rare case). It's also an ideal introduction.

● Hyperion CDA66039 ● 1 CD ● Full price ● DDD ● 1983 ✪

If you get hooked on Hildegard and want to try further, there's also a good recording by the vocal group Sequentia of her morality play *Ordo Virtutum*. The singing isn't quite as ethereally magical as Gothic Voices', but it's still fascinating.

● Harmonia Mundi GD77051 ● 2 CDs ● Special price ● DDD ● 1990

PLAINCHANT AND HILDEGARD'S MUSIC

Plainchant, as I've said, uses a single melodic line, sometimes sung by a soloist, sometimes by a larger group all singing together. There is no vocal harmony, no different vocal line. Mostly the music follows the speech rhythms with a single note to each syllable, but certain syllables are assigned a group of notes (an effect sometimes called a 'melisma'). Syllables given such treatment aren't necessarily more important or more significant than others; this is part of the devotional effect, and the nearest that plainchant gets to artistic flourishes.

The question of how this music was performed is, ultimately, unanswerable. A lot of our views on 'authentic' performance are, to be honest, educated guesswork, and it's hard enough for us to recreate the performing conditions of 90 years ago, so much have musical instruments, styles of playing and practices of singing changed over the years. It's quite possible that plainchant was, on occasion accompanied by a drone played by medieval instruments (rather like the drone which lies below all bagpipe music), and on the best introductory disc to Hildegard's music, this option

is pursued on some tracks, but not on others.

DISCOGRAPHY
There are now lots of recordings featuring 'traditional' plainchant. The best of these tend to place the music in some kind of context, whether it be thematic (e.g. music dedicated to the Virgin Mary) or liturgical (music recorded as though an actual celebration of the Mass or other service were taking place). In no particular order of preference, here are a couple of 'taster' discs.

Gregorian Chant: a selection from various feasts of the church year, sung by the Choir of Liguge Abbey.
● Studio SM1216.68 ● 1 CD ● Full price ● DDD ✪

Gregorian Chant: a larger, more extensive selection sung by the Choir of Clervaux Abbey.
● Philips 432 506-2 ● 2 CDs ● Full price ● ADD

ORGANUM, POLYPHONY AND PÉROTIN

A single line of melody is obviously limited as to what it can achieve. However beautiful it may be, it can't produce harmony, and the kind of speech-dictated melodic flow of much plainchant tends to prevent it from suggesting the regular kind of rhythmic patterns which we expect from most music.

These limits upon the music's potential soon led to the practice of adding an extra vocal line, complementary to that carrying the main melody. Often this would be a descant at a higher pitch rather than a kind of harmony underpinning the main melodic content. Usually the main melody would be something traditional, along the lines of Gregorian Chant; when an extra line was added to an established, traditional musical form used to set part of the religious liturgy the result was called 'organum'. In organum, it was perfectly possible to have the vocal parts moving at different rhythms and speeds. As yet the system known as 'tonality', the 'major' and 'minor' keys, which formed the bedrock of the harmony of Western music between 1600 and the twentieth century, hadn't been dreamt of; so harmony, in the sense that we know it from Mozart or Beethoven, wasn't a consideration for composers like Pérotin. They wanted the whole effect to produce a pleasant blend, of course; but they didn't put their music together thinking about chords and keys in the way that most later composers did.

The independent vocal lines of organum formed an important stepping-stone to the system of 'polyphony' (literally, 'many voices') and, subsequently, to the whole concepts of harmony and tonality as we know them. The earliest surviving piece of written music for four different vocal lines is a piece of organum by Pérotin or Perotinus the Great (dates unknown; we know he was particularly influential around the end of the twelfth century). Pérotin was a choirmaster at the Cathedral of Notre-Dame in Paris who lived in the latter part of the twelfth century. This earliest four-part work, *Viderunt omnes*, may well have been written for Christmas 1198; of similar vintage is *Sederunt principes*, possibly composed for St Stephen's Day (26 December) 1199. Pérotin was the pupil of Léonin (who lived between approximately 1163 and 1190), a man influential in his day (he wrote a major musical text-book) but little of whose actual work has come down to us today. It's also worth remembering that we can't be 100 per cent sure that the music we call Pérotin's was actually written by him. Still, *Viderunt omnes* definitely occupies the proud position of being the earliest extant piece of European four-part music.

A few years ago, Pérotin's music was really only of interest to specialists, and it's not perhaps as immediately accessible as the melodic lines of Hildegard of Bingen. But Pérotin has been a great influence on many modern composers, particularly those interested in 'Minimalism', people like Steve Reich, Philip Glass, Steve Martland, and you can also detect something of Pérotin's influence in a popular modern composer like John Tavener, who draws a great deal of inspiration from the Greek Orthodox musical tradition. It's worth bearing in mind that Pérotin lived within 150 years of the Great Schism between the Eastern and Western Churches, and is very close in musical time to that tradition. It is also fair to say that anyone who likes Tavener's work (such as *The Protecting Veil*) or that of Arvo Pärt or Steve Reich, may find Pérotin extremely rewarding.

In Pérotin, the apparently independent vocal lines blend together to produce a constantly moving, almost liquid sound, of which the harmonies are both more primitive and yet strangely more sophisticated than 'classical' Western tonality. Usually the music seizes obsessively on one syllable, not necessarily a very significant one, of one word of the text and extends it on an endless run. With different rhythmic patterns going on in the various voices, the overall effect is something like a shifting kaleidoscope of sound.

When we talk of Pérotin's music as having been 'written down', this naturally doesn't mean that it is all neatly written out in modern notation. Medieval musicians up to the late fourteenth/early fifteenth centuries didn't go in for writing things down except as a sort of prompt. So what was written down may be only a part of what was actually sung, and written manuscripts don't necessarily provide a coherent whole. This is equally true, in some cases, of music right through to Schubert; as with old books, there are 'doubtful' passages where we have to make an educated guess at what was originally intended.

DISCOGRAPHY
The Hilliard Ensemble, directed by Paul Hillier, offers undoubtedly the best introduction with a disc which includes beautiful performances of both the early pieces mentioned in the main text, as well as various other works by Pérotin in slightly different, less ground-breaking styles, and also some anonymous works of around the same era. The Hilliard Ensemble is another vocal group which specialises in music up to the Baroque, although they do complete the musical circle by recording modern composers clearly under the influence of early music, such as Pärt.
● *ECM New Series* ● *ECM 1385* ● *1 CD*
● *Full price* ● *DDD* ● *1989* ✪

An earlier stab at Pérotin's music can be found on *Sacred Music from the 12th–14th Centuries* by the Deller Consort under the leadership of Alfred Deller, the pioneering counter-tenor (falsetto male voice capable of singing a low soprano range, but producing a much more eerie, unearthly sound than either a woman or a boy). In 1960, modern understanding of medieval music was rather less sympathetic (there was still a tendency to regard it as something unformed in the wake of Handel, Mozart, Beethoven, and so on), but Deller was a fine, ground-breaking musician. The disc also includes later works by the fourteenth-century composer Machaut and a piece by Pérotin's contemporary and fellow countryman, Philippe the Chancellor.
Pérotin's *Viderunt omnes* is also included on *Music of the Gothic Era*, a 1976 recording by David Munrow and his Early Music Consort of London, another trail-blazing ensemble. For a fuller review of this disc, see below.

● ● ● ●

THE GOTHIC ERA
(c. 1200–1400)

The years of the late Middle Ages (itself a not particularly helpful term) have attracted the label 'Gothic' mainly because of a misguidedly snooty attitude to the architecture of the period (considered by self-styledly 'Enlightened' Classical attitudes to be

hideous). Musically, the term 'Gothic' takes us through to the fourteenth century or so, and most of the best-known, most often performed and recorded, music of this era is French.
In fact, between the years 1200 and 1500, the various countries and areas of Europe rather shared around the musical supremacy, but it was undoubtedly in France that all the groundwork for European music was laid. A fourteenth-century treatise, *Ars Nova* by Philippe de Vitry (who lived between about 1291 and 1361), proposed a system by which it became possible to write much more complex music than had been the case until then; if the actual written music is merely a kind of prompt, there are obviously limits as to what can be composed and committed to memory. A singer can remember his or her own part, but assembling a group of singers with the right communal memory of the music's precise and exact details inevitably becomes difficult as time progresses.

DISCOGRAPHY
The following recordings give a fair sample of music from the twelfth to the fifteenth centuries.

The disc I mentioned earlier, *Music of the Gothic Era* by the Early Music Consort of London directed by David Munrow, includes music by anonymous French composers of the thirteenth and fourteenth centuries, as well as Léonin, Pérotin, Adam de la Halle, Petrus de Cruce, Philippe de Vitry, Machaut. This is an edited version of a three-LP set devised by a man who helped to put 'authentic' performances of early music (i.e. performances which try to reproduce the vocal traditions and instrumental practices of the music's time) in the centre of public consciousness. The disc forms an excellent introduction to the music of the period, a natural 'sampler' of 200 years of music, and the performances leave you in no doubt that this is virtuoso music every bit as much as a nineteenth century concerto. There's also a smattering of the instrumental tradition, as well as a kind of chronological guide to the development of that central vocal work, the motet. Instructive, but, above all, entertaining.
● *Archiv 415 292-2* ● *1 CD* ● *Full price*
● *ADD* ● *1976* ✪

Gothic Voices' *Music for the Lion-Hearted King* offers music which *could* have been heard (no evidence that any of it ever *was*) by King Richard I, including a couple of items by the famous French troubadour Blondel de Nesle (fl. c. 1200). An illuminating survey of the early troubadour/chanson secular tradition.
- *Hyperion CDA66336* ● 1 CD ● *Full price*
- *DDD* ● *1989*

The Service of Venus and Mars by the same ensemble includes music by Philippe de Vitry, Dunstable, anonymous English composers of the fourteenth and fifteenth centuries, Pycard and Power, in a well-balanced mixture of the sacred and secular which reveals just how significant a figure Dunstable was (probably the most influential British composer in the history of music). It also includes the carol composed to celebrate Henry V's victory at Agincourt. Gothic Voices have come close to cornering this market.
- *Hyperion CDA66238* ● 1 CD ● *Full price*
- *DDD* ● *1987*

Le Banquet de Voeu 1454 by the Ensemble Gilles Binchois directed by Dominique Vellard includes music by Binchois, Dufay, Vide, Fontaine, Grenon and anonymous fifteenth-century French composers. It is a recreation of a great Burgundian feast of 1454 designed to laugh in the face of disaster (the loss of Constantinople to the Turks) and to launch a new Crusade (it never happened). Again, a mixture of the sacred and secular, giving a very good idea of what (nominally) motivated the chivalry of the age (religious piety and sexual desire, with an odd mixture of the two at moments), the whole recording is remarkable, carefully reconstructed and performed with feeling.
- *Virgin Classics Veritas VC7 91441-2* ● 1 CD
- *Full price* ● *DDD* ● *1991*

GUILLAUME MACHAUT (1300–1377)

The first major composer to follow and use Vitry's theories was Guillaume Machaut, another figure whose use of harmony strikes perhaps more resonance in a modern age used to challenging, abrasive harmonic figures than in the more 'temperate' Classical era. Machaut's *Messe de Nostre Dame* is the first surviving setting of the Mass with all the pieces of the liturgy set by a single composer; it may not have been designed as a single, integral setting, like masses by Palestrina or Lassus, but this doesn't alter its status.

DISCOGRAPHY
A disc featuring the Taverner Consort and Choir directed by Andrew Parrott pits a plainsong setting of the Mass against Machaut's *Messe de Nostre Dame*, and places both in a full liturgical context with bells, priests, and so on. For various reasons, the singing is a bit heavy; it's sung at a low pitch, with more than two singers to most lines, with only tenors and basses used as soloists. Interesting, but not ideal.
- *EMI Reflexe CDC 7 47949-2* ● 1 CD
  - *Full price* ● *DDD* ● *1983* ✪

The Hilliard Ensemble's Machaut has a lighter texture, which may be (at a guess) closer to the composer's intentions. The disc also offers two of Machaut's sacred songs. Probably the better introduction of the two.
- *Hyperion CDA66358* ● 1 CD ● *Full price*
- *DDD* ● *1990*

WAS ALL MUSIC SACRED?

Although there's a tendency to assume that everything medieval is theocentric, in fact, the thirteenth and fourteenth centuries seem to have produced at least as much secular music as sacred. Much medieval secular music is by unknown hands, and some of it parodies its sacred counterpart (the *Carmina Burana*, of which the original medieval texts were later destroyed by Hitler's favoured composer Carl Orff, is probably the best-known example). There was also the 'troubadour' tradition, with its love lyrics and tales of adventure and – quite often – political propaganda. Quite a few popular tunes of the later Middle Ages found their way to posterity via sacred music, as it became more and more common to use well-known tunes as the basic organisational principle of a setting of the Mass, putting that tune through endless variations and changes and inversions. In this the composers of the time rather foreshadowed the way in which many twentieth-century composers worked after they abandoned the Classical concepts of harmony and tonality.

There was also a fairly thriving instrumental tradition, although most of the instruments were only distantly related to what was to come. One popular instrumental form was the 'hocket', in which two instrumental players rapidly alternated notes and chords, creating an effect which twentieth-century Minimalists have sometimes tried to recreate (as in Steve Martland's *Drill*).

THE STORY CONTINUES

The musical centre of Europe shifted around through the Gothic era, from Paris, to Italy, to England, to Burgundy, then to the Low Countries. Significant names following on Machaut include Francesco Landini (c. 1325–1397), who worked on French principles but had an especial talent for melody; John Dunstable (c. 1390–1453), who was instrumental in creating integrated settings of the Mass, and in using already familiar material as a basis for these settings: Dunstable also made heavy use of the new concept of 'canonic' imitation, that is, melodies being repeated at regular, offset times in different voices at different, transposed pitches; Gilles Binchois (c. 1400–1460) and Guillaume Dufay (c. 1400–1474), two Burgundians whose chansons (popular secular songs) and sacred music contain sounds which at times seem to look back to the Middle Ages, and at other times to belong in the Renaissance; Johannes Ockeghem (c. 1410–1497), a Flemish composer who went on from where Dunstable had left off. But somewhere in the middle of all these began the life and career of the great Josquin Des Près, possibly the earliest great genius in Western music.

JOSQUIN DES PRÈZ
(c. 1440–1521)

'Other composers do what they can with the notes; Josquin alone does what he wants to.' This was the judgement of Martin Luther (himself quite a useful writer of tunes), and it gives some idea of the phenomenal reputation Josquin enjoyed during his own lifetime, a reputation which has been almost entirely restored in the past two decades.

By the time of Josquin, the idea of music being subservient to the texts it set, especially religious texts, had been left far behind. The notion of music as something to be enjoyed in itself, which had begun with Hildegard, developed over four centuries, until composers whom one would still consider essentially 'medieval', like Binchois and Dufay, were producing melodically complex lines which interwove and created sophisticated harmonic structures. In the 300 years since Pérotin created that earliest surviving four-part work, serious music using four and more melodic lines had increasingly become the norm, and what is demonstrated by musicians like Philippe de Vitry onwards is the development of the very idea of 'the composer'.

As we've seen, there was a fair number of composers around at the end of the fifteenth century, and the concept of one composer's work influencing another's had become something of which we may legitimately speak. Josquin, like every genius, absorbed all the influences around him, assimilated them, and added something peculiar to himself.

Josquin was originally from northern France, but his musical life took him all over Europe; in particular, he spent several formative years (from around 1474 to about 1503) in Italy, living first in Milan, where he was employed by an extremely powerful cardinal, then working in the Papal Chapel in Rome, finally becoming composer-in-residence to Duke Hercules of Ferrara. This was very much the ideal way of life for a composer until, really, the nineteenth century – to find a rich patron who would either subsidise and commission work or provide a full-time job which allowed plenty of room for composition. Although France had been a great and dominant musical influence in the Gothic era, it was during and after Josquin's lifetime that composers began naturally to gravitate towards Italy, which was where all the main cultural action of Europe was then to be found (Josquin's contemporary Heinrich Isaac – c. 1450–1517 – probably the composer closest to him in stature, spent much of his working life in Florence in the service of the most famous patrons of all, the Medici family).

Josquin was especially famous for developing and refining the way in which composers incorporated into their work extraneous material like popular tunes, well-established plainchant settings, or motets and chansons by other composers. Josquin was fond of using only brief allusive snatches of these, sometimes inverted or reversed, scattered through the course of a piece, especially through a complete setting of the Mass. With Josquin, the idea of the thematically unified mass-setting reached a new level of sophistication, and he showed how the same piece could be used to produce works and settings that sound entirely different and radically removed from each other.

WHY IS JOSQUIN SO REMARKABLE?

Whatever the scholarly tomes might say, the real reason for Josquin's continuing and revived reputation is the sound his music makes (this, at least until the twentieth century, usually turns out to be the main reason for a composer's success). All the 'parody' and the imitative entries of his polyphony are governed by the most extraordinary sense of melody and harmony, even if 'harmony' in the sense in which we understand it was still being developed during Josquin's lifetime. It's possible to get highly – and frighteningly – technical about Josquin's achievement, but basically it's the way that the individual voices add up to amazing, echoing slabs of sound that ensures that he remains popular. Allied to this, Josquin was also famous in his own time for matching words and music and making music express the meaning of the words set. There's no sense, as there can be with Hildegard or Pérotin or a whole host of names who come between them and the end of the fifteenth century, that the relationship between the words' meaning and the music is a tenuous thing. Josquin is arguably *the* first expressive musical genius of Europe.

DISCOGRAPHY
Josquin
The recording which put Josquin back on the map in a big way, after it won the *Gramophone* Record of the Year Award in 1987, was the combination of the masses *Pange lingua* and *La Sol Fa Re Mi* by Peter Phillips's superb Tallis Scholars, who combine purity of tone with an expressive sense so that the meaning of the words is clear, but not in some operatically histrionic manner. The quality of the recording, too, is quite exemplary, with the chapel of Merton College, Oxford, providing a perfect acoustic ambience. The inclusion of the *Pange lingua* plainchant at the beginning of the disc helpfully allows those who want to to detect how Josquin used pre-existing material in his music. If you never listen to

another Josquin recording, try this one, if this kind of music holds even the slightest attraction.
● *Gimell CDGIM 009* ● *1 CD* ● *Full price*
● *DDD* ● *1986* ○

The Tallis Scholars' recording of two of Josquin's masses based on the popular Burgundian tune 'L'Homme Armé' (see pp. 21–2) starts by presenting the tune in its own right. Again, the performances are absolutely right, and the sound lovely.
● *Gimell CDGIM 019* ● *1 CD* ● *Full price*
● *DDD* ● *1989*

Although there are nineteen singers in the Paris Chapelle Royale Choir (here directed by Philip Herreweghe), they produce a very refined sound. Philip Herreweghe is another doyen of the early/Renaissance/Baroque performance world, and this disc of Josquin motets does him proud.
● *Harmonia Mundi HMC 901243* ● *1 CD*
● *Full price* ● *DDD* ● *1987*

Heinrich Isaac
I can't end this series of discs without putting in a fervent word for a favourite recording of music by Heinrich Isaac. Not a lot of his music has survived, and he doesn't exhibit quite the same musical ingenuity as Josquin – his settings fall back on conventional plainchant modes. However, anyone who isn't thoroughly enchanted by the mass setting and motets on *Missa de Apostolis*, another offering from Peter Phillips and the excellent Tallis Scholars, probably has no real taste for the music from that nebulous period which is both early Renaissance and late Middle Ages.
● *Gimell CDGIM 023* ● *1 CD* ● *Full price*
● *DDD* ● *1991* ○

RENAISSANCE MUSIC

The religious upheavals of the sixteenth century cut Britain – and especially England – off from continental Europe, making it more difficult for new influences to break through. Simple geography would doubtless have contributed to this; Portugal and Spain also remained locked into somewhat archaic styles. And we should beware of assuming that Protestantism changed the course of England's musical history; the two greatest English composers of the sixteenth and early seventeenth centuries, Thomas Tallis (1505–1585) and William Byrd (1543–1623), both remained Roman Catholics despite the personal risk involved. Also,

Henry VIII and Elizabeth I both took a great deal of pleasure in music, and to some extent in ritual and religious music. For them the Reformation was simply a question of politics and finance, part of the European power game which still goes on today.

Unfortunately, the dissolution of the monasteries during Henry VIII's reign, an exercise in money-grabbing rather than theology, did lead to the abolition of several choral foundations; it also killed off the 'Marian' tradition (the veneration of the Virgin Mary) popular in the Roman Church, and therefore threw out quite a large number of texts and elements of the liturgy which had been popular with pre-Reformation composers.

THE ETON CHOIRBOOK

Anyone who wants to get some idea of what musical compositions were like in England immediately before the break with Rome can find out through three excellent recordings by Harry Christophers and his vocal ensemble The Sixteen.

The Eton Chapel (or, to give it its full name, the Chapel of the College Royal of Our Lady of Eton) kept a huge collection of anthems, motets and other music for daily use in its services, and two-thirds of this has survived; it will give some idea of how comparatively large a collection this is that the missing third contains about 98 pages. Many of these pieces were written for other venues than Eton, and occasionally they directly address or refer to members of the Tudor Royal Family; sometimes these references are more oblique and emblematic.

The music of the works in the Eton Choirbook occasionally seems a good deal more old-fashioned than that of Josquin or Isaac, who were contemporary with most of the composers represented here. It was all written at a time when England's relations with continental Europe were tolerably good: one could argue that the high point came with Henry VIII's much publicised, though ultimately ineffectual, 'Field of the Cloth of Gold' encounter with François I of France, and his being titled by the pope in 1521 as 'Defender of the Faith' for putting his name to a pamphlet rebutting Luther. From then on the whole succession/divorce issue began to dominate the diplomatic world and Henry, ever on the look-out for more cash to spend, began to eye up the possessions of the monasteries and other religious foundations. Still, though, influences are hard to detect in the Choirbook; a good deal of the music has a spikier, thinner, sound than most of Josquin or Antoine Brumel (c. 1460–c. 1520), another French/Flemish composer. You could describe some of the music as 'introverted' (in other words, the voices cover a narrow range and the expression tends towards the subdued), but very often that's dictated by the subject matter.

DISCOGRAPHY

Harry Christophers and The Sixteen did, before undertaking to record the entire surviving contents of the Choirbook, record a selection from it, which might serve anyone who wants to sample this music without really enjoying its full range. *Music from the Eton Choirbook* offers pieces by all the 'better-known' names – John Browne, William Cornysh, Richard Davy – but I don't think this disc, dominated by very conventional religious settings (Stabat Maters, Ave Marias, Salve Reginas and the like) quite gives a full sense of the range of music and styles which this very important English collection has to offer.
● *Meridian* ● *CDE 84175* ● *1 CD* ● *Full price*
● *DDD* ● *1989* ◎

There are early music 'experts' who feel that some music is too 'inaccessible' for those who haven't given quite a bit of study to the subject, but I

think this is nonsense. Some of the strangest stuff in the Eton Choirbook is amongst the most intriguing and remarkable of its day, and I think anyone wanting to get a real sense of the variety should try one of the three later compilations, especially the first.

The Rose and the Ostrich Feather: Music from the Eton Choirbook, Volume 1, not only contains one of Browne's typically gloomy religious pieces describing the Passion (*Stabat iuxta Christi crucem*), it also runs a gamut from formal religious 'praise' music of a distinctly Marian strain (the Magnificat and the Salve Regina) to almost folk-like music (a song called 'From Stormy Windes' and an anonymous song, close in spirit to medieval chanson, entitled 'This day day dawes'). And hiding behind almost everything is the presence of the Tudor Royal Family; hence the disc's title, provided by the texts of two of the works recorded. The rose isn't merely the Tudor Rose, it's Elizabeth of York, Henry VII's wife, and 'This day day dawes' is a song in her honour, in which she is described in Marian terms. *The Ostrich Feather* – here written and pronounced 'Estridge' – is an emblematic reference to Prince Arthur (Henry VIII's elder brother, who died young in 1502), and 'From Stormy Windes' is essentially a prayer for Arthur's safekeeping by a fairly obscure figure called Edmund Turges (born some time around 1450). Where things start getting subtle is in Browne's piece, which ostensibly describes the grief of Mary at the foot of Christ's cross, yet quotes phrases from Turges's song, and is clearly a tribute to Arthur after his death and a description of Elizabeth of York's grief. And the music is very fine, beautifully sung, with the full variety of styles represented being given full rein. The disc won the 1992 *The Gramophone* Early Music Award, and I don't see how this could be too 'difficult' for anyone who likes the music of this period.
● *Collins Classics 13142* ● *1 CD* ● *Full price*
● *DDD* ● *1991* ◎

The Crown of Thorns: Music from the Eton Choirbook, Volume 2, is probably the least accessible of the three discs in this series to date. As the title indicates, its music is all connected with Passiontide, and of the five tracks, no fewer than three are settings of the great hymn 'Stabat Mater' (a much used traditional medieval Latin description of Mary at the Crucifixion; the most famous settings are undoubtedly by Pergolesi in the Baroque era and Rossini in the early nineteenth century). Three of the four composers represented here are real heavyweights; Browne (who has two pieces), Davy and Cornysh, three men who clearly knew and respected each other's work. The three Stabat Maters are works on a large scale vocally, but inevitably introverted in terms of mood. There are also two more song-like pieces, Browne's 'Jesu, mercy' and 'Ah gentle Jesu' by a completely unknown figure called Sheryngham; these are smaller, more intimate works, aimed more at period specialists than the others in the series.
● *Collins Classics 13162* ● *1 CD* ● *Full price*
● *DDD* ● *1991*

The Pillars of Eternity: Music from the Eton Choirbook, Volume 3, is dominated by Richard Davy; again it's full of religious music strung around the loose theme of fear and admiration of the divinity. The opening 15-minute epic hymn of praise (*O Domine caeli terraeque*) is an impressive enough piece, but it's two particularly bizarre pieces which make this a recording to investigate. One is a song by Davy, setting a terrifying poem about human decay and misery ('Ah blessed Jesu, how fortuned this?'), in which the music mirrors the words quite remarkably. However, the prize of the disc is the $5^1/_2$-minute work described in the booklet notes as 'the most bizarre . . . in the Eton Choirbook', 'Jesus autem transiens' by Robert Wylkynson (who lived from the middle of the fifteenth century until some time around or slightly later than 1515). This takes a piece of plainchant setting of the words 'Jesus autem transiens' ('Jesus, however, passing through the midst of them') and builds up around it, voice by voice, twelve singers, each taking a phrase of the Creed (the statement of belief at the centre of the Mass), until there's a strange, hypnotic musical wall of sound symbolically representative of Christ and the Twelve Apostles. Nothing develops, all is static, until the voices just fade away, almost like a palindrome. This is among my favourite five minutes of music of any period. Wylkynson (another shadowy figure) was clearly ambitious about the use of voices, as he also wrote a nine-voice setting of the great Marian hymn of praise Salve Regina, with which this impressive recording ends.
● *Collins Classics 13422* ● *1 CD* ● *Full price*
● *DDD* ● *1992*

THE MASS

It may help to outline briefly the five or six (depending upon how you define it) elements of the Mass. Obviously these were, once upon a time, common currency, but it would be foolish to imagine that this continues to be the case. The parts of the Eucharist liturgy, centring around Holy Communion, which were traditionally sung in elaborate settings were:

i) Kyrie: the one part of the Mass which remained in Greek, it is a threefold plea for mercy, three calls upon the 'Lord' (the word *kyrios* carries overtones almost of feudalism), three upon Christ, and three more on the Lord.

ii) Gloria: a hymn of praise to God in three persons, beginning and ending with an optimistic strain of praise and a prayer for peace, with a more reflective plea for mercy in the centre.

iii) Credo: the Creed, the basic statement of belief in the doctrines of the Church, which also briefly describes the life of Christ.

iv) Sanctus and Benedictus: sometimes these are separated out (they have become completely detached in certain Church of England traditions). The Sanctus proclaims God's holiness, the Benedictus simply states 'Blessed is he who comes in the Name of the Lord'. Each part ends with a cry of 'Hosanna'.

v) Agnus Dei: the most introverted, peaceful part of the Mass (usually), which immediately precedes Communion, and constitutes a twofold plea for mercy and finally a prayer for spiritual peace.

JOHN TAVERNER
(c 1495–1545);
ROBERT CARVER
(c. 1485–c. 1568)

The major English composer at the time of the Reformation, more highly regarded than all those featured in the Eton Choirbook, was John Taverner. He was the first choirmaster at Cardinal Wolsey's new Oxford college (later the College and Cathedral of Christ Church), where his Protestant sympathies got him into trouble. Later he became an agent of Thomas Cromwell who, as Henry VIII's Vicar-General, carried out the dissolution of the monasteries. Taverner's music was renowned for its sheer melodiousness and its extreme sensitivity to the texts it set. He was one of the last English composers to have much exposure to Continental influence, as his *Missa Gloria tibi Trinitas* shows; after Henry VIII broke with Rome, England became culturally and politically isolated.

Robert Carver was the dominant musical figure in Scotland through much of the sixteenth century, and some of his works are as ambitious in their use of polyphony as either of his two more famous English counterparts, Tallis and Byrd. Of especial interest are his motet *O Bone Jesu*, written in the 1520s, which employs nineteen separate vocal lines (Tallis later eclipsed this). The nineteen aren't constantly singing together; but when they do it certainly grabs the attention. Another of Carver's greatest works is the mass *Dum Sacrum Mysterium*, written for ten voices (the average would be four, five or six); this is a grand, elaborate piece, possibly composed for the coronation of the infant King James V of Scotland in 1513.

DISCOGRAPHY
Taverner
Inevitably, the Tallis Scholars have come up trumps with a first-rate recording of the *Missa Gloria tibi Trinitas*, which also offers a motet and a setting of the Kyrie.
● *Gimell CDGIM004* ● *1 CD* ● *Full price*
✓ ●*DDD* ● *1984* ✪

Carver
Carver's two great works have been well recorded by a Scottish-based ensemble, Capella Nova, on *Scottish Renaissance Polyphony: Robert Carver, Volume 1*.
● *EASV Gaudeamus CDGAU 124* ● *1 CD*
● *Full price* ● *DDD* ● *1991* ✪

A boxed set containing Carver's complete surviving works is available by the same ensemble.
● *ASV Gaudeamus CDGAU 124/6/7* ● *3 CDs*
● *Special price* ● *DDD* ● *1991–2*

THOMAS TALLIS
(c. 1505–1585)

Tallis's musical career bears witness to the developing range of musical practices in sixteenth-century

- England; even before the Reformation there was a tendency towards more succinct, less extravagant motets such as the early four-part piece *Sancte Deus* (which bears the imprint of Taverner's influence). Mary's reign saw a flourish of extravagant Marian tributes (the fact one could both praise the Virgin Mary and toady to the Queen in the same text was politically useful), and the lengthy six-voice *Gaude gloriosa*, a ninefold invocation to the Virgin, shows how Tallis could elaborate and trade echoing choral work against more melodic solo or two-voice sections. Pieces from the reign of Elizabeth, like the two different settings of *Salvator mundi, salva nos*, show a return to the more compact tendencies of the earlier work, in which polyphony has given way a little to the idea of chordal progression – that is to say, instead of the parts moving principally along independent but imitative melodic lines composed, as it were, horizontally, the composer is clearly interested in composing vertically, thinking of each line as contributing to a series of chords. It is this approach to music which makes for the 'diatonic' system which prevailed through to our own century and which gave rise to the system of key signatures (C major, A minor, and so on) so familiar through music from the Baroque era onwards.

Undoubtedly the most popular of Tallis's works is the massive 40-part motet *Spem in alium*, which combines both the polyphonic and the chordal, building up from single voices at the outset to enormous slabs of sound. Tallis wasn't the first person to write for such huge choral forces – a composer called Striggio, who visited London in 1567, wrote a 40-part piece, and as we have seen Carver wrote a

Thomas Tallis

c. 1505–1585

By the accession of Queen Mary (1553), Tallis had become the dominant figure in English musical life, the most important and respected of the composers attached to the Chapel Royal. There is every indication that Tallis's supremacy actually dates from earlier, but it was the reign of the devoutly Catholic Mary which helped make his fortune. His will had some fairly substantial legacies in it for the age, and it's clear that England's reversion to Protestantism under Elizabeth didn't affect his standing (although he died before the national anti-Catholic paranoia induced by the Armada in 1588).

Throughout his life, Tallis maintained a strong connection with Greenwich, where he owned a decent-sized house, and the parish church of St Alphege, where he was buried.

19-voice motet. Josquin wrote a motet for 24 voices, Ockeghem for 36, while the late seventeenth/early eighteenth-century Bohemian Heinrich Biber is believed to have composed a mass for 56 voices. But of all these ambitious projects, Tallis's *Spem in alium* was definitely the most successful. What inspired it isn't known; it may have been written for Queen Mary's 40th birthday (1556), or perhaps for Elizabeth's (1573); one scholar firmly believes that the piece dates from 1570/1 and was essentially a plea to Elizabeth for tolerance of Catholicism. This is an attractive idea, given that the text set for the piece is concerned with mercy and with hope in the clemency of a powerful Lord. Whatever its occasion, *Spem in alium* is a massively powerful work, which combines the pathos of an intimate piece in its more polyphonic sections with the splendour and grandeur of 40

- separate, but harmonised vocal lines
- raising the roof. It's an enormously
- accessible work, and has curious
- echoes in popular twentieth-century
- pieces by composers who specialise in
- works based around static chords, like
- John Tavener or – above all – the
- astonishingly popular 3rd Symphony
- of Henryk Górecki.
- Another well recorded Tallis work
- is his lengthy setting of part of the
- Lamentations of Jeremiah, in which,
- despite the need to observe certain
- decorums – one can hardly go over
- the top with thrilling, bouncy music
- in settings of Lamentations – the
- composer makes this Lenten work
- fascinating and riveting by use of
- expressive, plaintive music to bring
- out the full drama of a lengthy text
- describing the desolation and
- destruction of Jerusalem. Settings of
- texts from Lamentations were popular
- in the Renaissance and Baroque
- periods, and at least one

twentieth-century English religious composer, Edward Bairstow (an organist and choirmaster at York Minster), has tried his hand. Tallis's *The Lamentations of Jeremiah* also underlines the extent to which, by the reign of Elizabeth, English music had adopted the diatonic system of major and minor keys; Tallis very effectively moves (or modulates, to use the technical term) from one to the other and back. *The Lamentations* also highlights one of the favourite English expressive devices of the time, a trick called 'false relation' in which discordant notes, either of which could fit into the harmony on its own, are sung together or so close together as to emphasise the music's pathos. This is a trick also found a great deal in William Byrd's music.

DISCOGRAPHY
Tallis's vocal music has done very well on disc, and there are also a few discs of his instrumental music available. However, it's the vocal music which hooks most people.

Although this book is beginning to read like a Tallis Scholars publicity hand-out, there is little doubt that their disc including *Spem in alium* makes an excellent introduction and features the single most compelling performance of that work. All the works mentioned above, except *The Lamentations of Jeremiah* (see below), are featured here, and given the usual excellent, thoughtful Tallis Scholars treatment based on scrupulous research as to period performance, all enhanced by excellent recording. The only reservation is that it's a bit on the short side (43 minutes).
● *Gimell CDGIM 006* ● *1 CD* ● *Full price*
● *1985* ✪

The recording of *The Lamentations of Jeremiah* includes several other anthems which illustrate various different techniques of composition; but you don't have to notice the technicalities if you don't want to.
● *Gimell CDGIM 025* ● *1 CD* ● *Full price*
● *DDD* ● *1992*

One of the side-effects of the Reformation was that composers started setting music to texts written in languages other than Latin. The English church music tradition is one of the finest and most consistently continuous in the world, and these anthems represent a very

important foundation of that heritage. The Tallis Scholars' *The Complete English Anthems* contains lots of small masterpieces like the Whitsuntide work *If Ye Love Me*, which show that Tallis worked as well on a small scale as on a 40-part showcase.
● *Gimell CDGIM 007* ● *1 CD* ● *Full price*
● *DDD* ● *1986*

Winchester Cathedral Choir's selection of *Sacred Choral Works* makes a good comprehensive introductory disc, which has the merit of including both *Spem in alium* and *The Lamentations*, both *Salvator mundi* and a little gem entitled *O nata lux* (although no *Gaude gloriosa*). This is a good example of the strengths of the traditional English choral style, solid, if a little underplaying the expressive aspects of the music, and not perhaps touched by quite the same genius as the Tallis Scholars (particularly as they perform Tallis's work on the first of the three discs cited above).
● *Hyperion CDA 66400* ● *1 CD* ● *Full price*
● *DDD* ● *1990*

The Hilliard Ensemble's Tallis disc is a fairly lenten, sombre selection, and perhaps a bit one-dimensional in mood to recommend to the first-time buyer. But anyone a little further into Tallis will find not only a very distinguished, beautifully considered version of *The Lamentations* and a superbly simple account of the austere Mass for Four Voices, with several other penitential pieces thrown in. The singing is stylish and expressive without ever resorting to unnecessary histrionic devices, stressing an element of Tallis's music which can often be overlooked – its clarity.
● *ECM New Series 833 308-2* ● *1 CD*
● *Full price* ● *DDD* ● *1988*

The Taverner Consort and Taverner Choir's selection of Latin anthems by Tallis lasts over two hours and offers another well-performed anthology. *Spem in alium* is supported by instrumental accompaniment. The gem of this selection is a tremendously exciting version of *Gaude gloriosa*, which really gets to grips with the character of this terrific piece. The Taverner Choir makes a nice noise, although with the slightest touch of vibrato-ridden strain in the upper voices at times.
● *EMI Reflexe CDC7 49555-2* ● *2 CDs*
● *Full price* ● *DDD* ● *1989; discs also available separately*

One general complaint is that almost all discs of medieval and Renaissance music seem to be full price, making life difficult for those who want to experiment. This would seem a useful juncture, then, to recommend two discs which aren't exclusively Tallis, but on which he features strongly.

Pro Cantione Antiqua's *Renaissance Masterpieces* has *Spem in alium* and *The Lamentations* supplemented by the famous early-seventeenth-century setting of the Miserere (Psalm 51) by the Italian choral composer Gregorio

Allegri (1582–1652). Pro Cantione Antiqua's style is very colourful, some would say old-fashioned, and perhaps a little on the dense side, but this disc is a very useful introduction, very enjoyable, with the two Lenten pieces nicely placed around the exuberant *Spem in alium*.

● *IMP/Pickwick PCD 806* ● *1 CD*
● *Budget price* ● *DDD* ● *1986*

The budget label Naxos offers some of the most attractive best-value bargains in the shops, and their venture into early music has been especially welcome and most distinguished. This imaginative disc includes Tallis's two sets of Lamentations alongside settings by another Elizabethan English composer, Robert White, as well as by Palestrina and Lassus (see below) and a Portuguese composer, Estevao de Brito. Quite apart from the opportunity this release gives to compare different national styles, Jeremy Summerly's ensemble Oxford Camerata (many of whom, including Summerly, can be found on earlier releases by all the other leading British early music groups) have a vocal manner which combines purity of tone with passion of delivery. A bargain for a fiver; this is a series to watch with interest.

● *Naxos 8.550572* ● *1 CD* ● *Budget price*
● *DDD* ● *1991*

●●●●

WILLIAM BYRD

Until the 1580s, Byrd's music had an exuberantly outgoing style. From then on, however, the increasing persecution of Catholics led him to look for inspiration in texts describing the Babylonian exile of the Jews in the sixth century BC. One of his greatest works, *Infelix ego*, is a long and complex motet written in the 1580s and based on the writings and sayings of the ultra-fundamentalist Florentine Catholic preacher Savonarola (who had been strangled and burnt in 1498 for posing awkward questions about worldly possessions and political influence to the princes of the Roman Church). *Infelix ego* combines the best of Byrd's more exuberant style, the ability to criss-cross, like Tallis, from small, intimate 'horizontal' writing involving only two or three of the

voices at his disposal, to chordal, 'vertical' writing that grips and leads you all over the place, occasionally (in a harmonic sense) completely up the garden path and back again.

Byrd's best-known Mass settings, the Masses for Four and Five Voices, (which are probably his most recorded works) were written after the 1580s, and the darker tone which entered his music is clearly detectable; there's a great reliance on minor keys, which are often used to depict turmoil or conflict, whether internal or external, and more reflective moods. Comparing Byrd's music written in adversity to anything by Palestrina (1525–1594), you can easily detect a more restrained, inward-looking technique, mirroring the private, furtive nature of English Catholicism in the late sixteenth and early seventeenth centuries.

None the less, Byrd also provided settings and anthems which have proved, alongside Tallis's, to be the cornerstone of the Church of England tradition. He was also an instrumental composer of some distinction, especially prolific in his dances for keyboard instruments of the time. Much of his instrumental music dates from his time as a more 'public' composer, a good deal of it commemorative of contemporary military campaigns. A large nine-section keyboard piece such as *The Battle* (probably dating from the 1570s) is intended as a vivid, musically realistic, and extremely virtuoso depiction of an entire sequence of events from summons of soldiers to the retreat of the defeated. As an instrumental composer who helped establish in England a concept of music specially dedicated to virtuosity, Byrd was second only to John Dowland (c. 1563–1626), whose

William Byrd

(1543-1623)

◖◗

Byrd was Tallis's natural successor in more ways than one. Like Tallis he remained a Roman Catholic, something which had a direct impact on his work during the nearly forty years he lived on after Tallis's death. He worked with Tallis at the Chapel Royal and shared with him the monopoly of music publishing to the Queen; but from the 1580s onwards, life became more difficult for English Catholics, and Byrd and his family found themselves regularly penalised for non-attendance at Church of England services.

As a result, Byrd gradually withdrew himself from the public life of London and the Royal Court, and concentrated on providing settings of the Roman liturgy and motets for performance at private ceremonies in Catholic households.

songs and compositions for string ensemble have an affecting, if rather predominantly gloomy, power.

OTHER ENGLISH SIXTEENTH-CENTURY COMPOSERS

If you get pleasure from Byrd, Tallis and all the names mentioned up to now, it might be worth pursuing some of the following (in no particular order): Thomas Weelkes (1576–1623), a composer of some excellent and highly ornamental church music which points the way to the late arrival (compared with most of the rest of Europe) of the Baroque in England; Thomas Tomkins (1572–1656), mentioned above, a Welshman who wrote some wonderfully dark-hued material; Thomas Morley (1557 or 1558–1602), one of the earliest setters of songs from Shakespeare's plays; Robert Jones (exact dates unknown, but at the height of his career between 1597 and

- 1615), who combined a fine poetic
- talent (rather along the lines of John
- Donne) with a fine melodic sense in
- both secular and religious songs.
-
- DISCOGRAPHY
- **Byrd**
- Anyone wondering where to start in the whole
- area of early/Renaissance music would be well
- advised to begin with this superb bargain (a
- personal favourite) – 65 minutes of sheer beauty
- for only a fiver. The Masses for Four and Five
- Voices are, I think, Byrd's most instantly
- accessible pieces, and placed as they are around
- the superb *Infelix ego*, this selection gives an
- admirable sense of Byrd's vocal range and style.
- Jeremy Summerly's Oxford Camerata are excellent
- throughout. The recording ambience (the chapel of
- Hertford College, Oxford, was the location) is quite
- eerily beautiful.
- ● *Naxos 8.550574* ● *1 CD* ● *Budget price*
- ● *DDD* ● *1992* ✪
-
- The Tallis Scholars' collection of Byrd's masses
- and motets is one of their earliest recordings, and
- a very good one too, also made in an Oxford
- college chapel (the older Merton College) resulting
- in exceptional acoustic quality. This is very much
- one dimension of Byrd, though, with only one
- four-part motet and three mass settings (for Three,
- Four and Five Voices) all of which exemplify the
- composer's more inward nature.
- ● *Gimell CDGIM345* ● *1 CD* ● *Full price*
- ● *DDD* ● *1984*

The Tallis Scholars also tackled the other side of the coin, with several English works, including the *Great Service* (an eight-voice setting of the Anglican liturgical canticles like the Magnificat and Nunc Dimittis from Evensong) and English extrovert anthems like *O sing joyfully unto God our strength*. You may have gathered by now that there's no such thing as a bad Tallis Scholars disc.
● *Gimell CDGIMO11* ● *1 CD* ● *Full price*
● *DDD* ● *1987*

Many of the best other recordings of Byrd's choral music comes on anthology discs not devoted to a single composer.

16th Century Motets featuring the Choir of King's College, Cambridge, directed by David Willcocks, contains music by Palestrina, Lassus, Giovanni Gabrieli, Victoria and others, as well as by Byrd. Since Byrd's music is very much part of the English church tradition (however ironic this may seem), it's worth hearing the most traditional of English church choirs bring their special touch to the music. Boys' voices have a very different, somehow more ethereal, quality, but inevitably there's less emotional understanding of what's being sung. Also, all English church tenors feel obliged to imitate the influential and nasal tones of Sir Peter Pears. This bargain disc offers a good chance for the most direct comparison between Byrd and Palestrina, as both versions of the anthem for St Peter's Day, *Tu es Petrus*, are included.
● *Classics for Pleasure CD-CFP4481* ● *1 CD*
● *Budget price* ● *ADD* ● *1975*

Tudor Anthems by the Oxford Christ Church Cathedral Choir, directed by Simon Preston, also contains music by Tallis, Weelkes, Tomkins, Gibbons, Mundy and others, and places Byrd very much in his English context (only Tallis's great Mariolatrous contemporary, Christopher Tye, is missing) with fine performances from Oxford's answer to King's (with respect to New College). One of the best pieces here isn't, in fact, by Byrd but by his younger Welsh contemporary, Tomkins, the exquisitely heartbreaking *When David heard that Absalom was slain*.
● *Gamut GOUPCD153* ● *1 CD* ● *Full price*
● *DDD* ● *1990*

Byrd's instrumental music

There's a fair selection, again placed in the context of English keyboard writing up to the end of the seventeenth century, on *Music of the English Virginalists*, Z. Ruzickova (virginals).
● *Orfeo C139661A* ● *1 CD* ● *Full price*
● *DDD* ● *1989* ○

Dowland

The Dowland Consort's recording of *Lacrimae or Seven Teares* has been described very fulsomely by the *Good CD Guide*: 'If Renaissance music were to be represented by only one disc it should perhaps be this one.' I can't quite go along with that view – Dowland's music for four viols (forerunners of the violin) and lute is too one-dimensionally miserable, as the title suggests.

Beautifully done, though; perhaps if Dowland were to be represented by only one disc . . .
● *BIS CD315* ● *1 CD* ● *Full price* ● *DDD*
● *1986* ○

Robert Jones

For Robert Jones's distinctive talent, try *The Muses Gardin*, another display of the talents of Emma Kirkby and Anthony Rooley.
● *Virgin Classics VC 7 91212-2* ● *1 CD* ● *Full price* ● *DDD* ● *1991* ○

● ● ● ●

CONTINENTAL EUROPE

BRUMEL (1460–1520) TO PALESTRINA (1525–1594)

Contrary to what we might assume, composers in sixteenth-century Europe were a much-travelled lot, and so we find the French/Flemish Orlando Lassus or Orlando di Lasso (1530 or 1532–1594), a man from what is now Belgium working in Munich after a spell in Rome; the Spaniard Tomas Luis de Victoria, sometimes known by the Italian spelling of his name as Vittoria (c. 1548–1611), carving a path from his native Avila to Rome and back, and eventually to Madrid; whilst in Rome, more conventionally static at the centre of the web, is the most famous of all sixteenth-century composers (and himself the subject of a twentieth-century opera by the German composer Hans Pfitzner), Giovanni Perluigi da Palestrina (c. 1525–1594).

We've already seen that, in the course of its development, English music had tended away from horizontally composed polyphony towards more chordal music based around the system of major and minor keys. The music of Europe, and especially of the Italians and Victoria, went in the same direction, only perhaps a little faster – more so in some places than in others. The Baroque era, in which the whole musical system became fixed, had already arrived in Venice by the end of the sixteenth century.

Because of the haphazard nature of the survival of printed manuscripts – composers of this era usually had their work printed in large volumes, but the dates of publication can often be misleading as to the dates of composition – more than a few pieces highly regarded by contemporaries have been lost. We know, for instance, that most of Heinrich Isaac's music has disappeared. And it's only with the recent enormous revival of interest in music of the sixteenth century and earlier that certain reputations have started to be reclaimed from oblivion, reputations which were very high in their own day.

ANTOINE BRUMEL
(c. 1460–c. 1520)

Antoine Brumel was a Frenchman and pupil of Josquin des Prèz (indeed, he took over Josquin's job in Ferrara) who enjoyed the high regard of his own and the next generation. Like other composers he led a fairly itinerant life, moving between Chartres, Paris, Geneva and Rome, involved (again, like most of his colleagues) in the religious musical life of Europe. Until 1992, the only works of Brumel available on record were a small instrumental chamber work, a motet and a chanson. Now, happily, there's a choice of versions of Brumel's absolute masterpiece, a twelve-voice setting of the Mass called *Missa et ecce terrae motus* (based around a small plainsong fragment) or the 'Earthquake' Mass. (The only surviving sixteenth-century copy was made, incidentally, by Lassus.) The mass is a relatively huge and lengthy

work, full of great static, harmonic slabs, a kind of forerunner of Tallis's *Spem in alium*, even though it's based on polyphonic principles of composition. Again, it's a piece which will appeal to lovers of a certain type of modern music, powered as it is by the same kind of spiritual faith and inspiration that motivates twentieth-century composers like Tavener and Górecki.

The Franco-Flemish tradition in the wake of Josquin – of which Brumel was a part – was very much the dominant musical school of Europe at the start of the sixteenth century, and figures like Clemens non Papa (c. 1510–1555 or 1556), whose strange nickname defies explanation (did people confuse him with the Pope, or some other Clemens? It doesn't seem likely). He's another figure whom the Tallis Scholars are currently in the process of rescuing, a rather complex, slightly less accessible, but ultimately very worthwhile composer (try *Missa pastores quidnam vidistis*, Gimell CDGIM013, 1 CD, Full price, DDD, 1987). However, the centre of musical power began to tilt with the Reformation, as northern Europe and the Flemish lands became swamped in the conflicts and wars which led to the establishment of countries like Holland. The musical appointments in the influential Catholic courts became more the prerogative of the southern Europeans from countries remaining loyal to the Faith, with Lassus (born around 1530) proving one of the last major Flemish composers.

DISCOGRAPHY
Without doubt, one of the discs of 1992 was the Tallis Scholars' version of Brumel's *Missa et ecce terrae motus*, astonishing even by their usual high standards. The recording manages to achieve both the drenching overwhelming sound of great forces without sacrificing the clarity of a single line. The addition of a set of Lamentations and a Magnificat

is a welcome bonus, showing Brumel working with more conventional polyphonic forces.
● *Gimell CDGIM026* ● *1 CD* ● *Full price*
● *DDD* ● *1992* ✪

It's rough luck for Paul van Nevel and his Huelgas Ensemble that the Tallis Scholars followed quickly in their footsteps in recording Brumel's mass, because this is an excellent disc of great power and with only slightly less clarity and firmness of tone than the British group. And it may be that if you find the Tallis Scholars a bit impossibly 'pure' in their tone, this highly expressive version might seem to have a bit more 'oomph'. Nice to be spoiled for choice, though, rather than making the best of a bad job.
● *Sony Vivarte SK46348* ● *1 CD* ● *Full price*
● *DDD* ● *1991*

GIOVANNI PERLUIGI DA PALESTRINA
(c. 1525–1594)

Given his role in the politics of the period, it's hardly surprising that all Renaissance music seems to lead to Palestrina. Evidently his contemporaries had a fairly high opinion of him; two years before he died, sixteen of them got together to compose, in his honour, settings of the evening psalms used in the church service vespers.

Dedicated to one of the shortest-lived popes in history (Marcellus II lasted about three weeks), the *Missa Papae Marcelli* is direct and unadorned, more chordal than polyphonic; yet lurking somewhere in the main melodic themes of the work, several commentators have detected the lurking shadow of the popular Burgundian tune 'L'Homme Armé'. As one of the most 'impure and lascivious' influences on masses was popular song, Palestrina may have been playing a dangerous game, although he managed to get away with it.

Palestrina is one sixteenth-century composer whose reputation has never really suffered eclipse. Part of the reason for this must be his proficiency in writing outgoing music based around major key tonalities, both in

his motets (the beautiful *Tu es Petrus* for instance) and in his masses (*Missa Assumpta est Maria*, one of his later works, has been performed consistently); perhaps also his generally conservative avoidance of subversive sensual expressive games has helped to keep him in favour with the Church establishment. A work like *Missa sicut lilium*, though, has a much more inward and brooding nature; perhaps that's why it has only recently been resuscitated.

DISCOGRAPHY
Palestrina
The Tallis Scholars won another of *The Gramophone*'s Awards for their Palestrina disc combining the masses *Assumpta est Maria* and *Sicut lilium*. You couldn't ask for more thoughtful, well-sung, atmospheric, haunting performances of them than you get here. Each mass is prefaced with the music on which Palestrina is drawing (in both cases motets by himself, although *Assumpta est Maria* ultimately derives from plainchant), so the listener can, if desired, get some idea of the technical composition methods. But whether that interests you or not, this is one of those touchstone discs; if you don't like it, you won't like Palestrina or, in all probability, Renaissance music. And if you do like Renaissance music, you shouldn't be without it.
● *Gimell CDGIM020* ● *1 CD* ● *Full price*
● *DDD* ● *1989* ✪

The Oxford Camerata under Jeremy Summerly has recorded the masses *Papae Marcelli* and *Aeterna Christi Munera*. The second of these is a late four-part mass based on plainsong, in which Palestrina produces a conservative, smooth work with few complications. This isn't perhaps quite as indispensable as the other Oxford Camerata discs, but it's still fairly fine value, and a very good, precise account of *Missa Papae Marcelli*, a work which no Palestrina collection should be without.
● *Naxos 8.550373* ● *1 CD* ● *Budget price*
● *DDD* ● *1992*

Papae Marcelli turns up again along with the eight-part *Stabat Mater*, sung by all the all-adult male Pro Cantione Antiqua directed by Bruno Turner. A rich experience.
● *Pickwick PCD 863* ● *1 CD* ● *Budget price*
● *ADD* ● *1978*

L'Homme Armé
One of the most popular tunes used as the basis for settings of the Mass in the fifteenth, sixteenth (and even the seventeenth) centuries was a Burgundian song entitled 'L'Homme Armé' and possibly written by a Flemish composer called

Giovanni Perluigi Da Palestrina

c. 1525–1594

Palestrina's musical life was lived almost exclusively in religious circles; he graduated through a series of church appointments to become director of the Julian Chapel Choir at St Peter's in Rome before his 30th birthday. The list of religious establishments where Palestrina had jobs reads like an itinerary of the major tourist spots in Rome; St John Lateran, St Maria Maggiore, and back to St Peter's again. He must have been comfortably off; quite apart from influential jobs, his second wife was a wealthy widow. Dating Palestrina's music with any certainty can be a difficult task, as much of it was published late, even posthumously; his first book of masses came as early as 1554, and over his life he composed more than 100 mass settings and nearly 200 motets. Politically, the papacy saw him and his music as a key weapon in the Counter-Reformation, the great 'Catholic Empire Strikes Back' movement in the face of the rising tide of Protestantism. Palestrina's career occupied a crucial moment in European musical history; there was a faction in the Church which felt that polyphony in church music, with all its expressionist devices, had gone far too far and that all should be purged, and a severe regime of plainsong and nothing more elaborate reintroduced. Eventually the Church rulers decided to issue a warning against 'impure and lascivious' influences in religious music; and one of Palestrina's most consistently popular works, the *Missa Papae Marcelli* (1567) may have been his contribution to the debate about the 'new' spirit of church music. Certainly it was Palestrina who was primarily responsible for saving the whole idea of church music; when the issue came to a head at the Council of Trent (1567), it's doubtful whether, without a figure of his musical genius and political sensitivity, the die-hard anti-music faction could have been stopped.

Antoine Busnois (who died in 1492). It's a jolly, skipping tune whose words we know but whose meaning is utterly out of our reach. The frequency with which it turns up in the works of composers from Dufay, Josquin and Ockeghem right through to Giacomo Carissimi (1605–1674) suggests that it must have been popular on a very widespread scale. Anyone interested in hearing a whole load of variations of 'L'Homme Armé' in different parts of the Mass should sample an excellent disc by Paul van Nevel and his Huelgas Ensemble in Sony's early/Renaissance/Baroque series *Vivarte: La Dissection D'un Homme Armé*.
● *Sony Vivarte SK45860* ● *1 CD* ● *Full price* ● *DDD* ● *1991* ✪

ORLANDO LASSUS OR ORLANDO DI LASSO (1530 OR 1532–1594)

Lassus's life ran parallel to Palestrina's in more than just years. Lassus occupied the post at the Church of St John Lateran immediately before Palestrina, and his religious music bears strong similarities to Palestrina's, although he tended towards more sensual reflection of the text in his use of melody and harmony. Most of Lassus's creative life, though, was spent not in Italy but at the Munich court of Duke Albrecht V of Bavaria.

Lassus was, in the earlier part of his life, a fairly jolly soul prone to writing drinking songs and secular love chansons; however, in middle life he developed a tendency to illness and depression, which had the inevitable effect of making him compose more music on religious themes in the hope of salvation.

One Lassus motet in particular, *Timor et tremor* ('Fear and trembling') is remarkable for its use of 'chromaticism', a term which literally means 'colouring' and refers musically to the introduction of lots of notes completely outside the range of the harmonies implicit in the tonality being used. Chromaticism is a favourite destabilising device as it makes the listener's sense of a 'home key' much less certain; it was much used by late-Romantic composers, and the ultimate in chromatic works are probably Wagner's opera *Tristan and Isolde* and Schoenberg's orchestral/chamber tone-poem *Verklärte Nacht*. The usual effect of chromaticism is to give an exotic, strange, rather hot-house feel to music.

Lassus would mirror the meaning of a text very closely in his music using every means at his disposal; his changing harmonies and above all his rhythms pick up every detail and nuance of the words being set. This detailed attention to expressiveness makes him a pivotal figure in the development of the 'Baroque', where expressiveness becomes so significant that music develops a new, imitative, ornamental strain. Lassus's role is particularly emphasised by the fact that in 1560 he was visited in Munich by Andrea Gabrieli (c. 1510–1586), one of a family of great Venetian composers, who took many of Lassus's techniques back to Venice where they wound up in the 'care' (as it were) of the first great modern composer, Claudio Monteverdi (1567–1643).

DISCOGRAPHY

The Tallis Scholar's recording of the recently rediscovered *Missa Osculetur Me* – a work for double choir, a device which was to become a favourite Venetian Baroque tactic – is an expressive, haunting and utterly melodious experience. The motet *Timor et tremor* is also here, although the disc is still slightly short measure.

● *Gimell CDGIM 018*   ● *1 CD*   ● *Full price*
● *DDD*   ● *1989* ●

Although based on a setting of a love poem by Petrarch, the *Missa Qual Donna* is a late work, full of pathos, depression and religious despair, a mood carried even further by *De profundis* ('Out of the depths'), one of the two motets to be found here. The other mass is a cheery affair, known as the 'Hunting' Mass. The recording by Christ Church Cathedral Choir is a good, inspired disc for most of the time, except when the trebles sound a bit weedy.

● *Nimbus NI5150*   ● *1 CD*   ● *Full price*   ● *DDD*
● *1989*

■■■   ■■■   ■■■

TOMAS LUIS DA VICTORIA or VITTORIA (c. 1548–1611)

Like Vivaldi a hundred years later, Victoria was a composer-priest, although there seems every sign that he took his priestly orders a good deal more seriously than the red-haired Venetian. When young he probably knew Saint Teresa of Avila (he was born near Avila), and he was sent to Rome to prepare for the priesthood by no less a religious devotee than King Philip II of Spain. While in Rome he studied under Palestrina, succeeding him his post at the Seminary. Victoria's music has a certain archaic sound about it; sometimes its deep expressiveness gives it almost a claustrophobia that seems peculiarly Spanish (it's detectable in the later Portuguese music which he influenced so greatly). Yet Victoria was a very 'modern' composer; his use of repeated notes for emphasis was a relatively new device; his expressive music was more overtly pictorial and graphic than that of any of the composers yet discussed; he was one of the first composers to provide separately written organ parts; and in his music the sense of the diatonic major and minor key system is more or less complete.

DISCOGRAPHY
The Tallis Scholars' recording of Victoria's *Requiem* is another great achievement.
● *Gimell CDGIM012* ● *1 CD* ● *Full price*
● *DDD* ● *1987* ○

The Tenebrae are Biblical quotations which form part of the liturgy for Holy Week, and Westminster Cathedral Choir, the foremost British Catholic cathedral choir, here conducted by David Hill, definitely have the edge over the competition in performance of Victoria's *Tenebrae*, as they sing these small antiphons with every sense of their place in the larger scale of things. All the drama is nicely judged, but with nothing out of place or tasteless; a truly Christian recording.
● *Hyperion CDA66304* ● *1 CD* ● *Full price*
● *DDD* ● *1989*

Victoria's music wasn't so layered and complex as Palestrina's or Josquin's, and so it requires a special kind of performance to bring out its strengths. Once again the Westminster Cathedral Choir put their liturgical practice to good use in a splendid recording of the masses *Q Quam Gloriosum* and *Ave Maris Stella*.
● *Hyperion CDA66114* ● *1 CD* ● *Full price*
● *DDD* ● *1984*

● ● ● ●

PORTUGAL: CARDOSO AND DUARTE LÔBO

At this time in history, Spain was the dominant force in the Iberian Peninsula and Spanish musical styles reigned supreme in Portugal until well into the seventeenth century. Recently two remarkable requiems by Portuguese composers active in the

first half of that century have been resurrected; the composers in question are Frei Manuel Cardoso (c. 1566–1650) and Duarte Lôbo (c. 1565–1646). Both composers wrote in movingly intense styles, and their music repays constant and detailed listening. Of the two, Lôbo is probably the more instantly appealing; there's something of that dense layered quality in some of his more chordal passages which is reminiscent of Brumel and Tallis.

DISCOGRAPHY
The resurrection job on Cardoso and Lôbo has been done, inevitably, by the Tallis Scholars. The Cardoso recording also contains several of his motets, whilst Lôbo's *Requiem* is complemented by a mass setting. Both discs are on Gimell.
● *CDGIM021 for Cardoso* ● *CDGIM028 for Lôbo* ○

● ● ● ●

DON CARLO GESUALDO, PRINCE OF VENOSA (1560–1613)

It would be impossible to end this introductory chapter without reference to one of the weirdest figures in the history of music. Gesualdo was a Neapolitan nobleman who in 1590 ordered the murder of his unfaithful wife and her lover. He spent the rest of his life tortured by guilt, and represented his warped state of mind in bizarrely chromatic music which has no real precedent in his time; indeed, there is nothing like it until the late nineteenth century. Gesualdo pushed chromaticism to the extreme, so much so that the concept of keys and major and minor tonality in his compositions seemed doomed before it had really got going. He also made his music entirely disjointed, ruining its mellifluous flow, thus going against every contemporary style. Gesualdo was lurid and extreme in every sense, and I think everyone ought to try him once. As you may gather, he's a bit of a personal favourite.

DISCOGRAPHY
The Hilliard Ensemble have made a formidable recording of Gesualdo's *Tenebrae* responses. For once the Tallis Scholars (who've done a perfectly up-to-standard Gesualdo recording) have to yield pride of place to one of my own potential 'desert island discs'. The Hilliard get right inside the drama, and, without any tasteless histrionics, bring Gesualdo's own personal life right into the centre of this penitential music (the moment when the text prophesies Judas's suicide is especially memorable). With a setting of the Miserere and the canticle Benedictus as well, this is a guided journey round one of the most extraordinary and peerless (literally – there were no contemporary composers like Gesualdo) musical minds.
● *ECM New Series 1422/23* ● *2 CDs* ● *Full price* ● *DDD* ● *1991* ✪

A selection of five part madrigals sung by Les Arts Florissants directed by William Christie, is equally convincing, although without quite the claustrophobia of religious penitential music. I'm not entirely sure about the advisability of using keyboard accompaniment on some items, but apart from that this is fine stuff from one of the best Baroque-music ensembles currently operating. A good introduction.
● *Harmonia Mundi HMC90 1268* ● *1 CD* ● *Full price* ● *DDD* ● *1988*

II

The Symphony

INTRODUCTION

The symphony is probably the most celebrated of all classical musical forms. Anyone wanting to give themselves highbrow airs in more popular music tends to invoke the symphony; there's the song 'Tenement Symphony'; Diana Ross and the Supremes claimed to 'Hear a Symphony' back in the 1960s; nineties 'rave music' group Primal Scream offered a 'Dub Symphony in 2 parts' of their song 'Higher than the Sun' on their 1991 album *Scream-adelica*; most memorably of all, Cole Porter used the symphony to epitomise the height of classical taste and sophistication in his song 'You're the Top', although his wilful misattribution of the form – 'You're a melody from a symphony by Strauss' – seems odd in such a musically knowledgeable person. In fact, the symphony is a relative parvenu amongst musical genres. Until the eighteenth century the term 'sinfonia' (which is merely the Italian word for 'symphony') referred principally to an instrumental passage in an opera or other piece of vocal music. Thus Monteverdi's operas all have instrumental sinfonias at the start of each act; Henry Purcell's longer and more elaborate church anthems are punctuated by instrumental sinfonias. Handel was writing opera in the first half of the eighteenth century, and his operas use sinfonias where we would expect overtures; and that's exactly the pedigree of the classical symphony: it's an operatic overture which has grown out of its surroundings, got a bit too big for its boots, perhaps. In fact, some early symphonies sound more like overtures than the great, dense pieces Bruckner and Mahler were to write in the late nineteenth and early twentieth centuries.

The sinfonia developed a simple shape; two fast passages, with a short, slower interlude for balance. It's the simplest form imaginable: A-B-A, fast-slow-fast, easy to follow for any audience. Wealthier patrons liked a chance to show off what their musical ensembles could do together; concertos are all very well, but they tended, through most of the eighteenth century, to emphasise the virtuosity of the soloist, or soloists, rather than allow full rein to all the instrumental players. As the technical capacity of wind instruments became more and more sophisticated, both audiences and composers were curious to hear new sounds derived from new instrumental blendings; and obviously more primitive valve instruments like horns, trumpets and trombones (especially) were of more use as ensemble instruments than as things on which to display virtuosity.

The symphony, slow to arrive, was very quick to take off, which is simply illustrated by the fact the no one thinks at all of symphonies written by Johann Sebastian Bach (died 1750) or Handel (died 1759), both of whom wrote concertos by the yard. Yet J. S. Bach's second son, Carl Philipp Emanuel (1714–1788) was one of the great influential figures in establishing the symphony as a form; indeed, one of his symphonies, written in 1756 and published in 1759, was described by a forgotten composer of the time as 'the best symphony' he had ever heard.

The symphony developed very quickly over the next 50 years, thanks mainly to the enthusiasm which both Franz Joseph Haydn (1732–1809) and Wolfgang Amadeus Mozart (1756–1791) showed for the form. Haydn was the first great symphonic experimenter, and it was he who fixed the standard four-movement form which prevailed for a century or so.

Most Haydn symphonies open with a brief slow passage, designed to grab the attention of – and thus shut up – the audience; musical recitals of the era were, literally, as much social as artistic events. The slow passage leads to the first movement proper (usually

in 'Sonata form' – see below), in which one or two musical themes are introduced and worked over, taken through various different musical keys, but always eventually returning to the 'home' key – the one that the title tells you the symphony is 'in', as Mozart's 40th Symphony is 'in' G Minor. If a symphony is in a major key, its second movement will often be in a more mournful minor key, as second movements are predominantly slow; marked either 'andante' ('walking pace') or 'adagio' ('slow'). Usually, slow movements are simple in structure; an opening musical theme, a more agitated middle section, then a return to the material of the first section. This is often called 'ternary form' (as it has three sections). Third movements were usually based on dances, often the minuet, although a later symphonist like Mahler was drawn to a folk dance called the Ländler. A minuet movement would also be ternary, with a straightforward minuet, followed by a section in a slightly different tempo – the 'trio' – then a reprise of the original minuet. As the symphony developed, some composers preferred to make the third movement a 'scherzo' (literally, 'joke'), a fizzy fast movement which serves as a contrast to the elaboration of the first movement and the reflective pathos of the second. The most popular form of finale was the 'rondo', in which a main theme, usually very catchy and instantly identifiable, comes round and round again, separated by melodically related episodes which take the music through various modulations (changes from one key into another).

SONATA FORM

One of Haydn's great achievements was to establish the form known as 'sonata form' as the basis for almost all first movements, whether in the symphony, the concerto or the instrumental sonata itself. The term can seem a bit daunting, but for all the grandiose technical things that are written about it, sonata form is just another ternary A-B-A form. Most listeners to music don't need to know exactly when the 'transition' or the 'bridge' or the 'secondary development' begin; but it is quite useful to have a general sense of direction. Even some of the most apparently elaborate and complex symphonic movements are rooted in sonata form. So, very simply, what happens is this.

Exposition

There are two 'subjects' in sonata form. A subject is often simply a tune, but it can be just a rhythmic idea or a motif. The opening three notes of Beethoven's 5th Symphony could be called that movement's 'first subject'. The first subject is stated and the music moves on to the second, very often seeming to start the symphony over again as it does so but moving away from the home key. This is the crucial thing about the second subject – it's almost always in a different key, and it usually introduces a new contrasting mood. When you've heard this, there's a little flourish which either leads to a repeat of everything you've heard so far, or into the 'development'. Repeats were more or less *de rigueur* in Mozart's and Haydn's time, although they didn't always specify them in the score, and opinions vary about observing them.

Development

This central part of sonata form, unsurprisingly, develops material which has gone before, usually starting with the little flourish that led out of the exposition. It's in this section that tension starts to build up and the composer has fun taking the music through all sorts of keys. The effect on the listener is (or should be) excitement, as you begin to lose sight of the home key. As things build up, the first subject material comes back (in a hopelessly wrong key) and things begin to make more sense; the tension is defused gradually until it's time for the . . .

Recapitulation

In essence the recapitulation does exactly what you might suppose; it recalls the exposition, starting with the first subject (in the right key) and working through to the second subject, then heading towards a brief ending flourish. However, there's usually some suggestion of what went on in the development thrown into the transition between first and second subjects, although the home key is always kept well in sight.

Not all of Haydn's 100-plus or Mozart's 40-plus symphonies follow this form; but the majority of their more mature works do, so that by the end of their careers the form was established as *the* orchestral genre. Thus it was the symphony in which the great Romantic revolutionary Ludwig van Beethoven (1770–1827) felt he could express many of his central ideas about music and what it could achieve. Within 75 years of Bach's death, Beethoven's nine symphonies, which form probably the most famous symphonic cycle, had been written. From his 3rd Symphony ('Eroica') onwards Beethoven used the form as a kind of autobiographical depiction of emotions; from this point on, too (generally), symphonies became longer; so that in the 1820s, both Beethoven's 9th ('Choral') and the 9th (and last) Symphony of Franz Schubert (1797–1828), lasted for over an hour.

After Beethoven, the symphony became almost a challenge of machismo for any serious composer who didn't intend to stick purely to opera; if you couldn't write a symphony, you weren't a 'real' composer. Composers like Robert Schumann (1810–1856) and Johannes Brahms (1833–1897) took Beethoven's model very seriously; although non-Germanic composers like Hector Berlioz (1803–1869) and, later, Peter Tchaikovsky (1840–1893) took the idea of the symphony as a means of personal autobiographical expression to extremes.

Through the nineteenth century, the symphony went on getting longer, until two composers – Anton Bruckner (1824–1896) and Gustav Mahler (1860–1911) – took it to new proportions. Bruckner stuck with the four-movement form, writing exceptionally long movements; Mahler also wrote very long movements but varied the number in each of his symphonies, ranging from two to six.

Bruckner and Mahler were perhaps the last of the great Germanic symphonists; after them came the 'Modernist' movement known as the 'Second Viennese School', headed by Arnold Schoenberg (1874–1951), which reacted both against the length and the musical style of Bruckner's and Mahler's works. However, the symphony's survival in the twentieth century was assured first by such 'Nationalist' composers as Jean Sibelius (1865–1957) and Carl Nielsen (1865–1931), who both sought to combine the mainstream musical tradition with a sound redolent of their native countries (Finland and Denmark respectively). The single greatest corpus of twentieth-century symphonies is probably formed by the fifteen works of Dmitri Shostakovich (1906–1975), who always had to walk the tightrope between his own artistic ambitions and the constraints of musical life in the Soviet Union. There's also a fair-sized body of British symphonic writing, mainly of a Romantic, melodic nature, by composers like Edward Elgar (1857–1934) and Ralph Vaughan Williams (1872–1958); whilst Michael Tippett (1905–   ) and Robert Simpson (1921–   ) have both, in different ways, kept the symphony very much alive as a mode of intellectual expression.

C. P. E. BACH

CPE wrote nineteen symphonies, and the fact that many were published in full in his lifetime is testimony to their enormous popularity. Publishing a large-ensemble work in its entirety was then – as it remains now – an expensive business which no publisher would undertake without being sure that it would pay. We can be sure that CPE's popularity as a composer of symphonies was widespread, because copies of at least one of his best-known works in the genre, the E Minor Symphony written in 1756, have been found all over Europe from England to Russia.

CPE wrote symphonies at a time when Germanic culture was beginning to take on board the ideas of Romanticism, and a spirit called *Sturm und Drang* – 'storm and stress' – was abroad. It's perhaps from the prevalence of *Sturm und Drang* in the latter part of the eighteenth century that the belief has developed that *Angst* (fear, anxiety) is an essential element of the German character. Be that as it may, the effects of *Sturm und Drang* on the music of CPE and,

C. P. E. Bach
1714-1788

Carl Philipp Emanuel Bach, whose music often gets lost amidst his father's vast output, was regarded during his lifetime as 'the great Bach'. He had everything going for him, of course; his father's reputation stood him in good stead, and his godfather was Georg Philipp Telemann, probably the most celebrated German composer of the time. At about the age of 25 CPE was appointed court harpsichordist to Frederick the Great, a post in which he remained for almost 30 years, performing and writing music. After such a lengthy appointment, CPE was rather glad to get away in 1768 when he took up the post of City Director of Music for the five major churches of the City of Hamburg. Away from the ever-interfering Frederick (who rather fancied himself as a musician), Bach was able to compose more in the style of his choice; and it was in Hamburg that he wrote his most important symphonies. He also wrote music to commissions by Baron Gottfried van Swieten, a figure who subsequently did much to help Mozart; indeed, Haydn, Mozart and Beethoven all looked upon him as a major influence (both Mozart and Beethoven explicitly referred to him in writing as a 'father').

>> *Concerto* 100

more importantly, of Haydn shouldn't be confused with the kind of Romanticism to be found in Berlioz, Tchaikovsky, Mahler or even – to some extent Beethoven and Schumann. Just because CPE and Haydn developed a fondness for depicting something relatively stormy (relative to their time, that is) doesn't mean they're hanging their souls and emotions out on their musical washing-lines for public inspection, trying to tell the stories of their lives in symphonic form. For CPE and Haydn, the minor-key-orientated *Sturm und Drang* was an interesting way of varying the unremittingly cheery major-key sound.

The best of CPE's nineteen symphonies show a real interest in

- exploring and developing the textures
- of orchestral sound, as well as a new
- approach to establishing basic
- tonalities, harmonic progression, and
- the use of unusually dislocated
- rhythms. Some of the best examples of
- these tendencies in CPE's work can be
- found in four symphonies he wrote in
- Hamburg, composed in the 1770s and
- published in 1780. These have the
- catalogue number Wq183/1-4 (like
- many composers of this period,
- including his father, Johann Sebastian
- Bach, and Haydn and Mozart, CPE's
- music was never given opus numbers
- by the composer himself, but
- catalogued at a later date). These
- works are symphonies 'for 12
- obbligato parts', combining strings
- and woodwind on more or less equal

terms; they are delightfully lively, typical in length and shape of the earlier sinfonia (none lasts very much longer than ten or twelve minutes). The first, in D major, is a particularly good example of CPE's work, starting off with a daringly vague tonality and rhythmic patterns which don't immediately establish a straightforward 'four in a bar'.

DISCOGRAPHY

The best introduction to CPE's symphonic skill is a disc made some quarter of a century ago, which combines the four 'Hamburg Symphonies' (as Wq183/1-4 are often known), the 1756 piece hailed as 'the best symphony ever written' (catalogued as Wq177), and a C minor work from the early 1770s (Wq182/3), of which one critic once said 'hardly has ever a more noble, daring or humorous musical work issued from the pen of a genius'. The disc is simply titled *Carl Philipp Emanuel Bach: Six Symphonies*, and the performers are the English Chamber Orchestra conducted by Raymond Leppard. This is an excellent example of the 'old style' of performance on modern instruments which has full regard for scholarly investigation of performance tradition, yet doesn't seek to abandon the idea of musical phrasing.
● *Philips 426 081-2* ● *1 CD* ● *Mid-price*
● *ADD* ● *1968* ✪

If you don't have any problem with period instruments (personally, I find it depends on the orchestra/ensemble/conductor involved) there are three other CPE symphonic discs worth pursuing. Trevor Pinnock's The English Concert are leading exponents of this era's music, and their recording of six earlier symphonies written in Hamburg (Wq182) won a *The Gramophone* Award in 1980. I actually think Pinnock is more exciting when heard live, but his recordings are all extremely proficient and polished.
● *Deutsche Grammophon Archiv 415 300-2*
● *1 CD* ● *Full price* ● *ADD* ● *1980*

Gustav Leonhardt is much spikier, and there's a great deal of verve about his direction of the Orchestra of the Age of Enlightenment's performance of the four Wq183 pieces (plus the fifth of the Wq182s).
● *Virgin Classics Veritas VC7 90806-2* ● *1 CD*
● *Full price* ● *DDD* ● *1990*

Dutchman Ton Koopman is one of the really classy performers in both Classical and Baroque repertoire. He uses a fairly small ensemble, but he's so good at getting interesting and diverse tone (often a bit of a problem with the thinner sound of period instruments) from comparatively small numbers. His Amsterdam Baroque Orchestra gives colourful performances of the four later

'Hamburg' works (Wq183), though at 43 minutes this isn't exactly the best bargain in the shop.
● *Erato 2292 45361-2* ● *1 CD* ● *Full price*
● *DDD* ● *1989*

● ● ● ●

FRANZ JOSEPH HAYDN

'Papa' Haydn has a vast symphonic output. The 'official' numbers credit him with 104; actually he wrote 107, although in the following discussion I shall stick to conventional numbering. The classifications can be rather misleading, as the numbers, unlike those of Beethoven or Brahms, were stuck on after Haydn's death for identification purposes; the various nicknames were sometimes assigned by the composer or his friends, sometimes by publishers.

Leaving dry musicological considerations aside, Haydn's symphonies have sometimes been in danger of being the subject of praise which amounts to little more than mere lip-service, with all but a very small number consigned to a relative oblivion. As long as extrovert Romanticism remained in the musical ascendant, Haydn's subtle wit would always struggle to attract an audience; his musical games are a long way from Mahler's life-and-death struggles. Even under the influence of the *Sturm und Drang* movement of the mid-eighteenth century, a German artistic trend which, as I've said earlier, prized overt emotional expression, Haydn remained urbane and civilised, but never boring. His symphonies are full of jokes; most famously, Symphony No. 45 in F Sharp Minor, the 'Farewell', has a finale which instead of building up to the usual buoyant ending, winds down to the sound of two lone violins because, in the first performance, all the other orchestral players left one by

Franz Joseph Haydn

1732–1809

Haydn's life revolved around music from the age of about six – quite late by Mozart's standards, but still pretty impressive. He was a boy chorister at St Stephen's, Vienna (there's a story that the authorities had designs upon transforming him into a 'castrato'), spent nine years from the age of seventeen as a freelance musician, and obtained his first proper job as a music director and court composer to a Bohemian count in 1758. During his first year in Bohemia he wrote his very first symphony, and amongst the audience who heard it was the wealthy Austro-Hungarian nobleman Prince Paul Anton Esterházy. The Prince lured Haydn into his employment, and although he died within a year, the accession of the new Prince, Nicholas Esterházy, assured Haydn's future. For almost 30 years Haydn was based at the court of the art-loving Nicholas, free to develop his music; first as deputy court music director, then, after five years, as the chief director. Prince Nicholas delighted in art in all its forms, and he expected Haydn to produce symphonies, concertos, operas, choral works, everything. By 1776, Haydn was well enough established to appear in the Austrian equivalent of *Who's Who*. In 1781 he met Mozart, who regarded him with veneration as a father figure ('Papa Haydn'); Haydn, for his part, respected the younger man and felt greatly protective towards him. In 1790, Prince Nicholas died, and his successor dismissed most of the court musicians (although not Haydn), leaving the composer free to travel; he took up a long-standing invitation to England where he spent much of the next five years. In the early years of the nineteenth century, around 1802 or 1803, Haydn's creative energies dried up and he lived more or less in retirement (giving credence to a premature report of his death in an English magazine in 1805). He died nineteen days after Napoleon's troops began their bombardment of Vienna.

>> *Concerto* 100, *Chamber* 218, *Choral* 256

one, which was Haydn's way of dropping a hint to Prince Nicholas Esterházy that his instrumentalists were badly in need of a holiday. Symphony No. 64, the last Haydn symphony influenced by *Sturm und Drang*, written in 1772, bears the title 'Tempora Mutantur' – 'Times Change' – which may hint that this influence had run its course, but has more to do

- with the slow movement, which keeps
- changing pace with an almost neurotic
- unpredictability. This may have been
- designed to deter the Prince from his
- perpetual habit of tapping his feet to
- the rhythm of the music.
- Such details of context fill out one's
- appreciation of Haydn's music, but
- they aren't essential for musical
- enjoyment pure and simple. Through

his whole output Haydn uses subtle rhythmic variation; alters musical phrases slightly, suddenly cutting them short when they return; he also takes pieces through a bewildering variety of keys and tonalities which – according to the textbooks – he shouldn't have gone anywhere near. He's even witty in his silences and pauses; in the third movement of No. 104 he leaves a phrase of the minuet hanging in mid-air; in No. 90 he apparently brings the symphony to a conclusion, only to start up again, almost infuriatingly.

HAYDN AND THE SYMPHONY

Haydn is the first great symphonist, and the symphonic form that we know perhaps owes more to him than any other single composer. It is Haydn above all who transforms the three-part overture into a work which is conceived as a thematic unity, a form which can work on several levels at once. Remarkably, Haydn's primary motivation seems to be intellectual, an interest in the form and music for its own sake; almost everyone else who takes the symphony through a new twist is usually spurred on by some autobiographical impulse that one might call (in an entirely uncritical sense) 'self-indulgent'. And very often the 'new ideas' of symphonists like Beethoven, Tchaikovsky and Mahler are foreshadowed in small experiments Haydn has conducted. Mahler's five- and six-movement epics are anticipated in No. 45 (the 'Farewell'), with five movements, and No. 60, with six. No fewer than seven of Haydn's symphonies begin with complete slow movements (as opposed to a declamatory slow introduction to a conventional fast movement),

- something which is regarded as the
- hallmark of the late Romantic
- symphony. The kind of descriptive
- scene-painting to be found in
- 'programme' symphonies (that is,
- works whose music depicts events in
- a narrative 'programme' devised by
- the composer), such as Berlioz's
- *Symphonie Fantastique* and
- Beethoven's 6th ('Pastoral'), are found
- throughout Haydn's work, as in No.
- 55 ('The Schoolmaster') or the
- 'hunting scenes' of Nos. 65 and 73
- (musical descriptions of hunting were
- especially popular with Vivaldi, the
- most famous being the finale of
- 'Autumn' in *The Four Seasons*).

- **The symphony that Haydn created**
- From Symphony No. 31 ('Horn Signal',
- a very devious and enjoyable piece)
- onwards, and with the exceptions
- mentioned earlier, Haydn settled on
- the classic four-movement structure
- described at the outset of this chapter.
- In Haydn's work, the first movement
- was always the most complex and
- developed; although even after
- Beethoven shifted the balance of the
- symphony (and other forms) to the
- finale, the opening movement of most
- symphonies almost always follows the
- sonata form, a pattern which Haydn
- did much to fix and establish. In
- establishing sonata form (which he did
- in his works in many forms in the
- 1770s), Haydn made a significant
- contribution to music which would
- have ensured him a place in the
- textbooks even if he hadn't happened
- to be a great composer. But he also
- pointed the way as to how the form
- could be a platform for the composer
- to show off from; just as he showed
- how the symphony could be a
- showcase for the composer's ideas
- about orchestral textures, for melody,
- for wit.

Haydn's symphonies: the nicknames

The 'nicknamed' Haydn symphonies are amongst his more famous, possibly because the nicknames provide a useful handle for the listener. Nicknames often have a bearing on only one movement ('Farewell' refers only to the finale, for example), or sometimes have nothing to do with the music itself (No. 48 becomes 'Maria Theresia' because it's believed to have been played when the Archduchess of Austria visited Esterház, although we know it to have been written well before that visit took place; others like the 'Oxford' or 'London' Symphonies take their names from the places where they were written). Here, for handy reference, are all Haydn's nicknamed symphonies, together with their numbers and keys:

No. 6 in D Major – 'Le Matin'
No. 7 in C Major – 'Le Midi'
No. 8 in G Major – 'Le Soir'
No. 22 in E Flat Major – 'The Philosopher'
No. 26 in D Minor – 'Lamentatione'
No. 30 in C Major – 'Alleluja'
No. 31 in D Major – 'Hornsignal'
No. 43 in E Flat Major – 'Mercury'
No. 44 in F Minor – 'Trauersinfonie' ('Funeral Symphony')
No. 45 in F Sharp Minor – 'Farewell'
No. 48 in C Major – 'Maria Theresia'
No. 49 in F Minor – 'La Passione'
No. 53 in D Major – 'Imperial'
No. 55 in E Flat Major – 'The Schoolmaster'
No. 59 in A Major – 'Fire'
No. 60 in C Major – 'Il Distratto'
No. 63 in C Major – 'La Roxelane'
No. 64 in A Major – 'Tempora Mutantur'
No. 69 in C Major – 'Loudon'
No. 73 in D Major – 'The Hunt'
No. 82 in C Major – 'The Bear'

No. 83 in G Minor – 'The Hen'
No. 85 in B Flat Major – 'La Reine'
No. 88 in G Major – 'Letter V'
No. 92 in G Major – 'Oxford'
No. 94 in G Major – 'Surprise'
No. 96 in D Major – 'Miracle'
No. 100 in G Major – 'Military'
No. 101 in D Major – 'Clock'
No. 103 in E Flat Major – 'Drumroll'
No. 104 in D Major – 'London'

To say that these nicknames allow a more accessible approach to Haydn isn't to say that these symphonies are 'superior' to the unnamed works; eventually there's enough material in the 107 symphonies for any convert to Haydn to spend years losing themselves in the composer's ingenuity. Conductors have tended (until the advent of period instruments) to perform the later symphonies – especially the last twelve, written on Haydn's very lucrative visit to England – more than the earlier, which is a shame. Smaller-scale work though it be, No. 26 has an emotive power to equal anything in the more mature pieces. There has always been some interest in the *Sturm und Drang* works, precisely because they have always remained more open to the kind of subjectively Romantic approach which many great conductors prefer, but it is the last twelve or so symphonies which attract the largest entry in the catalogue of available recordings.

DISCOGRAPHY
If you're not familiar with Haydn's symphonies, but are tempted to dip your toes in the water, then once again the excellent Naxos label is on hand. There are six separate discs of 'famous' Haydn symphonies, all very attractively and intelligently done; five feature the Slovak Orchestra Capella Istropolitana under British conductor Barry Wordsworth, while the sixth is performed by the Northern Chamber·Orchestra conducted by Nicholas Ward. All six offer excellent value for money; performances that would be good at any price for about a fiver. A good starter is a

selection which spreads itself across the 'types' of Haydn symphony, like the release combining the 'London' (No. 104) with the *Sturm-und-Drang*-ridden 'Funeral' (No. 44) and the witty 'Letter V' (No. 88) for counterbalance.

● *Naxos 8.550287* ● *1 CD* ● *Bargain price*
● *DDD* ● *1988* ⊙

The latest, which balances two angst-ridden works, 'Lamentatione' (No. 26) and 'La Passione' (No. 49), with the more genial No. 35 is also excellent.

● *Naxos 8.550721*

Some critics believe that Haydn can only be properly played on instruments of the period (either originals or re-creations); this is the so-called 'authentic' or 'period' lobby. The best period-instrument Haydn recordings were masterminded in the early 1980s by Londoner Derek Solomons with his ensemble L'Estro Armonico (which features some of the most accomplished period instrumentalists). Solomons never completed the full cycle (for reasons which aren't exactly clear), and of the 50 symphonies he did record, only 13 ever appeared on CD, and Sony, now masters of CBS, seem to have only two of these (relatively) easily available in the shops. These two, Nos. 45 ('Farewell') and 48 ('Maria Theresia'), must have some claim to be the best available performances; Solomons not only manages a great deal of fizz and fire in the faster outer movements, something which a lot of the period lobby are good at, he also shapes slow movements so that they remain interesting and aren't reduced to the condition of lift-muzak.

● *Sony Masterworks MK46507* ● *1 CD*
● *Mid-price* ● *DDD* ● *1985*

If these performances appeal, you might be lucky to find the only other Solomons set recently sighted in shops, *Haydn Symphonies*, Volume 7 (Nos. 35, 38, 39, 49, 58 and 59 'Fire').

● *Sony Masterworks M2K 37861* ● *2 CDs*
● *Mid-price* ● *DDD* ● *1982/4*

Of the ongoing Haydn projects, the most applauded is Roy Goodman's with the Hanover Band; at its best it is very exciting (the outer movements of some of the *Sturm-und-Drang* works are pulsating), but Goodman, like so many of his school, believes that the conductor's role in shaping phrases should be minimal, and this has an inevitable effect on the slower movements. This series is beautifully recorded, with clarity and a certain warmth.

● *Hyperion* ● *Full price* ● *DDD* ● *1990 onwards*

One of the great 'authentic' pioneers in this repertoire is Christopher Hogwood (and he has a barrow-load of awards to prove it), although his Haydn has to my mind a certain flatness and sameness of delivery. The Academy of Ancient Music is a fine ensemble of great players, and the Haydn cycle to date is superbly recorded.

● *L'Oiseau-Lyre* ● *Full price* ● *DDD* ● *1990 onwards*

Adam Fischer's cycle for Nimbus uses modern rather than period instruments, but stakes its claim for authenticity on being recorded in the Esterházy Palace at Eisenstadt. Actually, this isn't entirely authentic, given the number of later works written for venues in Paris and London. Again, there's a lot of lively playing from the Austro-Hungarian Orchestra, but Fischer either overdoes the phrasing in fast movements or doesn't phrase at all in slower movements. Still, this cycle has some very prestigious fans. Nimbus has a very 'purist' attitude to recorded sound, which can sound truthful and exciting, but can also echo a bit.

● *Nimbus* ● *Full price* ● *DDD* ● *1990 onwards*

I'd put in a few words of praise for Frans Bruggen's very colourful accounts with the Orchestra of the 18th Century, the only problem being that they're rather short measure (only two symphonies to a disc). I'd particularly recommend Nos. 90 and 93 ● *Philips 422 022-2* ● *Full price*
● *DDD* ● *1987*
and 99 and 102 ● *Philips 434 077-2* ● *Full price*
● *DDD* ● *1991*

There's much to be said, too, for Sigiswald Kuijken's issues, even if he does have an eccentric approach to rhythm (which means that he never gets boring). The disc combining Nos. 26, 52 and 53 is especially worth a listen.

● *Virgin Classics Veritas VC7 90743-2* ● *1 CD*
● *Full price* ● *DDD* ● *1988*

Trevor Pinnock and the English Concert have recorded all the nineteen *Sturm-und-Drang* symphonies; very polished as always, although my reservations about his C. P. E. Bach performances apply even more strongly here.

● *Archiv 435-001-2AX6* ● *6 CDs* ● *Full price*
● *DDD* ● *1988/90*

There is only one complete Haydn symphony cycle available, and that is performed on modern instruments by the Philharmonia Hungarica conducted by Antál Dorati. Unlike most of his current rivals as conductors of Haydn, Dorati has interpreted music right across the ages, and this versatility shows in the colour and tonal variation he manages to get out of his orchestra. The entire 32-CD set is rather a large financial commitment, though, and the sub-packages are still quite hefty. But especially recommended separate boxes are Nos. 84–95 ● *Decca 425 930-2DM4* ● *4 CDs*
● *Mid-price* ● *ADD* ● *1969–73*,
96–104 (plus three unnumbered) ● *Decca 425 935-2DM4* ● *as before*,
and Nos. 17–33 ● *Decca 425 905-2DM4* ● *as before*

A similar style to Dorati's, though recorded more recently, can be found in any of the 1970s/1980s releases featuring Sir Colin Davis conducting the Royal Concertgebouw of Amsterdam. This orchestra has some claim to be the most versatile in Europe, and Davis has a lively rhythmic sense matched by a keen view of how to phrase music. Particularly good are the effects in Nos. 82 ('The Bear') and 83 ('The Hen').

● *Philips 420 688-2* ● *1 CD* ● *Full price*
● *DDD* ● *1987*

I can't leave Haydn without mentioning a couple of recordings which don't form part of a cycle or part-cycle. First is a good, charming, mid-price release, from the late Sir Charles Groves and the English Sinfonia, of Nos. 92 and 104; excellent lightness of touch is the hallmark of these performances.
● *Pickwick IMP Classics PCD916* ● *1 CD*
● *Mid-price* ● *DDD* ● *1989*

Second is an inspirational rendering of No. 102 which might horrify the 'authentic' purists, as it is performed by the Vienna Philharmonic under the baton of Leonard Bernstein. This live-concert version is the kind of intense performance that has music critics using pretentious words like 'incandescent'.
● *Deutsche Grammophon Vienna Philharmonic 150th Anniversary Edition 435 322-2* ● *1 CD*
● *Mid-price* ● *ADD* ● *1971*

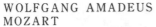

WOLFGANG AMADEUS MOZART

Mozart did compose very easily, as easily as the myth had it, and he would often be writing several things at once. He was also given to scatological humour, and had a great deal of self-confidence, bordering on downright arrogance, which didn't help his popularity with the dominant Italian clique in Vienna's musical life, or the aristocracy, or either of the Emperors – Joseph II, then Leopold II – who ruled between 1781 and 1791.

Mozart was, obviously, one of the greatest composers who ever lived, but this doesn't mean that every note he wrote was sheer genius. Such a thing is true of scarcely no composer, certainly not one who spent a lot of his life writing music to order, as Mozart did. I don't believe that his greatest genius is to be found in his symphonies, extraordinarily beautiful and enjoyable though many of them are. Most were written before he left Salzburg, and the last three were all

written in three weeks in 1788; so in some senses he seems to have abandoned the form. Had Mozart enjoyed a longer life and gone to England, as he was planning to do at around the time he died, then things might have been different; after all, if he'd lived to be 47, he'd have heard Beethoven's 'Eroica', and what might that encounter have stimulated? We can only dream.

Mozart's symphonies

Mozart's last symphony is No. 41, but there are at least 45 symphonies of one sort or another attributed to him. Some are very early and may possibly be the work of his father Leopold; authorities differ and some of the earliest, shortest pieces weren't included in the 'official' Mozart catalogue by Ludwig van Köchel, who gave Mozart's works their 'K numbers', which do the service of the opus numbers found in the works of later, more self-conscious composers.

All of those written before No. 35 belong to his 'pre-Vienna' career. Music historians tend to regard these ten Viennese years as 'the true blossoming of Mozart's genius' (or something similar in like words), but this doesn't mean that all symphonies prior to No. 35 are merely competent. Works like No. 29, No. 30, No. 31 ('Paris') and No. 32 (a mere eight minutes or so long, and more like an old-fashioned overture) are all, when played in the right spirit, enjoyable, melodic, with subtle orchestral textures; in the right performance, Mozart's use of woodwinds and trumpets and horns becomes something to marvel at. But it's the later symphonies that have most substance;

Wolfgang Amadeus Mozart

1756–1791

There's so much myth wrapped around Mozart's life now, especially after the (generally) excellent film *Amadeus*, that disentangling the truth isn't always easy. Wolfgang Amadeus Mozart was a child prodigy who had toured all the major courts and musical venues of Europe before he was ten, performing with his astute, slightly pushy, father Leopold and his elder sister (known in the family as Nannerl). From very early on he had a gift for writing down music he had heard only once; he also showed an early inclination to compose, and was already a recognised, seasoned composer by the time he was in his early teens. The Mozarts were principally employed by the most important man in their home town of Salzburg, the Cardinal Archbishop; unfortunately Cardinal Colloredo, elected in 1771, was, although an enlightened and liberal man, extremely frosty and not gifted with a great ear for music. During his adolescence, Mozart fretted more and more in the Archbishop's employment, tempted away by the success he enjoyed in Paris in the 1770s and by his glimpses of the imperial capital, Vienna. And so, around 1780, he broke away from Salzburg (very much against his father's advice) and thus became more or less without a patron, but based in Vienna. For a while everything went well; the Viennese (always ready to embrace novelty) took to Mozart and he tailored his music to suit popular taste. But around the middle of the 1780s, the Viennese got bored with him. However, the idea that it was all downhill from there doesn't fit the facts; Mozart had a lot of success in Prague, and much of his financial trouble stemmed from the fact that neither he nor his wife Constanze were brilliant managers of money (although after Wolfgang's death, Constanze showed herself to have bucked up in this department a little), rather than from any inherent lack of income or because a 'Philistine world' had turned its back on him. In his last year or so Mozart was doing rather well, and his being buried 'in a pauper's grave' tells us more about the burial traditions of 1791 Vienna (where individual graves had been banned as a hygiene measure) than about his finances.

>> *Concerto* 100, *Opera* 144, *Chamber* 220, *Choral* 257, *Orchestral* 275

quite apart from the fact that they're just longer, they also have more *gravitas*.

- **Nicknamed symphonies and No. 37**
- A few of Mozart's symphonies were named after the places where they

were first performed, and his final essay in the genre earned the sobriquet 'Jupiter' from English audiences for reasons which aren't entirely obvious. The 'named' works are:

Symphony No. 31 in D Major – 'Paris'
Symphony No. 35 in D Major – 'Haffner' (after its patron)
Symphony No. 36 in C Major – 'Linz'
Symphony No. 38 in D Major – 'Prague'
Symphony No. 41 in C Major – 'Jupiter'

Symphony No. 25 in G Minor is often known as 'the little G Minor', to distinguish it from the very famous 40th Symphony in G Minor (whose opening is one of Mozart's best-known tunes).

One quirk of the numbering of Mozart's symphonies is that there's no No. 37; for a long time it was believed that a symphony by Michael Haydn, which Mozart had copied by hand for a patron at the same time as writing the 'Linz' Symphony, was in fact his 37th.

MOZART AND SYMPHONIC FORM

Three-movement symphonic form persists in Mozart's symphonies almost until the end; even the relatively mature 'Prague' Symphony, written towards the end of 1786, sticks to the ternary form, although the first movement alone (with repeats observed) is twice as long as the whole of the 32nd Symphony, and the slow movement is also slightly longer than that entire piece. Haydn's influence can be detected in several of the later symphonies, especially in the way that the opening movement of No. 39 uses detailed development of its

• original thematic material; Mozart,
• with his great gift for melody, is
• rather prodigal with his invention in
• many of his symphonies, whereas
• Haydn liked to pursue a single theme.
• This influence can also be detected in
• the first movement of No. 35 ('Haffner').
• But the popularity of Mozart's
• symphonies, especially the last two,
• isn't due merely to hype; after all, an
• instrumental version of the beginning
• of the 40th (with a hideous
• guitar-and-drum beat) reached the top
• five of the Singles Chart in 1971,
• testimony to its enduring melodic and
• dramatic power. And it's in those
• words 'melodic' and 'dramatic' that
• you can define the appeal. Mozart is
• above all a 'dramatic' composer, which
• is why, I think that his true genius is
• to be found in the operas and the
• concertos. Opera is, of course, a
• dramatic form; so, too, is the concerto,
• consisting as it does (the way Mozart
• handles it) of both dialogue between,
• and dramatic opposition of, soloist and
• orchestra. Mozart made a lasting and
• remarkable impact upon the structure
• of both forms; as a symphonist he was
• not a notable revolutionary.

• DISCOGRAPHY
• Anyone shopping for Mozart is so spoiled for
• choice, especially after the glut of releases to mark
• the bicentenary of the composer's death, that the
• prospect becomes daunting. I should start this
• survey by saying that some of the cheapest
• Mozart symphony recordings are also the best;
• once again the excellent Naxos label rides to the
• rescue. Barry Wordsworth and Capella
• Istropolitana have recorded the 'fifteen greatest' on
• five separately available discs; very sensibly, Nos.
• 40 and 41 are also combined on a single disc,
• although they are also to be found elsewhere in
• the series, programmed with slightly earlier works.
• So if you don't want both together, or if you want
• more than two symphonies to a disc (typical of
• Naxos's value for money), your wish can be
• granted. Wordsworth's judgement of how faster
• and slower tempos interrelate in the symphonies
• (part of Mozart's dramatic technique) is almost
• impeccable. Symphonies Nos. 25 and 27–41 are
• available in this series; all the best Mozart
• symphonies for around £25 – need I say more?
• *Nos. 25, 32 and 41* ● *Naxos 8.550113;*

Nos. 29, 30 and 38 ● Naxos 8.550119;
Nos. 28, 31 and 40 ● Naxos 8.550164;
Nos. 34, 35 and 49 ● Naxos 8.550186;
Nos. 27, 33 and 36 ● Naxos 8.550264;
Nos. 40 and 41 ● Naxos 8.550299 ● all
Bargain price ● DDD ● 1988–90 ✪

Any 'completist' after all the forty-however-many symphonies has three main candidates. For my money, the finest cycle currently available offers the best of both worlds: awareness of Mozart's own performance traditions and ensemble size, played on modern instruments with modern concepts of phrasing and shaping of structure. The Australian conductor Sir Charles Mackerras and the Prague Chamber Orchestra bring out all the rhythmic and tempo excitement in Mozart's writing in their ten-disc set; the earlier works are given their due weight but aren't treated as though they're more significant than they really are; whilst the fresh playing and the precise rhythms make the more familiar works like the 40th and the 'Jupiter' seem new again. I always believe that a good performance of a familiar work makes it sound fresh, exciting, and even a bit dangerous, and Mackerras and the Prague Chamber Orchestra pass that test with flying colours. I strongly recommend the whole set.
● Telarc CD-80300 ● 10 CDs ● Special price ● DDD ● 1986–90

However, more cautious buyers, or people who aren't obsessive about full cycles, won't fail to enjoy the pairing of Nos. 40 and 41,
● Telarc CD-80139 ● 1 CD ● Full price ● DDD ● 1986

and may also want to try Nos. 38 ('Prague') and 36 ('Linz').
● Telarc CD-80148 ● 1 CD ● Full price ● DDD ● 1986

Period instrument devotees will be delighted with Christopher Hogwood's pioneering recordings made in the 1970s and early 1980s with the Academy of Ancient Music. Hogwood was one of the first conductors to record all the earlier works complete with harpsichord continuo accompaniment, employing an ensemble of something like the size Mozart would have written for. The results were a revelation, making 'the little G Minor' (No. 25) and other pieces from the early 1770s seem more substantial. However, I find the later symphonies a little thin in orchestral texture and the longer slow movements are, as in many 'authentic' performances, a bit lacking in phrasing and structure. Hogwood has also performed valuable scholarly service by recording the 40th Symphony twice, in the different scorings, one of which uses oboes, the other clarinets. This cycle is available in one large set or in smaller boxed sets; the best combines the second version of the 40th (using clarinets) and a host of earlier works, some possibly not Mozart's, as well as Michael Haydn's symphony long believed to be Mozart's 37th.
● L'Oiseau-Lyre 421 135-2 ● 3 CDs ● Full price

I'm also quite a fan of American conductor James Levine's recent cycle with the Vienna Philharmonic Orchestra, a traditionalist counterblast in the face

of the authentics. Inevitably, an orchestra of the size of the Vienna Philharmonic is less sprightly in the earlier works, but Levine is clearly aware of what has been going on in the musical world over the past couple of decades or so, and where he really comes into his own is, perhaps surprisingly, in works like Nos. 29 and 30 and others of that period. The excellent state-of-the-art recording makes every note clear, and the use of brass is astonishingly exciting. Perhaps Levine is a bit too 'Romantic' in No. 40, but that's forgivable. The notes to the later symphonies include a splendidly pugnacious essay by the conductor. The eleven-disc set is divided into two separate boxes: Early Symphonies ● Deutsche Grammophon 431 711-2 ● 5 CDs ● Special price ● DDD ● 1989–90, and Late Symphonies ● Deutsche Grammophon 435 008-2 ● 6 CDs ● Special price ● DDD ● 1984–9

There are countless excellent recordings of individual or paired (or larger combinations) of Mozart's symphonies. There's great pleasure to be had (and great value for money, too) in the releases from Jane Glover and the London Mozart Players; fresh, crisp, dramatic performances with no aggravating mannerisms, especially of the works from the 1770s. Best in this series is the disc combining Nos. 26, 27, 28, 30 and 32.
● ASV CDDCA 762 ● 1 CD ● Full price ● DDD ● 1991

Günter Wand is a German conductor of the old school, and his large-orchestra approach to Mozart is 'old-fashioned' in the best sense of the phrase – warm phrasing, carefully shaped; relaxed tempos; a plush sound. I wouldn't want to hear the earlier symphonies done like this, but his live Hamburg recording of Nos. 39 and 41 with the North German Radio Symphony Orchestra is gloriously enjoyable.
● RCA Victor Red Seal RD60714 ● 1 CD ● Full price ● DDD ● 1990

Going further back into 'traditional' music-making, one of the finest Mozartians of the grand old 'maestro' school of conductors was the Austrian Bruno Walter. His name will keep on cropping up in these pages, as several of the recordings he made towards the end of his life (he died in 1962) are classics. His gift for bringing out Mozart's natural melodic flow, especially in slow movements, is shown beautifully in his early-1960s renderings of the last six symphonies with the Columbia Symphony Orchestra.
● CBS/Sony M2YK 45676 ● 2 CDs ● Budget price ● ADD ● 1960–1

The next generation of the grand tradition which produced Walter (and figures such as Otto Klemperer and Wilhelm Furtwängler) was headed by Leonard Bernstein and Herbert von Karajan (its last surviving members are Sir Georg Solti and the reclusive German Carlos Kleiber). Bernstein can take Mozart outrageously slowly (and wait until we get to him doing Beethoven), but however slow, he's always dramatic in the extreme, full of power, especially on live recordings; if you prefer your Mozart done by large orchestras with a

• BEETHOVEN •

Romantic edge, his 1980s versions of the last six symphonies with the Vienna Philharmonic will give you hours of pleasure.
● *Deutsche Grammophon 419 427-2* ● *3 CDs*
● *Full price* ● *DDD* ● *1984–6*

Karajan is most often associated with the Berlin Philharmonic Orchestra, and all his virtues (and one or two of his vices) are evident on a 1970s version of Nos. 32, 33 and 36.
● *Deutsche Grammophon 429 804-2* ● *1 CD*
● *Mid-price* ● *ADD*

Another member of the 'maestro' school was Karl Böhm (who died in 1981); he made some fine Mozart recordings, and the budget-label reissue of Nos. 35, 36 and 38 with the Berlin Philharmonic has a lot of warmth to it and manages to keep the tempos flowing nicely and naturally.
● *Deutsche Grammophon 429 521-2* ● *1 CD*
● *Bargain price* ● *ADD* ● *1960–6*

The authentic lobby may feel a bit overlooked; after all, three of the greatest British stars of the movement – Trevor Pinnock, John Eliot Gardiner and Roger Norrington – have all made Mozart symphony recordings, and the great founding father of the concept, Nikolaus Harnoncourt, has recorded Mozart with the modern-instrument-playing Concertgebouw of Amsterdam. All have their good points, but I don't think any of these recordings quite makes it into the fairly exalted company I've described above. However, I've enjoyed recent Mozart symphonic releases by Sir Colin Davis for their determinedly old-fashioned approach (Davis's releases can be found on Philips, but they represent poor value for money in playing time).

━━━ ━━━ ━━━ ━━━

TAKING THE SYMPHONY INTO THE NINETEENTH CENTURY: BEETHOVEN

Beethoven's attitude to composition was signally different from that of his great predecessors. Mozart could turn out three symphonies in as many weeks; Haydn had a similar approach to such work. But for Beethoven the symphony – indeed almost all composition – was something to agonise over, to plan, and to labour on; each symphony had to be an artistic statement, a manifesto. With Beethoven, the symphony developed a form which became a proper arena for ambition.

Symphonies Nos. 1 and 2

The 1st Symphony eventually appeared, almost over-symbolically, in the year 1800; taking Haydn as a model, it sought to take stock of what had gone before and yet move the form forward. Although it is in the 'natural' key of C major ('natural' because it can be played on the piano using only the white notes; C major doesn't need any sharps or flats), the piece opens with a discord, almost posing a question. It is possible to talk about Beethoven's symphonies in such terms; the concept of rhetoric and grammar in music would have been something which he had studied in depth, and one of the best recent recordings of Beethoven's symphonies draws very much on this area of learning. By retaining a slow, declamatory introduction Beethoven is consciously looking back to Haydn's symphonic practice, but Beethoven allows his 'introduction' to go on for a surprising length of time, developing its own material. Already in this work Beethoven is concerned to play around with short, motif figures, drawing what he can out of these, interweaving them through the whole orchestra, creating a new kind of drama in music, one which combines Haydn's methods of construction with Mozart's delight in dramatic expression. It's easy to regard the 1st and 2nd Symphonies as 'apprentice' works which don't have quite the same overt 'revolutionary' nature as the great odd-numbered later symphonies (Nos. 3, 5, 7 and 9); but the mood-dramas in both these works draw on greater extremes than are found in the works of Haydn or Mozart, while the economy of material, the obsessive pushing and working-out of a single idea, reaches its first great culmination in the

41

Ludwig van Beethoven

1770–1827

▰

Early in his musical career, at the start of the 1790s, Beethoven studied for a while under Haydn, whom he respected enormously; yet he was disappointed at the progress he made with Europe's musical elder statesman. However, later in the 1790s Beethoven began to establish himself; there were two piano concertos, six string quartets, piano sonatas, violin sonatas, as well as a long, complex septet. Beethoven was based in Vienna for most of his life; while Haydn was on his travels in the 1790s, his new music found its way back there, and it was when Beethoven encountered Haydn's 'London' symphonies (the last twelve) that he started planning a symphony of his own. It took him five years to realise this ambition. During Beethoven's career old-style patronage of the arts began to crumble; Beethoven did have patrons, but strove in his music to please himself first and foremost.

It was in the early 1800s that Beethoven's hearing began to deteriorate, and in 1802 he faced the great crisis in his soul which resulted in the written document known as the 'Heiligenstadt Testament' (so-called because of the spa town Beethoven was visiting). This was a letter to his brothers expressing the full despair and trauma of a composer and musician doomed to lose the most important of his five senses. The astonishing thing is that Beethoven somehow drew artistic and spiritual strength from this crisis; his music after 1802 experienced a 'quantum leap', with major personal musical statements like the 3rd 'Eroica' Symphony (1805). After several rocky financial years, scarcely helped by the fact that Europe was undergoing the turmoil of the Napoleonic Wars all around him, Beethoven managed to consolidate himself at around the time when the tide turned against Napoleon (1812 or so), and from the middle of that decade he lived in semi-retirement, dedicating himself to music designed to stretch the limits of whichever form he was employing, culminating in the 9th 'Choral' Symphony (1824).

His reputation suffered a bit of an eclipse around 1820 or so, with the advent of 'Rossini-mania' in Vienna, but the 'Choral' Symphony was a great success; none the less Beethoven felt rather cut off from the world. To survive into one's 50s was rare in early-nineteenth-century Vienna; and apart from being deaf, he also had major problems with his bowels which rather preoccupied his conversation (held via a notebook).

>> *Concerto* 106, *Opera* 149, *Chamber* 222, *Choral* 258

repeated chords of the opening movement of the 'Eroica'.

The 1st Symphony was first performed in April 1800 and was respectfully received, although it took a while to become truly popular. A year later Beethoven began work on a 2nd Symphony in D Major, doing the most detailed composition in 1802 round about the time he wrote the 'Heiligenstadt Testament'. It's quite remarkable that in the face of encroaching deafness he produced the 2nd Symphony, which traditionally attracts epithets like 'genial' and 'good-humoured', and is written in a key associated with optimism and happy endings. Actually the work does have a tragic undertow; the first movement has several unexpected, slightly threatening changes of key, right from the slow introduction, which at first is lyrical and melodious, but then suddenly drops into the altogether less jolly D minor (not a natural modulation this; D major's 'relative' minor key is in fact B minor). As with the 1st Symphony, Beethoven uses sonata form in both the first and second movements, showing a desire to elaborate the symphony through its whole course; once again, this allows him to darken the mood at surprising moments. Where his 1st Symphony conventionally stuck to the minuet for its third movement (Beethoven never wrote a symphony with fewer than four movements, and the 6th, the 'Pastoral', has five), the 2nd uses the less specific scherzo, retaining, though, the shape of the Haydn-esque third movement with a central Trio section. The Finale is perhaps the most consciously backward-looking movement in either of the first two symphonies; although it picks up the high spirits of the

Scherzo, it shifts to a kind of orchestral writing which owes a great deal to polyphony, paying tribute to the fugal writing of Johann Sebastian Bach, and even to the vocal music of the Renaissance. The 2nd Symphony was premièred in April 1803, and whilst its critical reception was again lukewarm, Beethoven actually made a great deal of money out of it. This symphony could be called a kind of summation of life and personal influences up to that point; with his next symphony, Beethoven altered the rules and took symphonic form a great deal further.

Symphony No. 3 ('Eroica')
A lot of picturesque, and mainly true, stories surround the composition of the 'Eroica'. Principally there's the business of the dedication to Napoleon, whom Beethoven (and thousands of others in the early years of the nineteenth century) still saw as a friend to democracy and republicanism, the man to overthrow an old, effete order. Supposedly, when he heard that Napoleon had proclaimed himself Emperor, Beethoven tore up the dedication to the symphony with the cry 'Now he will trample on all human rights'. The symphony, written in 1803 and early 1804, emerged in April 1805 with the dedication '*Sinfonia eroica, composta per festeggiare il sovvenire d'un grand' uomo'* ('Heroic symphony, composed to celebrate the memory of a great man'). The Napoleon story is a nice one, and possibly partly true; but the 'heroism' of the symphony is probably much more enormous than that of one man at one specific time, and at least one of the 'heroes' Beethoven is celebrating is himself. In some ways, the 'Eroica' is the first Romantic symphony.

What makes the 'Eroica' different?

To begin with, its sheer size is something new. Not only are the opening and second movements massive, Beethoven also elaborates the Finale, shifting much of the symphony's dramatic weight to the end. In our day and age, we're used to end-directed music; it was, in truth, Beethoven who pioneered this concept, in works such as this and the 'Choral' Symphony (No. 9), as well as the piano sonatas and string quartets. The Finale is, in some ways, its own drama, with English and Hungarian music combining to 'win' a victory over the movement's other material.

The first movement takes sonata form and frees it from the classical straitjacket; not for Beethoven simple statements of theme, with tame recapitulations and all drama and excitement confined to the development. Beethoven uses the form as a vehicle for constant development, constant elaboration and rethinking of thematic material. Nothing stands still here, and at moments it seems as if Beethoven is trying to find a new way forward; in a good performance of the piece, when the repeated chords hammer away, it's as though the composer is trying to batter down the whole idea of tonality. There are references here and elsewhere to music Beethoven had written for a 'heroic ballet' about Prometheus, the Titan of Greek myth who gave mankind fire and thus, by implication, the civilising impulse. It's quite possible that in devising the structure for his music, Beethoven had a specific narrative 'programme' in mind. Certainly with the Funeral March of the second movement, it's possible to imagine the progress of a cortège in the music; the conductor Nikolaus Harnoncourt is convinced that Beethoven had a specific poem in mind when he wrote this movement (though Harnoncourt is reluctant to reveal which poem). Likewise in the Scherzo, the most conventional movement here, there's a reference to a scene from the Prometheus ballet involving the god Pan, and the music developed from this reference frames material reminiscent of hunting music. In the Finale, with its contending musical styles, Beethoven allowed himself remarkable freedom of form; fugal music interweaves with references to English and Hungarian folk music (intended as a tribute to the nations in league to defeat Napoleon), with the English dance theme especially representative of democracy and freedom.

The progress of the 'Eroica' is one from uncertainty in the opening movement and funereal grief in the second to exultation and rejoicing at the end. This emotional pattern became deeply ingrained into the consciousness of ambitious symphonists; we find it a century later in Mahler's 5th, and again in the later twentieth century in the symphonic writing of Sir Michael Tippett. Size, subjectivity and a nice Romantic legend, all have conspired to elevate the 'Eroica' in the musical pantheon, but what matters most, of course, is that it's one of the most challenging, stimulating and uplifting symphonies ever written. Naturally the 1805 audiences were rather perplexed by it, and even reviewers normally sympathetic to Beethoven resorted to terms such as 'garish' and 'bizarre'.

Symphonies Nos. 4 and 5

From the 'Eroica' onwards, there's a traditional belief that Beethoven wrote 'great' symphonies with odd numbers

and 'smaller' ones with even numbers.
It's true that the odd-numbered pieces
are more intense and immediately
dramatic, but ignore the even-numbers
– especially Nos. 4 and 8, which are
often overlooked – and you'll miss out
on some of Beethoven's most deeply
enjoyable and witty music. Symphony
No. 4 in B Flat Major, written mainly
in 1806 but finished in 1807/8
(opinions differ as to whether the first
performance was in the earlier or latter
year), does draw to some extent on the
styles and models of Haydn and
Mozart (especially in the elaborate
writing assigned to woodwind in the
second movement), but it also has the
personal stamp of Beethoven, the same
mingling of comic and tragic at
surprising moments in a way that's
quite disruptive at times. In the first
movement, Beethoven plays tricks
with sonata form once again, making
it 'difficult', towards the movement's
end, for the first subject to return; in
the Finale he uses what will become a
favourite game (particularly in the 7th
Symphony) of having a reprise which
keeps on starting up over and over
again, preventing more tranquil music
talking hold.

At the time he composed the 4th,
Beethoven was enjoying a period in
which he consolidated his popularity
(the same period also saw the
composition of the 4th Piano Concerto
and the Violin Concerto), and its
composition was comparatively easy.
To write it, he temporarily broke off
work on a symphony which he had
first begun to sketch in 1800, and
which finally appeared before the
public in December 1808. This was his
5th Symphony in C Minor, whose
opening notes are possibly the most
famous four notes in classical music,
perhaps the most famous in all
Western music.

**So why is Beethoven's 5th so
famous?**

Something about this symphony has
always seized the imagination of
writers, poets and others. The (to my
mind, rather twee and nauseating)
passage in E. M. Forster's *Howards
End*, in which the piece's progress is
seen in terms of goblins and other
spirits, like some latter-day fantasy
novel, is one of literature's best-known
examples of music 'explained' by a
programme assigned by a (not
especially musical) author. One of
Beethoven's earliest devotees, E. T. A.
Hoffmann (the man whose stories and
life inspired Offenbach's *Tales of
Hoffmann*) also wrote a long exegesis
of the 5th Symphony as descriptive of
another, dark realm of the imagination
('The lyre of Orpheus opens the gates
of the Underworld', was one of
Hoffmann's oft-repeated maxims).

The 5th Symphony doesn't mess
around with slow introductions; it gets
straight on with things, and that
opening four-note phrase is in many
ways the basis of everything else that
happens in all four movements.
Musically, this motivic use is very
exciting; not only is the whole first
movement obviously built out of the
phrase (both the sonata form's two
subjects use it very obviously), it's
also there, slowed down, as the main
rhythm of the second movement; it's
present in the ghostly horn calls in the
central section of the Scherzo; and
eventually it's inverted in the fanfare
figure of the triumphantly martial
Finale. Romantic writers have liked to
see this motif as symbolic of 'Fate
pounding on the door', although one of
Beethoven's more prosaic
contemporaries, the composer Carl
Czerny (who wrote one of the greatest
piano technique exercise manuals),
thought it represented 'the call of the

yellowhammer'. The rhythm of the motif is, of course, more or less that of the Morse code for the letter 'V', which was why the BBC used the opening phrase for its broadcasts to Occupied Europe during the Second World War; this fact, and the work's triumphant ending, have sometimes earned the symphony the sobriquet 'Victory'. Beethoven, however, may well not have seen it in such an obvious light, as he originally planned a more downbeat Finale. C minor is quite a neurotic, intense key, as well (the most neurotic work Mozart composed was in C minor, his 24th Piano Concerto).

Right from its first performance the 5th has had audiences in ecstasies (although quite a few critics considered it the work of a madman); my belief is that it's precisely the economy of material, this persistent, almost maniacal, working over again and again of this simple motif to profoundly dramatic effect, which accounts for the near-instantaneous grip the work can take (when properly performed). Here a complex representation of the depths of the human spirit is formed out of the simplest musical idea; a slightly 'Pseuds' Corner' explanation, I know, but quite possibly true for all that.

The 6th Symphony ('Pastoral')

It's often been suggested that Beethoven may have worked to a definite 'programme', a specific story or narrative, when composing. Be that as it may, only the 6th Symphony in F Major actually offers the audience any semblance of a story-line; each of its five movements has a descriptive 'title'. The first is 'Awakening of joyful feelings on arrival in the country', the second 'Scene at the brook', the third 'Merry-making of the country folk', the fourth simply

- 'Thunderstorm', and the Finale
- rejoices in the title 'Pastoral song.
- Feelings of happiness and gratitude
- after the storm'. The first two
- movements and the Finale fit fairly
- neatly into Beethoven's usual
- symphonic plan, and it's possible to
- see the third and fourth movements
- together as an elongated scherzo with
- a surprisingly dramatic ending.
-     All this specific descriptive
- instruction to the listener might look a
- bit like a throw-back to descriptive
- Haydn symphonic nicknames like 'La
- Chasse' and 'The Hen', but not a bit of
- it. Beethoven was after something a
- bit deeper than descriptive musical
- realism, even though the 'Pastoral'
- abounds in it (he'd been doing musical
- sketches of murmuring brooks since
- 1803, and there's birdsong interwoven
- with rustic peasant-like music); he was
- actually trying to push the
- symphony's territory a bit further, into
- 'not tone-painting, but feelings
- awakened by one's enjoyment of the
- country'. This was essentially inner
- description, precisely the kind of
- attitude to artistic scene-painting that
- was central to Romantic poets all over
- Europe (it's particularly like William
- Wordsworth's approach to his poetry).
- As such, the 'Pastoral', far from being
- a nice classical bit of mock-rusticity, is
- the direct forerunner of elaborate
- subjective programme music like
- Berlioz's *Symphonie Fantastique*,
- Liszt's 'Faust' Symphony, and the
- tone-poems of Richard Strauss. 'Scene
- at the brook' may seem a long way
- from the depiction of the evolution
- towards the *Ubermensch* ('superman')
- in the latter's *Also Sprach Zarathustra*,
- but the line relating the two is bold
- and clear.
-     The 6th Symphony was premièred
- at the same concert as the 5th, in
- December 1808, and enjoyed

immediate popularity. It is, perhaps, the most naturally melodious of Beethoven's symphonies, and it's long been a favourite of the advertising industry, which often uses parts of it to enhance 'idyllic' rural scenes.

The 7th and 8th Symphonies

After 1808, Beethoven went into a sort of 'semi-retirement'; in any case, the constant warring in Europe had such financial repercussions in Austria that music became a bit of an expensive luxury. In 1811, the Austrian currency was devalued by 80 per cent in order to finance the war that eventually drove Napoleon's forces out of Vienna. Beethoven retired to another spa town, Teplitz, and spent 1812 writing, amongst other things, his 7th Symphony in A Major, which was premièred in December 1813 on the same programme as his tone-poem *Wellington's Victory*. Both were amongst the most immediate and lucrative successes of Beethoven's career.

The 7th is one of Beethoven's most energetic symphonies, and has been described as 'the apotheosis of the dance'. Some critics have even suggested that the Finale, with all its madcap reeling, is descriptive of a drinking session. Whatever the truth of that, this symphony quickly makes its impact, after a stately introduction, with a lively first movement making great use of precise, springing rhythms, based on a Sicilian dance, and a second theme making advanced use of syncopation. And even the funereal second movement has a joyful second section (actually, as recent advertisement soundtracks have shown, even the funeral march of this movement lends itself to a dance beat). However, it's the Scherzo which often dominates memories of this symphony,

with its lurching Trio that refuses to lie down, even forcing its way into the Finale.

The 8th Symphony in F Major has always been overshadowed by its immediate 'neighbours' in Beethoven's symphonic output. It is a short work (it can, with certain conductors, be the briefest of all the symphonies), but Beethoven himself referred to it as a 'great' symphony. And, I have to say, it's one of my absolute favourites, full of jokes about rhythms and melodic and harmonic movement. It's been suggested, rather credibly, that part of its inspiration came from Beethoven's on-off friendship with Johann Maelzel, the inventor of the metronome. Although the instrument we know wasn't developed until 1815, Maelzel had produced an earlier version, and in all the movements of this work you can hear the thing ticking away, sometimes apparently distracting the music so that it tails off into nothing, as in the second movement, or almost stultifying the rhythmic freedom, as in the very precise Minuet. The first movement makes use, like the 'Eroica', of repeated chords which seem to be trying to break through a musical traffic jam; yet somehow the effect in the 8th Symphony is altogether more humorous and gentle. There's also a good deal of pure melodic material here; the first movement swings straight into a glorious, expansive, irresistible tune. I suspect that the work's comparative unpopularity lies in its resistance to Romantic myth-making, but in the right hands it's one of the sunniest pieces of music I know. It's extraordinary to think that Beethoven wrote it more or less simultaneously with the 7th, and that while working on both of them he had initial ideas for another symphony on a new and larger scale.

The 9th Symphony (the 'Choral' Symphony)

Beethoven's last symphony was as major an advance in the form as the 'Eroica' had been. Once again, proportions were increased, creating the first symphony to take more than an hour in performance. The logic of 'finale-directed' music was also taken to what was then its greatest extreme, and the 'Choral' became the first symphony to be completely dominated by its last movement; not simply because it's the longest movement of the four, but because of its role in surveying the thematic material of the three previous movements, rejecting each in turn for something else, and eventually lighting on the famous 'Ode to Joy' theme. And as with his 1st Symphony, Beethoven starts the work in a kind of tonal limbo, although rather than a discord he uses an indeterminate, unbased 'misty' atmosphere before allowing the D minor which is the symphony's home key to take root.

Beethoven had been planning a D minor symphony since 1811; and sketches for the piece's Scherzo have been found in notebooks dating from 1817. It was in 1818 that the composer conceived the idea of a symphony with a part for singers, but work on such a piece took a back seat to the composition of the huge *Missa Solemnis*. It was a £50 commission from the London Philharmonic Society which forced him back to the symphony, working on it through 1823 and the early part of 1824; in 1822 he had already decided to set words from Friedrich Schiller's 'Ode of Joy' as a chorus for part of this new symphony, thus fulfilling a long-cherished ambition to put this poem to music (the idea had first occurred to him in 1793).

- Many critics – some as
- distinguished as the composer Richard
- Wagner, on whom the 'Choral'
- Symphony was a major and vitally
- significant influence – have written
- 'programme' narratives for this
- symphony; but what we can be certain
- of is that Beethoven intended it as a
- universal message to mankind.
- Schiller's words, towards which the
- symphony is always working, are
- about universal brotherhood, and
- musical harmony is an obvious
- symbolic representation of that idea;
- we can see the first three movements
- as an attempt to reach a 'great musical
- statement', Beethoven's way of
- working out different musical forms.
- In the first movement, the music is
- constantly on the verge of
- disintegration and dissonance
- (discordant music) perpetually
- intervenes. There's a hint of the
- Finale's big tune on the woodwind,
- but this is always being overwhelmed.
- ‑ Beethoven brought the Scherzo
- forward to the second movement,
- which opens like a pistol shot and
- seems very exciting, until the listener
- gets the sense of this rhythmically
- vibrant music running out of control
- (Stanley Kubrick's decision to use it in
- his violent film *A Clockwork Orange*
- may give some idea of the threatening
- undercurrents), with calmer, sweeter
- music struggling to establish itself,
- and eventually the whole thing ending
- as abruptly as it begins. The slow
- third movement is an apparently
- tranquil (often called 'pastoral') theme
- and variations, but to create confusion,
- Beethoven uses two themes, and the
- listener becomes gradually less certain
- as to what the theme originally was.
- And any sense of harmony is
- destroyed by the crashing discord
- which opens the Finale, leading to that
- brief reprise of each of the themes of

the previous movements. Even when the orchestra has arrived at the great 'Joy' theme, it is disturbed by that initial discord again, and only the concord of four solo voices, a chorus, and the full orchestra, manages to gain control of the music and establish harmony – at last.

Although the Philharmonic Society had commissioned the work, Beethoven chose to première it in Vienna, with himself as conductor. The occasion, in May 1824, was a huge success; the story is that the crowd went wild with enthusiasm, whilst Beethoven, unable to hear their cheers, stood facing the orchestra until friends turned him round to face the audience.

With this final symphonic work, Beethoven had set new standards and created in composers' minds the concept of the 'important ninth symphony', a concept which was to endure like a superstition (it had an immediate impact on Franz Schubert who, when composing his own 9th Symphony, felt duty bound to create something of equal proportions and significance). Beethoven did make sketches for a 10th Symphony, but how long this might have taken, or what resemblance a finished 10th might have borne to the fragmentary stuff of the first movement we have, is highly debatable; the case for 'Beethoven's 10th' as part of the repertoire is in no way as persuasive as the case for the much more detailed plan of Mahler's unfinished 10th. And it is difficult to know how Beethoven could have followed the 'Choral'; it has a certain finality about it, even though Beethoven lived for three more years. A finality for Beethoven's work, that is; for the symphony itself, the 'Choral' represents a new starting point.

DISCOGRAPHY

Anyone building a serious classical music disc collection will almost certainly want at least one complete set of Beethoven symphonies – unless, of course, they don't find the works too enjoyable (and there's no rule that you have to; personal taste is personal taste, and there are no rights and wrongs, not even where Beethoven, Mozart and Bach are concerned). So the first part of this discography looks at the best (and one or two not so wonderful) complete Beethoven cycles; while the second picks out single recordings (some of which are part of complete cycles) of various symphonies that are worth hearing and/or having, offering a kind of eclectic, multi-component cycle.

The complete cycles

One of the most recent complete Beethoven cycles is also one of the most exciting; the much garlanded Nikolaus Harnoncourt cycle, winner of *The Gramophone*'s Recording of the Year Award for 1992. Harnoncourt was for a long time synonymous with period-instrument performance, having more or less invented it back in 1953. He combines the studious attention to detail derived from spending hours combing autograph manuscripts and immersing himself in both the musical thinking and, more importantly, the intellectual ambience of the composer's world, with the inspirational fervour of a maestro like Klemperer or Furtwängler (as an orchestral musician in Vienna since 1952, Harnoncourt has been conducted by all the greatest names). The Chamber Orchestra of Europe play modern instruments, except here the trumpets are old-fashioned 'natural' instruments without valves, making a much more exciting noise than the modern instrument. These recordings were taken from a cycle of live performances at the annual music festival at Graz in Austria in 1990; there have been no subsequent 'corrections' added in the studio (more or less standard practice for modern live recordings), although you'd never guess that. What Harnoncourt has achieved is to restore the excitement to Beethoven, as well as the wit and the humour; these performances have verve and sparkle. They go quite fast, although not uniformly, Harnoncourt is not a slave to the metronome, and he believes that the conductor's job is above all to shape the music. The sound is breathtakingly clear; the 5th becomes that nearly mad piece we read about in contemporary accounts; the 8th emerges from the shadows; the 'Eroica' is positively vertiginous. Only the 'Choral' is a bit of a let-down (oddly, because Harnoncourt conducted it marvellously live); so, rather than buying the boxed set, you may prefer to buy just Nos. 1–8 (which is possible; the component discs of this cycle, like all those discussed here, can be bought separately). I should say that one or two fellow critics whose opinions I respect have failed to be quite as overwhelmed; one, Michael Tanner, has called this cycle 'great fun, but not one to live with'. On the other hand, *The Gramophone* panel was ecstatic, and Hugh Canning of the *Sunday Times* has labelled it 'the best of the Beethovens'. I wouldn't be without it.
● *Teldec 2292-46452-2* ● *5 CDs* ● *Full price*
● *DDD* ● *1990* ○

On the other hand, the safest basic choice (and none the worse for being the safest) is the second of Karajan's Beethoven cycles; his 1960s recordings with the Berlin Philharmonic, now at budget price. Karajan was very good on Beethoven's grandeur, on the stormy drama, and the sheer scale of the works is well reflected in his versions. What I miss, and am prepared to pay a bit more for, is the wit and the reflective side. There's also a sense in which these performances are, once you know the music, a bit too conventional; the revolutionary Beethoven is lost, the raw edges rubbed smooth. Still, fine value for money.

● *Deutsche Grammophon 429 036-2* ● *5 CDs*
● *Bargain price* ● *ADD* ● *1960 onwards*

One traditionalist conductor of the old school whose Beethoven is well worth trying is Otto Klemperer. His wonderfully luxurious interpretations from the late 1950s/early 1960s were, when I was growing up, synonymous with Beethoven. The down side for some people is his famously slow speeds, but they never sound dull; they're simply natural, and surprisingly they don't detract from the humour of the 4th or the 8th; nor do the 5th or the 7th come across as any less exciting for being taken at a more measured speed than almost any other conductor would use. The playing of EMI's house orchestra, the Philharmonia (1945–64, succeeded by the self-governing New Philharmonia Orchestra), has splendid precision, and Klemperer's sense of the music's structure is completely sure; these versions of the 'Eroica' and the 'Choral' have some claim to the title 'best on record'.

● *EMI CDM7 63354/5/6/7/8/9-2* ● *6 CDs*
● *Mid-price* ● *ADD* ● *1958–61*

There are critics whom I greatly respect who regard Bernstein's cycle with the Vienna Philharmonic as essential listening. Personally, I find Bernstein's slow speeds in Beethoven the exact opposite of Klemperer's; they're wilful and inconsistent, pulling the music all over the place and re-creating Beethoven in the image of Bernstein. But if that's what you want . . .

● *Deutsche Grammophon 423 481-2* ● *6 CDs*
● *Mid-price* ● *ADD* ● *1970s*

There are also good, sound old-fashioned cycles from Günter Wand and the North German Radio Symphony Orchestra

● *RCA Victor Red Seal RD60090* ● *6 CDs*
● *Full price* ● *DDD* ● *1980s*

and, excellent value for money, from Wyn Morris and the London Symphony Orchestra.

● *Pickwick IMP BOX D2* ● *Bargain price*

These are to be much preferred to better-known names like Georg Solti and Claudio Abbado, who don't bring anything individual to Beethoven. Fans of the City of Birmingham Symphony Orchestra will be well satisfied with that orchestra's performances for Walter Weller (which includes a re-creation of the first movement of the 10th Symphony); the CBSO sounds almost Viennese in this set.

● *Chandos CHAN 8712/7* ● *6 CDS* ● *Full price*
● *DDD*

And the super-bargain LaserLight label's cycle is competitive in musical terms; Janos Ferencsik is an efficient conductor, even if the Hungarian Philharmonic aren't quite as refined as most of the orchestras mentioned hitherto.

● *LaserLight 15 900* ● *5 CDs* ● *Bargain price*
● *DDD*

As long as you don't have ideological objections to mono recordings, you should try to experience Beethoven in the hands of the century's two greatest conductors. Arturo Toscanini (1867–1957) brought a tension and power to Beethoven which led to the better-sounding of his two available cycles using suprisingly fast speeds. Some people find these performances so tense as to lack any evidence of Beethoven's human side, or his wit; others find them powerful.

● *RCA Victor Gold Seal GD 60324* ● *5 CDs*
● *Mid-price* ● *ADD* ● *1949–52*

There's another, much more horrible sounding, Toscanini set taken from old pre-war (and practically prehistoric) acetate discs; but if you can get through the crackles this actually has more variety and more humanity.

● *Nuova Era 2243/48* ● *6 CDs* ● *Mid-price*
● *ADD* ● *1939*

There are sound problems, too, with EMI's boxed set which constitutes a cheat of a 'cycle' conducted by the great Wilhelm Furtwängler (1886–1954); 'cheat' because these performances weren't recorded at the same time. Such problems are well worth enduring, as Furtwängler's vision of Beethoven has some claim to being one of the greatest. Both the Vienna and the Stockholm Philharmonic Orchestras are involved here (the recording of No. 2, the worst for sound, with the Swedish orchestra, is the only surviving Furtwängler recording of the symphony), but Furtwängler could inspire a school orchestra to sound like the world's best players. His Beethoven is seen very much through the spectacles of Wagner; these are graphic, dramatic performances, but Furtwängler also has a great sense of the power of melodic playing and gentle phrasing. This version of the 9th, recorded live at the 1951 Bayreuth Festival, has some claim, for all its problems of ensemble in the Finale, to be regarded as the most powerful recording of the piece ever made.

● *EMI CHS7 63606-2* ● *5 CDs* ● *Mid-price*
● *ADD* ● *1948–51*

And now for the authentic lobby. Inevitably, Christopher Hogwood and the Academy of Ancient Music are there (L'Oiseau-Lyre), as are the Hanover Band under Roy Goodman (Nimbus), although both sets strike me as distinctly thin and weedy. The most convincing authentic Beethoven, and the most controversial, is that of Roger Norrington and the London Classical Players. Norrington has taken all Beethoven's metronome marks, which the composer, at around the time he composed the 8th, inserted into the earlier symphonies as a favour to Maelzel, at their exact values. This leads to exceptionally fast tempos, except for one notorious moment in the Finale of the 'Choral' where the exact metronome mark is

about half the usual speed for the section. Norrington supposedly believes that the conductor's function is more or less that of the metronome. The result can be very exhilarating, and I have a great affection for his version of the 'Choral'; the sound the orchestra makes, despite smallish numbers and period instruments, isn't at all weedy, but the business of metronome marks is a bit suspect, to say the least. Debussy once said that he considered the metronome marking valid for about the first bar of any piece he wrote, and other composers have indicated a similar attitude. The danger of Norrington's approach is that the spiritual grandeur which Beethoven clearly intended flies out of the window. Still, it's worth hearing, the recording quality is astonishing, and in some moods it's great fun.
● *EMI CDS7 49852-2*   ● *6 CDs*   ● *Full price*
● *DDD*   ● *1986 91*

Individual symphonies
If you wanted to put an eclectic Beethoven symphony cycle together, it would be possible to make an excellent one by 'mixing and matching' from all the above. There are, however, a few non-cycle releases which really demand to be heard (and, in an ideal world, bought and cherished). First and foremost are three recordings by the reclusive conducting genius Carlos Kleiber. Kleiber, the son of a contemporary of Furtwängler, Klemperer *et al.*, conducts very rarely (these days his live performances are mainly confined to major opera houses, where he gives an electrifying account of Verdi's *Otello*; and his studio recordings can be numbered on the fingers and toes (the most recent was made more than ten years ago). He has recorded three Beethoven symphonies, Nos. 4, 5 and 7, unfortunately, these are all on separate recordings without any couplings. If they weren't so musically astonishing, they'd represent appalling value for money. Best of the three is the 5th; he draws from the Vienna Philharmonic a truly revolutionary, exciting, urgent performance – rarely has the orchestra sounded quite this athletic.
● *Deutsche Grammophon 415 861-2*   ● *1 CD*
● *Full price*   ● *ADD*   ● *1975* ☺

In the 7th, Kleiber keeps the exuberance tightly under control, another cunning twist. This, too, is an edge-of-the-seat performance, although the rhythms of the funereal second movement can be a bit disconcerting.
● *Deutsche Grammophon 415 862-2*   ● *1 CD*
● *Full price*   ● *ADD*   ● *1976*

The performance of the 4th, with the Bavarian State Orchestra (Kleiber's local band, so to speak; he lives near Munich), is a live recording, but there's no fall-off in quality; this is probably the single best available version of the 4th.
● *Orfeo C10084-2*   ● *1CD*   ● *Full price*   ● *DDD*
● *1982*

For versions of the 'Choral', it's hard to better Klemperer, Furtwängler or, in certain moods, Norrington, but there's a lot of liveliness and a good deal of the spiritual resonance the work demands in Sir Charles Mackerras's recording with the excellent Royal Liverpool Philharmonic

Orchestra, featuring the wonderful voice of the new star baritone, Bryn Terfel.
● *EMI Eminence CD-EMX2186*   ● *1 CD*
● *Mid-price*   ● *DDD*   ● *1991*

This consumer's guide can only begin to scratch the surface, but I'm pretty sure that anyone could put together, by careful sampling of all the recordings I've mentioned, a decent Beethoven cycle, with a few reserve versions to suit changes of mood.

━━━ ━━━ ━━━ ━━━

THE SYMPHONY AFTER BEETHOVEN: SCHUBERT

Beethoven's impact on the symphony can be clearly detected in the symphonic output of his near-contemporary Schubert. But it's Schubert's exceptional gift for melody which is the hallmark of the early symphonies (Nos. 1–6; there was for a long time a distinct problem in the numbering of Schubert's symphonies, and there is, by conventional numbering nowadays, no 7th Symphony; the piece sometimes referred to as Symphony No. 7 is only a realisation of a series of sketches).

Effortless, easy melodies are indeed the hallmark of Symphony No. 3 and, above all, the 5th Symphony in B Flat Major, probably the most recorded of the earlier works. Schubert wrote his first six symphonies between 1813 and 1818, that is, between the ages of 15 and 21; they are charming works, of similar proportions to the later Mozart and Haydn symphonies and to Beethoven's 1st. This is not to say they are unambitious; Schubert strives for interesting effects with dynamics, moving quickly from extreme loudness to extreme softness, while employing unusual combinations of high- and low-pitched instruments. Many of his original intentions have been submerged under a welter of 'improvements' by Schubert-lovers like Brahms, who felt that it was their duty to smooth out rough edges and

Franz Schubert
1797–1828

━━━

S chubert was born in Vienna and lived near Beethoven, whom he knew in most of Beethoven's later years, and whom he survived by less than a year. He was friendly with many of the leading intellectual figures of his day, including quite a few poets, and it was partly his involvement with writers that led to his fascination with the small 'art-song' (or 'Lied', to use the German term by which these works are often known), which concentrates on setting short (or relatively short) poems. He was tutored in his teens by none other than Antonio Salieri (1750–1825), Mozart's supposed great rival (although very definitely *not* his murderer); the job Salieri did on Schubert suggests that he can't have been quite the talentless hack the film *Amadeus* would have us believe. In the first part of his musical career Schubert found composition effortlessly easy, but in the early 1820s something changed; a whole range of incomplete works, including the famous 'Unfinished Symphony', show that he was trying to reach deeper within himself in all forms in which he wrote (especially the symphony) and produce music which was somehow more 'momentous'. It was at about this time, too, that he was first ill with the syphilis which was eventually to kill him. Much of Schubert's work was unheard during his short life, especially after the Rossini craze hit Vienna around 1820, although his very supportive friends organised evenings known as 'Schubertiades' devoted to his music.

>> *Opera* 159, *Chamber* 227, *Choral* 260

emend unusual effects, so that Schubert's symphonies conformed to the way Brahms (or whoever) would have written them. Unfortunately, these Schubert-lovers weren't above adding their 'improvements' to the original autograph manuscript, which has made life difficult.

Whatever the originality of the first six symphonies, Schubert clearly developed 'symphonic ambition'. In 1822 he began work on the B Minor Symphony, known to us as his 8th, but better known as the 'Unfinished' Symphony. After two, comparatively long, movements, he abandoned it,

- leaving a full draft in piano score of a
- scherzo third movement, but never
- bothering to return to it. This
- abandonment has been subjected to
- Romantic interpretation, and is the
- punchline of hundreds of comedy skits,
- but no one knows why it happened.
- Schubert left a lot of work unfinished
- at this time, symptomatic, possibly, of
- a sea-change in his approach to
- composition. There are unfinished
- songs, two more false symphonic
- starts, an incomplete piano sonata, and
- other smaller fragments, all dating
- from around this period of 1822–4.
- Perhaps it was the lack of a suitably

impressive and grandiose Beethovenian finale which led Schubert to leave the symphony at two movements. However, he clearly thought of it as a self-sufficient work, because he presented these movements to two friends who had given him a diploma on behalf of a music society (although the 'Unfinished' wasn't made public until 1836).

In fact, the 'Unfinished' might have turned out, if completed, to have been monstrously large. The kind of scale Schubert had in mind can be gauged from his last symphony, No. 9, the 'Great' C Major (so called to distinguish it from No. 6, also in C major, a piece which stands as a kind of riposte to the dominant popularity of Rossini). He wrote the piece between 1825 and 1826 (much of the initial writing was done while on holiday in Upper Austria), but revised it again in the year of his death. This is a work altogether different, deeper and bigger than any other Schubert symphony, although there are critics who are in two minds about the work's greatness. It seems fairly likely that the composer believed that all future symphonies would be judged against Beethoven's, especially after the appearance of the 'Choral' in 1824. Schubert's 9th retains the four-movement form, in the conventional order (Scherzo third), but the Scherzo is enlarged to more or less the same length as the outer movements; and whilst the Schubertian melodic flow is present through the whole work, there's an almost conscious tribute to Beethoven in the way that Schubert uses rhythmic figures as motivic and thematic material from which the movements are built. As with the earlier symphonies, Schubert tries to make unusual alliances of instruments, unusual sound combinations,

something which particularly attracted Schumann to the work when he began to write symphonies some twelve to fourteen years later.

DISCOGRAPHY
One complete Schubert symphony cycle stands head and shoulders above the rest; unfortunately, it's also more expensive than the others, not just because it's full price, but because it includes two complementary overtures and an orchestration of the Grand Duo. Like Harnoncourt's Beethoven cycle, it features the Chamber Orchestra of Europe, this time conducted by (probably) the most prestigious conductor alive at the moment, Claudio Abbado. Abbado is something of a Schubert scholar, and prepared for this cycle by going back to the manuscripts and trying to locate Schubert's original intentions. The result is something quite startling, especially in the earlier symphonies, always fresh and exciting; the traditional Schubertian charm is there, but something a little more challenging too. The whole set won a *The Gramophone* Award in 1989; the 'Unfinished' and the 9th (the 'Great' C Major) are available separately at mid-price.
● *Deutsche Grammophon 423 651-2* ● *5 CDs*
● *Full price* ● *DDD* ● *1988* ○

There aren't any other Schubert cycles I could recommend quite as fully, although at the time of writing a full set is expected from Nikolaus Harnoncourt (this time with the Concertgebouw) whose researches are likely to produce something quite different. Meanwhile, at bargain price, there's a very enjoyable, if slightly old-fashioned, set from Istvan Kurtesz and the Vienna Philharmonic; there's a welcome lightness of touch in the earlier symphonies, but the bigger works aren't quite as convincing. Good value and excellent sound, though, all in all.
● *Decca 430 773-2* ● *4 CDs* ● *Bargain price*
● *ADD* ● *1962–71*

Karl Böhm and the Berlin Philharmonic are better with the later works, although arthritic with the earlier ones, and it's very much smoothed-down Schubert – which may of course be to your taste.
● *Deutsche Grammophon 419 318-2* ● *4 CDs*
● *Mid-price* ● *ADD* ● *1963–73*

Individual symphonies
Testimony to both Schubert's genius and the greatness of one of the most colourful figures ever to grace the British music scene is the reissue of Sir Thomas Beecham's performances of Nos. 3, 5 and 6 with the Royal Philharmonic Orchestra. Beecham (1879–1961) had a real feel for Schubert's melody and his rhythmic sense, and three symphonies on one mid-price disc is a bit of a steal.
● *EMI CDM7 69750-2* ● *1 CD* ● *Mid-price*
● *ADD* ○

Most people are likely to want the 8th Symphony in B Minor, the 'Unfinished', more than any other symphony, and there are several very attractive versions available on single discs, in various combinations with other symphonies. The most remarkable comes from Carlos Kleiber and the Vienna Philharmonic, with all the work's dramatic contrasts reinforced but none of the lyricism lost; there's also an extraordinarily fast, but beautifully shaped version of No. 3.

● *Deutsche Gammophon 415 601-2* ● *1 CD*
● *Full price* ● *ADD*

There's a fully up-to-date, state-of-the-art digital version of the 'Unfinished' featuring the San Francisco Symphony conducted by Herbert Blomstedt. I wonder whether it isn't more of a triumph of the recording technician's art than musicianship, but both the 'Unfinished' and the accompanying No. 5 are given performances which marvellously balance the light and shade from this highly accomplished outfit under a very versatile conductor.

● *Decca 433 072-2* ● *1 CD* ● *Full price*
● *DDD* ● *1992*

Various versions of the 'Unfinished' by Herbert von Karajan are highly praised in some CD guides, but I find him a bit heavy-handed for Schubert; what we get is Karajan's idea of what Schubert *should* have written. A more contemporary conductor, one who can be idiosyncratic to the point of wilfulness, is Giuseppe Sinopoli; his version of the 'Unfinished', though, is amazingly concentrated and very detailed, with some lovely sound-recording.

● *Deutsche Grammophon 427 818-2* ● *1 CD*
● *Mid-price* ● *DDD*

Turning to the 9th (the 'Great' C Major), various competing versions offer different strengths. I have a great affection for Roy Goodman and the Hanover Band's atmospheric performance, where the period instruments seem to serve to prevent the orchestral sound becoming too stodgy, while the sound of the natural horns is quite ravishing. The problem is that Nimbus's 'natural' recording sound and the acoustics of All Saints' Church, Tooting, create an echo overhang which is either charming or appalling, depending upon your point of view.

● *Nimbus NI 5222* ● *1 CD* ● *Full price*
● *DDD* ● *1990 – also available at Mid-price in the Woolworths 'Classics' Series*

Roger Norrington has recorded the Schubert symphonies, and if you like his 9th, you may want to follow the experience further; it's the usual rapid-tempo chase (much quicker than the Hanover Band), superbly recorded.

● *EMI CDC7 49949-2* ● *1 CD* ● *Full price*
● *DDD* ● *1988*

One of the best authentic Schubert combinations is Sir Charles Mackerras and the Orchestra of the Age of Enlightenment; Mackerras has conducted works from all periods, and so he shapes, phrases, and serves the music with greater sensitivity.

● *Virgin Classics VC7 90708-2* ● *1 CD* ● *Full price* ● *DDD* ● *1988*

The versions by Sir Georg Solti (Decca) and Sir Adrian Boult (EMI) also have their fans. But I reserve a lot of affection for a live performance from 1957 featuring the Vienna Philharmonic under Hans Knappertsbusch. Known mainly as a Wagnerian, yet not always the most authoritarian of conductors, Knappertsbusch leads the orchestra through a lyrical, slowish, yet always exciting account. They don't make them like this any more.

● *Deutsche Grammophon Vienna Philharmonic 150th Anniversary Edition 435 328-2* ● *1 CD*
● *Mid-price* ● *ADD* ● *1957*

THE PERSONAL VISION: BERLIOZ AND THE *SYMPHONIE FANTASTIQUE*

Hector Berlioz (1803–1869) produced the *Symphonie Fantastique* in 1830, but in many ways it belongs outside the mainstream of the history of the symphony, so strongly personal a work is it. Beethoven put himself and his own struggles into the symphony, and so, in his later works, did Schubert; Berlioz, though, bled his life and his personal problems all over the music, even to the extent of providing a story-line based on his despair at ever getting the woman he loved. It was in 1827 that he saw the Irish actress Harriet Smithson perform the role of Ophelia at Covent Garden, and fell in love at first sight (Berlioz did everything headlong and on a grand scale – before encountering Smithson in this role he had already identified strongly with Shakespeare's unstable Dane). The resulting frenzy of ecstasy, depression, drug-taking, and morbid self-preoccupation precipitated the *Symphonie Fantastique*.

Quite apart from the overt programme Berlioz provided, the work had some musical innovations which were to prove of immense importance, although not necessarily imediately, to the development of the symphony. The immense variety within certain movements, especially the violent Fantasy of the Finale, followed on from the tempo and mood swings found in Beethoven's longer movements (especially the Finale of the 'Choral' Symphony); the concept of the *idée fixe*, though, looked forward to the operas of Wagner. The *idée fixe* (literally 'fixed idea') is a musical phrase or motif which occurs early in the first movement and then recurs unchanged through the rest of the symphony, at least once in each movement, denoting the object of the composer's devotion. But, so as to be larger than life, and to depict the scale of his grandiose love, Berlioz decided that his symphony would be in five rather than four movements; instead of a Beethovenian scherzo or a Haydn-esque minuet, he would have a waltz and also a march, and these two movements would surround the slow movement, which would provide the symphony with a centre of repose.

Berlioz originally wanted to distribute his massive narrative description of the work at its première, although he relented and limited the descriptive elements to the movements' titles, as long as these were printed in full. The whole story is supposed, ultimately, to be a drug-induced fantasy (opium-taking was *de rigueur* for the Romantic artists of the 1820s and 1830s). The first movement, 'Rêveries – Passions', is about drifting memories, vague impressions and the establishment of the *idée fixe* which, here, is a long violin melody. 'Un bal' ('A ball') places the lovers in a sumptuously elegant setting; Berlioz's Waltz is a most accomplished piece of dance music, and its use of four harps is entirely new to symphonic form. In fact, a lot of Berlioz's specific instructions about the placement of musicians and such things as the angles at which drums were to be hit, or the type of material from which

- both drumskin and drumstick-head
- were to be made, were all novel and
- revolutionary. 'Scène aux champs'
- ('Scene in the country') is an intimate
- movement, conversational, drawing on
- effects similar to those of Beethoven's
- 'Pastoral' Symphony. It's in the fourth
- movement, 'Marche au supplice'
- ('March to the Scaffold') that Berlioz's
- imagination begins to run riot; the
- lover has killed his beloved out of
- frustration; the music denotes jeering
- crowds, and the central march
- represents the triumph of a grim and
- ruthless justice. At the crucial moment
- before execution, the *idée fixe* turns up
- very briefly (a vision in the lover's
- dying moment). The music has a
- sardonic quality born of deep
- self-expression which is unrivalled in
- the symphony until the unsettling
- scherzos found in Mahler's
- symphonies. The Finale ('Songe d'une
- nuit de Sabbat' 'Dream of a witches'
- Sabbath') depicts just such a sabbat,
- and includes the medieval requiem
- chant 'Dies Irae' (also used by Liszt in
- his work for piano and orchestra,
- *Totentanz*, 'Dance of the Dead'). This
- is mayhem on a grand scale; the arty
- way of putting it is, I believe, 'Grand
- Guignol'.
- Berlioz's *Symphonie Fantastique*
- prepared the way for the musical
- vocabulary of the form to be extended;
- you could be vulgar, way over the top,
- in a symphony, although in some
- ways this lead wasn't really followed
- up until Tchaikovsky began writing
- symphonies. Certainly more than a few
- of Berlioz's immediate contemporaries
- were less than impressed; while
- Schumann described him as 'a
- virtuoso of the orchestra' (although
- backhandedly then suggesting that the
- symphony didn't require any great
- virtuosity from its players), Rossini
- was highly dismissive of the piece,

and Mendelssohn called it 'loathsome and indifferent drivel'. However, the work always had its devotees from the start, and is deeply popular today. And did he get the girl? Yes, after Harriet Smithson had spent about two years throwing all his love letters in the bin, she and Berlioz eventually married in 1833. And a complete disaster it was, too.

DISCOGRAPHY
The *Symphonie Fantastique* has done well on record, and there's been a recent glut of new recordings as the period-instrument lobby have grabbed hold of it eagerly. Even more than with Mozart, Haydn and Beethoven, there are two attitudes to this; the welcome with open arms, and the feeling that period instruments, however 'authentic', are not what the composer would choose in preference to modern instruments, with their fuller, richer tone. Still, the period lobby have to acknowledge that one of the most consistently exciting conductors of this work on record over three decades has been Sir Colin Davis, and his latest version – with the Vienna Philharmonic – not only employs state-of-the-art digital recording technology, but is his most profound, most powerful, most expressive reading yet. Obviously the calibre of the orchestra has something to do with this, but not all conductors manage to bring out the subtlety and pathos of the reflective moments as well as the vulgar excitement. Davis's earlier versions are good, too, but this is the best.
● *Philips 432 151-2* ● *1 CD* ● *Full price*
● *DDD* ● *1991* ○

If you like period instruments, then you might be tempted by John Eliot Gardiner's recent version (also Philips), though it's a bit one-dimensional and thin. The period recording of this work which works best is Roger Norrington's; surprisingly the final two movements manage not to disappear in a fluster of breakneck tempos.
● *EMI CDC7 49541-2* ● *1 CD* ● *Full price*
● *DDD* ● *1988*

In a Romantically imaginative work like this, a Romantically imaginative conductor can either be a great bonus or an utter liability. In his 1976 recording with the French National Orchestra, Leonard Bernstein shows his great conducting genius, producing a flamboyant, illuminating version with every loud and soft part of the score really underlined. This is a performance which suggests that Berlioz was probably totally mad. Brilliant.
● *EMI CDM7 69002-2* ● *1 CD* ● *Full price*
● *ADD* ● *1976*

Another imaginative performance, although with a slightly different orchestral timbre, comes from Sir Georg Solti and his highly polished Chicago Symphony Orchestra. Due to various recording

techniques there's a great emphasis on the lower-pitched instruments, and that has a tremendous effect. Solti also brings out the picture-painting in the 'Country Scene' of the third movement more effectively than almost anyone else.
● *Decca Ovation 417 705-2* ● *1 CD*
● *Mid-price* ● *ADD* ● *1977*

Finally, the energetic side of the work comes out well in a bargain-price version by the Royal Philharmonic Orchestra under the Mexican conductor Enrique Bátiz. The weakness is the third movement, which, as a more subtle, slower section, doesn't play to the conductor's strengths, but the Finale is really ghastly (in the way the composer intended).
● *ASV Quicksilva CD QS 6090* ● *1 CD*
● *Bargain price* ● *DDD* ● *1987*

● ● ● ●

THE RESPECTABLE ROMANTIC SYMPHONY (1830–1860): SPOHR, MENDELSSOHN, SCHUMANN

Symphonic composition until 1840 was dominated by the erstwhile child prodigy Felix Mendelssohn (occasionally Mendelssohn-Bartholdy, 1809–1847), who wrote five symphonies for full orchestra, as well as twelve early shorter pieces for string orchestra only which are known as the 'String Symphonies'. The next major composer whose symphonies still enjoy a place in the repertoire is Robert Schumann (1810–1856), although it's fair to say that the dominant, most influential symphonic force through the active careers of both composers was the now neglected Louis Spohr (1784–1859). Spohr's nine symphonies, written between 1811 and 1850 (from well inside Beethoven's lifetime to the point at which Brahms was getting launched on his musical career) were of two distinct types: five traditional, Classical four-movement works, on a scale similar to early Beethoven or late Haydn/Mozart symphonies; and four titled programmatic works, which attempted to portray vast cosmic questions and ideas in musical terms (not for Spohr the self-centred programme of a Berlioz) – the 7th rejoices in the name 'Earthly and Divine in Human Life', with movements entitled 'The World of Childhood', 'The Age of Passion', and 'Final Victory of the Heavenly'. This symphony, composed in 1841, inspired Schumann to say of Spohr 'Let us follow him in art, in life, in all his striving . . . May he stand with our greatest Germans as a shining example.' In his 'programme' symphonies, Spohr attempted to break free of the four-movement form (a friend had suggested this might be a good idea, as it might head off too many comparisons with Beethoven), or at least to change the way the movements worked; less rigid sonata form, less clinging to the shape Beethoven and Schubert employed.

Spohr's music doesn't sound so amazingly revolutionary to our ears; in fact, it has just the slightest edge of hackneyed contrivance every now and again. However, there's a great deal of melodic pleasure to be had from his music, and given the influence it had on figures like Wagner, it's amazing that it has become so neglected. After all, in Gilbert and Sullivan's *The Mikado* Spohr is mentioned in the same breath as Bach and Beethoven.

DISCOGRAPHY
Some of Spohr's symphonies have been released on the specialist Marco Polo label; for a sample I'd suggest Nos. 7 (discussed above) and 8 (a conventional, charming work in G major).
● *Marco Polo 8.223432* ● *1 CD* ● *Full price*
● *DDD* ● *1991* ✪

Others are available on Orfeo. It would be interesting to see a really top-flight orchestra and conductor get hold of Spohr's symphonies and subject them to state-of-the-art recording; it would certainly be more interesting than yet another uneventful stroll through Mozart, Beethoven or Brahms.

MENDELSSOHN: CAN YOU TELL SCOTLAND FROM ITALY?

Mendelssohn's symphonies, of which there are five, are deeply conventional, entirely safe Romantic works, which go in for lots of impressionistic scene-painting inspired by his travels and, to a lesser extent, by his personal beliefs. Written between 1824 and (about) 1840, they were subject to quite a few revisions, so that more than one contemporary became confused about the numerical sequence, with comic results, as will be seen.

Mendelssohn's mastery of melody is enviable, and it's thanks to that, rather than any deeply revolutionary quality, that two of his symphonies in particular – the 3rd ('Scottish') and 4th ('Italian') – remain very popular. Mendelssohn's 2nd Symphony, 'Lobgesang' ('Song of Praise'), uses voices as well as orchestra; but, impressive though this piece can be, it's fair to say that it's the 3rd and 4th Symphonies which are most immediately accessible. Each was inspired by travel and seeks to capture the atmosphere of the country described; the opening tune to the 'Italian' must be one of the most infectiously catchy, uplifting beginnings to a symphony ever written. The Scottish aims for a gloomier, darker atmosphere; it was partly inspired by the ruins of Holyrood and the tragic story of Mary, Queen of Scots. However, let critics beware: these works appeared before the public out of numerical order, so that No. 4 was premièred before No. 3, and Robert Schumann wrote a glowingly warm review of a symphony which to him reeked of 'old melodies sung in beautiful Italy' – and, of course, it turned out that he

Mendelssohn

1809–1847

Mendelssohn was a formidably popular composer from his youth, loved by rich people all over Europe, and always a welcome guest with the British Royal Family – he and Queen Victoria and Prince Albert used to have delightful musical evenings together. Some of his best, most adventurous music was written before he was twenty (the Octet for Strings, one of the greatest of all chamber works, was composed when he was a mere stripling of sixteen). His older sister Fanny was a gifted pianist, and her early death, a few months before his own, affected him deeply. Quite apart from the music he composed himself, Mendelssohn was also responsible for reviving interest in Johann Sebastian Bach, who was very neglected in the first years of the nineteenth century.

>> *Concerto* 112, *Chamber* 230

was writing about the 'Scottish' Symphony. These two pieces frequently turn up on the same recording, and naturally complement each other as the 'Scottish' is in A minor, whilst the 'Italian' is in A major.

For me, Mendelssohn's greatest symphonic achievement, and a key work in the Germanic repertoire which is so central to music, is his Symphony No. 5 in D Minor, the 'Reformation', which, whilst it hasn't exactly been ignored, tends to be a bit overshadowed by the 'Scottish' and 'Italian'. The 'Reformation' seeks to enshrine the Lutheran tradition of German choral music in instrumental symphonic form (Mendelssohn doesn't use a choir), starting with a chord sequence which subsequently reappears as the basic thematic material for Wagner's final, massive opera *Parsifal* (1882); Mendelssohn's use of the sequence here, some 40 years before Wagner got hold of it, is eloquent and passionate. The symphony proceeds

from this point to a triumphant Finale centring on 'Ein' feste Burg', a hymn tune attributed to Martin Luther (and used by Bach as the basis for his Cantata No. 83). Although Mendelssohn clearly couldn't know what Wagner was going to do, this symphony stands as a turning-point in German music, drawing on the past with Romantic fervour, and achieving a sense of spiritual depth which is perhaps missing from (and perhaps was never intended in) the rest of Mendelssohn's symphonies.

DISCOGRAPHY
The one outstanding complete Mendelssohn cycle can fairly claim to offer the top version of Symphony No. 2 ('Lobgesang'), and its accounts of the 'Scottish', 'Italian' and 'Reformation' are hard to beat. This is Claudio Abbado's second cycle with the London Symphony Orchestra, and is much more colourful than his earlier performances with the same orchestra (available at Mid-price on Decca). In the recent recordings Abbado avoids the temptations to sentimentality which have, perhaps, driven the 2nd and 5th Symphonies underground (in some performances they can sound like out-takes from the TV programme *Songs of Praise*, which fatally misunderstands their nature). Abbado also judges the atmospherics of the

'Scottish' and 'Italian' very pleasantly; taken either as a set, or as individual component discs, these are well worth the time and the money. The complete set includes excerpts from the eternally popular incidental music to *A Midsummer Night's Dream*, and such eternally popular works as *Fingal's Cave* ('The Hebrides' Overture), to ensure good value.
● *Deutsche Grammophon 415 353-2* ● *4 CDs*
● *Full price* ● *DDD* ● *1983–5* ⊘

There are plenty of pairings of Nos. 3 and 4 around, but good ones are harder to find than one might expect. The two Abbado performances from the set discussed above are generously available very cheaply.
● *Deutsche Grammophon 3D Classics 427 810-2*
● *1 CD* ● *Bargain price* ● *DDD* ● *1985*

For sheer effervescence with an interestingly neurotic edge, I have a great deal of affection for James Levine's performances with the Berlin Philharmonic. This is vast-scale Mendelssohn; it bounces along at driving speeds, and the effect is an excitement I've not encountered anywhere else.
● *Deutsche Grammophon 427 670-2* ● *1 CD*
● *Full price* ● *DDD* ● *1988*

Employing more or less the same tactics, Roger Norrington and his period-instrument London Classical Players have won great praise from some, but the orchestral sound is a bit too thin for my taste; the atmosphere of Scotland and Italy are a bit lost – watery mists and thin watery sunshine. But for those who like this sort of thing . . .
● *EMI CDC7 54000-2* ● *1 CD* ● *Full price*
● *DDD* ● *1990*

In the same sort of vein, and not to all tastes (but very much to mine) Nikolaus Harnoncourt and the Chamber Orchestra of Europe have attempted these two works, preoccupying themselves with rhythm and precise dynamics (loudness and softness). The result is a bit dry for some, but I find it grows and works on its own terms.
● *Teldec 9031-72308-2* ● *1 CD* ● *Full price*
● *DDD* ● *1991*

For No. 5 (the 'Reformation'), apart from the Abbado version mentioned above, there is a good deal of lobbying for a Mid-price recording of Karajan and the Berlin Philharmonic, which is supplemented by an excellent performance of Schumann's No. 3 (the 'Rhenish'). Karajan tries too hard to turn the Mendelssohn into something Wagnerian, although at least he avoids the *Stars on Sunday* approach, but the work's inner warmth is a bit mislaid.
● *Deutsche Grammophon 419 870-2* ● *1 CD*
● *Mid-price* ● *ADD* ● *1973*

My favourite 'Reformation' is a glorious performance framed by assaults on No. 4 and the Overture to *A Midsummer Night's Dream*, and features the English Chamber Orchestra under Raymond Leppard. This is a beautifully judged, warm account, which understands the scale of the

work; you don't have to blaze away like the Berlin Philharmonic to get the listener's attention. Although the rest of the disc isn't of quite the same quality, at this price, that's less important.
● *Erato Bonsai Collection 2292-45932-2* ● *1 CD*
● *Bargain price* ● *ADD* ● *1977*

━━ ━━ ━━ ━━

ROBERT SCHUMANN

Is Schumann a Classical or a Romantic composer? To some extent he shows how easily these labels can get blurred. His life is an extremely Romantic affair; sometimes his work shows traces of the kind of flamboyance with which the term 'Romantic' is usually associated in music. But he belongs much more to a kind of Classical tradition of Romanticism, like his great idol Beethoven, especially when put next to figures like Tchaikovsky, Rachmaninov, Richard Strauss or Mahler.

Schumann wrote two of his four symphonies before the end of 1841; confusingly, these were No. 1 in B Flat Major ('Spring') and No. 4 in D Minor, which was subsequently revised ten years later. No. 2 in C Major was written during 1845–6, with No. 3 in E Flat Major, the 'Rhenish', appearing in 1850. The symphonies are often disparaged because of Schumann's supposed lack of talent for orchestral writing. In fact, like Schubert, he was rather keen on trying to achieve new sounds and new combinations in his orchestration, although the best examples of this are in his piano concerto. Symphony No. 1, as its title, 'Spring', suggests, aims at picturesque tone-painting; it and No. 4 are perhaps the more accessible works, although the right performance of No. 3 brings out a grandeur which anticipates Wagner. The 'Rhenish' nickname for the 3rd Symphony arose because Schumann wrote the work as a response to the landscape of the Rhine and the

Robert Schumann

(1810–1856)

Schumann's life is a decidedly 'Romantic' affair; it includes madness, despair, attempted suicide, and delirious joy. Originally he wanted to be a virtuoso pianist, but he deformed his hands with some bizarre technical experiment designed to make them stronger (a typically Schumann piece of excess); it's quite likely that syphilis (an occupational hazard for artists of this period) helped to weaken him physically, too. His piano tutor, Friedrich Wieck (1785–1873), had a daughter called Clara, and Schumann spent most of the 1830s pursuing her and writing solo piano music intended for her. After various complications they were married in 1840; as things turned out, Clara became one of the most important musicians of the nineteenth century, an internationally celebrated pianist and friend to every important figure in musical life. Once he and Clara were married in 1840 Schumann wrote a glut of blissful (and brilliant) song cycles and turned his attention fully to writing for orchestra. Unfortunately, within five years he had succumbed to a very serious bout of depression, and the rest of his life was a battle against this, a battle he ultimately lost; he died in an insane asylum.

>> *Concerto* 113, *Chamber* 230, *Choral* 262

Rhineland; it's an interesting coincidence that when Wagner depicted the Rhine in *Das Rheingold,* the first part of his massive four-part opera known as '*The Ring Cycle*' (*Der Ring des Nibelungen*), which he began in 1853, he chose to do it in the same key – E flat major. The 'Rhenish' is a five-movement work, shaped, in its tempos, rather like Berlioz's *Symphonie Fantastique*, although it's a good deal shorter and the fourth-movement March becomes a solemn ceremonial procession. It's a mark of how Schumann felt about the soul-baring sort of Romanticism that originally he had entitled that movement 'In the manner of the accompaniment to a solemn ceremony', but modified this to simply 'Solemnly', in the belief that he should not 'bare his heart to the people' and that it was better for them to have just 'a general impression of the work'. In this work above all, Schumann sought to link his movements together; he preferred movements to flow one from another rather than ending and then restarting, since this enabled the thematic material to blend more easily. The 'Rhenish' is, I think, his most ambitious and interesting symphony, with an immediately appealing first movement.

DISCOGRAPHY
Sadly, good Schumann symphony recordings aren't exactly plentiful; too many conductors give routine, uninteresting, unshaded performances and don't seek to play up the strengths of the orchestration. The best performances of all four come, by and large, in one cycle, featuring the Staatskapelle Dresden Orchestra and its long-time conductor Wolfgang Sawallisch. After twenty years these versions haven't really been bettered, or even equalled. The string sound of the Dresden orchestra is quite ravishing, and Sawallisch clearly has a great deal of sympathy with the music; his

tempos are nicely judged, never rushing, always keeping the undercurrent of rhythm going nicely, and never overplaying the Romantic edge of Schumann.
● *EMI CDM7 69471/2-2* ● *2 CDs* ● *Mid-price* ● *ADD* ● *1974* ● *available separately as Nos. 1 and 4, Nos. 2 and 3* ✪

One of the few more recent, fully digital discs, to do Schumann a service is by the excellent Concertgebouw Orchestra and Riccardo Chailly, a conductor who is generally exciting in whatever he chooses to perform, and whom one would normally more readily associate with the very late Romantic music of Mahler and the young Schoenberg. Here he treats Schumann's two light symphonies – Nos. 1 ('Spring') and 4 – with respect, and produces something quite lovely to belie the reputation for 'poor orchestral writing' which has dogged the composer.
● *Decca 425 608-2* ● *1 CD* ● *Full price* ● *DDD* ● *1989*

A favourite version of the 3rd Symphony (the 'Rhenish') is a surprisingly restrained account by Leonard Bernstein with the Vienna Philharmonic. Bernstein is, of course, superb with the sombre sonorities of the third and fourth movements, but his opening to the Rhine flows majestically. This comes with a fresh performance of Schubert's 'Unfinished'.
● *Deutsche Grammophon 431 042-2* ● *1 CD* ● *Mid-price* ● *DDD* ● *1985*

━━━ ━━━ ━━━ ━━━

THE ANXIETY OF INFLUENCE: BRAHMS

Brahms didn't produce his 1st Symphony until 1876, so in the strictest chronological sense he should come after Dvořák and Tchaikovsky, both of whom started writing symphonies in the 1860s. But as Brahms agonised about his 1st Symphony for around two decades, it really merits pride of place. Besides which, the whole story of the symphony to this point has been, as you will have noticed, essentially Germanic (Berlioz aside), and the symphonic forays of Tchaikovsky and Dvořák represent, to some extent, personal nationalistic reactions against that tradition. This isn't to belittle their work; but it's Brahms who takes the step forward which unites the deeper purposes of Beethoven with the more melodic tendencies of Mendelssohn; it's

Brahms who achieves fully the effect after which Schumann is striving in a more ambitious work like the 'Rhenish'.

The genesis of the 1st Symphony was a protracted business. Brahms sent Clara Schumann the first movement of a symphony in 1862, eight years after he had first mentioned that he was working in the form (one of his earliest attempts turned into his 1st Piano Concerto). To 'help' Brahms get a move on his friends started scheduling this symphony for performance in the 1860s, but he gave up on the idea again until around 1870, concentrating most of his effort around the years 1873–6. Clara Schumann's response to the eventually finished work was scarcely helpful. 'I am bitterly disappointed', she wrote.

Actually, the Symphony No. 1 in C Minor was probably the most substantial and self-consciously intellectual work in the form since Beethoven's 'Choral', and it has often 'enjoyed' the nickname 'Beethoven's Tenth', partly because of a vague similarity between part of the big tune in the Finale and a line of the 'Ode to Joy' (this may very well be an overt and deliberate reference). However ambitious or effective the symphonies of Schumann and Mendelssohn had been, they had essentially been organised around the idea of melody, more on Mozartian lines, than around obsessive examination and working out of small fragmentary ideas, as in Beethoven's 5th, the first movement of the 'Choral', or much of Beethoven's more mature work. Brahms, who was more of a natural melodist than Beethoven, wanted to try to reconcile the two elements; he felt the ghost of Beethoven keenly, and on occasion referred to the strain he endured at having such a predecessor in his chosen field (oddly, he found Bach a

Johannes Brahms

1833–1897

Brahms had a colourful early musical life. In his late teens he earned his living as pianist in a brothel, then he became the accompanist to Hungarian self-styled 'gypsy' violinist Eduard Reményi (1830–1898), going with him on tours of Austria and Germany. (Brahms never left mainland Europe; he had a morbid fear of sailing, which led to him never visiting England or America, despite invitations to do so, and the great popularity of some of his works outside his native Germany.) Through Reményi he met the Hungarian violinist Joseph Joachim (1831–1907), who was to the violin in the nineteenth century what Clara Wieck-Schumann was to the piano: inspirer of several great works, introducer of many more, friend to the famous, and so on. Brahms was also, like Joachim, friendly with Clara and with her shared many of the agonies of composition. And composing was often, for Brahms, an agonising business; he would spend years over something like his 1st Symphony, frequently feeling himself to be pressurised by the influence of Beethoven. His work often met with initially lukewarm responses, too, although by the end of the 1870s he was a deeply respected pillar of the musical establishment, paraded by his (rather conservative) friends as the antithesis of figures like Wagner. He had a constant cheerleader in the figure of the deeply influential critic (and Wagner-hater) Eduard Hanslick.

>> *Concerto* 114, *Chamber* 234, *Choral* 262

much more benign influence). The influence of Beethoven was particularly profound on the way in which Brahms's use of sonata form became, like Beethoven's, 'development-led' (as opposed to the theme-dominated usage of Mendelssohn and Schumann) – in his symphonies, at any rate. All Brahms's four symphonies are blessed with beautiful and noble melodies (the most famous is probably the main tune from the Finale of the 1st, which had the misfortune to be appropriated by the Labour Party in the 1987 British General Election); his first movements, in particular, all possess 'first subjects' of a grave yet melodious and flowing seriousness. These movements also

- have long passages in which the
- thematic material is subjected to deep
- reworking in a manner which isn't
- always instantly dramatic. It's a
- measure of a good Brahms symphonic
- performance how much this fascinates
- the listener and how much it strikes
- him or her as note-spinning in search
- of greater length; obviously, any
- version that has the latter effect can
- scarcely be deemed successful.
- Once he started writing symphonies,
- Brahms produced all four magnificent
- works within a decade (the 4th, in some
- ways the loveliest and most accessible,
- was composed in 1884–5). He stuck
- faithfully to the four-movement form, to
- some extent redressing the balance

back to the first two movements; in his 4th Symphony in E Minor, though, he created a 'tragic' ending, a minor-key Finale which, for all its marking of 'Allegro energico e passionato' ('Energetically and passionately fast'), has a static quality compared to the joyfully dramatic, almost martial, major-key Scherzo which precedes it. Brahms quite enjoyed putting little coded messages into his music; the 3rd Symphony (which was for many years the most popular of the four) has a first movement whose main theme and grandiose opening is built out of two contrasting three-note motifs; the notes F-A-F and F-A-E, the initials of mottos adopted by Brahms and his friend the violinist Joachim. Brahms's was *'Frei aber Froh'* ('Free but happy'), Joachim's *'Frei aber Einsam'* ('Free but lonely').

DISCOGRAPHY
I have strong views on recordings of Brahms's symphonies. I doubt whether there are more than two conductors alive today who quite have the measure of the works; or have the ability to do justice to Brahms's grandeur and lyricism at one and the same time; or have the understanding to make the musical argument of the development passages coherent, lucid and entertaining, especially in the first three symphonies. Plenty of critics would disagree with me quite violently; for instance, there's particularly wide support for Claudio Abbado's recently finished complete cycle, with the Berlin Philharmonic. I'd agree that Nos. 1 and 2 are competent, although Abbado is mainly happier with the melodic side of the symphonies, so that the development work is a shade routine, but I find his performance of No 3 entirely unappealing, thoughtless, directionless, and surprisingly sloppy in execution. That said, some critics believe this to be the best version ever recorded. Which goes to show that critics can't be relied on. No. 3 apart, the Abbado discs are certainly well recorded, and I acknowledge that mine is a minority view.
● *Deutsche Grammophon 435 683-2* ● *4 CDs*
● *Full price* ● *DDD* ● *1988–90, also available on 4 separate discs with various complementary Brahms works*

For splendour of recording, and also for execution, the Abbado set is, I think, far outclassed by another Deutsche Grammophon release, the final Brahms recordings made by Herbert von Karajan. In particular, his performance of No. 1 is dazzling; there's none of Karajan's sometimes idiosyncratic, self-serving messing around with the music, just a tenacious commitment to the work's structure. Fantastic.
● *Deutsche Grammophon 423 141-2* ● *1 CD*
● *Full price* ● *DDD* ● *1987*

Excellent cheaper versions of the 1st Symphony come from some of the best known of conductors. Otto Klemperer with the Philharmonia doesn't have particularly brilliant sound, but his slow tempos, rather than making the work drag, manage to achieve an intensity which serves the music well.
● *EMI CDM7 69651-2* ● *1 CD* ● *Mid-price*
● *ADD* ● *1958*

Sadly, Sir Adrian Boult's much praised 1970 recording with the London Philharmonic was unavailable at the time of writing; I hope that EMI will put it out again soon. The slightly less famous Eugen Jochum has also produced a marvellous account with the same orchestra, rather similar in spirit to Klemperer's in places, but with a better-recorded sound and a richer orchestral timbre.
● *EMI CDZ7 62604-2* ● *1 CD* ● *Mid-price*
● *ADD* ● *1976*

As for the 2nd; rather perversely, my favourite version is a 1945 radio broadcast, which has surprisingly good sound, all things considered, but scarcely pristine digital clarity, and certainly not in the class of Karajan's last series. It features the Vienna Philharmonic conducted by Wilhelm Furtwängler, who makes the long first movement a superbly clear structure; even under the crackles you can tell that this is one of the greatest orchestras playing with intelligence and passion.
● *Deutsche Grammophon Vienna Philharmonic 150th Anniversary Edition 435 321 2* ● *1 CD*
● *Mid-price* ● *ADD* ● *1945*

The best Karajan performance of the 2nd is actually quite an old one, too, recorded in 1955 (but in very clear early stereo). It's a remarkably exuberant version.
● *EMI CDM7 69227-1* ● *1 CD* ● *Mid-price*
● *ADD* ● *1955*

Good recordings of the 3rd are as rare as winter thunder, and my favourite, by Bruno Walter (CBS/Sony, 1960) isn't currently in the catalogue. Once again, I hope this will be remedied. Failing that, I rather like the *'gravitas'* and sense of melody on the undemonstrative version by Günter Wand and the North German Radio Symphony Orchestra.
● *EMI CDC7 47872-2* ● *1 CD* ● *Full price*
● *DDD* ● *1983*

There's also much to be said, again, for Sir Adrian Boult (happily still available in this case).
● *EMI CDM7 69203-2* ● *1 CD* ● *Mid-price*
● *1970*

The best version of the 4th is lousy value for money; but as the conductor is Carlos Kleiber and the orchestra the Vienna Philharmonic, such considerations might be of slightly less account. Kleiber, who is so tense and high-voltage in Beethoven, takes an entirely different approach to Brahms, shaping the phrases lovingly, melodically, and yet always producing the same excitement as his Beethoven recordings.
● *Deutsche Grammophon 400 037-2* ● *1 CD*
● *Full price* ● *DDD* ● *1980*

There is another, cheaper (older) version of the symphony almost as good. For high-octane excitement, especially in the final two movements, Charles Munch and the Boston Symphony Orchestra's 1958 recording is as good as Kleiber's, and the sound quality is amazing.
● *RCA Silver Seal 09026 61206-2* ● *1 CD*
● *Bargain price* ● *ADD* ● *1958*

MEANWHILE IN EASTERN EUROPE: TCHAIKOVSKY AND DVOŘÁK

Just after the mid-point of the nineteenth century, a number of Russian composers, whose leaders included Alexander Borodin (1833–1887) and Mily Balakirev (1837–1910), both members of a group called 'The Five', tried to inject a degree of Russian nationalism into the course of Western music and to break the Germanic stranglehold on musical theory and practice. Peter Ilyich Tchaikovsky (1840–1893) was greatly influenced and encouraged by these slightly older figures, and tried to follow their practice of incorporating something distinctly Russian in his work, especially in his symphonic work.

Tchaikovsky wrote six symphonies, of which the last three have always been terrifically popular with audiences, although critics have become less kind over the years. In fact, if you look up Tchaikovsky in the average musical encyclopaedia written at any time up to the 1980s, you'll find a distinctly patronising and lukewarm account of most of his music, and especially of the three best-loved symphonies. Why? Well, basically because the successful Tchaikovsky symphonies are flamboyantly emotional works, metaphorically wearing their hearts on their sleeves. Borodin's symphonies have been much more flatteringly treated by critics, ironically not so much for their 'nationalist' content as for their Beethoven-like manner of developing a musical argument. But whatever the

critics may have written or thought, the fact remains that very few concert promoters got rich in the twentieth century by staging concerts that included a Borodin symphony, while Tchaikovsky's 4th, 5th and, especially, the 6th ('Pathétique'), can usually be guaranteed to pack the audiences in.

Tchaikovsky's first three symphonies are rather in the nature of attempts to find himself in the form; he was another constant reviser of his work. They have their *longueurs*, but they also have some terrific melodies; Tchaikovsky was another of the great tune writers. In the 2nd (the 'Little Russian') he tries to follow the precepts of Borodin and his circle by basing the symphony around Russian (or Ukrainian) folk music; but one of the problems Tchaikovsky faced in composing symphonies was the struggle he felt between the coherent, developed form on the one hand, and the freer, more expressive, more disparate, ballet suite on the other. Ballet music was especially the province of Russian composers (the Russian ballet tradition goes back well into the nineteenth century, and was, of course, to provide some of the most shattering music of the early twentieth century Modernist movement in Stravinsky's *The Rite of Spring*), and Tchaikovsky is, of course, famous for such works as *Swan Lake*, *Sleeping Beauty* and *The Nutcracker*. Some distinguished critics have seen the early symphonies as being confused by the pull of proper 'form' on the one hand and the attractions of the dance on the other.

Tchaikovsky's tortured personal life naturally plays a large part in his emergence as a fully fledged symphonic composer. The immediate outcome of his marriage crisis was the 4th Symphony in F Minor, a work which begins with a Fate motif and which is ultimately about heroism –

Peter Tchaikovsky

1840–1893

Tchaikovsky had so painful and confused a personal life that Ken Russell felt compelled to make a film of it. His early career seemed conventional enough, based around Moscow and the musical life of the Moscow Conservatoire. He had a conventional affair with a French singer, but all the time he grew increasingly prone to despair and neurosis, principally because he recognised more and more clearly that he was, in fact, homosexual. As Russia in the late nineteenth century wasn't an ideal setting for a gay lifestyle, he tried to solve the problem in 1877 by getting married. Unsurprisingly, this didn't work; he fled the country, tried to kill himself, and then set about writing the music which has ensured his lasting popularity. From this point on not only was he more liberated about his sexual preferences, it was as though something in his creative make-up had also been liberated. To add to the ease of his life, he acquired a patroness, Nadezhda von Meck, who offered to fund him completely; Tchaikovsky agreed to this, on the sole condition that the two should never meet face to face. Amazingly, she agreed. This arrangement sustained him through much of his life; by the time he and Nadedzha fell out, he was so established a figure that money was less of a problem to him. Tchaikovsky's death is still surrounded by mystery; officially he died of typhoid, but the story persists that he was forced by the Russian Court aristocracy to kill himself after an indiscretion with a young member of the Tsar's family. The jury is still very much out on this one.

>> *Concerto* 118, *Opera* 185, *Chamber* 235, *Orchestral* 279

above all Tchaikovsky's own heroism. The 4th was a major breakthrough, for the first time Tchaikovsky was able to reconcile his different artistic impulses, to use his talent for dance music in a way that worked with the logic of the symphony, rather than making it seem more disjointed. And, like many other great symphonies of personal discovery, the material from which the work develops seems quite meagre and fragmentary – unusual in such a great tune-writer, but a sign, perhaps, that he now understood how the

- symphony could work.
- The intensity of the 4th centres
- mainly on the first movement; No. 5
- in E Minor, written some eleven years
- later, centres on its slow movement.
- These two works are both popular
- for their melodic content, and
- perhaps even more for their dramatic
- impact; but it's the 6th in B Minor,
- the 'Pathétique', written not long
- before his death in 1893, which is
- the most characteristic and best-
- loved Tchaikovsky symphony. Its
- blend of melodic invention and drama
- is so deeply and personally felt that,

however sniffy critics might have been about it, it has been impossible for audiences not to respond, right from the big tune of the first movement through to the elegiac ending. In the 6th, Tchaikovsky felt the confidence to alter the traditional ordering of symphonic movements, so that this extraordinarily emotional work ends with a passionate and tragic slow movement that comes as a great emotional release after a febrile Scherzo which, although full of wit and excitement, never quite settles down; in a great performance, the impact of the Finale's first chord after the Scherzo can be tremendous. The confidence Tchaikovsky felt with dance forms is also evident in the Waltz of the second movement; only a master of the craft would dare to write a waltz with five rather than three beats to each bar. Great music with five beats in a bar is in any case rare before the twentieth century (and in it, to be truthful; the most famous five-beat piece is probably not some classical piece, but jazz musician Dave Brubeck's 'Take Five'), and the Waltz in the 'Pathétique' has some claim to being unique in this respect.

DISCOGRAPHY

If you want a full Tchaikovsky cycle, then it would be hard to better Karajan's 1970s recordings, economically forced onto only four discs (although this does lead to inconvenient breaks in the middle of a couple of symphonies). At his best, Karajan is superb at bringing out the structure of a work, but never so concerned to admire the musical architecture that he doesn't let rip with a vengeance at the passionate moments. The performances here of the three early symphonies are the most likely to make you warm to them; the gifts Karajan could display for the subtlety of dance rhythm are all extremely well displayed. Listening to these performances, you understand why Karajan and the Berlin Philharmonic enjoy such elevated reputations.
● *Deutsche Grammophon 429 675-2* ● *4 CDs*
● *Mid-price* ● *ADD* ● *1976–79* ❍

One other recording of the first three symphonies might convince listeners of their merits: Bernard Haitink with the Concertgebouw. Haitink was this orchestra's principal conductor for a longish period and he helped it to become a pre-eminent force, developing its sound. He takes these three symphonies on their own terms, looking for the merits they contain in themselves, not as forerunners of what was to come; no attempting to invent huge passionate musical events which don't exist.
● *Philip 420 751-2* ● *2 CDs* ● *Mid-price*
● *ADD* ● *1979–81*

If, as is quite likely, you want only the last three symphonies, then I don't think you can find more 'authentic' (in the proper sense) performances than the classic, full-blooded live recordings by Eugene Mravinsky and the Leningrad Philharmonic Orchestra. Energy, passion, rhythm; they're all here in spades, and the Russian orchestra has a dark-coloured sound which confers perhaps that extra degree of excitement, getting just that bit nearer to Tchaikovsky's heart.
● *Deutsche Grammophon 419 745-2* ● *2 CDs*
● *Full price* ● *ADD* ● *1961*

Maris Jansson's series of all six symphonies won a lot of plaudits as it was released: I'm afraid I find it on the drab side, underplayed throughout, but once again I'm in a minority, and the sound quality is excellent. Anyone who wants the febrile Tchaikovsky toned down a bit could do worse if they want state-of-the-art digital sound. The symphonies are available separately; especially praised has been No. 4. ● *Chandos CHAN8361*
● *1 CD* ● *Full price* ● *DDD* ● *1985, No. 5*
● *Chandos CHAN8351* ● *1 CD* ● *Full price*
● *DDD* ● *1984, and No. 6 ('Pathétique')*
● *Chandos CHAN8446* ● *1 CD* ● *Full price*
● *DDD* ● *1986*

Anyone wanting the 5th separately, though, will probably find a better bargain in Sian Edwards's electrifying rendering with the London Philharmonic.
● *EMI Eminence CD-EMX 2187* ● *1 CD*
● *Mid-price* ● *DDD* ● *1991*

As for the 'Pathétique', I am unique (among critics, anyway) in not being bowled over by Mikhail Pletnev's outing with the Russian National Orchestra; where I found it choppy, contrived, unmellifluous and ultimately heartless, my fellow critics to a person regarded it as 'amazing', 'passionate', and 'the best since Mravinsky, possibly the best ever'.
● *Virgin Classics VC7 91487-2* ● *1 CD* ● *Full price* ● *DDD* ● *1991*

But then I'm rather fond of Sir Georg Solti's intensely febrile and downright unsettling account, even if it does skimp on the work's 'nobility'. What you get here is the Chicago Symphony Orchestra blazing away on the edge of hysteria, some fabulous brass noises in the third movement (which to my mind should be hysterical rather than noble), and a real sense of emotional catharsis.
● *Decca 430 442-2* ● *1 CD* ● *Mid-price*
● *ADD* ● *1976*

FROM BOHEMIA TO THE 'NEW WORLD'

For a long time the average non-enthusiast listener knew Dvořák principally for one movement of one symphony – the second movement of his last symphony, No. 9 in E Minor, 'From the New World'. In Britain, that state of affairs was perpetuated by the appropriation of the tune by advertisers keen to promote the delights of old-fashioned brown bread, so that a tune with (probably) Czech roots, based (according to the composer) on a sketch for a melody to be part of an opera based on Longfellow's American-Indian epic *Hiawatha*, became associated with cobbled streets and early-twentieth-century Britain.

Well, there's a lot more to that symphony than just that movement, and there's a lot more to Dvořák than just that symphony. Dvořák's symphonic career covers almost exactly the same period as Tchaikovsky's; his 1st Symphony appeared one year earlier (1865), and the 'New World' was premiered in December 1893, within two months of Tchaikovsky's death. Although usually classified as 'Romantic', Dvořák's music is almost entirely free of the kind of emotional turbulence which characterises Tchaikovsky at his best; whilst it's become something of a cliché to refer to works like the 5th Symphony, or the 8th, as 'sunlit' and 'full of the spirit of the Czech countryside', the reason these descriptions have become clichéd is because it is pretty difficult to avoid them. Dvořák's music is the natural Romantic development of Beethoven's 'Pastoral' Symphony. Recently, the other 'mature' symphonies (usually reckoned from No. 5, written in 1875, onwards) have begun to emerge from

the shadows of the 'New World' as works in their own right, and there's a general consensus (to which I'd happily subscribe) that the real gem of Dvořák's symphonic career is No. 8 in G Major, written in 1889. It's a work in which Dvořák often playfully suggests that something more disturbed and dramatic is lurking in the offing; the introduction to the work is a solemn passage in the minor key which is immediately dispelled by a flute melody, suggesting musical picture-painting of birdsong, which in turn ushers in something earthier and more robust. This procedure, of making something solemn give way to a more joyful spirit, also turns up again in the Finale, and is inherent in little rhythmic touches which undercut the more reserved nature of the slow movement. But the third movement, a sort of slow folk waltz, has a claim to be one of Dvořák's loveliest melodies.

Symphony No. 9 in E Minor ('From the New World')

Actually, the 9th Symphony is a rather intricate piece of work, although the composer himself has managed to obfuscate people's views of what really went into it. The story at the time of its appearance, one that Dvořák fostered by copious 'programme'-like comments, was that the music was intended to be entirely American, depicting American-Indian festivals and so on. Yet seven years later he described this view of the music's basis as 'nonsense' and 'a lie'. 'Whatever I have written, wherever I have written it, it always remains Bohemian music,' he said. Quite possibly the acrimonious end of his American sojourn may have coloured his view of the American influences.

Antonin Dvořák

1841–1904

▬

It's perhaps mildly ironic that Dvořák has become best-known to the musical public for a product of his two-year sojourn in America; ironic because he was above all responsible for helping to put the Czech Bohemian musical tradition on the map. It was because of his determined missionary work for the folk tradition of his native country that Dvořák was invited to America in the first place, in the hope that he would educate American composers and musicians in the value of 'native traditions'. The son and grandson of a butcher, Dvořák was originally destined to follow the family trade, but between the ages of twelve and sixteen he exhibited amazing musical talent, and so he went off to Prague to train as an organist. He began composing in his early twenties, and his nationalist works greatly impressed Brahms, who promulgated Dvořák's reputation in the rest of Europe. Dvořák spent a lot of time travelling and arguing with publishers; he wasn't above giving pieces misleading opus numbers in order to get round contractual obligations. He had six children to support, so his concerns about money are understandable; his acceptance in 1891 of an invitation from the wife of a millionaire grocer, Mrs Jeanette Thurber, to become the Director of the National Conservatory of Music in New York, which she had founded a few years before, was primarily motivated by his need for hard cash. Although his time in America (1892–1895) resulted in the 'New World' Symphony and one of his best-loved string quartets, the appointment ended in tears, as Dvořák wanted more money. He returned to Prague; when he died he was considered enough of a national hero to be buried alongside many great Bohemian statesmen.

>> *Concerto* 121, *Opera* 201, *Chamber* 236

The first movement employs Dvořák's favoured tactic of threatening darkness and then breaking out instead into sunshine and folk-dance-style music; as with the 8th Symphony, this tactic is used again in the Finale. However, Dvořák's awareness of symphonic complexity makes the Finale a reprise of all the thematic elements of the rest of the symphony, mixed up together in a subtly tempestuous *mélange*

- threatening total crisis. The artless
- artfulness of the work's structure is
- probably one of the things that has
- contributed to its popularity; that and
- the profusion of memorable tunes.
-
- DISCOGRAPHY
- There is a first-rate, cheapish complete Dvořák
- cycle which is, as far as cycles go, unbeatable; and
- most of the individual symphonic performances
- are at least on a par with the best, if not actually
- top of the list. The conductor here is the Czech
- Rafael Kubelik; one of the notable things about the
- best Dvořák recordings is that often they feature

Czech conductors (and sometimes Czech musicians) who have a natural affinity with the music. Kubelik, in some cases here in charge of the Berlin Philharmonic, at others conducting the Bavarian Radio Symphony Orchestra, has a way of making the music both fresh and 'spring-like', while still bringing out all the drama, the threatening storm-clouds. The performances of Nos. 8 and 9 (New World) are delightful, and this would be the ideal way to get familiar with the earlier works.
● *Deutsche Grammophon 423 120-2* ● *6 CDs*
● *Mid-price* ● *ADD* ● *1967–78*

There's an excellent version of the 8th Symphony which comes along with the 7th – another good bargain, and the 7th is a work worth getting familiar with, encompassing as it does a surprising variety of moods. Sir Colin Davis gets a lot of vitality and a lot of fine textures out of the Concertgebouw and the whole sound is beautifully warm.
● *Philips 420 890-2* ● *1 CD* ● *Mid-price*
● *ADD* ● *1976–9*

My absolutely favourite performance of the 8th is rather bizarrely coupled with music from Wagner's *Parsifal* (the Prelude and 'Good Friday Music') – beautifully performed though the Wagner is, it's not the most obvious choice to go with Dvořák. The symphony is played by the Columbia Symphony Orchestra under the great Bruno Walter, and this recording simply exudes warmth, with some marvellously precise touches and, above all, the right kind of passion – nothing showy, just a great love of the music.
● *CBS/Sony MYK 44872* ● *1 CD* ● *Mid-price*
● *ADD* ● *1961*

There are a lot of excellent versions of the 9th Symphony, 'From the New World', around, but the best is a superb bargain, with a fine performance of the orchestral piece 'Symphonic Variations' added on to boot. Zdenek Macal's recording with the London Philharmonic balances every aspect of the work perfectly; the recording is excellent. There are no over-Romantic touches in the famous slow movement, the timing and rhythm is spot on, and the Finale has just the right flash of fire.
● *Classics for Pleasure CD-CFP9006* ● *1 CD*
● *Bargain price* ● *DDD* ● *1982*

Another London orchestra, under Istvan Kertész, is almost as good, although the age of the sound is just a slight drawback. This is an exuberant performance, with an extra element of yearning and a real sense of mystery at moments in the Finale.
● *Decca Ovation 417 724-2* ● *1 CD*
● *Mid-price* ● *ADD* ● *1966*

Mainly the performances which try to play Dvořák as though he belonged in the German mainstream aren't so wonderful, but there's one great exception. The Hungarian conductor Ferenc Fricsay (1914–1963), whose reputation is finally being restored (and a good thing too), brought his talent for interpreting symphonies – primarily through an understanding of their structure – to the 'New World' at a time when it was still mainly

regarded as a rag-bag of folk tunes. Fricsay uses more tricks of tempo than most other conductors; and what he seeks from the Berlin Philharmonic is a long way from what Kubelik demands. This is a grandiose performance, perhaps not always in the right tradition, but always intensely involving.
● *Deutsche Grammophon 423 384-2* ● *1 CD*
● *Mid-price* ● *ADD* ● *1959*

GERMANIC VASTNESS: BRUCKNER AND MAHLER

Bruckner's career as a writer of symphonies is more or less exactly contemporary with those of Tchaikovsky and Dvořák, yet in theoretical attitude and musical style his music is so removed from either of these two as to seem to belong to a different age.

Why? Well, a partial answer would simply be to say 'Richard Wagner'. By the time Bruckner came to composing symphonies – and as nothing came easily to Bruckner, this was at a relatively late age – Wagner's music was beginning to make its influence felt in the Germanic world. It is often assumed that this means vastness in all senses – huge length, huge orchestral forces, huge noises – but in fact an awful lot of Wagner's music employs remarkably small sections of a *potentially* enormous orchestra, and Bruckner in his later symphonies tries for something of the same technique. And the huge length of Wagner's works bred in his admirers and followers a new and different attitude to musical time; new, at any rate, in post-Renaissance music, but perhaps more akin to medieval ideas of 'time suspended'. Bruckner, a devotee of Wagner and also familiar with the entire tradition of religious music back to the Middle Ages, felt that this more spacious temporal architecture offered him his best means of expression. He preferred to work out his ideas over

Anton Bruckner

1824–1896

Bruckner was a complex man whose life was fraught with difficulties; he had to undergo some fairly strict (if advanced for the time) medical treatment in order to cure a psychological disorder which led to him having, amongst other things, a habit of compulsive and point-less counting. But he was also a man of profound religious faith, and this is central to his music. However much despair and doubt his music may reflect, it always has this unshakeable core of belief; another reason, perhaps, why our age has been slower to take to him than to the doubting, questioning, and ultimately despairing Mahler. Bruckner actually earned his living for a time within the religious tradition, as organist of Linz Cathedral; this was the time at which he finally came to music and studied the subject, and it is no exaggeration to say that an echo of the Germanic chorale tradition (Bruckner was Austrian) permeates his music. However, he was so racked by self-doubt that he didn't start composing until he was 40, and even then he was a compulsive, even neurotic reviser. As his music became famous, he came into contact with figures like the young Gustav Mahler, who both respected and faintly despised him. Self-doubt and religious faith: that is Bruckner in a glib nutshell.

long movements, and his musical phrases are long, arching things which often slow up in the middle or towards their ending. This makes Bruckner a very difficult composer to conduct; too difficult, in fact, for Bruckner himself, who made a shambles of it on the occasions he tried.

Wagner's influence on Bruckner is incalculable, especially on the 7th Symphony (perhaps the most instantly accessible of all), which was finished in the year that Wagner died and was, to some extent, transformed into a tribute to him (although it was his 3rd Symphony that Bruckner actually dedicated to the 'Lord of *The Ring*'). But Bruckner's purposes in writing music were very different from

- Wagner's, and Bruckner never tried to
- achieve the operatic drama of his
- admired master. Perhaps a part of the
- reason why Bruckner has always
- remained something of an acquired
- taste (although his star has definitely
- been on the rise for a couple of
- decades) is that he prefers to make his
- drama inward, and very rarely opts
- for the flamboyant gesture.
- There is no short cut to
- understanding Bruckner; the only way
- to get into his music is to listen to it.
- That may seem self-evidently true of
- any composer, but with most others
- there is some external key that will
- let you in, or some immediate hook
- on which to hang your attention.
- Bruckner's music is proportioned

rather like a spacious cathedral, and very often makes huge movements out of apparently ridiculously small motifs. The slow movement of the 7th, for instance, is a 20-minute or so (depending on who performs it; on my favourite recording it lasts for nearly 22 minutes) Adagio (that is, properly slow, not just leisurely) based more or less around a three-note rising pattern. And there is only one enormous climax (and that comes some five minutes from the end); much of the time the music is slow, if not stationary. On the other hand, in the textures Bruckner achieves by his use of brass (instruments known as 'Wagner tubas') in harmony, in the selectivity of his orchestration, and in his sheer intensity – there is nothing overtly passionate about it, but the sense of submerged excitement is awesome. Awesome (in its proper meaning) is a word that Bruckner inspires a lot in his admirers. And the deep-feeling, yet static, nature of this movement seems perfectly in keeping with the following Scherzo, the main theme of which is a restless, questing figure, a bit like a hunting-call.

I would say that the 7th (in E Major) is the Bruckner symphony to start with, if you are not already familiar with his music. The incomplete 9th (he died after he had completed three movements, thus inspiring a fearful superstition in a lot of composers of the next generation) is also readily accessible, as is the slightly less popular 5th. The 4th (known as the 'Romantic' Symphony) has a great deal of charm, but does not quite reach the heights and plumb the depths as do the last three symphonies (or two and three-quarters, to be pedantic). No. 6 is emerging from the shadows again, and many keener

Brucknerians than I would argue that it deserves to be ranked with Nos. 7, 8 and 9. The real challenge, though, is No. 8 in C Minor. It is massive (so much so that in many recordings it lasts longer than the 80 minutes generally accepted to be the time-limit of a CD if its quality is to be preserved, and, on first hearing, can easily seem to meander, especially in the massive slow movement which lasts for nearly half an hour; yet when it works and takes a grip on the listener, it is one of the most exciting and uplifting pieces of music.

There was a time when Bruckner's symphonies were considered 'shapeless' by critics, partly because, like the works of Haydn, they get into some odd keys relative to the home key. Some might suggest that this is a Wagnerian trait; after all, Wagner's opera *Tristan und Isolde*, which was completed in 1865, was a landmark in music in that it broke down the idea of tonality, moving chromatically through the whole tonal spectrum. However, Bruckner's music is steeped in traditional tonality (in a way which distinguishes him from Mahler, with whom he is so often and erroneously compared); very often the logic of his movement from one key to another can be found in the lines of the low-pitched instruments in the bass register. The music lecturer and critic Roderick Swanston believes that this is connected with Bruckner's professional involvement with the church organ – that this instrument, with its demanding pedal work, gave Bruckner a keener sense of the role of the musical 'bottom line' than many other composers.

Symphony No. 0?
Yes, Bruckner really did write one; and, even more oddly, it seems quite

likely that at least part of it was written after his 'official' Symphony No. 1. The official Bruckner symphonic canon consists of nine consecutively numbered works, including the three-quarters-complete No. 9 (the first four were revised at least once, the 4th revised twice); but around the same time that he wrote No. 1 in C Minor, Bruckner also wrote a Symphony in D Minor (and possibly wrote at least the Trio section of the third movement after he'd completed No. 1), to which he subsequently assigned the title 'Die Nüllte' ('the Noughth'), evidently implying that he didn't wish it to be officially regarded as part of his symphonic output. And actually there's another symphony written just before either No. 0 or No. 1, the 'Schul-Symphonie' (either 'Study Symphony' or 'Apprentice Symphony' catches the sense) in F Minor. Bruckner took the idea of being a symphonist so seriously that he felt that he had to have the right 'official' 1st Symphony. Bits of the 0th turn up in the later symphonies.

DISCOGRAPHY

There are five complete Bruckner cycles currently available, two featuring the same conductor, Eugen Jochum, though with different orchestras. For me it's Jochum who holds the key to Bruckner; it was through his first cycle with the Berlin Philharmonic that I came to know and love Bruckner, and I find his approach to the music entirely selfless and full of understanding. Every phrase has the right kind of excitement and seems logical, although there are those who feel that his tempos are occasionally on the fast side. However, Jochum comes from a tradition which understands that a snail's pace and depth are not necessarily synonymous. The component discs of the cycle are available separately, and this is one of the few performances of the 8th to fit onto one disc, which means that you can pick it up at somewhere around £5–6 if you shop around. The Bruckner neophyte will of course want the individual performances of Symphonies No. 7–9 first, but eventually the whole cycle will be well worth tracking down.

● *Deutsche Grammophon 429 079-2* ● *9 CDs*
● *Mid-price (although various individual symphonies available separately at Bargain price)*
● *ADD* ● *1958–67* ✪

There are a lot of cheers raised for Karajan's versions with the Berlin Philharmonic recorded in the late 1970s/early 1980s, but I feel that Karajan sometimes treats Bruckner a bit too brashly, especially in the 8th, and likes to push and pull the tempos around to suit his own version. This Karajan cycle, though, will always have some very devoted admirers, and it may open the door to Bruckner for you.

● *Deutsche Grammophon 429 648-2* ● *9 CDs*
● *Mid-price* ● *ADD/DDD* ● *1976–82*

Of individual symphony performances, I prefer to concentrate on Nos. 7–9. The classic version of the 7th comes from one of the greatest Brucknerians ever – Otto Klemperer. Although his treatment of slow movements was stately (to say the least), by the time he made his famous recordings in the late 1950s and the 1960s, Klemperer always demanded of his orchestral players an intensity which never loses the thread of the music. This version of the 7th has the right Wagnerian dimensions, but never loses track of the fact that this is Bruckner and *not* Wagner. The slow movement is exactly right, while the more neurotic Scherzo never collapses into ill-judged film-music hysteria. A great recording.

● *EMI CDM7 69126-2* ● *1 CD* ● *Mid-price*
● *ADD* ● *1960*

I've already mentioned Jochum's account of the 8th, well worth having separately even if you don't want the rest.

● *Deutsche Grammophon 431 163-2* ● *1 CD*
● *Bargain price* ● *ADD* ● *1964*

There is, however, a superb, newer version of the 8th, recorded live, which for many Brucknerians is a treat surpassing all others. The conductor Günter Wand did record all the symphonies in the studio with the Cologne Radio Symphony Orchestra; good though those discs are, the passage of time has lent a greater understanding to his view of the architecture and structure of the composer's music. Nowhere is this shown to better advantage than in Wand's majestic, deeply felt performance of the 8th with the North German Radio Symphony Orchestra, full of subtlety, always aware exactly where the music demands to go, and never drawn towards the vulgar effect. The only snag is that Wand's tempos mean, inevitably, that the recording is split over two discs.

● *RCA Victor Red Seal RD60364* ● *2 CDs*
● *Full price* ● *DDD* ● *1987*

As for the 9th, there is of course a fine version by Klemperer (sadly he never recorded the 8th), but this must yield to the powerful recording made by Bruno Walter. His is a full-bodied performance with rich string sounds and stirring brass, but never touching vulgarity. As with all the truly great Bruckner performances, the music's logic is inescapable, and the way that Walter conducts the slow third movement leaves the listener not with a sense of the work's incompleteness, but a deep spiritual satisfaction.

● *CBS/Sony MYK 44825* ● *1 CD* ● *Mid-price*
● *ADD* ● *1961*

There is also a new, superbly recorded version which almost matches Walter's. In his performance with the Berlin Philharmonic, Daniel Barenboim reveals depths of understanding which bode well for future Bruckner recordings in the same series. One devoted Brucknerian critic actually described this recording as 'humbling in its magnificence', and frankly, if this doesn't get you, don't bother with Bruckner.

● *Teldec 9031-72140-2*   ● *1 CD*   ● *Full price*
● *DDD*   ● *1990*

Bruckner cycles don't include the 0th; anyone interested in hearing it (and it *is* interesting for anyone who gets into Bruckner) might like to try Riccardo Chailly's version with the Berlin Radio Symphony Orchestra.

● *Decca 421 593-2*   ● *1 CD*   ● *Full price*
● *DDD*   ● *1989*

● ● ● ●

DESPAIR, IRONY AND TACKY TUNES: MAHLER

Probably no composer has enjoyed a greater boom in the last 25 or 30 years than Mahler. From being a recondite taste enjoyed only by a few, with scarcely any recordings made of his work, he's become one of the 'big banker' names, and it now seems as if every conductor feels he (or she) has to record all nine-plus (the 10th is unfinished) Mahler symphonies (and you do rather wish a lot of them wouldn't). Part of Mahler's late success has certainly been due to the advocacy of certain influential figures, amongst whom Leonard Bernstein (1918–1990) must be granted pride of place; Bernstein recorded a symphony cycle in the 1960s when Mahler was still deeply unfashionable. Bernstein also preached the 'modernity' of Mahler and hit a deeply responsive chord; a liberal society becoming increasingly less sure of itself, yet simultaneously increasing in sophistication and so deepening its sense of irony, found Mahler's vast explorations of the uncertainty of human life in the face of mortality very much in tune with the times. Mahler feared that posterity would make his work sound like nonsense; so although he perhaps

wouldn't recognise every conductor's style, he would doubtless be relieved.

From very early in his career Mahler was drawn towards traditional Germanic poems and legends, especially a collection known as *Des Knaben Wunderhorn* (*The Magic Horn of Youth*). Like several composers at the turn of the century, Mahler set several of these traditional ballads and nature poems, all of which were very concerned with the landscape of Austria, particularly its rural mountain areas. It was the influence of these songs that Mahler took with him to his early symphonies; in fact, all his symphonies up to the 5th bear something of the imprint of his *Des Knaben Wunderhorn* settings, often quoting melodies directly.

But this Dvořák-like rusticity was only part of Mahler's world. He was also a sophisticated Viennese intellectual, and he desired his music to be at the cutting edge; to this end he tried to extend the symphony's resources (especially in the range of percussion used) and also the kind of music it could contain, trying to show that a symphony could employ Beethovenian sophistication of argument alongside folk-dance forms like the Ländler, parody serenades, grand choruses, gentle arias . . . From his very first symphony, Mahler developed a tactic of building scherzo movements out of cheap, nasty tunes and bullying them, ironically and sardonically, to create a mood of ironic and bitter despair; sometimes he opted for happy endings, although this tendency died away as his career went on, leaving most conductors and performers fairly ambivalent about the mesmerically slow and quiet ending to the 9th, his last completed symphony; does it represent serenity, acceptance, resignation and something spiritual, or

Gustav Mahler

1860–1911

Mahler is one of the pivotal figures in music between the nineteenth and twentieth centuries; his symphonies dominate the last decade of the old century and the first decade of the new. He lived in the thick of musical life in Vienna, acting for a while as principal conductor to the Vienna Philharmonic Orchestra, and he knew everybody who was anyone in artistic life; he had studied under Bruckner and his own pupils included Arnold Schoenberg; his friends and acquaintances included the composer Richard Strauss, conductors like Bruno Walter and Otto Klemperer, influential artists, and architects such as Walter Gropius (with whom his wife had an affair). Mahler came from an Austrian-Jewish family which had converted to Catholicism (his origins meant that his music was banned by the Nazis), but he had no conventional religious faith; much of his creative mainspring was doubt and fear, and he fretted endlessly about mortality and the meaning of life. He was over 40 when he met his wife, the ferociously intellectual Alma Schindler; she was a composer in her own right, although it seems that Gustav stifled her talent somewhat. It was never an easy relationship, marked by infidelity on both sides, although it seems that her infidelities had a more profound effect upon Mahler than did his upon her. Certainly his love for Alma provoked much of the great music of his later symphonies. It was during the last decade of his life that Mahler discovered that his hold on life was more tenuous than he had imagined. He had had a brief brush with death in the early 1900s, when a bowel disease almost killed him; later, a routine check-up revealed a heart disorder which enforced a severe change in his lifestyle, ending the great long walks in mountainous Austrian countryside that had been such an inspiration to a great deal of his earlier music. Eventually this heart problem killed him, leaving Alma free to marry several famous artistic figures (including Gropius) in turn.

>> Choral 266

is it the despairing cry of someone whose voice has almost faded? A lot of Mahler has this ambivalence, and it was this quality which attracted figures like Leonard Bernstein, who always liked to feel he was recomposing any piece as he conducted it.

Four of Mahler's symphonies make fairly extensive use of vocal music: No. 2 ('Resurrection'), No. 3, No. 4 and No.

- 8 (sometimes known as the
- 'Symphony of a Thousand' because it
- takes almost that many people to
- perform it). The 8th, in fact, is an
- almost entirely choral work. There's
- also a symphonic song cycle which
- sets German translations of ancient
- Chinese poetry, called *The Song of the*
- *Earth* (or, more properly, *Das Lied von*
- *der Erde*). It's thought that Mahler

thought of this as a symphony but deliberately didn't number it because of a superstition (bolstered by Bruckner's death before his 9th Symphony was completed) about a composer's life being limited to nine symphonies. In this prescience he was proved quite correct, for he died with only one movement of his 10th Symphony completed, although the existence of full sketches has led to some quite effective realisations, though certain conductors will have no truck with this work apart from the movement which Mahler wrote himself. Mahler did alter a great deal during composition, so their argument has a certain force.

Mahler was open to all kinds of influences; listening to his music you can, of course, hear all the great Germanic writers lurking in there, but you can also hear the countryside, fairgrounds, military bands, and incompetent local musicians. Around the time he wrote his 5th Symphony (1901–1902; the work includes the movement which became famous as the music central to Luchino Visconti's film *Death in Venice*) he was walking with two friends in the country when they heard a bad, tinny military band playing, which caused the friends to wince. 'If you like my symphonies as much as you say,' Mahler remarked, 'then you ought to enjoy that performance.' A joke, maybe, but a joke with a point (Mahler wasn't exactly a laugh a minute). Actually, he found the influence of bad barrel-organ-like music sufficiently disconcerting to agree reluctantly to a consultation with Sigmund Freud, when both were in the Dutch town of Arnhem, to try to sort out why such comparative trash had such a grip on his intellectual processes. Freud delved around and discovered that Mahler's unhappy childhood contained a submerged memory of a family quarrel, during which the young Gustav ran out into the street where a barrel-organ was playing the folk tune 'Ach! du liebe Augustin'. This didn't clear the problem, which from our point of view is just as well; it's precisely the clash of the elevated and the banal which gives Mahler's music its modern appeal.

MAHLER AND SYMPHONIC FORM

In his desire to expand the form, Mahler was quite happy to deploy extra movements and move away from traditional structure. All but two of his symphonies (Nos. 1 and 4) could fairly be described as enormous; No. 2 has five movements, including a vast Choral Finale depicting 'Resurrection'; No. 3 has six, No. 5 has five, as does No. 7; and although Nos. 6 and 9 have a conventional four, they too are huge. Tempos are rarely constant in a Mahler movement, either, and usually move through vast mood swings, although the use of motif and formal logic is always impeccable, even where despair and irony predominate (much of Mahler is a tussle between head and heart of this kind). No. 8 has only two movements, but the scale of resources and the length are enormous too. In works like Nos. 2 and 5, Mahler divided the whole into parts, grouping certain movements together and indicating that there should be longer gaps between these parts than is traditional simply between movements (his wishes are fairly rarely observed in this).

The variety of influence in his music and its apparent lack of stability does give Mahler some claim to the title of 'First Modern Symphonist' (certainly people like Pierre Boulez regard him as such); so too does his attitude towards tonality. Mahler is the first composer we've looked at with whom it's no great help, or no great relevance to the progress of the music (away from the first movement), to say that a given symphony is 'in D Minor', or whatever. Not that Mahler is given to the kind of endless chromatic winding around the place you find in *Tristan und Isolde* or in early Schoenberg; tonality, however, is something of a secondary consideration, and there's every sign in what we have of the 10th Symphony that he was intending to move yet further away from it.

Mahler's music aroused a lot of hostility in his own lifetime; however, the last of his symphonies that he was to conduct at its première (1910), the 8th, was a rousing success. By the time the 9th was performed, the composer had died of a heart-related infection. The première, in 1912, of the 9th was conducted by Bruno Walter (1876–1962), who lived to record it twice. Mahler's music always divided the great conductors of the century; Walter and Klemperer happily performed it with affection, but Furtwängler considered it nihilist, and Toscanini, although he studied it, never performed it. And it was to be quite a long time after the demise of the Nazi regime before Mahler's music returned to the standard concert repertoire.

DISCOGRAPHY

If you find Mahler greatly appealing, then it probably is well worth having a Mahler cycle, and this is one of those happy occasions when, as far as cycles go, the cheapest is also the best. The Austria Mahler lived in included most of what became the Czech Republic, and, like Mozart, he always had an affinity with Czech musicians (he had, in any case, been born in Bohemia). The Czech conductor Rafael Kubelik has, as no other living conductor quite has, a link with Mahler; his instrumentalist father, a virtuoso player in Prague, played Mahler's own work under the composer himself. Kubelik's excellent cycle from the late 1960s/early 1970s brings a freshness and vitality to the nature-inspired movements, and yet retains

a full awareness of the darker depths. The heroic No. 1 ('Titan') is beautifully done, as is the deliberately Haydn-modelled No. 4, but of the more complex works, Kubelik also produces a No. 7 which has only very recently been even equalled. In the right shop, you can get this whole cycle for around £50/60; good value for anyone's money. The long Adagio of No. 10 – the one movement of that symphony Mahler completed himself – is also included.

● *Deutsche Grammophon 429 042-2*   ● *10 CDs*
● *Bargain price*   ● *ADD*   ● *1967–71* ○

Most of the other boxed sets available are patchy at best; the 'live' Bernstein cycle done with various orchestras (mainly the Vienna Philharmonic and the Concertgebouw) in the 1980s has some wonderful things in it, but these are best obtained separately. Sir Georg Solti did a lot to help put Mahler on the map, and people who got to know the symphonies exclusively through his performances tend to defend them loyally, but they really are completely untrue to the spirit of Mahler, seeking to make his music all of one glossy, sleek piece, and to smooth out the quirks. Klaus Tennstedt's studio performances again have some superb accounts amongst them, but he's gradually producing live versions which far outstrip what he did before (his brush with death seems to have given him a particular hot-line to Mahler, something which was true also of Karajan).

In fact, one of these superb live Tennstedt performances is of No. 1; it's a daring performance which goes right to the extremes of irony and plays lots of time tricks, though as such it perhaps represents one facet of the piece more fully than others. But it's a blistering sound from the Chicago Symphony Orchestra, even if at moments Tennstedt does seem to be doing such strange things with time that ensemble (orchestral 'togetherness') is threatened.

● *EMI CDC7 54217 2*   ● *1 CD*   ● *Full price*
● *DDD*   ● *1990*

The alternative view of the 1st Symphony comes in another live performance of similar vintage. Claudio Abbado draws a kind of freshness out of the Berlin Philharmonic which I never dreamed them capable of, and this is a tightly bound reading, full of youthful bloom and beauty.

● *Deutsche Grammophon 431 769-2*   ● *1 CD*
● *Full price*   ● *DDD*   ● *1989*

Some feel that the two views are reconciled in Bernstein's 1987 live performance with the Concertgebouw, and that certainly does have both elements as well as an enormous amount of Bernstein's personal interpolation. The result can strike one as either contrived or glorious, depending at least partly on the listener's own mood. Demands to be heard, though.

● *Deutsche Grammophon 431 036-2*   ● *1 CD*
● *Mid-price*   ● *DDD*   ● *1987*

The best digital No. 2 ('Resurrection') is probably Simon Rattle's, although Rattle is still improving almost daily with Mahler, and I hope he'll come back to this work with slightly more experience of life. Still, the sound is marvellous and the performance well thought out; the Finale has a

real terror and grandeur about it, and the
recording won a *The Gramophone* Award in 1988.
- *EMI CDS7 47962-8* ● *2 CDs* ● *Full price*
- *DDD* ● *1987*

My favourite 'Resurrection' has the advantage of
appearing all on one disc; although the long first
movement is perhaps slightly uncertain in
direction, the rest of Otto Klemperer's
magnificently intense conducting produces both
mystery and excitement – and Elisabeth
Schwarzkopf fans should note that she appears in
the Finale.
- *EMI CDM7 69662-2* ● *1 CD* ● *ADD*
- *Mid-price* ● *1961-2*

Good recent performances of No. 3 are hard to
come by; no one seems quite to have got the work's
measure since the late Jascha Horenstein over two
decades ago. Horenstein is a favourite Mahler
conductor; he tends towards the nihilistic side of the
composer (not so evident in this more 'nature-
inspired' work), but he never loses sight of the deep
human tragedies and triumphs lurking in there.
Really, no other recording quite matches this one.
- *Unicorn-Kanchana UKCD2006/7* ● *2 CDs*
- *Mid-price* ● *ADD* ● *1970*

There are some lovely versions of the neo-Classical
4th Symphony, and it's well worth trying this
piece on spec., as it's probably Mahler's friendliest
symphony. A good recent version features the
lovely voice of Felicity Lott in the two songs
which make up the Finale, and conductor Franz
Welser-Möst, despite the occasional controversially
slow tempo, has the advantage of the LPO,
regarded by some Mahlerian conductors as a good,
even great, Mahlerian orchestra.
- *EMI Eminence CD-EMX2139* ● *1 CD*
- *Mid-price* ● *DDD* ● *1988*

A recent issue from the archive offers another
(there are several available already) chance to hear
Bruno Walter conduct this lovely music, and this
'new' issue is arguably the best of all his excellent
versions. The Vienna Philharmonic really was
Mahler's 'own' orchestra at the time he was
composing this work, and the soloist Hilde Gueden
(a beautiful singer of Mozart) has the right kind of
voice for the neo-Classical effect Mahler wanted to
achieve. As a bonus piece of jewel-setting, the disc
also contains Walter's affectionate rendering of
Mozart's Symphony No. 38 ('Prague').
- *Deutsche Grammophon Vienna Philharmonic
150th Anniversary Edition 435 334-2* ● *1 CD*
- *Mid-price* ● *ADD* ● *1955*

Due to the appropriation of the fourth movement
('Adagietto') as the main theme for the film *Death
in Venice*, the 5th has some claim to be Mahler's
most popular symphony at present. Once again
Klaus Tennstedt leads the way with an
electrifying live performance which reaches deep
into the music's soul; the third movement, which
Mahler feared posterity would regard as the work
of a madman, has a particularly urgent ferocity
here. An entirely brilliant and yet ultimately really
rather compassionate performance, with the LPO
living up to their reputatation.
- *EMI CDC7 49888-2* ● *1 CD* ● *Full price*
- *DDD* ● *1988*

Almost as good is Leonard Bernstein's hugely
powerful and emotional performance with the
Vienna Philharmonic; a real roller-coaster, this one.
- *Deutsche Grammophon 431 037-2* ● *1 CD*
- *Mid-price* ● *DDD* ● *1987*

One of Mahler's earlier champions in Britain was
Sir John Barbirolli (1899–1970), and his 1960s
recording of the 5th, for all its slight threats of
failing ensemble at times, has a real vision way
ahead of what many Mahler performers (Solti, for
instance) were achieving at the time. This is a disc
for which collectors have real affection, based both
on respect for the conductor and (more
importantly) esteem for a great performance.
- *EMI CDM7 69186-2* ● *1 CD* ● *Mid-price*
- *1969*

For Symphony No. 6, some admire Karajan, but I
find him a bit dry and flat. Two recent releases
have very good points; Simon Rattle with the City
of Birmingham Symphony Orchestra manages to
put across much of this complex work's
affectionate side, though I'd like to hear more bite.
- *EMI CDS7 54047-2* ● *2 CDs* ● *Full price*
- *DDD* ● *1990*

Riccardo Chailly brings out more of the work's
bitter irony and despair in his performance with
the Concertgebouw; conversely, the passion in the
larger outer movements isn't quite what one would
wish for.
- *Decca 430 165-2* ● *2 CDs* ● *Full price*
- *DDD* ● *1990*

Both these performances are worth hearing, and
are probably the best in glorious digital sound.
But the greatest of all is Horenstein's again, this
time with the inauspicious Stockholm
Philharmonic, from whom he extracts a
performance of great terror, beauty, irony,
affection, and warmth. I don't know a 6th to
match this, and I'm prepared to live with slightly
inferior sound for the quality of this musicianship.
- *Unicorn-Kanchana 2024/25* ● *2 CDs*
- *Mid-price* ● *ADD* ● *1966*

Few recordings of the 7th, apart from Kubelik's
mentioned above (and not, alas, available
separately), manage to grasp the nettle of the
sardonic first movement contrasting with the two
'Nachtmusik' ('Night music') movements placed
second and fourth. This movement is a work of
telling contrasts, with a weird, whispering, shady
third movement at its centre. Far and away the
best single recording is a recent live performance
by Simon Rattle and the City of Birmingham
Symphony Orchestra; although Rattle takes the
first, more famous, 'Nachtmusik' section
surprisingly briskly (which at least gets the piece
onto a single CD), his grasp of the rest, especially
the latter three movements, is outstanding.
- *EMI CDC7 54344-2* ● *1 CD* ● *Full price*
- *DDD* ● *1991*

Klaus Tennstedt has actually made a live
recording of the 8th which hasn't yet been issued
on CD; why not? Meanwhile his studio recording
stands as a masterpiece of technology and a pretty
good reading of the symphony – it won a *The*

Gramophone Award in 1987.
● *EMI CDS7 47625-8* ● *2 CDs* ● *Full price*
● *DDD* ● *1986*

There are some classic versions of the 9th available; pride of place must go to Bruno Walter's historic live recording in Vienna made in March 1938, only a few weeks before the Nazi takeover of Austria forced Walter himself out of the country and suppressed Mahler's music. Perhaps certain parts are a bit scrappy, but this is a beautiful and instructive account. Walter was, after all a friend of Mahler, and had conducted the première in 1912; by no means the speediest of conductors, he takes it enormously faster than anyone would nowadays.
● *EMI CDH7 63029-2* ● *1 CD* ● *Mid-price*
● *ADD* ● *1938*

The essence of modern interpretation of the 9th Symphony can be found in the deeply magisterial Karajan live rendering, in which the Berlin Philharmonic achieves a quietness that almost glows.
● *Deutsche Grammophon 410 726-2* ● *2 CDs*
● *Full price* ● *DDD* ● *1982*

The Czech connection with Mahler continues with a finely thought out version, especially good in the dance-based central movements, by Libor Pešek and the Royal Liverpool Philharmonic Orchestra. The recording also has a good, intense account of the Adagio from Symphony No. 10.
● *Virgin Classics VCDS7 91219-2* ● *2 CDs*
● *Full price* ● *DDD* ● *1990*

THE SCANDINAVIAN EXPERIENCE: SIBELIUS AND NIELSEN

Sibelius is another composer who's become something of a growth industry, and his seven symphonies have come to be seen as important works in the development of the form during the twentieth century. He was, in his own way, something of a revolutionary; not an austere radical like Schoenberg or Webern or other members of the so-called 'Second Viennese School', the group which laid down the rules which for a long time dominated 'Modern' music; but a radical within a Romantic tradition, with a fine sense of drama and melody. And like many of the more overt radicals, Sibelius sought to make symphonic form something altogether more manageable and compact than it

had become with Mahler and Bruckner, eventually writing, in 1924, a one-movement symphony that was truly a one-movement work (as opposed to Schumann's 4th, which was merely a four-movement work without breaks between movements).

Sibelius was also important as a nationalist composer. Strong currents of nationalism ran throughout Europe at the turn of the nineteenth and twentieth centuries (rather as at the turn of the twentieth and twenty-first), and music had a decisively political role to play. Sibelius's *Finlandia*, written in 1900, became an act of defiance against the occupying Russians; whistling it in the street was a provocative act. (Finland was ceded to Russia by Sweden in 1809, and declared itself independent in 1917 with the collapse of Russia. She was invaded by Russia again in 1939, and in 1940 and 1947 was forced to cede large tracts of her land to the USSR.) Sibelius's music had this political dimension; and even when Finland was a free, independent country (of a sort), Sibelius's instincts were always to promote its nationhood and self-perception through his art.

Which said, his first symphony (1899) owes something, ironically enough, to Russian music, and possesses quite a lot of Tchaikovskian overtones. But with the ever-popular 2nd Symphony in D Major (1901), Sibelius discovered an individual voice, a distinct melodic style which is especially reflected in the big tune of the Finale. There's a Sibelian technique here of starting a tune in a tentative manner and only gradually allowing it to force its way through; not a new idea, of course, very reminiscent, in fact, of Beethoven's 'Choral' Symphony. Although desirous of creating a 'Nordic' musical voice, Sibelius wasn't such a fool as to want

Jean Sibelius

1865–1957

‍S‍ibelius is, of course, the composer of *Finlandia*, and the musician who helped to give a small, poor, occupied country a distinctive national musical style. Yet he spent much of his life forced to eke out his existence by writing trashy 'salon music', pot-boiler stuff aimed at the popular music market; so desperate were his finances that he parted with the rights to one of his most popular orchestral works, the *Valse Triste*, for a completely risible sum. It's clear from this that he also had little real sense of the value of money. Like any composer born in the late nineteenth century, Sibelius studied in the great Germanic capitals, Vienna and Berlin, but he found a lot of inspiration in the more overtly nationalist styles of Borodin and Tchaikovsky (although he outgrew this as his life went on). Although he lived to be 92, Sibelius stopped composing around 1926.

>> *Orchestral* 278

to alienate people whose main musical experience was Germanic or Italianate; and what the 2nd Symphony does so successfully, and which makes it one of the composer's three most popular symphonies, is to blend his own technical (and highly formalised) approach to the symphony with something more immediately graspable. A few critics have put the high melodic 'warmth quotient' of this piece down to the fact that Sibelius wrote it while visiting Italy; in fact, he visited Italy during the winter, which can be a depressingly cold experience.

Apart from the one-movement 7th Symphony which, although in a very Romantic musical idiom (there are even little touches that are almost Spanish lurking in its texture), looks towards the kind of compression that an entirely 'Modern' composer like Webern sought to achieve in his one-movement symphony (completed in 1928, some two years after

- Sibelius's 7th appeared); apart from
- this and the 2nd, the most enduring –
- and these days the highest-rated by
- some – of the symphonies is the 5th.
- Its popularity is slightly surprising,
- given that only in its third, final,
- movement is there any immediately
- appealing melody. The work is a
- piece of formal genius; Sibelius bases
- all three movements around a single
- chord, whose individual notes he
- spells out in a horn call at the
- opening.
- Sibelius was not, as you will have
- realised, especially committed to a
- 'classical' concept of the
- four-movement symphony;
- occasionally he cut complete
- movements which he felt didn't work
- in practice (the 5th was originally a
- four movement piece). His is an
- individual approach to the form,
- something which characterises many
- of the more nationalist composers;
- although his intellectualism has often

been underrated. In the midst of this output he produced his recondite (but powerful when familiar) 6th Symphony and his quietly revolutionary 7th. Fortunately he had devoted and influential friends amongst conductors, of whom the great Serge Koussevitzky was the most determined to promote Sibelius's symphonies into the regular repertoire.

DISCOGRAPHY
It's pretty easy to make Sibelius sound like a craggy old bore; he didn't always make it simple for conductors because important passages aren't always 'signposted' (as they are in Tchaikovsky) by enormous sound effects or massed orchestral resources. And sometimes, as in the 5th Symphony, when Sibelius is working out an idea, a conductor who hasn't really got the measure of the piece can make it seem an awful trial. Even the 2nd can, in the wrong hands, sound like a stop-go tune that never gets going. But it must *never* sound like some smoothed-out Brahmsian experience; the logic of Brahms is there, but the evenness most certainly isn't. That's why the 2nd as performed by Leonard Bernstein and the Vienna Philharmonic is one of the most wrong-headed experiences ever; Finland occupied by Austria, as it were, and with Bernstein's odd tendencies to play havoc with tempo, to boot.

There's little reason to pay full price for more than one Sibelius disc, I'm happy to report, and several complete cycles are well worth the money. My marginal preference goes to the excellently recorded, well thought out, performances from Sir Alexander Gibson (a devoted Sibelian) and the Royal Scottish National Orchestra. Some find that Gibson doesn't quite scale the peaks of excitement or plumb the troughs of despair in the manner of some other conductors, but I think he has a depth and undercurrent which matters more than superficial effects.
● *Chandos Collect CHAN 6559* ● *3 CDs*
● *Mid-price* ● *DDD* ● *1982–4* ○

The next best cycle is Russian pianist-turned-conductor Vladimir Ashkenazy's rich and luscious, deeply colourful set with the Philharmonia Orchestra. Perhaps the recordings reflect Ashkenazy's Russian-ness as much as Sibelius's Nordic nature, but this makes for a warm, accessible entry to the works, with a beautifully passionate (in the right way) 2nd. The only drawback is that the performances spread over four discs.
● *Decca 421 069-2* ● *4 CDs* ● *Mid-price*
● *ADD/DDD* ● *1980–6*

For slightly more immediate and vivid colouring, though, either Simon Rattle with the City of Birmingham Symphony Orchestra,
● *EMI CMS7 64118-2* ● *4 CDs* ● *Mid-price*
● *DDD* ● *1985–8; contains two other orchestral works*

or Lorin Maazel and the Vienna Philharmonic will provide all the thrills. Maazel especially is a man who loves to chase the immediate effect.
● *Decca 430 778-2* ● *3 CDs* ● *Mid-price*
● *ADD* ● *1963–8*

The one absolutely indispensable full price Sibelius symphony disc features the 5th and the 7th, both played with an unsurpassed depth of understanding by the Berlin Philharmonic under Karajan. The sound, although almost three decades old, is marvellous, and Karajan really shows why he acquired his reputation in a carefully considered, utterly logical, yet always gripping performance. The recording of the 5th, in particular, remains a first choice.
● *Deutsche Grammophon 415 107-2* ● *1 CD*
● *Full price* ● *AAD* ● *1965*

Anyone who fancies lashing out the full whack on just the 2nd will probably get a great deal of pleasure from Sir Colin Davis's sturdy version with the Boston Symphony Orchestra;
● *Philips 420 490-2* ● *1 CD* ● *Full price*
● *DDD* ● *1986*

but if you're prepared to put up with some surface noise, recordings of the 2nd don't come any more thrilling than the same orchestra about half a century earlier under the great Sibelius promoter Koussevitzky.
● *Pearl GEMM CDS 9408* ● *1 CD* ● *Mid-price*
● *ADD* ● *1935*

THE GREAT DANE: NIELSEN

There are still critics who write Nielsen's music off as 'provincial' (the same critics get incensed if Europeans make similar comments about Edward Elgar). Certainly Nielsen sought to create a voice as individual and 'Danish' as Sibelius's was 'Finnish', but to my mind there seems to be little room for argument with the view that most of Nielsen's music seeks, like Mahler's, only in a much more compact way, to examine enormously global issues. His Symphony No. 5 (written between 1920 and 1922) has some claim, with Mahler's 9th, to the title 'Greatest Symphony of the Twentieth Century'. The names Nielsen gave to three of his six symphonies give some idea of the

Carl Nielsen

1865–1931

Carl Nielsen was born on Funen, a rural Danish island, and his first professional musical job was as a brass player in a military band at the age of fourteen. It wasn't until 1905, when he was 40, that he decided to concentrate on composing; he was appointed musical director of the Royal Theatre in Copenhagen and became the most famous musical figure in Denmark. This didn't mean, though, that his reputation travelled (even though he did); he didn't become known outside Denmark until relatively recently. He remained passionately committed to his home country, fearing for its future both from the expansionist policies of its larger neighbours and from industrialisation.

In a book he wrote, Nielsen insisted that his emotional life was lived in his music rather than in his actual existence, which makes him sound more grim and humourless than he probably was; after all, the idea for his 2nd Symphony, 'The Four Temperaments', came from seeing some pictures in a Danish pub.

scale of his imagination: No. 2, 'The Four Temperaments', seeks to depict the psychological make-up of the human species; No. 3, 'Sinfonia Espansiva', is a portrait of 'the world in general'; No. 4, 'The Inextinguishable' (written between 1914 and 1916), was an attempt to depict the unquenchable strength of the forces of Nature, even in the face of the dreadful conflict of the First World War. Even the 'Simple Symphony', No. 6, is ironically titled, for it may be one of the most despairing works of music ever written; when Nielsen wrote it in 1924–1925 he was suffering repeated heart-attacks.

Nielsen's music is extremely expressive, and whilst his command of melody isn't perhaps Tchaikovskian or Sibelian, the excitement of his work makes it readily accessible, especially to anyone who enjoys Mahler for these

- same qualities. But Nielsen is, like
- Mahler, a deeply intellectual composer,
- creating whole works out of simple
- relations of intervals between notes,
- out of very simple ideas that you don't
- need to know to enjoy the music, but
- which form subtle and ever more
- complex blueprints. Nielsen had an
- uncommon instrumental grasp; he
- could play cornet and trombone as
- well as, more conventionally, the violin
- and piano (on the latter instrument he
- was unusual in being almost
- self-taught). His military band
- experience gave him a deeper feel for
- what the sometimes neglected brass
- instruments can achieve. His most
- famous work, the 5th Symphony,
- revolves around the drama of two
- opposing musical ideas (broadly, one
- represents good, the other evil). Nielsen
- subdued form very much to meet his
- own ends – if 'conventional'
- symphonic form worked for him in his

music (as it more or less does in the 1st, or in No. 2, 'The Four Temperaments') he used it; his 5th Symphony, however, is in two vast movements. Ideas of tonality are less fixed, too; Nielsen's symphonies can't usefully be said to be 'in' any particular key. He most emphatically doesn't reject tonality in favour of the 'twelve-note system' that the new Viennese composers of his lifetime were employing, but the relations between keys are more complex, even when based around simple intervals.

DISCOGRAPHY
There is a complete Nielsen cycle which should meet every requirement; the playing by the London Symphony Orchestra is almost faultless through all six pieces, conductor Ole Schmidt has an absolute understanding of the music, and the notes to the music, by the distinguished contemporary British composer Robert Simpson, are peerless. Schmidt and the LSO encompass a vast range of moods, intense where necessary, relaxed and almost pastoral at other moments; the 5th and 6th Symphonies are especially gripping. This was the first complete Nielsen cycle recorded; the first to be conceived as such; and even superior technology and more flamboyant studio playing can't beat it.
● *Unicorn-Kanchana UKCD 2000/1/2* ● *2 CDs*
● *Mid-price* ● *AAD* ● *1973–4* ✪

If you were interested only in Nielsen's masterpiece, the 5th, and wanted the best that modern studio practice can offer, along with a finely directed performance, then look no further than Herbert Blomstedt and the San Francisco Symphony Orchestra. This is a dynamic, driven recording that you can blast from your stereo, with rarely a foot put wrong (there's a blast from a side-drum at one crucial moment of the 5th that could have been more terrifying, but that's about it). The 5th is paired with the 4th, also very well done.
● *Decca 421 524-2* ● *1 CD* ● *Full price*
● *DDD* ● *1988*

THE BRITISH LINE:
ELGAR, VAUGHAN
WILLIAMS AND OTHERS

So far, British and American names have been noticeable in the history of the symphony only by their absence.

- There were British symphonists at the
- start of the nineteenth century –
- Cipriani Potter (1792–1871), William
- Sterndale Bennett (1816–1875), to name
- two – who were writers of
- inoffensively pleasant work (although
- Beethoven ranked Potter very highly)
- which, thanks to the CD boom, is all
- becoming available to the public again
- after between 150 and 200 years. But
- British symphonies of great impact
- and power had to wait until the
- twentieth century; it does rather look
- from our perspective as though British
- music stopped with the death of Henry
- Purcell in 1695, and only started up
- again at the beginning of the twentieth
- century with Elgar's leap into 'serious'
- musical status.
-

SIR EDWARD ELGAR
(1857–1934)

- Of course, until recently Edward Elgar
- was damned by his 'Pomp and
- Circumstance' Marches and the
- associations of 'Land of Hope and
- Glory'. It was only with the
- extraordinary increase of interest in
- his Cello Concerto that a change in the
- perception of him took place. This
- work, written in 1919, after the Great
- War, reflects the elegiac, nostalgic part
- of Elgar's character; his two
- symphonies, written in 1907/8 and
- 1909/11, are equally complex, mingling
- a sound which can only be described
- as 'English' with a real sense of the
- symphony's Germanic history. Until
- the Great War, in fact, Elgar was
- taken more seriously as a composer in
- Germany than in England.
-   Elgar was a deeply conservative
- composer, and his melodic
- symphonies, with strongly
- euphonious harmony, are very much
- in the style of Brahms and, like
- Brahms's, contain a great deal of
- working-out and development of

thematic material. Perhaps they don't add to the genre, but the pleasure they bring is great and music would definitely be poorer without them.

DISCOGRAPHY

We actually have recordings of Elgar conducting his own works, and the recent reissue of the symphonies on CD has led to a certain reassessment of other recordings. There's no indulgent, wistful slowing of everying up in Elgar's own versions, nor is there any stultifying pomp or stodge in the more 'stately' passages. The sound quality isn't bad considering the date, but, important though these recordings are, they're probably more aimed at the Elgar buff. Quite a few other works are featured apart from the two symphonies.
● *EMI CDS7 54560-2* ● *3 CDs* ● *Full price*
● *ADD* ● *1927–30* ○

Anyone wanting to sample an Elgar symphony for the first time can try an excellent economical version of the 1st, in which conductor James Judd has clearly learnt lessons from Elgar's own performances.
● *Pickwick PCD956* ● *1 CD* ● *Bargain price*
● *DDD* ● *1991*

There are classic performances by Sir Adrian Boult (1889–1983), too, considered by many to be the finest Elgar conductor of all; his performances with the London Philharmonic have a simple, straightforward grandeur which many listeners still prefer to anyone else's.
● *No. 1: EMI CDM7 64013-2* ● *1 CD*
● *Mid-price* ● *ADD* ● *No. 2: EMI CDM7 64014-2* ● *details as before*

The best modern new Elgarian, though, is American. A few American and European conductors are (at last) taking Elgar seriously; long may this continue. The man to beat is Leonard Slatkin, whose performances with the London Philharmonic have a real understanding of the music. No overstated climaxes, no loosening of the thread during development sections; deep, enjoyable performances which yield more on each hearing. They can sound understated at first, but that's part of Slatkin's subtlety.
● *No. 1: RCA Victor Red Seal RD60380* ● *1 CD*
● *Full price* ● *DDD* ● *1990; ● No. 2: RCA Victor Red Seal RD60072* ● *details as before*
● *1988*

━━━━ ━━━━ ━━━━ ━━━━

RALPH VAUGHAN WILLIAMS (1872–1958)

The last word in English Romanticism must go to Vaughan Williams, whose music (best-known in the haunting orchestral piece *Fantasia on a Theme*

by Thomas Tallis) probably defines what most people mean when they talk about music having a peculiarly 'English' feel. This is achieved through the use of lush strings which move in blocks by steps from chord to chord (Vaughan Williams had some trouble passing formal harmony exams when young, because of his love of keeping all the notes at the same distance from each other and having music move by means of these great chordal-block processions). Between 1903 and 1958 he wrote nine symphonies, of which the most rewarding are Nos. 5 and 6. The 5th, which was first performed in 1943, shows off VW's traditional gifts to their best advantage – long, plangent melodies which tear at the heart (and cunningly deployed on woodwind as much as on the sometimes overdone VW strings). The 6th Symphony, conceived and begun during the Second World War, is often regarded as a 'War Symphony', which the composer strenuously denied. However, the contending forces of major and minor tonality in the grandiose opening movement, allied with the sarcastic and rather surprising use of a saxophone in the sardonic Scherzo and the almost nihilistic, flattened, unmoving sound of the Finale, do all suggest that the composer was thinking of a world very much out of joint when he wrote the piece.

DISCOGRAPHY

A Vaughan Williams neophyte could do no better than get hold of Andrew Davis's recent superb recording of the 6th Symphony, which comes with the *Fantasia on a Theme of Thomas Tallis* and a beautiful version of *The Lark Ascending*, an instantly enjoyable work for solo violin and orchestra. Davis's 6th is quite the most outstanding for years, getting the moods of the different movements exactly right and showing the BBC Symphony Orchestra, perhaps for the first time on record, to be every bit the equal of their German broadcasting counterparts.
● *Teldec British Line 9031-73127-2* ● *1 CD*
● *Full price* ● *DDD* ● *1991* ○

There's a version of the 6th almost as good on a recent recording by Leonard Slatkin (he seems to have a gift for English Romantic music). This has the advantage of coming with the 5th; excellent performances both.
● *RCA Victor Red Seal RD60556* ● *1 CD*
● *Full price* ● *DDD* ● *1991*

A good cheaper 5th, for those who might want to try that on its own, is provided by Vernon Handley and the Liverpool Philharmonic.
● *EMI Eminence CD-EMX9512* ● *1 CD*
● *Mid-price* ● *DDD* ● *1987*

And if any of these inspire you to try the full Vaughan Williams cycle, Bryden Thomson's series for Chandos Records, recorded in the late 1980s, is full of superbly considered, deeply felt performances which don't lay the string syrup on with a trowel. For the two last symphonies, the 8th and 9th, a new release from Leonard Slatkin is quite irresistible; full of passionate, eloquent grandeur.
● *RCA Victor Red Seal 09026 61196 2* ● *1 CD*
● *Full price* ● *DDD* ● *1993*

THE FRENCH: CHAUSSON, FRANCK, ROUSSEL

No French composer or work has turned up in these pages since Berlioz and his *Symphonie Fantastique*. This is principally because the French genius lies elsewhere than the symphonic form, and few of the very great French composers have used the form, preferring instead to work with the picture-painting concept of the tone-poem. There was, though, a 'French Symphonic Revival' towards the end of the nineteenth century, centring around symphonies by Ernest Chausson (1855–1899) and César Franck (1822–1890; and in fact a Belgian), who each wrote one. Both are three-movement works, aiming at a grandiose Classical effect, even going firmly back to the old tradition of the slow introduction; both have fairly large first movements, working through complex developments, and long, stately, slow movements. Sadly, both can, in the wrong hands, sound like titanic bores, and I'm afraid neither has ever really worked its way into my essential mental furniture.

A slightly later, but more likeable, French symphonist was Albert Roussel (1869–1937), whose 3rd and 4th Symphonies (of four) were written in the 1930s. They're firmly cast in the German mould, complete with use of motif-like material. Roussel was a composer with a light touch, and these pieces are deeply engaging.

DISCOGRAPHY
Both Chausson's and Franck's symphonies have been very sympathetically recorded by one of the great Gallic conductors of the century, Ernest Ansermet (1883–1969), with the Orchestre de la Suisse Romande; the sound isn't always the greatest, and the orchestra (very much the conductor's own creation) sometimes sounds thin, but that prevents the kind of tedious stodginess which is much more threatening to this music.
● **Franck:** *Decca 433 718-2* ● *1 CD*
● *Mid-price* ● *ADD* ● *1962*
● **Chausson:** *Decca 433 715-2* ● *1 CD*
● *Mid-price* ● *ADD* ● *1962*

For Roussel, try Ansermet again.
● *Decca 433 719-2* ● *1 CD* ● *Mid-price*
● *ADD* ● *1956*

RUSSIANS: ROMANTICISM TO REVOLUTION

One important strand of 'Modern' music as we know it came out of Russia – Igor Stravinsky's rhythmic, neo-primitive *The Rite of Spring*. However, this doesn't belong to the symphonic tradition, but to the music of the dance. The Russian symphonic tradition continued in the early part of the twentieth century with Serge Rachmaninov (1873–1943), more famous, of course, as a pianist and composer for the piano. His three symphonies are quite impressive in their scale, but I always feel as though I'm waiting for the piano to come in. The music has all the same qualities, melody and passion, but lacks that final

Sergei Prokofiev

1891–1953

━━

Prokofiev was probably the last composer to make his reputation in pre-Revolutionary Russia; he was a celebrity in St Petersburg (Petrograd; later still, Leningrad) in the years up to 1917. But after the Bolsheviks won control he left for Western Europe, living in Paris for fifteen years, and also spending a great deal of time in the United States. He acquired a taste for the good life, becoming a gourmet and a jazz-lover, but eventually homesickness got the better of him and, in the late 1930s, he decided to go back to his native land. Unfortunately, Prokofiev walked straight into Stalin's first round of artistic repression; although he was – cautiously – welcomed back, his past always made him suspect and he lived in fear. His wife was sent to Siberia; his children made 'wards of the state' (that is, they were held hostage); and in Stalin's second artistic purges, Prokofiev found that he had to grovel, alongside Shostakovich, and accept a reduction in his status. He died, ironically enough, on the same day as Stalin.

>> *Opera* 204

clinching touch which Rachmaninov's own instrument, of which he was such a master, confers. However, it was left to two other Russian composers to create a distinct Russian symphonic tradition in the twentieth century – something they achieved under the least promising circumstances.

━━ ━━ ━━ ━━

THE MAN WHO WENT BACK: PROKOFIEV

Prokofiev's symphonies are characterised by the basic conflict in his musical personality, the conflict between conservative conformity and the desire for adventure. His most popular symphony is his 1st, known as the 'Classical', a melodic, slightly tongue-in-cheek work produced in 1917. The rest of his seven symphonies vary profoundly in tone, but usually with a respect for melody, and often using

- quotation from and pastiche of other
- composers. Inevitably the final three
- symphonies, written after his return to
- the Soviet Union, show a darkening of
- tone, even where he was supposedly
- 'repenting' his 'artistic crimes'.

DISCOGRAPHY
For Prokofiev symphonies, you generally can't go wrong with Neeme Järvi's recordings with the Scottish National Orchestra. The combination of the 1st with the 4th is quite appealing.
- ● *Chandos CHAN8400* ● *1 CD* ● *Full price*
- ● *DDD* ● *1985* ✪

Järvi's recording of Prokofiev's most intense symphony, the 6th, won a *The Gramophone* Award and is also well worth investigating.
- ● *Chandos CHAN8359* ● *1 CD* ● *Full price*
- ● *DDD* ● *1984*

Rachmaninov
There are solidly exciting and passionate versions of all three Rachmaninov symphonies in a set by pianist/conductor Vladimir Ashkenazy and the Concertgebouw.
Decca 421 065-2 ● *3 CDs* ● *Mid-price* ● *DDD*
● *1981–3*

Also, there's a sparkling newer version of the most popular, No. 2, by Andrew Litton and the Royal Philharmonic Orchestra.
Virgin Classics VC7 90831-2 ● *1 CD* ● *DDD*
● *Full price* ● *1989*

THE PUBLIC FACE AND THE PRIVATE AGONY: SHOSTAKOVICH

The symphony was never quite Prokofiev's métier in the same way that it became of such profound significance for Shostakovich, whose fifteen symphonies were all expected to be the public pronouncements of a Soviet artist in a Soviet state. The 4th Symphony (1935–6) was withdrawn by the composer before it could be performed, and it's easy for us to see why, because it's a work clearly written out of anger, bitterness and resentment. This makes it exciting listening for us, but not the sort of thing Stalin wanted his state composers to be producing. The 5th (1937), subtitled 'An Artist's Response to Justified Criticism', was Shostakovich's public grovel to Stalin; supposedly a portrait of the 'Great Leader', it is Romantic yet modern, and can be played without a hint of irony (the trouble is, though, that with Shostakovich it's very easy to read irony into some of the more pompous moments). The 7th, or 'Leningrad', was officially hailed (1941) as Shostakovich's great tribute to the fight for the Motherland, his depiction of Soviet heroes fighting Nazi invaders; actually we now know that originally the cruelties depicted were Stalin's, not Hitler's, but obviously the composer wasn't going to risk his neck by making this point at the height of the work's popularity. For a long time the 7th was regarded as the 'great' Shostakovich symphony, but even with the knowledge of what it's really about, it still has something of the hollow clang of fake grandiosity about it. Shostakovich was next in trouble for his 9th; confidently, the Soviet authorities had hoped for some work to set alongside Beethoven's 9th,

Schubert's 9th, Bruckner's 9th, Mahler's 9th. Shostakovich deliberately wrote a witty, lightweight work, full of humour, which not only failed to be the 'great Soviet 9th' but also seemed doubly inappropriate, coming as it did at the end of the war (1945), when something so memorable was expected. His 10th Symphony, which really is the kind of passionate, serious piece the authorities might have hoped for, couldn't appear until 1953, the year of Stalin's death; and Shostakovich's rehabilitation as a Soviet artist continued with Symphony No. 11, 'The Year 1905' (1957), a tribute to the failed 1905 Revolution (although it may very well be a condemnatory response to the Soviet invasion of Hungary in 1956). Symphony No. 12 (1960–1) commemorated 'the Year 1917' (although we now know that the composer was close to suicide at this time); but Symphony No. 13 ('Babi Yar', 1962), a work including a bass and chorus singing words by the poet Yevgeny Yevtushenko, daringly attacked Russian anti-Semitism. The 14th (1969) is a glorious, dark, beautiful song cycle for soprano and bass; with its variety of styles and tones, but its passionate eloquence, it is a very personal statement. Shostakovich's final Symphony, No. 15 (1971), is an obliquely personal work, making ironic use in its first movement of the famous theme from Rossini's *William Tell* Overture (and thus offering a rather bleak commentary on the nature of heroism). It also quotes Wagner's 'Fate' motif from *The Ring Cycle*, a short but poignant harmonic sequence which is full of meanings connected with death, the acceptance of death, the acceptance of one's allotted role in life, and free will. Private

Dmitri Shostakovich

1906–1975

Shostakovich was the first composer of the Russian Revolution, and was hailed in the 1920s as the 'Great Red Hope'. Unfortunately, at the time that Shostakovich started composing, Stalin began slaughtering anyone who got in his way, and the optimistic, celebratory nature of Shostakovich's music was deeply affected, to the extent that two of his works, the 4th Symphony and *Lady Macbeth of the Mtsensk District* (the original title of his opera *Katerina Ismailova*) attracted direct criticism from Stalin himself. Shostakovich publicly grovelled, but devised a code on which all his music became based; on the surface his work said what Stalin and his cohorts wanted it to say, but those in the know could detect despair and criticism of the regime. When Shostakovich's 9th Symphony, premièred a few months after the victory over Germany in 1945, failed to be the titanic artistic achievement Stalin expected, a new wave of artistic repression was launched and the regime invented the crime of 'Formalism' (never properly defined). Shostakovich was sacked from his teaching job and forced to write film music. Under the apparent thaw of the later regimes, he was restored to his position of pre-eminence, but his spirit was inwardly governed by despair, and his health broken by a combination of terror and a poor diet.

>> *Opera* 204, *Chamber* 243

undercurrents in public statements; always the hallmark of this important corpus of twentieth-century symphonies.

DISCOGRAPHY
Neeme Järvi's recording of Shostakovich's 4th with the Scottish Symphony Orchestra exemplifies exactly why Stalin would have hated it. Fortunately, Stalin's aesthetic criteria are not ours, so we can enjoy this biting, vivid, almost paranoid performance.
● *Chandos CHAN 8640* ● *1 CD* ● *Full price*
● *DDD* ● *1989*

There are loads of rather good 5ths around; Järvi and the Scottish Symphony again, as well as Ashkenazy firing on all cylinders with the Royal Philharmonic.
● *Decca 421 120-2* ● *1 CD* ● *Full price*
● *DDD* ● *1987*

Järvi gives as good a performance as any of the 7th ('Leningrad'),
● *Chandos CHA.N 8623* ● *1 CD* ● *Full price*
● *DDD* ● *1987*

and is also your man for the 9th.
● *Chandos CHAN 8567* ● *1 CD* ● *Full price*
● *DDD* ● *1987*

For the 10th, try Karajan, who really gets every ounce out of this serious work.
● *Deutsche Grammophon 413 361-2* ● *1 CD*
● *Full price* ● *DDD* ● *1981*

A very good combination of No. 11 ('The Year 1905') and No. 6 comes from Bernard Haitink and the Concertgebouw.
● *Decca 411 939-2* ● *2 CDs* ● *Full price*
● *DDD* ● *1983*

The same conductor's recording of No. 15 really gets to grips with both the ironies and the depths of this allusive symphonic swansong.
● *Decca 417 581-2* ● *1 CD* ● *Full price*
● *ADD* ● *1976*

Naxos also do a Shostakovich cycle; several discs have been conducted by Ladislav Slovák, a conductor who worked with Shostakovich. Good tasters here are the 4th and the 14th, both passionately and convincingly done.
● *No. 4: Naxos 8.550625* ● *1 CD* ● *Bargain price* ● *DDD* ● *1988; No. 14: Naxos 8.550631* ● *1 CD* ● *Bargain price* ● *DDD* ● *1991*

THE BRITISH ROMANTIC TRADITION: SIR MICHAEL TIPPETT (1905–)

The great modern British symphonist has undoubtedly been Sir Michael Tippett, whose four symphonies are among the most ambitious modern compositions. Tippett has used the formal basis of the symphony as a way of packing together all the writing styles which have interested him; from the formal, structured, technically challenging 2nd Symphony (1956–7), through the apparently looser, blues-dominated 3rd, with its great soprano solos (1970–2), to the tightly organised 4th (1976–7), which opens with a wind machine seemingly depicting birth, and moves, through one highly organised movement, from birth to death. The 4th is a more brass-dominated work than its predecessors, sharper, too, than anything in Tippett's work which had gone before.

DISCOGRAPHY
Tippett's four symphonies come in a cheap three-disc set, the first three in superb versions by Sir Colin Davis with the LSO, the 4th by its original dedicatees, Sir Georg Solti and the Chicago Symphony Orchestra.
● *Decca 425 646-2* ● *3 CDs* ● *Mid-price*
● *ADD/DDD* ● *1970s-1984* ○

There is, I gather, a new cycle with Richard Hickox being planned as this book goes to press; watch this space.

SIMPSON, LLOYD, ARNOLD

A whole group of British composers has kept determined faith with the Romantic concept of the symphony, and all its members have been highly prolific within the form. Robert Simpson (1921–) had reached more than ten symphonies at the last count; he has been highly influenced by Nielsen and his works combine a

certain passionate, melodic approach with Nielsen's fascination with simple intervals. Both George Lloyd (1913–), with over twelve symphonies, and Malcolm Arnold (1921–) with ten, have determined to hold onto the form's Romantic sweep; Arnold's work, in particular, is unashamedly autobiographical, with the 8th Symphony being written at the time of, and describing the mental conditions which contributed to, a suicide attempt. Both these composers fell from fashion because of their determined respect for tonality. Havergal Brian (1876–1972) wrote more than twenty symphonies in his own inimitable style; atmospheric, enigmatic, strange – these are just three words which describe Brian's style.

DISCOGRAPHY
Simpson
For Robert Simpson, try either the combination of Symphonies No. 6 and 7, very well conducted by Vernon Handley (one of the most underrated conductors around),
● *Hyperion CDA66280* ● *1 CD* ● *Full price*
● *DDD* ● *1988*

or the 9th, with the same conductor and a talk about his music by the composer himself.
● *Hyperion CDA66299* ● *1 CD* ● *Full price*
● *DDD* ● *1988*

Lloyd
You can catch both early and late George Lloyd on a disc combining his 1st Symphony (from the 1930s) and his 12th (1989); the composer himself is the conductor and the effect can be most enjoyable.
● *Albany TROY032-2* ● *1 CD* ● *Full price*
● *DDD* ● *1990* ○

Arnold
Malcolm Arnold's 7th and 8th Symphonies, two remarkable autobiographical pieces full of his 'dark night of the soul', have been superbly realised by Vernon Handley and the Royal Philharmonic.
● *Conifer CDCF177* ● *1 CD* ● *Full price*
● *DDD* ● *1990* ○

Brian
If you want to sample Havergal Brian, then Sir Charles Groves's combination of the 8th and 9th Symphonies has a lot going for it.
● *EMI CDM7 69890-2* ● *1 CD* ● *Mid-price*
● *ADD*

And the exuberant 'Gothic' Symphony No. 1, compete with soloists, brass band and chorus, is well worth a dabble.
● *Marco Polo 8 223280/1* ● *2 CDs* ● *Full price*
● *DDD* ● *1990*

THE MOST SUCCESSFUL MODERN SYMPHONY: HENRYK GÓRECKI (1933–)

The most successful piece of modern music has been a symphony, the 3rd Symphony (or 'Symphony of Sorrowful Songs') by the Polish composer Henryk Górecki. Written in 1976, this work employs the Minimalist style which has proved especially popular with American composers like Philip Glass and John Adams, a style which tends to be static and repetitive, with little or no harmonic movement. Górecki, though, differs from the Americans in that his Minimalism is much denser, producing a thick, enchanting, string-dominated sound whose impact is much more visceral than the thinner sound of the American composers. The additional element in Górecki's 3rd Symphony is

* a soprano voice, singing traditional
* Polish texts (some of which were
* found in the Warsaw Ghetto where, in
* 1943, an uprising by Jews was
* savagely put down by the Nazis),
* which adds an intensely plaintive edge
* to the music, making its 'Sorrowful
* Songs' all the keener in their impact.
* Whether this is a style which can
* succeed over and over again, or
* whether Górecki's hit symphony is a
* one-off, time will tell; so far there
* hasn't been too much public interest in
* Górecki's first two symphonies (which
* weren't even available on CD at the
* beginning of 1993).

DISCOGRAPHY
The recording which put Górecki on the map is David Zinman's with the London Sinfonietta; it is, above all, Dawn Upshaw's mesmerising soprano voice that has worked the trick here.
● *Elektra Nonesuch 7559-79282-2* ● *1 CD*
● *Full price* ● *DDD* ● *1991*

III

The
Concerto

INTRODUCTION

As soon as musical technology developed far enough to create truly euphonious instruments, a natural desire arose in the players of instruments to show off their ability. This is part of what the concerto is about: a soloist or, in some cases, a group of soloists, showing off. By showing off when supported by a larger ensemble, it is possible to create sound contrasts which are probably more interesting for the listener than the unrelieved sound of, say, the solo violin, cello, trumpet, oboe.

The concerto is most usefully defined as a piece for soloist(s) and orchestra. The way the form developed led to it becoming, through the works of first Mozart and then Beethoven, a sort of symphonic dialogue between soloist(s) and orchestra, with the rivalry between the individual or small group and the larger forces creating intense competition. But the symphonic form familiar from the great Classical and Romantic concertos isn't the whole story, because the greatest era of the concerto, if numbers composed were the major criterion, could be said to be the Baroque.

BAROQUE MANNERS AND THE DEVELOPMENT OF CONCERTO FORM

At around the end of the sixteenth century and the beginning of the seventeenth, the most advanced musical centre in Europe was Venice,

- then an independent republic. It was
- in Venice that the great instrumental
- composing family, the Gabrielis,
- flourished; Venice gave employment to
- Monteverdi; and for something like
- 100 years Venice was the place which
- counted. It was only in the eighteenth
- century, after Vivaldi's star had
- waned, that the city went into a
- decline as an artistic centre, and even
- then it exercised a spell over figures as
- diverse as Wagner, Diaghilev, Thomas
- Mann, and Stravinsky.
- Out of the predominantly vocal
- music of the Renaissance, and with the
- advance in technology of musical
- instruments, there arose a desire to
- formalise musical structure and
- develop the role of the ensembles of
- viols, lutes and mandolins which had
- become increasingly popular as the
- sixteenth century wore on. Around the
- end of that century, instruments were
- a strange mix of things we'd broadly

recognise as quite close to what we have today (violins, violas, cellos) and others which were to be abandoned (viols, the cittarone, keyboard instruments like the clavichord). The ones that survived did so largely because of beauty and versatility of tone; the ones that didn't were felt to be 'inferior' because of their limits in these departments.

The Baroque is often supposed to be characterised by lots of 'frilly bits' and it was a time in which ornament and decoration was of great importance. The term 'Baroque' was originally an architectural one, and it applied to a style of buildings from the seventeenth century characterised by elegance and harmoniousness of form, with a certain amount of surface decoration rounding off angles and points. It's important to realise that the Baroque valued the underlying form just as much as the decoration. Other terms which can be applied to the Baroque are 'rococo' and 'mannerist' (with something of the affected sense of 'mannered' as we use the word today).

The underlying structure of the concerto, as it quickly became established, owed something to the dance suite, which remained an eminently popular form right through to the middle of the eighteenth century and beyond. Dancing was a major social accomplishment at the courts of the sixteenth and seventeenth centuries (which is where most musicians and composers not earning a living through the Church would have been employed), and it's natural that the main requirement of players and composers should have been to provide an accompaniment. Dancing is a lot easier with music, after all. Dancers of the age liked to vary the pace, mixing stately slow measures like the saraband with more up-tempo

numbers such as the gigue. When separate instrumental pieces of any length designed to be listened to (or eaten and drunk and gossiped over), rather than danced to, began to emerge, the variety of tempo of the dance suite, with the same kind of ratio of quick to slow, seemed to form a natural basis; so the three-part quick-slow-quick form, a kind of shrunk-down dance suite structure, was evolved.

Actually, at the start of the Baroque era (which we can loosely label the early 1600s to somewhere in the early to mid-1700s, depending on the country), the term 'concerto' was flung around pretty indiscriminately, as was 'sonata'. Look at one of the great choral masterpieces of the early Baroque – indeed of all time – Monteverdi's *Vespers for the Blessed Virgin* of 1610, and you'll find a couple of concertos and a sonata, all with voices, none really relating to our current ideas of the form. 'Concerto' simply relates to the English word 'concerted' or together.

FATHERS OF THE CONCERTO: TORELLI, SCARLATTI AND CORELLI

It was in the latter part of the seventeenth century that concertos, as we understand the term, started to appear in vast profusion. The first major contributors to the form whose work still attracts any attention today were Giuseppe Torelli (1658–1709), Alessandro Scarlatti (1660–1725) and, above all, Arcangelo Corelli (1653–1713), a highly influential composer whose memory has been honoured by composers as diverse in time, style and temperament as J. S. Bach and Sir Michael Tippett. A great deal of Corelli's vast output has been lost (preserving music of the past only started in earnest when Mendelssohn decided to resurrect J. S. Bach's *St Matthew Passion* in 1829).

Right into the 1690s, the concerto was exclusively (we believe) the province of stringed instruments. There were two kinds of concerto: the solo concerto, which, self-explanatorily, featured a single soloist accompanied by a group of musicians (quite often twelve in number; the precise size of the forces would depend on what the sponsoring patron or society paying for the composition and the performance had at his or their disposal); and the concerto grosso (literally 'big concerto'), which frequently featured a small ensemble of soloists, quite often four or more string-players, as well as the larger orchestral group. Sometimes a group in a concerto grosso would not include violinists, but a work with only two or three soloists wouldn't be deemed a concerto grosso (not grosso enough).

In the concerto of this period, there wasn't the same interaction between soloist(s) and orchestra as subsequently became the genre's hallmark. Instead, the main faster movements would make use of the 'ritornello', a regularly repeated section played by the full orchestra, almost a self-sufficient melodic passage which could be transposed up and down the scale where necessary to fit in around the more elaborate virtuoso work of the soloist(s). The solo material would sometimes offer a contrast with the ritornello, or sometimes it would develop it, working out quite elaborate variations. You might say that the ritornello passages offered a chance for the soloist to relax and take a short break. Slow movements at this point (and for quite a long time) were somewhat rudimentary and brief; some (as in Vivaldi's famous and overrated

Four Seasons) just successive chords with an underlying slow pulse.

DISCOGRAPHY
Corelli
While the music of Corelli, Torelli and their like makes for quite pleasant background stuff, I wouldn't say that, unless you're an obsessive Baroque fan, it makes for gripping front-of-the-attention listening. The best Corelli on offer contains twelve concerti grossi played by Trevor Pinnock and his English Concert, who achieve a nice clean sound on forces of just about the right size. Corelli does sound ludicrously overblown on modern instruments, especially played by orchestras of modern size. This Pinnock collection may seen a bit steeply priced for anyone just wanting a sampler of the Baroque concerto, but then I wouldn't recommend anyone wanting just that to go for Corelli in the first place. This Pinnock recording won a 1990 *The Gramophone* Award.
● *DG Archiv 423 626-2* ● *2 CDs* ● *Full price*
● *DDD* ● *1988* ○

THE CONCERTO IN THE EIGHTEENTH CENTURY: ALBINONI AND TELEMANN

Round about the beginning of the eighteenth century, composers began to use wind and slightly less orthodox stringed instruments for solos in the concerto; Scarlatti wrote concertos for flute and strings and an oboe concerto, Torelli wrote two trumpet concertos, as well as a guitar concerto. Younger composers like Tomaso Albinoni (1671–1751) and Antonio Vivaldi (1678–1741) showed greater interest in new possibilities for the concerto, although it was outside the hitherto dominant Venice that the true potential of wind instruments as concerto soloists were fully recognised; it was Georg Philipp Telemann (1681–1767), working as a Kapellmeister in Hamburg, who really went to town on different combinations of oboes and trumpets. Generally Venice preferred strings, Hamburg and other towns in northern Germany oboes and trumpets, although the Venetians began to follow the German taste at some point in the middle of the second decade of the eighteenth century. Albinoni's first collection of concertos to make extensive use of one and two oboes (the twelve works under the heading Opus 12) comes in the middle of the 1710s and is dedicated to a Venetian nobleman and patron, but clearly has its eyes on lucrative sales in North Germany.

DISCOGRAPHY

As for other Baroque concertos of this ilk, I have a great admiration for a double-disc set of Albinoni's twelve Opus 7 concertos, a recording which brings together the formidable talents of the baroque ensemble I Musici and oboist Heinz Holliger.
● *Philips 432 115-2* ● *2 CDs* ● *Full price*
● *DDD* ● *1990–91*

Christopher Hogwood, stalwart of the period instrument world, has produced what is, I think, the most persuasive Telemann recording, full of surprising folk-rhythm influences and freshness, and revealing Telemann as a cosmopolitan soul. The works offered include a D major concerto for three trumpets, an E minor recorder and flute concerto, a Concerto Polonois, among others.
● *L'Oiseau-Lyre 411 949-2* ● *1 CD* ● *Full price*
● *DDD* ● *1982*

CONCERTO FACTORIES

Telemann, Vivaldi, Albinoni and others turned out concertos like factory hands to meet demand. They were used to turning music out by the yard, working very much within clearly defined rules and parameters. Occasionally they'd try something new, such as bringing in different solo instruments, but the Albinonis, Vivaldis and Telemanns of the world never wanted to start any serious or deeply disturbing revolutions. Usually change would be introduced for the sake of novelty, to keep the audience's attention. All three enjoyed huge popularity, even if it did eventually wane in Vivaldi's case, and they reaped

the rewards of writing music which was exactly in keeping with their times. Telemann – one of the most prolific composers of all time – was so highly regarded that J. S. Bach was considered a very poor second choice (in fact, he was thought a poor third choice; the otherwise-engaged second choice is now scarcely remembered at all) for one of his musical appointments. Yet it's clear, given our hindsight, that Bach was a significant figure in the history of music, whose mastery of various forms (including the early concerto) was both more rigorously intellectual and more far-reachingly consequential than Telemann's. Ironically, Bach would possibly have agreed with his contemporaries' 'ranking'; all clear proof that we shouldn't assume that our own estimates will persist through all eternity.

VIVALDI

Of all the Venetian composers of this period, Vivaldi enjoys far and away the most enormous popularity today, and there does seem to be some logic to this. He produced sets of concertos, supposedly organised around principles, with titles like *The Trial of Harmony and Invention* and *The Extravaganza*. Bach took Vivaldi extremely seriously, and arranged several of his violin concertos for harpsichord; Vivaldi also took Vivaldi extremely seriously, which led to him being less than popular with his fellow musicians. They also rather sneered at his work for one of the reasons that has led to its now enjoying a resurrection – the sheer extravagance of the virtuosity in the solo writing. Some of Vivaldi's contemporaries felt that the kind of pyrotechnic violin displays at what was then the edge of known playing technique (and all designed to show what a talented

Antonio Vivaldi

1678–1741

Vivaldi was, for almost all his life, based in Venice; for much of that time he was fantastically popular. He was known as 'the Red Priest' because for a while he was in minor canonical orders, although there's little or no sign that he ever regarded the Church with any seriousness from a religious point of view. At the peak of his popularity, Vivaldi's reputation – like that of many of his fellow Venetian-based composers – extended through much of Europe; consequently when, in the 1730s the fickle Venetian public, bored with a familiar name, got bored with his music too, Vivaldi thought he'd try and restore his flagging fortunes in Vienna, then rapidly developing as an artistic centre. He left Venice in 1740, but his health, never good at any time, collapsed, and he died in poverty and obscurity in Vienna. In fact, Vivaldi can more truly be said to have died the death of a pauper in Vienna than can Mozart.

>> *Choral* 251

violinist Vivaldi himself was) were trivial and outside the bounds of musical decorum.

Actually, Vivaldi's reputation, which waned in his own lifetime, was only restored fairly recently. Even half a century ago he was held in sufficient disregard for Stravinsky to remark that Vivaldi wrote the same concerto 400 times (more like 500, in fact). But one work above all has restored him to the repertoire and ensured that the Vivaldi section in the record shop spreads over a (to be honest, ludicrously) vast area.

The Four Seasons

Le Quattro Stagione, *The Four Seasons*, comprises the first four concertos in the twelve-strong collection *The Trial of Harmony and Invention*. Vivaldi published a poem with each concerto, depicting a 'seasonal' scene; the poetry is probably bad enough to have been the composer's own. In fact, *The Four Seasons* is an early example of programme music, the ancestor of Beethoven's 'Pastoral' or Berlioz's *Symphonie Fantastique*, but whether that's why it now enjoys the popularity it does is dubious. *The Four Seasons* is highly melodic, undemanding, easy to relate to the pictures the concertos depict, characterful (especially the frissons in the first movement of 'Winter'). It's not at the cutting edge of Vivaldi's art, not even at the edge of his virtuosic writing. Not a single major composer has ever been influenced by it. Yet it is one of the most recorded works in the current catalogue, and the concertos are extremely infectious and enjoyable. You may gather that I'm a bit mystified by the vogue for the piece, although I always enjoy a characterful version.

DISCOGRAPHY
Finding your way around the maze of *Four Seasons* recordings can be difficult. I believe that *The Four Seasons* usually benefits from the thinner, more precise tones of period instruments (and if you cast elsewhere around this book, you may gather that I'm not always the biggest fan of 'authenticity'). There's a cracking version by Nils-Erik Sparf and the Drottningholm Baroque Ensemble; clear but robust, rhythmically exciting and original. There's also some interesting phrasing, which you don't always get with period performers. The old value-for-money problem rears its ugly head, but this version can also be found in the UK in branches of Boots at bargain price. Otherwise it's a pricey piece of excitement.
● BIS BIS-CD275 ● 1 CD ● Full price ● DDD ● 1985 ○

When considering recordings of this work, Nigel Kennedy seems to loom large. In fact, his version is a rather old-fashioned approach, quite close to the Romanticism of the interpretation by Ann-Sophie Mutter and Herbert von Karajan, which is scarcely along the lines of the period-instrument lobby. Kennedy has some interesting ideas about the music (if you cut through all the guff about nuclear holocausts) and his is a very strong performance which takes some risks both in style and technique; there's lots of subjective mood changing, even in an overtly descriptive moment like 'The Hunt' (the third movement of 'Autumn'). But at a mere 40 minutes, this is lousy value for money.
● EMI CDC7 49557-2 ● 1 CD ● Full price ● DDD ● 1988

Better value for money and almost as good musically as the Drottningholm version is Claudio Scimone's lively reading with I Solisti Veneti. This also offers four more works from *The Trial of Harmony and Invention* and makes a good sampler of slightly more Vivaldi than just *The Four Seasons.*
● Erato Collection Bonsai 2292-45945-2 ● 1 CD ● Bargain price ● ADD ● 1973

Anyone wanting to branch out further into Vivaldi could try the highly enjoyable performances of his Opus 3 set – *L'Estro Armonico* ('Harmonic whimsy') – by Sir Neville Marriner and his Academy of St Martin-in-the-Fields. Marriner's performances might appear slightly thickset next to those played on period instruments, but they still have great style, wit and verve.
● Decca 430 557-2 ● 2 CDs ● Mid-price ● ADD ● 1971

BACH

The Brandenburg Concertos
While Bach was based at Cothen, he encountered (on a trip to Berlin in 1818, where he also gave a performance) the Margrave Christian Ludwig of Brandenburg (musical life in Germany in those days seems to have been nothing but an endless round of aristocratic encounters; that was how you tried to make money, in any case). The Margrave asked if Bach would compose something for him.

It took Bach about three years to get around to responding to the Margrave's request, and even then he didn't offer him a series of specially composed works. One of the interesting aspects of the six Brandenburg Concertos is that they represent a selection by JSB himself from compositions he had to hand (or which he composed around that time) which he obviously felt made an interesting 'manifesto' of the concerto's possibilities. Bach was always interested in exploring the possibilities of musical form to their utmost limits; hence his exhaustive keyboard works, such as *The Art of Fugue* and *The Well-Tempered Clavier.* Although the six Brandenburgs are just a small percentage of Bach's concerto output, they exhibit a range of techniques and approaches to the form which are both of their time, in line with the concerti grossi of Corelli, Vivaldi and Albinoni, and forward-looking, sowing the seeds of the more familiar concerto. The solo keyboard antics of the 5th Brandenburg, and the extended virtuoso passage which sounds very much to modern ears like a cadenza, anticipate the Mozartian piano concerto, which laid the ground rules for all the enduring piano concertos that followed.

The style of the six Brandenburgs ranges from the publicly festive and celebratory mood of the 1st to the private, almost chamber-music timbre of the 6th; this doesn't represent any kind of progression, as the 6th was

Johann Sebastian Bach

1685–1750

From a distance, Johann Sebastian Bach can look a bit grim and forbidding. He wrote so much religious music that it's hard not to imagine him as highly pious, while so much of his music seems organised around academic, intellectual principles that he must have been a dry old stick. But he once walked 200 miles to hear an organist; he was married twice, producing twenty children in all; and his employers discovered that he didn't always want to toe the 'establishment line'. Life could be distinctly uncomfortable for composers in those days. Dependent upon wealthy and aristocratic patrons for employment, if the conditions failed to suit the composer, he would often face starvation – or even worse. In 1717, Bach decided that employment with Duke Wilhelm of Weimar wasn't working out to his advantage and asked to be released from his job. The Duke's response was straightforward; he threw Bach in prison for six weeks, and then dismissed him. Bach fortunately went on to more congenial employment with Prince Leopold of Anholt-Cothen, who was pleased to appoint a figure such as JSB as his Kapellmeister (despite the apparent religiosity of the title, the job basically meant Director of Music and, in some cases, Composer in Residence; the kapellmeister tradition is one of the noblest in the Germanic world and several conductors working today – Günter Wand, Kurt Masur, Wolfgang Sawallisch – have come through it). Leopold was a Calvinist and therefore didn't approve of church music, which left Bach free to work, for the first time for many years, on secular and instrumental music (although the bulk of his religious cantatas were written in the 1720s). Bach lived for long enough to become something of a 'back number'. In his last decade his music was unfashionable, though he didn't allow this to worry him; he just kept on composing music which has outlasted most of the more 'fashionable' stuff which his younger contemporaries were producing. And his influence on subsequent composers has been incalculable.

>> Chamber 215, Choral 253, Orchestral 274

either the first or second of the set to be written (while Bach was still in Weimar). All but the 1st are three-movement works; the 1st was originally a three-movement work, which was slightly odd in that it consisted of an Allegro, an Adagio and a Minuet; when Bach subsequently added a conventional second Allegro, he placed it before the large, seven-sectioned Minuet. The celebratory style of the 1st is achieved by its use of brass and woodwind, the prominence given to the horns; he also rewrote the score to include an instrument called the 'violino piccolo', a small, higher-pitched violin, which engages in solo dialogue with the oboe in the Adagio. The 2nd Brandenburg Concerto reflects the taste and practice of the time; a group of soloists à la Vivaldi or Telemann, mixing a solo violin with oboe and recorder, but allowing, in three movements, a specially dazzling role for a solo trumpet. The third concerto is probably the most famous (its opening is used as the theme for BBC1's popular *Antiques Roadshow*) and is almost a purely orchestral piece. It makes much play of groups of three (three violins, three violas, three cellos), allowing one player from each group to stand out as soloist at different times (in the original performance, there would probably have been only one player to each line). The slow movement consists of only two chords – whether or not some improvisation at the accompanying keyboard would have been expected isn't known. The fourth concerto features a violin and two recorders as solo instruments; in the outer movements the piece seems almost like an early violin concerto (as we understand the term), although the recorders are always present. The fifth, which is the most forward-looking, was also (probably) the last to be written; although it is technically a concerto grosso using a standard(ish) group of soloists – flute, violin and harpsichord – it gives a prominence and virtuoso freedom to the harpsichord that was unheard of then in concerto writing. Bach went on to write harpsichord concertos after this. The 6th Brandenburg Concerto, for all its earliness, is unique amongst concertos of this era in not using violins, employing instead lower-pitched strings such as the viola (which Bach himself played);

two violas are the soloists. This piece has an extraordinary intensity and intimacy, because of the difference of its sound.

BACH AND OTHER CONCERTOS

Bach wrote (and rearranged) a large number of concertos apart from the Brandenburgs, for instruments as diverse as harpsichord, oboe, violin, double (that is, two) violins, flute. The 'Double Violin' Concerto (Concerto for Two Violins in D Minor) has proved particularly popular, as again it anticipates the modern concerto in more than just form and structure; it has the same kind of 'symphonic' feel, a sense that soloists and orchestra are engaged in a dialogue rather than a series of alternating monologues. Written around the time Bach wrote/compiled the Brandenburgs, it has adapted rather well to the sound of the larger Romantically-based modern orchestra. It was reworked by the composer as a double harpsichord work (pitched a tone lower in C minor); reworking one concerto for another instrument or group of instruments was a favourite Bach tactic – his oboe concertos were originally written for harpsichord.

Bach wrote so many concertos that it's possible to get lost exploring them all; while some are perhaps slightly more perfunctory than the Brandenburgs or the Double Violin Concerto, it's fair to say that Bach rarely wrote a dull note. He was such an intellectual composer that he was always looking for a new twist on music, and this is perhaps why he was the first composer to enjoy a significant 'revival' in the early nineteenth century, and why he has proved such a major influence on so many other composers.

DISCOGRAPHY
The Brandenburgs
By common consent, the leading version of the
Brandenburg Concertos currently available is by
Trevor Pinnock and his English Concert; it's on a
recording like this that you realise why Pinnock's
stock is so high. Occasionally a dry interpreter, he
here phrases everything with a great deal of
character and drive, although the slower
movements sing beautifully and melodically. The
boxed set includes some of the orchestral suites;
hence the number of discs.
● *Deutsche Grammophon Archiv 423 492-2* ● *3
CDs* ● *Mid-price* ● *DDD* ● *1987* ✪

The concertos are also available on 2 separate discs.
● *Nos. 1–3 DG Archiv 410 500-2* ● *Nos. 4–6 DG
Archiv 410 501-2* ● *both Full price*

Period-instrument playing has revolutionised our
view of the Brandenburgs; much admired though
the works were before 'authentic' performances
became the norm, scholarly attention to details of
the original styles of performance brought out the
clarity and subtlety of Bach's structures and
experiments. The trail-blazing recording has
recently been reissued on CD; it features Nikolaus
Harnoncourt and his 'authentic' ensemble of 40
years' standing, Concentus Musicus Wien.
Listening again to Harnoncourt's interpretation, it's
interesting how he is, at times, quite leisurely in
his tempos (one of the criticisms of period
performances is that they're often ridiculously
fast), sounding almost Romantic. There is, too, a
certain thinness at times which some of the more
recent period ensembles, abetted by digital
recording, avoid, but this is an important disc; and
a very good one, too.
● *Teldec 9031-77611-2* ● *2 CDs* ● *Mid-price*
● *ADD* ● *1964*

Very often in this kind of music (late
Baroque/early Classical) if you don't want period
instruments then your best bet is Raymond
Leppard. Leppard's direction of the English
Chamber Orchestra in the Brandenburgs is full of
wit, lightness and drive; one of the recorder
soloists is the early music scholar David Munrow;
and I honestly don't believe that modern
instruments have ever played this music better.
● *Philips 420 345/6-2* ● *2 CDs* ● *Mid price*
● *ADD* ● *1974: available separately*

Other Bach concertos
There are quite a few enjoyable versions of the
Double Violin Concerto, which come with a variety
of complementary programmes. A favourite
version of mine pairs the J. S Bach's Double with
two violin concertos and a cello concerto by
C. P. E. Bach (whose dimensions are much more
those of the Romantic concerto). The Scottish
Ensemble under Jonathan Rees plays modern
instruments, but with crispness, clarity and drive.
The tonal colouring throughout is superb; the
recording is vivid and biting, and the 66-minute
disc is a great bargain, ideal for anyone wanting
to try the music for the first time.
● *Virgin Virgo VJ7 91453-2* ● *1 CD* ● *Bargain
price* ● *DDD* ● *1991* ✪

Tevor Pinnock's English Concert is in the frame
again, with a disc of violin concertos (two solo and
the Double) played brightly and vigorously,
although perhaps at times the whole effect is on
the academic side.
● *Deutsche Grammophon Archiv 410 646-2* ● *1
CD* ● *Full price* ● *DDD* ● *1983*

Another period specialist, Christopher Hogwood,
has recorded a disc of Bach's double concertos (the
Double Violin, plus two double harpsichord works
and a violin and oboe concerto). This is very
much period performance aimed at
deromanticising the music it plays; the slow
movement of the Double Violin isn't allowed any
kind of elegant polish. A good, sound, beautifully
recorded release.
● *L'Oiseau-Lyre 421 500-2* ● *1 CD* ● *Full price*
● *DDD* ● *1988*

For the richer flavour that a more traditional
modern-instrument approach brings, but
sacrificing not a whit of musical sensitivity, I'd
recommend a disc featuring the Academy of St
Martin-in-the-Fields conducted by the
distinguished violinist (particularly expert in
chamber music) Gidon Kremer, and featuring the
oboist Heinz Holliger in the Violin and Oboe
Concerto. This full-blooded sound wouldn't appeal
to the Hogwood purists, but it gives me a great
deal of pleasure.
● *Philips 432 036-2* ● *1 CD* ● *Bargain price*
● *DDD* ● *1982*

And finally, there's an excellent Bach oboe
concerto disc, with one of the best solo oboists
around, Douglas Boyd (he'll be cropping up again
later in this chapter). Perhaps not a primary
requirement, but if you find yourself getting into
Bach's concerto idiom, you'll love this.
● *Deutsche Grammophon 429 225-2* ● *1 CD*
● *Full price* ● *DDD* ● *1989*

●   ●   ●   ●

THE CONCERTO MOVES
ON: J. S. BACH TO
MOZART
The concerto remained a popular
form throughout the eighteenth
century, and the balance tipped more
and more towards the use of a
single solo instrument, although
generally the idea of complex
interaction and dialogue between
soloists and orchestra didn't catch on.
A soloist then expected to be able to
show off uninterrupted, with
relatively little clutter surrounding
him or her.

All the major composers of the period used the form extensively, whether they composed solo parts to play themselves or for accomplished virtuosi to perform, or slightly simpler parts for patrons who wanted to shine in their own specially written concerto. It became quite commonplace for composers performing their own solo concerto parts not to bother writing them out in advance. George Frederick Handel (1685–1759) composed a series of organ concertos which were performed in the intervals of his operas; quite often he would devise the solo part during the act before he was due to play. At a time when music was more stylised and there were fewer options open, this was, of course, easier; it was also how Mozart worked with some of his piano concertos.

Organ concertos were very popular in the eighteenth century; apart from Handel, Haydn also wrote a set. Haydn, in fact, wrote some very enjoyable concertos, although it's not a form in which he's usually celebrated; his two cello concertos (No. 1 in C Major and No. 1 in D Major) both suggest the direction the form was taking, with the soloist blending into the orchestra at times, and also have a great deal of clever melodic virtuosity. His Trumpet Concerto in E Flat Major, too, is considered one of the great staples of the trumpet repertoire; it's a bright and brilliant piece; in fact, great fun (a word not always associated with Haydn).

C. P. E. Bach, as we've already seen from one of my recommended J. S. Bach recordings, was a dab hand at concertos; his oboe works are particularly enjoyable, and by the time he was writing them, the oboe concerto was (although no one knew it) on the verge of becoming an endangered species. The number of major oboe concertos between that of Mozart (1777) and Richard Strauss (1946) can be counted on the fingers of one hand.

DISCOGRAPHY
I feel that Handel's organ concertos are a bit of an acquired taste; anyone wanting to acquire it should turn (yet again) to Pinnock, whose recordings boast the organist Simon Preston.
● *Deutsche Grammophon Archiv 413 465-2*
● *2 CDs* ● *Full price* ● *DDD* ● *1983*

Haydn's Trumpet Concerto, played well by the very trendy Wynton Marsalis, can be found on the same disc as the 2nd Cello Concerto – a superb performance by Yo-Yo Ma – and a skilful rendition of a C major violin concerto.
● *CBS/Sony Masterworks CD39310* ● *1 CD*
● *Full price* ● *DDD* ● *1984*

There's also a disc of Yo-Yo Ma, who has a real gift for Haydn's cello writing, playing both works with the English Chamber Orchestra.
● *CBS/Sony Masterworks CD36674* ● *1 CD*
● *Full price* ● *DDD* ● *1984/6*

And the current idol of the trumpet, Håkan Hardenberger, gives a suitably sparkling rendition of the Trumpet Concerto well backed by Sir Neville Marriner and the Academy of St Martin-in-the-Fields.
● *Philips 420 203-2* ● *1 CD* ● *Full price*
● *DDD* ● *1987*

Two of C. P. E. Bach's oboe concertos are available with another that has become part of the oboist's repertoire, the D Minor Concerto by Alessandro Marcello (1684–1750), as well as an unaccompanied oboe sonata by CPE. The soloist József Kiss has a way of making the instrument's tonal range (which can seem narrow, thin and dull) colourful and vastly inventive, and this superb bargain is a good way to get hold of some music which may not perhaps be 'basic library' material, but will none the less brighten up dark days or nights.
● *Naxos 8.550556* ● *1 CD* ● *Bargain price*
● *DDD* ● *1991*

MOZART

Bach was the first genius of the concerto; Mozart was the second and perhaps the greatest of all. There are 42 concertos in the catalogue against his name; 27 for piano (or pianos), 5 for violin, 4 for horn, 2 for flute and 1 each for clarinet, oboe and bassoon, as well as 1 for flute and harp combined.

The first five of the works for piano were in fact transcriptions of pieces by other composers (most of whom now are largely remembered for the fact that Mozart arranged their pieces for solo piano or orchestra into concertos while still quite young). The Oboe Concerto, discovered in 1920, is in fact a transcription of the 2nd Flute Concerto and may very well not have been done by Mozart at all, but by an oboist desperate to invent a concerto for his instrument written by a significant name after the Baroque era. The piano concertos earlier than No. 11 (the numerical order for the piano concertos is, for once, the same as the chronological order), the two flute concertos, the bassoon concerto, and the flute and harp work were all written before Mozart's break from the Archbishop of Salzburg and his move to Vienna where, partly by choice, and partly by force of circumstance, he was mainly a freelance composer.

THE CONCERTO AS MOZART FOUND IT

As Baroque had become Classical, the concerto had developed in length and absorbed the idea of sonata form, in a slightly modified 'concerto-sonata' form which was almost invariably used for first movements; both first and second subjects would usually be laid out in a long orchestral introduction, and the soloist would appear only when the development started. The soloist would usually be supported by only part of the orchestra, and such decorative material as the orchestra would be allowed was designed not to distract from what the soloist was doing. The weight of the first movement was biased towards a section, usually occurring as part of the recapitulation, called the 'Cadenza', an extended improvisation by the soloist without any orchestral accompaniment, and (probably) based on the material used earlier in the movement. Once the cadenza was over, the orchestra would take up the strain and (without the soloist) carry the movement to its end. Cadenzas were vital in first movements, but quite often were used in finales and even in slow movements, always occurring at a point just before the movement was about to be wrapped up. Although the soloist usually developed melodic material introduced by the orchestra, the amount of interplay between the two was limited; and in the finale, usually a fast rondo, the orchestra would give out the main theme, while the pianist was kept to intervening decorative episodes.

MOZART THE DRAMATIST

Mozart's greatest concertos (and there are at least fifteen which can vie for this extremely enviable title) often draw comparison with his operatic writing. This is a very illuminating comparison, and gives some idea of why Mozart's concertos are both so lastingly attractive and so vitally important in the development of the form. Just as Mozart the operatic composer had little time for set piece bits of solo singing which held up the action of the drama, and wanted even his most showy arias to progress the story and shed light on the character of the 'person' singing; just as he made more use than any operatic composer before him of ensemble numbers during which the plot actually unfolds; so with his concertos, and above all with his piano concertos, he sought to bring the soloist and the orchestra together, to make them interact and react to one another, to bandy phrases and melodies, even to change roles. As early as his Piano

Concerto No. 9 in E Flat Major (K271, written in 1777, also known as 'Jeunehomme' as it was written for a Mademoiselle Jeunehomme), Mozart tore up the conventional rules. The piano enters with the second half of the very first musical phrase, and when its more conventional time for entry arrives, later in the movement, rather than coming in with a bang, as soloists usually did then, it glides in on two extended trills, playing supporting role to the orchestra; and even then carries on trading half-phrases for much of the rest of the movement.

A nice little earner: Mozart's piano concertos
It is in the piano concertos that Mozart's greatest contribution to the genre can be found. His heart was never in the works for flute (he hated the sound of the flute); the horn concertos are full of delightful melody, as are the earlier violin concertos; and his most sophisticated essay in the form away from the keyboard was the Clarinet Concerto, his very last concerto of all (written in the year he died, 1791), and the first really important work for that relatively newly developed instrument.

First of all, the piano concertos weren't really *piano* concertos; most of them were written not for the pianoforte which we are used to but an earlier version of the instrument called the 'fortepiano'. It has an altogether thinner, damper sound, and smooth melodic playing on it is much more difficult; in fact, so much more difficult that one can be forgiven for believing (as I partly do) that Mozart was, half the time, writing for an idealised keyboard instrument which hadn't been invented in his own time, something more like our own

pianoforte with its greater tonal range and its ability to produce smooth, rippling runs. 'Authentic' performers would disagree with me violently about this.

In writing piano concertos, Mozart had to perform a rather neat little balancing act, especially after he'd moved to Vienna. Some were commissioned by and therefore written specifically for certain patrons to play; No. 7 (K242), for three pianos, was written for a Countess Lodron and her daughters, and the ability of each of the players is reflected in the difficulty of each of the three solo parts (the third part is really ludicrously easy for anyone with a modicum of skill at the piano). Most, we know, were written with the composer himself as the designated soloist; No. 10 (K365), the last he wrote in Salzburg, is a two-piano work which was written for Mozart and his sister Nannerl to perform. After he moved to Vienna, the concertos became a lucrative source of income for Mozart, as he would compose them each year for a series of 'subscription concerts' that were to take place during Lent, when performances at the opera house were forbidden for reasons of religious observance. Mozart – or a patron, on his behalf – would canvass all the aristocracy in advance, asking them to pay a fixed sum which would entitle them to attend a series of concerts at which Mozart would perform a new set of concertos. When the overheads of a performance (the other musicians' pay and, where appropriate, the hire of the venue) had been paid off, the rest would be clear profit for the composer. In his first five years in Vienna, Mozart raked in money at an ever-increasing rate in this way. But suddenly, in 1786, his concertos fell out of fashion. Perhaps it was the genre as a whole rather than Mozart's in particular which the audiences grew tired of; it's certainly fair to say that the Viennese, like the Venetians of Vivaldi's time, liked novelty and fairly easily grew bored.

But it's also possible that Mozart's concertos had become too 'difficult' for them: that they didn't offer enough soloist pyrotechnics; that they developed too much into works which blended the role of soloist and orchestra together; that they were in some way too inward. Five years before his concerto style fell from grace, Mozart had written to his father that he sometimes found it difficult to maintain a balance between writing music which he (and other connoisseurs) would value, and music which would find favour in the eyes of the public. Certainly the year in which his piano concertos failed saw three of the greatest of all: the outwardly melodic No. 23 in A Major (K488), whose sunny outer movements frame a dark and rather disturbing slow movement; the completely neurotic No. 24 in C Minor (K491), one of only two Mozart piano concertos in a minor key and one which keeps winding in on itself, the piano-writing asking the soloist for great gifts of control rather than overt displays of brilliance (this concerto was much admired by Beethoven, and its echo can be heard in practically every C minor piano work he wrote); and No. 25 in C Major (K503), which in some ways displays the reverse side of the coin, though it is equally self-controlled. After these three masterpieces failed in commercial terms, Mozart wrote only two more piano concertos, one for the coronation of the Emperor Leopold II in 1790 (generally agreed to be a more perfunctory work than any since

his move from Salzburg), and the last, deceptively simple, superficially rustic, No. 27 in B Flat Major (K595).

The best of the best: eight 'desert island' Mozart piano concertos

Like Beethoven's symphonies, I could quite happily recommend the reader to start anywhere with Mozart's piano concertos and work through them at their leisure. However, time doesn't always allow such luxury; and so I here offer my eight 'desert island' concertos, the ones I believe to be essential. If you don't get on with at least one of these, then you're not going to like Mozart's piano concertos – or, quite possibly, Mozart in any shape or form.

No. 9 in E Flat Major (K271), 'Jeunehomme'
Apart from the rule-breaking opening movement discussed above, it also has a slow movement quite different from anything which had gone before, in which Mozart manages to freeze time. This concerto stands with the best for its musical content, not merely for its 'historical' importance.

No. 17 in G Major (K453)
Part of a set regarded by Mozart himself as 'grand' concertos, this, one of his successful Viennese compositions, is full of the easy-going warmth and melodic invention for which Mozart is famous. Irresistible.

No. 20 in D Minor (K466)
The first of two minor-key works, full of overt Romanticism and tempestuousness, yet actually a very confident and playful work demanding technical bravura in its frenetic Finale. A pussycat disguised as a tiger.

No. 21 in C Major (K467), 'Elvira Madigan'
The tacky nickname derived from the use of the slow movement in a tedious 1960s Swedish art film. The slow movement is actually a *tour de force*, demanding complete evenness from both soloist and orchestra, another exercise in suspended time. A fine example of how Mozart could create great music from the simplest material.

No. 23 in A Major (K488)
As discussed above. The opening movement has one of his most winning tunes; the Adagio (the only slow movement he ever marked 'adagio', a genuinely slow marking, rather than 'andante', which literally means 'at a walking pace') is surprisingly introspective.

No. 24 in C Minor (K491)
As discussed above. The only truly neurotic concerto, with everything kept under an ordered surface. My favourite.

No. 25 in C Major (K503)
As discussed above. Very formal and unshowy, but deceptively difficult for, and demanding of, the soloist, and using quite a lot of surprising tonal twists and turns.

No. 27 in B Flat Major (K595)
Deceptively childlike in its simplicity, you can tell it was written at the same time as *The Magic Flute*. The slow movement is possibly the greatest of all his considerable slow movements.

Mozart didn't invent the keyboard concerto; what he did was to take a fledgling form, started by Bach and developed a little by Haydn, and turn it into a mature and challenging musical genre. Once Mozart had finished with the concerto (and added his superbly melodic Clarinet Concerto for good measure), he had created the 'modern' form.

DISCOGRAPHY
Piano concertos: full and near-full cycles
I first learnt the concertos from a classic series of recordings made in the 1960s by Hungarian pianist Gèza Anda. Perhaps nostalgia sways my choice, but to my mind these versions are still better than anything else you can get, especially in the mature, great works. Anda and the orchestra he directs (the Camerata Academica des Salzburger Mozarteums, one of the greatest Mozart orchestras in the world, both then and now) use modern instruments, but the lucid quality of both his playing and conducting and the orchestra's technique never allow for any heaviness; nor does Anda see Mozart through Romantic glasses. His touch and tone are perfect throughout; some of his tempos are so brisk that Roger Norrington would be proud of him; phrasing is exquisite; every time I come back to Anda's set I find myself gushing about its qualities. It offers all 27 works except No. 7 for Three Pianos and No. 10 for Two Pianos, the recording quality is excellent (though with the slightest surface hiss at times), and above all you can get the whole set for between £50/60. If Mozart's piano concertos interest you at all, you won't regret buying this.
● *Deutsche Grammophon 429 001-2* ● *10 CDs*
● *Bargain price* ● *ADD* ● *1961–9* ○

Staying with modern instruments for a while, there have been four major Mozart piano concerto projects in recent(ish) years. One, Daniel Barenboim's (Teldec), is a second-time-round affair and, sadly, doesn't quite match up to the pianist/conductor's first attempt back in the late 1960s/early 1970s. Whereas on his first time round (EMI), Barenboim brought an unashamed Romantic perspective to the music, in his fully digital incarnation, which is backed by the might of the Berlin Philharmonic, there's a lacklustre dryness of approach, and he has a tendency to break up long melodic phrases.
No, much better – if you want something more modern than the Anda recordings – is to go with the man who for many is the King of Mozart, Murray Perahia. He is the soloist/conductor with the English Chamber Orchestra on a series recorded in the 1970s and 1980s; possessed of a flawless technique and a poise which merits the word 'Olympian', Perahia delivers some of the most clear, cool Mozart ever recorded. My only reservations are that he is a little too perpetually 'cool'; Mozart does at times demand warmth, and Perahia isn't perhaps the sprightliest of conductors, so that sometimes the orchestra doesn't match his touch.
● *Sony CD46441* ● *12 CDs* ● *Special price*
● *ADD/DDD* ● *1976–84*

If Perahia is the reigning King of Mozart, the Queen must be the breathtakingly brilliant

Mitsuko Uchida. Her touch and tone on a piano are of the kind that make everything sound easy, and she delivers run after run so that you wonder just how she does it. Mozart is something of a special gift with her, and you won't find recordings with the solo parts better played. Sometimes though, she's just a little too reserved, a little too polished; although my great reservation about this series is, alas, the conducting of the otherwise excellent Jeffrey Tate, who seems altogether too solid and loud at times.

● *Philips*   ● *available on separate discs*   ● *each*
Full price   ● *DDD*   ● *1983–9*

My personal favourite amongst recent Mozartians, though, is András Schiff, whose partnership with conductor Sándor Végh is well-nigh perfect in its sympathy and its approach to the music. Like Anda's 1960s recordings, Schiff and Végh use the Salzburg Camerata Academica, and the delicacy of their playing is an added bonus. But, above all, the triumph of the series is Schiff's precise, pointed, excellently phrased playing which manages to run the full gamut from the Olympian and detached to the warm and committed, showing, in a piece like No. 20, a surprising amount of pyrotechnics.

● *Decca*   ● *available on separate discs*   ● *each*
Full price   ● *DDD*   ● *1987–92*

There are, of course, several 'authentic' Mozart cycles performed on fortepiano, most of which, I'm afraid, rather fail to appeal to me. But one fortepiano cycle strikes me as being way ahead of the opposition; it features Dutchman Jos van Immerseel as soloist/director of his own ensemble Anima Eterna. Van Immerseel has the technique to make the fortepiano sing (a rare accomplishment), and his tonal range on the instrument seems so much wider than any other performer's. His direction of the orchestra, too, is subtle, clever, and entirely in keeping with his own studious views on rhetoric and structure in the works. The notes which come with the recordings are some of the most detailed and interesting I've ever read.

● *Channel Classics CCSBOX10*   ● *10 CDs*
● *Special price*   ● *DDD*   ● *1990; also available separately*

There are great lobbyists for the soloist Malcolm Bilson's versions with John Eliot Gardiner and the English Baroque Soloists, and there are some fine moments to be found there (especially the slow movement of No. 9), but in the mature works the sound is, in the end, a bit thin.

● *Deutsche Grammophon Archiv 431 211-2*
● *9 CDs*   ● *Special price*   ● *DDD*   ● *1985–9*

The same also goes for Melvyn Tan's current project with Roger Norrington (EMI), though some period-instrument lovers adore what's gone so far, especially the disc coupling Nos. 24 and 25.

Piano concertos: individual recordings
There are a few recordings of individual concertos which entirely deserve the status 'classic'. Sir Clifford Curzon (1907–1982) was one of the greatest of pianists, and his partnership with Benjamin Britten (1913–1976) and the English Chamber Orchestra in Nos. 20 and 27 is not only a meeting of great musicians; it also reveals both sides of Curzon's ability in the fiery D minor work and the deceptively simple No. 27.

● *Decca 117 288-2*   ● *1 CD*   ● *Full price*
● *ADD*   ● *1970* ✪

A columnist wrote in the *Guardian* recently named the Rumanian Dinu Lipatti (who was born in 1917 and died tragically young of leukaemia in 1950) as 'Pianist of the Century'. That's a debatable point, but what we have of Lipatti's artistry on disc persuades that he was a genius of the instrument. His live recording of No. 21 at the 1950 Lucerne Festival (with the Festival Orchestra conducted by Herbert von Karajan) gives no sense of the pain he must have been suffering, and despite the imperfect sound remains one of the great moments in recording. It's coupled with an earlier studio recording of Schumann's concerto (see page 114) which is staggeringly brilliant.

● *EMI References CDH7 69792-2*   ● *1 CD*
● *Mid-price*   ● *ADD*   ● *1948/50*

I'm also rather fond of Stephen (Bishop–) Kovacevich's stylish performances of the two mature C major works, Nos. 21 and 25; Kovacevich has a fine touch, especially in slower movements.

● *Philips 426 077-2*   ● *1 CD*   ● *Bargain price*
● *ADD*   ● *1973*

Other Mozart concerto recordings

Clarinet, oboe, bassoon, horn
The Clarinet Concerto was originally written for a slightly different instrument, the basset clarinet, although the solo part adapts easily enough to the modern instrument. There are excellent recordings using both original and modern clarinets; Antony Pay makes a fine and sensitive soloist and Christopher Hogwood's direction of his Academy of Ancient Music is balanced and nicely judged. There's also a decent version of the Oboe Concerto.

● *L'Oiseau-Lyre 425 643-2*   ● *1 CD*   ● *Full price*
● *DDD*   ● *1984* ✪

An excellent Hyperion release combines the Clarinet Concerto with one of Mozart's most interesting pieces of chamber music, the Clarinet Quintet. Thea King uses a basset clarinet, backed by the modern instruments of the English Chamber Orchestra under Jeffrey Tate (in much more characteristic form than in the cycle with Uchida).

● *Hyperion CDA66199*   ● *1 CD*   ● *Full price*
● *DDD*   ● *1985*

One of the greatest clarinettists of the century has been Jack Brymer, and of his many recordings of the Mozart concerto, the most magical is his 1950s collaboration with Sir Thomas Beecham. It's a deeply Romantic, expansive view of the work, a million miles from Hogwood, but no less inspired by a devotion to Mozart and his inner truths. This great bargain also contains a radiant version of

the Bassoon Concerto, played by the great Gwydion Brooke, and of the 3rd Violin Concerto.
● *EMI CDM7 63408-2* ● *1 CD* ● *Mid-price*
● *ADD* ● *1949/58*

Whether or not Mozart really wrote the Oboe Concerto, there is one recording that really demands to be heard; a characterful, yet light, feathery, reading by Scotsman Douglas Boyd, given superbly complementary support by the Chamber Orchestra of Europe under Paavo Berglund. The work is paired with Richard Strauss's neo-Classical concerto – the next major oboe piece – given probably its best recording to date.
● *ASV CDCOE808* ● *1 CD* ● *Full price*
● *DDD* ● *1986*

There are two superb versions of all four horn concertos, one classic, one from the digital age. The classic performance, inevitably, comes from the great Dennis Brain (killed in a car crash in the late 1950s at the age of 36), a horn player who achieved a range of tone, subtlety and melodic phrasing that will probably never be bettered. His humanity and wit rubbed off on his conductor here, Herbert von Karajan (never the securest Mozartian).
● *EMI References CDH7 61013-2* ● *1 CD*
● *Mid-price* ● *ADD* ● *1954*

The nearest equal to Brain in recent years has been Barry Tuckwell, whose versions with the English Chamber Orchestra (under the soloist's direction) come closest to providing an acceptable digital substitute (or back-up) to Brain.
● *Decca 410 284-2* ● *1 CD* ● *Full price*
● *DDD* ● *1984*

Violin concertos
Perhaps surprisingly, the world isn't bursting with great versions of the Mozart violin concertos. Enjoyable though these pieces are, they aren't quite essential and, very sensibly, most record companies pair the two best – Nos. 3 and 5 – together. The excellent Naxos provides a combination that's about as good as any; the names of soloist Takako Nishizaki and conductor Stephen Gunzenhauser may hardly be familiar in every household, but they certainly deliver the goods.
● *Naxos 8.550063* ● *1 CD* ● *Bargain price*
● *DDD* ● *1989* ○

But if you want famous names, then I suggest you try the excellent, supple but steely, Anne-Sophie Mutter, Karajan protégé, in concert with her master when she was only fourteen years old; a fine, radiant, if slightly Romantic (but none the worse for that), reading.
● *Deutsche Grammophon 429 814-2* ● *1 CD*
● *Mid-price* ● *ADD* ● *1976*

For superb sound and spirited performance with a sparkle, Isabell van Keulen is your woman. As soloist/director of the Concertgebouw, she delivers a really cheering performance.
● *Philips 426 715-2* ● *1 CD* ● *Full price*
● *DDD* ● *1990*

She's pretty good on the other three concertos too, if you want to branch out to those.
● *Philips 432 100-2* ● *1 CD* ● *Full price*
● *DDD* ● *1990*

I can't leave the violin concertos without commending the great David Oistrakh, soloist/conductor with the Berlin Philharmonic in a series recorded in the early 1970s. Unfortunately, however, EMI has separated No. 3 and No. 5 (which used to appear on the same LP), but his versions of Nos. 1–3 have a real grandeur and technical dazzle, even if they're not what Mozart himself might have expected.
● *EMI CDM7 69176-2* ● *1 CD* ● *Mid-price*
● *ADD* ● *1972*

And, finally, there's a typically stunning, lightly delivered but technically breathtaking account of No. 5 by the twentieth century's greatest violinist – Jascha Heifetz (1901–1987), in his sole recorded appearance as conductor/soloist. The 'Turkish' Finale is astounding.
● *BMG/RCA GD87869* ● *1 CD* ● *Mid-price*
● *ADD* ● *1954*

THE SYMPHONIC CONCERTO: BEETHOVEN

Beethoven's seven concertos, written over a period of twelve years between 1797 and 1809, are (with the possible exception of his first two works for piano) typical of the man's struggle with music and form. Never a natural melodist, Beethoven tested the genre's dramatic possibilities to the utmost. Even more than Mozart's piano concertos, Beethoven's essays in the genre are conceived symphonically and make enormous technical demands of the soloist without necessarily providing the opportunity to show off that (earlier) Vivaldi, or (later) Liszt or Mendelssohn would have regarded as the essence of concerto form.

With Beethoven we arrive at a point where concertos have become rarer in a composer's work than symphonies (or, in Beethoven's case, string quartets and piano sonatas). Also, the dawning of the nineteenth century saw the piano and violin assume supremacy as concerto instruments. The piano was, of course, getting closer to the prodigiously exciting and noisy instrument of our own time (it hadn't quite developed to that point when Beethoven wrote his five piano concertos, but I rather hear him, like Mozart, writing for the instrument of the future as much as that of his own day), and Beethoven brought to the form his own special vision of what a symphonic orchestra could achieve. His four great concertos – that is, No. 4 in G Major, Opus 58, and No. 5 in E Flat Major, Opus 73 ('Emperor'), both for piano, the Violin Concerto in D Major, Opus 61, and the 'Triple' Concerto for Violin, Cello and Piano in C Major, Opus 56 – were all written as Beethoven was seeking to advance symphonic form and proportions through Symphonies No. 3 ('Eroica') to No. 6 ('Pastoral'). So, as one might expect from Beethoven, the size of movements suddenly makes a quantum leap, with the first movement of his last concerto (the 'Emperor') lasting almost twenty minutes. This all adds to the piece's heroic qualities; it's tempting to see the 'Emperor' as a defiant gesture by its pianist composer, who was unable to play the work in public himself as he was completely deaf by the time he wrote it. The last two piano concertos also bring the solo instrument in at the very beginning; indeed, No. 4 must have sounded revolutionary, with its opening hushed solo piano chords to which the orchestra replies in a key some way distant from 'home'.

Beethoven's concertos: works to admire or to love?

Sometimes, Beethoven's concertos can become a bit pompous or abstract in a way that his symphonies rarely do, even in the least sympathetic hands.

- The slow movements of the two last piano concertos both have a tentative pattern; that of No. 4 has often been likened to 'Orpheus taming the wild beasts by the power of music', as its dramatic rhetoric is organised around a soft solo part gradually coming to dominate some rough, threatening minor-key orchestral music, all of which subsides into a gentle nothingness and then erupts in the surprisingly skittish Finale. Again, the long opening movements of both the 'Emperor' and the Violin Concerto sometimes seem to be dominated simply by the basic chord of the home key, requiring special insight from both soloist and conductor to find the drama and the right tonal colouring.
- The 'Triple Concerto' was for a long time something of an 'Ugly Duckling' amongst the concertos; while it may seem to hark back to the Bach and Vivaldi concept of a group of concerto soloists, in fact it's more like a bizarre, slightly unpredictable mixture of a symphonic work and a chamber trio.

Beethoven's approach to the concerto seems to us, with hindsight, to be a logical development from Mozart's and by no means as radical as his contribution to the development of the symphony. At the time, however, it was an approach which found little favour, especially in the years immediately after the composer's death, when the more flamboyant, soloist-dominated pieces by Liszt and Mendelssohn became the order of the day. When, in 1841, Robert Schumann looked to Beethoven as a model for his own piano concerto, it seemed suicidal; and it took the determined championship of the greatest virtuoso of the century (possibly ever), Joseph Joachim, to establish the virtues of Beethoven's Violin Concerto, and he gave his first significant performance of the piece in 1844 (at the age of thirteen). The 'Triple Concerto', too, has proved a hard act to follow; to the extent that when Michael Tippett produced a similar piece in the 1970s it was regarded as daring in several ways.

I've not devoted much space to the first three piano concertos since the first two are fairly conventional works, while the 3rd, in C Minor, is a classic example, as I've said, and particularly in the way it opens, of the influence of Mozart's Piano Concerto No. 24 in C Minor. This doesn't mean that it's an inferior work (it's extremely enjoyable), and it's recognisably Beethoven rather than Beethoven trying to be Mozart. However, it isn't in the same imaginative league as the four concertos he wrote after it.

DISCOGRAPHY
Piano concertos

If you want to splash out on all five and still not spend too much, then Wilhelm Kempff's early 1960s recordings have a good deal of love and thoughtful playing in them; Kempff was a great Beethoven pianist, even if his technique wasn't quite of the highest (one eminent critic of pianists has described him as the 'worst of the greats', if that makes sense).
● *Deutsche Grammophon 427 237-2* ● *3 CDs*
● *Bargain price* ● *ADD* ● *1960–2* ❂

Barenboim also recorded an interesting, slightly odd set in the 1960s with Otto Klemperer; the conductor, of course, tended to take everything at a measured pace, while the young Turk Barenboim (still in his early twenties at that time) has different ideas. Compelling, though again with some fluffed technique along the way.
● *EMI CMS7 63360-2* ● *3 CDs* ● *Mid-price*
● *ADD* ● *1967–8*

Meanwhile, closer to the present, Murray Perahia's Olympian poise brings out one side of Beethoven's piano writing superbly, and Bernard Haitink, his conductor, has a fine grasp of these works. The coupling of Nos. 3 and 4 won a *The Gramophone* Award in 1985.
● *CBS/Sony Masterworks M3K 44575* ● *3 CDs*
● *Mid-price* ● *DDD* ● *1984–6*

I ought, too, to mention a recently released cycle by another outstanding Beethoven pianist, John Lill. His way with this composer is mercurial, fascinating, sometimes wilful (he likes his slow movements slow and he attacks some of the

quicker movements with real bite), but never dull, and together with the City of Birmingham Symphony Orchestra under the clever, informed direction of Walter Weller, he has produced a cycle which makes *all* the concertos sound fresh and new. Good accompanying notes, too.
● *Chandos CHAN9084/6* ● *3 CDs* ● *Full price*
● *DDD* ● *1992*

You could also put together your own coherent cycle simply by buying three discs by one of the best Beethoven pianists around; Stephen Kovacevich (who was originally Stephen Bishop, became Stephen Bishop-Kovacevich, and has subsequently dropped the Bishop). He recorded all five concertos with Sir Colin Davis and the BBC Symphony Orchestra in the late 1960s/early 1970s, and these versions are all top recommendations. I urge you to hear them.
● *Nos. 1 and 2: Philips 422 968-2* ● *1 CD*
● *Bargain price* ● *ADD* ● *1970* ● *Nos. 3 and 4: Philips 426 062* ● *1 CD* ● *Bargain price*
● *ADD* ● *1969* ● *No. 5: Philips 422 482-2*
● *1 CD* ● *Bargain price* ● *ADD* ● *1969*

But recently Kovacevich made a new, live recording of the 'Emperor', this time conducting himself – and it's even better.
● *EMI Eminence CD-EMX 2184* ● *1 CD*
● *Mid-price* ● *DDD* ● *1989*

If you want to stick just to Nos. 4 and/or 5 (occasionally with No. 3 thrown in), I have a great deal of affection for the ultra-intellectual, yet never aridly dry, Alfred Brendel, whose No. 4 (with Bernard Haitink) has been, as a record, a long-time favourite. On CD it comes with No. 3.
● *Philips 420 861-2* ● *1 CD* ● *Mid-price*
● *ADD* ● *1978/9*

Recently BBC Radio 3's regular *Building a Library* feature chose Maurizio Pollini's account of No. 4 as its top choice, part of the recommendation being its coupling with his performance of the 'Emperor'. Oddly, I remember the same programme being decidedly sniffy some thirteen years ago about Pollini's 'Emperor', which just goes to show how tastes change. Pollini is one of the greatest technical pianists alive today, although sometimes it seems there's more technique than feeling going on; he's a fine interpreter of twentieth-century music, certainly, but I wonder whether these recordings, with Karl Böhm (not always the most spirited of conductors) are the best testament to his ability. Still, their highly intellectual approach to the music (which for my taste lacks smoothness of phrasing; Beethoven may not always be tuneful, but his phrasing usually was carefully planned) may suit some people down to the ground.
● *Deutsche Grammophon 435 098-2* ● *1 CD*
● *Mid-price* ● *ADD* ● *1976/80*

There are some classic performances of the 'Emperor' – Kovacevich apart – which throw in one of the long, late sonatas (or something similar) for good measure. I remember being rather cool when reviewing French pianist Robert Casadesus's version on its reissue in 1990; more fool me, as

time has made it one of the more enduring, searching performances of this deeply difficult piece. Some of the timing in the slow movement is exquisite, and Hans Rosbaud, the conductor, really makes something fresh of the score.
● *Philips 426 106-2* ● *1 CD* ● *Mid-price*
● *ADD* ● *1961*

Vladimir Horowitz is one of the greatest of 'Romantic' pianists; players who recast everything they touch in some brilliant, bravura mould of their own. His live 1952 performance of the 'Emperor' with Arturo Toscanini (1867–1957) may have slightly dodgy sound quality, but it's a thoroughbred genius piece of music-making (and all the better for being coupled with the same pair's 1943 live Tchaikovsky 1st Concerto, one of the greatest recordings ever made).
● *RCA Victor Gold Seal GD 87992* ● *1 CD*
● *Mid-price* ● *ADD* ● *1952*

And again, perhaps a few shortcomings in the sound quality, but inspiration and excitement aplenty come in the pairing of Edwin Fischer (1886–1960) and conductor Wilhelm Furtwängler. One of the most powerful performances ever made of this extraordinary work.
● *EMI References CDH7 61005-2* ● *1 CD*
● *Mid-price* ● *ADD* ● *1951*

'Authenticists' will doubtless wonder why I've omitted any of the period-piano versions of the Beethoven concertos; simply, I don't think there are any yet recorded which do the works justice, rather than merely thinning the pieces down and playing them far too peremptorily and perfunctorily.

Violin Concerto, Triple Concerto
Nigel Kennedy, accompanied by the usual merchandising hype, garnered a lot of praise for his version of the Violin Concerto; and I'm happy to say every word of it was deserved. He always sounds spontaneous and this is truly a 'live' performance (Kennedy refused the opportunity for studio 'corrections'). He and Klaus Tennstedt make a remarkable team here; Romantic interpretation at its outer edges and well worth anyone's time and money.
● *EMI CDC7 54574-2* ● *1 CD* ● *Full price*
● *DDD* ● *1992* ○

A little down the price range there's an excellent performance featuring Herman Krebbers, the leader of the Concertgebouw, with his home orchestra and their long-time conductor Bernard Haitink. They too make a formidable but less showy team; and the rich, yet never heavy, sound of the Dutch orchestra has been one of the most pleasing in Europe over the last two or three decades.
● *Philips 422 971-2* ● *1 CD* ● *Mid-price*
● *ADD* ● *1974*

The Beethoven Violin Concerto has attracted all the greatest players, and for sheer high-voltage drive, taking the work as close as it will go to a purely virtuoso work, you can't beat the great

Heifetz. It cracks along, making the concerto something new, and different from almost any other performance.
● *RCA/BMG RD85402* ● *1 CD* ● *Full price*
● *ADD* ● *1951*

Wolfgang Schneiderhahn's 1962 performance with Eugen Jochum and the Berlin Philharmonic has a spiritual intensity in the second movement which has probably never been matched, leading the *Penguin CD Guide* to give this bargain one of its rare rosettes for excellence.
● *Deutsche Grammophon 427 197-2* ● *1 CD*
● *Bargain price* ● *ADD* ● *1962*

The greatest living violinist (arguably), Itzhak Perlman, made a truly spirited live recording with Daniel Barenboim; Perlman can hold both the Classical and Romantic aspects of Beethoven in perfect balance, and Barenboim is a conductor who suits him ideally, having the same dual perspective on the music.
● *EMI CDC7 49567-2* ● *1 CD* ● *Full price*
● *DDD* ● *1986*

Yehudi Menuhin has recorded the work several times, always superbly, but perhaps never better than his 1953 essay with the great Furtwängler. The allegations of Nazism (never proved, but never completely dispelled) hurled at Furtwängler will always cloud his reputation in some eyes, but here, with one of the greatest, best-loved, Jewish musicians of our time, he shows an uncanny sympathy and rapport.
● *EMI CDH7 69799-2* ● *1 CD* ● *Mid-price*
● *DDD* ● *1953*

Bargain-hunters should keep an eye out for the deeply satisfying, entirely reliable version by Oscar Shumsky.
● *ASV Quicksilva* ● *CD QS 6080* ● *1 CD*
● *Bargain price* ● *DDD* ● *1988*

Truly great recordings of the Triple Concerto are a bit thin on the ground. One of the best is a star-studded feast, featuring the pianist Sviatoslav Richter (for many, the greatest of the twentieth century), the cellist Mstislav Rostropovich, and the violinist David Oistrakh; add to them the Berlin Philharmonic and Herbert von Karajan and you've got either brilliance or a recipe for egomaniacal disaster. Fortunately, you get brilliance; the three soloists hit a real vein of sympathy in the more 'chamber' moments of the piece, and Karajan turns out the kind of delicate reading he isn't especially renowned for.
● *EMI CDM7 69032-2* ● *1 CD* ● *Mid-price*
● *1970*

Even cheaper is a recording by that underrated conductor (and former Prime Minister) Edward Heath, who reveals a surprisingly solid grip on the expansive work's structure, and an ability to make a studio work sound live. In this he's greatly helped by the cellist of the Trio Zingara.
● *Pickwick PCD 917* ● *1 CD* ● *Bargain price*
● *DDD* ● *1989*

There's also a fine, beautifully recorded version with three young American soloists and Sir Alexander Gibson running a tight, impressive ship; the support here is a fairly convincing performance (by Walter Weller) of the attempted reconstruction of the first movement of Beethoven's 10th Symphony.
● *Chandos CHAN 6501* ● *1 CD* ● *Mid-price*
● *DDD* ● *1984*

THE CONCERTO AS SHOWPIECE: LISZT, CHOPIN AND MENDELSSOHN VERSUS SCHUMANN

Beethoven's great 'symphonic' concertos weren't fashionable during the composer's lifetime; at the première of the Violin Concerto the soloist, realising that both he and the audience needed some distracting at the end of the slow movement, turned his violin round and played an amusing series of virtuoso pieces to lighten the 'monotony'. This gives some idea of public taste in the early nineteenth century; and nothing much changed for an awfully long time as long as there were plenty of composers around to 'give the people what they wanted'. Many of these composers have now passed from view (rightly so in more than a few cases), but it would be a real intellectual killjoy who tried to pretend that every bit of bravura, soloist-dominated concerto writing in the first half of the nineteenth century was to be sneered at.

LISZT

Only a fool would argue that Liszt had no intellectual structure behind his two extraordinary virtuoso piano concertos, written in the 1830s. In his own way, he was every bit as interested as Beethoven in using small motifs and ideas as bases for whole

works, and he followed this through to a much more logical conclusion, transforming his concertos (and his piano sonata, which is gradually coming to be seen as not only one of the most technically challenging ever composed, but also one of the most deeply intellectual) into long, single-movement pieces without a break, everything deriving from ideas put forward in the first bars. Liszt brings the piano in from the very start, as had Beethoven; unlike Beethoven, however, he doesn't then play along with convention by making the soloist withdraw as the orchestra works out the opening thematic material. The soloist is the dominating presence all the way through, and very often the solo part seems like a succession of written-out cadenzas, designed to allow the soloist to show off endlessly, with lots of decorative, pointless running scales. Liszt also, though, liked playing around with orchestral sounds, and the instrumental textures of the parts around the soloist are really very exciting, sometimes unashamedly vulgar (for instance the blaring trumpets all over the 1st Piano Concerto). Long out of fashion, Liszt is now back in a big way, and rightly so.

DISCOGRAPHY
There are two outstanding discs containing both the Liszt piano concertos; one is ostensibly better value than the other, but the shorter actually has the greater musicianship. The brilliance of Sviatoslav Richter brings an extra dimension to Liszt's music, and the accompanying orchestra, the London Symphony, plays with great verve and passion under conductor Kirill Kondrashin.
● *Philips 412 006-2* ● *1 CD* ● *Full price*
● *ADD* ● *1961*

Alfred Brendel is one of the best Liszt pianists around, and his recordings with Bernard Haitink and the London Philharmonic have a fierceness and vivacity which drives the music home. This disc also contains Liszt's piano and orchestra piece *Totentanz* (*Dance of the Dead* or *Danse Macabre*),

Franz Liszt

1811–1886

L iszt is one of the most flamboyant of all musical figures, the archetypal Romantic. He was perhaps the most famous musician of the nineteenth century, and his influence was much greater and more widespread than has often been allowed. He was one of the great sex symbols of his day, too; the word 'Lisztomania', used as the title of Ken Russell's rather fanciful film biography, was actually coined during Liszt's own lifetime. The son of a minor court official and musician from Hungary, Liszt first showed talent as a pianist when he was about six, and in 1822, when his family moved to Vienna, he was taught by some of the leading figures of his day (including the ageing Salieri); legend even has it that he was kissed by Beethoven. At sixteen he settled in Paris, and as he grew up he met all the important figures of his day; Victor Hugo, Heinrich Heine, Berlioz, Niccolò Paganini, Schumann, and Frédéric Chopin. He began a scandalous affair with a married Parisian aristocrat by whom he had three illegitimate children (one of whom, Cosima, became Wagner's second wife). To escape the moral censure, Liszt undertook a major musical tour of Europe, and was received with adulation everywhere he went. He had several affairs with quite prominent women (including Lola Montez, later mistress to King Ludwig I of Bavaria). It was another married woman, the cigar-smoking, religious Caroline von Sayn-Wittgenstein, who took Liszt in hand in the late 1840s, and helped him set himself up with a court position at Weimar, where for ten years he composed a great deal, as well as promoting the work of his friends. In 1861 he moved to Rome, where he spent the rest of his life, taking minor clerical orders a few years later (which is why he is sometimes known as Abbé Liszt). This was not some affectation; despite his wild life, Liszt had from an early age taken a deep interest in religious philosophy.

>> *Chamber 232, Choral 262, Orchestral 276*

based, like the last movement of Berlioz's *Symphonie Fantastique*, on the medieval setting of the Dies Irae section of the Requiem mass.
● *Philips 426 637-2* ● *1 CD* ● *Mid-price*
● *ADD* ● *1972* ❂

FRÉDÉRIC CHOPIN
(1810–1849)

If Liszt was the greatest pianist of the century, then Chopin must be the runner-up. He's another of the great 'Romantic' figures of musical history;

- he didn't just write some of the most
- affecting music for solo piano, he also
- had a tempestuous affair with one of
- the most notorious women of the time,
- the French transvestite novelist George
- Sand, and died the proper Romantic
- death, of TB (then much more
- beautifully called 'consumption'). Born
- in Poland, he made his reputation in
- Paris, although he remained
- ferociously patriotic about the
- oppressed country of his birth,

incorporating its dance rhythms into a great deal of his solo piano music. It was Schumann and Liszt who first recognised his genius; hearing Chopin play the variations he'd written on a duet from *Don Giovanni*, Schumann exclaimed 'Hats off, gentlemen! A genius.'

Look up 'Romanticism' in a musical dictionary and there's bound to be a reference to Chopin. Oddly, his two piano concertos, both curiously underrated pieces written around 1829/30, aren't much like Liszt's; they hold much more of a balance between soloist and orchestra, sticking more to conventional pathways, and setting the soloist rather a different challenge than do the more flamboyant works of the Abbé. The slow movement of Chopin's 1st Piano Concerto is one of the most teasingly taxing and entirely beautiful movements ever written, demanding a subtlety of technique from the performer, the kind of playing which allows the music to flow gently, falling like a silent cascade. If this all seems a bit lyrical and over the top, go and listen to it; it's a piece of music to wallow in unashamedly, and it's a good deal more thoughtful and cunning in its orchestration than Chopin is sometimes given credit for.

DISCOGRAPHY
Quite a few excellent discs combine both Chopin piano concertos, and if you just wanted to sample them cheaply, you could do no better than get hold of the Naxos release featuring Istvan Szekely and the Budapest Symphony Orchestra conducted by Gyula Nemeth. This unstarry combination delivers one of the best accounts of the music around; Szekely's technique is fine and he's not ashamed to be rhythmic in the dance-inspired movements, while the orchestral accompaniment is extremely sympathetic, finding a refinement which some big names don't seem capable of.
● *Naxos 8.550123* ● *1 CD* ● *Bargain price* ● *DDD* ● *1989* ✪

The very best performance of both concertos on a single disc costs about three times as much as the Naxos release, but it is excellent. Krystian Zimerman is a pianist whose technical ability is

awesome, and he provides a youthful zest which contrasts well with the magisterial 'maestro' command of conductor Carlo Maria Giulini.
● *Deutsche Grammophon 415 970-2* ● *1 CD* ● *Full price* ● *DDD* ● *1985*

Murray Perahia's cool detachment actually works rather well with Romantic composers; for Chopin he has a special gift, combining elegant touch and melodic phrasing with the taste to avoid over-milking the music. The only slight drawback of his Tel Aviv performances with the Israel Philharmonic is the heavy-handedness of conductor Zubin Mehta (famous for conducting the 'Three Tenors' concert in Rome in July 1990, given by José Carreras, Placido Domingo, and Luciano Pavarotti).
● *Sony SK44922* ● *1 CD* ● *Full price* ● *DDD* ● *1989*

If you want, or can afford, the pieces on separate discs, or you only want No. 1, the recording to go for is definitely Maurizio Pollini, who brings many of the same qualities as Perahia to the music, but has the edge, I think, for spontaneity.
● *EMI CDM7 69004-2* ● *1 CD* ● *Mid-price* ● *ADD* ● *1973*

I can't leave the Chopin concertos without mentioning a remarkable historic document; performances of the two works featuring the celebrated Polish pianist Josef Hofmann (1876–1957), who enjoyed superstar status from the end of the nineteenth century (as a child prodigy) to the middle of the twentieth. He was the one pianist whom Rachmaninov acknowledged as his superior. These performances are taken from 1930s radio recordings and accordingly the sound isn't great, but the listener can still appreciate Hofmann's genius. The slow movement of No. 1 will break your heart.
● *VAI Audio VAIA/IPA 1002* ● *1 CD* ● *Full price* ● *ADD* ● *c.1939*

MENDELSSOHN
Felix Mendelssohn also wrote piano concertos, which are attracting a growing band of champions (of whom I am not one), but it is above all his Violin Concerto in E Minor, which appeared in 1844, that marks his contribution and attitude to the genre. Mendelssohn's violin concerto set a benchmark (along with the Joachim-resuscitated Beethoven work) by which future attempts for that instrument were judged; a partisan pro-Brahms critic writing after the première of Brahms's concerto in 1879

described it as 'the most important violin concerto since Beethoven and Mendelssohn'. Compared with Brahms and Beethoven, Mendelssohn's work is a soloist-orientated piece; but then, compared with the great show-off virtuoso Niccolò Paganini's six violin concertos (written between 1815 and 1830) it's positively symphonic and orchestra-bound. And the important contribution of the orchestra, added to the melodic brilliance of the solo part, is probably why the work has survived so triumphantly, even at times when Mendelssohn's reputation has fallen. It may not be the most intellectual of works, but it's one of the most enjoyable; and its influence on the famous Violin Concerto No. 1 in G Minor by Max Bruch (1838–1920), first performed in 1868, is clear and indelible.

DISCOGRAPHY
If you fancy trying out the piano concertos, there's a good cheap recording which doesn't remotely show its age (nearly 40 years) with soloist Peter Katin.
● *Pickwick PWK 1154* ● *1 CD* ● *Bargain price*
● *ADD* ● *1955*

But if nothing less than digital will do, try either Murray Perahia,
● *CBS/Sony MK 42401* ● *1 CD* ● *Full price*
● *ADD* ● *1978*

or András Schiff.
● *Decca 414 672-2* ● *1 CD* ● *Full price*
● *DDD* ● *1985*

With the Violin Concerto we're in the same position as with the Beethoven; everyone has recorded it and you really are spoilt for choice. My personal vote goes by a short head to Kyung Wha Chung, who combines a suprisingly up-tempo approach with a great deal of warmth, flair and superbly melodic tone.
● *Decca 410 011-2* ● *1 CD* ● *Full price*
● *DDD* ● *1981* ❂

The most popular pairing for Mendelssohn's concerto seems to be Bruch's 1st Violin Concerto in G Minor. Amongst the excellent Mendelssohns which bring an excellent Bruch in its wake is Nigel Kennedy's striking and vivid performance.
● *EMI CDC7 49663-2* ● *1 CD* ● *Full price*
● *DDD* ● *1988*

There's also a very attractively done bargain version by Jaime Laredo, which is in the same class as all these others.
● *Pickwick PCD 829* ● *1 CD* ● *Bargain price*
● *DDD* ● *1986*

The celebrated and historic Menuhin/Furtwängler Beethoven concerto comes with an equally electrifying Mendelssohn performance of the same vintage (for details see above p. 109). And I can't possibly ignore Arthur Grumiaux.
● *Philips 422 473-2* ● *1 CD* ● *Bargain price*
● *ADD* ● *1973; comes with the Tchaikovsky violin concerto*

SCHUMANN'S COUNTERBLAST

'The person holding sway at the piano must be given the opportunity to exploit the riches of his instrument and to display his art, while the orchestra, not relegated to the role of mere spectator, has the chance artfully to enliven the scene with the diversity of its sonoric capabilities.'

These were the words of Robert Schumann, reviewing one of Mendelssohn's piano concertos (and one by the Czech-German composer Ignaz Moscheles [1794–1870]), and they formed part of Schumann's manifesto for the concerto which he attempted to embody in his own Piano Concerto in A Minor (begun in 1841, completed in 1845). Schumann idolised Beethoven, but was also, inevitably, deeply touched by the influence of the overtly Romantic composers who formed part of his circle. In his first-movement-dominated concerto, Schumann sought to hold the two forces of Romanticism and Classicism in balance, enlarging the orchestra's role, giving it a more dominant force in stating thematic material (and most of the concerto's thematic stuff emanates from a four-note pattern played by the woodwind immediately after the opening piano flourish) and developing that material; and, as in Beethoven's concertos, the piano often finds itself in a supporting rather than leading role. The orchestration is some of the most subtle that Schumann ever wrote, blending high and low-pitched instruments, surprising combinations of woodwind and strings. Yet the brilliance of much of the piano writing (bearing witness to Schumann the thwarted virtuoso), and the overt emotional nature of the music, belong completely to Romanticism. Liszt knew what he thought; 'a Concerto without piano', he called it, and critics in the 1840s insisted that it was more of 'an instrumental fantasy with piano' than a concerto. Clara, Schumann's virtuoso wife, loyally declared it a 'bravura work', but she was in something of a minority at the time; yet the concerto's influence can be clearly seen in the four concertos by Brahms (who was very friendly with Clara Schumann), and in Edvard Grieg's piano concerto (also in A minor).

From this point on in the concerto's history these two schools of thought battled the matter out; solo flamboyance (later represented by Tchaikovsky and Rachmaninov) versus symphonic integration (led by Brahms).

DISCOGRAPHY
What applies to the Mendelssohn Violin Concerto could also be said of the Schumann Piano Concerto, at which every pianist of every persuasion has had a go. The competition amongst the finest versions is truly intense, but the pianist who manages best to hold the two sides of the work's personality most cleverly in balance is Stephen Kovacevich, aided by an orchestral reading of some subtlety and distinction conducted by Sir Colin Davis.
● *Philips 412 923-2* ● *1 CD* ● *Full price*
● *ADD* ● *1970* ✪

Sir Colin Davis also features on another good version, Murray Perahia's; Perahia has all the qualities necessary for this concerto.
● *CBS/Sony MK 44899* ● *1 CD* ● *Full price*
● *DDD* ● *1988*

Two versions from lower down the price range are worth considering; many critics rate Radu Lupu's recording with André Previn as the best;
● *Decca 417 728-2* ● *1 CD* ● *Mid-price*
● *1973*

and the restoration of the Mercury Living Presence series to the CD catalogue brings back the really warm, vibrant performance by Byron Janis.
● *Mercury Living Presence 432 011-1* ● *1 CD*
● *Mid-price* ● *ADD* ● *1962*

These all pair Schumann's concerto with Grieg's; ever since the advent of the LP, these two piano concertos seem to have been bound hand and foot. Grieg doesn't feature, however, on two fascinating and extraordinary historical recordings of the Schumann. One has cropped up already; Dinu Lipatti's luminous 1947 recording, which is paired with his live performance of Mozart's Concerto No. 21 (see above for details).

Fanny Davies (1861–1934) was a pupil of Clara Schumann, and in the 1920s she recorded the concerto, which she would have learnt from the person who inspired it. With all respect to period-instrumentalists, this is the nearest one can come to true authenticity, and for that reason alone her recording would be fascinating. But it's also actually a stunning performance, full of drive and poetry, and with none of the unfortunate 'milking' and playing around with tempo that some pianists have tried to inflict on the work. The sound isn't quite the disaster you'd expect. Obviously a collector's item rather than a basic library choice, but quite a revelation.
● *Pearl GEMM CD 9291* ● *1 CD* ● *Full price*
● *ADD* ● *1928*

THE APOTHEOSIS OF THE SYMPHONIC CONCERTO: BRAHMS

Johannes Brahms wrote only four concertos; two for piano, one for violin, and one 'double' for violin and cello. To my mind these works represent the absolute apex of the concerto as a 'symphonic' form; like Schumann's piano concerto, they blend classical elegance and structure with Romantic flamboyance, but manage to create from this blending an opposition which makes them the most satisfyingly dramatic concertos ever written. The tension within them between these two apparently disparate elements to some extent reflects Brahms's own view of himself as a man 'born too late'.

The first of Brahms's concertos, Piano Concerto No. 1 in D Minor, Opus 15, predates the others by at least twenty years. Written in 1854/8, it comes less than a decade after Schumann's; in one sense it's very much the work of a young man (Brahms was aged 21 to 25 during its composition, and the athletic demands the first and last movements make on the soloist are perhaps designed to display the prowess of youth; indeed, the two piano concertos were written for the composer to play himself). Yet when you first hear this D minor concerto, you could be forgiven for assuming that you've stumbled upon a symphony; the opening is a declamatory, dramatic orchestral passage and the soloist doesn't appear until after about four minutes of the performance (even longer on some versions). Even when he or she does appear, the entrance is meek and mild compared to the bold, brash stuff which has gone before, gliding in softly and melodically. Brahms took much further in all his concertos, but especially his piano concertos, the idea of the soloist acting sometimes as accompanist to the orchestra rather than dominating it entirely, and very often there seems to be the dramatic tension of a battle for supremacy going on. This means that sometimes the demands on the soloist aren't always as overt as those of, say, Tchaikovsky's or Rachmaninov's or Liszt's works. Nevertheless, even the simplest chordal passages in a Brahms concerto (such as those in the slow movement of No. 1) make real and heavy demands on the pianist's inner resources, while some of the solo passages in the two outer movements are amongst the most difficult ever written, so that simply getting the notes right is a major challenge for the most gifted of pianists.

Twenty years after the 1st Piano Concerto, Brahms undertook to fulfil a promise made to one of his closest musical associates, the violin virtuoso Joseph Joachim; the result was the Violin Concerto in D Major, Opus 77 (1878). The choice of D major as a

base key seems to refer back deliberately to Beethoven's concerto, which was Brahms's conscious model. Again he gave the work a long orchestral introduction, underlining the crucial role the orchestra held in his conception of the concerto; again he wrote whole sections for the soloist, calling upon the latter's abilities to produce a range of tones and generate a kind of inner excitment, rather than just perform Paganini-esque contortions up and down the instrument at violently fast speeds; and again he made enormous technical demands of the soloist. (All these factors led one violinist of the time to describe the piece as 'a Concerto not for but AGAINST the Violin', while a child prodigy whose performance of the piece in the 1890s Brahms found moving – uncharacteristically, for he hated child prodigies – turned this remark round by saying that the concerto was for 'Violin against the Orchestra – and the Violin wins!')

One deviation from 'classical' concerto form which Brahms had originally planned for the Violin Concerto was to give it four (rather than three) movements; however, his ideas for an additional scherzo to add to the traditional fast-slow-fast pattern were abandoned, only to reappear three years later in his next major work, Piano Concerto No. 2 in B Flat Major, Opus 83. This, the most expansive of his four works in the form, is in some ways the perfect expression of his view of the genre. It's perhaps the most overtly Romantic, too (although Romanticism in the sense of emotional impact is stamped through all four concertos like 'Brighton' or 'Blackpool' through the proverbial stick of rock), bringing the solo instrument in at the very outset, playing with a languorous, wistful first theme followed immediately by some grandiose, testing chordal passages. (For all his idolatry of Beethoven and Bach, Brahms is really one of the greatest melodic writers in the whole of classical music, even if he does sometimes construct his melodies out of fragmentary motifs.) The extra scherzo brings a new dimension of fire and verve, in an energetically dramatic movement which culminates (daringly) with the roles of soloist and orchestra being exchanged, so that supporting and leading roles become entirely confused. This contrasts with a superbly beautiful and melodic slow movement which also prominently features a solo cello (another daring move at this stage in the concerto's history). The Finale is both skittish, with its rhythmic delays in both main themes, and somehow rather wistful, containing the kind of sad tunes you can go away whistling.

The Double Concerto for Violin and Cello in A Minor, Opus 102 (1887), is very much *not* a harking back to the days of the concerto grosso; nor does it go in for the cross-breeding of chamber music with symphony which is to some extent the hallmark of Beethoven's Triple Concerto for Piano, Violin and Cello. Both solo instruments get their cadenza, and the presence of two of them merely adds to the tension and drama; each soloist has to play against the other as well as against the orchestra. The grave, dramatic, and powerful opening sets the mood pretty accurately for what follows; back to conventional three-movement form, Brahms once again allows the Classical side of his nature to predominate, but as usual the melodic and dramatic quotient of the work is startlingly high. After all, there's no such thing as a dull or 'second-rank' Brahms concerto.

The Brahms concertos have enjoyed a kind of love-hate relationship with various critics; obviously the lack of immediately apparent virtuosity in the Violin Concerto led to it being 'respected' rather than loved by its first audiences (oddly enough, by the time it was popular, Brahms had rather taken against it). And in the early part of the twentieth century, when Brahms-knocking was quite fashionable, it was common to criticise him for his orchestration, for his Germanic earnestness, for his appeal to Classical values. Which is fair enough, if that's your taste; but I've always found the Brahms concertos as essential a part of my life as the Mozart piano concertos, Beethoven's symphonies, and Bach's Passions.

DISCOGRAPHY
Piano concertos
The catalogue isn't as crammed with recordings of the piano concertos as one might suppose; they are such daunting works, after all. The finest versions ever committed to disc are now both available at Mid-price. They feature pianist Emil Gilels, one of the greatest of all masters of Brahms, and conductor Eugen Jochum in charge of the Berlin Philharmonic. The gifts which Jochum had for Bruckner's symphonic form are ideal for Brahms; a sure sense of form and structure, and a knowledge of how to get an orchestra to sound exciting and stirring at more inward moments as well as at overtly dramatic points. Gilels's technique is outstanding, but his phrasing and his understanding of the music are even more important, even more moving. These were great events in the history of recorded music.
● *No. 1:* ● *Deutsche Grammophon 431 595-2*
● *1 CD* ● *Mid-price* ● *ADD* ● *1972*
● *No. 2:* ● *Deutsche Grammophon 435 588-2*
● *1 CD* ● *Mid-price* ● *ADD* ● *1972* ○

A version of No. 1 which takes a slightly different view, with slower tempos and even greater intensity, combines the talents of Daniel Barenboim (always a good Brahms performer) and Sir John Barbirolli. The warmth and passion this performance generates has transferred amazingly well from vinyl LP to CD; there's terror and beauty in this recording.
● *EMI CDM7 63536-2* ● *1 CD* ● *Mid-price*
● *ADD* ● *1968*

I tend to prefer older versions of the piano concertos; one performance of No. 1 which shows

signs of its age in its recorded sound, but none in its musical insights, matches the aristocratic technical poise of Sir Clifford Curzon with the authoritarian conductor George Szell (1897–1970). Brilliant stuff.
● *Decca 417 641-2* ● *1 CD* ● *Full price*
● *ADD* ● *1962*

Individual versions of No. 2 are harder to recommend. I got great pleasure for many years from Maurizio Pollini's performance with Claudio Abbado and the Vienna Philharmonic, but it seems to have lost some of its sheen and majesty in the transfer from vinyl to CD; still pretty good, though.
● *Deutsche Grammophon 431 596-2* ● *1 CD*
● *Mid-price* ● *ADD* ● *1977*

There's a classic old(ish) version by Sviatoslav Richter which is in some ways self-indulgent, but is still an experience of greatness.
● *BMG/RCA GD 86518* ● *1 CD* ● *Mid-price*
● *ADD* ● *1960*

The best of more recent recordings is probably Stephen Hough's; he has the technique for Brahms, although I'm not sure that Andrew Davis is quite the right conductor.
● *Virgin Classics VC7 91138-2* ● *1 CD* ● *Full price* ● *DDD* ● *1990*

Rather good bargain buys are John Lill's performances of the two concertos, with James Loughran and the Hallé Orchestra. Lill occasionally takes some strange liberties with tempo, but never for pure self-indulgence; his Brahms is as well considered as his Beethoven, and Loughran has a fine sense of Brahmsian structure.
● *No. 1:* ● *ASV Quicksilva CD QS 6083*
● *1 CD* ● *Bargain price* ● *ADD* ● *1978*
● *No. 2:* ● *ASV Quicksilva CD QS 6088* ● *1 CD*
● *Bargain price* ● *ADD* ● *1982*

Violin Concerto
As with Beethoven and Mendelssohn, one is spoilt for choice; however, I have a clear favourite. Herman Krebbers's performance with Bernard Haitink and the Concertgebouw combines every element of warmth, fire, melody and virtuosity, and he manages some extraordinary variation of tone, early in the pseudo-gypsy Finale, melodic in the slow movement. Haitink makes a fine complementary partner. The transfer to CD is lovely; the violin is distinctly forward in the recording, but it works terribly well.
● *Philips 422 972-2* ● *1 CD* ● *Bargain price*
● *ADD* ● *1973* ✪

A beautifully lyrical view of the piece comes from Arthur Grumiaux, a subtle reading which draws you in and then holds you firmly in its gentle, caressing grip. Sir Colin Davis's conducting is up to his usual stalwart standard.
● *Philips 420 703-2* ● *1 CD* ● *Mid-price*
● *ADD* ● *1971*

Itzhak Perlman has recorded this concerto live with Daniel Barenboim. The performance is titanic, a real emotional cauldron with lots of distinctive technical touches; speed and clarity (not always to be found in the same place), and warmth too.
● *EMI CDC7 54580-2* ● *1 CD* ● *Full price*
● *DDD* ● *1991*

The great Jascha Heifetz made a dazzling recording of this piece whose speeds must be very close to those originally used by Brahms and his friend Joachim, to judge from their estimate of the time the work should take to perform. Heifetz is simply amazing; notes pour from his bow at an astonishing rate and the clarity of his style is astounding, though just a shade of warmth and earthiness is lacking at times.
● *RCA/BMG RD 85402* ● *1 CD* ● *Full price*
● *ADD* ● *1954*

One vintage version which should be heard is by Ginette Neveu, a French violinist killed in a plane crash in 1949 at the age of 30. Neveu clearly had the most impressive musical imagination; this is such an exciting performance that the sound-blemishes inevitable with a recording of this age soon fade into nothing. Coming with one of the best recordings ever made of Sibelius's demanding concerto, this is one of the great recorded documents around.
● *EMI References CDH7 61011-2* ● *1 CD*
● *Mid-price* ● *ADD* ● *1948*

Nigel Kennedy's version was subjected to a great deal of hype; it's a highly considered performance, but far too slow and drawn out.
● *EMI CDC7 54187 2* ● *1 CD* ● *Full price*
● *DDD* ● *1990*

Double Concerto
The most exciting recording of the Double Concerto may be over 30 years old, but it has all the drive and tension of a live performance. Much of the credit for this rests with conductor Bruno Walter (whose recorded versions of the Brahms symphonies are classics, though the transfer to CD makes them sound a little claustrophobic); but soloists Zino Francescatti (violin) and Pierre Fournier (cello) live up to every demand of both the music and Walter's conducting. A fine and noble piece of work, it comes with a decent version of Schumann's piano concerto.
● *CBS/Sony Maestro MYK 44771* ● *1 CD*
● *Bargain price* ● *ADD* ● *1960*

The most favoured recent version boasts the cello playing of the great Yo-Yo Ma and violinist Isaac Stern, as well as Claudio Abbado. This version is sound rather than thrilling, but you can't do better if you want a fully digital version.
● *CBS/Sony Masterworks CD42387* ● *1 CD*
● *Full price* ● *DDD* ● *1987* ✪

FLAMBOYANT DRAMA: TCHAIKOVSKY

Considering that two of Tchaikovsky's four (or, to be strict, three and a third) concertos are staples of the repertoire, it's odd to reflect that he wasn't particularly interested in the form as such. Early in his career he expressed a strong dislike for music which combined the piano and an orchestra; despite which in 1874 he set about writing a large-scale piano concerto. The result was his Piano Concerto No. 1 in B Flat Minor, Opus 23, whose opening bars are amongst the most famous in classical music – possibly *the* most famous after those of Beethoven's 5th Symphony.

When, on 5 January 1875 (Russian Orthodox Christmas Eve), Tchaikovsky first played his concerto to the man he wanted to be the soloist at its première, Nikolai Rubinstein (1835–1881), the reaction wasn't quite what the composer was looking for. 'Worthless, unplayable, clumsy, plagiarised' were some of the pianist's kinder comments; he felt that possibly 'two or three pages might be saved'. Tchaikovsky acted defiant – 'I won't change a single note' – but actually he was devastated, for he was hyper-sensitive to any critical response to his music. Although the concerto went ahead as planned, and was a huge success at its première in Boston (although a total flop initially inside Russia), over the next few years Tchaikovsky did revise it to some extent. In any case, Rubinstein evidently changed his mind, because he began to incorporate the piece in his repertoire and eventually became its most persuasive advocate.

The 1st Piano Concerto is a deeply dramatic work; melodic, like so much of Tchaikovsky, and with a nod to the idea of employing Russian (and Ukrainian) folk melodies (or tunes which could pass for folk melodies). Purists of musical structure have often been sniffy about the work because its

- opening seems to bear no relation to
- anything elsewhere in the piece's three
- movements; Tchaikovsky's fullest
- biographer, David Brown, has
- suggested that actually there is a
- motivic reference in there to
- Tchaikovsky himself, and that it's
- possible to see, behind this, the kernel
- of the rest of the fruit. Be that as it
- may, one thing that is definite is that
- the second movement is based partly
- on a French song which was popular
- with the singer Desirée Artot, with
- whom Tchaikovsky had had an affair.
- By the time he wrote his Concerto
- for Violin in D Major, Tchaikovsky
- had been through his marriage and
- great sexual crisis, and at least a part
- of the inspiration for the concerto was
- a handsome young ex-pupil (at that
- time a student with Joachim), Josef
- Kotek. Tchaikovsky, atypically, took
- only a month to complete the Violin
- Concerto, and a few more days to
- replace the original second movement
- with the beautifully melodic
- Canzonetta. Reaction to the piece was
- again extreme; the critic Eduard
- Hanslick, who was then the world's
- greatest champion of Brahms,
- famously referred to the piece as
- 'stinking music'.
- This isn't surprising in that
- Tchaikovsky and Kotek had been
- deeply unimpressed by Brahms's own
- violin concerto, which had appeared at
- the beginning of that year (1879); the
- biggest influence on Tchaikovsky at
- this time had been a piece by the
- French composer Edouard Lalo
- (1823–1892), the *Symphonie Espagnole*,
- which for all its name is actually a
- five-movement quasi-violin concerto
- (it's one of the very few pieces by Lalo
- to get a regular outing today), but it
- had become wildly popular after its
- appearance in 1873 (something I find a
- bit baffling to understand, to be

truthful). Tchaikovsky praised Lalo's work for its 'freshness, lightness . . . and beautiful melodies', which is a fair summary of what you find in his own concerto, if you mix in a good helping of drama and fire.

These are Tchaikovsky's two major contributions to the concerto; he did write a 2nd Piano Concerto, and one movement of a 3rd (his death stopped its completion, although whether he would have gone on and finished it properly is a moot point) which, because of its length, is often allowed to stand as a complete one-movement work in itself. (Tchaikovsky's pianist friend Serge Taneyev did in fact write two more movements based on the composer's own sketches.) These pieces, although they undoubtedly have their moments, have never quite caught on; Nikolai Rubinstein declined the opportunity to première the 2nd Piano Concerto, and this time he didn't have second thoughts about his decision. One reason for the 2nd's unpopularity was the prominence in its second movement of a solo violin and solo cello, which most pianists found far too limelight-stealing, and which too many performances have tended to underemphasise.

DISCOGRAPHY
Anybody who is anybody has had a crack at 'Tchaik 1' (the 1st Piano Concerto), but a lot of great names have never quite caught it. Some capture the drama, but miss the poetry of the quieter, more melodic moments; some are just too restrained when they should be prepared to let rip with all the vulgarity of the big moment. Conductors can be a liability, too. It's not a music critic's affectation to say that, for all its age and sound problems, the 50-year-old recording by Vladimir Horowitz with Toscanini (a live performance staged at a concert staged to sell, of all things, US War Bonds) can't be beaten. It's hypnotic and spell-binding.
● *RCA Victor Gold Seal GD 60321* ● *1 CD*
● *Mid-price* ● *ADD* ● *1943* ✪

There's a digital version featuring András Schiff, who turns out not to be too genteel for this sort of thing (which comes as a bit of a surprise); the fact that Sir Georg Solti is the conductor may have something to do with this, although he too surprises with his instinct for the poetry and melody.
● *Decca 417 294-2* ● *1 CD* ● *Full price*
● *DDD* ● *1986*

There are lots of good violin concerto recordings around; my winner by a short head is a fiery reading by the young Chinese player Xue-Wei. This is, I should say, a young man's reading of the piece, all fire and intensity, but none the worse for that.
● *ASV CD DCA 713* ● *1 CD* ● *Full price*
● *DDD* ● *1989*

Kyung Wha Chung's recording (which comes with her Mendelssohn) has a real lyrical beauty, a sense of the piece's inner virtues (for details see p. 113 above).

If you want to try the two 'ugly duckling' piano concertos, you won't find them better done than by Peter Donohoe with Rudolf Barshai and the Bournemouth Symphony Orchestra. The other solo parts (violin and cello) in the second movement of the 2nd are taken very seriously by Nigel Kennedy and Steven Isserlis; their beautifully intense playing makes more sense of the movement's balance. Donohoe is brilliant throughout. The recording of the 2nd won a *The Gramophone* Award in 1988, but both concertos are available on the one disc.
● *EMI CDC7 49940-2* ● *1 CD* ● *Full price*
● *DDD* ● *1986/7*

● ◁▬▶ ◁▬▶ ◁▬▶ ◁▬▶

THE CONCERTO APPROACHES THE TWENTIETH CENTURY

The concerto of around the turn of the nineteenth/twentieth century is principally distinguished by its use of melody rather than by any extraordinary formal developments. Oddly, even the composers of the Second Viennese School who used the concerto tended to be conservative with the actual shape of the genre; in fact, their concertos make a good introduction to the work of modern composers like Alban Berg and Béla Bartók.

KINGS OF MELODY: GRIEG AND BRUCH

This is to leap ahead, however. Two of the most popular concertos of the 1860s have already cropped up as CD pairings for works already discussed; the A Minor Piano Concerto by Edvard Grieg (1843–1907) and the Violin Concerto No. 1 in G Minor by Max Bruch (1838–1920). Grieg is the outstanding Norwegian composer; he is to Norway what Sibelius is to Finland and Nielsen to Denmark. His piano concerto is Grieg's one enduring major orchestral work of any length (there is a C minor symphony which can hardly be said to be a repertoire perennial), and although it naturally forms a pair with Schumann's, it has always attracted praise and interest from the virtuoso players who have looked askance at Schumann's work. Liszt, in particular was a great admirer of the piece from an early stage of its composition ('Go on, I tell you,' he encouraged Grieg after sight-reading the manuscript, 'you have the stuff!'). It was an immediate success and earned Grieg the nickname 'The Chopin of the North', but there's more to it than just flamboyance and virtuosity. The orchestral part is fully integrated, the melodic content is superb (there's another of those second movements to break your heart with its sheer beauty), and, played properly, it's always an exciting piece.

DISCOGRAPHY
Grieg
Most of the versions paired with the recommended Schumann recordings are outstanding, but my particular favourite is Murray Perahia's; poise, elegance, and a singing melodic touch which reaches the parts other interpretations cannot reach. Sir Colin Davis's conducting is ideal, too. (For details, see p. 114 above.)

A ONE-WORK COMPOSER?: MAX BRUCH (1838–1920)

There are around forty versions of Max Bruch's 1st Violin Concerto currently available, compared with two of his 2nd and one of his 3rd. And the simple fact is that the G Minor work (on which Bruch sought the advice of Brahms's friend Joachim; most major concertos written for the violin around the middle of the nineteenth century tend to have Joachim lurking somewhere in their gestation) is a much more memorable and instantly attractive work. In his lifetime Bruch was most famous for church music; a small irony, because another of his works whose popularity has survived is a piece for cello and orchestra entitled *Kol Nidrei*, based around Hebrew melodies to the Jewish prayer on the eve of Yom Kippur. The Nazi regime assumed that a man who wrote a piece called *Kol Nidrei* must himself be Jewish, so Bruch's music was banned in his native country between 1933 and 1945. (By such logic the Nazi regime must presumably have believed that he was a Scottish Jew, since one other work of his which retains its place as a violin showpiece and popular concert item is another violin and orchestra piece, the *Scottish Fantasy*.)

Bruch's G Minor Concerto isn't a piece to get intellectual about; it's something to lie back and enjoy, especially for the glorious and haunting melody in the second movement (the first movement could almost be described – indeed, Bruch himself did describe it – as a 'Prelude' to that central and beautiful movement). And *Kol Nidrei* and the *Scottish Fantasy* are well worth hearing, too (the latter especially when played by Jascha Heifetz with Sir Malcolm Sargent [RCA]).

DISCOGRAPHY
Almost all the versions of Bruch's 1st Violin Concerto which come with the recommended Mendelssohns are good; especially fine is Jaime Laredo (see p. 113 above). However, an alternative of some merit is Tasmin Little's lovely, plaintive recording (with Vernon Handley), which pairs the piece with Dvořák's violin concerto.
● EMI Classics for Pleasure CD-CFP4566
● 1 CD ● Bargain price ● DDD ● 1990 ○

And the distinguished critic Edward Greenfield hailed another recording of the Bruch by Cho-Liang Lin as 'one of the most radiantly beautiful violin records I have heard for a long time', which, given the number of violin releases that have crossed Mr Greenfield's path, is saying volumes. And it's pretty damn fine, a melodic treat, with superb support from Leonard Slatkin and the Chicago Symphony Orchestra – and the Scottish Fantasy as a supporting programme
● CBS/Sony Masterworks CD42315 ● 1 CD
● Full price ● DDD ● 1987

A final word, too, for Kyung Wha Chung, who brings to this piece the kind of radiance she bring to Tchaikovsky and Mendelssohn; the coupling work here is Saint-Saëns's 3rd Violin Concerto. Camille Saint-Saëns (French; 1835–1921) is, frankly, a composer I can take or leave, but Kyung Wha Chung comes close to making me take him.
● Decca 417 707-2 ● 1 CD ● Mid-price
● ADD ● 1972

MELODY REIGNS SUPREME: DVOŘÁK

Finding their way back into popular favour now, Antonin Dvořák's concertos in many ways demand the same response as Bruch's; enjoy the melodies and don't look too deeply for some intellectual angle. Dvořák wrote three concertos, one each for piano, violin and cello (there's also an early and abandoned attempt at a cello concerto which has attracted little or no attention); of these the violin and cello concertos have enjoyed the greatest favour, particularly the latter (to some extent hitching a ride on the back of the

phenomenally popular Elgar work for the same instrument, making a natural pairing on both LP and CD). The Piano Concerto in G Minor, written in 1876, has been criticised for not being exactly sympathetic or alive to the piano's potential; on the other hand, both the Violin Concerto in A Minor (originally written in 1860 but revised in 1882) and the Cello Concerto in B Minor (written in 1894/5, a product of Dvořák's period of employment in the United States) have been praised for their melodic invention. I have to say that I find them a bit lacking in drama (especially the Piano Concerto, which has always struck me as a titanic bore), but in the right hands they can prove diverting.

DISCOGRAPHY
The most convincing version of the Piano Concerto united the remarkable talents of Sviatoslav Richter with those of conductor Carlos Kleiber. For some reason EMI has deleted this from the catalogue, leaving the palm of 'most persuasive advocate' to the talented Hungarian András Schiff, who brings all his qualities of delicacy, precision and superb phrasing sense to the piece; Christoph von Dohnányi is one of the most intellectual conductors around (sometimes almost too much so; not a note of the score doesn't have some part to play in a deeply systematised Dohnányi plan).
● Decca 417 802-2 ● 1 CD ● Full price
● DDD ● 1986 ○

One of the best introductions to the Violin Concerto is Tasmin Little's wonderful performance (for details see Bruch above); otherwise Kyung Wha Chung does exactly the kind of – brilliant – job you'd expect of her.
● EMI CDC7 49858-2 ● 1 CD ● Full price
● DDD ● 1988

The most impassioned account of the Cello Concerto can also be criticised for being slightly self-indulgent, but in my view the piece needs just that kind of committed, dramatic approach. The culprit/hero here is the great Mstislav Rostropovich (who has actually recorded this work, which is central to the cello's otherwise rather sparse repertoire, six times), kept in balance by some deeply authoritarian conducting from Herbert von

Karajan which never allows anything to get too far out of hand.
● *Deutsche Grammophon 413 819-2* ● *1 CD*
● *Full price* ● *ADD* ● *1969*

But if you want a cheap introduction to what is undoubtedly the greatest and most immediate of Dvořák's three concertos, there's rather a good Naxos version featuring cellist Maria Kliegel, which also offers a finely considered account of the more famous Elgar work.
● *Naxos 8.550503* ● *1 CD* ● *Bargain price*
● *DDD* ● *1991*

RACHMANINOV

For many years Rachmaninov was considered more significant as a performer than as a composer; the musical dictionaries had some perfectly awful things to say about the music he wrote ('ninth-rate' was one comment). Born and educated in the great Russian virtuoso tradition of Nikolai Rubinstein (see Tchaikovsky in this section, pp. 118–19), he quickly became famous as a pianist throughout Europe and indeed America, but his ambitions as a composer were always important to him, and the hostile reception of some of his early work led to his being one of the first well-known composers to have any truck with psychoanalysis. After the Russian Revolution of 1917 he abandoned his native country and settled in America, eventually taking American citizenship.

Rachmaninov may have added nothing new to the concerto, and his solo parts may have been partly intended as showpieces for himself, but this hasn't prevented two of his four concertos and one quasi-concerto (the *Rhapsody on a Theme of Paganini*) becoming some of the best-loved classical music ever written. Even the authors of the musical couldn't crush the sheer dramatic impact and popular appeal of his 2nd Piano Concerto in C Minor, known

through the musical world as 'Rach 2', and also known to film-lovers as the score to the classic 1945 weepie *Brief Encounter*. This particular concerto has a knack of tugging at the heartstrings like few other pieces of music, and one of its great secrets is knowing when to stop, knowing how to vary the tone, knowing how to mix up the threatening, angst-ridden music of the opening with more plaintive, melodic material. That's the secret, too, of the *Rhapsody*, where Rachmaninov blends what could be a rather arid academic exercise designed to show off the pianist's skill and his own ability to write in the variations format, with his extraordinary gift for memorable tunes; just as it's all seeming very showy, quite fun but ultimately a bit dry, he throws in the 18th Variation, the work's single most famous passage, a quiet, reflective, passionate few minutes.

Now that knocking Rachmaninov isn't so fashionable, the 'in' concerto has become the 3rd in D Minor; in truth, both it and the 2nd (as well as the *Rhapsody*) do represent the apex of Rachmaninov's achievement in the form, although for all its structural cunning, the 3rd doesn't quite have the same visceral impact as the 2nd. Or perhaps it does, depending upon your viscera; the great thing about much of Rachmaninov's music is its entirely subjective impact. In being possessed of such a subjective quality, it serves as a warning to music critics and scholars alike that music is first and foremost designed to please, to impress the mind and the heart together.

DISCOGRAPHY
For a bargain and a good, impressive performance, you can do no better than Vladimir Ashkenazy's coupling of the 2nd Piano Concerto with the *Rhapsody on a Theme of Paganini*; both performances have some claim to be the finest available and Ashkenazy brings a Russian instinct

to the music, whilst André Previn's dramatic sense (finely honed through working on film scores in Hollywood) is ideal.

● *Decca Ovation 417 702-2* ● *1 CD*
● *Mid-price* ● *ADD* ● *1972* ○

The same combination of pieces comes even cheaper, and is almost as excellent, on Naxos with the pianist who features on many Naxos releases, Jenö Jando – and very fine he is too.

● *Naxos 8.550117* ● *1 CD* ● *Bargain price*
● *DDD* ● *1989*

There's also a surprisingly un-Romantic version which works very well for 'Rach 2' and for the 3rd Concerto. The American pianist Earl Wild can be a great showman; in a recording originally issued through *Reader's Digest* he keeps himself very much in control, and with Jascha Horenstein (1898–1973) conducting, the sense of structure in these two works becomes clearer than perhaps anywhere else.

● *Chandos Collect CHAN6507* ● *1 CD*
● *Mid-price* ● *ADD* ● *1966*

Sviatoslav Richter makes of 'Rach 2' a dark, brooding thing with a hidden inner centre; a marvellously passionate performance hinting at both pleasures and terrors lurking. This version comes with a superb performance of Prokofiev's 5th Piano Concerto.

● *Deutsche Grammophon 415 119-2* ● *1 CD*
● *Full price* ● *ADD* ● *1960*

For the 3rd Concerto, Ashkenazy and Previn again offer a good-value release which digs deep into the piece's potential, making much of its more introspective nature, yet never teetering over into awful self-indulgence. The added Preludes for solo piano are a delightful bonus.

● *Decca Ovation 417 764-2* ● *1 CD*
● *Mid-price* ● *ADD* ● *1972*

━━━ ━━━ ━━━

ELGAR

On the surface, Elgar's life isn't all that interesting, he spent much of it around Worcester, and success arrived rather late, at the very end of the nineteenth century, with the *Enigma Variations* (1899). Before this he had had to scrape a living partly out of composing pot-boiler melodies. In the public mind he is for ever associated with 'Land of Hope and Glory' (words set to part of his 1st 'Pomp and Circumstance' March); in private he was far from being the jingoistic, triumphalist patriot this piece might suggest. He was a rather melancholy man, who greatly

admired German music and who was greatly appreciated by the Germans until the Great War interrupted all commerce between the two countries. After the war his melancholy dominated, and composition became more difficult for him.

Although his Violin Concerto in B Minor (1909/10) and his Cello Concerto in E Minor (1919) were both written after Sibelius's violin concerto, Elgar belongs with the great melodists. I mean it as only a compliment to say that for sheer drama and emotional impact his cello concerto belongs with 'Rach 2' – and since the 1970s at least it has had the same grip on the popular imagination. It is the single work amongst his entire output which helped to transform Elgar's image in the public mind from that of a jingoistic old buffer to an elegiac, thoughtful man mourning the passing of decent English values, a million miles from imperialism. From its very opening chords, the Cello Concerto sounds a note of pathos, of loss, of mourning, and continues in this mode with one of the great cello melodies of all time. This concerto succeeds in being both an instrumentalist's showpiece and a superbly melodic, listener-friendly work.

The Violin Concerto, too, was a deeply personal work; Elgar was himself a violinist and he perhaps sees the soloist's part as his own voice doing combat with the world (represented by the orchestra); he was deeply insecure for much of his life. Many soloists found this work too daunting when it first appeared, deterred mainly by the length of the Finale which balances the rather long opening movement. Like the Cello Concerto, it's both technically demanding and melodically inventive, and its increasing popularity is good to behold.

DISCOGRAPHY

The Violin Concerto's popularity was very much on the up in any case when the young Nigel Kennedy got hold of it, but the service he performed the music was a truly great one, as his version is one of the best available. This is Kennedy the musician at his very finest, superb tonal command of his violin, no disturbing tendencies to go for rather drawn-out tempos, backed by a very good, and underrated, conductor in Vernon Handley.

● *EMI Eminence CD-EMX 2058* ● *1 CD*
● *Mid-price* ● *DDD* ● *1984* ✪

It's fair to say that the Cello Concerto's leap in popularity was at least partly due to its association in the public's mind with the tragic career of Jacqueline du Pré (1945–1987), the British cellist (wife to Daniel Barenboim) whose playing talents were destroyed by multiple sclerosis. Her recordings of the Elgar have long stood as classics, the better of the two being the earlier with Sir John Barbirolli (a man with a natural gift for Elgar's elegiac vision) and the London Symphony Orchestra. Listening to this performance, you realise just how tragic was the loss of du Pré.

● *EMI CDC7 47329-2* ● *1 CD* ● *Full price*
● *ADD* ● *1965* ✪

Two other versions are also worth investigating; one older, one more recent. The more recent features the very talented Steven Isserlis, who, like du Pré, can make the cello do amazing things – make it both emotional, a burning, exciting thing, and then, in almost the next phrase, sound skittish. Isserlis became very well known to many as the soloist on John Tavener's highly successful cello and orchestra piece *The Protecting Veil*; in a more three-dimensional work than Tavener's, Isserlis's true talents are allowed more range.

● *Virgin Classics VC7 90735-2* ● *1 CD* ● *Full price* ● *DDD* ● *1988*

The earlier recording I mentioned again features Sir John Barbirolli as conductor (although here with his beloved Hallé Orchestra rather than the LSO, as on the du Pré recording) with the cellist André Navarra. This performance (which has transferred excellently to CD) hits a nerve that even du Pré doesn't quite reach; there's also arguably the best recording available of Elgar's *Enigma Variations* on the disc, to boot.

● *EMI CDM7 63955-2* ● *1 CD* ● *Mid price* ● *1957*

TWO CONCERTOS IN ONE: SIBELIUS

Jean Sibelius's Violin Concerto in D Minor has been recognised for some time now (certainly since the Second World War) as one of the great works in the form, a concerto to stand with Beethoven, Brahms, Mendelssohn and Tchaikovsky, with all of which works it has something in common, as well as an individual style of melodic phrasing which is unique to Sibelius. It's Sibelius's only concerto; and actually it took him two goes to get it – as he saw it – 'right'.

The first version of this D minor concerto was written in 1903/4, and when it was premièred the leading Finnish music critic of the day, Karl Flodin, was devastating. The piece was, he wrote, 'a mistake' and 'boring, something which could not hitherto be said of a composition by Jean Sibelius.' The première was a fiasco, a novelty to Sibelius, who had become used to his major works being hailed as triumphs of particular national significance. The problem was, in fact, that the piece was just too difficult; in particular, the first movement had not one but two cadenzas (two and a half if you count a short cadenza-like burst immediately after the opening of the piece), and the soloist at the première made a complete dog's breakfast of the whole thing. There have been suggestions that Sibelius might deliberately have been asking too much; he had wanted at one stage of his career to be a violinist and hadn't quite made the grade – could this have been his revenge? Well, given his reaction to Flodin's criticism, scarcely. In the event, he took the concerto and went through it, cutting and rewriting it very much in line with Flodin's criticisms, scaling down both the first movement and the Finale so that about five minutes' music was lost.

All of which would be just academic if it hadn't occurred to someone to dig up the original version and give it another whirl. In fact, it turned out to be a remarkable piece – difficult, yes (but then the revised version still poses spectacular technical problems), but somehow possessed of a rugged grandeur; a work with perhaps more rough edges than the familiar revised version, but something which managed somehow to incorporate in some measure a homage to all the great violin writers preceding Sibelius. It's the same work, but different enough to constitute a whole new challenge to soloists. How many will decide to take it up in the future?

DISCOGRAPHY
The recording which brought us the original version of the Violin Concerto also includes a very fine performance of the more familiar revised version. For this superb disc we have to thank the head of BIS Records, Robert van Bahr, whose devotion to Sibelius and to certain principles of recording have yielded other great results apart from this. The recording, which eschews the editing techniques common to most other recordings, is a fantastic showcase for the talents of the young Greek violinist Leonidas Kavakos, who tackles the difficulties of the extra cadenza like a thoroughbred. The Lahti Symphony Orchestra and conductor Osmo Vänskä may not be star names, but they certainly make a fine contribution to this disc, which deservedly won a *The Gramophone* Award in 1991.
● *BIS CD 500* ● *1 CD* ● *Full price* ● *DDD*
● *1991* ❍

I've already mentioned Ginette Neveu's amazing 1946 recording, which had a singular impact in helping to promote the concerto to a wider audience. This is one of those pieces of violin-playing that merits terms like 'incandescent'. (For details, see p. 117 above.)

Another Sibelius performance that won a *The Gramophone* Award comes from Cho-Liang Lin, who brings the work together, logically enough (though very rarely), with Nielsen's slightly neglected but very interesting violin concerto. One reviewer feels that this disc will 'take its place among the classic concerto recordings of the century', and he has a point.
● *CBS/Sony Masterworks CD44548* ● *1 CD*
● *Full price* ● *DDD* ● *1988*

THE EMPHASIS SHIFTS BACK TO WIND: STRAUSS

Concertos rather neatly frame Strauss's career. He wrote only four; one for violin, two for horn and one for oboe, of which the three for wind instruments have found enormous popularity. The violin and first horn works came early (in 1882 and 1883 respectively); the second horn and oboe pieces were late works (1942 and 1945). In between the 1st and 2nd Horn Concertos came great upheavals and cataclysms, both in the musical world (the arrival of Modernism) and in the world at large. Strauss the alleged Nazi seemed a far cry from the radical 'young Turk' whose early tone-poems and operas had seemed to be the rallying cry of the avant-garde.

Actually, Strauss had never been quite the fearsome prophet of Modernism some liked to think him. Even where his music seems to flirt with the abandonment of traditional tonality, of major and minor keys, in reality it always stays rooted there, even in stupendously chromatic passages like some of those in his opera *Elektra* (1908). His 'reactionary' streak was responsible for one of his greatest successes, the opera *Der Rosenkavalier* (1910) and after this his work mainly espoused the style known as 'neo-Classical', much of Strauss's music deliberately cultivates the sound and style of the eighteenth century. He tended to work well within the bounds of his ability, and it was only the traumatic effect of the ruin of Germany and the revelation of the nature of the regime he had served which seemed to unlock Strauss's deepest abilities once more in a final flurry of brilliant works, of which the Oboe Concerto was undoubtedly one.

The Oboe Concerto was actually written for one of the American

Richard Strauss

1864–1949

R ichard Strauss was one of the most colourful figures in the musical
world at the beginning of the twentieth century. He made his name
in the German-speaking world with a series of orchestral pieces (symphonic tone-poems) which told vivid, lurid stories, often taking the
composer himself as a hero figure. Never especially modest, Strauss was
a brilliant self-publicist, and he quickly became regarded as some kind
of *enfant terrible*, a reputation which persisted until he was well into his
40s. He wrote a vast amount of vocal music, partly because he married
a singer. The success of his early pieces, and an early horn concerto, was
followed by a string of celebrated operas, but after *Der Rosenkavalier*
(1911) Strauss became something of a conservative figure, both musically
and politically. When the Nazis came to power he was offered a major
job under the new regime, a job he accepted possibly out of ignorance of
the regime's real nature; certainly he numbered a large number of Jewish
musicians amongst his friends, and his use of a Jewish librettist (the writer
Stefan Zweig) on one of his operas led him into conflict with the Nazi
leadership. None the less, he remained in Germany throughout the Second
World War, and after it inevitably faced accusations of being a Nazi. The
music of his last years, which includes some of his most famous work,
is imbued with an autumnal sense of shock at what had gone on under
his nose, while he had lived in secluded splendour at his luxurious villa
in the German countryside.

>> *Opera* 193, *Choral* 265, *Orchestral* 276

soldiers occupying the land, post-war, near Strauss's villa in Germany. John de Lancie, an oboist with the Pittsburgh orchestra, took the opportunity to meet the 81-year-old composer, despite the stigma of Nazism attaching to him. He suggested that Strauss might care to write an oboe concerto, an idea that didn't take hold immediately, but which the composer later acted on. The dedication was more than obscure; Strauss mistook de Lancie's home town and didn't mention him by name, and when the piece was

- premièred in the US, it wasn't de
- Lancie who got to play the solo part,
- but his senior, Mitchell Miller. Mitchell
- Miller became an international
- celebrity with his hit-single version of
- 'The Yellow Rose of Texas' in 1955.

DISCOGRAPHY
The three most popular and effective concertos, the two for horn and the one for oboe, are all available on one very good and competitively priced disc with fine, fluent performances by soloists Peter Damm (horn) and Manfred Clement (oboe). The conductor, Rudolf Kempe, has a special talent for Strauss's orchestral writing, which can be thick and glutinous in the wrong hands, and for the rhythms which underpin it.
● *EMI CDM7 69661-2* ● *1 CD* ● *Mid-price*
● *ADD* ● *1976* ○

Strauss's horn concertos, like Mozart's, became the special property of the great Dennis Brain, and his performance on a 1950s recording with conductor Wolfgang Sawallisch is excellent, however, the orchestral sound hasn't transferred too well to CD, coming across rather flat and thin.
● *EMI CDC7 47834-2* ● *1 CD* ● *Full price*
● *ADD*

We've already encountered the best recording of the Oboe Concerto; Douglas Boyd's characterful performance with Paavo Berglund and the Chamber Orchestra of Europe, very cleverly set against the Mozart concerto (for details see p. 106 above).

It's well worth checking out John de Lancie's own, fairly recent, recording, which has a delightful fluency, while the use of a fairly small chamber orchestra (which is the kind of delicacy the work demands) strikes some listeners as thin, but seems to me to be dead right.
● *BMG/RCA Gold Seal GD 87989* ● *1 CD*
● *Mid-price* ● *DDD* ● *1987*

For many years the earliest recording of the concerto was also considered to be the best; that by the great oboist Leon Goossens with the Philharmonia Orchestra under Alceo Galliera. It has finally appeared on CD, showing its age a little and with a surprising number of technical awkwardnesses, but still lit up by a great musicianship, especially in the slow movement and the lively Finale. This disc also offers an alternative performance by Dennis Brain of the 1st Horn Concerto, as well as the great bassoonist Gwydion Brooke playing the minor, but charming, concerto for this instrument by the early-nineteenth-century composer Carl Maria von Weber (1786–1826).
● *Testament SBT 1009* ● *1 CD* ● *Full price*
● *ADD* ● *1947*

The one available version of Strauss's neglected Violin Concerto is something of a gem; a fiery and loving performance by the Chinese virtuoso Xue-Wei
● *ASV CD DCA 780* ● *1 CD* ● *Full price*
● *DDD* ● *1990*

THE MODERN CONCERTO

Many of the concertos discussed in recent pages could be called Modern works, yet the spirit of their music is essentially Romantic (Strauss's neo-Classicism was always Romantic at heart). As I've already hinted, the truly 'Modern' composers, those who embraced the breakdown of the old system of major and minor keys, adopted a reverentially formal approach to the concerto, and I feel that these could offer one of the most fruitful approaches to the sometimes apparently daunting prospect of 'modern music'. In particular, the concertos of Béla Bartók and the Violin Concerto by Alban Berg are eminently accessible to anyone who enjoys Sibelius or Richard Strauss.

DRAMA AND DISPLAY: BARTÓK

Much of Bartók's best music involves some form of drama, whether it stems from writing directly for the stage, or from the internal tension of competition between various orchestral instruments. He wrote three piano concertos, of which the first two are the more significant. The 3rd, although pleasant, is essentially lightweight; Bartók wrote it in the hope that it would make money for his widow after he had died. He also wrote two violin concertos, a double piano concerto (which is an arrangement by the composer himself of his Sonata for Two Pianos and Percussion), an incomplete viola concerto and, most remarkable of all perhaps, a 'concerto for orchestra'.

Although the years immediately preceding his death saw Bartók compose some of his greatest music (including the Concerto for Orchestra), it was only after his death, through the championship of figures like Pierre Boulez and Yehudi Menuhin, that he eventually came to be perceived as one of the major and most innovative figures of twentieth-century music, possessed of a whole range of expression and technique way beyond the scope of the 'twelve-note' orientation of the Second Viennese School.

In writing for the piano, Bartók tried

Béla Bartók
1881–1945

Bartók was Hungarian, and the folk tradition of his country, especially its dance forms, permeates much of his music. One of the most significant composers of the twentieth century, he wasn't directly involved with the 'twelve-note' experiments of Schoenberg, Berg and Webern; he sought a new way forward for music through the potential of musical instruments themselves, promoting percussive elements (especially of the piano) and driving, insistent rhythms. After the First World War, Bartók left Hungary and eventually settled in New York, where he wrote music for, amongst others, the jazz clarinet player Benny Goodman; but although highly regarded by some musical figures, he found it difficult to earn a living, and died in near poverty.

>> *Opera* 201, *Chamber* 236

to exploit the instrument's percussive possibilities; after all, the piano is essentially a percussion instrument, given that its workings depend upon hammers striking strings. He invented a whole new piano tuition system, his six volumes called *Mikrokosmos*, designed to promote the values in piano-playing he wished to advocate. Indeed, a strong percussive presence is one of the hallmarks of Bartók's music; one of his most celebrated pieces is entitled 'Music for Strings, Percussion and Celesta' (the celesta being a keyboard, and therefore essentially percussive, instrument); and his interest in rhythm as a driving force in music demands that all players, solo and orchestral, make the effort to understand the percussive nature, the rhythmic force, of what they are playing.

But there's much more to Bartók than endless (if inventive) drum-banging. His music is fiendishly demanding, calling for technical

- prowess and display, often very
- exciting; but there's also a strongly
- Romantic streak, to be heard
- particularly in the opening of the 2nd
- Violin Concerto, or in the delicate
- pauses and silences of the slow
- movement of the 1st Piano Concerto.
- He also has a great and strong sense
- of play, of fun; it is this which
- dominates the charming second
- movement of the five-movement
- Concerto for Orchestra, entitled 'Giocco
- delle coppie' ('Game of the couples'), a
- piece which both in spirit and in the
- texture of its orchestration could have
- come straight out of Tchaikovsky's
- ballet *The Nutcracker*. Eclectic
- influences pop up everywhere in
- Bartók; the beginning of the 2nd Piano
- Concerto definitely attests to his
- interest in Baroque music. Above all,
- Bartók is a highly melodic composer;
- not melodic perhaps in the way that
- Mozart or Mendelssohn are, but I defy
- anyone not to find melodic joys
- a-plenty in any of his great concertos

(especially the 2nd for Violin). He may not be easy, but he's not 'difficult' in the way that some people like to make out that modern music always is. Above all, he's not joyless.

Bartók mainly stuck to three-movement concerto form, varying this in the extended Concerto for Orchestra. And why a concerto for orchestra? To allow, I think, each section of the orchestra to revel in its own ingenuity and to create a larger drama by having a contest between not a single soloist and the orchestra as a whole, but between sections of the orchestra.

It's very sad that Bartók didn't complete his viola concerto; even what we have stands as an important part of the repertoire for that neglected instrument.

DISCOGRAPHY
It's possible to experiment with Bartók and not break the bank. A very good place to start would be a two-disc set which features not only the three piano concertos, but two other pieces he wrote for piano and orchestra; there's a superb version, too, of the Concerto for Orchestra. The soloist and conductor are both Hungarians, which helps, as they have a head start in comprehending one of Bartók's major influences. And as the soloist is the excellent Géza Anda and the conductor the underrated Ferenc Fricsay (1914–1963, and whose reputation is gradually climbing again), a pupil of Bartók's, all the more reason for trusting this combination.
● *Deutsche Grammophon 427 410-2* ● *2 CDs*
● *Mid-price* ● *ADD* ● *1957–61* ✪

Alternatively, all three piano concertos are available on a single disc, played by the highly intelligent and technically superb Stephen Kovacevich. Sir Colin Davis's conducting is good, if not perhaps the absolute best Bartók conducting around, but this is fine value for money.
● *Philips 426 660-2* ● *1 CD* ● *Mid-price*
● *ADD* ● *1969–76*

If you want to throw financial caution to the winds, though, you can get entirely brilliant performances of the first two piano concertos by one of the greatest pianists in twentieth-century repertoire – Maurizio Pollini – and Claudio Abbado, conducting music for which he has an instinctive feel, in a recording which brings out every nuance. Winner of a *The Gramophone* Award and quite right too.
● *Deutsche Grammophon 415 371-2* ● *1 CD*
● *Full price* ● *ADD* ● *1977*

You can't do any better, either in terms of performance or of value for money, than Kyung Wha Chung's fine recording of the two violin concertos. The conductor here is another ex-pupil of Bartók's, Sir Georg Solti, and these performances are inspired.
● *Decca Ovation 425 015-2* ● *1 CD*
● *Mid-price* ● *ADD/DDD* ● *1978–84*

For the Viola Concerto, I'd suggest trying Yehudi Menuhin's 1960s recording with Antál Dorati; Menuhin understood Bartók well, being so closely associated with him, and this performance burns with the soloist's 'mission to explain' the composer to a sometimes indifferent world. You also get the 1st Violin Concerto (a rather tricky work) and two wonderfully folksy Rhapsodies for Violin and Orchestra, in which Menuhin's earthiness is intriguingly balanced by a dry, clinical approach from conductor Pierre Boulez.
● *EMI CDM7 63985-2* ● *1 CD* ● *Mid-price*
● *ADD* ● *1965*

There is definite spoiling for choice when it comes to the Concerto for Orchestra. Apart from Fricsay's version (see above), there are two excellent versions by Sir Georg Solti, both at less than Full price, the better of which is probably the earlier recording with the London Symphony Orchestra, a dazzlingly spontaneous performance.
● *Decca 425 039-2* ● *1 CD* ● *Mid-price*
● *ADD* ● *1965*

Dorati, also with the LSO, turns in a scorcher in the old Mercury Living Presence series, with a lot of generous additional tracks which will help the new listener explore further in the wonderful world of Bartók.
● *Mercury 432 017-2* ● *1 CD* ● *Mid price*
● *ADD* ● *1962*

For the Music for Strings, Percussion and Celesta, if it's got to be fully digital, and with the added bonus of a first-rate performance (possibly the best on record), then Charles Dutoit and the Montreal Symphony will fulfil your every need. A wonderfully warm, witty, clear and exciting recording.
● *Decca 421 443-2* ● *1 CD* ● *Full price*
● *DDD* ● *1987*

A VIOLIN CONCERTO FOR AN ANGEL: BERG

Berg is one of the three great figures of the musical movement known as the Second Viennese School, the movement which rewrote the rules of music, formally and publicly abandoning the whole idea of tonality for a twelve-note system. Briefly, the

Alban Berg

1885–1935

Berg was a highly intellectual composer who lived in Vienna at a time when it was a hot-bed of new movements in all the arts. He was taught composition by Arnold Schoenberg, and was soon drawn to the new ideas about tonality which Schoenberg formulated over the first decade of the century. Berg's career was interrupted by the Great War, in which he served as a conscript; his experiences upset him greatly, and must have contributed to his great operatic masterpiece *Wozzeck* (the partly true story of a downtrodden soldier). Berg's personal life was highly complex; for many years the legend of a faithful, loving husband was fostered by his widow, but it is clear that he had at least one significant extramarital dalliance. His death from blood poisoning at the age of 50 was totally unexpected, and led to his second opera, *Lulu*, remaining incomplete.

>> *Opera* 197, *Chamber* 241, *Choral* 268

idea was this: in major and minor key structures, based on a scale of eight notes (do re mi fa so la ti do), some notes are less important as not 'properly belonging' to the key. In a twelve-note system, based on the idea that in any one octave there are in fact twelve notes each a semitone apart, each note is treated as of equal value with an equal potential, and music should therefore be constructed from patterns ('tone rows') which use all of the twelve notes once in turn. Of course, it gets more sophisticated than that, but that's the basic premise; and the use of all twelve notes in this way creates a stranger sort of melody than one rooted in the kind of harmonies we're used to in music from Mozart to the Beatles.

The great father-figure of all this was Arnold Schoenberg (1874–1951); his most prominent disciples were Berg and Anton Webern (1883–1945).

- To begin with there was a 'small is
- beautiful' attitude amongst these
- composers (which Webern adhered to
- throughout his life), and the
- 'legitimate' concerto was the 'chamber
- concerto'; Berg wrote one for piano,
- violin and thirteen wind instruments
- in 1923–5, Webern wrote a 'concerto'
- for nine instruments (essentially a
- chamber piece) between 1931 and
- 1934. But in 1935 Alban Berg tore
- himself away from work on his
- second and enormous opera, *Lulu*, to
- fulfil a commission which he had
- previously been neglecting, a
- commission to write a violin concerto.
- It was the death of the daughter of
- the architect Walter Gropius by
- Mahler's widow which inspired him
- finally to attempt the work he'd been
- letting slip. He dedicated his
- two-movement work 'to the memory
- of an Angel', and the result was
- twofold; a great twentieth-century

masterpiece, and *Lulu* never being finished, for Berg died in December 1935, before he had time either to finish the opera or to hear a performance of the concerto.

In rejecting the conventional concerto structure, Berg didn't then set out to create something entirely shocking. He was always regarded (and still is) as something of a reactionary amongst the Second Viennese School, the one whose music most clearly refers back to old habits and influences; indeed, in parts of *Lulu* and the Violin Concerto you can hear the shadow of an earlier dominant Viennese figure, Johann Strauss II (1825-1899), the 'Waltz King' (something pointed out to me by the conductor Nikolaus Harnoncourt). The structure Berg went for was a basic two-movement one which formed a simple mirrored pattern; the first movement goes from quite slow to quite fast, the second from fast to slow. And while the approach to melody isn't what you get in Brahms, the whole piece, right from its ethereal, hesitant beginning, is steeped in a kind of Romanticism reflected in various markings Berg used to indicate how the music should be played – 'Religioso' and 'Amoroso'. There's a quotation (complete with harmonies) from a Bach chorale; there's an Austrian folk-tune lurking in there somewhere; and whilst Berg's use of the tone-row is scrupulously in accordance with the rules of the Second Viennese School, the effect is so far from academic or arid, and so steeped in love and beauty that once a listener has come to terms with the loss of the old harmonic system, then it would take a very hard heart indeed not to succumb to the rapture of the experience.

DISCOGRAPHY

Once again Yehudi Menuhin and Pierre Boulez make a fine combination, each providing a complementary quality, Menuhin's loving Romanticism drawing inspiration from Boulez's precision and definition. Just occasionally, though, the orchestra could be a shade warmer. Still, in all a lovely recording.
● *EMI CDM7 63989-2* ● *1 CD* ● *Mid-price*
● *ADD* ● *1968* ○

Arthur Grumiaux's lovely recording also includes Stravinsky's Violin Concerto – not, in my view, a work in the same class as Berg's, but still well worth making an effort with. Grumiaux's Berg brings out all the pathos, the elegiac nature of the piece, and the orchestral support is rather more loving than the Menuhin/Boulez.
● *Philips 422 136-2* ● *1 CD* ● *Mid-price*
● *ADD*

Another excellent Mid-price option is Henryk Szeryng's passionate version; as conductor, Rafael Kubelik has a sympathy for this music to rival his talent for Mahler's symphonies. You also get Schoenberg's violin and piano concertos.
● *Deutsche Grammophon 431 740 2* ● *1 CD*
● *Mid-price* ● *ADD*

But why not spoil yourself and get the rapturously beautiful new recording by Anne-Sophie Mutter? She had planned to record this piece with Karajan (who then died), and James Levine proves to be an exciting, inspired substitute. His warmth and phrasing, and, above all, Mutter's amazing gift for being both lyrical and tough in her playing, make this a superb experience.
● *Deutsche Grammophon 437 093-2* ● *1 CD*
● *Full price* ● *DDD* ● *1992*

WRAPPING UP THE CONCERTO: SOME MORE MODERNS AND A FEW CLASSICAL BYWAYS

I've given such prominence to Bartók's and Berg's concertos over Stravinsky's and Schoenberg's because I believe the listener can plunge more easily into them, and that they are, ultimately, greater, more rewarding pieces of music. However, there are plenty of other twentieth-century concertos well worth the time and trouble; Walton's concertos for viola and for violin; Schnittke's Viola Concerto (and his revival of the old concerto grosso form makes a good introduction to this well-marketed, but probably rather slight, modern composer). It's good to see the viola being revived as a concerto instrument; after the 6th Brandenburg, its fortunes took a nosedive and it's still the butt of orchestral jokes today.

Sir Michael Tippett has always had a strong interest in the concerto, as opposed to Britten, who wrote a very fine violin concerto and a rather nugatory piano concerto. Tippett's Triple Concerto and Piano Concerto are both important works; while his Concerto for Double String Orchestra is an easily accessible joy, full of life and vitality.

Among minor but charming works from various earlier periods, Delius's cello, violin and double concertos all have their advocates, being as they are such strong examples of the English 'Romantic' school of the early part of the century. The eighteenth century yielded Weber's clarinet concertos, two of the most delightfully pleasurable pieces ever written for that warm and mellow instrument, and Hummel's piano concertos, on which the English pianist Stephen Hough did such a wonderful rescue job a few years ago. These may be 'minor' works, but they're very enjoyable. Concertos are still being written, too; but then gifted musicians will always want to show off, and what better vehicle than the concerto?

- DISCOGRAPHY
- **Final Thoughts**
- For Walton's viola and violin concertos, try Nigel
- Kennedy's excellent recordings.
- ● *EMI CDC7 49628-2* ● *1 CD* ● *Full price*
- ● *DDD* ● *1987*

- There is no better version of Schnittke's Viola
- Concerto than Yuri Bashmet's.
- ● *RCA Victor Red Seal RD 60446* ● *1 CD*
- ● *Full price* ● *DDD* ● *1991*

- For Schnittke and the concerto grosso, try No. 1.
- ● *Deutsche Grammophon 429 413-2* ● *1 CD*
- ● *Full price* ● *DDD* ● *1988*

- Tippett's Triple Concerto and Piano Concerto are
- available on the same disc, conducted by the
- composer.
- ● *Nimbus N15301* ● *1 CD*

- A better performance, however, also comes with
- the Concerto for Orchestra, and is conducted by
- Sir Colin Davis, a Tippett expert.
- ● *Philips 420 781-2* ● *1 CD* ● *Full price*
- ● *ADD* ● *1965/80.*

- Try also his superb Concerto for Double String
- Orchestra, best in its performance by Sir Neville
- Marriner and his Academy of St
- Martin-in-the-Fields.
- ● *Decca 421 389-2* ● *1 CD* ● *ADD* ● *1972*

- For Delius's Violin Concerto, try the collection by
- Ralph Holmes with Vernon Handley conducting
- the Royal Philharmonic.
- ● *Unicorn-Kanchana DKPCD 9040* ● *1 CD*
- ● *Full price* ● *DDD* ● *1985*

- The Cello and Double Concertos come together on
- one excellent disc, with Sir Charles Mackerras
- conducting the Royal Liverpool Philharmonic, with
- soloists Raphael Wallfisch and Tasmin Little.
- ● *EMI Eminence CD-EMX 2185* ● *1 CD*
- ● *Mid-price* ● *DDD* ● *1991*

- There's a lovely period-instrument recording of
- Weber's clarinet works, featuring Antony Pay as
- soloist and conductor of the Orchestra of the Age
- of Enlightenment.
- ● *Virgin Classics VC7 90720-2* ● *1 CD* ● *Full*
- *price* ● *DDD* ● *1988*

- Stephen Hough's great Hummel disc also features
- the English Chamber Orchestra conducted by
- Bryden Thomson.
- ● *Chandos CHAN8507* ● *1 CD* ● *Full price*
- ● *DDD* ● *1986*

IV

Opera

INTRODUCTION:
BEGINNINGS OF OPERA

Opera is probably best defined as music drama in which the drama is provided through, and emphasised by, the music. This distinguishes it from the stage musical, where the music embroiders rather than pushes forward the action, although a good musical will use the music to push the drama forwards every bit as much as opera.

'Opera certainly takes its time', a character in a Martin Amis novel remarks. While there's plenty of boring opera around (and not a few boring productions and recordings of opera which shouldn't be boring at all), the best opera – and there's a lot of it – is all about drama. After all, it was drama which gave birth to opera. In fact it was the sixteenth-century fascination with Ancient Greek literature which (accidentally) gave opera to the world. Greek drama was known – or at least assumed – to have had a strong musical component, making use of both singing and dance, and a group of Florentine noblemen ran some experiments to see how this might actually have worked. This partly explains why so much early opera took Greek myth and history (and Roman to a lesser, though significant, extent) as its proper subject. These experimental pieces had a certain relentless earnestness in their attempt to match speech and musical rhythms, and the evidence of those which have survived suggests that they were, in the main, stultifyingly dull both musically and dramatically.

JACOPO PERI (1561–1633)
Jacopo Peri is the man credited with 'inventing' opera, and it's standard practice to describe his *Dafne* (1597) as 'the first opera'. Sadly *Dafne* has been

- lost to the world, and the earliest
- surviving work by Peri is *Euridice*
- (1600), based around the myth of
- Orpheus (Orfeo), whose wife Eurydice
- (Euridice in Italian) is bitten by a

snake and dies. Orpheus goes down to Hades to win her back from the King of the Dead by the power of his musical skill, and, in the traditional version, is granted his wish on condition that he can lead her to the gates of the Underworld without once looking back; unfortunately, he can't manage this, looks back, and she vanishes back to Hades for ever. Peri allowed himself the licence to alter the end of the story (Orfeo succeeds in his mission) as a celebration of the status of Art in general and Music in particular. A lot of modern scholars delight in finding parallels between the kind of semi-natural speech rhythms Peri used and the relationship between music and words in Schoenberg, in Debussy's *Pelléas et Mélisande*, and even in Wagner. You can see what they mean, but it doesn't make *Euridice* a more accessible or lovable piece. It's something of a statuesque star vehicle for Orfeo (probably originally played by Peri himself), yet without asking him to use a very wide vocal range or offering much in the way of melody. But perhaps it's fitting that the first opera to survive should have been a treatment of the Orpheus story: not only did that story about the Triumph of Art enjoy something of a vogue amongst the musicians of the 1600s, but the first operatic masterpiece also happens to be a setting of the same story.

CREATING AN ART FORM: MONTEVERDI

Three of Monteverdi's operas have survived, and two of these are amongst the greatest operas of any age. *La Favola di Orfeo*, more often referred to as *L'Orfeo* (1607), has all the drama which Peri lacks – you actually care about his characters as

human beings (or gods, or whatever they happen to be) – and Monteverdi's exploitation of the human voice makes for a much more exciting piece of music. Indeed, some of the demands made on the voice, the urgently repeated notes, swooping and soaring melodic lines which lack the smooth charm of the Italian grand operas of Verdi and Puccini, have a curiously Modernist sound. Although the lion's share of the action rests with Orfeo, the minor characters, especially the Messenger who announces Euridice's death and Charon, the Ferryman of the Styx, are fully realised musically. This version of the legend reverts to a fallible Orfeo who loses his love for a second time through his own lack of self-control, and has all the more dramatic tension and energy for it, although the myth's possibilities as a paean to Art and Music are still exploited. The work ends in an apotheosis hymning the power of Music, who is the personified god who initiates the action. (When Gluck came to treat the same myth 150 years or so later, Love – Amor – becomes the initiator, and the happy ending is restored.)

Most of Monteverdi's other operas have been lost, except for two masterpieces of his old age. *Il Ritorno d'Ulisse in Patria* ('Ulysses's Return to his Homeland') tells of the Greek hero's homecoming after ten years' wandering and his plans to outwit the unwanted suitors of his wife Penelope, faithfully following the plot in Homer's *Odyssey* almost to the letter. Written around 1640, it's the most neglected of the three surviving Monteverdi pieces, but it can be startlingly dramatic, and the ending of the second act is like a cliffhanger from *Dr Who* or something similar; all of which stands as testimony to the

Claudio Monteverdi

1567–1643

Monteverdi is associated mainly with Venice, where he wrote some of the greatest Baroque religious music including the famous *Vespers* (1610). However, he was born in Cremona, and for a significant portion of his creative career he was employed at the court of the Duke of Mantua, in that city. From the 1580s he wrote many madrigals, and in Mantua his job was to devise court entertainments; although he did well enough to be promoted in 1601, from about 1604 the Mantuan court became rather irregular in paying his salary. None the less, it was for that court that Monteverdi wrote the first operatic masterpiece, his *L'Orfeo*, in 1607. By a rather macabre coincidence, in the same year that this opera about a man who has lost his wife appeared, Monteverdi's own wife died. Three years or so later, Monteverdi was offered the prestigious job of musical director of St Mark's, Venice; he seized the chance to get out of Mantua with both hands. He flourished in Venice (at that time one of the greatest artistic centres of Europe) and continued to write music of genius until his death, creating in his last decade two further operatic masterpieces.

>> *Choral* 249

fact that no one wrote operas as dramatically exciting as Monteverdi's for another century and a half.

Monteverdi's third operatic masterpiece, and possibly the most remarkable opera written before Mozart's prime, is *L'Incoronazione di Poppea* (1642). This large piece, which has a huge cast of principals, was written for the general public rather than for a specialist court audience, as most opera had been until then. The story describes how Nero manipulates Roman politics and gets rid of his enemies for the love of Poppea, so that he can marry her and have her crowned as Empress. The portrait of Nero (sung by a soprano, as was usual in those days of castrati) is

- surprisingly subtle: this Nero is a
- character of real emotion and depth
- who gets some of the best music in
- the opera. The libretto (the text) – and
- its musical treatment – are
- reminiscent of Shakespeare: comedy
- and tragedy are juxtaposed in a
- manner which operatic writers a
- century later would have frowned on
- greatly. One moment the noble Seneca
- is preparing himself for suicide, the
- next debauched courtiers are making
- passes at one another. This calls for a
- variety of musical styles; Monteverdi
- makes great use of dramatic recitative
- – words sung at the speed and
- rhythm of ordinary speech to light
- accompaniment, usually on a
- keyboard instrument – but creates

some truly haunting arias and duets. Remarkably, this is all done using an almost chamber-sized orchestral ensemble under the voices, although one never feels that the musical effects are thin. This opera may demand some concentration, on first acquaintance, but it works very well on disc, and can become dangerously addictive. Certainly most opera written over the following century seems pallid and static by comparison.

DISCOGRAPHY
La Favola d'Orfeo
Despite some of my prejudices, I happily concede that the best recordings of *Orfeo* all use period instruments. Top choice is probably John Eliot Gardiner's, which is imaginative, witty, crisp; Anthony Rolfe Johnson in the title role gives a fine, clear, intelligent performance.
● *Deutsche Grammophon Archiv 419 250-2*
● *2 CDs* ● *Full price* ● *DDD* ● *1985* ○

Nigel Rogers has twice recorded the role of *Orfeo*, and his self-directed attempt (in conjunction with Charles Medlam) with Chiaroscuro and the London Baroque Orchestra features a tour de force of wide-ranging expression in the title role and a real sense of the opera's darkness in some of the Underworld scenes.
● *EMI CDS7 47142-8* ● *2 CDs* ● *Full price*
● *DDD* ● *1983*

It was, inevitably, Nikolaus Harnoncourt who set the original standard with period instruments back in the 1960s, and this recently reissued version still strikes the listener as fresh even if it isn't quite as shocking as it was 25 years ago. Then it seemed more acidic than anyone was used to; now it can be appreciated for some remarkable performances, not least by the late Cathy Berberian as a messenger.
● *Teldec 2292-42494-2* ● *2 CDs* ● *Mid-price*
● *ADD* ● *1968*

Il Ritorno d'Ulisse in Patria
This is quite a long work, so listen before you buy, but I really love Harnoncourt's pioneering version, not least for the singing of Nigel Rogers (as one of the suitors) and Rotraud Hansmann (as Minerva).
● *Teldec 2292-42496-2* ● *3 CDs* ● *Mid-price*
● *ADD* ● *1970* ○

✓*L'Incoronazione di Poppea*
The top choice is undoubtedly Richard Hickox's genuinely dramatic performance, featuring fine singing from the late Arleen Auger and from Della Jones. A brilliant set, even if it is a bit costly.
● *Virgin Classics VCT7 9055-2* ● *3 CDs* ● *Full price* ● *DDD* ● *1989* ○

AFTER MONTEVERDI

Monteverdi had developed opera to a point where it was genuinely dramatic; where character was reflected and expounded through the music rather than simply through the words of the libretto; where the setting of words to music bore some relation, within musical limits, to real speech patterns; and where vocal virtuosity was kept within limits which didn't allow it to take over and dominate proceedings. All these gains were immediately thrown away by his successors, and it wasn't until the advent of Christoph Willibald Gluck (1714–1787) over 100 years later that anyone thought about reclaiming these virtues.

The opera of the mid-seventeenth to late eighteenth century is, I think it's fair to say, a fairly acquired taste, although an awful lot has been done in recent years to restate the cases for Handel and some of the French operatic composers. But I don't think the reputation of a composer like Francesco Cavalli (1602–1676), a Venetian-based composer of over 40 operas, is ever really likely to rise again, so changed is public taste.

In this era two things happened; in 'serious opera' (*'opera seria'*) a taste was cultivated for high-minded plots describing the actions of mythological heroes and heroines, with a background of gods organising the mortals' behaviour in highly schematic stylised ways. Comic opera (*'opera buffa'*) was something of an infra dig. affair, revolving around farcical love confusions, and so on.

FRENCH BAROQUE OPERA: LULLY, RAMEAU ET CIE

France in the time of Louis XIV (who reigned for most of the seventeenth century and on into the eighteenth) was a hive of musical activity and, as I've said, the French Baroque is coming back into fashion at the moment, at least partly due to the pretty-pretty (but in my view utterly dull) film *Tous Les Matins du Monde*. The dominant figures in French opera at this time, and through into the reign of Louis XV (as Baroque yielded to Classical) were Jean-Baptiste Lully (1632–1687) and Jean-Philippe Rameau (1683–1764).

The most popular type of opera was *'tragédie lyrique'*, aimed primarily at the King and his court at Versailles, but also popular with the public at the Paris Opéra. *Tragédie lyrique* was, like *opera seria*, all about courtly ideals, and was packed with gods; it also went in for spectacular stage effects and lavish scenery and costumes, which is where much of the excitement for the public lay. The French were also very given to 'opera-ballet', essentially the forerunner of modern ballet, telling stories through dance; and ballet remained a part of opera through into Mozart's time (anyone who's seen the film *Amadeus* will remember the fuss about Mozart including a ballet in *The Marriage of Figaro* at a time when the operatic powers of Vienna were trying to get the dance out of opera).

Lully was, basically, the inventor of French opera; his works stressed the importance of the chorus and of dance, and paid a fair respect to the libretto. His operas were very much in the static Classical mould of the plays of Corneille and Racine, with much attention paid to *'bien séance'*, the idea that awful things could only happen off the stage, as in Greek tragedy (it was Shakespeare's ease of presentation of gruesome events in front of the audience which made the French so dismissive of him). Lully's dramatic form rather eclipsed the Italian operatic forms in France; his works *Atys* (1676), *Bellerophon* (1679)

and, above all, *Armide* (1686), his final opera and, according to many, his masterpiece, set the standard for French opera over the next century, and spawned imitators such as Marin Marais (1656–1728; the musical 'star' of *Tous les Matins du Monde*).

Rameau added to Lully's form a more developed sense of harmony and a richer use of orchestral instruments (living through a time when, of course, instruments were developing technologically). If Lully's music is ornate in typical Baroque style, Rameau's cubes the effect. His particular masterpieces are considered to be *Hippolyte et Aricie* (1733), *Dardanus* (1739) and, most notably and accessibly, *Castor et Pollux* (1737).

DISCOGRAPHY
Lully's *Armide* prefigures much future opera by being a tale of love and death in which the lovers' passion brings its own destruction, indeed, somehow seems to necessitate that destruction. There was an excellent recording of the opera conducted by Philip Herreweghe (Erato), but that is, sadly, currently unavailable. There is a fine recording of the epic *Atys* by the doyen of this repertoire, William Christie and his ensemble Les Arts Florissants, and, happily, there's a very good disc of extracts from that recording which preserve all the moments of high drama.
● *Harmonia Mundi HMC90 1267* ● *1 CD*
● *Full price* ● *DDD* ● *1986* ❂

Rameau recordings are a bit of a growth industry; *Castor et Pollux* is a good and natural starting-point. No excerpts disc as yet; a brand new version from Christie and Les Arts Florissants is typically absorbing and sumptuous (Christie isn't afraid, as some practitioners of Baroque are still inclined to be, of being expressive and overtly dramatic).
● *Harmonia Mundi HMC90 1257* ● *3 CDs*
● *Full price* ● *DDD* ● *1992*

Slightly down the price range there is – again inevitably – one of the first period-instrument recordings of the piece by Nikolaus Harnoncourt.
● *Teldec 2292 42510-2* ● *3 CDs* ● *Mid-price*
● *ADD* ● *1971*

● ● ● ●

ENGLAND'S ONE GREAT CONTRIBUTION: PURCELL

When opera took off in England, it was mainly through Handel's Italian

Henry Purcell

1659–1695

D uring his tragically short life, Henry Purcell managed to establish himself as one of the (if not *the*) greatest of all British composers. His life encompassed a lot of upheaval, and in 1665 the six-year-old Londoner would have been confronted with all the scenes of the Great Plague, followed the next year by the Great Fire of London. His reputation wasn't affected by the change of regime in the so-called 'Glorious Revolution' of 1688 (when the Catholic Stuart King James II was supplanted by the Protestant William III and his wife, Mary II), even though he was a leading writer of church music (involvement in church affairs of any kind could lead to political trouble), and he was called on to provide funeral music for Queen Mary when she died in 1694; in a macabre coincidence, the music was able to do service at Purcell's own obsequies the following year.

>> *Choral* 253

operas (after the composer came over from Germany with George I, who was by no means the Germanic boor he's often been depicted as), which were then eclipsed by ballad-based works like John Gay's *The Beggar's Opera* (1728). The late seventeenth century saw a great flood of 'semi-operas', dramas by leading figures such as the poet John Dryden, and which included musical 'numbers' by major British composers such as John Blow (1649–1708; most famous for a quasi-operatic masque, *Venus and Adonis*; 1681) and, above all, Purcell.

Much of Purcell's musical career was taken up with the theatre; he wrote countless sets of incidental music (one of his single most famous tunes comes from this source; a rondeau from *Abdelazar, or the Moor's Revenge*,

- which was appropriated in an
- unpleasant arrangement by Andrew
- Lloyd-Webber by the Conservative
- Party during the 1992 British General
- Election), several semi-operas, the odd
- masque (a courtly entertainment,
- basically lacking in drama, somewhat
- akin to a series of tableaux rather than
- the continuous narrative of a play), and
- in 1689 a work which can fairly claim
- to the first British opera, written well
- before the advent of Italian opera to
- these shores. And it's a masterpiece, a
- miniature treasure of incalculable price.
- 'It' is, in fact, *Dido and Aeneas*,
- telling the story related in Virgil's
- *Aeneid* of the doomed love affair
- between Aeneas, Prince of Troy and
- destined to become the forefather of
- the Roman race, and Dido, widowed
- Queen of Carthage. Aeneas is forced
- by the gods to abandon her in order to

fulfil his mission and Dido, heartbroken, wills her own death. To add to the drama, the libretto, taken from Virgil by the very proficient hack writer Nahum Tate, mixes in a band of malicious witches determined to cause Dido's downfall.

Dido and Aeneas was written originally for the 'young gentlewomen' of a girls' boarding school, and accordingly it isn't too difficult either to play or to sing (the orchestral part is for stringed instruments only). However, Purcell created several memorable, entirely singable choruses and, in the role of Dido, one of the greatest of operatic parts; Dido's Lament in the final act has become a popular 'excerpt' in the repertoire, understandably so, for it is simply a sublime melody, set over a simple repeated bass line and orchestration, demanding the most subtle performance from the singer. And the great thing about *Dido*, as opposed to much French and Italian Baroque opera, is that it recognises the advantage of brevity; even taken outrageously slowly it can't last much above an hour, and yet it's ten times as affecting and memorable as many works ten times its length. Even I, a confirmed Wagnerian, have to admit that size isn't everything. This is one of the great English masterpieces.

DISCOGRAPHY
Although the French accents of some of the singers may seem odd to English ears (although no odder, I dare say, than German or Italian sung by English-speakers), the version of *Dido* which gives me the most joy is, once again, the brainchild of William Christie and Les Arts Florissants; sumptuous, loving, beautifully and purely sung, yet full of drama.
● *Harmonia Mundi HMC 905173* ● *1 CD* ● *Full price* ● *DDD* ● *1985* ○

If you absolutely insist on English accents, but you still want an 'authentic' performance, then you can't do any better than Andrew Parrott's version, featuring the beautiful tones of Emma Kirkby in the role of Dido.

● *Chandos CHAN 8306* ● *1 CD* ● *Full price* ● *DDD* ● *1990*

Entirely non-authentic, but of great appeal to Jessye Norman fans in particular, is the version conducted by Raymond Leppard featuring Ms Norman as Dido; as I've said, Leppard is usually the best of the non-period performers in this repertoire.
● *Philips 416 299-2* ● *1 CD* ● *Full price* ● *DDD* ● *1985*

But the greatest of all interpreters of the role of Dido must remain the great Dame Janet Baker, and her 30-plus-year-old recording is still a classic; her range of tone in a part which moves from a quite high soprano to dark, lower contralto is superb. Conductor Anthony Lewis takes some fast speeds, but it all works brilliantly.
● *Decca 425 720-2* ● *1 CD* ● *Mid-price* ● *ADD* ● *1962*

A COMPOSER OF ITALIAN OPERAS: HANDEL

Although most of his best work was written for a London audience, Handel's operas typify 'Italian opera' of the early eighteenth century. Mythological and Classical Greek and Roman stories predominate, although the drama of the operas (probably) depended upon stage effects, which is why some less than spectacularly staged versions of Handel operas in recent years have proved (to be polite) rather less than gripping. The main purpose of the works was to provide long vocal showpieces (although Handel kept his soloists under better, more dramatically logical, restraint than many other composers) which seldom involved duets until moments of rare high tension: for example in *Xerxes* (*Serse*, 1738) it isn't until the final act that two singers are involved in the same number, a witty, entirely civilised, yet by no means dispassionate lover's argument.

What makes Handel's operas stand out from the herd is their sheer melodic invention. I don't think we'll ever be able to recapture whatever it

George Frederick Handel

1685–1759

To most casual listeners to music, George Frederick Handel (1685–1759) is known as the author of the oratorio (sacred choral work) *Messiah*, and of the instrumental suites, the Water Music and Music for the Royal Fireworks. We've touched on Handel's career as a copious composer of concertos; but if you'd asked the man himself just what he did, he'd probably have replied that he was 'a composer of Italian operas'. He came to England in 1714 with the Hanoverian George I, and quickly established his operatic style on the English stage, as well as his sacred oratorios in English concert halls. For a decade and a half all was well, but the success of John Gay's *The Beggar's Opera* in 1728 caused Handel severe problems. Gay's work was very much more accessible through being based on tunes and songs already popular with the public, and because it dealt with real, if undesirable, people, rather than the high-minded heroes and mythological figures who populate the scene of Handel's works. Through the 1730s Handel's reputation waned, but an invitation to Ireland in 1742 led to his writing *Messiah*, which made for rather a spectacular comeback.

>> *Concerto* 100, *Choral* 255, *Orchestral* 274

was that made them memorable stage experiences in their day, but quite a number have been recorded to good effect, and they make very good listening. And when the requisite special effects can be managed in a piece revolving around magic, such as *Alcina* (1735 – probably the most enduring of all), they can be pleasing to the eye too.

John Gay's *The Beggar's Opera* (1728) dealt a severe blow to the lofty ideals of Handel's operas, and in the 1730s Handel tried to make his pieces lighter and wittier, with limited success. This taste for the ballad-opera was almost exclusively an English phenomenon, but since Handel was based in England, this shift in taste was extremely relevant to him.

DISCOGRAPHY

Finding good, well-performed representative excerpt selections from Handel operas is fairly difficult, and my advice would be to treat yourself to a distinguished but not very 'authentic' recording of *Alcina* (in a botched-up version in which various arias have been reappropriated to the starrier roles), which also includes highlights of *Giulio Cesare in Egitto (Julius Caesar in Egypt)*. The great 'plus' of this particular set is the presence of the great Joan Sutherland (who in the 1960s was at least partly responsible for rescuing *Alcina* from oblivion), with a supporting cast including two other great sopranos, Teresa Berganza and Mirella Freni. *Alcina* is a story about an enchantress on an island deflecting a knight from his heroic destiny until the knight's true love comes along and rescues him; *Giulio Cesare in Egitto* (1724) is loosely based on the historic carryings-on of Caesar, Ptolemy and Cleopatra in their jockeying for political power – and with a bit of love interest thrown in – in the first century BC. These excerpts feature not only Sutherland as Cleopatra, but another great singer of this and the early-eighteenth-century bel canto style, Marilyn Horne (recently the star singer at President Clinton's 1993 inauguration ceremony).
● *Decca 433 723-2* ● *3 CDs* ● *Mid-price*
● *ADD* ● *1962/63* ○

If you're impressed by this and want to know how *Alcina* ought to sound, there's an excellent version by Richard Hickox.
- *EMI CDS7 49771-2* • *3 CDs* • *Full price* • *DDD* • *1988* ✪

Amidst the ever-growing racks of Handel operas, two are particularly noteworthy (if expensive); a fine recording by Christopher Hogwood of *Orlando* (1733), another story about a hero struggling to assert his manly nature,
- *L'Oiseau-Lyre 430 845-2* • *3 CDs* • *Full price* • *DDD* • *1990*

and *The Gramophone* Award-winning latest version of *Giulio Cesare in Egitto* by Baroque expert René Jacobs
- *Harmonia Mundi HMC90 1385/7* • *3 CDs* • *Full price* • *DDD* • *1991*

REFORM: CHRISTOPH WILLIBALD GLUCK (1714–1787)

As the eighteenth century progressed, opera became more and more about showpieces for star singers and less and less about character, plot and drama. By 1762, one prolific German operatic composer, Christoph Willibald Gluck, had had enough of this; he wanted to write operas in which the music contributed to the drama and worked with the text, rather than using his works as a pretext for vocal pyrotechnics. Gluck set out to reform the whole business, and the subject he chose for his first 'reform opera' (as his mature works became known) was, appropriately enough, opera's original starting-point, the story of Orpheus and Eurydice, first performed in Vienna in 1762.

Restraint is the hallmark of Gluck's style in *Orfeo ed Euridice*. The excessive decoration of the late Baroque has vanished to give way to a style in which the music is designed to mirror what is actually being sung; Classical 'decorum', in other words. There's also much more attention in the music to making things continuous; the first chorus anticipates in some way the great climactic aria of the lovelorn Orfeo, the very famous and beautiful 'Che farò?' ('What shall I do without Eurydice?'), and throughout the chorus, soloists and orchestra are given music which brings all the forces involved together, emphasising dramatic unity and purpose. Gluck was forced to give the piece a happy ending and to stick an overture on the front, but these were the only concessions to pre-reform taste. In the original Viennese version of the work, the part of Orfeo was taken by a soprano.

By the time Gluck wrote his *Orfeo*, Vienna was one of the two great cultural centres of Europe, Paris being the other; although, outside France, Italian was still the accepted operatic language. Gluck's reforms had a fairly instantaneous effect and their influence continued well into the nineteenth century (in fact, much of what is in Wagner's operas is a direct consequence of what Gluck started), and when he presented a revised and expanded version of *Orfeo* in Paris in 1774, it had as big an impact on French opera as the original version had had on Italian. This *Orfeo* had the principal role rewritten for tenor and incorporated a greater amount of ballet music, as ballet was still of great significance in Paris. This has led to some confusion about which version of the opera is more 'authentic', as some of the ballet music is most effective and enjoyable. There is a successful 'compromise' version prepared by Berlioz in 1859, which most often employs a female Orfeo.

Gluck continued as an influential figure in Vienna and Paris, the most enduring of his other operas being (probably) *Iphigénie en Tauride* ('Iphigenia in Tauris', 1779), a story about the reunion of Orestes with his sister Iphigenia, whom he believes dead, full of human drama and noble sentiments about self-sacrifice, revolving around inner feelings and lyrical expression of psychological states.

DISCOGRAPHY
Recently the best version of *Orfeo ed Euridice* was reissued on CD; it's based on the Berlioz compromise, and taken from the Glyndebourne production which was Dame Janet Baker's last operatic performance. She took the title role and gave a magnificent, compelling performance, with telling and subtle support from conductor Raymond Leppard and a beautiful-voiced Euridice in Elisabeth Speiser. A great recording.
● *Erato 2292-45864-2* ● *2 CDs* ● *Mid-price*
● *DDD* ● *1982* ○

And there's an excellent compilation of Gluck arias, again featuring Dame Janet and Leppard.
● *Philips 422 950-2* ● *1 CD* ● *Mid-price* ● *ADD*

OPERATIC GENIUS: MOZART

Gluck's *Iphigénie en Tauride* appeared two years before Mozart's first mature opera, and what one might call his only true essay in the *opera seria* form, *Idomeneo, Re di Creta*. There were plenty of highly popular operatic composers around at this time whose work hasn't travelled through time especially well, people like Giovanni Paisiello (1740–1816), composer of the original version of *The Barber of Seville* (1782 – ten years before the birth of Rossini, composer of the great version of the same work), and Domenico Cimarosa (1749–1801), whose *opere buffe* (the most famous now being *Il Matrimonio Segreto, The Secret Marriage*) are proof positive that humour dates in a big way. The popularity of Antonio Salieri (1750–1825) as a composer of operas was enormous in the last decades of the century, especially in court circles. Haydn too wrote operas, big serious

affairs which are very much to a specialist's taste. But from our perspective, although not in his own lifetime, the dominant operatic figure was unquestionably Wolfgang Amadeus Mozart. Mozart composed at least three operas which have a claim to be considered the greatest ever written – *Le Nozze di Figaro* (*The Marriage of Figaro*, 1786), *Don Giovanni* (1787), and *Così Fan Tutte* ('That's how all women behave', 1790); and he also effectively founded German opera, first with *Die Entführung aus dem Serail* (*The Abduction from the Harem*, 1782), then with *Die Zauberflöte* (*The Magic Flute*, 1791 – a fourth Mozartian candidate for the title of 'best opera').

Idomeneo (1781), the first of the mature operas, doesn't quite belong in the big league; it owes more allegiance to the stylised kind of opera, full of high thoughts, noble sentiments and mythological characters, which Mozart's contemporaries (and especially Salieri) excelled in. *Die Entführung*, which is not a 'through-composed' opera, in that the characters speak the dialogue rather than sing it, is remarkable not merely for being in German, but also for its complete abandonment of lofty, god-like mythological figures. It belongs to a genre known as the 'rescue opera' (because its plot involves a rescue) and the setting – a Turkish harem – owes something to a long-lasting craze of the day for 'Turkish music' (which meant the inclusion of a lot of jingling percussion and the use of strong martial beats). Another fine example of both the 'rescue' craze and the taste for 'Turkish' music (although in a non-Turkish setting) is Rossini's *L'Italiana in Algeri* (*The Italian Girl in Algiers*, 1813). Mozart's *Die Entführung* contains some quite brilliant passages of vocal writing, especially for the soprano heroine Konstanze, and much more vivid characterisation than in many operas by Mozart's contemporaries. However, it was with his next major opera that Mozart created something new, different and remarkable.

Le Nozze di Figaro (The Marriage of Figaro)

The problems that surrounded *Figaro*'s première form an amusing episode in the film *Amadeus*, and, unlike much else in that film, are pretty accurately depicted. Beaumarchais's original play had been banned from production in Vienna, and the Emperor Josef II had declared ballet scenes in operas unacceptable, so that it required much political manoeuvring to get round these obstacles. Still, it was all well worth it, for in *Figaro* Mozart's genius for comedy, drama and pathos found its most perfect subject. Some of the credit must go to the librettist, Lorenzo da Ponte (1749–1838), in the first of three remarkable collaborations (see also *Don Giovanni* and *Così Fan Tutte* below). But for all da Ponte's subtlety and economy, the opening scene of *Figaro* is conclusive proof that Mozart could make the music provide the drama. In that scene Figaro tries to measure the room, accompanied by solid purposeful music; Susanna, his fiancée, attempts to distract him, accompanied by decorative fluttering twiddles. The more urgent she gets and the more he tries to concentrate, the more the music characterising the woman predominates, until Figaro gives up and does as he's told. A shrewd and subtle portrayal of domestic sexual politics, and typical of what follows over four acts. *Figaro* is one of Mozart's greatest works, and the most listener-friendly of operas.

Figaro, technically an *opera buffa*, but touching a level of psychological realism undreamt of in the works of Cimarosa, as well as including a remarkable amount of pathos in the character of the Countess Almaviva, is a complex farce, full of disguise and deceit. Basically it tells of how Count Almaviva tries – and fails – to exercise *droit de seigneur* over Susanna on her wedding day, and, thwarted, attempts to prevent the wedding, whilst Susanna plots with her mistress the Countess to return the errant husband to his devoted wife. Minor comic characters are also out to get Figaro for various reasons, and matters are further confused by Figaro himself and a permanently randy page called Cherubino (a mezzo-soprano role), but eventually Figaro marries Susanna, the Count gets his comeuppance, and all ends in happiness (just).

What makes *Figaro* special?

Figaro is one of the most subtle psychological and dramatic operas ever written, much of which is due to Mozart. Even the smallest role (Antonio, a drunken gardener) has its own characteristic musical style, and Mozart interweaves his principal voices in a manner more or less unheard-of in opera up to that point. Every act is crammed with famous arias and duets ('Voi che sapete', 'Non più andrai', 'Dove sono', 'Se vuol ballare', 'Porgi Amor'), tunes which have been heard by countless people who've never actually sat through the opera itself. *Figaro* is also that rare thing, a *genuinely* funny comic opera, but one which, for all its comedy, touches at times a tragic level of pathos: the Countess comes close to being a truly tragic figure in the midst of all the frenetic farce. The one lie the film *Amadeus* does tell about *Figaro* is that it was a terrible flop: although it got only nine performances in Vienna in 1786, it was quite well received, but it was a smash hit in Prague, where Mozart's later work was always more popular. If Mozart's music moves you at all, *Figaro* could be every opera you'll ever need.

Don Giovanni

Don Giovanni (1787), fruit of another collaboration with da Ponte, was premièred in Prague, further testament to Mozart's great popularity there. The opera, described as a *'dramma giocoso'* (technically more sophisticated than *opera buffa*), tells of the notorious aristocratic Spanish seducer Don Giovanni (better known as Don Juan) and his abortive attempts to get off with a peasant woman (Zerlina) despite her jealous fiancé (Masetto), whilst pursued by two of his former victims (Donna Elvira and Donna Anna) and Anna's ineffectual fiancé (Don Ottavio). If Giovanni's progress with Zerlina were typical, then the list of conquests declaimed by his servant Leporello during the famous catalogue song (the list culminates in the relevation of 1,003 women in Spain) would scarcely be credible. Eventually the ghost of Anna's father (killed by Giovanni at the piece's beginning), in the form of a graveyard statue, comes to dinner and drags the unrepentant Don to hell. Out of this morality tale, Mozart and da Ponte fashioned a farce in which the Devil has almost all the best tunes and the good characters teeter on the edge of self-caricature and tedium (despite Ottavio's two great arias, 'Dalla sua pace' and 'Il mio tesoro'). There's a sense in which

- Mozart's treatment of the characters
- flirts with amorality, and the idea
- peddled in *Amadeus* that he saw the
- statue-ghost as his father stands little
- close scrutiny. In combining the
- morally serious and the farcical like
- this, *Don Giovanni* broke new ground.

Così Fan Tutte

- *Così Fan Tutte* ('That's how all
- women behave', 1790) is the last and
- in some measure the most intriguing
- of Mozart's collaborations with da
- Ponte. It's also my personal favourite.
- *Così* tells the story of two pairs of
- lovers, Ferrando and Dorabella and
- Guilelmo and Fiordiligi; the two men
- are so convinced of their lovers'
- fidelity that they make a bet with the
- cynical Don Alfonso that the women
- cannot be swayed in their affections.
- Don Alfonso arranges for the men to
- seem to leave for war, precipitating the
- beautiful trio 'Soave sia il vento' ('May
- the breeze blow gently'), probably the
- single best-known item in the opera,
- after the men have gone. Then
- Alfonso disguises Guilelmo and
- Ferrando as Albanian strangers and
- introduces them to the two women,
- bribing their maid Despina to help
- convince Dorabella and Fiordiligi to
- get amorous with the 'strangers'. They
- become tempted; each going for the
- other's man. All ends happily (of
- course), but the lesson is learnt that
- *così fan tutte.*
- Some people find *Così* deeply
- cynical; others find it lacking in a
- centre, because it is a work without a
- hero (which may explain why it has
- found greatest appreciation in the
- twentieth century, which places less
- value on heroism). The six principal
- characters share an equal burden of
- responsibility both in singing and
- acting; in terms of the plot, all six
- share an equal blame (although

ultimately the plot isn't about the apportioning of blame). Since much of the action is inward and psychological, the burden falls on performers to make the drama work (although there is some delightful high comedy and some conventional farcical 'hiding'). Being an ensemble piece, there aren't many set-piece solo arias (although Dorabella's 'Amore e un ladroncello' – 'Love is a little thief' – is one of Mozart's catchiest). There's some deeply subtle music; for instance, the use of a surprising discord in 'Soave sia il vento' indicates that all is not as it seems. This is one of the most civilised, melodic, witty operas ever written, and once its appeal grabs you, it becomes a piece to wallow in and enjoy more and more.

MOZART'S LAST YEAR

In 1791 Mozart produced two operas; one was a conventional, almost retrogressive by his own standards, *opera seria*, *La Clemenza di Tito* (*The Clemency of Titus*), a tale of skulduggery redeemed by aristocratic good behaviour in Ancient Rome. It was designed to win favour with the new Emperor, Leopold II, and as such was an abject failure. Part of the problem was that Mozart kept trying to turn the formal, static text into something more exciting, and *Tito* is a deeply melodic piece (better listened to than seen, I think).

Die Zauberflöte (The Magic Flute)

The other opera from 1791 isn't really an opera at all. *Die Zauberflöte* is an elaborate musical pantomime, a spoken drama with lots of sung bits and a juicy comic role in the first performance for the librettist, the vaudevillian Emanuel Schikaneder (1751–1812), who created the part of

- Papageno. The story is loaded with
- Masonic symbolism and tells of
- Tamino's quest to rescue Pamina,
- daughter of the Queen of the Night,
- from Sarastro. It transpires that
- Sarastro is in fact a force for profound
- good and the Queen is evil, and so
- Tamino undergoes symbolic ordeals to
- exhibit his commitment to truth and
- goodness. Meanwhile the bird-catcher
- Papageno (the comic turn), Tamino's
- press-ganged aide, decides against
- ordeals and settles down with
- Papagena. The evil Queen and her
- servant Monostatos are destroyed.
-   Many critics see *Zauberflöte* as a
- profound analysis of the human
- condition, although I find this hard to
- go along with. To work properly on
- stage it needs stunning visual effects
- in a way that no other mature Mozart
- opera does and in a manner more
- reminiscent of the most stately of
- Italian *opera seria*. Some of the
- musical writing is dazzling, and the
- vocal resources demanded of the
- Queen of the Night are spectacular
- (few of the sopranos to record the role
- manage to respond successfully to the
- challenge). *Zauberflöte* is exceptional
- amongst German Singspiels ('plays
- with singing', i.e. musical shows), but
- this is to damn with faint praise.
- Musically, some of the melodies are
- amongst Mozart's most infectious
- (Papageno's song is probably the
- best-known item), but the symbolism
- can get wearing if you aren't a
- Freemason. And it's hard to resist a
- sneaking sympathy for the much
- more entertaining forces of evil as
- opposed to the tediously bullying
- Sarastro. On the other hand, a
- well-staged production can provide a
- visual feast. A full recording will
- include a lot of spoken dialogue
- which the listener at home can
- probably live without.

DISCOGRAPHY

The best recording of *Idomeneo* is John Eliot Gardiner's; very pricey, but a cut above every other version available; yet, given the nature of the piece, it's probably for connoisseurs only.
● *Deutsche Grammophon Archiv 431 674-2*
● *3 CDs* ● *Full price* ● *DDD* ● *1990*

Karl Böhm's version of *Die Entführung* features some fine singing.
● *Deutsche Grammophon 429 868-2* ● *2 CDs*
● *Mid-price* ● *ADD* ● *1974; highlights available with those of* Don Giovanni
● *Deutsche Grammophon 431 181-2* ● *2 CDs*
● *Bargain price*

Le Nozze di Figaro
By a short head, the best fully digital version available is conducted by Riccardo Muti, with all the acting perfectly judged and some delightful singing – especially Kathleen Battle (Susanna) and Ann Murray (possibly the most delightful of all Cherubinos).
● *EMI CDS7 47978-8* ● *3 CDs* ● *Full price*
● *DDD* ● *1987* ✪

Daniel Barenboim's recent version is almost as good; it's his second recording, using some surprisingly slow speeds which work very effectively in building the drama. John Tomlinson makes one of the best Figaros to date, and Lella Cuberli is a most affecting Countess.
● *Erato 2292 45501-2* ● *3 CDs* ● *Full price*
● *DDD* ● *1991*

Bernard Haitink conducts a reliable and at times excellent set using the cast of a Glyndebourne production. Gianna Rolandi is a little too aristocratic-sounding to be completely convincing as the maid Susanna, but the recording as a whole has a sense of theatre which an awful lot of studio recordings lack.
● *EMI CDS7 49753-2* ● *3 CDs* ● *Full price*
● *DDD* ● *1985*

The best older version features Erich Kleiber (1890–1956; the father of Carlos, also a conductor). It's transferred beautifully to CD, and has some clever performances: Alfred Poell's Count is a thoroughly vindictive piece of work, Hilde Gueden's Susanna brilliantly mixes shrew and coquette. Still many people's favourite, and very good value.
● *Decca 417 315-2* ● *3 CDs* ● *Mid-price*
● *ADD* ● *1959*

No music-lover can afford to miss the great bargain of Vittorio Gui's marvellous version. Slightly abridged (it fits on two discs), this 1950s Glyndebourne version has a great deal of sparkle and is a very good option for anyone not wanting to venture more than £11 or so.
● *EMI Classics for Pleasure CD-CFPD 4724*
● *2 CDs* ● *Bargain price* ● *ADD* ● *1955*

For collectors of really vintage performances, there's a compilation of recordings of two 1930s

Glyndebourne performances and featuring Glyndebourne founder John Christie's wife Audrey Mildmay as Susanna, with Fritz Busch conducting.
● *Pearl GEMM CDS 9375* ● *2 CDs*
● *Mid-price* ● *ADD* ● *1934/5*

For period-instrument addicts, there's a well sung, if rather fast and orchestrally thin, version on L'Oiseau-Lyre conducted by Arnold Östman. This version also includes all the extra 'alternative' arias Mozart wrote for later performances, and has an extremely helpful booklet.
● *L'Oiseau-Lyre 421 334-2* ● *3 CDs* ● *Full price* ● *DDD* ● *1988*

Anyone wanting highlights only will find an excellent bargain in Deutsche Grammophon's 'Compact Opera' series, where *Figaro* is paired with *Così Fan Tutte* in performances which feature Gundula Janowitz, one of the finest of all post-1945 sopranos.
● *Deutsche Grammophon 427 712-2* ● *2 CDs*
● *Bargain price* ● *ADD* ● *1968*

Don Giovanni
Don Giovanni is difficult to bring off both on stage and on disc, and makes great demands on its 'serious' characters if they aren't to seem like three monotonous prigs spoiling everyone's fun. Undoubtedly the best combination of cast and conductor is still to be found on the 30-plus-year-old version by Carlo Maria Giulini; Eberhard Waechter, often thought of principally as a Wagnerian, makes a youthfully attractive, if slightly hammy, Giovanni; Elisabeth Schwarzkopf is a forceful Elvira, slightly eclipsing Joan Sutherland's Anna; Giuseppe Taddei is an intelligently comic Leporello. This recording was described by polymathic operaphile Stephen Fry as 'one of the greatest recordings of anything there's ever been'.
● *EMI CDS7 47260-8* ● *3 CDs* ● *Full price*
● *ADD* ● *1960* ✪

On the fully digital front, it's hard to better the 'authentic' Arnold Östman version; the singing is first-rate all round, the acting clever, and only the slightly fast speeds (which can make the music sound perfunctory) prevents this from being a top recommendation.
● *L'Oiseau-Lyre 425 943-2* ● *3 CDs* ● *Full price* ● *DDD* ● *1989*

There's much to be said for the stage-based teamwork of another Bernard Haitink Glyndebourne set. Thomas Allen's Giovanni is rather chilling, and Haitink's pacing of the drama is striking. This set won a *The Gramophone* Award.
● *EMI CDS7 47037-8* ● *3 CDs* ● *Full price*
● *DDD* ● *1985*

Much to be enjoyed, too, is Daniel Barenboim's version; a thoughtful approach, with some fine singing, especially from Lella Cuberli as Anna and Waltraud Meier (more normally a Wagnerian) as Elvira.
● *Erato 2292-45588-2* ● *3 CDs* ● *Full price*
● *DDD* ● *1991*

Further down the price range, Sir Colin Davis's version, now part of the admirable Philips Complete Mozart Edition, features some glorious singing (including Kiri te Kanawa in top form as Donna Elvira), and displays Davis's unerring instincts for the drama of Mozart's music.
● *Philips 422 541-2* ● *3 CDs* ● *Mid-price*
● *ADD* ● *1977*

The dark and disturbing voice of baritone Cesare Siepi takes on the title role in a vibrant, exciting performance from the 1950s conducted by Josef Krips; this set features a particularly debauched Leporello and Hilde Gueden as a marvellous Zerlina.
● *Decca 411 626-2* ● *3 CDs* ● *Mid-price*
● *ADD* ● *1955*

Cosi Fan Tutte

The greatest modern conductor of *Cosi* is, without a doubt, Nikolaus Harnoncourt, who has as much of the measure of the work as any one man can of a work of genius. I've seen him conduct a magical version in the opera house, and his recording is a constant delight, full of little surprises. Some of his chosen tempos are surprisingly fast (his 'Soave sia il vento' is nearly a minute shorter than one from about 30 years before by Karl Böhm). The orchestra is the Concertgebouw on peak form, and the six principals make a varied, well characterised bunch (especially Charlotte Margiono as the more reflective Fiordiligi and Anna Steiger as the perky Despina). A great recording.
● *Teldec 9031-71381-2* ● *3 CDs* ● *Full price*
● *DDD* ● *1991; highlights available on 1 CD* ✪

Karl Böhm's mid-price version on EMI is very highly rated by the *Penguin CD Guide* writers, and it does have a very starry cast, headed by Elisabeth Schwarzkopf.
● *EMI CMS7 69330-2* ● *3 CDs* ● *Mid-price*
● *ADD* ● *1962*

I should also once more plug the Deutsche Grammophon bargain double set of highlights which matches *Figaro* with *Cosi* (a fine pairing). Once again the superb and breathtaking Gundula Janowitz is singing in her prime, with another of my favourite singers, mezzo Brigitte Fassbaender. (For details see above p. 148.)

La Clemenza di Tito

The best version of *La Clemenza di Tito* is rather expensive; John Eliot Gardiner's fine, crisp, clean and intelligent version.
● *Deutsche Grammophon Archiv 431 806-2* ● *2 CDs* ● *Full price* ● *DDD* ● *1990* ✪

Either Colin Davis in the complete Mozart Edition
● *Philips 422 544-2* ● *2 CDs* ● *Mid-price*
● *ADD* ● *1974*

or Karl Böhm again
● *Deutsche Grammophon 429 878-2* ● *2 CDs*
● *Mid-price* ● *ADD* ● *1971*

offer good-value, lower priced alternatives.

Die Zauberflöte

A great mid-price bargain is Otto Klemperer's recording, featuring Lucia Popp as a stunningly beautiful Queen of the Night and Gundula Janowitz as Pamina. This version has all the necessary ceremonial pomp, but manages to get quite a lot of passion into the work, too.
● *EMI CMS7 69971-2* ● *2 CDs* ● *Mid-price*
● *ADD* ● *1964; highlights available on 1 CD* ✪

There are lots of good recent digital versions; a splendidly sumptuous and exciting recording from Sir Georg Solti, one of his best encounters with Mozart in the studio, and one which has a brilliant young Queen of the Night in Sumi Jo.
● *Decca 433 210 2* ● *2 CDs* ● *Full price*
● *DDD* ● *1991*

There's also a very good 'authentic' reading by Roger Norrington, whose Pamina, Dawn Upshaw, is famous as the soloist in the chart-busting Górecki 3rd Symphony.
● *EMI CDS7 54287-2* ● *2 CDs* ● *Full price*
● *DDD* ● *1991*

Beethoven's Solitary Opera: *Fidelio*

Whatever the popular success of *Die Zauberflöte*, and however celebrated Mozart was in Prague, the dominant figures in opera at the end of the eighteenth century remained Haydn, Paisiello and Cimarosa. Although Vienna was one of Europe's cultural centres, with Salieri and a host of Italian cohorts based at the court of the Holy Roman Emperor, opera still largely came out of Italy, from Venice, Rome and Naples. Those who believed in a German culture tried various forms of fight-back over a couple of decades, of which the first was Beethoven's only foray into opera. *Fidelio* first appeared in Vienna in 1805, and was subject to two revisions, the final form eventually emerging in 1814.

Beethoven didn't write a vast amount of vocal music; the most famous piece, of course, is the Finale to the 9th Symphony ('Choral'), and the most intriguing the enormous *Missa Solemnis*. Both were written well after *Fidelio*, a story of freedom and tyranny and the triumph of the human spirit, supposedly based on a true incident in the French Revolution (which is hard to believe) and, technically, a 'rescue opera'. Leonore, the heroine, believes that the tyrannical prison governor Pizarro has imprisoned her husband Florestan because of his constant denunciations of despotism. So she disguises herself as a young man called Fidelio, gets a job in the prison, and becomes involved in rescuing a political prisoner who may or may not be her husband. She tries to bring a little humanity to the prison regime, winning the prisoners the right to go outside into the yard. There's a lot of suffering, Pizarro prepares to gloat over Florestan before he kills him (the mistake megalomaniacal villains always make), but Right triumphs over all.

Fidelio is definitely one of those works which is more respected than loved. It's not a through-composed opera, but, like Mozart's *Die Entführung* and *Die Zauberflöte*, a Singspiel; that is, a work with musical numbers separated by speech, as opposed to a 'number opera', in which the musical numbers are separated by sung recitative, as in *Figaro*. The sense of drama in *Fidelio* is deeply peculiar. The early scenes, which are basically about domesticity, often seem rather stilted, contrasting oddly with the dungeon scenes towards the end, which are intensely melodramatic. The demands on all the principal singers are astronomic. *Fidelio* does contain some wonderful music; there's a sublime quartet in Act 1 based around a 'mistaken' love (the gaoler's daughter falls in love with the 'young man' Fidelio); the Prisoner's Chorus is one of the most extracted and anthologised of operatic choruses (up there with the Anvil Chorus from Verdi's *Il Trovatore* and the Chorus of the Hebrew Slaves from the same composer's *Nabucco*); and Beethoven imbues the music with a radiant kind of symbolism at the moment when Leonora (in disguise) presents her imprisoned husband with

bread and wine (deeply symbolic sustenance). Beethoven had several attempts at writing the Overture (there are various 'Leonore' Overtures scattered through his output), wanting to strike exactly the right tone, and it seems that the opera's lack of conventional drama is at least partly due to his desire to do something rather different. I've talked about opera having an interest in 'psychology' and 'states of mind', but in *Fidelio* Beethoven attempted a breakthrough, an opera where the music actually does as much work as the set designer, where all the effects are implicit in the music.

Whatever Beethoven's intentions, though, *Fidelio* can seem stultifyingly dull in the wrong hands, although in the right hands it may feel like the greatest opera you've ever heard. A lot of lip-service is paid to it ('one of the signal works of Western culture', and so on) but actually *Fidelio* is hard work, much more so than operas by supposedly 'difficult' composers like Wagner and Richard Strauss. But it's the kind of hard work which is ultimately extremely rewarding.

DISCOGRAPHY
Two relatively elderly *Fidelio*s knock spots off more recent attempts. First is Otto Klemperer's dignified, 'still-waters-run-deep' performance, with outstanding singing from Jon Vickers (one of the great Florestans), Christa Ludwig and Gottlob Frick.
● *EMI CMS7 69324-2* ● *2 CDs* ● *Mid-price*
● *ADD* ● *1961* ○

The CD transfer of Wilhelm Furtwängler's 40-plus-year-old account has clarified the sound so much that it becomes clear that this is one of the most noble versions of this elusive opera. Frick is the villain once again, and the great Wagnerian tenor Wolfgang Windgassen gives a deeply moving reading of Florestan. Leonore is played by Martha Mödl, an intelligent singer who made up in subtle understanding what she sometimes lacked in beautiful tone, and who always worked well with Furtwängler. The Vienna Philharmonic play at their remarkable best.
● *EMI CMS7 64496-2* ● *2 CDs* ● *Special price*
● *ADD* ● *1953*

ITALIAN DOMINATION CONTINUES: ROSSINI

Rossini is most celebrated for his *opera buffa*, his highly civilised comedies, which are characterised by an extraordinary degree of melodic invention and some entertaining vocal display. His greatest works belong to a style called 'bel canto' (literally, 'beautiful song'), which dominated Italian opera through to the development of true 'grand opera' typified by the works of Giuseppe Verdi. Bel canto lays great stress on vocal showpieces and includes many arias in which the singers can show off their expertise; unlike some of the worst Baroque excesses, however, this is always done within a framework of melody and – at its best – within the bounds of characterisation and attention to the text. There's a slightly erroneous idea that bel canto involves a lot of ornate, twiddling and fiddling twittering at the upper end of the soprano register; in fact, many of the greatest bel canto roles were written for the mezzo-soprano voice and demand, within character, a certain toughness and sinew behind the prettiness of tone. Many Rossini heroines are, as we shall see, tough and resourceful women who know how to get what they want, rather than helpless nightingales, and the greatest moments of bel canto combine vocal showcase and astute characterisation with a touch of comedy, to superb effect. Rossini did also write in the *opera seria* mould, although his serious operas have endeared themselves less to the repertoire than his comedies; still, they have provided some memorable arias (especially in his version of *Otello*), as well as one of his most famous pieces of music (which, ironically enough, is non-vocal), the *William Tell* Overture.

Rossini's operas are (usually) through-composed, although they tend to revolve around numbers separated out and joined by recitative. Although Rossini became for the best part of a century the benchmark by which Italian operatic composers were judged, and because of which he is rightly seen as the progenitor of a tradition, he is essentially, in his comedies, the heir of Mozart. The same civilised graces, the same wit, characterise the works of both composers, and it's not merely coincidence that each was drawn to the sophisticated satires of Pierre Augustin Caron de Beaumarchais (1732–1799) (*The Marriage of Figaro* in Mozart's case; its predecessor *The Barber of Seville* in Rossini's) for some of their greatest music. Rossini was also, like Mozart, a great writer for ensembles (his talent in this area is often overlooked); the last scene of *L'Italiana in Algeri* is quite masterful in its staging, indeed that whole opera is full of cunning and witty ensemble pieces. To what extent he was consciously influenced by Mozart is a moot point, but it's impossible not to hear strong overtones of a rootedly ensemble work such as *Così* in his greatest music.

L'Italiana in Algeri (*The Italian Girl in Algiers*)

One of Rossini's first popular successes was an *opera seria* entitled *Tancredi*, but it was later the same year, 1813, that he produced *L'Italiana in Algeri*, his first great comic masterpiece, and one of his most enduring and appealing works. It tells the story of Mustafa Bey, who has decided to repudiate his wife and appropriate for himself an Italian mistress at just the moment when, as

Gioacchino Rossini

(1792–1868)

▬

G ioacchino Rossini was, like Mozart, something of a prodigy, and he was only 21 when he became an established, celebrated operatic composer. He first made his name in Venice in 1813 with *L'Italiana in Algeri*, and international fame followed very quickly; the rest of Italy, Vienna, Paris, all succumbed to the charms and infectious melodies of his operas, and he became as much a name to be reckoned with in French opera as in Italian. Then, suddenly, in 1829, at the age of 37, and after the enormous success of the huge historical epic *William Tell* in Paris, Rossini abandoned composition. Despite a reputation for gourmandising – his name is celebrated in the culinary world, principally in Tournedos Rossini, medallions of steak topped with pâté – he was, in fact, prone to severe depression, which dominated the first two decades of his retirement. This lifted sufficiently for him to begin composing again late in his life, although he wasn't drawn back to opera; he also coined the famous comment on Wagner – 'Some marvellous moments, but some terrible quarters of an hour'. When his depression lifted he returned to Paris (where his stock remained as high as ever) and instituted his famed musical evenings known as the '*Samedi soirs*'.

>> *Choral* 261

luck will have it, a young woman (*l'Italiana* of the title) called Isabella has been shipwrecked and captured on the Algerian shore. She has been looking for her fiancé Lindoro, who is held captive by Mustafa. From the moment she meets the Bey, Isabella can twist him around her little finger, and the opera proceeds to describe how she makes a fool of him, forcing him in the end to be reconciled with his wife, and frees both herself and Lindoro. The final scene is a comic classic, as Mustafa is hoodwinked into ignoring the Italians' escape after he has been unwittingly initiated into a 'secret society' of *pappataci* (compliant cuckolds who eat, drink, sleep and say nothing, regardless of their wives' behaviour).

- *L'Italiana* is packed with brilliant
- arias; Isabella's first great solo,
- 'Crude sorte' ('Cruel fate'), is one of
- *the* showpieces of the bel canto
- mezzo repertoire. The carefully
- planned ensembles, full of farcical
- comedy and witty characterisation,
- are hilarious, and make for good
- listening as well as (when staged
- properly) diverting viewing. There's
- a patriotic song addressed to all
- Italians (Italy was then under
- Napoleon's rule); Rossini wasn't
- afraid of mixing his genres a bit and
- he was quite happy to borrow a
- tune – or a good deal more – from
- an *opera seria* and stick into an
- *opera buffa* (or vice-versa). *L'Italiana*
- is one of three or four operas each of
- which makes an excellent introduction

to Rossini; you can make his acquaintance through compilation discs, but there's nothing quite like a great opera of this standard heard properly all the way through.

Rossini followed up *L'Italiana* the following year with a similar, role-reversed, piece, *Il Turco in Italia* (of which there's a very fine recording with Maria Callas playing the heroine); but his next truly great opera came two years later.

Il Barbiere di Siviglia (The Barber of Seville)

Another of Rossini's enduring achievements, *Barber* was written in 1816 and first produced in Rome later that year. It actually suffered a disastrous first night, but it quickly became a massive popular success and confirmed Rossini's reputation in Italy (and, when it travelled, everywhere else) for good.

It's always tempting to see *Barber* as a 'prequel' to *Figaro*, forgetting that the playwright, Beaumarchais, did actually write *Barber* first. The story tells of the Count Almaviva, who is in love with the beautiful Rosina, the ward of Dr Bartolo who himself wants to marry her. The Count, posing as Lindoro, enlists the help of Figaro, the Barber of Seville, and together (with some co-operation from Rosina herself) they outwit Bartolo and his henchman Don Bastilio.

Once again, *Barber* manages to be a truly comic opera simply by its melodic sparkle, another work of sheer brilliance. It contains another of the great bel canto mezzo showpieces, 'Una voce poco fa' (possibly the perfect Rossini aria), as well as Figaro's famous 'Largo al factotum' with its cries of 'Figaro là, Figaro qua' ('Figaro there, Figaro here', one of the best-known of all operatic numbers).

La Cenerentola (Cinderella)

The year after *Barber* Rossini produced the third of his three great comic masterpieces, a work based on the Cinderella story, but taken out of the world of fairytale into a very real human setting. In this version, the Prince and Dandini have changed places before the work starts, so that the Prince can discover for himself people's real worth. The Cinderella figure falls for the Prince (whom she thinks to be a groom) and so rejects the testing advances of Dandini (whom she believes to be the Prince). It all ends happily and morally, yet is slightly less of a farce than the other great Rossini comedies, having a moral point to drive home, and setting up Cinderella's position in her step-father's, Don Magnifico's, household with some pathos. This makes *Cenerentola* hard to categorise in precise terms; but it's an enchanting entertainment – naturally very popular at Christmas.

Rossini wrote a good many operas in the *seria* tradition, most of which are a little more stylised and a little less immediate in their appeal than these three comedies, although several of them have yielded good arias which make their way onto Rossini collections. His last Italian opera, the tragic *Semiramide* (1823; based on a play by Voltaire), is one of the most impressive, and looks forward to grand opera in the way that the recitative between arias and ensemble numbers is less routine and springs more naturally from the numbers themselves. The heroine Semiramide's extravagant aria 'Bel raggio lusinghier' ('A beautiful, enchanting ray of light') has remained, whatever the whole opera's popularity, one of the most popular showpieces in Rossini's mezzo output.

Quite a few of Rossini's less popular Italian operas are making it back into the catalogue (and onto the stage); so anyone wanting to get deeply acquainted with, say, *Elisabetta, Regina d'Inghilterra* (1815) or *Maometto II* (1820; later revised for Parisian audiences as *La Siège de Corinthe*), can now do so.

Rossini conquered Vienna in a period spanning the late 1810s to the early 1820s, but the rest of his operatic career was based around Paris, culminating in the final, enormous *William Tell* (1829). One opera which seemed at the time the most disposable and ephemeral was *Il Viaggio a Reims* (*The Journey to Rheims*; 1825). This, despite its Italian title, was a firmly French entertainment about the coronation of King Charles X of France in 1824, who (rather foolishly, in retrospect) restored the old pre-Revolutionary habit of being crowned at Rheims (no wonder he was forced out in a second revolution only six years later). Rossini himself clearly regarded the work as ephemeral, for he revamped most of it three years later as an opera called *Le Comte Ory*.

By the time Rossini came to write his epic *William Tell* in 1829, he had more or less arrived at the verge of grand opera as we know it (although one sense of 'grand opera' simply refers to the scale of the productions, and all Parisian productions tended to be vast, with huge crowd scenes), producing a massive-scale sung-through piece which revolves as much around ensembles as solo virtuosity. However, virtuosity remained the order of the day with Rossini's principal competitors in the bel canto school.

DISCOGRAPHY

L'Italiana in Algeri

There's an outstanding, and cheap, version of *L'Italiana* which should convince the most hard-hearted critic of the work's sheer genius, both for melody and for comedy. It stars Marilyn Horne, one of the greatest singers in this repertoire (and unusual in that she can sing both soprano and mezzo), with the delightful Kathleen Battle as Elvira, Mustafa's wife, as well as Samuel Ramey, an imposing yet comic Mustafa; while the less starry Domenico Trimarchi is excellent in the buffoon role. Conductor Claudio Scimone times and paces the whole thing marvellously, his orchestra I Solisti Veneti play with verve and sparkle. A beautiful recording, easily the best available of the work; a friend once gave it to me as a birthday present, and I owe that friend an eternal debt of gratitude.
● *Erato 2292-45404-2* ● *2 CDs* ● *Mid-price*
● *ADD* ● *1980* ○

Il Barbiere di Siviglia

Again, there's an admirable, outstanding, complete version which I can recommend with a whole heart even to the listener completely new to Rossini. Conducted by the great Vittorio Gui, it's based on an early 1960s production at Glyndebourne and stars as Rosina the utterly enchanting Victoria de los Angeles, whose pure, appealing voice has just the right element of sex appeal and allure. Luigi Alva's Count is the perfect blend of youthful ardour and aristocratic poise, Sesto Bruscantini's Figaro hits the right note, while Ian Wallace and Carlo Cava make great buffoons as Bartelo and Basilio. Another glorious recording which must be a top recommendation.
● *EMI CMS7 64162-2* ● *2 CDs* ● *Mid-price*
● *ADD* ● *1962* ○

The recent version with Placido Domingo, cast slightly against type and certainly against voice in the baritone role of Figaro, is actually rather good, despite the slightly gimmicky selling point; certainly Claudio Abbado is one of the best Rossini conductors around, and here he finds an astonishing amount of colour in the score. Kathleen Battle, a true rather than mezzo-soprano, makes a charming if slightly lightweight Rosina.
● *Deutsche Grammophon 435 763-2* ● *3 CDs*
● *Full price* ● *DDD* ● *1991*

La Cenerentola

Claudio Abbado's early 1970s version, with the very intelligent, fine-toned Teresa Berganza in the title role and Luigi Alva as the Prince, is an excellent, generally recommendable recording, although a bit on the pricey side.
● *Deutsche Grammophon 415 698-2* ● *3 CDs*
● *Full price* ● *ADD* ● *1972* ○

One of the great Rossini mezzos of the 1970s/1980s was the Greek singer Agnes Baltsa, a marvellously tough-voiced, resonant, vibrant-toned singer; she features on Sir Neville Marriner's very fine recording which has the spring and vitality of a live performance.
● *Philips 420 468-2* ● *2 CDs* ● *Full price*
● *DDD* ● *1987*

A great money-saving bargain is another Deutsche Grammophon Compact Opera double set, with highlights from Claudio Abbado's early 1970s *Barber* and the *Cenerentola* mentioned above. Teresa Berganza has long been one of the finest of bel canto singers, and she's at her best in both sets here.

● *Deutsche Grammophon 427 714-2* ● *2 CDs*
● *Bargain price* ● *ADD* ● *1972*

Il Viaggio a Reims

The return of *Il Viaggio* to the repertoire is mainly due to an imaginative staging in 1984, which yielded a *The Gramophone* Recording of the Year, and confirmed Claudio Abbado as the great Rossini conductor of this era.

● *Deutsche Grammophon 415 498-2* ● *3 CDs*
● *Full price* ● *DDD* ● *1984* **✪**

Rossini recital disc

Anyone who wants to dip their toes very gently in Rossini's Italian waters won't find a better introduction than the recital disc by Cecilia Bartoli, currently one of the hottest properties in the classical recording business and, if all goes well, the first great mezzo of the twenty-first century. Her disc, *Rossini Heroines*, is a gem.

● *Decca 436 075 2* ● *1 CD* ● *Full price*
● *DDD* ● *1991* **✪**

BEL CANTO REIGNS SUPREME: BELLINI AND DONIZETTI

Rossini's immediate successors as the masters of Italian operas were Gaetano Donizetti (1797–1848) and Vincenzo Bellini (1801–1835), masters of the bel canto style, both composers of comic and serious operas. Donizetti worked at an incredible rate; although he died when he was 50, he composed 66 operas. Of these a high proportion are most emphatically *not* works of genius; but as a composer of both tragedies and comedies he dominated his contemporary scene, producing successful works in Italy and France. Bellini, whose life was even shorter, wrote ten operas of a distinctly Romantic nature; all essentially, like Donizetti's, vehicles for the star singers of the day (both composers would have had specific individuals in mind when writing).

English history was a surprisingly fertile ground for opera plots at this time (a sort of revenge for the number of Italian-based plots in Shakespeare, perhaps?). I've already mentioned Rossini's *Elisabetta, Regina d'Inghilterra*, based on a remotely true event; and one of Donizetti's first significant works was all about the tragic fate of Anne Boleyn – *Anna Bolena* (1830) – and Henry VIII's determination to supplant her with Jane Seymour (Giovanna) by making use of Anna's former lover Percy. It was in this piece (before which he had written about 30 operas) that Donizetti found a personal musical style and manner of working out the drama; of his four principals, one, Henry (Enrico), has no arias but is a purely ensemble figure against whom everyone else reacts. Anna gets an awful lot of bel canto singing. This dramatic style developed in *Lucia di Lammermoor* (1835), probably Donizetti's dramatic masterpiece, based on Sir Walter Scott's *The Bride of Lammermoor* (and the opera which is performed, in distinctive local turn-of-the-century Italian style, during the course of E. M. Forster's *Where Angels Fear To Tread*). The story of Lucia, forced into marrying a man she doesn't love, and her descent into madness, provides one of the greatest of all bel canto moments in the celebrated 'mad scene', in which Lucia loses her grip on reality and stabs her husband. Actually when *Lucia* first appeared it was the quality of the tenor writing which drew most admiration. *Maria Stuarda* (also 1835) gives a highly romanticised version of the doom of Mary, Queen of Scots (and her highly improbable and imaginary love affair with Elizabeth I's favourite, Leicester); it's not quite in the same class as *Lucia*, although the drama of the confrontation between Maria and Elisabetta crackles with tension (Donizetti loads the dice by giving Maria all the good tunes), and again the romantic tenor writing (for Leicester) is lovely. The other great Donizetti serious opera, *La Favorita* (1840), was actually written for Paris, using a French libretto; a historical drama about a king and his mistress, it is especially notable for the way in which Donizetti and his librettist portray the king, a human being faced with difficult choices rather than a dramatic 'heavy'. *La Favorita* clearly prefigures the work of Verdi (whose first works were appearing around the same time).

Donizetti's Comic Operas

Three of Donizetti's comic operas rank amongst his great achievements. *L'Elisir d'Amore* (1832), a kind of parody of the story of Tristan and Isolde, revolves around quack doctors and fake love philtres. Donizetti wrote the piece in a fortnight and it was a smash hit; he put in only a few arias, but all of them are highly memorable. It's all very stylised, *commedia dell'arte* (Italian Renaissance comedy) characterisation, but very effectively set to music; and the inclusion of a truly heartfelt aria of some pathos ('Una furtiva lagrima', 'A furtive tear') looks forward to the way that one of Puccini's most heartrendingly sincere arias ('O Mio babbino caro', 'O my beloved father') comes bang in the middle of the slapstick *Gianni Schicchi* (1918). Donizetti's *La Fille du Régiment* (1840) was written to a French libretto for Parisian performance, and tells the story of a man (Tonio) who joins a foreign enemy's regiment in order to be accepted as a suitor for Marie, the 'Daughter of the Regiment' (an

abandoned baby the regiment has brought up as a daughter/mascot). Of course, she turns out to be of noble birth, but in a very funny scene the soldiers all explain about the rough-and-tumble vulgarity of army life to Marie's real mother, so that she won't insist on a noble marriage – and Love Triumphs. This opera has some of the most exciting tenor writing in the whole of Donizetti's output, including Tonio's 'Ah! mes amis', the famous 'High Cs' Aria (it includes nine high top Cs, and was the piece that made Pavarotti internationally famous when he first performed it at the New York Metropolitan Opera House); it's also genuinely funny, and in a more realistic way than the rather stylised *L'Elisir* and *Don Pasquale*. The French thought so highly of *La Fille du Régiment* that until 1917 it was one of only two possible works with which the Paris Opéra-Comique celebrated Bastille Day.

Don Pasquale (1843), written in Italian although first performed in Paris, is out of the same stable as *The Barber of Seville*, ridiculing an old man seeking a young wife. It's another *commedia dell'arte*-style piece, full of great tunes and some witty orchestration. Many consider it to be Donizetti's masterpiece.

BELLINI

Three of Bellini's operas are particularly attractive and noteworthy. *La Sonnambula* (*The Sleepwalker;* 1831) was the work which made his reputation throughout Europe. Basically a lightweight tale about a woman who appears to be unfaithful but who has actually sleepwalked her way into someone else's bed, and then somnambulates into peril to prove her love (but all ends well), the way that Bellini treats this as a Romantic work which teeters on the brink of tragedy shows just how vastly he differed in his approach from Donizetti, who would surely have portrayed the whole thing as farce. To us the story seems ludicrous (somnambulism was a great fascination in the nineteenth century); its great charm lies in two tenor arias, and in the challenge to the leading lady to make her performance credible while 'sleeping'.

Norma (1831) is Bellini's greatest tragic opera, a tale of self-sacrifice in Roman-occupied Gaul; the eponymous heroine is a Druid priestess who eventually sacrifices her life, torn between her Gaulish patriotism and the aftermath of her affair with a Roman proconsul, the father of her children. The scene involving Norma's aria 'Casta diva' is an opera classic; and the portrayal of the heroine is extremely well rounded. Norma is, in fact, one of the first heroines of an opera to have to die for love.

Sonnambula and *Norma* were both written for performance in Milan, then emerging as one of Italy's great opera centres (with the famous opera house La Scala, which opened in 1778), but Bellini's final great work, *I Puritani* (1835), was first performed in Paris. Like some of Donizetti's works it was based on a period in English history (the Civil War), a far-fetched extravaganza about love across the Roundhead-Cavalier divide, owing something to one of Sir Walter Scott's novels. Writing as he was for Paris, Bellini created a piece on a larger scale and with more chorus work than his earlier operas. The treatment of the heroine's (temporary) madness signals how far opera had come from the Baroque; rather than something to be feared, a mad character becomes an object of sympathy for whom the audience weeps.

DISCOGRAPHY
Donizetti's Serious Operas
Although bel canto isn't always the most immediate or gripping of operatic styles, two of its greatest exponents have been two of the great and best-known sopranos: Maria Callas and Joan Sutherland. It was largely thanks to Callas and a series of astonishing performances in the early 1950s that much of Donizetti and Bellini got back into the international repertoire; and Sutherland made her name standing in for Callas in precisely this repertoire after an early flirtation with Wagner (from which her husband, the conductor Richard Bonynge, deflected her).

I can't put my hand on my heart and say that any serious collector must go out and buy *Anna Bolena*. Interesting though it is historically, it has *longueurs* for the non-specialist. The best introduction to Donizetti's serious opera is either a full set or a highlights disc of *Lucia di Lammermoor*, and you don't have to pay full price for any of the best on offer. There are two Callas versions; one is the 1955 recording with Herbert von Karajan, which features the ultimate diva on top of her form, in complete control of her voice. It was never a conventionally beautiful voice; Callas prided herself on her acting (it was she who brought the idea of acting back to the centre of operatic performance), and the harsh self-discipline she inflicted on her body (a series of crash diets), as well as a highly tense emotional life and a demanding performance schedule, took their toll of her voice quite early. This version has the added dimension of some inspired conducting from Karajan, who makes something altogether meatier and more colourful of the score than most.
● *EMI CMS7 63631-2* ● *2 CDs* ● *Mid-price*
● *ADD* ● *1955* ✪

Perhaps even more formidable, although with occasional thinness of sound, is the earlier Callas recording with conductor Tullio Serafin (a man who understood Italian opera brilliantly), the same tenor (Giuseppe di Stefano, always better in 1950s recordings than later, when a dissolute lifestyle had ruined his voice), and the superb Tito Gobbi, one of the outstanding portrayers of 'heavies'.
● *EMI CMS7 69980-2* ● *2 CDs* ● *Mid-price*
● *ADD* ● *1953*

And then there's Joan Sutherland; a more delicate characterisation than Callas's, as Sutherland's voice is capable of sounding sweeter (though she occasionally loses her consonants). Her earlier recording has an innocence in its performance which is unique.
● *Decca 411 622-2* ● *2 CDs* ● *Mid-price*
● *ADD* ● *1961*

There is also a highlights disc featuring Callas (again with Serafin as conductor) taken from a slightly later full recording; although her control isn't quite as great, the performance is still full of character.
● *EMI CDM7 63934-2* ● *1CD* ● *Mid-price*
● *ADD* ● *1959*

The new version of *Lucia* starring Cheryl Studer (one of my favourite voices currently performing) and Placido Domingo, excitingly conducted by the

young Romanian Ion Marin, is superb and, if you love the work and want to splash out, a great treat.
- *Deutsche Grammophon 435 309-2* ● *2 CDs*
- *Full price* ● *DDD* ● *1992*

The best recording of *Maria Stuarda*, all in all, is a full-price affair starring Edita Gruberová, one of the best singers around at the moment in this kind of repertoire.
- *Philips 426 233-2* ● *2 CDs* ● *Full price*
- *DDD* ● *1989*

However, this is a bit expensive, and most would be happy, if they want full Donizetti collections and so decide to go for this opera, with Joan Sutherland, ably supported by Luciano Pavarotti (who turns Leicester into a hot-blooded Italian). Sutherland's husband Bonynge is a bit of a dull conductor, and this is one of his less inspired moments.
- *Decca 425 410-2* ● *2 CDs* ● *Mid-price*
- *ADD* ● *1971*

Donizetti's Comic Operas
L'Elisir d'Amore is available in two fine versions, both of which feature one of the world's greatest and most famous tenors. Pavarotti gives a surprisingly gentle performance in the Romantic role of a shy farmer, with Sutherland in great form and Spiro Malas very good as Dulcimara, the comic quack. Bonynge is much more alert and lively here.
- *Decca 414 461-2* ● *2 CDs* ● *Full price*
- *ADD* ● *1975* ○

The recording of *La Fille du Régiment* with Sutherland and Pavarotti is one of the best recordings that either singer has ever made, and Bonynge is sparkling; really, no one can sing the part of Tonio quite like Pavarotti.
- *Decca 414 520-2* ● *2 CDs* ● *Full price*
- *ADD* ● *1968*

A slightly different line-up produces far and away the best *Don Pasquale*. Mirella Freni as the heroine Norina and Sesto Bruscantini as the old buffoon Pasquale are delightful, and conductor Riccardo Muti paces the opera superbly.
- *EMI CDS7 47068-2* ● *2 CDs* ● *Full price*
- *DDD* ● *1987*

The best general Donizetti sampler emphasises that his writing for the tenor voice was exceptional. *Pavarotti: Donizetti* is a collection of arias from complete operas sets, with a few oddities and rarities unavailable elsewhere, all made early in Pavarotti's career when his voice, and his control of it, were at their freshest. Lovely.
- *Decca 417 638-2* ● *1 CD* ● *Full price*
- *ADD* ● *1968–75*

Bellini
Again, the newcomer to Bellini will wish to test the water before diving all the way in – which proves to be trickier than it ought. The greatest versions recorded of all three operas mentioned above star Maria Callas at her mid-1950s peak; she was more or less singlehandedly responsible for the revival of Bellini. However, they're all full-price sets; and the only fair and representative Bellini highlights disc is taken from a slightly later, less satisfactory recording of *Norma* (although being a Callas recording it has, as everything she did has, great fascination).
- *EMI CDM7 63091-2* ● *1 CD* ● *Mid-price*
- *ADD* ● *1960* ○

The other great Norma of our age, Joan Sutherland, is available on a mid-price complete set, and very good it is too, if not quite Callas.
- *Decca 425 488-2* ● *3 CDs* ● *Mid-price*
- *ADD* ● *1965*

For the record, the three great Callas Bellini recordings are:
Norma – ● *EMI CDS7 47304-8* ● *3 CDs*
- *Full price* ● *ADD* ● *1954*
La Sonnambula – ● *EMI CDS7 47378-8* ● *2 CDs* ● *Full price* ● *ADD* ● *1957*
I Puritani – ● *EMI CDC7 47308-8* ● *3 CDs*
- *Full price* ● *ADD* ● *1953*

Rossini, Donizetti, Bellini recital
A really excellent introduction to all three great Italian operatic composers of the first half of the nineteenth century is available on a disc compiling various arias sung by the great American diva Marilyn Horne, which shows as well the freak effect of her true and mezzo-soprano double life. All the great arias are there except 'Casta diva' – 'Una voce poco fa' from *Barber*, 'Cruda sorte' from *L'Italiana*, and 'Bel raggio' from *Semiramide*. A generous and luscious portion.
- *Decca 421 891-2* ● *1 CD* ● *Mid-price*
- *ADD* ● *1964–66* ○

THE GERMANS IN ECLIPSE: HOFFMANN, SCHUBERT, WEBER

German and Austrian composers didn't give up trying to establish a truly 'German' operatic tradition in the first two decades of the nineteenth century. One of the greatest opera theoreticians of this period was Ernst Theodor Amadeus Hoffmann (1776–1822; usually known as 'E. T. A.' Hoffmann) the man who wrote the stories from which Offenbach's last great opera, *Tales of Hoffmann* (1881), took its libretto and title. Hoffmann was a wild eccentric, a bureaucrat who was actually passionate about art, a talented writer and caricaturist as well as a musician of some ability. He deeply resented all the operatic practices of his day; at this time there was no question of dimming the house lights during a performance, people often talked and gossiped all the way through, came and went as they pleased. He hated the bel canto tradition, regarding it as deeply intrusive in the truly dramatic. A lot of Hoffmann's ideas, expressed in his music criticism *Kreisleriana* (all written in the persona of the deeply eccentric Kapellmeister Kreisler) were influential on Wagner (Hoffmann was friendly with Wagner's uncle). He wrote one opera himself, *Undine* (1816), which met with some success, but all his further attempts to get something staged successfully were thwarted by the popularity of the Italians.

Hoffmann wasn't at all friendly with his contemporary Carl Maria von Weber (1786–1826); which is ironic, really, since their ideas about opera were all along the same lines. Opera, they thought, should first and foremost promote drama and attain some kind of thematic unity. Indeed, in *Der Freischütz* (*The Marksman*; 1821), Weber seeks to promote unity by something not unlike the 'leitmotif' which would become the staple of Wagner's enormous *Ring Cycle* – a musical phrase intended to characterise and refer to either some character or some element of the plot. Weber's orchestration in *Freischütz*, too, is something much more subtle in tone colouring; given that the plot of his opera mixes the rural and domestic with almost satanic magic, the subtlety of the musical colouring (especially compared with most Italian contemporaries) is remarkable. *Freischütz* is an important step along the road to German operatic greatness (even though it isn't through-composed), and was

immensely influential on the Germanic composers later in the century. It was a big popular success, too, and Weber followed it two years later with *Euryanthe*, another artistically ambitious work. Unfortunately, by this time the Italians had grabbed everyone's attention and *Euryanthe* flopped completely. This had a knock-on effect on Schubert, who had composed a large and noble piece called *Fierrabras* to follow *Euryanthe* into the opera house. But with Rossini all the rage, no opera-house management wanted to take the risk with some humourless piece of high-minded nobility, and Schubert's opera was never performed in his lifetime; it took a revival in 1988 to make anyone realise that it contained music of considerable merit.

Weber, meanwhile, fled to London; he was used to things going wrong for him just when they looked set to go right, for that had been the persistent pattern of his life. Like J. S. Bach, he had been flung into prison at one stage by a dissatisfied patron, although he had exacerbated the situation by an extravagant lifestyle. He had been bred to a musical life practically from the cradle, and his ambitious father had often lied about his son's age, lowering it to make him seem more of a prodigy than he really was. Composing great and serious opera had always been Weber's main ambition; he had a marvellous gift for lyrical melody allied, as I've mentioned, to some forward-looking ideas about structure and orchestration (he was one of the finest writers for the clarinet ever). It was doubly cruel, then, that he ended up in 1820s London, where opera was seen as a peculiar mixture of vocal showing-off and pantomime, working to a libretto by James Robinson Planché. Planché

(1796–1880) was a prolific dramatist of the day; sadly, he treated the idea of a story about Oberon as an opportunity for a series of feeble comedy sketches and some laborious slapstick, added to a bit of reactionary sermonising and some uncomplicated love interest. But Weber needed the money, and Rossini's popularity had driven him out of mainland Europe; terminally ill, with a family to provide for, he needed the fee Covent Garden was prepared to stump up. *Oberon* appeared successfully in 1826; Weber lived only two months more after its première. Even on Planché's appalling libretto he had conferred some dignity, with some superbly evocative 'faerie music'.

Neither Hoffmann nor Weber appreciated the impact they made on opera; it was a very delayed impact, but enormous when it eventually made itself felt.

DISCOGRAPHY
Very little of Hoffmann's music is currently available (record companies please note). Schubert's *Fierrabras* was recorded from the 1988 live production, and a fine recording it is too; there's a soprano duet with Cheryl Studer taking one part which is absolutely divine. The full set is good, but a bit pricey unless you absolutely can't live without it; surely this is a case where a highlights disc would be very welcome?
● *Deutsche Grammophon 427 341-2* ● *2 CDs*
● *Full price* ● *DDD* ● *1988* ✪

Weber's *Der Freischütz* has done well on disc, even attracting the attention of the great recluse Carlos Kleiber. His version is interesting, but eccentric. A good cheap set is conducted by Joseph Keilberth.
● *EMI CMS7 69342-2* ● *2 CDs* ● *Mid-price*
● *ADD* ● *1955*

Anyone wanting to pursue Weber and see how he wasted his genius on scripts which might politely be termed *merde* should try Rafael Kubelik's brilliantly paced and dramatic *Oberon* (with some fine singing by the great Swedish Wagnerian soprano Birgit Nilsson);
● *Deutsche Grammophon 419 038-2* ● *2 CDs*
● *Mid-price* ● *ADD*
and Marek Janowski's *Euryanthe* starring Jessye Norman.
● *EMI CMS7 63509-2* ● *3 CDs* ● *Mid-price*
● *ADD*

THE GREAT ITALIAN: VERDI

The two greatest operatic composers of the nineteenth century (perhaps simply the two greatest ever) were born within six months of each other in the year 1813; May saw the birth of Richard Wagner, October that of Giuseppe Verdi. Both had an incalculable impact on operatic form and style; neither left the form as he had found it.

For many, the name Verdi is synonymous with opera; and with Verdi we discover the first (reasonably) long-lived composer whose achievement continued to develop even in old age, so much so that some consider the two works of his old age, *Otello* (1887) and *Falstaff* (1893), to be his masterpieces.

The struggle for Italian unification and national identity forms a very important backdrop to Verdi's work. Throughout his operatic career you can see again and again the recurring themes of heroism in the face of tyranny, and the unprincipled nature of despots and tyrants, all of whom very often pay lip-service to some concept of devout religious (sometimes Catholic) observance. As he wasn't operating in an atmosphere necessarily happy about freedom of speech, Verdi often had to make his political points allegorically, in some suitable historical setting; and even when 'Italy' was established he found it easier to deliver messages using this distancing technique. Occasionally it was forced upon him; the great *Un Ballo in Maschera* (*A Masked Ball*; 1859) was originally about the downfall and assassination of the artistic eighteenth-century Swedish King Gustavus III, but the censors were adamant in refusing to allow the depiction on stage of the murder of a

Giuseppe Verdi
1813–1901

By the time he was 30, Verdi had lost a wife and two children (a son and a daughter had both died in infancy in 1838 and 1839; followed the next year by their mother, a victim of encephalitis), and had become a central figure in the Italian nationalist struggle. Although depressed by his personal tragedies, when he was beginning to establish himself on the Italian music scene in the early 1840s, he couldn't help but respond to the libretto offered him entitled *Nabucco*. Verdi's interest in the politics of his country and the politics of the libretto led to the opera causing riots when it was staged in Milan; and Verdi became a nationalist figure in the struggle for Italian unification and freedom from foreign domination. (Following the collapse of Napoleon in 1814, Italy had been 'de-unified' once more, reverting to a collection of states split among Austria, the Pope, the kingdoms of Sardinia and Naples, and four smaller duchies. The nationalist struggle of the 1840s to 1860s was concerned with driving out foreign rule and unifying the country as a single kingdom, finally achieved in 1861.) Even Verdi's name was useful as an acronym, for it spelt out 'Vittorio Emanuele, Re d'Italia' (the name of the monarch designated by the nationalists); crowds would chant it at performances of his operas, the authorities unaware of the true meaning. He hit his stride as a composer around the early 1850s, and had developed an international reputation by the end of that decade; as a sure sign of this he was invited to Paris in the 1860s, where he presented revised versions of some of his Italian successes and also produced a sprawling, flawed masterpiece, *Don Carlos* (1867). Even when he slowed down his rate of composition, Verdi remained the dominant Italian musical figure, producing two great works in his old age, and his death provoked public demonstrations of grief.

>> Choral 264

king who was still, for some people, just about in living memory. Verdi and his librettist, Antonio Somma, therefore switched the plot to colonial Boston (making *Ballo* one of the first operas to be set in America), and converted the King into Count Riccardo, Governor of Boston.

So Verdi was a political operatic composer, both in the sense that he

- was motivated by his own idealism
- and beliefs, and also in that he was
- clearly fascinated by stories about the
- operation and exercise and nature of
- power and authority. Even in less
- 'public' subjects, like his very famous
- *La Traviata* ('The Woman Gone
- Astray', i.e. 'The Prostitute'; 1853),
- there is an interest in what we now
- call 'sexual politics', the balance of

power in relationships and the power exerted by a family patriarch. Verdi's range of female characters is particularly interesting. Not only did he write some superb soprano music for his conventional heroines (Gilda in *Rigoletto*, Violetta in *La Traviata*, two Leonoras, one in *Il Trovatore*, the other in *La Forza del Destino*, Elisabetta in *Don Carlos*, Desdemona in *Otello* – the list is endless), he also created a whole range of mezzo-soprano figures whom one might call 'sympathetic villainesses', very often in some way akin to that stock figure 'the tart with the heart' (Maddalena in *Rigoletto*, Preziosilla in *Forza*, Princess Eboli in *Carlos* to name but three). Some of these roles develop the bel canto style, making it more dramatically serviceable. Although it's conventional to regard Verdi and Wagner as in some way opposites, one thing both have in common is a burning desire to make opera dramatic in an almost Classical sense; to make the necessary vocal display a part of the drama and not an obstacle to it. With Verdi, the idea of 'number opera' has gone; although one can talk confidently about arias, duets and so on in Verdi, these are not one-mood pieces separated by plot-developing recitative, as in so many composers of the eighteenth and early nineteenth centuries; they are essential elements of the drama, and depict subtle modulations of mood, event and character. They also offer a lot of cracking good tunes. No wonder that so many Verdi operas have remained stalwarts of the repertoire since their first appearance.

The early operas: *Nabucco*

Verdi's earliest works are quite slight, but a romantic-comic piece like *Un Giorno di Regno* (*King for a Day*; 1840)

shows behind its plot of disguises and mistaken identity some of Verdi's concern with heroism; staged and performed well, it's a very enjoyable experience.

It was with the performance of *Nabucco* in 1842 that Verdi really established himself as a national – and nationalist – figure. The most famous piece in the opera, the Chorus of the Hebrew Slaves, easily explains why it was such a sensation; an exiled and enslaved people sing a hymn to their *patria si belle e perduta* ('country so beautiful and lost'). There's a sense in which the chorus may be said to be the central character in this opera; although even this early in his career Verdi and his librettist, Temistocle Solera, offer us a villainess, Abigaille, who turns out to have an unexpected depth of feeling. There is, however, a certain backwardness in Nabucco's bout of madness, which has less conviction and sympathy in its depiction than that in Donizetti's *Lucia* or Bellini's *I Puritani*.

VERDI THROUGH THE 1840s AND 1850s

One thing that's remarkable about Verdi is the way that he just seemed to keep on turning out masterpiece after masterpiece; and as time goes by and we begin to appreciate some of the more neglected pieces (such as *Stiffelio*; 1850) more fully, he comes to seem all the more remarkable. The list of acknowledged masterpieces over the twenty years following *Nabucco* is quite something: *Macbeth* (1847), *Luisa Miller* (1849), *Rigoletto* (1851), *Il Trovatore* (1853), *La Traviata* (1853), *Simon Boccanegra* (1857), *Un Ballo in Maschera* (1859). Seven great works in about twelve years – an excellent average by anyone's reckoning.

Macbeth

Macbeth was the first sign of Verdi's
enduring interest in Shakespeare (the
two masterpieces of his old age were
both Shakespearian, and one of Verdi's
unrealised ambitions was to write an
operatic version of *King Lear*). It was
first staged in Florence in 1847 at
which time it was a piece primarily
designed to convey the tragedy of the
central character and his relationship
with his wife (for whom Verdi wrote
music designed to bring out the
rougher side of the female voice; he
refused to cast a very famous
'box-office name' soprano as Lady
Macbeth on the grounds that her voice
was far too pure for the part). Later
Verdi revised the opera for
performance in Paris (1865) where, in
keeping with the Parisian taste for
having large crowds milling around a
lot of the time, he placed the Macbeths
in a more overtly political context and
ended the opera not with the tyrant's
death but with a chorus of triumph
sung by the people. But the original,
too, inevitably had its political side; as
Macbeth establishes himself as a
tyrant, there are great appeals to
patriots to rescue their oppressed
country (the chorus 'Patria oppressa').
The individual characterisation is
fascinating, though, especially in the
feast at which Banquo's ghost appears
(Lady Macbeth's unconvincingly jovial
drinking song keeps getting shoved
out of the way by Macbeth's demented
recitative), and in Lady Macbeth's
sleepwalking scene.

Luisa Miller

Luisa Miller (1849) is probably the least
remarkable of the works mentioned
above; and yet this tale of blackmail
and love across class lines is a superb
drama. Verdi's abiding interest in
family relationships is well reflected; a

father and daughter (the latter being
Luisa Miller) are involved with a father
and son (the Count and his son
Rodolfo); Rodolfo loves Luisa, but the
Count will have none of it and so takes
revenge upon Miller *père*; while
manipulating everyone is the scheming
aide Wurm. Again, there is a madness
interlude (quite common in these early
Verdi operas), and all ends in death
and despair. Verdi actually gave his
three acts titles; 'Love;', 'Intrigue', and
'Poison'. Musically, he used small
unifying devices of some sophistication,
including the occasional repetition of
the first notes of the Overture, in
ever-darkening variants. The
orchestration is lavish, making the one
ensemble sung unaccompanied (or 'a
cappella') even more effective. All that's
really missing are the types of
memorable 'hit tune' you find in
abundance in Verdi's next successful
opera (the underrated *Stiffelio*, recently
revived to much acclaim and another
piece for which José Carreras has always
shown a particular talent, followed *Luisa
Miller* almost immediately, in 1850, but
flopped; after its initial failure, Verdi
recast a lot of its material in *Aroldo*,
first performed in 1857).

Rigoletto

Rigoletto (1851) is one of the most
abiding and accessible operas ever
written by anyone. It contains one of
the most famous arias for tenor, 'La
donna é mobile' ('Women are fickle'),
the not very convincing but entirely
tuneful justification offered by the
tyrannical Duke; one of the best-loved
of soprano arias ('Cara nome', 'Dear
name'); and its central themes are such
that the piece can be dressed and
redressed in different historical
costumes and periods, from the
original medieval setting (which was
in any event a deliberate compromise)

to the New York underworld to Fascist Rome, and so on. Again, a father and daughter lie at the centre – Rigoletto the hunchback jester and his beautiful daughter Gilda – as well as a brother and sister: the assassin Sparafucile and his prostitute sister (often the bait in his traps) Maddalena. The characterisation of the Duke, a careless womaniser, is a memorable portrait of sardonic, unscrupulous power, given almost all the best tunes (a witty twist thus to transform the Romantic tenor here into a villain); in a very dark view of the world by librettist Francesco Maria Piave underlined by Verdi's music, the most villainous character gets off scot-free, while the most innocent (Gilda) dies to save the life of her faithless seducer, the Duke. The opera is dominated by a curse, which is given some musical force in the Prelude. The music all serves to move the drama on, nothing drags, nothing is ill-judged, even the daring placing of a formal Quartet before the final climax works superbly, just as the storm music of the Finale is original and effective. If you can't get on with *Rigoletto*, then it's quite likely you're completely allergic to opera.

Il Trovatore (*The Troubadour*) and La Traviata (*The Wayward Woman*)

Rigoletto was the first of Verdi's three great Romantic early operas; the next two, *Il Trovatore* and *La Traviata*, both appeared in 1853, in Rome and Venice respectively. *Trovatore* has survived almost entirely on its musical and dramatic merits (especially the famous Anvil Chorus, much appropriated by TV advertisements); its plot – it is the only one of these three operas not to have a libretto by Piave, one of Verdi's regular collaborators – is a typical operatic confusion over children, almost

like some modern bodice-ripper bestseller. It's extremely fast and furious, and with a very complicated plot, but at the centre is (surprise, surprise) a parent-child relationship of some substance, this time between the mother Azucena and son Manrico. Except that the son proves not to be a son, but brother to the villainous Count di Luna. Another revenge story, whatever the romantic interest (the soprano heroine, Leonora, gets some fine arias), the real focus of interest is Azucena. The violent drama (it is set against the backdrop of a fifteenth-century civil war) of *Il Trovatore* makes for an extreme contrast with *La Traviata* (a version of Dumas's famous novel *La Dame aux Camélias*, perhaps best known from the Garbo film *Camille*), a domestic tale of love, self-sacrifice, and consumption. And it is remarkably domestic, with only three central characters (including a father and son, Giorgio and Alfredo Germont). The heroine, Violetta, is in many ways (possibly along with Mimi from Puccini's *La Bohème*) everyone's idea of the typical operatic heroine; doomed by a love that can't be accepted by society and, of course, by a fatal disease (which still allows her to sing some well-known arias). The social background against which these characters move is subtly depicted (the famous Drinking Chorus); Violetta herself combines the old bel canto idea of soprano musical line with the romantic heroine, the 'tart with the heart' figure.

Simon Boccanegra and Un Ballo in Maschera (*A Masked Ball*)

Simon Boccanegra (1857, revised and re-presented in 1881) is a more elusive piece, less easy to love, for it lacks a central hero figure, being more about the entwined political life of fourteenth-century Genoa. Verdi obviously cared deeply about the opera, though, as he worked on it at different times with both of his favourite collaborators, Piave and Arrigo Boito (1842–1918; a composer himself, his version of the Faust story, *Mefistofele* – 1868 – has retained a permanent place in the repertoire). However, even if *Boccanegra* is difficult (though it has some glorious duets), the final great opera of the 1850s, *Un Ballo in Maschera* (1859), is a deeply accessible work of genius; like *Traviata*, it is about unacceptable love against the background of a highly watchful society (Count Riccardo is in love with his best friend's wife), with the paranoid screw turned a few notches by the presence of a group of conspirators and would-be assassins, as well as a supernatural fortune-teller who really does (as they always do in operas) know everything. Again centring on three figures, again without a real 'villain' (as everyone is in the grip of something they cannot manipulate), *Ballo* contains some fabulous ensemble pieces, and the love duets in the second act are quite sublime. The 'brotherly' friendship between the two leading male figures looks back in some degree to the estranged brothers of *Trovatore*, and forward to the friends-turned-rivals in *Forza del Destino*.

VERDI IN MATURITY AND OLD AGE: THE INTERNATIONAL CELEBRITY

La Forza del Destino (*The Force of Destiny*)

By the 1860s Verdi was internationally celebrated, and his great operas of that decade were written initially for opera houses outside Italy. *La Forza del*

Destino was first performed in St Petersburg in 1862; Verdi changed the ending (making it much more sanctimonious than the bleak suicidal conclusion he and Piave originally concocted) for the Milanese première in 1869. It's another tale of a brother and a sister and a surrogate brother; the brother of Leonora accidentally becomes friendly with her would-be lover and unintentional murderer of her father, ensuring disaster all round, although the epic action takes several years (not, thankfully, in real time) to develop, against a background of European wars. There's even a question of racism here, as the would-be lover, accidental murderer, Alvaro, is 'coloured', being of Peruvian Inca ancestry. In this opera, as in the two great epics which followed it, Verdi had completely left behind the idea of 'numbers'. This is through-composed, unified drama on a grand scale, with single musical phrases carrying a lot of dramatic work; the composer felt that this opera was 'modern' in its use of musical ideas, rather than being a string of arias, duets, and so on.

Don Carlos

Verdi also believed that he had made great advances with *Don Carlos*, which was originally written for performance in Paris in 1867, but was then revised twice for Italian performances in 1884 and 1886. This is perhaps Verdi's great epic political-historical masterpiece, a tale of love, betrayal, power, tyranny and religious oppression, set in the sixteenth-century court of Philip II of Spain and allowing Verdi to lambast the Church again in the terrifying persona of the Grand Inquisitor. Philip's relationship with his son Carlos is perhaps the ultimate father-son relationship in

Verdi, complicated by Carlos's love for his stepmother Elisabetta. Unfortunately the final – and very often performed – Italian version omits the original first act, which set up the love story and clarified the background to Carlos's relationship with Elisabetta. Although far from perfect in its structure, in its original five-act version *Don Carlos* contained some of Verdi's most powerful and affecting music, especially in the last act (which contains the heroine's aria 'Tu che la vanità', as well as the confrontation between Philip and the Inquisitor); it also has his ultimate 'fascinating temptress', the Princess Eboli, heir to the mezzo bel canto tradition with her famous, almost erotic, 'Song of the Veil'.

Aida

Verdi was such a celebrity that he was the inevitable choice to write an opera to commemorate the opening of the Suez Canal in 1869 and to inaugurate the new Cairo Opera House in the same year; that was the famous *Aida*, although it was not first performed until 1871, because of delays in transporting the production to Egypt caused by the Franco-Prussian War. Fittingly, Verdi took a story from Egyptian history, packed with self-sacrifice, patriotism and pyramids, as well as lots of spectacular scenery; hence the most famous piece of the opera is an instrumental Grand March and its following Chorus. Again, a father-daughter relationship fuels much of the action, as the eponymous heroine is torn between her love for her country and her love for the head of the Egyptian forces. *Aida* (which I have to admit I find a curiously uninvolving, cold work) is clearly the achievement of a man in control of his abilities.

Otello

But *Aida* is a million miles from the greatness of the first of the masterpieces of Verdi's old age, *Otello* (1887), in which he and Boito took Shakespeare's play and made from it an equal masterpiece in another form (losing Shakespeare's first act, it retains the main points of his plot). Verdi hadn't written an entirely new work since the early 1860s, and in *Otello* he created something special, something which managed to grasp, as clearly as do most Shakespeare plays, the fully rounded, multi-sided nature of human behaviour, marrying music of great psychological cunning to enormous melodic and orchestral flair. In Verdi's characterisation, Otello combines great love, passion and jealousy, and his madness is something so human and moving that he never becomes an alien figure to the audience. When Verdi wrote this piece, Wagner had been dead for four years; his claim had been that Italian opera was finished. This was one of Verdi's two responses.

Falstaff

The other response was the Italian comic masterpiece *Falstaff* (1893), based on Shakespeare, this time on *The Merry Wives of Windsor*. Comedy wasn't something Verdi ever went in for on a large scale, which may be exactly why *Falstaff* is suffused with a warmth and human understanding that is missing from, say, Rossini at his best. There's a lot of sending-up of tragic attitudes; technically, like *Otello*, *Falstaff* is testimony to the fact that Verdi had arrived, through purely Italian means, at a form of opera in which everything, arias, recitatives, ensembles, are all interwoven seamlessly.

At the end of his life, Verdi was aware of (but did *not* participate in) a lot of partisan argument between his own supporters and those of Wagner's 'music-drama'. He was the personification of Italian opera, and the competition to be recognised as 'the new Verdi' was, in the last decade of the century, intense. In many ways his successors, like Puccini, succeeded only in doing what the master had already done, only slightly more crudely, and to greater excess (excess was very much part of the 'modern' taste, as Richard Strauss's operas testify).

Apart from the operas discussed in detail here, Verdi wrote several works, like *I Vespri Siciliani* (originally written in French, his first opera for Paris, 1855) and *Attila* (1846), which have yielded either good performances or favourite arias. A couple of general Verdi selections, ranging as far and wide as possible, are recommended in the discography.

DISCOGRAPHY
Early operas: *Nabucco*
The only complete version of *Un Giorno di Regno* available stars the young José Carreras in superb voice, and remains one of the best things he's ever recorded.
- *Philips 422 429-2* ● *2 CDs* ● *Mid-price*
- *ADD* ● *1973*

You have to be a pretty devoted Verdi fan to want a full set of *Nabucco*, so most listeners would, I think settle for one of the two highlights discs available. The more expensive is the better; not only does it feature Placido Domingo (in a fairly small role), it also has some imaginative conducting from the ever thoughtful Giuseppe Sinopoli.
- *Deutsche Grammophon 413 321-2* ● *1 CD*
- *Full price* ● *DDD* ● *1983*

Riccardo Muti is the conductor on the other extracted selection; his singers aren't quite into their roles and generally the performance isn't as exciting.
- *EMI CDM7 63092-2* ● *1 CD* ● *Mid price*
- *ADD* ● *1978*

If you must have the full *Nabucco*, then the complete Sinopoli set is probably your best bet.
- *Deutsche Grammophon 410 512-2* ● *2 CDs*
- *Full price*

Macbeth
A complete *Macbeth* may be a bit prohibitive in cost; there is, however, a superb highlights disc from an excellent 1970s set conducted by Claudio Abbado. The quality of singing is vital in Verdi, and this set features Placido Domingo and the formidable Shirley Verrett in *Macbeth*.
- *Deutsche Grammophon 435 414-2* ● *1 CD*
- *Full price* ● *ADD* ● *1971* ✪

The full set of these highlights is, of course, very fine; but on three CDs is a bit costly.
- *Deutsche Grammophon 415 688-2* ● *3 CDs*
- *Full price* ● *ADD* ● *1971*

The same is true of the excellent sets conducted by Giuseppe Sinopoli and featuring the only Italian baritone of note, Renato Bruson.
- *Philips 412 133-2* ● *3 CDs* ● *Full price*
- *DDD* ● *1984*

And cost is a consideration in the Riccardo Muti version, rated by many as the best of the lot.
- *EMI CDS7 47954-8* ● *3 CDs* ● *Full price*
- *ADD* ● *1976*

Luisa Miller
There isn't, alas, an excerpts disc taken from the best set of *Luisa Miller*, although the next best does offer a pretty fine substitute, as the title role is taken by Katia Ricciarelli, a delicate-voiced singer whose tones sometimes teeter on the edge of a nervous breakdown, with both Domingo and Bruson also in the cast. Conductor Lorin Maazel, one of the smoothest operators around, makes every detail of the orchestration tell.
- *Deutsche Grammophon 435 413-2* ● *1 CD*
- *Full price* ● *ADD* ✪

The best complete set features one of Pavarotti's most nicely judged Verdi performances, as well as the great, sweet-voiced Montserrat Caballé, the final act is superbly intense here.
- *Decca 417 420-2* ● *2 CDs* ● *Full price*
- *ADD* ● *1976*

Rigoletto
There are many recordings of *Rigoletto* on offer, with two prominently featuring Pavarotti as the Duke. It is one of his finest roles on stage, but I don't think any recording has ever quite caught him at his best; the less good of the two is definitely the more recent, where his voice sounds quite uncharacteristically strained. The earlier recording also boasts Joan Sutherland, but is badly let down by the flaccid timing of conductor Richard Bonynge (although this set has its fans).
- *Decca 414 262-2* ● *2 CDs* ● *Full price*
- *ADD* ● *1972*

It perhaps fares better as a set of highlights.
- *Decca 421 303-2* ● *1 CD*

If you must have a fully digital version of the work, then Giuseppe Sinopoli's boasts not only some excitingly dramatic timing, but a fine vocal performance by Edita Gruberová, whose control of high tone is wonderful, as well as the utterly marvellous and very colourful mezzo Brigitte Fassbaender as Maddalena.
- *Philips 412 592-2* ● *2 CDs* ● *Full price*
- *DDD* ● *1985*

I can't put my hand on my heart and say much in favour of any other post-1960s version, except possibly for the vivid English-language recording of the celebrated English National Opera 'gangster' production; try the highlights disc.
● *EMI CDM7 63723-2* ● *1 CD* ● *Mid-price*
● *DDD* ● *1984*

The great version of *Rigoletto*, though, stars Maria Callas as Gilda, with Tito Gobbi in the title role, and Giuseppe di Stefano, still then in good voice, as a fine Duke. These characterisations will probably never be beaten for insight, intelligence and dramatic understanding, backed by excellent conducting from Tullio Serafin which brings real passion out of the La Scala Orchestra. A classic, and one of those recordings which shows just why people make such a fuss about Callas.
● *EMI CDS7 47469-8* ● *2 CDs* ● *Full price*
● *ADD* ● *1956* ✪

Il Trovatore
There's also a fine Callas recording of *Il Trovatore*, with some impressive conducting by Karajan, as well as another good serviceable bit of tenor work by di Stefano (it took Callas to get the best from him).
● *EMI CDS7 49347-2* ● *2 CDs* ● *Mid-price*
● *ADD* ● *1957* ✪

And an even earlier classic performance, starring one of the greatest of this century's tenors in this kind of repertoire, Jussi Bjoerling (1911–1960), has yielded an eminently worthwhile highlights selection.
● *RCA Gold Seal GD 60191* ● *1 CD*
● *Mid-price* ● *ADD* ● *1952*

Don't be misled by Sutherland and Pavarotti here; the two great versions of recent years are Carlo Maria Giulini's and Zubin Mehta's. Giulini has Brigitte Fassbaender making a most distinguished interpretation of the role of Azucena, as well as a powerful performance as Manrico from Domingo;
● *Deutsche Grammophon 423 858-2* ● *2 CDs*
● *Full price* ● *DDD* ● *1984*

also a highlights disc.
● *Deutsche Grammophon 421 310-2* ● *1 CD*

Domingo is also on an earlier recording by Mehta, almost as good, but the real star of the later disc is Leontyne Price's Leonora, a full-blooded performance from a singer whose voice is like the most delicious cream. This version gets a rare *Penguin CD Guide* Rosette.
● *RCA Victor red Seal RD 86194* ● *2 CDs*
● *Full price* ● *ADD* ● *1976*

La Traviata
With *Traviata*, too, one is spoiled for choice; again, there's a classic Callas recording.
● *EMI CDS7 49187-8* ● *2 CDs* ● *Full price*
● *ADD* ● *1958* ✪

But listen also to the finely paced conducting of Carlos Kleiber, with a vivid performance by Ileana Cotrubas as Violetta.
● *Deutsche Grammophon 415 132-2* ● *2 CDs*
● *Full price* ● *ADD* ● *1976*

Simon Boccanegra and Un Ballo in Maschera
Simon Boccanegra is perhaps best enjoyed in Abbado's excellent version, based on a production at La Scala which made a very successful trip to London; José Carreras is very good indeed here.
● *Deutsche Grammophon 415 692-2* ● *2 CDs*
● *Full price* ● *ADD* ● *1977*

Meanwhile *Ballo in Maschera* has two great recordings I particularly like; again (inevitably) there is Callas.
● *EMI CDS7 47498-8* ● *2 CDs* ● *Full price*
● *ADD* ● *1957*

Of more recent vintage is the sumptuous version conducted by Sir Georg Solti, with Margaret Price outstanding as the heroine Amelia, drawing from Pavarotti one of his best performances on record during the 1980s.
● *Decca 410 210-2* ● *2 CDs* ● *Full price*
● *DDD* ● *1985*

Forza del Destino
As before, there is Callas in supreme form, perhaps the best of all her great Verdi performances, with Tullio Serafin interpreting the score superbly.
● *EMI CDS7 47581-8* ● *3 CDs* ● *Full price*
● *ADD* ● *1955* ✪

Of more modern recordings, the combination of Domingo and Leontyne Price, as well as the thrusting, dynamic conducting of James Levine, is quite outstanding.
● *RCA Victor Red Seal RD 81864* ● *3 CDs*
● *Full price* ● *ADD*

Don Carlos
Don Carlos hasn't been recorded on the same scale as most other great Verdi operas, and for various textual reasons, no recording is entirely satisfactory. The best is Carlo Maria Giulini's, starring Domingo, although Monserrat Caballé could be a little more fully rounded as Elisabetta. Perhaps a case for a highlights disc only?
● *EMI CDM7 63089-2* ● *1 CD* ● *Mid-price*
● *ADD* ● *1970* ✪

Aida
There are loads of *Aida* recordings, and I must first commend two vintage classics. Callas, of course; her unique acting brings this heroine to life like no one else.
● *EMI CDS7 49030-8* ● *3 CDs* ● *Full price*
● *AAD* ● *1955* ✪

One of the greatest of Verdi conductors was Arturo Toscanini; his iron discipline and command of rhythm concealed a very warm approach to the music, and his timing is superb. His *Aida* is one of the great recordings of the opera.
● *RCA Gold Seal GD 60300* ● *3 CDs*
● *Mid-price* ● *ADD* ● *1949*

For a modern *Aida*, many regard James Levine's version with Domingo and Aprile Millo, based on a highly acclaimed performance at the New York

Metropolitan Opera, as quite dazzling. I don't, but then a lot about this opera misses me completely.
● *Sony CD45973* ● *3 CDs* ● *Full price*
● *DDD* ● *1990*

Otello

On the other hand, I think Levine's *Otello* is the recording of that work, with astonishingly realised performances by Domingo and Renata Scotto, with Sherrill Milnes an ideal Iago. This recording comes closer than any other (and is certainly far, far preferable to the recent overrated and shallow assault on the work by Pavarotti and Solti) to grasping the full nature of this masterpiece.
● *RCA Gold Seal GD82951* ● *2 CDs*
● *Mid-price* ● *ADD* ● *1978* ❂

Falstaff

It has long been generally agreed that the greatest conductor of *Falstaff* was Toscanini, whose grasp of the ensembles and the comic timing was almost immaculate (even if the sound quality isn't).
● *RCA Gold Seal GD 60251* ● *2 CDs*
● *Mid-price* ● *ADD* ● *1950* ❂

Better sound quality, and a version to choose for Tito Gobbi's performance in the title role, found on the titanic recording with Karajan; Gobbi is agreed to be one of the great Falstaffs since 1945.
● *EMI CDS7 49668-2* ● *2 CDs* ● *Full price*
● *ADD* ● *1961*

Verdi recitals and compilations

Some listeners may prefer to find a general way into Verdi by listening to various well-known (and occasionally not quite so well-known, but usually extremely rewarding) arias sung by a favourite or famous singer. They don't come any more favourite or famous at the moment than Luciano Pavarotti; he's generally better in the earlier Verdi operas, where the tenor roles are more ardent and passionate. He actually recorded a dedicated Verdi recital quite early in his recording career which has now been reissued on CD (with a few other pieces recorded at other times added), and it's an excellent testimony to his voice at its greatest; all the favourites from *Rigoletto* (including 'La donna è mobile') are there, as well as 'Celeste Aida' and the big tenor solos from *Macbeth*, *Traviata*, *Trovatore* and *Luisa Miller*, and there are also some lesser-known operas thrown in (e.g. *I Due Foscari*). This is a generous, good-value buy.
● *Decca 417 570-2* ● *1 CD* ● *Mid-price*
● *ADD* ● *1969–00* ❂

I've said some fairly enthusiastic things about the dark, sensual, creamy voice of Leontyne Price, and the collection *Verdi Heroines* sung by her is well worth the money. Price is as good as anyone, and brings her own unique vocal qualities to the big numbers from *Aida*, *Ballo*, *Forza* and *Traviata*, and is particularly acute and mesmerising in the sleepwalking scene from *Macbeth*, as well as the Willow Song followed by the Ave Maria from *Otello*. All these recordings were made when Price's voice was at its absolute best around the turn of the 1960s/1970s.
● *RCA Victor Red Seal RD 87016* ● *1 CD*
● *Full price* ● *ADD*

And then, of course, there's Callas; there are countless Callas compilations, but one of those dedicated to Verdi is especially fine, not least for her staggering rendition of the great aria from the final act of *Don Carlos*, 'Tu che la vanità' (considered by some to be one of the finest things Verdi ever wrote). That alone would be worth the price of the disc, but her illuminating account of arias from (amongst others) *Aida*, *Ballo*, *Macbeth* and *Nabucco* makes this a Verdi disc to treasure. It complements the Price disc well, as few items are duplicated.
● *EMI CDC7 47730-2* ● *1 CD* ● *Full price*
● *ADD*

● ● ●

EPIC AND CONTROVERSY: WAGNER

When Wagner began writing opera in the 1830s, the dominant German figure was Giacomo Meyerbeer (1791–1864), whose long and spectacular pieces like *Robert le Diable* (1831) and *Les Huguenots* (1836) were enormous successes in Paris. Meyerbeer's operas represent the apex of the French taste for the long, crowded, diversely-entertaining musical show; they're almost more truly the ancestor of the modern stage musical than of anything we might call operatic. Meyerbeer was popular throughout Europe, and it was against this background that Wagner sought to make his breakthrough with a very traditional grand opera *Rienzi, der letzte der Tribunen* ('Rienzi, last of the Tribunes'; 1842), an Ancient Roman story of pomp, sacrifice and the usual stuff. It's a competent work but no more than that; one aria in particular, 'Allmacht'ger vater' ('Almighty Father', known as 'Rienzi's Prayer'), has quite often been anthologised.

Der Fliegende Holländer (The Flying Dutchman)

It was in *Der Fliegende Holländer* (1843) that Wagner began to show his true colours. This is one of the most

Richard Wagner

1813–1883

Wagner is one of the most controversial figures in musical history; people tend either to love or to hate him (very few are indifferent). Born in Leipzig, he began writing music when still quite young, and some fairly juvenile symphonies and piano pieces brought him to the attention of Franz Liszt, who became something of a guide and mentor (until Wagner began his affair with Liszt's daughter Cosima). In the 1830s Wagner turned his attention to opera, the form which fascinated him most. He became involved in Dresden's revolutionary politics, and narrowly escaped capture and imprisonment after an abortive 1848 anti-monarchist rising. He went into exile in Switzerland, where he worked on *The Ring Cycle*, earning no money, running up huge debts, and making his wife miserable.

Things seemed desperate by the early 1860s, but in 1864 Ludwig II, the eccentric King of Bavaria (a great admirer of Wagner's music), offered to pay all the composer's debts and to finance him until his masterpiece was complete. Ludwig also offered to fund the staging of *The Ring*, a huge commitment on the public purse given that Wagner had ambitions of building a new opera house with special features. After a year Wagner was driven out of Bavaria, but Ludwig remained committed to the cause; meanwhile, the composer began his affair with Cosima. When, in 1874, the Bayreuth Festival Opera House was built and *The Ring* at last performed, Wagner was anything but satisfied; eventually he retired to Venice.

concentrated pieces Wagner ever wrote; it's also probably the most compact libretto he ever devised. From the word go Wagner was determined to write his own libretti, which was all part of his desire to create what he called the *Gesamtkunstwerk* – the 'complete work of art'.

Dutchman is probably Wagner's most accessible work; it tells the story of the cursed Dutch sea captain and his ghost ship, doomed to roam the seas for eternity unless he can be redeemed by love. Redemption by love is one of Wagner's favourite topics

- from first to last. Senta, daughter of
- the mercenary Norwegian captain
- Daland, has always been obsessed
- with the legend of the Flying
- Dutchman; so when her father appears
- with a mysterious stranger who has
- promised him a fortune in return for
- his daughter, she's happy to forget her
- boyfriend Erik, who tries his best to
- ruin things. In the end, however, Love
- Triumphs – and Senta and the ghostly
- Dutchman drown together.
- Thematically, the work looks forward
- to Wagner's main preoccupations;
- musically, too, it looks forward to the

style of his very greatest works, a completely blended and varied, quite often orchestra-led, structure in which the importance of motivic melodies and phrases is paramount. Wagner doesn't quite hang the opera entirely on the skeleton of these motifs, but the themes stated in the long Overture are the backbone of the opera, and the way that he allows these themes to confront one another gives some idea of his future method. The concept of 'numbers' still lurks behind such extraneous elements as the 'Spinning Song' (which, taken out of context, sounds more like something by Sullivan than Wagner), as it continued to lurk in *Tannhäuser* (1845) and *Lohengrin* (1848, performed in 1850).

Tannhäuser and *Lohengrin*

These next two operas are both based on stories from Arthurian legend. The pivot of *Tannhäuser* is the opposition of sacred and profane love; a diffuse and rambling work, it's probably Wagner's least coherent opera. It is best known for its Pilgrim Chorus, and is scarcely the ideal starting point for the would-be Wagnerian. In *Lohengrin* (which is most famous for its Bridal March), the development in Wagner's music towards long 'paragraphs' which build gradually is even more pronounced than in *Dutchman* and *Tannhauser*. These 'paragraphs' transform old-fashioned recitative into something integral to the unity of the drama as a whole, surrounding it with orchestral music as significant as that in the set-piece choruses and arias. Although, given the way Wagner wrote libretti, the concept of fast recitative exchanges vanished, his habit of composing in musical 'paragraphs' was at least partly necessitated by his parallel habit of writing poetry in long declamatory paragraphs.

- *The Ring Cycle: Das Rheingold*
- *(The Gold of the Rhine)*; *Die*
- *Walküre (The Valkyrie)*;
- *Siegfried; Götterdämmerung*
- *(Twilight of The Gods)*
- Originally Wagner planned simply to
- write an opera about the
- Germanic/Norse hero Siegfried; but as
- he devised the libretto, it became clear
- that his story required more than one
- opera. Writing the libretto was a
- massive undertaking in itself. In 1853,
- Wagner finally got down to work on
- the music.
- To tell the story of *The Ring Cycle*
- (properly, *Der Ring des Nibelungen –*
- *The Ring of the Nibelung*) in detail
- would fill a book in itself. The four
- operas tell of the creation and
- destruction of the world, of the arrival
- and supremacy, and then decline and
- death, of the gods of Valhalla; it is
- about free will and determinism,
- about love and self-sacrifice, about the
- psyche of man. The highly complex
- plot revolves around a Ring of Power
- made from gold stolen from the Rhine
- Maidens by the Nibelung dwarf
- Alberich; when he is tricked out of
- the Ring by Wotan, King of the Gods,
- he lays a curse on it so that it will
- bring the downfall of its owner. The
- opposition between Wotan and
- Alberich is one of the pivotal
- elements of the opera; Wotan wishes
- to regain the Ring but cannot be seen
- to do so himself, nor can he grant
- favour to a mortal hero. Hence he is
- forced to abandon his human son,
- Siegmund, although his immortal
- daughter, the Valkyrie Brünnhilde,
- rescues Siegmund's twin sister
- Sieglinde, who is pregnant by
- Siegmund (incest is not a great crime
- in this world). Brünnhilde is the
- heroine of the cycle; abandoned by
- Wotan and left to sleep on a rock
- surrounded by fire, she continues to

act on Wotan's behalf when awakened by Siegfried, the son of Siegmund and Sieglinde. Once Siegfried gains the Ring and gives it to Brünnhilde as a love-token, this ought to end the matter, but Alberich's son Hagen, the dominant plotter of the final opera, *Götterdämmerung*, adds a final twist by duping Siegfried into betraying Brünnhilde and then snatching the Ring from her. Hagen brings about Siegfried's death, but Brünnhilde takes control, and in the final scene she joins Siegfried on his funeral pyre, whose fire will spread to Valhalla and give Wotan the peaceful rest of oblivion which he has been urgently seeking through most of the cycle. The Rhine overflows and the Rhine Maidens reclaim the Ring; the Ring has, as it were, come full circle.

Wagner didn't write all the music at once; between 1853 and 1856 he wrote the whole of *Das Rheingold* and *Die Walküre*, and then the first two acts of *Siegfried*. But by this time he had developed other interests and feelings, and so he put *The Ring* aside for twelve years. It was during these dozen years that he wrote two completely contrasting operas; *Tristan und Isolde* (which appeared in 1865), the ultimate celebration of romantic love as religion, and *Die Meistersinger von Nürnberg* (*The Mastersingers of Nuremberg*, 1868), a celebration of music and song with Germanic nationalist overtones.

The music of *The Ring Cycle* was unlike anything heard before. The orchestral resources demanded at various points are vast, and this has led to the misapprehension that all of Wagner's music consists of vast orchestras blazing away en masse all the time. The score to *Rheingold* asks for six harps; but that doesn't mean

- that six harps are playing all the time.
- Quite often Wagner uses small,
- chamber-like combinations of
- instruments, and although his music is
- orchestra-led, he did also place an
- enormous roof over the orchestra pit in
- the Bayreuth Festspielhaus, designed
- to prevent the orchestra dominating
- the voices. Which doesn't alter the fact
- that sometimes the voice must be
- surrounded by the orchestra, a very
- different balance of power from that in
- Rossini's or Verdi's music.
- Wagner's use of the leitmotif was
- also unlike anything else; other
- composers had used phrases or
- melodies to refer to individuals or
- objects in dramas, but Wagner built
- his entire work out of these phrases,
- some of which consist only of two
- notes, others of whole melodies, others
- again of a single chord or an arpeggio
- based on the constituent notes of a
- single chord. The leitmotifs work
- through all four operas, taking on
- new meanings as they go on, and by
- the time we arrive at
- *Götterdämmerung* the motifs are so
- loaded with meaning that each
- occurrence refers the listener back to
- each previous occurrence. For this
- reason, many of the motifs are
- musically related, assisting the whole
- scheme to seem organic. For this is
- one of the great achievements of *The
- Ring*; a work based on these
- compositional processes could so
- easily have been soulless and
- schematised, whereas the growth of
- *The Ring* is entirely natural.
- When Wagner resumed work on *The
- Ring* in 1868, it was as though some
- new spirit were possessing him, as the
- intensity of the cycle from the Prelude
- of the third act in *Siegfried*, through to
- the end of *Götterdämmerung* is
- astonishing, even by the standards of
- the first two and two-thirds operas.

Tristan und Isolde

The two operas written while Wagner was taking time off from *The Ring* were scarcely light relief, even if one of them was a 'comedy' of sorts. But in *Tristan* Wagner created perhaps his greatest single opera, a work whose theme and subject-matter have had a major influence on art ever since, and whose musical style heralded one of the great revolutions in musical theory.

In *Tristan* Wagner takes the great romantic-love myth which has dominated Western thought and art and raises it to the level of religion. The story tells of Tristan and Isolde, enemies with a fatal attraction, who must betray everything they stand for and believe in if they acknowledge their love. Telling the story of the opera does nothing to explain what it's about; in the second act the lovers sing endlessly of submerging their individual identities in one another and of blissful extinction. Tristan is fatally wounded in a fight with a disloyal friend; after his death and a series of almost casual murders and suicides, the opera culminates in Isolde's famous 'Liebestod' (an untranslatable word meaning 'love's-death', but carrying senses of 'death in love', 'love of death', 'love in death'), which, along with Brünnhilde's 'Immolation Scene' from *Götterdämmerung*, is one of Wagner's great pieces of soprano writing.

Musically, *Tristan* is remarkable for its use of chromaticism and the way it never quite lands in a 'home key'. This is often seen as the first decay of tonality; the endless use of unresolved chords has an important dramatic function as it mirrors the endless yearning of the lovers, never satisfied (or not, at least, until both are dead at the end of the opera), and it also creates a kind of 'hothouse' atmosphere of erotic sensuality.

Die Meistersinger von Nürnberg (The Mastersinger of Nuremberg)

The fake medieval nature of *Meistersinger* is a long way from the chromatic yearning of *Tristan und Isolde*; a tale of a song contest, it's something of an obliquely autobiographical work on Wagner's part. The opera is about a search for an ideal song, and, as so often in his life, Wagner lays out the rules and then breaks them. This is essentially a chorus opera, an ensemble work, and to a certain extent it represents something that Wagner needed to do before he could write the terrifyingly ominous chorus scenes in *Götterdämmerung*, although the atmosphere of this opera is hundreds of times lighter than the culmination of *The Ring*. In the persona of Beckmesser, the caricature of a critic, Wagner was getting his own back on certain figures who had consistently attacked him, not the least of whom was Brahms's friend Eduard Hanslick.

Parsifal

Wagner's final opera, which appeared in 1882 at Bayreuth, was different again (although once more it draws on Arthurian legend). With his life's work done, Wagner returned to the same canon of legends that had provided much of his early work, and produced an opera about religion, but religion treated as though it were myth. *Parsifal* revolves around the Knights of the Grail; it is a sort of version of the Fisher King legend, except that instead of becoming sterile the King, Amfortas, has been wounded through his own folly. The figure of Parsifal, the Holy Fool, is an inversion of the concept of heroism, as Parsifal's heroism must consist of refusing to act. The figure of Kundry, a cursed, wandering Jewess in search of redemption, when memorably played, often steals the opera. If *Meistersinger* is an ensemble piece, *Parsifal* often belongs to the orchestra; there are transformation scenes, there is the Good Friday Music, above all there is the one central theme of the music, the great Dresden 'Amen' chord sequence, out of which Wagner fashions this extraordinary coda to his work. Even some Wagner-lovers find *Parsifal* tedious; those who don't often regard it as the pinnacle of his work.

DISCOGRAPHY
Der Fliegende Holländer
Dutchman is an excellent place to get acquainted with certain Wagnerian idioms, and the Overture is justifiably famous. Happily the three best versions of the opera are all quite cheap. The best is probably Otto Klemperer's highly symphonic reading, with dignified tempos which emphasise the mythic side of the story rather than the high drama. Unfortunately, Klemperer's speeds are so slow that the work spreads onto three discs; and there is a bit more drama in the piece than you might gather from this recording.
● *EMI CMS7 6334-2* ● *3 CDs* ● *Mid-price*
● *ADD* ● *1968* ✪

There's drama in abundance in Antál Doratai's ferocious reading, with some nice delicate touches too, and one of the great Wagnerian singers, George London. This is possibly the most newcomer-friendly recording of them all.
● *Decca 417 319-2* ● *2 CDs* ● *Mid-price*
● *ADD* ● *1960*

More modern, and recorded live in the opera house Wagner himself designed at Bayreuth, Waldemar Nelsson's recording boasts a scene-stealing Daland in Matti Salminen, and an unconvincing Dutchman. A respectable, occasionally thrilling experience.
● *Philips 434 599-2* ● *2 CDs* ● *Mid-price*
● *DDD* ● *1985*

Tannhäuser and Lohengrin
The Philips Richard Wagner Edition, issued in 1992, isn't universally excellent. Where it's most successful is with the earlier operas; it boasts the best *Tannhäuser* around and a very good *Lohengrin*. The earlier opera is superbly integrated by Wolfgang Sawallisch, who draws on some fantastic singing from Wolfgang Windgassen.
● *Philips 434 607-2* ● *3 CDs* ● *Mid-price*
● *ADD* ● *1962* ✪

The *Lohengrin* is a modern recording, with good singing from Paul Frey as the hero and Cheryl Studer, and competently held together by conductor Peter Schneider.
● *Philips 434 602-2* ● *4 CDs* ● *Mid-price*
● *DDD* ● *1990*

If you should be a *Lohengrin* addict, then you'll need to experience the classic set conducted by Rudolf Kempe, featuring singers like Dietrich Fischer-Dieskau, Gottlob Frick and Christa Ludwig.
● *EMI CDS7 49017-8* ● *3 CDs* ● *Full price*
● *ADD* ● *1964*

✓ The Ring Cycle
If you get hooked on *The Ring* the chances are you'll want to own every recording ever made, so deeply obsessive does the work become. Good recordings are few and far between, especially good stereo recordings, not least because most of the great Wagner singers died decades ago. The tenor lines in Wagner are like no others; the 'Heldentenor' ('hero-tenor') is a special entity, and figures like Messrs Domingo and Pavarotti don't possess the right talents for the winding vocal lines, demanding vocal clarity, touches of tenderness, and great power. The same applies to the soprano lines; Brünnhilde's 'Immolation Scene' requires something like twenty minutes' singing from the performer and the control must be immaculate, which is difficult even in studio conditions.

I have reservations about facets of probably the most famous Wagner recordings, those made under Sir Georg Solti between 1959 and 1965. They were the first full recordings of *The Ring*, the first in stereo, and at times they are dazzling. The cast includes a number of great Wagnerians, and many people admire Birgit Nilsson's Brünnhilde, though for me it's a shade coarse. The great problem is Solti, who treats *The Ring* as a series of climaxes and sound effects punctuated by bridge passages. There's no real sense of an unfolding organic drama. Still, at its most exciting, it's a remarkable achievement. There is a compilation of extracts from this cycle, for which there is something to be said, but I'm a bit dubious about recommending 'bleeding chunks' of *The Ring*. Because of the dazzling sound, the Solti recording is a good place to get acquainted with the work; the less perfect-sounding but musically greater versions can come later. The cycle is available in four separate boxed sets, or in one giant box, which will set you back about £130 or so.
● *Decca 414 100-2* ● *15 CDs* ● *Mid-price*
● *ADD* ● *1959–65; extracts: Decca 421 313-2*
● *1 CD* ● *Mid-price* ● *ADD*

An alternative introduction to at least three of the four operas for those who want perfect sound can be found in James Levine's cycle based loosely around performances at the New York Metropolitan in the late 1980s. The recording of *Walküre* is fairly dull, but some of the music on *Rheingold* and *Götterdämmerung* is superb, and Levine's view of the piece gets, I think, closer to its heart than does Solti. Reiner Goldberg is a fairly inadequate Siegfried, especially in *Götterdämmerung*, and Hildegard Behrens sometimes sounds disturbingly like Lotte Lenya, but Matti Salminen's Hagen in *Götterdämmerung* is titanic and disturbing, a real villain.

Rheingold: ● *Deutsche Grammophon 427 607-2*
● *3 CDs* ● *Full price* ● *DDD* ● *1989*
Walküre: ● *Deutsche Grammophon 423 389-2*
● *4 CDs* ● *Full price* ● *DDD* ● *1988*
Siegfried: ● *Deutsche Grammophon 429 407-2*
● *4 CDs* ● *Full price* ● *DDD* ● *1991*
Götterdammerung: ● *Deutsche Grammophon 429 385-2* ● *4 CDs* ● *Full price* ● *DDD* ● *1990*

The English-language *Ring* (live 1970s performances at the English National Opera) is most remarkable for the extraordinary conducting of the late Reginald Goodall, the last truly great Wagner conductor. Goodall took his ideas about tempo and phrasing from Wilhelm Furtwängler and, above all, the Bayreuth regular Hans Knappertsbusch; his performances are phenomenally slow, but they do get close to the work's heart, and feature some fine singing from Norman Bailey (Wotan) and Rita Hunter (Brünnhilde). Because of Goodall's tempos, these do spread further than other recordings, but if Wagner gets a grip on you then you must hear them.
Rheingold: ● *EMI CMS7 64110-2* ● *3 CDs*
● *Mid-price* ● *ADD* ● *1975*
The Valkyrie: ● *EMI CMS7 63918-2* ● *4 CDs*
● *Mid-price* ● *ADD* ● *1975*
Siegfried: ● *EMI CMS7 63595-2* ● *4 CDs*
● *Mid-price* ● *ADD* ● *1973*
Twilight of the Gods: ● *EMI CMS7 64244-2*
● *5 CDs* ● *Mid-price* ● *ADD* ● *1977*

The greatest of all Wagner conductors since recording began was Wilhelm Furtwängler, but unfortunately he only ever made one studio recording of any part of *The Ring*. It was hoped it would be the start of a cycle, but the conductor died. The one opera recorded was *Die Walküre*, and a titanic set it is too; Martha Mödl is a fine Brünnhilde and Ludwig Suthaus (a good Heldentenor) makes a very charming Siegmund, whilst Ferdinand Frantz is a fine Wotan. Furtwängler's phrasing and paragraphing makes complete sense and this set, being reasonably cheap and of pretty good sound quality (even if it is mono) might make a good test of whether or not Wagner will appeal – if you don't enjoy this, he won't.
● *EMI CHS7 63045-2* ● *3 CDs* ● *Mid-price*
● *ADD* ● *1954*

There are two live Furtwängler complete cycles, both with dodgy sound and execrable orchestras. For political reasons, Furtwängler only ever conducted *The Ring* in Italy, and his 1950 cycle at La Scala was recorded by some means or other. It stars the greatest Wagnerian soprano, Kirsten Flagstad (1895–1962), as Brünnhilde; once you're into Wagner, don't miss this sublime performance, but don't start here whatever you do.
● *Virtuoso 2697282/2699102/2699092/2699112*
● *14 CDs* ● *Mid-price* ● *AAD* ● *1950*

The other Furtwängler set was also recorded with a poor Italian orchestra, the Italian Radio Orchestra, in a series of concert performances done, act by act, in 1953. Furtwängler gets the orchestra to play out of their skins (but they're

still dreadful at times), and his cast is excellent. The recordings were made live but under studio conditions; unfortunately the sound quality isn't as good as it should be. This is probably the one vintage set that everyone who has an interest in Wagner really ought to have.
● *EMI CDZM 67123* ● *13 CDs* ● *Mid-price*
● *ADD* ● *1953*

Of other dodgy-sounding discs of *The Ring*, I'd also recommend two of Hans Knappertsbusch's recordings very strongly. Shopping around you can find versions (again of doubtful provenance) of both his 1957 and 1958 Bayreuth performances, and in the *Siegfried* and *Götterdämmerung* from 1958 you will hear something extraordinary and even incandescent; Astrid Varnay's Brünnhilde is superb, in the same class as Flagstad. Knappertsbusch's tempos are always slow and steady, while his grasp of orchestral and vocal ensemble is sometimes unsteady; but his understanding of the phrasing is as good as Furtwängler's.
Siegfried: ● *Hunt 4 CDLSMH 34043* ● *4 CDs*
● *Mid-price* ● *AAD* ● *1958*
Götterdämmerung: ● *Hunt 4 CDLSMH 34044*
● *4 CDs* ● *Mid-price* ● *AAD* ● *1958. Both contain an extract from the 1957 performances*

Tristan und Isolde
Tristan is no easier to record well than any other Wagner work. The best recording is prohibitively expensive; Kirsten Flagstad plays Isolde to Ludwig Suthaus's Tristan, with brilliant control at the centre by Wilhelm Furtwängler. Even after more than 40 years it's an incomparable recording, but for many people almost £60 for a mono set is too much to ask.
● *EMI CDS7 47322-8* ● *4 CDs* ● *Full price*
● *ADD* ● *1952* ❶

There is a decent, if not quite as great, alternative for about £30 less; Karl Böhm's live recording, with tenor Wolfgang Windgassen and Birgit Nilsson giving, for my money, her best performance on disc. This version has drama, drive, passion, and only occasionally misses the absolute depths. I don't think Böhm has ever done better. It used to be on Deutsche Grammophon, but transferred over to Philips as part of the Richard Wagner Edition.
● *Philips 434 425-2* ● *3 CDs* ● *Mid-price*
● *ADD* ● *1966*

One *Tristan* worth hearing, although perhaps not buying, is Carlos Kleiber's, which features the most beautiful voice ever to record Isolde, Margaret Price's, and the worst Tristan, René Kollo. The main thing to hear it for, though, is some astonishing choice of tempos by Kleiber, sometimes positively vertiginous and almost too much.
● *Deutsche Grammophon 413 315-2* ● *4 CDs*
● *Full price* ● *DDD* ● *1982*

Die Meistersinger von Nürnberg
Recordings of *Meistersinger* are few and far between; perhaps the best is Karajan's (even though it features René Kollo), largely for the

controlling vision of the conductor and the late Sir Geraint Evans's Beckmesser.
● *EMI CDS7 49683-2* ● *4 CDs* ● *Full price*
● *ADD* ● *1970* ✪

Parsifal
One *Parsifal* is entirely outstanding, a live performance conducted by Hans Knappertsbusch at Bayreuth. George London is a noble Amfortas and Jess Thomas, an uneven Wagnerian tenor, gives his best recorded performance in the title role. Knappertsbusch's judgement of timing is transcendent. This is the real thing.
● *Philips 416 390-2* ● *4 CDs* ● *Full price*
● *ADD* ● *1962* ✪

I can't quite see how people put the 1980 Karajan recording, good though it is, in the same bracket; still, it won a *Gramophone* Award in 1981.
● *Deutsche Grammophon 413 347-2* ● *4 CDs*
● *Full price* ● *DDD* ● *1980*

The version conducted by James Levine in the Philips Richard Wagner Edition is generally shallow but has two things very much in its favour; superb sound, and Waltraud Meier's multi-dimensional Kundry.
● *Philips 434 616-2* ● *4 CDs* ● *Mid-price*
● *DDD* ● *1985*

● ● ● ● ●

GERMAN POTBOILERS: NICOLAI, FLOTOW, MARSCHNER

Wagner's achievement stands amongst the most titanic in art. This is all the more remarkable given that what small tradition of German opera there was prior to Wagner is – Mozart, Beethoven and Weber aside – pretty negligible. The most famous Germanic opera before Wagner is probably *The Merry Wives of Windsor* (1849) by Otto Nicolai (1810–1849). Nicolai's role in musical history is assured, as he was more or less responsible for the rise of the Vienna Philharmonic Orchestra and its development into a magnificent force both in the concert hall and the opera house. Which is just as well, for if his reputation had to be secured by this unspectacular bourgeois comedy of manners, a very feeble

Shakespearian adaptation made all the more pallid by inevitable comparison with Verdi's late masterpiece, it wouldn't amount to much. The Overture's pretty good, though.

Nicolai is a towering giant of a composer, though, next to figures like Friedrich von Flotow (1812–1883), a prolific composer of operatic potboilers probably at his peak in the late 1840s (his best piece, *Martha*, appeared in 1847). Of slightly earlier German Romantic operatic composers, claims have been made on behalf of Heinrich Marschner (1795–1861), who suffered the indignity of having one of his full-blooded Romantic works, *Der Vampyr* (1828), turned into a semi-comic BBC Television soap opera in 1992. Marschner is often cited as a 'halfway figure between Weber and Wagner', but whatever claims you make, his music is really best left to specialists.

Actually, the most famous and popular piece of Germanic operatic writing in Wagner's lifetime appeared in the year *The Ring* was finished (1974). It belongs, however, not to a truly Germanic tradition, but derives essentially from the French tradition of comic opera or operetta. Johann Strauss's immensely popular *Die Fledermaus* (*The Bat*) began its own tradition of 'Viennese operetta', but without the example set by the works of Frenchman Jacques Offenbach (1819–1880), Strauss probably wouldn't have bothered with the form.

DISCOGRAPHY
Nicolai
You'll find a fine performance of the Overture to Nicolai's *Merry Wives of Windsor*, along with lots of classic Johann Strauss waltzes, on the live recording of the 1992 New Year's Day Concert conducted by the great Carlos Kleiber.
● *Sony CD48376* ● *1 CD* ● *Full price* ● *DDD*
● *1992* ✪

THE FRENCH TRADITION: BERLIOZ, THOMAS, GOUNOD

The French taste for operetta, a sort of civilised type of *opera buffa* where drama was definitely a secondary consideration, seems the inevitable corollary of the popularity of the spectacular, crowd-packed works of Meyerbeer and, to some extent, Berlioz. There is a little doubt that of all the composers writing French opera in the nineteenth century, Berlioz was the greatest, but this isn't, I'm afraid, to say an awful lot. There's been a big cult for Berlioz's operas recently with new productions on stage of *La Damnation de Faust* (1846; described by its composer not as an opera, but as a *légende dramatique*) and *Les Troyens* (*The Trojans*; 1863/90). Although many make a case for the latter as Berlioz's masterpiece, in which he distils his Romantic essence through the classical forms of 'number opera', I find it an unwieldy work very much in the spirit of Meyerbeer. Of course, there are remarkable Berliozian touches, principally in the portrayal of Dido the abandoned woman in the penultimate scene. There is probably a greater case to be made for *La Damnation de Faust*, which, for all that it often gets treated as something akin to operetta, is a rather profound account of the Faust legend – much more profound, anyway, than the best-known French assault on the story, the *Faust* of Charles François Gounod (1818–1893), first performed in 1859.

Berlioz's final opera, *Béatrice et Bénédict* (1862), was a version of Shakespeare's *Much Ado About Nothing*; clearly Shakespeare was 'in' with French composers that decade, as one of the great successes was *Hamlet* by Ambroise Thomas (1811–1896), an opera which is actually more successful if one manages to forget the fact that Shakespeare wrote a play of the same name with a vaguely similar (but no greater resemblance than that) story-line. Thomas had made his name in 1867 with a piece called *Mignon*, and *Hamlet* (1868) confirmed his reputation. Thomas, as a setter of Shakespeare, was everything Verdi wasn't (or, perhaps, more strictly, wasn't everything that Verdi was). His music concentrates on the overtly dramatic and ignores the inner and psychological; rather strange when you consider that *Hamlet* is one of Shakespeare's most 'inward' plays.

Another Shakespearian setting of the 1860s came from Gounod, with his *Roméo et Juliette* (1867). Gounod is a simple composer, probably at his most effective when at his most simple. He was a fantastically popular composer in his heyday (through the 1850s and 1860s), and his most enduring work is probably *Faust*, with its famous Soldier's Chorus. Gounod's music is strong on tunes and short on depth, but to criticise it for its intellectual shortcomings is really to misunderstand the terms on which it was written and the way in which it was designed to appeal. After all, Gounod, like all these French composers, was writing at a time when Offenbach ruled the roost, and during the absurd musical comedy of the French Second Empire, when the ridiculous posturing figure of Napoleon III was the figurehead of the nation.

DISCOGRAPHY
This really is 'acquired taste' time with a vengeance. Berlioz's major operas have probably been best done by Sir Colin Davis (who has a real feel for this composer), and why Philips don't offer the public a highlights disc of either of Davis's sets of *Troyens* or *The Damnation of Faust* is beyond me. Try borrowing the full set of one from a library.
Troyens: ● *Philips 416 432-2* ● *4 CDs* ● *Full price* ● *ADD* ● *1970*
Damnation: ● *Philips 416 395-2* ● *2 CDs* ● *Full price* ● *ADD* ● *1974*

Ambroise Thomas's *Hamlet* has been pretty effectively recorded with conductor Richard Bonynge turning in one of his more dramatic performances, and Joan Sutherland as Ophelia. Sherrill Milnes is a bit monochrome in the title role, but the whole performance is good and solid, and almost persuades that there's something to the piece.
● *(Decca 433 857-2* ● *3 CDs* ● *Mid-price*
● *DDD* ● *1983*

For Gounod's *Faust*, they don't come much better than Georges Prêtre's version starring Placido Domingo in the title role and Mirella Freni, giving one of her best-judged performances on disc (so good it gives the character some depth), as Marguerite.
● *EMI CDS7 47493-8* ● *3 CDs* ● *Full price*
● *ADD* ● *1979*

THE OPERETTA KING: JACQUES OFFENBACH (1819–1880)

Jacques Offenbach more or less singlehandedly invented the operetta, and in doing so paved the way for the stage musical. His influence in Europe was quite widespread, and it was largely down to him that Johann Strauss II invented Viennese operetta and that Gilbert and Sullivan came together for the hugely successful 'Savoy Operas'. In the mid-1850s, Offenbach established a theatre company, Les Bouffes Parisiens, whose initial repertoire included Mozart and Rossini, as well as his contemporary Léo Delibes (1836–1891; whose remaining claim to operatic fame is the female duet, the 'Bell Song', from his 1883 opera *Lakmé*, which has found its way into several film soundtracks and TV commercials). At first Offenbach's own contributions were fairly short works, and the first major addition from the theatre's founder came in 1859 with a two-act version of *Orphée aux enfers* (*Orpheus in the Underworld*; a larger four-act revised version appeared in 1874). In choosing this legend as a subject Offenbach was, in many ways, and either consciously or unconsciously, taking on the whole concept of opera as a satirical subject; after all, *Orfeo* had been central to the original birth of opera and to its reform by Gluck. By dismantling the whole legend, turning Eurydice into a highly shrewish figure whom Orpheus is unwilling to rescue, and making his failure a cause for celebration all round, Offenbach is turning on their heads all the assertions which earlier composers had made using the myth about the power of love (he even quotes Gluck's famous aria 'Che farò'). Offenbach lived in a trivialising society where surfaces were more important than depth; *Orphée* was, in some ways, his manner of attacking that society, while giving everybody a good tuneful laugh into the bargain. *Orphée* is famous for its cancan, and it's a poor revival which doesn't win the audience over; as a new work, shorter than most, it consolidated the reputation of Les Bouffes Parisiens, and helped spread Offenbach's name throughout Europe (the opera appeared in Vienna in 1860).

Offenbach had a run of great satirical hit operettas (the best known, apart from *Orphée*, is probably *La Belle Hélène*; 1864), but at the end of his career he wished to prove himself capable of something greater. The subject he chose was the great and influential early German Romantic, E. T. A. Hoffmann; taking a libretto which used three of Hoffmann's tales to illustrate something about the artistic spirit, Offenbach created what is for many his masterpiece, *Les Contes d'Hoffmann* (*The Tales of Hoffmann*; 1881). Through this work, Hoffmann, disillusioned and on the verge of getting drunk, looks back and considers how he lost three great loves of his life (who were all in some way manifestations of the same woman), always through the agency of the same villain; at the end, thwarted again, he realises that the true love of the artist must always be his Muse. The libretto on occasion trivialises Hoffmann, but for the most part it is very much in his spirit; Hoffmann's female characters were almost always embodiments of the same woman, and his tales did always have some autobiographical component. Offenbach's score (about which there are huge problems as the work was incomplete when he died; even the order in which the acts should come has been disputed) is surprisingly profound, especially in its ensembles. The climactic trio 'Ta mère? Oses tu l'invoquer?' ('Your mother? Do you dare to invoke her?'), from the story concerned directly with music, in which the girl Antonia (one of Hoffmann's loves), the villain Miracle, and the spirit of Antonia's mother (conjured by Miracle in order to delude the girl and lead her to a tragic death) sing together, is a remarkable achievement; the writing for the three/one heroine(s) is of a quite inspired beauty (all the better if one singer can pull it off alone). Despite its incompleteness, *Hoffmann* is in many ways the great French opera of the mid/late nineteenth century, combining spectacle, excitement and melody with, occasionally, something just a shade deeper. Practically anyone who listens to any kind of music knows the famous Barcarolle ('Belle nuit, o nuit d'amour' – 'Beautiful night, oh night of love'), which was even transformed into a Top 3 single in 1969, Donald Peers's 'Please Don't Go'.

DISCOGRAPHY
With a mainly French cast, Michel Plasson's recording of *Orphée* (in its four-act version) captures the work's spirit and sense of fun (as well as its rhythmic spring and variety).
● *EMI CDS7 49647-2* ● *2 CDs* ● *Full price*
● *ADD* ● *1980* ○

There is one version of *Hoffmann* which towers above the rest. It is not, alas, the recent Philips release with Jessye Norman (although that's worth hearing for Norman's wonderful singing, as well as for its inclusion of every note Offenbach wrote in every version); rather it is the marvellous Domingo and Sutherland recording, which really gets inside the work's skin, finding every nuance, every possible profundity, and with both stars in top form as well as Richard Bonynge at his wittiest, most light-handed.
● *Decca 421 866-2* ● *2 CDs* ● *Mid-price*
● *ADD* ● *1971* ○

THE BAT AND THE WIDOW: JOHANN STRAUSS II (1825–1899) AND FRANZ LEHÁR (1870–1948)

Offenbach was a great encourager of other composers; and it was after encouragement from Offenbach that Johann Strauss II, a son and brother of composers, took up the story of *Die Fledermaus*, another satirical tale of social mores, and turned it into a vehicle for some great tunes. Strauss was, of course, the 'Waltz King' of Vienna, and inevitably the waltz form keeps on turning up in *Die Fledermaus*. Actually, there's a great deal more to composing (and performing) this kind of music than might be imagined; the grasp of rhythm needs to be tight, and one of the reasons that Strauss's operetta succeeds so often and so well is precisely because of that – its rhythmic drive – as well as Strauss's light touch with musical satire (for example, a mock-tragic trio in which all three singers are secretly enjoying the situation hugely). There's also a party scene, which quickly became established as an excuse for indulgent intrusive performances by guest-star artists, which is why the work has become so popular as a Christmas or New Year's Eve entertainment in opera houses; and there's a purely spoken part which sometimes attracts quite well-known character actors. All of which can get in the way of drama (which is surprisingly taut) to an overbearing extent; but then, the kind of indulgence which the opera characterises became the hallmark of Viennese operetta. *Die Fledermaus* set the standard which yielded, some 31 years later, Franz Lehár's roaringly successful *Die lustige Witwe* (*The Merry Widow*; 1905), an opera which you can't intellectualise about but which is one of the most irresistibly tuneful works in the genre (on a slightly sinister note, 'The Merry Widow Waltz' is said to have been Adolf Hitler's absolutely favourite piece of music; he much preferred Lehár to Wagner). Lehár's attempts to write serious music after *Widow* never caught on in the same way as his Straussian entertainment, which remains popular to this day precisely because of its lack of pretensions. It certainly belongs with Johann Strauss's operetta rather than any of the extraordinary and daring works by Johann's unrelated namesake Richard, whose greatest operas were all written in the same decade as *The Merry Widow*.

DISCOGRAPHY
Carlos Kleiber's set of *Die Fledermaus* seems to divide the critics; I find it brilliant and tightly controlled, with marvellous singing by Lucia Popp and Julia Varady; others feel that it is too controlled, that Kleiber kills the fun.
● *Deutsche Grammophon 415 646-2* ● *2 CDs*
● *Full price* ● *ADD* ● *1976* ○

Safer, probably, is Karajan's 1950s version, in mono but beautifully clear, with Elisabeth Schwarzkopf in good form.
● *EMI CHS7 69531* ● *2 CDs* ● *Mid-price*
● *ADD* ● *1955*

Another safe bet is the very crisp, jolly stereo version led by Willy Boskovsky, for years the presiding genius of the Viennese New Year's Day Concert.
● *EMI CMS7 69354-2* ● *2 CDs* ● *Mid-price*
● *ADD*

With Lehár's *The Merry Widow*, it depends a bit on how much you want to pay. At full price, there's a classic 30-plus-year-old performance from Schwarzkopf.
● *EMI CDS7 47178-8* ● *2 CDs* ● *Full price*
● *AAD* ● *1962*

Slightly cheaper is a more all-round performance, not quite as sparkling perhaps, but a very straightforward account, conducted by Heinz Wallberg.
● *EMI CMS7 69940-2* ● *2 CDs* ● *Mid-price*
● *ADD* ● *1980*

● ● ● ●

THE BRITISH SENSE OF HUMOUR: GILBERT AND SULLIVAN

Another composer doomed (as he might see it) to be remembered for lighter works when he was ambitious for higher things, is Sir Arthur Sullivan (1842–1900). Yet it is for the series of light operas (known as the 'Savoy Operas', as most were written for Rupert D'Oyly Carte's Savoy Theatre), created in partnership with Sir William Schwenk Gilbert, that Sullivan will be musically remembered. No other composer waltzes down to posterity hand in hand with his librettist (apart from da Ponte, Piave and Boito, it's hard to name too many other librettists); and the fact that Gilbert demands such billing (he even gets credited on the cover of a recent release featuring only the overtures, which, naturally, don't contain a word by Gilbert) says a great deal about the works the two men wrote together. It's Gilbert's satirical words which tend to dominate (and only one, the earliest, *Trial By Jury*, 1866, has no spoken dialogue); although without Sullivan's easy flair for melody and ability to write good pastiche Verdi (a lot of the more 'serious' moments of the music have a definite sub-Verdi touch), the words wouldn't have anything like as memorable a framework. One or two of the Savoy Operas haven't travelled down the intervening century-and-a-bit too well, but several, including *HMS Pinafore* (1878), *The Pirates of Penzance* (1879), *Iolanthe* (1882), *The Mikado* (1885), and *The Gondoliers* (1889), retain most of their humour, and make great, relaxing, tuneful entertainments. *The Yeomen of the Guard* (1888) aims to be slightly more serious and comes close to being a good, if not great, British Romantic opera, although it doesn't have quite the hold on the memory that the purely comic works, with their absurd plots (and their slight hints of sadism; the relishing of extreme punishments in *The Mikado* teeters on the brink of perversity) and their verbal dexterity manage, to exercise. As is true of Offenbach and Johann Strauss, Gilbert's and Sullivan's natural descendants are the stage-musical composers, although Sullivan's music, with its occasional subtle touch of orchestration, is of a higher order than that of most musicals. The works were so successful in their day that it became necessary to introduce a system known as 'queuing' when tickets were being sold; a system which, like most of the Savoy Operas, has lasted into our own time.

DISCOGRAPHY
Most of the best Gilbert and Sullivan recordings were made in the 1960s by the D'Oyly Carte company, the doyens of G&S performance. These sets, or extracts from them, are almost exclusively available on Decca at mid-price. However, there's also a fairly new recording of *The Mikado* which really sparkles and shines, and which has a great deal of wit; it's conducted by Sir Charles Mackerras and features members of the Welsh National Opera company in top form. With no dialogue, it just manages to cram all the music onto one very generous CD.
● *Telarc CD80284* ● *1 CD* ● *Full price*
● *DDD* ● *1991* ✪

FRENCH OPERA BECOMES SERIOUS: GEORGES BIZET (1838–1875) AND *CARMEN*

Bizet never lived to see *Carmen* become a work of phenomenal popularity; and, ironically, on its debut in 1875 French audiences regarded it as 'too Wagnerian' because of the prominent role of the orchestra. His earlier work, *The Pearl Fishers* (1863), has managed to survive in the repertoire almost entirely because of the duet between the two leading men (entitled 'Au fond du temple saint', but known to all and sundry as 'The Duet from *The Pearl Fishers*') – something of a rarity in opera, a duet between two male singers. Apart from this *The Pearl Fishers* has a desperately creaky libretto; it's a tale of love, jealousy and (eventual) self-sacrifice, with Eastern overtones. That it has survived is largely because of the quality of the music which has, as the famous duet shows, a passionate, almost erotic, style.

Carmen (1875) has become one of the greatest and most famous of all operas, and several of its numbers are known well beyond the bounds of classical music aficionados – the Toreador Song and Carmen's two great arias, the 'Habanera' and the 'Seguidilla', to name but three. Part of its popularity stems from the plot: a soldier, José, abandons duty and homely love to follow the exotic, sensual gypsy Carmen, only eventually to be abandoned by her for the toreador Escamillo, after which José's only course of action is to kill the love of his life. The story of a man ruined by loving 'not wisely but too well' is always appealing; and Carmen herself, with the music Bizet has given her, has become almost an archetype of the wayward but utterly dazzling temptress. Actually, I find José an unbearably wet character and can't imagine what Carmen sees in him (except that she needs to dupe him to win her freedom); I also must confess that when Carmen isn't dominating the action, the opera goes to sleep. But Carmen herself is a fantastic creation, and the Spanish setting is dazzlingly realised in the best-known numbers; Spanish music was very popular with French composers in the latter part of the nineteenth century (Lalo's *Symphonie Espagnole*, Chabrier's *España*, Debussy's *Images*, and a whole host of works by Ravel were part of this trend). Despite the outcry from the original audience about the orchestrally dominant, Wagnerian nature of the piece, it is, at heart, a 'number opera', although the Finale achieves a synthesis of dialogue, music and drama, for José, for about the only time in the opera, asserts himself to become a real and deadly character.

DISCOGRAPHY
There are lots of fairly good recordings of *Carmen* around, including two very colourful recordings conducted by Herbert von Karajan. Karajan reconciles the two sides of the opera – the festively exotic and the grimly tragic – quite magnificently, and Agnes Baltsa is a tough, demanding Carmen, while Carreras makes a good, ardent José.
● *Deutsche Grammophon 410 088-2* ● *3 CDs*
● *Full price* ● *DDD* ● *1982; single highlights disc available* ✪

For slightly less money, however, an earlier version has the sultrily enticing Leontyne Price, with Franco Corelli very passionate (if occasionally slightly coarse).
● *RCA Gold Seal GD 86199* ● *3 CDs*
● *Mid-price* ● *ADD* ● *1964*

Placido Domingo is probably the definitive José among current performers, and his recording with Tatiana Troyanos for Solti has some very good characterisation, even if Solti does sometimes go over the top on climaxes (and is that such a bad thing?).
● *Decca 414 489-2* ● *2 CDs* ● *Full price* ● *ADD*

As for *Les Pêcheurs de Perles* (to give it its French title), there aren't many great versions around; the only real star with Michel Plasson is Barbara

Hendricks and she's fine, but somehow the whole experience falls short of what you feel it should be.
● *EMI CDS7 49837-2* ● *2 CDs* ● *Full price*
● *DDD* ● *1989*

Much better, though, to comb the recital discs and find a version of the famous duet by singers you like.

Biblical Epic: Saint-Saëns's *Samson et Dalila*

If part of the appeal of both *The Pearl Fishers* and *Carmen* was a perceived exoticism in their setting, that can also be found in the one great achievement amongst the thirteen operas by Camille Saint-Saëns (1835–1921), a dominant figure in French music in the second half of the nineteenth century. His opera *Samson et Dalila* appeared in 1877; it had originally been conceived as a non-dramatic sacred oratorio, although it's hard to see how much of the music in the opera could have been suitable in that context (but then, the French had a highly theatrical approach to religious music at this juncture, as Fauré's *Requiem* and various religious works by Berlioz indicate). *Samson*, which follows the biblical plot (slightly simplified; the hair isn't quite so important), is by no means a complex opera; the characterisation provided through the music is pretty two-dimensional (the Jews get one type of music, the Philistines get a bacchanal), yet there is some delightful melodic stuff in there – Samson's aria when at the mill at the beginning of Act 3, for instance, and, above all, Dalila's song of temptation, 'Mon coeur s'ouvre à ta voix' (known as 'Softly awakes my heart'). This isn't a great intellectual opera, but it can be very effective. As a subject both for music and for plot, the plight of Jewish folk had proved a winner earlier in the century for the then phenomenally popular Jacques Fromental Halèvy (1799–1862), whose opera *La Juive* (*The Jewess*; 1835) remained popular for more or less 100 years, providing one truly magnificent tenor aria ('Rachel, quand du Seigneur', 'Rachel, when from the Lord') which becomes a running joke in Marcel Proust's novel *À La Recherche du Temps Perdu*.

DISCOGRAPHY

Samson has recently become particularly associated with José Carreras; it was the opera with which he chose to return to Covent Garden after his near-fatal leukaemia, and his first major release after the illness. That release, with Agnes Baltsa as Dalila and Sir Colin Davis conducting, definitely has some merits, although Carreras's voice is a little coarse at times and Baltsa is a somewhat stentorian Dalila.
● *Philips 426 243-2* ● *2 CDs* ● *Full price* ● *1989*

The best version is currently available on CD only as a series of highlights, and in many ways this opera is best enjoyed in that format. Recorded in the early 1960s, it stars Jon Vickers, who manages to be both strong and sensitive, and a sultrily exotic Rita Gorr, with some passionate conducting by Georges Prêtre.
● *CDM7 63935-2* ● *1 CD* ● *Mid-price* ● *ADD* ● *1962*

FRENCH OPERA AT THE TURN OF THE CENTURY: MASSENET AND CHARPENTIER

The dominant operatic figure of the end of the nineteenth century in France is scarcely a household name now. Jules Massenet (1842–1912) is still remembered for his operas *Manon* (1884), an earlier version of the same story through which Giacomo Puccini first made his reputation, and *Werther* (1892), which was an international success, premièred in Vienna. Massenet's is an essentially melodic musical style, and his interest in the psychology of the plots he set was

minimal. Still, the audiences lapped it up, so one shouldn't feel too sorry for Massenet simply because his music has lost a great deal of its interest. Spare your sympathy instead for Gustave Charpentier (1860–1956), who lived into the second half of the twentieth century and enjoyed his biggest success by far in 1900 with *Louise*. This was a story of lower-class Bohemian life in Paris, rather after the style of Puccini, and in a musical manner somewhat reminiscent of him, employing musical phrases not as leitmotifs in the Wagnerian sense, but as being representative of characters and moods, and designed to evoke these at crucial points in the action. Actually *Louise* is a good deal more realistic than the Puccini 'realism' (or *verismo*); it has a certain enduring charm, but to be honest I find it a bit of a worthy bore. In any event two years later the first great twentieth-century opera – written anywhere – appeared in Paris, the first opera to move on from Wagner; *Pelléas et Mélisande* by Claude Debussy.

THE GREATEST FRENCH OPERA: CLAUDE DEBUSSY (1862–1918)

Pelléas is Debussy's only opera, yet its value doesn't lie merely in its uniqueness. Based on a very popular play by the Belgian Symbolist Maurice Maeterlinck, it tells the story of an enigmatic heroine, Mélisande, who is discovered in a forest by Prince Golaud. She marries the Prince, only to discover that she loves (and is loved by) Golaud's step-brother Pelléas. Pelléas struggles with his passion (to no avail); Golaud broods jealously and threatens Pelléas (taking him, in one memorable scene, to a dungeon deep in the earth); Mélisande – well, what is her role? The ambiguity of character, the half-understood nature of psychology, all combine to make *Pelléas* a modern opera. Like Wagner's *Tristan und Isolde*, to which *Pelléas* owes a musical debt (Debussy even quotes from it at one point), there is a love which claims lives, which seems even to demand that the lovers embrace their own death. Debussy, taking on a Symbolist drama, evolved a remarkable musical style, which was a logical development of his orchestral tone-poems. Like *Tristan*, his opera is not music rooted in tonality; indeed, it seems based in the old medieval modal system and may even owe something to Russian operatic writing by composers like Modest Mussorgsky. The dialogue/recitative is set to natural speech rhythms, and the manner of timing and pace is altogether different from that found in, say, Verdi or Puccini, or Massenet or Saint-Saëns. There is a certain leitmotif-like touch about certain musical phrases, but these are more abstract than Wagner's and much more allusive than similar phrases in Puccini. All of which goes to make *Pelléas* a deeply allusive, sometimes very shadowy, work; which means that done badly it can be a total bore, but done well it's an absorbing experience, a sound world all of its own, and certainly a candidate for the title 'greatest French opera ever written'.

DISCOGRAPHY
Pelléas is a deeply demanding work; first the conductor must have a real sense of how the drama operates, of the psychological process of the piece; second, the singers must be able to act, to hint at nuances of character. Probably the most effective recent conductor of the piece on disc is Claudio Abbado, who manages to steer the middle course between poetic and dramatic without sounding as though everything's a compromise. Not all the singing is ideal; Francois le Roux sounds ineffably wet as Pelléas, making José van

Dam's colourful Golaud too attractive, although Maria Ewing's Mélisande is highly sensual.
● *Deutsche Grammophon 435 345-2* ● *2 CDs*
● *Full price* ● *DDD* ● *1991* ❂

Pierre Boulez's 1960s recording was ground-breaking in that it took *Pelléas* out of the traditional manner in which Debussy is treated; instead of being all lush and dreamy it's actually quite hard and brisk. The singing is uniformly good, and anyone who usually finds Debussy a bit insipid will be very surprised by this version.
● *Sony SM3K 47265* ● *3 CDs* ● *Mid-price*
● *ADD* ● *1969*

One of the best versions around, though, was recorded in the 1950s (despite which the sound is rich, full and gorgeous). Camille Maurane plays Pelléas, and some regard him as the finest singer ever to take the role; the rest of the cast (which includes the delicious voice of Rita Gorr) is up to his standard, and the conducting of Jean Fournet is quite magical.
● *Philips 434 783-2* ● *2 CDs* ● *Mid-price*
● *ADD* ● *1953*

●●●●

RUSSIAN OPERA: MUSSORGSKY, GLINKA AND TCHAIKOVSKY

Russian opera began to make an impact in the West with *Boris Godunov* (1874) by Modest Mussorgsky (1839–1881). It emerged out of comedies about village life, which were determinedly nationalistic reactions against the influence of Paisiello and Cimarosa in the late eighteenth century. Folk song had a major influence on Russian opera from the start, in a way that it never touched the Western European art, and it was in some measure the earthy, modal folk timbre which gave the tonality of Russian opera an extra dimension, the extra melodic and harmonic dimension drawn on by Debussy when writing *Pelléas et Mélisande*. Favoured Russian plots were from history and fairy tales, often mixing the two together; thus one of the first Russian operas, Mikhail Glinka's *Ruslan and Lyudmila* (1842), deals with a Kiev princess and the enchantments of a wicked witch. The first great opera in Russian, *Boris Godunov*, is in fact a highly advanced work deeply rooted in the psychology of its historical characters; in scale and length and subject matter it is a grand opera, but a grand opera shut into a claustrophobic world of Tsarist power politics, with the underlying message that whoever wins the political game, the Russian people go on losing. Russian opera was highly political long before the Revolution of 1917.

The best-known Russian operas are probably two by Tchaikovsky; *Eugene Onegin* (1879) and *The Queen of Spades* (*Pikovaya Dama*; 1890). Both are based on works by the great Russian poet Alexander Pushkin (1799–1837). *Onegin* is an intense love story, with, at its centre, an apparently cold man who learns to love too late; it is particularly famous for the heroine's (Tatiana's) 'Love Scene' as she writes her declaration of love to the unresponsive Onegin, and for the aria by Lensky before a duel he is to fight with his friend Onegin. *The Queen of Spades* involves elements of satanism (rather weakened by the libretto written by Tchaikovsky and his brother Modest) and questions of fate, as well as one of the few interesting parts for an older woman singer, the Countess, who has the secret of winning at cards. The music of both these pieces is typical of Tchaikovsky at times, with shadows in *Onegin* of what was to come in the later symphonies. *The Queen of Spades* is often sung in French (in which it is known as *La Pique-Dame*) and has some vivid orchestral music when the composer is depicting hell or nature outraged by the gambler around whom the story revolves.

DISCOGRAPHY
Mussorgsky
Not every all-Russian recording of *Boris Godunov* has been a great success, but you can get the flavour of the work admirably from one of the exceptions, under conductor Vladimir Fedoseyev.
● *Philips 412 281-2* ● *3 CDs* ● *Full price*
● *ADD* ● *1984* ○

Tchaikovsky
There's a very good, reasonably priced highlights disc of *Eugene Onegin* from the very enjoyable version with conductor James Levine, and Thomas Allen as an excellent Eugene.
● *Deutsche Grammophon 431 611-2* ● *1 CD*
● *Mid-price* ● *ADD* ○

With no highlights disc of *The Queen of Spades* around, it's probably worth trying to get hold of (from a library, preferably) the recent set by Seiji Ozawa, which has some magnificent signing by Maureen Forrester (as the Countess) and others.
● *RCA Victor Red Seal RD09026 60992-2* ● *3 CDs* ● *Full price* ● *DDD* ● *1991*

THE END OF ITALIAN OPERA: CATALANI, MASCAGNI AND LEONCAVALLO

During the last decade of Verdi's life, as I've said, several younger operatic composers vied for the title of the 'new Verdi'. An immediate successor might have been Alfredo Catalani (1854–1893), most famous for *La Wally* (1892), which has survived principally in the soprano aria 'Ebben? . . . Ne andro lontana', featured in the film *Diva*. Catalani's music often tried to combine the influences of Verdi and Wagner, but not always with great success, and the drama of his work is somewhat diffuse. In any case, his early death ruled him out of the 'next Verdi' race. Early contenders included Pietro Mascagni (1863–1945) whose *Cavalleria Rusticana* ('rustic chivalry', 1890) established the principle of *verismo*, or realistic (*relatively* realistic) presentation of life in the lower strata of society; *verismo* was a key element in Italian opera for the next decade or so. *Cavalleria Rusticana* is one of the most famous short operas in the repertoire; it tells a story, set in the passionate, vendetta-ridden world of Sicily, about the battle of two men for one woman in a peasant village. *Cavalleria* won Mascagni a prize and established his reputation, and has provided three famous excerpts; the Orchestral Intermezzo, the Easter Hymn, and the Drinking Song. It is almost always performed on a double bill with a contemporary short opera, *I Pagliacci* (*The Clowns*, 1892) by Ruggiero Leoncavallo (1858–1919), a work which originally was *Cavalleria Rusticana*'s rival. *Pagliacci* crosses *verismo* with characters drawn from the stylised world of *commedia dell'arte*, which, in the opera, the travelling entertainers use to earn their living; the point being that Art mirrors Life, and Canio, who plays the cuckold in the 'show within the show', is playing the cuckold in real life. Canio's aria 'Vesti la giubba' ('On with the motley') has become one of the single most famous tenor arias in operatic repertoire; the famous Neapolitan tenor, Enrico Caruso (1873–1921), sold a million copies of a recording of it only a decade or so after the opera's first performance. Because of the similarity of their themes; because their music, although distinct, shares a similar background; and because one of these pieces on its own would seem like bad value for money; *Cav'n'Pag* are now linked together, probably for eternity.

DISCOGRAPHY
Although Pavarotti has included 'Vesti la giubba' from *I Pagliacci* in his concert repertoire for many years, he isn't the ideal Canio in any complete set (not yet, anyway, and least of all on his brand-new recording). There is a combination of *Cav'n'Pag* featuring Maria Callas and Giuseppe di Stefano, both operas conducted by Tullio Serafin,

and with a terrifically well characterised performance as the hunchback Tonio by the great Tito Gobbi. The recording is slightly dry, but the singers create an atmosphere all their own.
EMI CDS7 47981-8 ● *3 CDs* ● *Full price* ● *ADD* ● *1953/4* ☉

Do it the cheap way; Naxos offer the two operas completely separately (which will still only cost around £10/11 for both), although the performances could be a little more vivid.
Naxos 8.66001/2-2 ● *Bargain price* ● *DDD* ● *1992*

There's an excellent version of *Pag* with Domingo and Monserrat Caballé which comes, unusually, not with *Cav*, but with part of Puccini's *Il Trittico*, the grim and melodramatic (yet terrifically done) *Il Tabarro*.
RCA Gold Seal GD 60865 ● *2 CDs* ● *Mid-price* ● *ADD* ● *1971*

● ● ● ●

MORE PRETENDERS TO VERDI'S THRONE: FRANCHETTI AND CILEA

Neither Mascagni nor Leoncavallo ever repeated their early success in quite the same way (Mascagni ended up a supporter of Mussolini's fascist regime, and thus an entirely discredited figure); but both were hailed as potential 'new Verdis'. Another contender was Alberto Franchetti (1860–1942), whose 1892 opera *Cristoforo Colombo*, written for the 400th anniversary of the discoverer's most celebrated voyage, was greeted with extreme enthusiasm; so much so that Franchetti was seen as the composer of the opera that would, inevitably, be based on the melodramatic play then generally considered the hottest property around; Victorien Sardou's *La Tosca*. Franchetti actually acquired the rights to the piece, but some devious manoeuvring a few years later made sure that he surrendered them. This is probably just as well; the revival of Franchetti's work to celebrate the 500th anniversary of Columbus's arrival in the West Indies didn't immediately commend it as the work of a master. But Franchetti had his supporters who saw him as 'the new Verdi'. So too did Francesco Cilea (1865–1950), although his most successful work, *Adriana Lecouvreur*, didn't appear until 1902, and even then was somewhat overshadowed by more sensational works in both Italy and Germany. Umberto Giordano (1867–1948) had some success with *Andrea Chenier* (1896), which is still performed today, but it's scarcely the most musically memorable of works.

SEX, VIOLENCE AND MELODIES: PUCCINI

Ironically enough, Puccini made his reputation with a setting of a libretto by his rival Leoncavallo. *Manon Lescaut* was based on the same story (the Abbé Prévost's novel *Manon Lescaut*) as Massenet's *Manon*, but is an altogether more remarkable work than the other opera, even if not in the same league as Puccini's later masterpieces. Passionate vocal writing, clever manipulation of the orchestra, multi-layered musical writing, with crowds and soloists engaged on different but reconcilable themes and melodies; all these facets of Puccini's later work are already in place. Either it all moves you completely or else you find it way over the top; but then, of course, you could say that of all of Puccini's work.

La Bohème

Most of Puccini's contemporaries had started with great success, only to find a sequel to that success elusive. Puccini was possibly taking a double risk in using a story which Leoncavallo had already set, *La Bohème* (although Leoncavallo's opera was not produced until fifteen months after Puccini's).

The result was a sensation, establishing Puccini as an international star in the musical firmament. Cunningly, he had descended to the *verismo* world of poor, Bohemian artists in an impoverished Parisian quarter, but instead of presenting this as some hard-hitting, tough world, and in a manner designed to shock, Puccini subtly sentimentalised his Bohemians, so that the whole work became one long, classic weepie. The love of Mimi and the poet Rodolfo in some way mirrors that of Violetta and Alfredo in *Traviata*; after initial happiness she leaves him, believing it is for his good, but then returns to his side to die of TB.

Alongside the tender, pathetic story of Mimi and Rodolfo is the on-off relationship of two other Bohemians, the painter Marcello and Musetta. *La Bohème* is an opera all about feeling and contains some of the best-loved show-stopping arias in the business, especially Rodolfo's big first-act number 'Che gelida manina' ('Your tiny hand is frozen', as it has been immortally translated). This set-piece meeting, in which Rodolfo and Mimi introduce themselves to one another, is fairly typical of the way Puccini works; lush but subtle orchestration underpinning melody which manages to encompass both natural speech rhythms and the declamatory passion of grand operatic arias. And, of course, being Puccini, there are big tunes galore; apart from 'Che gelida manina', there's Musetta's Waltz. *Bohème* is, like *Carmen*, one of those operas which rarely fails when staged, and has become a sure-fire box-office banker for opera companies.

Tosca

After *Bohème* had become such a huge success, Puccini cast around for a new

Giacomo Puccini
1858–1924

Compared with many of his contemporaries, Puccini was a slow starter. Hailing from the walled Tuscan town of Lucca, he was trained as a chorister and organist, but from the age of seventeen he set his sights on a career as an operatic composer. His early works *Edgar* and *Le Villi* (*The Witches*) signally failed to set the world alight; but after three consecutive successes between 1893 and 1900, he became accepted in both Italy and the rest of Europe as the leading composer of Italian opera. His career was rather interrupted after *Madam Butterfly* (1904) by a court case over the suicide of a servant girl whom Puccini's wife accused (falsely) of having had an affair with her husband.

Although the outcome of all this upheaval was in Puccini's favour, the rate of flow of his composition was slowed down by it; however, his work didn't take on a significantly darker hue. He died before he could finish his final opera, *Turandot*, which was then completed by the composer Franco Alfano (1876–1954), from sketches Puccini had left.

subject. He considered *Pelléas et Mélisande* (pretty hard to imagine, just as Debussy's *Tosca* can scarcely be contemplated), but his real interest lay with the melodrama that Franchetti owned the rights to. And so he and his manager laid a plot whereby they convinced Franchetti that *Tosca* would never make a decent opera; he gave up his rights, and Puccini stepped in. The result was a phenomenon in the history of opera; just how it is that Puccini had this hot-line to audience emotions is not something we can ever completely understand, but if *Bohème* hit the popular nerve, then *Tosca* dug even deeper (even though its first performance wasn't quite the sensation its predecessor's had been). Lots of composers were waiting for Puccini to fall flat on his face, and the circumstances of the Rome première

didn't help; *Tosca*, a deeply republican piece espousing an anti-clerical, anti-authoritarian view of Roman life in 1800, was subject to bomb threats on its opening night. In the audience were several people hoping to see a fiasco; Franchetti was there of course, as was Cilea, while Mascagni deliberately and spitefully entered his box after the curtain rose, so that he would draw some applause from his supporters in the theatre in the middle of the opening scene.

He was fighting a losing battle. *Tosca* may be, as one critic called it in the middle of this century, a 'shabby shocker', but it hits the guts every time (at least, when it's done properly). At its heart is the opposition between Scarpia, the corrupt Police Chief, infatuated with the opera singer Floria Tosca, and the atheist and republican artist Mario Cavaradossi, Tosca's lover. Scarpia tries to use the lovers' relationship for his own ends, first to trap Cavaradossi and another republican Bonapartist sympathiser, then to blackmail Tosca into sleeping with him. The scene at the heart of Act 2, where Tosca confronts Scarpia and eventually kills him, is the culmination of the opera; unfortunately she's under the misapprehension that her lover's execution will be faked. Scarpia, being Scarpia, reaches out even from beyond the grave and thwarts them, leaving Tosca to hurl herself, crying a curse on Scarpia, from the battlements of the Castel San'Angelo. Every act has its great aria or two; Cavaradossi's 'Recondita armonia' in Act 1 and the very famous 'É lucevan le stelle' in the third act; Tosca's 'Vissi d'arte', which, with its cry of 'I lived for art', is often regarded as the great soprano's self-justification (there are those who regard this aria as Maria Callas's theme tune); and Scarpia's sardonic, twisted asides during the memorable conclusion to the first act, a massive celebratory Te Deum, as well as his blackmail demand to Tosca in the second act. *Tosca* moves from climax to climax, from great aria to great duet to set-piece, and yet manages to keep continuous and organic dramatic unity, never seeming like a sequence of numbers; very often the asides are as telling as the arias, and the orchestral setting of the dialogue is remarkably cunning. The thing about *Tosca* is that although it is – and always should be – a great visceral experience, it's also got a great deal more going for it intellectually than is often allowed.

Madam Butterfly

Puccini said that he never found composing as easy again after *Tosca*, but this didn't stop him creating works which hold a more or less equal place with *Tosca* in the public affection. *Madam Butterfly* (1904) was at least partly inspired by a craze for Oriental art, history and culture which had spread over Europe around the turn of the century (although this was also informed by a fear of Japan as the territorially ambitious 'Yellow Peril'). The opera is said to have been based on a true story; certainly the idea that an American naval lieutenant like Pinkerton would have 'married' a geisha, given her a child, and then abandoned her to go back home and take up family life is more than credible. But Pinkerton's motives are never in doubt, even though he shares the burden of half of one of the most memorable elongated love duets in Italian opera towards the end of Act 1 (where it's noticeable that he wants to get Butterfly to bed, whereas she wants to admire the landscape). The centre of the opera is Butterfly; the tragedy of her devoted love and her abandonment of her native tradition; her isolation as she sings another of the great and famous Puccini arias 'Un bel di vedremo' ('One fine day', which has been turned into a chart hit by former Sex Pistols guru Malcolm McLaren); her hopeless delusion, and the inevitable but still harrowing outcome when she discovers her mistake and realises that Pinkerton and his wife wish to take away even her child. It adds something of a (not entirely pleasant) frisson to realise that Butterfly is supposed to be about fifteen years old at the start of the opera. Again the music is ravishing, and Puccini mixes in some fake Orientalism (using the same 'Japanese' melody which Sullivan appropriated for *The Mikado*), as well as the American tune 'The Star-spangled Banner'.

La Fanciulla del West (The Girl of the Golden West); Il Trittico (The Triptych)

If *Butterfly* was an 'exotic' opera, then so, technically, was *La Fanciulla del West* (1910), set in the California Gold Rush of 1849. Just as he'd tried to inject some kind of Orientalism into *Butterfly*, Puccini sought to work some American tunes into *Girl*, although he consciously aimed at a more realistic, less soft, depiction of his subject matter; which is probably why there are effectively no arias from this opera which have made it into the public's consciousness or into the general cultural frame of reference. The fact that Puccini had come to find writing less easy is plain in the lack of lyricism, although his melodic gift wasn't quite dead yet. The three one-act operas gathered together as *Il Trittico* (1918) showed something of a return to old form; first in the hard, stark *verismo* melodrama of *Il Tabarro* (*The Cloak*), another tale of adultery and revenge amongst the impoverished; then in the beautiful aria 'Senza Mamma' ('Without Mamma') in the second opera *Suor Angelica* (*Sister Angelica*), a story about sin and redemption set in a convent; and finally in the brilliant pacing of Puccini's one piece of *opera buffa*, *Gianni Schicchi*, a superb medieval pantomime set in Florence, with some brilliantly parodic music, a breakneck pace ideal for farce and, crashing in suddenly, the famous aria 'O Mio babbino caro' ('O My beloved father', featured in TV commercials and the film of E. M. Forster's novel *A Room With A View*), which has some claim to be one of the best tunes Puccini ever wrote. That aria apart, there's not otherwise an iota of sentimentality in *Gianni Schicchi*, making it unique in Puccini's output.

Turandot

Puccini's final opera also looked for an exotic setting; *Turandot* (first performed in 1926; Puccini didn't live to finish it and the final act was completed by Alfano) is set in China, and Puccini tried not only to create some fake chinoiserie, but also to include some genuine Chinese melodies. How he would have wanted the opera to end we don't know (as it is, it ends happily for everyone except the poor slave girl Liù, who dies under torture to preserve the secret of her master Calaf's name), and certainly the last act is something of a compromise musically. In the first two acts, however, Puccini's timing is again remarkable, and there are some nice orchestral colours, all part of the 'Oriental' effects. *Turandot* always works, though, because of the conflict between the 'Ice Maiden' Empress Turandot and the impassioned hero Calaf; an opposition surrounded by an atmosphere of sexual tension, threats, torture and violence, as Turandot beheads anyone who can't answer her riddles. This is, of course, the opera which contains the aria 'Nessun Dorma', which was such a massive commercial success in the UK in 1990 as a result of TV exposure during the Football World Cup; it is, interestingly, the one true piece of Puccini-esque lyricism in the opera, the only really Italian touch which marks this out as the work of the same composer as *La Bohème*.

DISCOGRAPHY
Manon Lescaut
Puccini's operas offer such marvellous tunes that most singers who specialise in the Italian repertoire want to perform and record them. Very often one is spoilt for choice, although in several cases there are clear favourites; and in the case of *Tosca* there is one absolute classic. But I doubt if any potential Puccini collector would want to start with *Manon Lescaut*; should I be wrong, however, there are two reasonably priced complete sets. One

stars Renata Tebaldi (who spent the peak of her career rivalling Maria Callas in Milan); Tebaldi has a beautiful voice, ethereal at times, but she's not a great actress, and her tenor on most recordings is Mario del Monaco, a man for whom the word 'stentorian' could have been invented.
● *Decca 430 253-2* ● *2 CDs* ● *Mid-price*
● *ADD* ● *1956*

A slightly earlier version doesn't have quite as good recorded sound, but does have the remarkable Jussi Bjoerling.
● *RCA Gold Seal GD 60573* ● *3 CDs*
● *Mid-price* ● *ADD* ● *1954*

Otherwise, the best aria from *Manon Lescaut* turns up on various compilations, being especially well done by Placido Domingo on an arias-and-duets collection also featuring Caballé, Bjoerling, Victoria de los Angeles, and quite a few other big names.
● *EMI CDZ7 62520-2* ● *1CD* ● *Mid-price*
● *ADD* ● *1957–71*

La Bohème
The 'most famous tenor in the world' helped establish his reputation by playing Rodolfo in *La Bohème*, and the recording he made at round about the same time, with Mirella Freni as Mimi and Herbert von Karajan conducting the Berlin Philharmonic, stands as the most rapturous and accomplished *Bohème* in the catalogue. Pavarotti's voice is magnificent here, and Freni makes a hugely appealing Mimi; Karajan's princely control of the orchestra makes for a superb all-round experience.
● *Decca 414 049-2* ● *2 CDs* ● *Full price*
● *ADD* ● *1971* ✪

A good second choice was recorded some 37 years ago and stars Jussi Bjoerling and Victoria de los Angeles, with Sir Thomas Beecham his usual stirring self with the baton.
● *EMI CDS7 47235-8* ● *2 CDs* ● *Full price*
● *ADD* ● *1956*

Tosca
When, in the 1950s, producer Walter Legge gathered into the studio Maria Callas, Tito Gobbi and Giuseppe di Stefano, along with the Orchestra of La Scala and conductor Victor de Sabata, I wonder if he realised quite how great a recording he was making. Callas insisted that she felt no special empathy for the part above other roles, yet her recorded performance on this set remains, over 40 years later, the greatest Tosca; an intelligent, passionate woman faced with the greatest dilemma and threat to her faith. Gobbi's Scarpia is the most consummate on record, too, not just a villain and a hypocrite, but possibly a man consumed with self loathing, most fascinated by what most repels him. Di Stefano gives arguably his greatest performance on disc, while de Sabata's conducting is subtle without losing passion. The sound, although mono, is excellent.
● *EMI CDS7 47175-8* ● *2 CDs* ● *Full price*
● *ADD* ● *1953* ✪

There are other good sets of *Tosca*; José Carreras's first recording of the role of Cavaradossi is his most persuasive, and Caballé makes a human and vulnerable Tosca. Ingvar Wixell is gruff as Scarpia, while Sir Colin Davis's conducting is sumptuous and lavish; the best stereo *Tosca*, and recently reissued as part of Philips's 'Two for the Price of One' series – a bargain.
● *Philips 438 359-2* ● *2 CDs* ● *Special price*
● *ADD* ● *1976*

A favoured mid-price alternative is Karajan's version with Leontyne Price. She is marvellous, her rich tones making something quite different of the title role (there has never been an earthier Tosca); Karajan, however, is eccentric in his tempos, full of showy melodramatic pauses which hold things up and get in the way.
● *Decca 421 670-2* ● *2 CDs* ● *Mid-price*
● *ADD* ● *1971*

Also at mid-price is what might seem like a historical curiosity: *Tosca* starring one of the century's greatest tenors, Beniamino Gigli (1890–1957), as Cavaradossi. Actually this recording, whose sound, although thin, has transferred surprisingly well to CD, is a memorable performance, not just for Gigli (who is magnificent), but for the orchestral precision and timing of conductor Olivier de Fabritiis.
● *EMI CHS7 63338-2* ● *2 CDs* ● *Mid-price*
● *ADD* ● *1938*

The super-cheap Naxos recording makes a decent alternative; the orchestral sound is perhaps a bit less sumptuous than one might like, but the radiant and beautiful voice of Nelly Miricoiu as Tosca is a treat well worth the cover price.
● *Naxos 8.660001/2* ● *2 CDs* ● *Bargain price*
● *DDD* ● *1990*

Please note that I wouldn't recommend any of the recordings featuring Domingo or Pavarotti; both make superb Cavaradossis, but never quite on record, for some reason.

Madam Butterfly
The most gorgeous *Butterfly* is great value for money. Renata Scotto may not have the most purely beautiful voice among sopranos, but she is a superb actress, well able to convey the emotional range of the part, while Carlo Bergonzi is a practised Pinkerton; in fact, there's not a weak link in the cast, while the conducting of Sir John Barbirolli is passionate and full of drama.
● *EMI CMS7 69654-2* ● *2 CDs* ● *Mid-price*
● *ADD* ● *1966* ✪

The Naxos version is very competitive, with conductor Alexander Rahbari bringing real passion and intensity to the score and Maltese soprano Miriam Gauci giving a performance of great distinction.
● *Naxos 8.660015/6* ● *2 CDs* ● *Bargain price*
● *DDD* ● *1991*

La Fanciulla del West

There's no need to get into the full-price bracket if you're after *La Fanciulla del West* either, as the Renate Tebaldi performance from the early 1960s has made a brilliant transfer to CD. This is one of those Tebaldi recordings where everything is right, even the sense of drama, even Mario del Monaco, and it gets a Rosette in the *Penguin CD Guide*.

● *Decca 421 595-2* ● *2 CDs* ● *Mid-price*
● *ADD* ● *1958* ○

Il Trittico

Likewise, anyone wanting the whole of *Il Trittico* shouldn't pay full whack; there's a good collection of three recordings of the opera (or three operas) made by conductor Giuseppe Patanè. The casting isn't always ideal, but the drama is always communicated, and *Gianni Schicchi* is very well done indeed.

● *RCA/Eurodisc GD 69043* ● *3 CDs*
● *Mid-price* ● *DDD* ● *1985* ○

However, all most people really want of *Il Trittico* is the aria 'O mio babbino caro', which is to be found on almost any Puccini anthology, including collections of soprano arias.

Turandot

The greatest *Turandot* is indeed the obvious one, with Pavarotti in quite superb form as Calaf, matched by a frightening performance from Joan Sutherland in the title role and a truly pathos-evoking Liù by Caballé. Zubin Mehta, always a showman, is terrific here; this is the side of his conducting personality that gets results, that achieves real drama. A great and abiding recording, well worth lashing out the full price for.

● *Decca 414 275-2* ● *2 CDs* ● *Full price*
● *ADD* ● *1972* ○

More than just a historical curiosity is a selection of highlights from a Covent Garden performance from the season celebrating the coronation of King George VI. Dame Eva Turner was one of the greatest interpreters of the role of Turandot, and Giovanni Martinelli was a fine Calaf; add in Sir John Barbirolli and an excellent CD transfer and you have a document of great artistic merit and fascination.

● *EMI CDH7 61074-2* ● *1 CD* ● *Mid-price*
● *ADD* ● *1937*

WHATEVER HAPPENED TO ITALIAN OPERA? BUSONI, DALLAPICCOLA

Apart from Puccini, Italians seem to have contributed little to opera in the twentieth century. Was it the overwhelming shadow of Verdi that inhibited progress? Was it the inevitably stifling force of fascism through the 1920s and 1930s? After the majority of Puccini's operas, one is thrown towards either the feeble one-act operetta *Il Segreto di Susanna* (*Susanna's Secret*, 1909; the 'secret' of the title is that the heroine smokes, and the whole thing was clearly sponsored by the tobacco industry in the days before commercialised snooker) by Ermanno Wolf-Ferrari (1876–1948); or else to the work of Ferruccio Busoni (1866–1924), who insisted that his music emanated entirely from German influences and who worked out of Germany for most of his life. Busoni is an interesting composer, a fascinating theorist who had a great fervour for Bach (he arranged various Bach organ works for piano) and wrote one great opera, *Doktor Faust*. This is a version of the legend which eschews the sentimentality and ultimate redemption offered (after the play by Goethe) in most of the late-nineteenth-century accounts, and leaves Faust defiant of God and goodness to his death. The characterisation of Mephistopheles is particularly vivid and memorable; unfortunately, however, this is another incomplete opera, finished by a student of the composer, so it does tail off a bit. This remains, though, the best operatic realisation of the Faust story (unless you cheekily include *Don Giovanni*), both musically and intellectually, and it has been revived recently on the stage to great effect.

The only subsequent Italian operatic composer of note is Luigi Dallapiccola (1904–1975), who was forced underground during the latter part of the fascist regime. Dallapiccola was always an unrepentant and determined Modernist, wedded to the technique of the twelve-note tone-row. Arid though that technique can sometimes sound (rooted as it is in the idea that every element of a piece of music must always be based on the particular tone-row and its inversions, reversals and other geometric alterations, and all done by a strict schema), Dallapiccola achieved some fabulously beautiful effects, full of drama, passion and, amazingly, lyricism, both in his one-act allegorical piece *Il Prigioniero* (*The Prisoner*; 1949) and in his masterpiece *Ulisse* (1968). These works are very accessible; some of Calypso's music in the latter is quite moving.

Unfortunately there are no recordings available at present, although there are rumours that some are forthcoming. The recording industry should attend to this gap immediately.

DISCOGRAPHY
Busoni
Busoni's *Doktor Faust* is an expensive purchase, but, again, a library borrowing of the best version, which stars Dietrich Fischer-Dieskau would prove more than worthwhile.
● *Deutsche Grammophon 427 413-2* ● *3 CDs*
● *Mid-price* ● *ADD* ● *1969*

GERMAN OPERA: ENGELBERT HUMPERDINCK (1854–1921)

The intellectual battle between Verdi and Wagner was waged with great ferocity by their adherents, although with hindsight it does seem that the Germanic lobby was the more forward-looking faction. Not that that case is necessarily proved by the operatic composer who emerged immediately from Wagner's entourage. Engelbert Humperdinck had worked as Wagner's assistant on *Parsifal*, yet he is best remembered for the comic fairy-tale opera *Hansel and Gretel* (1893), a charming, cunningly written, beautifully orchestrated entertainment, especially popular in opera houses at Christmas. Humperdinck mixed up children's jingles with the harmonic influence of his great master, and it all works very well; but it is, inevitably,

fundamentally lightweight – and therein lies the secret of his success. A later, more overtly dramatic, work like the melodrama *Königskinder* (*Royal Children*; 1897) comes over as rather heavy, over-egged cake.

DISCOGRAPHY
To experience *Hansel and Gretel* at its most subtle, and in the hands of a fine modern operatic conductor, listen to the recent recording with Jeffrey Tate.
● *EMI CDS7 54022-2* ● *2 CDs* ● *Full price*
● *DDD* ● *1990* ✪

FROM CONTROVERSY TO CONSERVATISM: RICHARD STRAUSS

The great German successor to Wagner was in fact Richard Strauss, who established his operatic reputation with two of the most controversial operas of the first decade of the twentieth century (the controversy was all carefully hyped), and consolidated it with a perennially popular piece that represented a backward step – but a very charming one. Strauss's earliest forays into opera, *Guntram* (1894) and *Feuersnot* ('fire disaster', sometimes given as *No Fire in the City*; 1901), didn't make much of an impression. But then he followed up a suggestion from Kaiser Wilhelm II that he should try writing something based on a biblical story; doubtless the fiesta of perversion, sexuality and terror which is *Salome* (1905) wasn't quite what the Kaiser had in mind (in fact we know it wasn't, for the Kaiser expressed his fear that *Salome* would do its composer nothing but harm). Nonetheless, by taking Oscar Wilde's stylised version of the story of the death of John the Baptist, Strauss found a subject ideal for his musical style, and turned Wilde's squib into a masterpiece.

Salome

Salome is a work straight out of the hothouse, full of chromatic sliding and slipping in and out of tonality. This is one of Strauss's most exciting ways of characterising; most of the personae of the opera are so out of kilter that every time they try to start off a beautiful singable melody, it slips out of tune, up or down the scale. Herod, obsessed with lust for his stepdaughter Salome, keeps setting off on tunes that might have been written by Strauss's namesake, the 'Waltz King', but the tune and rhythm always break up. Salome herself, in a most arduous soprano role (it may be only a one-act opera, but it's very intense and demanding to perform), is given music of great beauty, yet its beauty is outlandish, exotic, drenched and dripping with too much harmonic uncertainty. Only Jokanaan (John the Baptist) is capable of staying in a simple, melodic tonality, as he sings of Christ and salvation; yet much of his music is as monomaniacally weird as Salome's or Herod's, as he utters denunciations of Herod, his wife Herodias, and then finally, memorably, curses Salome. Her temptation of Jokanaan is a scene of ever-increasing climax; so too her fifteen-minute monologue at the end, as she sings her perverse love song to the prophet's severed head, requires a tour de force from its singer; it's certainly a tour de force as a piece of operatic writing. Strauss's use of motif is breathtaking; he doesn't build his opera out of these phrases like Wagner, but uses them to such dramatic effect that the screw of tension is turned and turned. All this and the orchestral showpiece, the 'Dance of the Seven Veils' . . . *Salome*, for all its perversity, is one of the great musical achievements of the twentieth century.

Elektra

So too is *Elektra* (1909), another intense one-act piece, which marked the collaboration between Strauss and the librettist Hugo von Hoffmansthal. Based on Sophocles's play about the daughter of the murdered King Agamemnon awaiting the return of her brother Orestes, in order to persuade him to exact vengeance on her mother Klytemnestra and her mother's lover, Aegisth, for their conspiracy to murder the king, *Elektra* is as steeped in blood and violence as *Salome* is in sex. The palace of Agamemnon is a diseased place, revolving around a diseased queen; Strauss's portrayal of Klytemnestra, who has only the one scene (although it is a stunning scene), is the most remarkable thing in the opera, and possibly the nearest thing to Modernist music that Strauss ever wrote. Klytemnestra is haunted by a 'dream which is not a dream', which threatens to suffocate her, and as she relates this dream in one of the great operatic monologues, the music slides around the whole tonal range. What makes this especially claustrophobic is that she drags the orchestral accompaniment with her (the orchestra's role is just as forward in Strauss as in Wagner) around the whole tonal possibility of the Western system. In this opera, Strauss betrays his (and Hoffmansthal's) essential conservatism by allotting stable tonality to passages in which Elektra's sister, Chrysothemis, sings of her desire to have children (although this pure tonality is later parodied when Elektra hits the same tonality to try to persuade Chrysothemis to carry out the murder which she is too weak to perform herself). *Elektra* is a powerful, brooding piece – and, like *Salome*, sometimes almost too exhausting to endure.

Der Rosenkavalier (The Knight of the Rose)

After *Elektra*, Strauss seemed to take a step back from the brink, and opted to set something altogether more 'civilised' and Classical. *Der Rosenkavalier* (1911) is a cod-eighteenth-century piece, even reviving the tradition of having a female voice singing the role of the romantic lead. Of course, what lay behind this tradition in the eighteenth century was the concept of the castrato male singer; used by Strauss in the twentieth century, however, it added a refined twist, a slight perversion, for when the curtain goes up the audience is confronted by the sight of two women in bed together, clearly in the afterglow of sexual passion. The story, again with a libretto by Hoffmansthal, has a civilised romantic plot, in which the middle-aged Marschallin realises that she must relinquish her toy-boy Oktavian to allow him to marry his new love Sophie, who is his own age. Around all this is a sub-plot of sexual identity-confusion (Oktavian has been masquerading as a girl) centring on the lusts of the country cousin buffoon Baron Ochs. In the opera's last act, buffoonery gives way to gentility as the Marschallin makes way for Sophie, in the celebrated and luscious harmonic Trio which, in terms of erotic and melodic beauty, is much more successful than the duet by the two young lovers.

Rosenkavalier is written in a musical language that is clearly post-Wagnerian, with lots of close, dense harmonies which, to a certain extent, slither around the tonal range. But it is also clearly influenced by the period in which the opera is set, although some of the musical devices used to heighten the lush Romanticism (most especially the Waltz), are clearly anachronistic. The use of three leading ladies adds something extraordinary to the vocal texture, while Ochs, as buffoon, is a more realistic character than some. In some ways this highly sophisticated work, with its slight overtones of decadence, is as much about the imperial societies of Germany and Austria at the time of its composition as about the eighteenth century; *Rosenkavalier* is to some extent a lavish champagne picnic on the edge of a volcano.

STRAUSS AFTER *ROSENKAVALIER*

Strauss's career didn't exactly go downhill after *Rosenkavalier*; in fact, he continued to make money at a phenomenal rate. After he'd seen how the backward-looking style of *Rosenkavalier* could succeed at the box-office, he chose to stay mainly within that style, or something very like it. He had little or no sympathy for the 'new music' of the slightly younger composers of the Second Viennese School, and perhaps his opting for musical conservatism was a reaction against their work. His next opera, *Ariadne auf Naxos* (*Ariadne on Naxos*, performed in 1912 and then re-presented in 1916 with a Prologue), could, however, be seen as a modernist, even Post-Modernist work in some sense, as it takes apart the whole business of mounting stage shows, again against an eighteenth-century background. In the opera's proportions, Strauss and Hoffmansthal had returned to the one-act shape; however, the angst of those earlier works was gone in this tale of a new *opera seria* being forced to combine with a *commedia dell'arte* entertainment to save the Patron's time, while the Composer fumes. There are some serious moments in the 'opera-within-the-opera', but these are undercut by the buffoonery of the Composer (another 'trouser', that is, woman-playing-a-man, role). In keeping with his neo-Classical theme, Strauss cut resources down to a chamber orchestra; very different indeed from his next work, which he had hopes would be both his *Zauberflöte* and his *Parsifal. Die Frau Ohne Schatten* (*The Wife without a Shadow*) is a huge setting of a fairy tale; the longest opera Strauss ever wrote, it goes in for special effects on a grand scale – the earth caving in, subterranean rivers, people turning to stone – all of which are given vivid life in the music. And yet something about *Die Frau* has never quite clicked; partly the conservatism of its message (that a woman who isn't prepared to have children is incomplete), partly the over-sympathetic portrayal of Barak the Dyer, the wronged husband whose wife is prepared to sell her shadow (which represents her child-bearing capacity), and partly the lack of any single truly memorable scene like the seduction scene from *Salome* or the Trio from *Rosenkavalier*.

In the rest of his operatic work, Strauss would look to explore various types of musical expression. *Intermezzo* (1924), for instance, for which he wrote his own libretto, runs the whole gamut of different methods of setting dialogue. His final opera, *Capriccio* (1942), described as a 'conversation piece', and again reverting to the one-act formula, dramatises the dilemma of whether words or music contribute more to an opera through the problems of the Countess, who cannot choose between a poet and a musician (the libretto was written by the great conductor Clemens Krauss [1893–1954]).

Capriccio, written in the depths of the Second World War, is set at the time of Gluck's opera reforms and incorporates a whole load of eighteenth-century dance styles. The music for it is, like all Strauss's fake-eighteenth-century café music, sumptuous, rich and highly enjoyable, like a Viennese cream cake.

DISCOGRAPHY

Salome

The demands Strauss's operas make on singers, conductors and orchestral players are vast. *Salome* has not often been recorded – indeed, Carlos Kleiber has frequently excused himself from the idea of conducting it either in the opera house or the studio by saying that there isn't a singer around to take the title role. That is no longer true of the studio, however; Cheryl Studer's interpretation for Giuseppe Sinopoli is without peer, managing to create a Salome who is enticing, obstreperous, and yet always young. Sinopoli's conducting, too, is supremely intelligent, and some of the supporting cast are outstanding; the young Welsh baritone Bryn Terfel gives the best ever Jokanaan, a sweetly lyrical performance which makes perfect sense of the syrup-like music given to the prophet, while losing none of the character's *gravitas*.

● *Deutsche Grammophon 431 810-2* ● 2 CDs
● *Full price* ● *DDD* ● *1990* ✪

Until Sinopoli came along, the best *Salome* around was Georg Solti's starring Birgit Nilsson; a superbly dramatic, rich experience, with some brilliant sound from the orchestra. Nilsson is a very strong, Valkyrie-like Salome (perhaps a shade too much so), but everyone is upstaged by Gerhard Stolze's amazing Herod, a character tenor who imagines he's a Heldentenor and can't measure up. This may no longer be the clear market-leader, but it's still a great recording.
● *Decca 414 414-2* ● 2 CDs ● *Full price*
● *ADD* ● *1962*

If the recordings I've mentioned seem too expensive, there's a good cheaper alternative starring Montserrat Caballé (a Salome to be heard rather than seen, with all respect to her), whose sweet voice does sound very young, although she's not entirely sure with the German pronunciation, and a good, clean reading of the score by the underrated Erich Leinsdorf.
● *RCA Gold Seal GD96644* ● 2 CDs
● *Mid-price* ● *ADD* ● *1969*

Elektra

For a long time Solti's was also the leading version of *Elektra*, although the relentless use of studio techniques was something of a *cause célèbre* in its day – was this music-making or just technology run rampant? Nilsson takes the lead again, and the strong-willed *Elektra* is a part to which she is more or less ideally suited, while Regina Resnik makes a colourfully evil Klytemnestra, especially at her supposed moment of triumph. Solti's reading of the score is certainly vivid, if a little over-given to assuming that it's simply a progression of exciting moments rather than a unified drama.

● *Decca 417 345-2* ● *2 CDs* ● *Full price*
● *ADD* ● *1968* ○

However, that version now has a rival, which is marked by a fierce and very clever reading of the score by Wolfgang Sawallisch. The leading role is taken by Eva Marton, who has shown a tendency to record too many roles which don't suit her, although she, like Nilsson, is an ideal, strong-voiced Elektra. Marjana Lipsovšekk is phenomenal as Klytemnestra, a performance alive to every subtlety, especially in her great monologue.

● *EMI CDS7 54067-2* ● *2 CDs* ● *Full price*
● *DDD* ● *1989*

Der Rosenkavalier
Der Rosenkavalier calls for rather different skills; more delicate and comic touches at times, with a greater overt lyricism. Two of the earliest complete recordings remain the most recommendable. The first is Erich Kleiber's inspired account, which only occasionally fails to suit modern taste in not pausing to admire the musical scenery along the way. Sena Jurinac and Hilde Gueden make a great pair as Oktavian and Sophie, although Maria Reining's Marschallin is a little too restrained.

Then there's the great Karajan recording with Elisabeth Schwarzkopf giving one of her best recorded performances as the Marschallin. Christa Ludwig and Teresa Stich-Randall are fine as the lovers, and Karajan gives one of those performances which helped to confirm his reputation to new generations of music lovers.

● *EMI CDS7 49354-2* ● *3 CDs* ● *Full price*
● *ADD* ● *1957* ○. *There is also a highlights disc: EMI CDM7 63452-2* ● *1 CD* ● *Mid-price*

Ariadne auf Naxos
One of the best recordings of *Ariadne* comes at mid-price; Karajan and Schwarzkopf again (both were, on record, protégés of the producer Walter Legge), and with such canny performers as Irmgard Seefried and Hugues Cuenod also in the cast. Another *Penguin CD Guide* Rosette-winner.

● *EMI CMS7 69296-2* ● *2 CDs* ● *Mid-price*
● *ADD* ● *1954* ○

Die Frau Ohne Schatten
The fortunes of *Die Frau Ohne Schatten* may well have taken an upward turn with the release of Sir Georg Solti's recording, starring Hildegard Behrens (cunningly husbanding her resources and turning in a fine performance) and Placido Domingo, unusually transferring to German repertoire with huge success, as well as a highly starry cast (the soprano Sumi Jo takes a more-or-less one-line part). Billed as the most expensive recording ever made, it could have ended up as a disaster; in fact, it's a titanically good recording, regarded by some critics as the best operatic recording ever made. Well . . . A *The Gramophone* Award-winner, naturally.

● *Decca 436 243-2* ● *3 CDs* ● *Full price*
● *DDD* ● *1989/91* ○

Intermezzo and Capriccio
Recordings of *Intermezzo* and *Capriccio* aren't exactly common; the best of both feature Wolfgang Sawallisch, with Lucia Popp and Dietrich Fischer-Dieskau in *Intermezzo*, bringing their skills – which encompass both operatic and the more intimate lieder style – to this exploration of dialogue techniques. Warning: no translation of the text is given.

● *EMI CDS7 49337-2* ● *2 CDs* ● *Full price*
● *ADD* ○

The version of *Capriccio* stars Elisabeth Schwarzkopf, with an all-star cast (Fischer-Dieskau again, Hans Hotter, Nicolai Gedda and many more).

● *EMI CDS7 49014-8* ● *2 CDs* ● *Full price*
● *ADD* ● *1957/8*

THE END OF GERMAN OPERA? PFITZNER, ZEMLINSKY

It's tempting to say that most German opera ended with a Richard Strauss, and some might agree. Strauss had overshadowed most of his contemporaries; these include Hans Pfitzner (1869–1949), now only remembered for *Palestrina* (1917), which is fairly undramatic, and Alexander von Zemlinsky (1872–1942), whose *Eine Florentinische Tragödie* (1917) takes leitmotiv to extremes. However, the composers of the 'new music' for which Strauss had such distaste contributed at least three masterpieces to the operatic stage, even if two of them were left incomplete by their composers.

THE EXPRESSIONIST MASTER: BERG

Wozzeck
That one complete work is *Wozzeck* (1925) by Alban Berg. This is one of the finest examples of Expressionism, an intensely emotional style which places a higher value on the expression of inner emotion than on some aesthetically and objectively viewed 'beauty'. In *Wozzeck* Berg

made partial use of serial techniques of composition, mixing these with more traditional and lyrical forms to create a portrait of a downtrodden man, the poor soldier Wozzeck, oppressed by all around him and betrayed by his wife, whom he stabs one night before drowning himself. A depressing story, made all the more vivid and intense by Berg's style and the compactness of the technique. Generally the vocal style tends towards 'Sprechgesang', a sort of pitched speech somewhere between singing and speaking, but the orchestral score is lush, dense; the orchestra takes an important role, having interludes between the brief, vividly characterised scenes. Along the way Berg throws in a lullaby, a march, a waltz, a ländler (the folk dance form so loved by Mahler), yet still manages to build up a picture of a man under pressure. *Wozzeck* is a terrific experience; not a jolly night out, perhaps, but a great work of twentieth-century art.

Lulu

Even unfinished, Berg's second opera *Lulu* still stands as a masterpiece. It wasn't until 1979 that a performance took place with the completed third act (the completion was by one Friedrich Cerha), although the first two acts were first performed in 1937, within two years of the composer's death. *Lulu* is the classic tale of the woman who, desired by every man, can make a fool of them all, yet is ultimately amoral herself. There's a vast cast of characters, most of whom are intended to be doubled (one actor taking more than one part) to make a point about the cyclical nature of life. Lulu destroys everyone who comes into contact with her, even the hapless

lesbian Countess Geschwitz; only Jack the Ripper, whom she encounters at the end of the opera, can withstand her. This tale of corruption and depravity, an extended satire about the nature of society, could have provided a showcase for music of severe atonal unpleasantness; what Berg provided, although atonal and based around twelve-note tone-rows, was a score of some lyricism, which in some of its orchestral interludes is even evocative of Johann Strauss. Almost all the dialogue is delivered in sprechgesang (or even spoken at some points), and is surrounded with complex, but, once you're into the idiom, utterly intoxicating, orchestration.

DISCOGRAPHY

Wozzeck
Although Berg recordings don't exactly grow on trees, *Wozzeck* has been lucky. Claudio Abbado's live recording has all the thrill of live performance. Abbado has a special empathy with Berg's music, and his singers excel.
● *Deutsche Grammophon 423 587-2* ● *2 CDs*
● *Full price* ● *DDD* ● *1989* ✪

Another fine performance, even though studio based, comes from conductor Christoph von Dohnányi, and has the added bonus of offering a fine version of Schoenberg's *Erwartung* (*Anticipation*). Anja Silja, who stars in both works, has a voice which catches perfectly the Expressionist nuance; and Dohnányi has a fine grasp of the orchestral idiom.
● *Decca 417 348-2* ● *2 CDs* ● *Full price*
● *DDD* ● *1979*

Lulu
There are two very strong versions of *Lulu* available. The original recording (the première of the completed work) by Pierre Boulez, a master of modern idioms, has Teresa Stratas in commanding form in the title role.
● *Deutsche Grammophon 415 489-2* ● *3 CDs*
● *Full price* ● *ADD* ● *1979*

Excellent, too, is Jeffrey Tate's live recording, of which the only weakness is the opening Prologue; Patricia Wise is a good Lulu, with Brigitte Fassbaender outstanding as the Countess and Hans Hotter, at 82, giving a consummate performance.
● *EMI CDS7 54622-2* ● *3 CDs* ● *Full price*
● *DDD* ● *1991*

WHERE MUSIC ENDS: SCHOENBERG

Like Berg (and Puccini and Offenbach, with whom he'd doubtless be less enthusiastic to be bracketed), Schoenberg left an unfinished opera, *Moses und Aron*, based on the biblical story of the Golden Calf. Schoenberg composed the first two acts of *Moses* between 1930 and 1932 (although they weren't staged until after his death), partly as a way of working out various complex ideas about the Jewish religion and his relation to it. He tried to compose Act 3, but eventually suggested that it should be spoken. That is, of course, an immensely symbolic gesture, indicating that he believed that opera was over, that it couldn't move forward any further (Schoenberg believed that art forms had to keep moving forward and developing or they would stagnate and become worthless). The composed acts of *Moses* in any case tend towards speech, as the use of sprechgesang is extensive, especially to depict the voice of God (Schoenberg had made a great deal of use of sprechgesang earlier in his career, in one section of his massive choral work *Gurrelieder* [1911] and his chamber work for voice and orchestra, *Pierrot Lunaire* [1920]). In many ways the centre of musical interest in *Moses* shifts to the chorus, as the instrumental texture, though colourful, is quite spiky (especially when compared with Berg's operas).

I should also mention a one-act, half-hour work, a 'monodrama' Schoenberg wrote in 1909 (but first performed in 1924), *Erwartung* (*Expectation*). This depicts the state of mind of a woman lost in a forest at night and searching for her lover; through the music Schoenberg seeks to illustrate not just her state of mind but the presence or absence of moonlight in the forest. It is, in many ways, the greatest single work of Expressionism, with a deliberately overstated intensity. Like much of Schoenberg's more avant-garde work, even now it doesn't make immediately easy or comfortable listening (Schoenberg probably wouldn't have approved of music being comfortable), but it is a remarkable, intense, dramatic work.

DISCOGRAPHY
Moses und Aron
There's only one recording of *Moses* available, by Sir Georg Solti, who seeks out what warmth there is in the score and places it right in the Romantic tradition. Philip Langridge gives a lovely, accurate performance as Aron.
● *Decca 414 264-2* ● *2 CDs* ● *Full price*
● *DDD* ● *1984*

GERMAN OPERA UP TO DATE: HINDEMITH, WEILL, HENZE, STOCKHAUSEN

The rest of the story of German opera in the twentieth century is quickly told. A blow was struck for tonalism in *Mathis der Maler* (*Mathis the Painter*, 1938) by Paul Hindemith (1895–1963), in which the composer faces the major question confronting German artists in the 1930s, the loyalty to the state and the loyalty to 'higher truths', all vaguely allegorised in a sixteenth-century setting. Mathis as a character has some ideological interest, but it's a slow business. Hindemith is going through a revival of interest (another of his seven operas, *Cardellac* [1926], now has a band of supporters), but his work can seem very flat and dull.

The 'revue-type' operas of Kurt Weill (1900–1950) are usually better when undertaken by performers from the world of musicals, and are largely hamstrung by the attitudinising and simplistic left-wingery of Weill's habitual collaborator, Bertholt Brecht (1898–1956). *Die Dreigroschenoper* (*The*

Arnold Schoenberg

1874–1951

A rnold Schoenberg established himself as a composer with a series of works very much in the style of Wagner – vast, drawing on chromatic harmonies, deeply emotional – yet he felt imbued with a mission to change the face of music. His view was that Wagner's music had sounded the death knell of tonality, and that Western music needed to rethink its entire foundation. From the middle of the first decade of the century through to the 1920s, he struggled to win converts to his beliefs; very often he was poor, scorned by the establishment, and at one point he had to approach his former teacher, Mahler, for a substantial loan (Mahler granted the request unhesitatingly). For a while Schoenberg even abandoned music for painting. In the 1920s and 1930s he was drawn to America, where he eventually settled to a series of teaching posts, offering waspish views on the musical world. Never an easy man, he did almost singlehandedly change that musical world, which he believed someone had to do. There's a story that he was once asked the question, 'Aren't you Arnold Schoenberg, the composer of modern music?' His reply was, 'Well, if it hadn't been me, it would have been someone else.'

>> *Chamber* 240, *Choral* 267, *Orchestral* 280

Threepenny Opera; 1928), an updating of *The Beggar's Opera*, still has some effective numbers (especially the internationally famous 'Moritat der Mackie von Messer' – 'Ballad of Mack the Knife'). Weill's later attempt to create a genuine 'opera of the people' in the American theatre (he left Germany for America to avoid the Nazis), *Street Scene* (1947), strikes me as an uneasy cross between an opera and a musical, and its allegiances are hard to detect. I'm old-fashioned enough to believe that a good stage musical need have no pretensions to the state of opera (and it's hard to think of one which benefited from such pretensions).

Whether the operas of Hans Henze (1926–) or Karlheinz Stockhausen

- (1928–) have any future is a moot
- point. Everyone knows Sir Thomas
- Beecham's comment when asked if
- he'd ever conducted any Stockhausen:
- 'No, but I once stepped in some'.
- That's not entirely fair, but now that
- the great vogue for Stockhausen's
- work has passed away, it's hard to see
- what will survive of the works we've
- had so far from his *Light* Cycle; there's
- little about *Donnerstag aus Licht*
- (*Thursday, from Light*, 1981) that a
- composer such as Harrison Birtwistle
- can't do a good deal better. And
- Birtwistle doesn't have any truck with
- devices like handclaps or
- tongue-clicks, nor with the kind of
- tired 1960s mysticism which is the
- hallmark of Stockhausen's opera.
- Henze has a more traditional musical

language, and his one act opera *The Bassarids* (using a libretto by W. H. Auden and his lover, Chester Kallman) mingles music of supreme rationale and order with something more sensuous. Will it survive? Time will tell.

CENTRAL AND EASTERN EUROPE: SMETANA, DVOŘÁK, JANÁČEK

It's sometimes been too easy for opera from the centre and east of Europe to be shoved to one side under the weight of the Italian/Germanic tradition. In fact, there's a good deal that's sharper about this other tradition, especially in a Czech master of the stage like Leos Janáček (1854–1928). Janáček didn't emerge from nowhere; Czech opera was 'founded' (as it were) by Bedřich Smetana (1824–1884), the composer of *Ma Vlast* (*My Country*), the enormous symphonic cycle from which the famous 'Moldau' is the best known section. Smetana's *The Bartered Bride* (1866, revised 1870) is a village opera, full of wit, folk song, dancing, and yet some genuine feeling. Antonin Dvořák wrote twelve operas, of which only one, *Rusalka* (1901), has made any impact in the West, and that largely for one glorious aria, Rusalka's 'Song to the Moon'. This piece doesn't, however, reveal the extent to which Dvořák was influenced by Wagner operatically, attempting to structure his work through leitmotifs.

Janáček's operas form a remarkably consistent corpus and they are now coming into their own as popular works. *Jenůfa* (1904, revised 1916), *Kátya Kabanová* (1921), *The Cunning Little Vixen* (1924), *The Makropolous Case* (1926), and *From the House of the Dead* (1930) have all found their way more or less into the repertoire, and others are following them there.

They all possess remarkable orchestration, going from raw, spiky, quite atonal sounds to something warmer, and often giving unusual prominence to odd instruments (there's a lot of xylophone noise in Act 1 of *Jenůfa*, for instance). Often based around Czech village society or Czech folk traditions, and occasionally steering clear of realism (as in *The Cunning Little Vixen*) their psychological accuracy (and the way that this is depicted in the music) is quite remarkable. They are modern in many senses, both musically and thematically, and yet the folk influence, allied to Janáček's own extraordinary sense of lyricism, has made them more accessible to modern Western audiences than many pieces from a tradition more sympathetic to Western ears.

DISCOGRAPHY
Dvořák
For a wonderful version of the 'Song to the Moon' from *Russalka*, try Lucia Popp's glorious singing in a rather good compilation with an unfortunate title, *Opera Goes Nuts*.
● EMI CDM7 63583-2 ● 1 CD ● Mid-price
● ADD/DDD ○

Janáček
The great pioneering work in recording Janáček was all done by Sir Charles Mackerras. *Jenůfa*, one of the most popular of these operas was particularly well done, with a cast that included Lucia Popp.
● Decca 414 483-2 ● 2 CDs ● Full price
● DDD ● 1982 ○

In fact, any of the Mackerras recordings of Janáček operas made in the 1970s and 1980s is worth investigating; as is Simon Rattle's outstanding version of *The Cunning Little Vixen*.
● EMI CDS7 54212-2 ● 2 CDs ● Full price
● DDD ● 1992

Bartók: *Duke Bluebeard's Castle*
One short but extremely powerful opera from the Eastern European tradition is Béla Bartók's *Duke Bluebeard's Castle* (1918), a one-act, two-person setting of the Bluebeard legend; except that here Bluebeard co-operates with his inquisitive new wife, opening seven

doors, one after another, to reveal not only his torture chamber, but his wealth and, at the blazing climax of the fifth door, his kingdom. The stage, which was dark at the outset, is flooded with light by this time; but the final two doors (the last reveals Bluebeard's two previous wives) blot out the light again and the new wife joins her predecessors. Bartók's music is extraordinary; it suddenly explodes into a C major chord at the climax of the fifth door, and the atmosphere it conjures is always telling. The vocal lines, too, have great beauty. This is an eminently accessible, utterly enjoyable work which, at only an hour or so in length, is quite easy to grasp.

DISCOGRAPHY
I have always been very fond of the Wolfgang Sawallisch version with Dietrich Fischer-Dieskau and his wife Julia Varady; both bring a chamber, lieder-like delivery to the vocal parts, while Sawallisch extracts great drama from the score without swamping the intimate singing.
● *Deutsche Grammophon 423 236-2* ● *1 CD*
● *Mid-price* ● *ADD* ● *1979* ✪

On a slightly larger scale, and equally successful, is Antál Doráti's 1960s version, a really vivid recording. Singers Mihály Székely and Olga Szönyi may not be household names, but they sound brilliant.
● *Mercury Living Presence 434 325-2* ● *1 CD*
● *Mid-price* ● *ADD* ● *1962*

TWENTIETH-CENTURY FRENCH OPERA: RAVEL AND POULENC

French opera may have started the century well with Debussy's *Pelléas et Mélisande*, but that was far and away its greatest impact. Maurice Ravel (1875–1937), of *Bolero* fame, wrote two operas, both of which have found a place in the repertoire, but both of which also show the composer's talent for what is essentially pastiche. Both operas are one-act pantomime affairs. *L'Heure Espagnole* (*The Spanish Hour*; 1911) is a stylised business about a bored unfaithful wife, a clockmaker husband, and a load of clocks. It has been described as 'sheer delight' and 'very funny', but I'm afraid the jokes are a bit lost on me, although the orchestration, as always with Ravel, gives one something to wonder at. Like much eighteenth-century comedy (of which this is an elaborate pastiche) the opera has no heart, none of the sense of humanity which makes Mozart's comic operas so appealing. *L'Enfant et les Sortilèges* (*The Child and the Spells*; 1925) is a short opera about a child attacked by objects on which he normally takes out his tantrums. Ravel claimed the music was a mixture of 'Monteverdi, Massenet, Puccini, jazz and the stage musical'; whatever the truth of that, it comes out as pure Ravel. *L'Enfant* is a more engaging work than *L'Heure*, and its appeal isn't entirely childish; it is that rare success, a 'child's opera' with definite adult appeal.

François Poulenc (1899–1963) was an accomplished *pasticheur* (it seems to be a particularly French talent), and wrote many enjoyable works in many genres, especially choral works. He wrote film scores in his time, and the dramatic skills he learned there certainly rubbed off onto his more important operas, especially his two contrasting late works, *Dialogues des Carmélites* (1957) and *La Voix Humaine* (1959). *Dialogues* is a great ensemble piece about a woman taking refuge from the terrors of everyday life in a Carmelite convent, until eventually the French Revolution catches up with them all. The opera ends with a brilliant if macabre scene where fourteen nuns die on the guillotine; Poulenc's timing is superb and the choral and orchestral writing most effective – *Dialogues* may have a great future. *La Voix Humaine* is a one-act work for a single singer; a young woman talking on the telephone to a lover who wants to end their relationship. She runs the gamut of emotions, threatening suicide; there is an undeniable whiff of 'camp' about certain parts (Jean Cocteau was responsible for the libretto, after all), but this really is a tour de force of both vocal writing (the melodic line is fascinating, easily commanding the attention) and orchestral accompaniment. Not an easy opera to bring off because of the demands on the singer, but terrific when it works.

DISCOGRAPHY
Ravel
The key Ravel opera conductor is Lorin Maezel; his style and slickness are exactly what's wanted. His two 1960s recordings both feature French casts, not particularly starry in international terms, but their performances are full of fine characterisation.
L'Heure Espagnole: ● *Deutsche Grammophon 423 719-2* ● *1 CD* ● *Full price* ● *ADD* ● *1965*

L'Enfant et les Sortilèges: ● *Deutsche Grammophon 423 718-2* ● *1 CD* ● *Full price* ● *ADD* ● *1961*

Poulenc
There's an outstanding new recording of Poulenc's *Dialogues des Carmélites* by one of the best conductors of twentieth-century opera around, Kent Nagano, who for a while was based at the Lyon Opéra (it's their orchestra and chorus which feature on several of his recordings, including this one). The cast includes some big names (Rita Gorr, José van Dam, to name two), and it's a joyful and brilliant performance by all concerned.
● *Virgin VCD 759227-2* ● *2 CDs* ● *Full price* ● *DDD* ● *1992*

Conductor Georges Prêtre has twice recorded *La Voix Humaine*, both versions are gorgeous, but I lean slightly to the later, which has a finely neurotic (yet somehow erotic) performance from Julia Migenes.
● *Erato 2292-45651-2* ● *1 CD* ● *Full price* ● *DDD* ● *1990*

THE OPERA AND STALIN: STRAVINSKY, PROKOFIEV, SHOSTAKOVICH

All three of the great Russian composers of the twentieth century have composed operas. Igor Stravinsky (1882–1971) did so as either a Frenchman or an American, having managed to avoid any contact with the then new Communist regime in his country. His two major dramatic works make for something of a contrast; *Oedipus Rex* (1927/28) is a highly stylised work which can be (and often is) performed purely as a concert piece, almost as a secular oratorio. To heighten the 'static' effect, Stravinsky got from his collaborator, Jean Cocteau, a libretto in Latin rather than any living language, precisely because Latin has, to use Stravinsky's phrase, 'turned to stone'. Harking back, like the original creators of opera, Stravinsky calls for masks to be worn by the chorus (who have a traditional Greek role, given that Cocteau's libretto is based on Sophocles's masterpiece). The music is full of thumping bass patterns, which give a strong sense of the inevitable destiny running through the play. Classical poise, though, is the order of the day; this isn't, most emphatically, the world of Richard Strauss's *Elektra* – if that was a hot-house, this is a deep-freeze, but a splendid work, nonetheless. Stravinsky's other major opera was written in America to a libretto by W. H. Auden and Chester Kallmann. *The Rake's Progress* (1951) was an attempt to portray Hogarth's great eighteenth-century engravings as a single coherent story; given the eighteenth-century provenance of the story, Stravinsky immersed his music in the neo-Classical style which by then had come to dominate his music (the guiding idea of 'Back to Bach'). Deliberately, he opted for a 'number opera', with harpsichord accompanying the recitative; there's some very atmospheric writing (especially in a scene set in a graveyard) and some quite melodic arias, although the whole thing is so shot through with incessant and insistent irony that occasionally one can get weary. It's still, though, one of the best examples of neo-Classicism, especially in the operatic field.

Sergei Prokofiev eventually returned to Russia in the 1930s after a stay in the West during the first couple of decades after the Revolution. After his return, he often ran into trouble, for he was another soul given to neo-Classicism and pastiche, which didn't always meet the requirements of Stalin's regime in Russia (1925–1953). His greatest operatic success outside his own country came with one of his earliest essays in the form, a work premièred in Chicago in 1921, *The Love of Three Oranges*. A comic fantasy of the old Russian style (characters include the King of Clubs, Fata Morgana, Truffaldino – need I say more?), Prokofiev's musical style is determinedly non-Romantic and sharp; there's little or no lyricism, and there are declamations and free recitative. The best-known part of the opera is its March, more famous from the Orchestral Suite Prokofiev derived from the work, and the orchestral score is generally spiky and colourful. It's either great fun or a bit of a pretentious bore, depending on your point of view. There's something of a vogue for some of Prokofiev's other operas, all of which are rather more serious: *The Gambler* (1929), based on Dostoevsky; *The Fiery Angel* (first performed in 1954 but composed much earlier, as his Symphony No. 3, dating from 1928, is based on music from this opera); and *War and Peace* (1944, and based, obviously, on Tolstoy's massive work), which is the Prokofiev opera above all written to appease the regime. Although Prokofiev is undoubtedly one of the great Russians of the twentieth century, whether opera is quite the form for his greatness is still in doubt; usually his opera music yields

- orchestral suites (or, in the case of *The Fiery Angel*, a symphony) which show
- it to better advantage.
-   Dmitri Shostakovich wrote the
- single greatest Russian opera of the
- twentieth century, but it got him into
- serious trouble. A prolific composer, he
- was always getting into trouble with
- the regime and having to re-ingratiate
- himself. It now seems that many of his
- works which supposedly 'celebrated'
- Stalin's regime contained within them
- little coded messages which effectively
- reversed the music's meaning. *Lady*
- *Macbeth of the Mtsensk District* (1934,
- revised 1963) may have a rather
- unpromising title, but it's a superbly
- dramatic, rather grim slab of Russian
- provincial low-life (almost *verismo* in
- its most shocking sense, rather than
- its sentimentalised Puccini form).
- Crime after crime, tragedy after
- tragedy; the Soviet regime found it
- deeply unedifying and far too true to
- life. Shostakovich's wide musical range
- goes from atonal discord and crude
- brass outbursts to some beautiful
- melodic writing for the voice, which at
- times comes close to being highly
- erotic in a most frenzied manner (the
- more-or-less open depiction of sex on
- stage can't have endeared the work to
- Stalin and his henchmen, either). A
- great work, worth everything else
- mentioned in this section.
-   Of current Russian (to use the term
- in its loose, pre-1992 sense) composers,
- the one who's made the biggest splash
- in the West is Alfred Schnittke
- (1934–), and his opera *Life With An*
- *Idiot* (1992) was received with some
- enthusiasm. Schnittke is another
- accomplished *pasticheur* and ironist,
- and his opera is a work of satire,
- sometimes a bit too much so, full of
- ironic usage of older forms such as the
- waltz. I have my doubts about the
- lasting worth of Schnittke's music, but

he's a fairly accessible composer, and a very public and prominent one.

DISCOGRAPHY
Stravinsky
Stravinsky's very illuminating recordings of his own operas are availiable only as part of a 22-disc boxed set and don't represent a realistic investment for any but the most devoted Stravinsky fan. There is, however, a good version of *Oedipus* conducted by Sir Colin Davis.
● *Orfeo CO71831A* ● *1 CD* ● *Full price*
● *DDD* ● *1983* ○

Quite an accomplished brand-new version of this opera comes from the young conductor Franz Welser-Möst.
● *EMI CDC7 54445-2* ● *1 CD* ● *Full price*
● *DDD* ● *1992*

There's also a fairly good version, very vivid, colourful and well characterised, of *The Rake's Progress* by Riccardo Chailly, starring Philip Langridge, Samuel Ramey and Sarah Walker.
● *Decca 411 644-2* ● *2 CDs* ● *Full price*
● *DDD* ● *1984*

Prokofiev
Love of Three Oranges hit the headlines a few years ago when Kent Nagano's recording, made with his Lyon Opéra Orchestra and Chorus, walked off with the *The Gramophone* Recording of the Year Award. It's certainly a vivid, living version of this opera, about which I have my doubts; if this recording doesn't persuade you (or me), then probably nothing will.
● *Virgin VCD7 91084-2* ● *2 CDs* ● *Full price*
● *DDD* ● *1989*

Shostakovich
Lady Macbeth of the Mtsensk District is well worth sampling, above all in Rostropovich's gloriously dark-hued and impassioned account with a Russian cast (including Nicolai Gedda). First-rate playing, singing, acting, conducting
● *EMI CDS7 49955-2* ● *2 CDs* ● *Full price*
● *ADD* ○

Schnittke
Schnittke's *Life with an Idiot* has already made it onto disc, in a very proficient recording again conducted by Mstislav Rostropovich and taken from the original production.
● *Sony SK52495* ● *2 CDs* ● *Full price* ● *DDD*
● *1992*

BRITISH OPERA: BENJAMIN BRITTEN

With all due respect to Frederick Delius (1862–1934) and Ralph Vaughan Williams, British opera essentially re-emerged from several centuries' sleep in 1945 with *Peter Grimes* by Benjamin Britten (1913–1976). Vaughan Williams's stage music is best remembered (when it is remembered) for its characteristically pastoral orchestral textures. Delius's opera *A Village Romeo and Juliet* (1907) was in any case originally designed for the German stage (it first appeared in Berlin), and, despite some fine orchestral set moments ('The Walk to the Paradise Garden' in particular, which is often played as a concert item), and the vivid characterisation of the Dark Fiddler, its strengths are scarcely dramatic. Its appeal lies, as does all of Delius's appeal, in the rich, hot-house harmonies, at the chromatic edge of tonality (but, like Richard Strauss's, always well within that border).

The Power of the Sea: *Peter Grimes*

Peter Grimes, though unashamedly English, has established itself as a major work, not least because of Britten's powerful sense of drama. Drawing on the poetry of George Crabbe, it portrays a small village community in the midst of which is the enigmatic outcast Grimes. Two of the community, a sea captain and Ellen (whom Grimes loves), seek to protect him, but Grimes's treatment of his boy apprentices (he is a fisherman) has always raised cause for concern, and the death of another precipitates the opera's final tragedy. Not only does Britten make the whole community a single character, he also manages musically to give each member of that community a separate identity. The opera is also held together by some powerful orchestral writing, not least the four Sea Interludes, which make the sea almost a character in the piece. The vividness of the writing is quite unlike anything in English opera since Purcell.

The Rape of Lucretia; Billy Budd; The Turn of the Screw

Britten's next stage work, *The Rape of Lucretia* (1946), wasn't perhaps as successful; written for small chamber forces, it has a rather heavy philosophical centre, proving perhaps that this kind of classical *opera seria* is dead. There are some fine things in it, but it's not Britten at his best. *Albert Herring* (1947) again portrayed a village community, but this time as comedy, albeit comedy that goes quite deep; as the hero is about to drink lemonade laced with rum, the music alludes to the 'love/death potion' in Wagner's *Tristan und Isolde*. *Herring* is great fun, but lightweight when compared with *Grimes* and with Britten's next opera, *Billy Budd* (1951, revised 1961). This is a setting of Herman Melville's story about a handsome and innocent sailor victimised by an oppressive authority-figure, but admired by a higher but powerless authority. You may detect a strong homosexual component in Britten's operatic subjects; Britten, homosexual himself, was often writing tenor lines with his long-standing lover Peter Pears in mind, and was also often using such subjects as a way of deflecting or examining his own homosexual impulses. This is particularly evident in his great chamber masterpiece *The Turn of the Screw* (1954), a dark and sombre, but utterly compelling version of Henry James's ghost story about the spiritual possession of two children (and possibly inspired in some measure by the Oscar Wilde trial). Britten's combination of stark, unadorned melody, cunning orchestral writing, and use of variation as a

- musical peg on which to hang his
- drama, is utterly telling and entirely
- effective. His writing for voice is
- completely natural, with speech
- rhythms which are always melodic yet
- never unnatural.
-
- ### A Midsummer Night's Dream; Death in Venice
- Britten wrote two more great operas;
- the first was his delightful, very
- characterful version of Shakespeare's
- *A Midsummer Night's Dream* (1960),
- in which musical irony is combined
- with orchestral brilliance, and with
- some darker hues emanating from his
- sinister – counter-tenor – Oberon. This
- is the modern opera that all people
- who think they don't like modern
- opera should see; it's one of the best
- Shakespearian operas outside of Verdi,
- actually catching the spirit of the play,
- and it manages to use music to make
- the jokes all the funnier.
- Britten's final opera, intended as a
- great love token for Peter Pears, was
- *Death in Venice* (1973), an elaborate
- setting of the Thomas Mann story
- about the novelist Aschenbach's
- obsession with a young boy whilst
- holidaying in Venice; an obsession
- that leads him to risk, and then
- contract and die of, cholera. The opera
- was designed to revolve around
- Aschenbach, with one supporting
- singer taking most of the other roles;
- the boy Tadzio, a non-speaking role, is
- represented in dance, and the opera
- becomes a representation of the
- struggle between Apollo (the ordered
- rational element in art) and Dionysus
- (the inspirational, frenzied side).
- Overtly homosexual at many points, it
- is none the less a fascinating, at times
- highly lyrical, piece; if it doesn't quite
- carry the intellectual baggage Britten
- loaded it with, it still retains a great
- deal of power.

DISCOGRAPHY
Delius
For a good, enjoyable recording of *A Village Romeo and Juliet*, try Sir Charles Mackerras's lush realisation, which has a finely sinister performance by Thomas Hampson in the one memorable role.
● *Argo 430 275-2* ● *2 CDs* ● *Full price*
● *DDD* ● *1990*

Britten
There are two classic *Peter Grimes* recordings. One is the composer's own, starring, inevitably, Peter Pears; this is a superb recording.
● *Decca 414 577-2* ● *3 CDs* ● *Full price*
● *ADD* ● *1958* ❂

But the alternative is fascinating; it features Jon Vickers, an individual singer free from the influence of Pears's distinctive nasal style, and has some fine pacing by Sir Colin Davis.
● *Philips 432 578-2* ● *2 CDs* ● *Mid-price*
● *ADD* ● *1962*

The composer's own mono recording of *Turn of the Screw* with the original cast is a great bargain version; apart from Pears, there's also the young boy treble David Hemmings.
● *Decca 425 672-2* ● *2 CDs* ● *Mid-price*
● *ADD* ● *1955* ❂

Peter Pears isn't in *A Midsummer Night's Dream*, but the cast does include the superbly characterful Owen Brannigan and the counter-tenor Alfred Deller. The composer again is the conductor. A delight.
● *Decca 425 663-2* ● *2 CDs* ● *Full price*
● *ADD* ● *1962*

Britten wasn't able to conduct the recording of *Death in Venice*, but stand-in Steuart Bedford is pretty fine and the whole thing is dominated – inevitably – by Pears's Aschenbach.
● *Decca 425 669-2* ● *2 CDs* ● *Full price*
● *ADD* ● *1976*

MYSTICISM AND TOPICALITY: TIPPETT

The other great statesman of British opera in the latter part of the century has been Sir Michael Tippett. He made his name as an operatic composer with *The Midsummer Marriage* (1955), a version of the Fisher King legend with lots of mystical accretion. Tippett writes his own libretti and is very keen on mystical accretion as well as topical allusion, although this leads inevitably to the music being given greater value than the words; rarely

has he written a libretto that does not have some squirmingly embarrassing moments. This first opera succeeds largely through the strength and warmth of its music – Tippett is a fine orchestrator, whose string writing, in particular, is often intense and passionate. His most successful opera, however, is probably his second, *King Priam* (1962), based, obviously, on Homer's *Iliad* (and for this reason, I suspect, Tippett's finest libretto), even though its musical style seemed, at the time of its first performance, a good deal cooler and spikier than *The Midsummer Marriage*. In fact, *Priam* achieves a real white-hot intensity and a forward dramatic thrust of extraordinary clarity, and the use of percussion, of a guitar, of the piano, as well as conventional instruments, is masterly.

The Knot Garden (1970) depicts a complex web of six people in, as the title suggests, a garden, being manipulated by an analyst. One of the characters is black – the concept of race and racism is one of Tippett's concerns in his three most recent operas – and two are overtly homosexual. The opera uses Shakespeare's *The Tempest* as a background and reference point, although only, I think, with limited success. The music is Tippett at his most concentrated, most tightly organised; gone is the lushness of *The Midsummer Marriage* or the (fairly) immediate clarity of *Priam*. In many ways, *The Knot Garden* is his most inaccessible work.

Tippett's shortest opera is *The Ice Break* (1977), a story packed with Soviet dissidents, black supremacists and bad language (the climax of the first act is a cry of 'You motherfucking bastard!'). The score employs an electric guitar and one character is designed to be sung by two voices (a soprano and a counter-tenor) using electronic devices. There is a 'love-in' (about a decade behind the times). Get through all this and what you actually find is some ravishingly beautiful music, some vivid orchestral writing, some writing for the voice which uses singing as perhaps only Tippett ever has in recent years; he is in many ways a modern bel canto composer. I think that *The Ice Break* can survive, but I have my doubts about *New Year* (1988), with its spaceships, time-travel and an abysmally embarrassing attempt to write a rap (which is precisely as awful as you would expect from a Classical composer in his eighties). Still, Tippett has always sought to expand both the styles and the themes of opera, and has established himself as a major figure, especially in the United States.

DISCOGRAPHY
Recordings of Tippett's operas are still fairly rare, and a good starting-point might be either *King Priam*, ably done by David Atherton with Tippett specialists like Philip Langridge and Heather Harper in the cast.
● *Decca 414 241-2* ● *2 CDs* ● *Full price*
● *ADD* ●

There's another David Atherton tour de force, a fine and exciting recording of *The Ice Break* (only don't read the libretto too closely).
● *Virgin VC7 91448-2* ● *1 CD* ● *Full price*
● *ADD* ● *1991*

BRITISH OPERA TODAY

And yes, there is British opera after Britten and Tippett. The best of it comes from Harrison Birtwistle (1934– ; the first composer to come out of Accrington), whose *Punch and Judy* was premièred at Benjamin Britten's Aldeburgh Festival in 1968, on which occasion Britten walked out. Using the children's puppet show with all its horrors and violence, Birtwistle

created a striking expressionist work with a vivid and violent score. It's a terrific, powerful place, but not full of tunes you can hum. *The Mask of Orpheus* (1986) seeks to add to the Orpheus legend as used by Monteverdi, Gluck, Offenbach, and others, by placing it within its framework as part of the Dionysian cult (Orpheus ends up torn to shreds by Dionysian women); it's a vast and complex piece using singers, mime and even puppets, and it received a rapturous reception. Birtwistle's music is always challenging, but he may well be a good bet as an enduring composer. *Gawain* (1991) had some wonderful female vocal writing, although its epic stylisation didn't always come off.

Other British names worth investigation are Peter Maxwell Davies (1934–), whose *Taverner* is a difficult but intriguing work about the sixteenth-century composer; John Casken (1949–), whose *Golem* (1989) is an award-winning morality opera; Oliver Knussen (1952–), whose *Where the Wild Things Are* is a children's fantasy (based on the famous book by Maurice Sendak) full of intricately beautiful, highly crafted music; and Mark Antony Turnage (1960–), whose *Greek*, a setting of Steven Berkoff's play, incorporates all the eclectic musical influences (such as jazz and TV themes) to which he has been exposed, yet bearing all the time the stamp of his unique vision.

DISCOGRAPHY
Birtwistle
Harrison Birtwistle's *Punch and Judy* is available in a *The Gramophone* Award-winning version, again directed by Atherton and also starring Langridge, as well as the excellent bass John Tomlinson. A fine way to get acquainted with Birtwistle.
● *Decca Headline HEAD 24/5* ● *2 CDs* ● *Full price* ● *ADD* ● *1979* ●

Casken and Knussen

John Casken's *Golem* also got a *The Gramophone* Award on its recording debut.
● *Virgin VCD7 91204-2* ● *2 CDs* ● *Full price*
● *DDD* ● *1989*

Oliver Knussen's *Where the Wild Things Are* has been well recorded, too.
● *Unicorn-Kanchana UKPCD 9044* ● *1 CD*
● *Full price* ● *DDD* ● *1983*

━━━   ━━━   ━━━   ━━━

AMERICAN OPERA: THOMSON, BERNSTEIN, BLITZSTEIN, GERSHWIN

America as we know it evolved when a series of European and other emigrés came together, and for quite a long time into the twentieth century separate groups preferred to huddle within their own cultural experiences, so that the evolution of some separate and definite 'American culture' was a relatively slow business. The great American contribution to twentieth-century musical culture has, in any case, been the Broadway and Hollywood musicals, and the great American composers are Duke Ellington, Richard Rogers, Cole Porter, George Gershwin (not wearing his pseudo-Classical hat; any song Gershwin wrote for an Astaire/Rogers film is worth the whole of *Porgy and Bess* or *Rhapsody in Blue*), and others of that ilk. Great, and uniquely American, creations like the musical *Guys and Dolls* could never be 'improved' in any way by dragging in opera singers to perform/sing them; and it was to the detriment of Leonard Bernstein's *West Side Story* (1957) that he insisted on making a recording which pretended that this high-class musical was a piece of opera (although the enterprise was almost justified by Marilyn Horne's glorious and entirely idiomatic rendition of 'Somewhere').

This may all seem like a prelude to rubbishing American opera. It isn't. I may say at the outset that I think that American operatic composers like Douglas Moore (1893–1969), Gian Carlo Menotti (1911–) and Virgil Thomson (1896–1989), have added little or nothing to the operatic experience; there is some cult following for Thomson's setting of Gertrude Stein's *Four Saints in Three Acts* (1934), and Menotti's *Amahl and the Night Visitors* (1951) has joined the ranks of charming and potentially enduring works about and for children, even though next to Knussen's *Where the Wild Things Are* it seems rather sentimental. Nor can I regard Leonard Bernstein (1918–1990) as an operatic composer; even *Candide* (1956, revised 1973/1982) is at most an operetta, and rather a dull one, as Bernstein is not a *pasticheur* great enough to carry off this ironic work, and gets rather heavy-handed. (The proliferation of authors who worked on the libretto doesn't help; not including Voltaire, there have been seven, including such talents as Lillian Hellman, Dorothy Parker, Stephen Sondheim and Bernstein himself, and such collaborations usually tend to decrease in merit in inverse proportion to the ability of those involved.) *Regina* (1949) by Marc Blitzstein (1905–1964), based on Lillian Hellman's play *The Little Foxes* (so memorably brought to the screen by Bette Davis), incorporates almost every kind of American popular music; but then, so does *The Music Man* (of the song '76 Trombones' fame), and that isn't usually called an opera. *Porgy and Bess* (1935) by George Gershwin (1989–1937) has also been dragged onto the operatic stage; I find its characterisation of black people vaguely offensive, and it's largely only redeemed by one or two songs (principally 'Summertime').

AMERICA'S GREAT CONTRIBUTION: MINIMALISM

In fact, the great American contribution to opera has come late, and in the form of that modern musical style known as 'Minimalism'. The principal behind Minimalism is, of course, simplicity, and the movement was intended very much as a reaction to the increasing intellectualisation of music, especially that of twentieth-century composers. The hallmarks of Minimalism are constant repetition of single phrases, and infrequent shifts of key or even of chord. Repeated patterns are hammered away in blocks, achieving an almost hypnotic effect, and each shift to another chord, even to the same chord arranged in a different way, becomes a moment of high drama. Obviously Minimalism wouldn't be suitable for the kind of dramatic operas composed by Mozart or Verdi or Puccini or Wagner, and its use in opera has tended to produce very stylised, almost ceremonial, tableau-like pieces. The 'symbolic-gesture' nature of Minimalist opera fits, really, quite well into the Minimalist root in Native American music, which has a high ceremonial function in its constant repetitions.

RITUAL AND CURRENT EVENTS: PHILIP GLASS (1937–) AND JOHN ADAMS (1947–)

The key Minimalist composers have all been Americans; Steve Reich (1936–) who has shown little interest in opera to date, Philip Glass and John Adams. Glass and Adams have both composed operas; the former showing a taste for ceremonial symbolic subjects set either well in the past, like *Akhnaten* (1984), about religious disputes in Ancient Egypt, or else in the distant future, like *The Making of the Representative for Planet 8* (1988). Adams has preferred 'topical' opera, embodied in his works *Nixon in China* (1987) or the opera about the hijacking of the liner *Achille Lauro, The Death of Klinghoffer* (1991). Glass's works are overtly ritualistic; his music tends to be dominated by the top end of the scale and his works are deliberately plotless, static and directionless, often opening with the same arpeggio lasting for five to ten minutes. Either you find it intoxicating – or else it's a pointless bore. Adams's music tends to chug along a bit more, with 'motorvating' bass lines; there's no overt sentiment or drama, and in *Klinghoffer* different groups of characters stand around different parts of an elaborate set giving an internalised commentary on the action, all very deadpan. In fact, Adams goes in for large sounds which can be quite impressive, as in 'The Day Chorus' in *Klinghoffer*. Both Glass and Adams go in for a lot of electronically generated musical sounds. How far Adams's topical interests can legitimately stretch is a moot point; *The Manson Family* (1990) by John Moran (in the recording of which the composer himself plays Manson, and Iggy Popp also stars) is a slick, thoroughly nasty, tasteless little piece, as Minimalist in its morality as in its music.

Minimalism has proved very popular to date, and in Adams's latest work there are signs that it can move on. Its appeal is visceral rather than intellectual, and the most famous work of Minimalism to date is Symphony No. 3 by Henryk Górecki which, not being an opera, doesn't belong here (see above, p. 89). However, Minimalism strikes me as being rather like the Emperor's New Clothes. Time, as always, will tell. The fact remains that Puccini's *Tosca* and Mozart's *Figaro* can still draw audiences in a way that most modern opera doesn't. So whether the 'opera explosion' of recent years is of any real or lasting artistic value is still open to debate; the jury is, as they say, still out.

DISCOGRAPHY
Philip Glass
Philip Glass has done quite well on disc; three of his operas, *Einstein on the Beach* (1975), *Satyagraha* (1980), and *Akhnaten* have all been

recorded. Either *Einstein* or *Akhnaten* probably makes the best introduction for new listeners.
Einstein: ● *CBS/Sony CD38875* ● *4 CDs* ● *Full price* ● *DDD* ● *1985*

Akhnaten: ● *CBS/Sony CD42457* ● *2 CDs* ● *Full price* ● *DDD* ● *1987*

John Adams
Nixon in China and *Klinghoffer* have both been recorded; I'd strongly recommend the latter as the best Minimalist opera, and in a brilliant recording by Kent Nagano and the Lyon Opéra.

Nixon: ● *Elektra Nonesuch 7559 79177-2* ● *3 CDs* ● *Full price* ● *DDD* ● *1988*

Klinghoffer: ● *Elektra Nonesuch 7559 79281-2* ● *2 CDs* ● *Full price* ● *DDD* ● *1992*

V

Chamber

& SOLO INSTRUMENTAL MUSIC

INTRODUCTION

This chapter deals with the small, intimate side of music; small groups of instrumentalists, or solo performers, in a room, or a chamber, delivering a performance which, while it may not be short on technical bravura, is none the less more intimate than the huge sound of the concerto or the symphony

Chamber music is usually designed for smaller venues than the large concert halls; that's partly how the name derives. Baroque music is full of sonatas 'a camera' for varying groups of instrumentalists; small music designed to entertain if the people in the room wanted to listen to it, but not to swamp and overawe if they didn't. Chamber music wasn't intended at that time to command the same attention as choral music (which was often religious in nature and therefore of profound importance), or opera (a spectacle to delight more than one set of senses in any case). So most Baroque composers turned out chamber music by the yard, usually written for whatever combination of instruments was available, although the supremacy of various combinations of stringed instruments rapidly became apparent. Chamber music, of course, has always had the great advantage of being comparatively cheap to stage. Solo instrumental music can be cheaper still, for even if you're paying for one of the greatest soloists, all you need is him or her and an instrument (which, unless it's a piano, the performer will usually bring), and a venue.

However, there came a point in the history of music (and relatively early, too) when chamber music became something a good deal more exalted than simple background noise. J. S. Bach was in good measure responsible for this, for he undoubtedly played a significant role in transforming solo instrumental performance into something that is truly 'high art'. But the man who elevated the string quartet to the status of more than merely background music was, in the first instance, Joseph Haydn, who can safely be said to have been the first composer to recognise the quartet's potential as a framework for exercises in style and experiment. Haydn, in fact, did for the string quartet exactly what he'd done for the symphony, turning it into something notable; and, as before, it was Ludwig van Beethoven who built on Haydn's foundations, using the quartet as an intimate and personal form of musical development and experiment. It was also Beethoven who, with Franz Schubert, made the solo instrumental sonata a force to be reckoned with. From this point on, chamber music as we understand it was established; in many ways, very little has changed since the 1820s.

The amount of chamber and solo instrumental music (counting as 'chamber music' anything which requires two or more instrumentalists, up to a group of about thirteen or so) is vast; simply to list it would take a book several times this size. Most composers tended to turn their hands to small forms, even if only as compositional exercises, early in their careers; there's even a piano sonata by Wagner, although it would take a valiantly diehard Wagnerian to pretend that it's of vital and lasting significance. To begin with there are, as I've already said, thousands of Baroque works which come under this heading, many quite charming (but all ultimately rather similar). This chapter, therefore, will adopt a somewhat ruthless approach, not because this kind of music is of any less worth; quite the opposite, in fact, for some chamber and solo music comprises the greatest items in the repertoire. However, chamber music is very often a taste acquired later rather than sooner, and very few if any chamber pieces will ever quite make it into the 'popular domain' in the way that certain pieces of Beethoven, Mozart or Puccini have. So this is a trip along the major roads of chamber and solo music, with only the occasional detour.

DEVELOPING THE KEYBOARD SONATA: SCARLATTI AND BACH

Haydn took and moulded the string quartet in the latter part of the eighteenth century. The keyboard sonata (and all sonatas developing therefrom) was first laid out by Domenico Scarlatti (1685–1757), who wrote (according to the catalogue of his works) 555 pieces in the form. Just as with the symphony, the three- or four-movement sonata form familiar in the Classical and Romantic ages emerged out of the short single-movement piece, and it was Scarlatti who gave that shortened single-movement form its first extended workout as it naturally developed into the fast-slow-fast sequence familiar from early symphonies and concertos.

Scarlatti, who came from a musical

family, was an Italian who also found a great deal of work and popularity in Spain. His keyboard sonatas (they would in fact have been written for the harpsichord, but they have adapted quite well to the modern piano) took the sonata further, in terms of both virtuosity and expression, than any of his contemporaries or predecessors. His influence was vast – especially on a range of English composers, including Thomas Arne (1710–1778), the all-purpose composer whose most enduring monument is the music for 'Rule, Britannia!' – and he also made somewhat unprecedented demands on performance technique. Scarlatti's work is altogether more showy, more overtly virtuosic, than that of his great German contemporary Bach. Many of the sonatas were written to test his pupils and stretch their ability.

DISCOGRAPHY
You can get the complete Scarlatti sonatas, well played by Scott Ross, but a 34-disc set (Erato) is probably more designed to appeal to the specialist/obsessive than the casual sampler. Gilbert Rowland has also committed a more or less complete cycle to disc, with each available separately.
● *Keyboard* ● *Full price* ● *DAD*
● *1989*

However, the best introduction to Scarlatti probably lies in the hands and technique of one of the great promulgators of 'authentic' technique, Trevor Pinnock, who offers thirteen well-chosen sonatas.
● *CRD CRD3368* ● *1 CD* ● *Full price* ● *ADD*
● *1981*

Another good buy is the selection of eleven sonatas from the devoted Scarlattian Valda Aveling.
● *EMI Classics for Pleasure CD-CFP4538*
● *1 CD* ● *Bargain price* ● *ADD* ● *1976*

Away from the harpsichord, but still dazzling, is a collection of seventeen sonatas recorded by the great pianist Vladimir Horowitz.
● *CBS/Sony Masterworks CD42410* ● *1 CD*
● *Full price* ● *AAD* ● *1963-9*

TAKING IT TO THE LIMIT: J. S. BACH

Bach's contribution to all kinds of solo instrumental music is quite phenomenal, and could easily (and has easily) filled whole books on its own. There are unaccompanied works for cello and for violin, as well as sonatas for flute and for violin and viola da gamba (the cello's ancestor), each with keyboard accompaniment. The unaccompanied cello sonatas, violin sonatas and partitas (pieces of music consisting of collections of dance movements) comprise some of the greatest, most intense music ever written for these instruments (a statement which stands just as true now as 250 years ago). Bach isn't always sufficiently celebrated for his melodic writing (some of the vocal melodies in the cantatas and Passions are beautiful too), but the combination of tunefulness and technique in these pieces is something remarkable. At various times Bach writes music designed to make the single soloist sound like more than one instrument; there is fugal writing, in which the same melody is repeated at a different pitch, the kind of thing normally only possible with a combination of instruments or voices, or on a keyboard. Perhaps the greatest example of all this comes in the D Minor Partita for Violin, which in its final movement demands that the player make his instrument sound as though it's in two different places (a kind of echo effect), as well as employing some fierce fugal writing.

However, it's for his keyboard writing that Bach is perhaps most celebrated as an instrumental composer. *Die Kunst der Fuge* (*The Art of Fugue*, written some time between 1745 and 1750), and the two books of *Das Wohltemperirte Klavier*

(*The Well-Tempered Klavier*, the first book appeared in 1722, the second was written between 1738 and 1742) stand as pinnacles in the keyboard repertoire.

Das Wohltemperirte Klavier

These two books exemplify perfectly Bach's habit of taking an idea and pushing it to its technical and intellectual limits. *The Well-Tempered Klavier* consists of 48 pieces (24 to each book) – for this reason it is often known amongst musicians as 'The 48' – which work systematically through each key available in the Western chromatic scale; twelve major, twelve minor. If Scarlatti's sonatas were designed (as pieces written often for pupils) to test the resources of the performer, Bach's collection is aimed at pushing music itself to its outside limits. These works comprise probably the first and most comprehensive exploration of the system of tonality, obeying strict rules of harmony, rules which have come to be seen as best exemplified by Bach's work (so much so that all students of harmony are expected to acquire various Bach techniques as part of their training). Each work consists of a prelude followed by a fugue; the preludes can often be deceptively simple (the most famous is a C major prelude, consisting of arpeggio phrases laying out the C major chord in various positions, with different notes of the chord being used as the bass note, and then modulating to all permissible related keys in similar manner; this prelude was used as the basis for Gounod's setting of the intercessional prayer Ave Maria). The fugues demand that the performer looks at the music as existing simultaneously on several different lines; they are in some ways the instrumental descendants of the vocal polyphony of the Renaissance, with imitative entries standing independently of each other, but each contributing to a euphonious sum. Bach was fond of making keyboard players think in this multi-linear manner; he also wrote sets of two-part and three-part 'inventions' for the keyboard, short, highly structured pieces working (as their description suggests) on two or three interdependent but distinct lines, and many of his keyboard partitas have movements which work in a fugal manner. It is in Bach's composition that you encounter probably the most consistently effective use of 'counterpoint', the use of two contrasting musical lines which none the less work together; a favourite fugal technique is to use two different lines in counterpoint, alternating their entries at different pitches, so that the four lines become two-plus-two or even two-versus-two. *The Well-Tempered Klavier*, or 'The 48', shows Bach at his most systematic and most ingenious.

Die Kunst der Fuge

The Art of Fugue, which was written for Frederick the Great of Prussia, presents slightly more problems from a textual point of view (certain things were left unfinished), and it is perhaps even more academic (though not in a very dry sort of way) than *The Well-Tempered Klavier*. The music takes several forms, being set for a small orchestra as well as for keyboard (and here it has been interpreted by pianists, harpsichordists and organists), and once again Bach pushes himself through the use of fugue and counterpoint, seeing just how far these forms can be taken. If the purpose of 'The 48' is to test the resources of tonality, then *The Art of Fugue* tests the composer's favourite forms.

Organ works

Bach is also undoubtedly the most famous composer ever to have written a substantial body of work for the organ, a difficult instrument to write for, as, despite its supposed resources of differing tones (the different stops are supposed to produce different noises imitative of different instruments), it is deeply inflexible. Bach's Toccata and Fugue in D Minor is without question the best-known organ work ever composed (a toccata is a short, showy, virtuoso piece). Moreover, he wrote not only more fugues for the instrument, but a whole series of 'chorale preludes', works based around famous Lutheran hymn tunes, which are subject to decoration and variation in the unique Bach style (a good many of the Lutheran tunes which have survived from the seventeenth century have done so largely because of Bach's use of them in his chorale preludes and in his cantatas, and in his two great Passions).

The Goldberg Variations

The most fascinating of Bach's keyboard works may, however, be the Goldberg Variations. This was his response to a request in 1741 for some easy-going bedtime listening from an insomniac diplomat, Count Keyserlingk; the request specified 'a few keyboard pieces of a placid but cheerful nature'. Bach in response took a simple theme of very little intrinsic interest and proceeded to base 30 variations on it; variations which took the original theme through every conceivable twist and turn, and which also made severe demands on the performer. At this time of his life, his final decade, Bach was beginning to find himself regarded as a rather stuffy old thing, and all his ideas of fugue, counterpoint and canon were seen as things of the past. His response in this decade included such works as *The Art of Fugue* and his B Minor Mass; the Goldberg Variations are perhaps part of his deeply intellectual counterblast. The 'Goldberg' of the title comes from the name of Count Keyserlingk's bedtime music master, Johann Gottlieb Goldberg (a fourteen-year-old prodigy), who is supposed to have played them often for his employer. Keyserlingk was evidently very grateful; the Variations earned Bach a golden goblet containing 100 louis d'or, a small fortune. What makes the Goldberg Variations more than just a set of interesting academic exercises is a spirituality in the music, evoked partly by the effortlessly melodic flow of many of the variations, but also by a quality best described as translucent, something no other Bach keyboard work quite achieves with this intensity. Very often with Bach, the level of invention makes for a very full, dense sound; in the Goldberg Variations, there's a rare, fascinating sense of space. Bach's keyboard writing is often compared to mathematics; if that comparison holds at all, the Goldberg Variations are at the cutting edge, the furthest reaches of pure mathematical theory.

DISCOGRAPHY
Violin and cello works
Of course, all the most famous instrumentalists have inevitably tried to prove themselves with Bach's music, some to very great effect, and there isn't room to list every great recording here. For solo violin pieces, including a fantastic performance of the D Minor Partita, Itzhak Perlman, the greatest living violinist (probably), offers a stupendous, dynamic account in modern digital sound which scales the heights of violin technique.
● *EMI CDS7 49483-2* ● *2 CDs* ● *Full price* ● *DDD* ● *1987* ○

The unaccompanied cello suites, too, feature on some very fine recordings; there's the rather Romantic, but delicious approach of the great Paul Tortelier, caught towards the end of his career.
● *EMI CDC747035-2* ● *2 CDs, also available separately* ● *Full price* ● *DDD* ● *1983*

Then there's the slightly less flamboyant but very rewarding Maurice Gendron.
● *Philips 422 494/5-2* ● *2 CDs also available separately* ● *Mid-price* ● *ADD*

Pierre Fournier is highly lyrical.
● *Deutsche Grammophon 419 359-2* ● *2 CDs* ● *Mid-price* ● *ADD* ● *1962*

Finally, there are the vintage performances, flawed, but spiritually beautiful, by Pablo Casals (1876–1973), who restored these cello works to the repertoire.
● *EMI CHS7 61027-2* ● *2 CDs* ● *Mid-price* ● *ADD* ● *1936–9*

Keyboard works: piano performances
When buying Bach keyboard works for anything other than organ, it's important to decide whether you prefer the 'authentic' sound of the harpsichord or the modern pianoforte. There are very good recordings whichever your preference; so if you feel the same way as did Sir Thomas Beecham about the sound of the harpsichord (he likened it to two skeletons copulating on a corrugated-iron roof) you needn't feel shut out from Bach's keyboard writing. In fact, all you do is invest in as much of András Schiff's recording of Bach's keyboard music as you want. His sets of the two books of 'The 48' are the best piano recordings available.
● *Book 1: Decca 414 388-2* ● *2 CDs* ● *Full price* ● *DDD* ● *1985*
● *Book 2: Decca 417 236-2* ● *2 CDs* ● *Full price* ● *DDD* ● *1986*

Schiff is also the best choice for a piano version of the Goldberg Variations; his technique is superb, his understanding of the music deep, and he observes all the repeats Bach marked.
● *Decca 417 116-2* ● *1 CD* ● *Full price* ● *DDD* ● *1982* ○

Of course, the most famous piano version of the Goldberg was made by the eccentric Canadian pianist Glenn Gould in the mid-1950s (his insistence on using the same beaten-up stool, his overcoats in summer, his tuneless humming through recordings, and his hypochondriac reliance on strange remedies, helped to make Gould a celebrity). Whether you respond to him depends on your view of his clinical, over-mannered style, which had technical expertise in spades but was sometimes decidedly short on poetry, especially with his insistence on treating every pianistic line as of equal import (fine in Bach, pretty depressing in Beethoven and Mozart). His Goldberg has stood up to the test of time pretty well, although the speeds are as eccentric as the man himself. Famous, but not for first-timers.
● *Sony MYK 44868* ● *1 CD* ● *Mid-price* ● *ADD* ● *1955*

Keyboard works: harpsichord performances
The Art of Fugue is best heard on harpsichord, and the elegant performance and superb annotations provided with the set make Davitt Moroney's *The Gramophone* Award-winner a clear first choice.
● *Harmonia Mundi HMC90 1169/70* ● *2 CDs* ● *Full price* ● *DDD* ● *1985* ○

The greatest harpsichord exponent of 'The 48' is Kenneth Gilbert, who adds a certain subtle sensitivity to his great knowledge to gain an edge on the competition.
● *Deutsche Grammophon Archiv 413 439-2* ● *4 CDs* ● *Full price* ● *DDD* ● *1984*

Gilbert is also very good on the Goldberg Variations, as is Trevor Pinnock (on the same label), but the two best harpsichord exponents are both female. Maggie Cole's single-disc performance loses five repeats, but is nevertheless a deeply felt, illuminating performance.
● *Virgin VC7 91444-2* ● *1 CD* ● *Full price* ● *DDD* ● *1991*

Virginia Black observes every repeat and offers an interesting supporting programme.
● *Collins 70032* ● *2 CDs* ● *Full price* ● *DDD* ● *1991*

Organ music
Anyone wanting a good, cheap introduction to Bach's organ music should snap up Marie-Claire Alain's selection, which includes the famous D Minor Toccata and Fugue and some of the finest chorale preludes. Alain is one of the best organists alive today, and makes the instrument work superbly.
● *Erato Bonsai Collection 2292-45922-2* ● *1 CD* ● *Bargain price* ● *ADD* ● *1981* ○

Quantity and quality: the string quartets of Haydn
Perhaps it's not entirely coincidental that the same composer was responsible for the development of both the symphony and the string quartet as musical genres. The quartet has often had a role as the intimate counterpart to the symphony, and several composers who have been significant in the one form have also been of major importance in the other (Haydn, Beethoven, Shostakovich, even Robert Simpson); the basic structure of the two forms, as evolved by Haydn, was similar, indeed almost identical.

Haydn wrote something like 83

quartets over a period of 40 years; many were written during the period of his employment at Esterház, when he was more or less bound to the Palace there (it was only after Prince Nicholas Esterházy died in 1790 that Haydn had greater freedom to travel). It is in his quartets that we actually see best Haydn's involvement with his two great younger contemporaries, Mozart and Beethoven. Some of his quartets from the 1780s are clearly influenced by Mozart (although Mozart was in no way a great string quartet composer when stood next to Haydn or Beethoven, and he in turn graciously acknowledged his debt in his greatest contributions to the genre, his six 'Haydn' Quartets of 1783 5). There's also an unfinished quartet by Haydn, begun in 1803, which may have been his response (less than enthusiastic) to Beethoven's first six quartets (Opus 18, written between 1798 and 1800).

Haydn's earlier quartets (from the late 1750s and early 1760s) are charming little suite-like affairs, usually with five short movements, deriving more from the incidental form of the divertimento (as its name suggests, not a work designed to tax the intellect). But Haydn took this lightweight form and turned it into something altogether more cunning. As often with concertos at this period, composers would sometimes be commissioned to write chamber music designed for the patron to perform (Mozart's Prussian Quartets, Opus 50, were dedicated to King Friedrich Wilhelm III, an amateur cellist who would have expected to find the cello parts within his grasp), and always specific groups of musicians would be in the composer's mind while he was working; yet despite these considerations, Haydn set out to

explore exactly how far he could take the simple combination of two violins, a viola and a cello. As with the symphonies, many of the quartets have nicknames, some of which hint at effects Haydn wished to achieve (Opus 76, No. 2 is called 'Fifths', because of its employment of the simple motif of a pattern of descending notes at the interval of a fifth), some of which have nothing to do with the music (one is called the 'Razor' Quartet, because of the loan of a razor while Haydn was writing the piece).

By the time Haydn wrote his later quartets, he had developed the role of the cello quite considerably, all part of making the form less top-line dominated. All the qualities to be found in his symphonies are present in the chamber music; the melodic invention and, to an even greater extent, the subtle and surprising shifts of key. The sound quality of just four string instruments playing together allowed Haydn to make greater use of rhythmic devices, too. It was he who first realised that with only four instruments playing, every note could be made to count, and that to combine two parts on the same line might create a special effect (one he uses to great effect in the 'Witches' Minuet', the third movement of the 'Fifths'). The drama that comes from the fleeting, quicksilver sound of a small instrumental group (as opposed to a larger orchestra) is something quite special, as Haydn realised, just as a composer can achieve a certain special form of tension in the quartet form.

Haydn's piano trios

What Haydn did for the quartet, he also did for the combination of violin, cello and piano known as the 'piano trio'. This form was, when Haydn first encountered it, often even more hampered by the amateurism of the patron for whom the work had been written, and such pieces were frequently commissioned for families to play together. The balance between piano (even the old fortepiano) and stringed instruments was often difficult to strike, and the cello's role in affairs was basically minimal, providing a simple, little-moving bass support. Haydn brought his special touch to this form, too (he could, as his cello concertos show, write superb cello music), and in some of his 43 trios he shows perhaps the greatest daring of all in his wide-ranging use of modulation to distant keys.

DISCOGRAPHY
String quartets
Becoming acquainted with Haydn's quartets is now one of the easiest and cheapest things that anyone interested in classical music can do. One of the most imaginative and successful (both artistically and financially) projects of the bargain Naxos label has been the Hungary-based Kodály Quartet's Haydn series, many of which offer simply the best interpretations around of these marvellous pieces, giving you three or four quartets per disc, digitally recorded, for only a fiver each, each disc being available separately. Any of these recordings is well worth the time and the money and won't disappoint; I'd particularly recommend the two discs with the Opus 76 Quartets; not only is there the marvellous 'Fifths' (No. 2), but No. 3, the 'Emperor', has a slow movement centred around the very famous tune 'Austria' (better known to the world as the German national anthem).
● *Nos. 1–3: Naxos 8.550314* ● *1 CD* ● *Bargain price* ● *DDD* ● *1989* ✪
● *Nos. 4–6: Naxos 8.550315* ● *1 CD* ● *Bargain price* ● *DDD* ● *1989* ✪

Three of these quartets, 'Fifths', the 'Emperor', and No. 4 ('Sunrise'), are also available by the Kodály in an earlier performance, and it's equally good.
● *Naxos 8.550129* ● *1 CD* ● *Bargain price* ● *DDD* ● *1988*

Piano trios
The pioneering versions of the piano trios are those recorded by the Beaux Arts Trio, a long-established ensemble and a superb example of the kind of musicianship which grows amongst chamber groups who become entirely familiar with each other's styles. The whole set, though marvellous, probably isn't what the first-time

buyer is after; however, an excellent compilation of four of the best mature trios, including the highly passionate (yet, of course, entirely civilised) F Sharp Minor Trio is available and makes an excellent taster.
● *Philips 422 831-2* ● *1 CD* ● *Mid-price*
● *ADD* ● *1970/2*

EASY-GOING ELEGANCE: MOZART

Piano and violin sonatas
Chamber music isn't an area in which Mozart made an indelible mark, although some of his instrumental sonatas are designed to give a great deal of pleasure. Haydn wrote piano (or rather keyboard) sonatas which, although highly influential at the time, aren't quite at the inspirational level of the quartets and trios and haven't found their way back into popular consciousness to the same extent; Mozart's sonatas contain some miniature gems which may not be quite in the experimental league of Beethoven's later sonatas, but which are nevertheless well worth time and effort spent in listening to them. The works in minor keys are especially interesting (No. 8, K310 and No. 14 K457); like much of Mozart's minor-key writing, they achieve a certain intensity of feeling, and the later work in C minor has a clear foreshadowing of the C Minor Piano Concerto, sharing some of its near-neurotic qualities. This work is usually performed with the virtuosic C Minor Fantasia (K475) as a prelude, and that outgoing piece makes a fine introduction to the sonata (which is also not without its element of display). Some of the violin sonatas are also extremely enjoyable, having almost the quality of song; the combination of violin (as leading

instrument) and piano accompaniment often achieves an effect similar to that of the lied or 'art-song', with the violin taking the role of the voice. Quite a number of the violin sonatas were written when Mozart was very young and such works have, whatever their charm, a limited interest; but the more mature works can be highly engaging, especially when given performances which manage to encompass the music's natural melody and its fine, crisp rhythms.

Responding to Haydn: Mozart's string quartets and String Trio

As I've already said, Mozart's finest moments with the quartet came in his gracious response to Haydn; perhaps the greatest of these works is the C Major 'Dissonance' Quartet (No. 19, K465), named for its slow opening discord, which builds up through the four members of the quartet, creating an ethereal, mysterious atmosphere. This piece, arguably Mozart's best-known and most substantial quartet, was composed in 1785; three years later he turned away from the symphony to produce chamber music which included what is probably his chamber masterpiece, the String Trio in E Flat Major (K563). This came at the same time as three enjoyable piano trios (though they are not quite in the same class as Haydn's). He originally called this work a divertimento (possibly in an attempt to sell it in what was, for him, a lean year; there's some evidence that his more mature chamber music frightened off both audiences and peformers); but it demonstrates Mozart's individuality in taking an unusual combination of instruments (violin, viola and cello) with which few great composers have even bothered, and producing a work

- which includes one of his most purely
- beautiful slow movements. The
- spareness of the musical texture
- which Mozart employs at times (and a
- trio doesn't always make for the
- fullest texture imaginable) is quite
- daring, almost revolutionary, and
- looks forward in some measure to the
- kind of sound-world Beethoven
- produced in his late quartets. Chamber
- music may be one of the less
- substantial elements of Mozart's output,
- but, as always, when he shines in a
- form the effect is sheer brilliance.
-
- ### Wind serenades and clarinet quintet
- Mozart also wrote some fine music for
- slightly larger ensembles, including
- some very fine serenades for wind
- instruments. The serenade was never
- intended to be too demanding, but in
- at least one of these works, the B Flat
- Major Serenade No. 10 ('Gran Partita',
- K361) for twelve wind instruments and
- double bass, he touches once more
- those special heights of genius. It was
- one of the movements from this piece
- that was used in the film *Amadeus* as
- the exemplar of Mozart's cunning
- simplicity; the almost laughable
- squeeze-box-like accompaniment figure
- over which a beautiful melody
- suddenly appears. The C Minor
- Serenade (No. 12, K388; despite its
- numbering, probably written earlier
- than the 'Gran Partita') is a wind octet
- of some economy and passion, an
- almost symphonic four-movement
- piece. Mozart's understanding of the
- sound potential of wind instruments
- was way ahead of its time. His
- Clarinet Quintet, another chamber
- classic, is also one of the first great
- pieces to combine a woodwind
- instrument with a string quartet, to
- marvellous effect – another example of
- Mozart's foresight.

DISCOGRAPHY

Piano sonatas

Undoubtedly the finest modern exponent of the piano sonatas is Mitsuko Uchida; should you want the full set, her versions were included in Philips's excellent Complete Mozart Edition. She brings superb temperament, fine technique, and real understanding to these works.
● *Philips 422 517-2* ● *5 CDs* ● *Mid-price*
● *DDD* ● *1984–6* ✪

András Schiff's complete set, which is more or less in the same league (Schiff shows slightly more delicacy at various moments, although this can sound to some ears like reserve or diffidence), is also now available at mid-price.
● *Decca 430 333-2* ● *5 CDs* ● *Mid-price*
● *ADD/DDD*

Janö Jendo's cycle on separately available discs makes for interesting dabbling if you don't want a full set.
● *Naxos* ● *Bargain price* ● *DDD*

To hear how some of Mozart's mature solo piano music must have sounded to the man himself, there's a fine fortepiano recording, which includes the well-known and deceptively simple C Major Sonata (K545) as part of a generous programme played by the normally non-authentic András Schiff on Mozart's own piano. A very fine disc, and perhaps a fine introduction to this music, even at full price.
● *L'Oiseau-Lyre 433 328-2* ● *1 CD* ● *Full price*
● *DDD* ● *1991*

Violin sonatas

There are quite a lot of extremely enjoyable violin sonata programmes available; again, it's worth starting with the maturer works, which contain more ideas and subtlety, and there's a very fine and reasonably priced selection of three with the thoughtful pianist Radu Lupu and violinist Szymon Goldberg.
● *Decca 425 420-2* ● *1 CD* ● *Mid-price*
● *ADD* ● *1975* ✪

String quartets

The six 'Haydn' Quartets are available either as a set or on three separate discs offering two quartets each, in thoughtful, extremely deep performances by the Chilingarian Quartet. They may not be quite the most virtuosic chamber ensemble, but they have a fine feeling for these six pieces.
● *CRD CRD3362/3/4* ● *3 CDs, also available separately* ● *Full price* ● *ADD* ● *1980* ✪

String Trio

The String Trio (Divertimento) in E Flat is also superbly done in the version by the Grumiaux Trio that forms part of the Philips Complete Mozart Edition. This double set also contains some other lesser-known Mozart chamber pieces, including the very beautiful duos for violin and viola; as an introduction to Mozart's chamber music this could scarcely be bettered, even if these aren't the composer's best-known works.
● *Philips 422 513-2* ● *2 CDs* ● *Mid-price*
● *ADD* ● *1967* ✪

Wind serenades

A recent live recording of the Wind Serenade 'Gran Partita' by Sir Colin Davis and the winds of the Bavarian Radio Symphony Orchestra also offers the lovely C Minor Wind Octet, both in vibrant, warm performances.
● *RCA Victor Red Seal 09026 60873 2* ● *1 CD*
● *Full price* ● *DDD* ● *1991* ✪

Clarinet Quintet

The Clarinet Quintet has done well on disc; sample Andrew Marriner and the Chilingarian ridiculously cheaply, along with a pleasant, if lesser, version of the Oboe Quartet.
● *Classics for Pleasure CD-CFP4377* ● *1 CD*
● *Bargain price* ● *ADD* ● *1981*

THE QUANTUM LEAP: BEETHOVEN

There was no musical form which Beethoven took seriously which he didn't somehow alter irrevocably. The string quartet and the piano sonata both became mediums for his intense struggle with music, and his progress in both forms reflects music's journey from the intelligent, formal world of Haydn to the outer edges of music's possibilities. The sonatas and quartets both show the typical Beethovenian progress; early Haydn-influenced music with great regard to formal nicety; 'middle-period' music of fire, drama and intensity which is trying to drive a way through to something new; and final 'end-period' music capable of exhibiting great passion, but full of strange, surprising twists and turns, ruminative (apparent) meanderings, and a new freedom with regard to form.

The early quartets; the Rasumovsky Quartets

It's easiest to separate out the quartets into the three periods just mentioned, as Beethoven's creative involvement with the form came at three distinct points of time. His first six quartets, all under the umbrella of Opus 18 (implying that the composer himself saw them as a related set, possibly for a specific venue), were written while Haydn was still an active composer, between 1798 and 1800. These are very Haydn-like works; they have the same thematic economy which is typical of the older composer, building whole movements out of five-beat phrases, with cunning use of counterpoint, yet essentially civilised, formally shaped in four movements of about the same dimensions as Haydn's. Between 1805 and 1810 Beethoven wrote five more quartets, of which the best known are the three Opus 59 works, written for a diplomat called Count Rasumovsky (and hence known as the 'Rasumovsky' Quartets). These began the process of taking the quartet into new territory; the very first opens with a long development of a cello theme (something Mozart had done, too), but this leads not to any ensemble tonal certainty but a wavering, harmonically uncertain passage and a movement in which the music moves in ever-weakening wave-like surges. In the first Rasumovsky Quartet Beethoven also extends the length of the quartet movement; and although through all three the traditional Classical style is always to be found somewhere, it's as though Beethoven were straining at its leash. In the Finale of the 3rd Rasumovsky (in C Major), he uses the old form of the fugue, creating a fugue out of two unremarkable subjects, using the extra fugal subject to increase the music's emotional intensity and build towards an overwhelming climax. This has its counterpart in the final quartets in the long 'Grosse Fuge', usually treated now as a separate piece, although originally intended as the Finale of the B Flat Quartet, Opus 130.

Beethoven's late quartets

The five late quartets (Nos. 12–16, Opuses 127, 130–2 and 135) were written between 1823 and 1826, a time when Beethoven was essentially writing music for himself. These works are now regarded as almost sacred, though this hasn't always been so; Sir Thomas Beecham, for one, had a dim view of them ('written by a deaf man and best listened to by a deaf man'). Two (Nos. 12 and 16) are of traditional four-movement form, although only the final one is of anything resembling Haydn-esque proportions. Throughout, the late quartets are altogether more fragmentary, more prepared to take risks with the shapes and forms of music, prepared sometimes to break down almost completely and turn into music which leaves as much silence between the notes as there are notes. Intensity is built out of diffusion, and at times Beethoven happily spreads his four instruments as far apart across their registers as is possible. Quartet No. 14 in C Sharp Minor (Opus 131) has as many as seven movements, the longest lasting for over quarter of an hour, the shortest less than a minute (yet still specified very clearly as a distinct movement), and Beethoven changes the moods and tones of the music. The A Minor Quartet (No. 15, Opus 132), arguably the greatest of all these great works (if one can make such comparisons), has as its central third movement a huge slow piece entitled 'Hymn of Gratitude from a Convalescent to the Divinity in the Lydian Mode' (Beethoven wrote it after recovering from an illness); this builds from a slow, transparent beginning, almost ridiculously static in its presentation, to something powerful, lyrical and intense, in which Beethoven's close studies of Palestrina's music have clearly been influential. It's not all slow stuff here, either; the scherzos, often marked 'presto' (very fast), are full of wit and bouncing rhythm. It is possible that the late quartets won't grab you at all; but if they hold the slightest appeal, you could easily end up thinking that they rank amongst the greatest music ever written.

The piano sonatas

Beethoven, who was himself primarily a pianist, wrote 32 piano sonatas over about 30 years between 1793 and 1822; as with many composers, piano sonatas were amongst his earliest works (more than one composer has a piano sonata as his Opus 1), and he abandoned the form before he wrote any of the late quartets. This latter fact may be more than mere coincidence, as there is a great sense in the last four sonatas (written from 1818) that Beethoven is testing the resources of the piano and eventually finding them wanting. Many of the most famous piano sonatas come surprisingly early in Beethoven's output; it was possibly at the piano that he first found his passionate and expressive style. Although the 5th Sonata (Opus 10, No. 1) in C Minor, written in the 1790s, has overtones of Mozart's C minor piano writing (the opening of C minor piano pieces seems almost to have been an established rhetorical gesture at this point in musical history), it already shows signs of the more expressive, personal Beethoven style which was fully developed by the next C minor sonata, No. 8 (Opus 13), the 'Pathétique', belonging still – just – to the eighteenth century, which is a formidable work technically and makes an immediate impact.

The most famous of the sonatas is, of course, No. 14 in C Sharp Minor

(Opus 27, No. 2), the 'Moonlight', whose nickname is a Romantic accretion derived from the atmospheric first movement. Beethoven intended this work (composed in 1801) to be a 'sonata quasi una fantasia' ('almost a fantasia'), allowing himself a certain distance and freedom from the constraint of the formal sonata. The Opus 31 sonatas, written the following year, show Beethoven moving even further forward, above all in the first movement of the D Minor No. 17, the 'Tempest', which alternates slow, hesitant, almost over-simple arpeggios of chords with helter-skeltering runs, making the sense of time in the movement constantly unsettled. Mature Beethoven piano writing, though, comes phenomenally early (perhaps not so surprisingly, since the piano was his instrument), with No. 21 in C Major (Opus 53), the 'Waldstein', (named for its dedicatee, his friend Count Ferdinand von Waldstein, and written between 1803 and 1804). The Waldstein opens with thirteen quick repetitions of a C major chord, and although it has only two movements it is still over 25 minutes long – a sign of Beethoven's typical development of dimensions, with the balance beginning to shift once again to the Finale. The 'Appassionata' (No. 23 in F Minor, Opus 57) managed a totally new combination of lyrical beauty with something approaching brute force, as Beethoven used crashing, very loud chords repeated, almost symbolic of his trying to force the music into a new dimension. This approach was taken even further in the 'Hammerklavier' (No. 29 in B Flat, Opus 106, the first of the final four masterpieces; it should be noted that the nickname here derives simply from the term – the old German word for piano as distinct from harpsichord – which Beethoven constantly used at this period to denote the piano, although inevitably, given the near-violence of some of the chordal work in the sonata's first movement, a misunderstanding about this has arisen), although the real challenge of this sonata was its meandering slow movement, an eighteen-minute adagio full of apparent dead-ends and travels along byways, made even more extreme and pointed by coming after a two-minute scherzo. It is this ruminating quality, this unpredictability, which marks the late sonatas, as they search out the forms they are using. The next, No. 30 in E Major, prefaces a long finale set of variations with two extremely short movements (the first of which swings wildly between two extremes of tempo); while the 32nd and last sonata continues this relaxed approach to form with a two-movement work ostensibly in C minor, but which works its way to a conclusive C major by the halfway point. The second movement literally goes nowhere, and at times Beethoven seems to be using the old ornament of the trill to find smaller divisions of musical time, and even to force the music's way between the notes of the Western scale. It seems almost as though, after this, Beethoven had nowhere left to go on the piano.

Other instrumental and chamber pieces

Beethoven also wrote ten violin sonatas of which the 5th ('Spring') and the 9th ('Kreutzer') have become particular classics of the repertoire. All but the last of these ten were written in the six years between 1797 and 1803, and they reveal in

Beethoven a surprising gift for melody, though there's more to the best of them than that; there are subtle little dynamic shifts, and in the Kreutzer we once again see Beethoven's taste for developing intimate works to lengths getting on for the epic. There are also cello, flute and horn sonatas, none quite in the same mould, but Beethoven's trio writing cannot be overlooked; amongst his piano trios are the 'Archduke' (Opus 97), with its noble opening melody, and the 'Ghost' (Opus 70, No. 1), whose ethereal slow movement with its stalking bass gives the work its nickname, whilst the 'Kakadu' Variations (Opus 121) have much melodic charm. Beethoven also wrote a septet in 1800, a six-movement divertimento-style piece, which is actually most effectively served by the rearrangement he made of it five years later for clarinet trio (clarinet, piano and cello).

The 'Diabelli' Variations

One solo piano work which Beethoven connoisseurs prize greatly is the 'Diabelli' Variations. Beethoven had been asked in 1822 to contribute to a set of variations, by about 50 different composers, on a waltz by Anton Diabelli (1781–1858). Initially he refused, but then had a change of heart and produced these 32 transformations, which put Diabelli's rather wretched little tune through the wringer, parodying it, improving it, and eventually achieving something of the atmosphere of Bach's Goldberg set. Beethoven always surprised at the piano; even when he wrote 'bagatelles' (supposedly meaning 'trifles') the results, especially in the final set (Opus 126, amongst the last works he wrote for the piano), are small pieces of great beauty, whose apparent simplicity sets a real technical challenge to the pianist.

DISCOGRAPHY

String quartets

Purists swear that the best recordings ever of the Beethoven quartets, especially the late ones, were made by the Busch Quartet back in the 1930s and 1940s. Surprisingly, only two Busch performances have so far made it onto CD, and even slightly hissy sound doesn't detract from their magnificent quality. You get a fair sample of Beethoven quartet writing, too; the first of the three Razumovsky Quartets and the six-movement B Flat Opus 130 (sadly with the alternative last movement, rather than the gigantic Grosse Fuge).
● *Sony Masterworks Portrait MPK 47687*
● *1 CD* ● *Mid-price* ● *AAD* ● *1941/2* ○

For the quartets in general, whose versions you should buy does depend upon which pieces you want. For the early works, the Alban Berg Quartet, often described as leading modern exponents of Beethoven, are probably best.
● *EMI CDC7 47127/8/9-2* ● *3 CDs also available separately* ● *Full price* ● *ADD/DDD* ● *1979/80*

The Italian Quartet (or 'Quartetto Italiano', as the record company always refers to them) are long-standing Beethoven interpreters in their several incarnations, and they have a particular flair for the Razumovsky Quartets, even if the CD transfer has shown up a slightly threadbare quality in the top registers. The set also includes the other two 'middle period' quartets.
● *Philips 420 797-2* ● *3 CDs* ● *Mid-price*
● *ADD* ● *1971–4*

Opinions are wildly divided about the merits of several of the sets of late quartets. For some, the Sheffield-based Lindsay Quartet are the last word in expressive and powerful performance; for others they're inaccurate, over-driven, given to irritating humming (chamber performers seem particularly given to humming along with their performance). Their Grosse Fuge is a chapter of disasters, but they do bring out certain qualities of the other quartets which can only too easily be overlooked, and as a force to be reckoned with in the chamber world they're worth hearing.
● *ASV CD DCS 403* ● *4 CDs also available separately* ● *Full price* ● *ADD* ● *1987*

The Italian Quartet are much more reliable than the Lindsays, but on occasion much duller too, just a little too safe. Stunning at times, though, and a relative bargain, although it would be nice if the discs were available separately.
● *Philips 426 050-2* ● *4 CDs* ● *Mid-price*
● *1971*

There is a more recent recording by the same ensemble of the 12th and 16th Quartets, and very fine it is too; another good introduction to this music.
● *Philips 422 840-2* ● *1 CD* ● *Mid-price*
● *ADD*

Piano sonatas

The Beethoven piano sonatas have been recorded by every serious pianist (and quite a few who don't merit that title); in my view the race is not always to the 'great names', some of whom don't always offer tremendous value for money. I'm a great admirer of the bargain releases by the occasionally wayward John Lill; sometimes he drives hard, sometimes he pushes slow tempos to extremes, yet he's never ever dull and he always brings the music home dazzlingly.
● *ASV Quicksilva* ● *10 CDs available separately*
● *Bargain price* ● *ADD* ● *1977–81* ○

Another excellent, if unfashionable, Beethoven performer is Bernard Roberts, whose second sonata cycle has some terrific things in it, a fine, unfussy technique, and some really intellectual yet passionate playing.
● *Nimbus NI5050-60* ● *11 CDs also available separately* ● *Special price* ● *DDD* ● *1982–5*

Among bigger, better known names, Wilhelm Kempff offers very good value, even if the technique is sometimes a little wayward.
● *Deutsche Grammophon 429 306-2* ● *9 CDs some available separately* ● *Bargain price*
● *ADD* ● *1964/5*

And once familiar with these pieces, everyone should at least hear the great Artur Schnabel, often hailed as the greatest Beethoven pianist.
● *EMI CHS7 63765-2* ● *8 CDs* ● *Mid-price*
● *ADD* ● *1932–5*

Amongst non-cycle discs (which aren't always great value), Emil Gilels's *The Gramophone* Award-winning recording of the 'Hammerklavier', one of his last studio sessions, is titanic, even if appallingly bad value, but then you can't buy great musicianship by the yard.
● *Deutsche Grammophon 410 527-2* ● *1 CD*
● *Full price* ● *DDD* ● *1983*

Another *The Gramophone* Award-winner, Maurizio Pollini's set of the last five sonatas, is a modern classic.
● *Deutsche Grammophon 419 199-2* ● *2 CDs*
● *Full price* ● *ADD* ● *1975/7*

Violin sonatas

A recent set of the violin sonatas featuring violinist Pinchas Zukerman and pianist Marc Neikrug, something of an established partnership, really finds new depths in these works, especially in familiar pieces like the 'Spring' Sonata.
● *RCA Victor Red Seal RD60991* ● *4 CDs*
● *Special price* ● *DDD* ● *1991* ○

The combination of Itzhak Perlman and Vladimir Ashkenazy makes for a fine single disc of 'Spring' and the 'Kreutzer'.
● *Decca 410 554-2* ● *1 CD* ● *Full price*
● *ADD* ● *1975*

Piano and clarinet trios
The best combination ever to take on the piano
trios also features Perlman and Ashkenazy, with
cellist Lynn Harrell; their full set is a bit pricey,
but the single disc including the 'Archduke' is well
worth having.
● *EMI CDC7 47010-2* ● *1 CD* ● *Full price*
● *DDD* ● *1982* ○

There's an excellent, solid recording with two
clarinet trios (including the rearranged Septet),
affordable and very winning, by the Dutch Trio
Dante.
● *Canal Grande CG 9105* ● *1 CD* ● *Mid-price*
● *DDD* ● *1989*

Diabelli Variations and Bagatelles
One of the century's greatest pianists has made a
fine recording of the Diabelli Variations; Sviatoslav
Richter offers a live performance – in every sense.
● *Philips 422 416-2* ● *1 CD* ● *Full price*
● *DDD* ● *1986* ○

But there's also a fine version by another great, if
slightly less celebrated, Beethoven pianist, Stephen
Kovacevich.
● *Philips 422 969-2* ● *1 CD* ● *Bargain price*
● *ADD* ● *1968*

And it was through listening to Kovacevich that I
first came to realise the greatness of the
apparently slight Bagatelles; his recording offers
all three sets, and he makes them a beautiful,
memorable experience.
● *Philips 426 976-2* ● *1 CD* ● *Bargain price*
● *ADD* ● *1974* ○

THE MELODIC WAY FORWARD: SCHUBERT

Schubert's chamber and solo
instrumental music was, in a lot of
cases, contemporary with Beethoven's,
and while it shares similar
preoccupations, it often finds different
ways in which to approach them. His
great string quartets (and two other
remarkable chamber works) and piano
sonatas came in the 1820s after
Schubert had been through the phase
of writing unfinished works, including
the Unfinished Symphony. There were
about ten false starts on piano sonatas,
and it took a fragmentary attempt at a
C minor quartet (usually listed as No.
12 and known as the 'Quartettsatz' or
'Quartet Movement') before Schubert

found quite the right vocabulary in
this form.

The 'Trout' Quintet

Schubert's first eleven quartets aren't
major contributions to the genre;
they're really student exercises, and
show some signs of having had a
helping hand from Schubert's
composition teacher, Antonio Salieri.
The first indication of Schubert's
greatness as a composer of chamber
music came in 1819 with the Piano
Quintet in A Major, known as 'The
Trout' because the fourth of the five
movements is a set of variations on
the melody of Schubert's song 'Die
Forelle' ('The Trout'). The
instrumentation of the quintet is piano
plus violin, viola, cello and
double-bass, written for these forces
because these were the musicians
around in the home where Schubert
was spending a holiday. The
Variations movement is the highlight
of the work, although throughout it
shows Schubert's great melodic
invention, as well as giving some sign
of the kind of chamber sound and
style he was to favour, one which
eschewed the detailed contrapuntal
techniques of Haydn or Beethoven and
aimed at an altogether more
melody-dominated sound, with lots of
harmonic variation.

The late string quartets

As befits a piece written while on
holiday, 'The Trout' has a genial feel
to it, which contrasts strongly with the
minor-key, near neurosis of four of the
five great quartets (including the
'Quartettsatz'), which often play bold
tricks by directly confronting major
and minor keys. In fact, this is most
effectively done in the opening
movement of the final G Major Quartet
(No. 15); but it is there too in the A

Minor Quartet (No. 13). The penultimate D Minor Quartet (No. 14) is known as 'Death and the Maiden', as once again Schubert makes a movement out of variations on one of his song melodies. This time, however, the song is, as the title suggests, much more forbidding, and the atmosphere of this whole quartet is dark, brooding and dramatic. Unusually, Schubert makes the work's short Scherzo a great focus of interest by reprising several themes from the first two movements, and by once again having major and minor keys confront each other. Perhaps the final quartet is the greatest of all, with its shimmering opening chords shifting constantly across tonalities and its density of sound (Schubert by now regarded quartet writing as 'paving the way' for writing a great symphony), all making for a spiritual ambiguity which looks forward the best part of a century to the moods found in Mahler's music.

The String Quintet

However, even the greatest of the quartets has to bow to the sheer genius of the String Quintet in C Major, written during the composer's final illness. The traditional quartet (two violins, viola and cello) are joined by an extra cello, which allows for a magnificent effect in the first movement, where a beautiful melodic theme is played by the first cello and shadowed by the second. Once again, Schubert's daring in modulating around unexpected keys is extraordinary, taking over where Haydn left off, and he remains unafraid to place directly contrasting and opposing moods next to each other. The String Quintet is a fitting climax to Schubert's extraordinary chamber music.

There are several trios as well, including a one-movement Nocturne ('night-piece') in E Flat which is something of a gem, and a series of early violin sonatas (always described, thanks to a publisher of the day, as 'sonatinas') which are very much in the melodic cast of Schubert's lieder.

Piano works: sonatas, impromptus, the 'Wanderer' Fantasy

It might give some idea of the extraordinary quality of Schubert's sonatas if I tell the story of how one of the greatest pianists of the first half of the twentieth century, Artur Schnabel (1882–1951), came to know these pieces, which in those days weren't at all in popular favour. In an age where virtuosity of a showy kind was considered of paramount importance, Schnabel's teacher one day told his pupil 'You will never make a pianist; you are a musician'. He followed this up by suggesting that he look at and learn Schubert's sonatas because of their difficulties, which are mainly inward rather than virtuosic. The only truly virtuosic solo piano work Schubert wrote is the 'Wanderer' Fantasy (written in 1822), a piece in four connected movements using a simple motto as a linking device and full of most un-Schubert-like display. In contrast, the piano sonatas are ruminative, with only No. 17 in D Major coming close to rivalling the 'Wanderer'. It, like the 'Trout' Quintet, was the product of a holiday, and it is quicker in both its opening movement and its slow movement (which is unusually marked 'Con moto' – 'with movement'). The final three sonatas were all completed by Schubert only two months before his death in 1828 (although sketches for them go back over a year before that). They form a remarkable trilogy, clearly written in the shadow of Beethoven's death, but showing an extreme and venturesome attitude towards tonal and key relationships which even Beethoven would have found extraordinary; the Finale of the last sonata has a theme which keeps on starting in the 'wrong' key, while the same work's slow movement takes the idea of static, timeless, suspended music to new levels. Quite why these pieces remained ignored for almost a century is a mystery to me.

Schubert also wrote a good many shorter piano works which have remained popular, and which are both eminently accessible and illustrative of his ability. The Impromptus (whose name implies that they are almost spontaneous emissions of no importance) are clever short pieces with a lot of rhythmic spring and the usual Schubert talent for melody. As Schubert's genius, which has been criminally underrated for almost 200 years in all but a handful of works, is gradually rediscovered to its fullest extent, various other apparent trifles (like the twelve Ländlers) turn out to be small masterpieces. If you find Schubert at all appealing, then I can guarantee that you will go on making new discoveries the further you go (and we haven't discussed the lieder yet).

DISCOGRAPHY
'Trout' Quintet
Once again, there's no need to splash out for full-price discs to get acquainted with much of Schubert's chamber music. An excellent version of the 'Trout' Quintet is available from Naxos with chamber stars the Kodály Quartet and the excellent Jenö Jando at the piano. Delicate playing, careful phrasing, a bargain.
● *Naxos 8.550658* ● *1 CD* ● *Bargain price* ● *DDD* ● *1991* ○

A slightly (but only slightly) pricier 'Trout' comes in a more vintage set with Yehudi and Hepzibah Menuhin and members of the now-disbanded Amadeus Quartet; this double set also features small gems like the Nocturne in E Flat, as well as two piano trios.
● *EMI CZS7 62742-2* ● *2 CDs* ● *Mid-price* ● *ADD* ● *1958–68*

String quartets
If you want to dabble before plunging into all the string quartets, then Naxos and the Kodály Quartet once again provide a very competitive and enjoyable route, in a disc combining the Quartettsatz and the 'Death and the Maiden' Quartet.
● *Naxos 8.550590* ● *1 CD* ● *Bargain price* ● *DDD* ● *1991* ○

For a full set of the great final four quartets, then the American-based Juilliard String Quartet offer the best all-round value, culminating in a dynamic and at times terrifying No. 15.
● *CBS/Sony Maestro M2YK 45617* ● *2 CDs* ● *Mid-price* ● *ADD* ● *1979–82* ○

String Quintet
Naxos also offer a distinguished version of the String Quintet played by the Ensemble Villa Musica with great musical insight and understanding, made even more of a bargain by the additional inclusion of a String Trio in B Flat.
● *Naxos 8.550388* ● *1 CD* ● *Bargain price* ● *DDD* ● *1990* ○

For a little more money there's the most complete version of this work ever recorded, made under studio conditions at a festival some 40 years ago, and featuring great names such as Isaac Stern and the two great cellists Paul Tortelier and Pablo Casals. A classic.
● *Sony Masterworks Portrait MPK 44853* ● *1 CD* ● *Mid-price* ● *ADD* ● *1953*

Piano music
Getting acquainted with Schubert's piano music is slightly more expensive. A good starter buy is Alfred Brendel's combination of the virtuoso 'Wanderer' Fantasy and the last piano sonata (No. 21 in B Flat). Brendel is one of the most intellectual musicians around, and Schubert is a composer he loves deeply and to whom he has done great service.
● *Philips 420 644-2* ● *1 CD* ● *Mid-price* ● *ADD* ○

Brendel's more recent fully digital recordings of the other sonatas are also full of love and understanding; he has real ideas about these works, and often imagines them as orchestral pieces as he plays. Try the D Major (No. 17) and A Minor (No. 14).
● *Philips 422 063-2* ● *1 CD* ● *Full price* ● *DDD* ● *1987*

And there's an excellent combination of miniature pieces, including four impromptus and the twelve Ländler, in deeply subtle readings by András Schiff.
● *Decca 425 638-2* ● *1 CD* ● *Full price* ● *DDD* ● *1989*

Eventually, though, you should try Schnabel's superb, if elderly, recordings.
● *Sonatas Nos. 17, 20 and 21, plus other smaller pieces: EMI CHS7 64259 2* ● *2 CDs* ● *Mid-price* ● *ADD* ● *1937/9*
● *Impromptus: EMI CDH7 61021 2* ● *1 CD* ● *Mid-price* ● *ADD* ● *1939/50*

A CHAMBER PRODIGY: MENDELSSOHN

Both Schubert and Beethoven were still alive when the much younger Felix Mendelssohn produced his most stunning piece of chamber music, the Octet for Strings in E Flat Major. Mendelssohn was only sixteen when he wrote this work, and some claim it to be the greatest piece he ever composed. The intensity he achieved with his eight string instruments, a simple double string quartet, is almost symphonic, and no greater work has been written for eight instruments (Schubert did write an octet which has its champions, but it's bland next to Mendelssohn's). As always with Mendelssohn there's a high quotient of melodic invention, but here the youthful composer blended that natural skill with a dramatic drive which isn't always present in his more mature work, and which makes the string symphonies sound pale by comparison. At a time when chamber musicians often felt at liberty to play like soloists, Mendelssohn included a specific note in his Octet demanding that they play as an ensemble.

There are also quartets and quintets by Mendelssohn; perhaps the greatest of these is the 6th (and last) Quartet in F Minor, written to commemorate the death of his sister and preceding his own by a very few months. This touches once again those heights of intensity to be found in the Octet, and was highly rated by contemporaries for its eloquence and 'gloomy foreboding'.

Mendelssohn also turned out piano music by the yard, most famously a series of 'Songs without Words', which are, as the name suggests, primarily melodic. Not deep music, but highly engaging when one is in the right mood.

DISCOGRAPHY

Two recordings of the Octet lead all the rest; one on modern instruments, one on period instruments of c. 1825. The modern-instrument recording is by the Academy of St Martin-in-the-Fields Chamber Ensemble, and it's really passionate stuff; eight very fine players blending superbly and producing a really full sound. This disc also includes the 2nd String Quintet, very well done.
● *Philips 420 400-2* ● *1 CD* ● *Full price*
● *ADD* ● *1979* ❂

The period ensemble involved are called Hausmusik (they include, in the Octet, the British exponent of 'authentic' violin, Monica Huggett), and while their reading is, inevitably given the nature of period instruments, less full-bodied, it is none the less a passionate, intelligent and committed performance. This disc also gives you the 1st String Quintet.
● *EMI CDC7 49958-2* ● *1 CD* ● *Full price*
● *DDD* ● *1989*

There's a very fine live performance of the 6th String Quartet (coupled with Brahms's 2nd) by the Lindsay Quartet. As so often with the Lindsay, there's huffing and puffing, and intonation slides a bit, but the spirit of the work is superbly communicated and the sense of occasion is terrific.
● *ASV CD DCA 712* ● *1 CD* ● *Full price*
● *DDD* ● *1988*

For a selection of the Songs without Words, try the cool and clear recording by the excellent András Schiff.
● *Decca 421 119-2* ● *1 CD* ● *Full price*
● *DDD* ● *1987*

THE GREAT PIANO COMPOSERS: SCHUMANN

At the heart of the nineteenth century lie three of the greatest composers of music for solo piano, two of whom were, of course, amongst the greatest virtuosos of all time on the instrument.

The exception was Schumann who, as I've said, ruined his hands with some hare-brained scheme of his own. Schumann's music is also perhaps more restrained, more touched by the Classicism of Beethoven, than either Liszt's or Chopin's; and certainly Schumann's piano masterpiece, the C Major Fantasia (Opus 17), draws on a

Beethoven melody for part of its thematic material. The Fantasia, like many of Schumann's earlier works for the piano, was written with the intention of pleasing Clara Wieck, his teacher's virtuoso daughter (and later his wife); hence its use of part of a Beethoven love song. It turns the usual expectations of the sonata inside out, placing the confident, outgoing movement at the centre, and surrounding this with two movements which create, through a technically challenging torrent of notes, a more shimmering atmosphere, prone to restraint and sudden doubt. Much of Schumann's piano music had an autobiographical edge to it; the 'Davidsbündlertänze' (literally 'David's-League dances') were connected with Schumann and his friends' artistic visions of themselves as a set of Davids fighting against the Philistines who didn't appreciate their talent; and in pieces like 'Waldszenen' ('Forest Scenes') and 'Kinderszenen' ('Scenes from Childhood'), although these are in one sense descriptive genre pieces with parallels in the visual art world, there is also a strong effect of Schumann recalling episodes of his own life. He also believed that solo piano music could be both virtuosic and yet, in some way, highly intellectual; hence he wrote a series of pieces called 'Kreisleriana', drawing on the artistic and critical theories of E. T. A. Hoffmann (who sometimes used the pseudonym 'Kreisler' for articles) for inspiration. Schumann's piano music is formidable, at times almost a little too daunting; and yet it has all the ecstasies of Romanticism, especially in the Fantasia. His two violin sonatas, written in four and six days in 1851, are also of a high order of invention, and actually show rather

well (almost as well as the Piano Concerto) how the two sides of Schumann's nature could combine; both his passionate and his melancholic aspects are on full view here.

CHOPIN

Chopin's piano music is some of the most purely Romantic ever written, and some of the most demanding. All of it is highly melodic, and much of it is heavily rhythmic. Chopin took dance forms – the mazurka and polonaise from his native Poland, and the then new and dangerous waltz – and worked through them exhaustively, creating works both brilliant and melancholic. He also wrote the most famous funeral march in the whole of music. It's probably for his less heavily structured and intellectually planned music that Chopin is best loved; the small, beautiful Preludes (which work through the major and minor tonal systems, rather like Bach's more elaborate and cerebral Preludes and Fugues). He even managed to make the 'étude' or 'study' – which could, in the hands of certain minor piano composers, be just the kind of boring exercise the name implies – a focus for brilliance, and never more so than in the so-called 'Revolutionary' Étude (written in 1831 when Chopin learnt of the fall of Warsaw to the invading Russians). The piano had developed from a five-octave instrument in Mozart's day to one of seven-plus-octaves (pretty close to the instrument we know today) in Chopin's heyday, and technical refinements meant that the range of tones was wider than before, so that the range of effects also became greater. Thus Chopin's music runs the gamut from the brilliance of the

Waltzes to the moody, suspended animation of the haunting Berceuse in D Flat (Opus 57) to the complex yet ethereal sound of several of the Nocturnes.

LISZT

All through Chopin's relatively short career (he was 39 when he died in 1849) the dominant musical figure in Europe was the flamboyant virtuoso Franz Liszt. For a long time Liszt's music for the solo piano was relegated to the position of second-rate showy trash, having no intellect whatsoever. This is rather far from the truth; in many of his piano pieces Liszt's music looks forward to styles and developments that lay a long way in the future. The music descriptive of various sights and phenomena in Italy and Switzerland of the three books of piano pieces, *Années de Pèlerinage* (*Years of Pilgrimage*) has, in places, all the subtle impressionism and colour of Debussy. The Mephisto Waltzes (especially the first of the four) are actually dramatic tours de force which take the piano's range to the very edge in order to portray something about Liszt's own psychological fascination with the Faust legend, anticipating on a small scale what Richard Strauss would do with an orchestra (Strauss was in many ways Liszt's natural successor, as we shall see). Of course, there are the technique-laden pieces full of exhilarating and exciting moments, like the Hungarian Rhapsodies. There are endless piano transcriptions of operatic themes and of orchestral works such as the Beethoven symphonies. There are quiet, haunting works (which also, like Chopin's Berceuse, achieve an effect of suspended animation) like the *Liebesträume* (*Love's Dreams*) and the six Consolations. But above all, at the centre of Liszt's work is the B Minor Piano Sonata, written in 1852/3 for Robert Schumann, but never seen by its dedicatee. This one-movement work (the boundaries of movements have broken down in it; again, Liszt anticipates much of what was to come in the 'Modern' music of the early twentieth century) is of course grand and rhetorical, but unlike many other of his works, it was not written to show off his own technique. By this stage of his career he had retired from giving public concerts and only ever played for small gatherings of friends and admirers. The Piano Sonata tries to take in the whole of musical history to that point, including the two composers whom Liszt dubbed the 'Old Testament' – Bach – and the 'New Testament' – Beethoven. Liszt's sonata takes three small figures, laid out at the very opening, and pushes them through a series of remarkable transformations, making something dark and mysterious sound warm and lyrical, and bringing back material from the start when least expected; the slow section suddenly recalls the beginning as the subject of a sort of fugue (homage to Bach). The piano's resources are tested to the full in what seems to be a bravura ending, but Liszt fools the listener completely with a superb, hushed recollection of the slower section's initial theme. By refusing to divide the sonata into distinct movements, each with its own ending, Liszt makes the form a series of unfolding moods; again a touch which looks forward to Debussy or even Schoenberg. The B Minor Sonata is one of the most complete piano works ever written, and once again shows why Richard Wagner held Liszt in quite such esteem.

DISCOGRAPHY
Schumann
We're dealing here with repertoire which some of the greatest pianists have touched with a little magic, and names such as Artur Rubinstein and Vladimir Horowitz are never dull and always worth hearing playing any piece I've mentioned above. And hopping back to Schubert as well, you can get an excellent, superbly poised performance of his 'Wanderer' Fantasy along with Schumann's Fantasia played by the Prince of Olympians, Murray Perahia.
● *CBS/Sony MK 42124* ● *1 CD* ● *Full price*
● *DDD* ● *1986* ✪

The excellent Alfred Brendel can be trusted here, too, combining the Fantasia with the smaller, spirited, diverse Fantasiestücke.
● *Philips 411 049-2* ● *1 CD* ● *Full price*
● *DDD* ● *1983*

And Rubinstein is subtle, poetic and philosophical by turns, giving us the Fantasia and the Kreisleriana.
● *RCA Victor Red Seal RD 86258* ● *1 CD*
● *Full price* ● *ADD* ● *1965*

Another, more modern, fine and all-embracing account of the Kreisleriana comes from Martha Argerich, a first-class Schumann player, with some beautifully observed subtle versions of the Kinderszenen.
● *Deutsche Grammophon 410 653-2* ● *1 CD*
● *Full price* ● *DDD* ● *1983*

Argerich is also the accompanist in a truly gripping recording of the violin sonatas, with the excellent chamber performer Gidon Kremer taking the other role.
● *Deutsche Grammophon 419 235-2* ● *1 CD*
● *Full price* ● *DDD* ● *1986*

Chopin
The Schumann recommendations I've listed are all a bit pricey (but artistically wonderful); however, you can save a great deal of money on Chopin's piano works simply by getting hold of as many as you want of Turkish pianist Idil Biret's complete Chopin on the Naxos label. As an all-round Chopin performer, Biret has the good taste and sensitivity not to turn the composer's work into a 'gloopy', over-Romantic syrup.
● *Naxos 8.550356-67/8.550508* ● *13 CDs also available separately* ● *Bargain price* ● *DDD*
● *1990–92* ✪

There's a rather elderly live performance of the two books of Études played by a young Vladimir Ashkenazy which is also well worth seeking out; really fiery stuff.
● *Saga Classics SCD 9002* ● *1 CD* ● *Mid-price*
● *AAD* ● *1950s*

Martha Argerich is as good at Chopin as at Schumann, and a selection played by her is

first-rate; a superb reading of the 24 Preludes, and with a few 'goodies' such as the Barcarolle in F Sharp Major and the famous A Flat Major Polonaise (possibly the definitive polonaise).
● *Deutsche Grammophon 415 836-2* ● *1 CD*
● *Mid-price* ● *ADD* ● *1967–77*

Chopin's piano sonatas, deeply complex works, aren't perhaps the most accessible pieces he ever wrote, but in the hands of Maurizio Pollini, the complexities of Nos. 2 and 3 are laid bare with style, wit and cunning.
● *Deutsche Grammophon 415 346 3* ● *1 CD*
● *Full price* ● *DDD* ● *1985*

Liszt
A good cheap selection of Liszt's piano music – and very generous at about 78 minutes – comes from the South Korean Kun Woo Paik; he includes a Hungarian Rhapsody, the 1st Mephisto Waltz, and the sublimely proto-Impressionist 'Les Jeux d'Eau à la Villa d'Este' ('Fountains at the Villa d'Este') from the *Years of Pilgrimage*.
● *Virgo VJ7 91458-2* ● *1 CD* ● *Bargain price*
● *DDD* ● *1990* ✪

Another Liszt selection, played by the underrated British pianist David Wilde, is also worth investigating; a different Hungarian Rhapsody, a fantasia on an aria from Wagner's early opera *Rienzi*, the deeply moving D Flat Major Consolation; this disc may come with a recommendation from Rick Wakeman and the naff title *Lisztomania*, but you shouldn't let that put you off.
● *Saga Classics SCD 9042* ● *1 CD* ● *Mid-price*
● *ADD* ● *1975*

One of the best versions of the Liszt Piano Sonata is by Peter Donohoe, an intellectual pianist with brilliant technique; unfortunately, EMI recently deleted this preparatory to reissuing it with a different set of pieces (a shame, because with sonatas by Alban Berg and Béla Bartók, this was rather a bargain). Louis Lortie's reading of the Piano Sonata has a strong sense of form, even if it does miss out slightly on the fullest excitement which the work can communicate.
● *Chandos CHAN8548* ● *1 CD* ● *Full price*
● *DDD* ● *1986*

Alfred Brendel has made several recordings of the piece; he has a fine sense of the sonata's architecture and brings excitement out of the music's intellectual properties. His *The Gramophone* Award-winning version has a good selection of smaller descriptive pieces.
● *Philips 410 040-2* ● *1 CD* ● *Full price*
● *DDD* ● *1982*

There's a stupendous, if elderly and crackly, recording by the great Annie Fischer which also has a fine account of Schubert's last sonata; a great document by a fine musician.
● *Hungaroton HCD 31494* ● *1 CD* ● *Full price*
● *1953/68*

DECEPTIVE SIMPLICITY: BRAHMS

Brahms was one of that select élite which heard Liszt play his own piano sonata; he went to one of the older composer's private recitals and reputedly fell asleep in the middle of it. Of course, Liszt's demonstrative piano music is, on the surface, a long way from the much more Classically orientated and restrained work of Brahms. Brahms's solo piano music actually treads a fascinating path, in some ways (inevitably, almost) rather similar to Beethoven's. The early pieces, culminating in the fiery, complex and remarkable 3rd Sonata (written in 1853, and only Opus 5 in the official Brahms numbering), are all very technique-on-sleeve, dynamic works; at the end of his life, however, he wrote a series of short, translucent piano pieces (intermezzi and 'Fantasiestücke' or 'fantasy-pieces'), deceptively simple, sometimes almost immobile, which are actually still quite technically stretching (although they don't sound it) but which demand spiritual depth if they are to come off properly. His chamber career, too, includes some fascinating pieces; only three quartets, but two string sextets, three piano quartets, three major violin sonatas, the greatest piano quintet in the repertoire, and a late flirtation with the clarinet, producing two superb sonatas (amongst the best works ever written for the instrument) and a clarinet quintet of profundity and genius.

The two quintets come more or less from opposite ends of Brahms's career; his latent interest in the clarinet stemmed from a meeting in 1891 with the instrument's greatest exponent in the latter part of the nineteenth century, Richard Mühlfeld (1856–1907). It was Mühlfeld's ability which convinced Brahms of the instrument's potential; his two sonatas for it have a superb combination of melody and elegy, while the Clarinet Quintet allows the instrument a freedom to roam over its range between that of the violins and the viola. Brahms lived at a time when chamber music was enjoying a resurgence of interest, and some of his earlier works, especially the piano quartets, were designed to expedite his introduction to Viennese audiences. Many were also intended to back up a public manifesto which Brahms and his friend, the violinist Joseph Joachim, drew up against Liszt's 'new German music.' The chamber music, in carefully organised Classical forms, was very much a part of this campaign. Also during this time, Schubert's music became a major influence. The benign nature of this influence was evident, as opposed to the ever-present shadow of Beethoven; for fear of Beethoven's precedents, Brahms claimed to have destroyed around twenty string quartets before finally producing one (which itself took seven years to write) in public. But chamber music didn't always cost him so much sweat; and the more mature works are of a beauty which places them amongst the greatest of solo instrumental and chamber music.

DISCOGRAPHY

Piano music

I can think of no greater recent disc of Brahms's piano music than the young French pianist Hélène Grimaud's magnificent version of the 3rd Sonata, a technical tour de force with real poetry and sensitivity; it has, too, as a total contrast, the six late Klavierstücke, to which she brings a superb gentleness of touch which is never wishy-washy. Grimaud completely outdoes such more-favoured modern masters as Perahia, and I greatly value this disc.
● *Denon CO-79782* ● *1 CD* ● *Full price*
● *DDD* ● *1991* ✪

Violin sonatas

There are four recordings of the violin sonatas worth considering, and two of them feature Daniel

Barenboim as pianist (a fine Brahmsian). The earliest of these four recordings has Pinchas Zukerman as soloist, and the performances are warm and spontaneous.
● *Deutsche Grammophon 431 599-2* ● *1 CD*
● *Mid-price* ● *ADD* ● *1975* ✪

A later disc stars the great Itzhak Perlman, captured live and, as always, skirting close to the edge in tonal experiment and timbre, with Barenboim a suitable partner.
● *Sony SK 45819* ● *1 CD* ● *Full price* ● *DDD*
● *1989*

The vintage choice pairs violinist Josef Suk and pianist Julius Katchen, who blend Classicism and Romanticism quite amazingly.
● *Decca 421 092-2* ● *1 CD* ● *Mid-price*
● *ADD* ● *1967*

And, most recent of the bunch, the exquisitely talented pianist Maria João Pires (who is at last being recognised for the great artist she is) and Augustin Dumay, partners on and off record, on a technically quite superb recording, produce something special, imbued with mystery, excitement and revelation.
● *Deutsche Grammophon 435 800-2* ● *1 CD*
● *Full price* ● *DDD* ● *1992*

Clarinet sonatas
My favourite recording of the clarinet sonatas comes bearing a delightful Weber work for clarinet and piano, the Grand Duo Concertant. The performers are Michael Collins and the Russian pianist Mikhail Pletnev; they are ideally matched, and I cannot recommend this disc too strongly.
● *Virgin Classics VC7 91076-2* ● *1 CD* ● *Full price* ● *DDD* ● *1988* ✪

Piano Quintet and Clarinet Quintet
There are many star names who have recorded both the quintets, but the first-time buyer won't do a lot better than the warm, spacious recordings, generously packed onto one disc, by the Allegri Quartet, with James Campbell (clarinet) and Rian de Waal (piano). Delightful performances, the equal of any of the better-known recordings, and at just over 80 minutes in total some kind of record for length on a single CD.
● *Cala CACD 1009* ● *1 CD* ● *Full price*
● *DDD* ● *1991* ✪

String quartets and sextets
The best recordings of the first two string quartets are by the Takács Quartet, who manage both the civilised aspect of Brahms's music and its more passionate, sorrowing elements. Excellent.
● *Decca 425-2* ● *1 CD* ● *Full price* ● *DDD*
● *1988* ✪

For the sextets, your best bet (by universal acclaim) is the delightful recording by the Raphael Ensemble.
● *Hyperion CDA 66276* ● *1 CD* ● *Full price*
● *DDD* ● *1988*

Piano trios and quartets
The Beaux Arts Trio (heroes of Haydn) also serve Brahms well, and their recording includes a posthumous work not found elsewhere.
● *Philips 416 838-2* ● *2 CDs* ● *Full price*
● *DDD* ● *1987* ✪

The piano quartets can be found in a very competitive cheap set, although 'cheap' describes only the price. The performances by the Eastman Quartet are classic.
● *VoxBox CDX5052* ● *2 CDs* ● *Bargain price*
● *ADD* ● *1968*

THE END OF THE NINETEENTH CENTURY: RUSSIAN CHAMBER MUSIC

Russian chamber music is often overlooked, and admittedly it's not the most fertile of traditions, but there are one or two pieces well worth hearing.

BORODIN, TCHAIKOVSKY

The Quartets and incomplete Sextet of Alexander Borodin (1833–1887) are pleasant, especially the two-movement Sextet fragment, in which Borodin blended his natural nationalism with a certain respect for the Germanic tradition. Tchaikovsky only once caught fire as a chamber writer, with his Piano Trio in A Minor, a work whose centre is the theme and variations of its second movement; his Sextet, 'Souvenir of Florence', has its moments, but he was not a composer ideally suited to the smaller scale. Certainly his best-known works for solo piano come under the heading 'salon music', a slightly dismissive term implying easy listening of the Radio 2 *Friday Night is Music Night* type.

ELEGIAC GEMS: ANTON ARENSKY (1861–1906)

The real gems of Russian chamber music come from the still relatively unknown pen of Anton Stepanovich Arensky, whom Tchaikovsky desperately tried to promote. In some ways the two composers were quite similar personalities, both depressive and obsessive, although Arensky never achieved any real fame and drank himself to death at the age of 44. He wrote two small masterpieces, both inspired by the deaths of friends. The D Minor Piano Trio (Opus 32) was dedicated to the memory of a cellist friend, and it is the leading role given to the cello which helps to bestow on this work its haunting and elegiac quality (Arensky was as good a tune-writer as Tchaikovsky at times). The A Minor String Quartet (Opus 35) was inspired by Tchaikovsky's own death, and one of the movements is a set of variations on a religious tune which Tchaikovsky had used.

DISCOGRAPHY
There's a very good, criminally underrated disc by a chamber group called the Arensky Ensemble, which gathers not only Borodin's interesting two-movement Sextet, but Tchaikovsky's 'Souvenir of Florence' and Arensky's quartet in memory of Tchaikovsky. The playing is nicely toned, and with that dark, Slavic edge carefully judged.
● *Meridian CDE84211*   ● *1 CD*   ● *Full price*
● *DDD*   ● *1990* ✪

Arensky's great Trio is available in surprisingly few versions (although the number is gradually creeping up). It makes a natural bedfellow with Tchaikovsky's Trio, and the American trio of Andres Cardenes, Mona Golabek and Jeffrey Solow pour on the passion and bring out the elegiac qualities to perfection.
● *Delos DE 3056*   ● *1 CD*   ● *Full price*   ● *DDD*
● *1989*

There's also a newish Naxos recording of these two pieces by the Ashkenazy Piano Trio, which is up to the usual high Naxos standard.
● *Naxos 8.550467*   ● *1 CD*   ● *Bargain price*
● *DDD*   ● *1990*

KEYBOARD VIRTUOSITY: RACHMANINOV

Of course, the great Russian instrumental writer is Sergei Rachmaninov, another piano virtuoso and composer, and his dazzling Preludes and Études-Tableaux challenge even the greatest players' techniques. The Études-Tableaux, a series of ornate and descriptive studies, are especially difficult, while his two piano sonatas are highly Romantic works, long but thrilling – everything you would expect from the composer of the famous 2nd Piano Concerto.

DISCOGRAPHY
Rachmaninov's music is always safe in the hands of Vladimir Ashkenazy, and his recordings of the 24 Preludes and the Piano Sonata No. 2 are amongst the best in his distinguished career.
● *Decca 414 417-2*   ● *1 CD*   ● *Full price*
● *ADD*   ● *1976/81* ✪

This would also seem an opportune juncture at which to plug one of my all-time favourite piano recital discs, Murray Perahia's *Aldeburgh Recital*, recorded at the Aldeburgh Festival in 1989. It includes four superbly done Études-Tableaux, alongside Liszt's Hungarian Rhapsody No. 12 and D Flat Major Consolation (the most heart-rending performance I know), with Schumann's *Carnival Jest from Vienna (Faschingsschwank aus Wien)* and a set of Beethoven variations. This is the kind of artistry which would be worth any price.
● *Sony SK 46437*   ● *1 CD*   ● *Full price*   ● *DDD*
● *1989* ✪

● ● ● ● ● ●

EASTERN EUROPE: DVOŘÁK, BARTÓK

Antonin Dvořák was actually devoted to the string quartet from early in his career; his Opus 2 is a quartet and he wrote fourteen works in the form in all, the most famous of which is probably No. 12 in F Major, the 'American' (written, obviously, during his time in the United States). Dvořák's quartets cross a certain reverence he felt for the

Germanic/Viennese musical tradition with his natural yen for folk and folk-like melodies, especially rhythmic dance tunes. The 'American' probably gave way to this tendency most obviously, but in the right hands many of the others cross-fertilise rhythmic spring (to an almost manic degree at times) with a lyricism which can – in the wrong hands – seem a bit over-sugary. Of the work of all the Eastern European composers, Dvořák's chamber music is the most obviously influenced by the 'great tradition'; the music of Bedřich Smetana and, later, his fellow Czech Leoš Janáček and Hungarians like Béla Bartók and Zoltán Kodály (1882–1967), departed much more from these traditions, while staying well away from the austerities of Schoenberg and the rest of the Second Viennese School. Bartók's chamber music draws much of its early impetus from folk rhythms, and the six string quartets – one of the great sets – explore the way that four-stringed instruments can exploit rhythmic drive, sometimes to the point of fury and mania, although with Bartók an under-belly of lyricism and elegy is never too far away. Bartók carved out a unique Modern path for himself, utterly different from anyone else's, and the intricate cross-weaving of the quartets, which are sufficiently clear (when performed properly) for the listener to follow more easily than some of his great orchestral writing, is perhaps, for some, a good way into this genius's musical vocabulary. His contribution to piano writing has already been touched upon – his extraordinary 'piano tutor', the six-album *Mikrokosmos*, stands as a major achievement both in theory and in practice; and anyone who finds their way into Bartók's music

shouldn't miss 'Contrasts', a curious piece for piano, violin and clarinet and written originally for the 'King of Swing', the jazz clarinettist Benny Goodman (1909–1986). It's a strange piece, by turns harsh and wistful, but a miniature masterpiece.

DISCOGRAPHY
Dvořák
There are a couple of highly recommendable Dvořák discs which give a good introduction to his quartets, and also his delightful smaller chamber pieces, the 'Cypresses' (which were originally for voice and piano and were then rearranged by the composer). The 'American' Quartet is given a fine outing by the Hagen Quartet, and not only do they add a bonsai forest of cypresses, there's a chance to sample the introspective, brooding world of Kodály's miniature 2nd Quartet.
● *Deutsche Grammophon 419 601-2* ● *1 CD*
● *Full price* ● *DDD* ● *1986* ○

On another recording, the 10th and 14th Quartets are admirably played by the Lindsay Quartet; they strike the right balance between lyricism and rhythmic motivation.
● *ASV DC DCA 788* ● *1 CD* ● *Full price*
● *DDD* ● *1991*

Bartók
An extraordinarily well performed set of the Bartók quartets by the Emerson Quartet won a *The Gramophone* Award in 1989. The musicians take each piece on its own terms, play with fire and subtlety, and really work together.
● *Deutsche Grammophon 423 657-2* ● *2 CDs*
● *Full price* ● *DDD* ● *1987* ○

There's a classic Bartók disc, featuring the composer himself, first as pianist in 'Contrasts' – with the line-up completed by Benny Goodman and the great violinist Joseph Szigeti (1892–1973) – then as soloist in excerpts from the *Mikrokosmos*. Bartók's piano style is surprisingly relaxed about percussion, even though he did believe in the piano's percussive potential, but he was something of a virtuoso. This is an invaluable recording, both as historic document and as artistic experience. The sound quality is fairly good, too.
● *Sony Masterworks Portrait MPK 47676*
● *1 CD* ● *Mid-price* ● *AAD* ● *1940*

THE INTIMATE MAVERICK: JANÁČEK

There's something distinctly maverick about Janáček, which is probably why he was such a great composer. His two string quartets came relatively late; the first, after Tolstoy's novel *The Kreutzer Sonata* (what a marvellously distorted genesis – a piece of Beethoven inspires a work of literature which in turn inspires a Janáček trio and then, fifteen years later, a quartet), was written in eight days in 1923 when Janáček was 69. There's no narrative in Janáček's work; it's expressive, sometimes to the point of seeming frustrated with the limitations of the instruments. The 2nd Quartet, 'Intimate Letters', was another speedy piece of work, written in three weeks in 1928, and almost certainly inspired by a crisis in Janáček's strange relationship with Kamilá Stosslová, who was about 50 years his junior. There's a moment in the 2nd Quartet which almost suggests sexual passion, hinting at an unconfirmed consummation of this unlikely match. Janáček's musical language is both frenetic and fragmentary, but utterly compelling.

Janáček's piano music is also waywardly brilliant; he has a way here, as in his operas and his quartets, of plucking melodies out of fragmentary stuff. The piano music is overtly descriptive; his Piano Sonata 1.X.1905 was a response to the murder of a Czech worker by Austrian troops engaged in putting down a demonstration (this was originally a three-movement work, but Janáček burned the Finale during rehearsals for the première); 'In the Mists' manages to be both physical and psychological; but some of Janáček's most interesting intricate piano writing comes in the two series *On the Overgrown Path*, full of small pieces with titles like 'A blown-away leaf', 'Words fail' and 'The barn owl has not flown away'. Enigmatic, but entirely gripping.

DISCOGRAPHY
I'm particularly fond of the recording of the two Janáček quartets by the Hagen Quartet; the music shines, bursts, excites, and does all the other unpredictable things that Janáček demands (with the less strenuous filler of the Italian Serenade by Hugo Wolf, best known for his lieder).
● *Deutsche Grammophon 427 669-2* ● *1 CD* ● *Full price* ● *DDD* ● *1988* ◉

And a fine introduction to Janáček's piano sound-world comes on the generous collection by young Norwegian heart-throb pianist Leif Ove Andsnes, which includes the Sonata 1.X.1905, 'In the Mists', and a generous dollop from the first set of *On the Overgrown Path*, all played with a certain rapt, dream-like intensity.
● *Virgin Classics VC7 91222-2* ● *1 CD* ● *Full price* ● *DDD* ● *1990*

DEFINING FRENCH MUSIC: CLAUDE DEBUSSY

Claude Debussy, while aware of music's Germanic heritage, was also ambitious to achieve a different kind of sound-world, one analagous to certain contemporary movements in painting (principally Impressionism) and literature (especially Symbolism). This gives his music, in all genres, a certain elusive, oblique quality, although he never quite abandoned the idea of tonality, even if he did do some strange things with it (but then so did Haydn and Schubert in their ways), and even if he did put together some surprising harmonics in the interest of 'colour'. Debussy thought a great deal in terms of colour, and the old set forms and formulas of music didn't interest him greatly. He did write a string quartet, which was praised in its day for its 'Impressionist' qualities, and it does indeed have a certain fleeting, melting, dissolving sensation, especially in its harmonies. Perhaps his greatest chamber works came at the end of his life, when, in the upheaval of the First World War, Debussy set out to write music which was definitively French as a riposte to the German invader. He projected a series of six sonatas, but only lived to complete three; one for piano and violin, one for cello and piano and, perhaps the best and most sublime of all, one for flute, viola and harp. This last has a lovely sound-timbre to it, something quite new, entirely enchanting. Debussy could make the flute sound immensely attractive; he was, after all, the composer of the best-known and best-loved piece of solo flute music, the haunting *Syrinx*. As a piano composer, Debussy seemed to find new potential in what is (as Bartók stressed) essentially a percussive instrument; and while his piano music, especially in his *Children's Corner* (which includes 'Golliwog's Cakewalk'), does have its rhythmic side, his most fascinating pieces, in his two books of Préludes, his Images and his Études, seem to drift above rhythm, picking notes sparsely from random areas of the piano and alternating these with dripping, rippling arpeggios. The Préludes and the Images were given suggestive, almost Symbolist titles (like 'The Drowned Cathedral' and 'Footsteps on the Snow'), although the Études, quite properly, were all described in terms of what pianistic skill they were supposed to exercise. One of Debussy's piano works, 'Clair de Lune' (part of his *Suite Bergamasque*) is strikingly famous, and rightly so; as an evocation of moonlight and the play of light and darkness it exploits the full resources of the piano like few other short pieces.

DISCOGRAPHY
There's a cheap(ish) double set of Debussy's chamber music, which has some slightly indifferent performances but a ravishing version of

the String Quartet and a fine account of the Cello Sonata, as well as a selection of all too rarely heard piano duets and the Dance for Harp and String Orchestra. A good basic kit.
● *EMI CZS7 67416 2* ● *2 CDs* ● *Mid-price*
● *ADD* ● *1962–82* ❂

You really should treat yourself to a fine French disc, available here, which has just the sonatas played by such great musicians as Pascal Rogé (the greatest of pianists in this kind of repertoire), flautist Philippe Bernold, and harpist Frédérique Cambreling. Marvellous.
● *ADDA 581103* ● *1 CD* ● *Full price* ● *DDD*
● *1988* ❂

One of the greatest Debussy piano recordings is Mitsuko Uchida's tremendous, intelligent, technically flawless, and poetic version of the twelve Etudes. Another treat.
● *Philips 422 412-2* ● *1 CD* ● *Full price*
● *DDD* ● *1989* ❂

For the Préludes, try the classic (and reasonably priced) recording by the great Walter Gieseking – lovely sympathetic playing, and with recording sound that still holds up.
● *EMI CDH7 61004-2* ● *1 CD* ● *Mid-price*
● *AAD* ● *1955*

The Images have been beautifully done (beautifully even unto a *The Gramophone* Award) by Zoltán Kocsis.
● *Philips 422 404-2* ● *1 CD* ● *Full price*
● *DDD* ● *1989*

For all the recording's brevity, you won't come across much greater musicianship than that displayed by the great Chilean pianist Claudio Arrau in one of the releases from his last collection, *The Final Sessions* (which was brought to an end by his death), which includes the *Suite Bergamasque*, complete with 'Clair de Lune'.
● *Philips 4334 622-2* ● *1 CD* ● *Full price*
● *DDD* ● *1991* ● *Limited Edition*

▬▬ ▬▬ ▬▬

PASTICHE AND CHARM: RAVEL, POULENC, SATIE

Maurice Ravel often strikes me as something of a pale imitation of Debussy; he tends also to get more immersed in pastiche. There was a vogue for 'Spanish'-sounding French music, and Debussy did contribute some remarkable pieces to it, which remain always recognisably Debussy; Ravel always seems more of a chameleon, although virtuoso works like his *Tzigane* (a gypsy reference) for violin and piano are highly entertaining. Debussy looked at the neo-Classical movement, the idea that music should return to the forms and qualities of Bach, and brought something of his own qualities to bear on all that; Ravel seems at times obsessed by this movement, and his finest piano work, *Le Tombeau de Couperin* (*The Tomb of Couperin*, a reference to one of the French Baroque's most prolific composers), is, as its title suggests, immured in neo-Classicism. Ravel is an 'easy-on-the-ear' sort of composer, but I do really feel that his reputation is grossly inflated.

There are other French keyboard writers: François Poulenc, whose Nocturnes and Mouvements Perpetuels are charming pieces; and the vastly overrated Erik Satie (1866–1925), a strange obsessive figure, perhaps as much given to posing as mad as being genuinely insane. His 'Gymnopédies' are simple little pieces with bitter-sweet harmonics which have reached almost cult status due to repeated use on advertisement and film soundtracks. Personally, if I never heard any more Satie again, it would be far too soon, but I'm definitely in a minority on this subject.

DISCOGRAPHY
Ravel
The same EMI double series that offers Debussy's chamber music also makes a good Ravel starter kit, complete with *Tzigane*, the Violin Sonata, a piano trio, the Quartet, and the lovely Sonata for Violin and Cello.
● *EMI CZS7 67217 2* ● *2 CDs* ● *Mid-price*
● *ADD* ● *1954–73* ✪

For Ravel's piano music, try Volume 1 of Vlado Perlmuter's series, which has the descriptive 'Jeux d'eau' as well as a piano version of the much-loved *Pavane for a Dead Infanta*.
● *Nimbus NIM5005* ● *1 CD* ● *Full price*
● *AAD* ● *1979*

For *Le Tombeau de Couperin*, the best around is over 40 years old and takes a few liberties with

tempo, but is really remarkable for most of its course; the player is Robert Casadesus.
● *Sony Masterworks Portrait MP2K 46733*
● *2 CDs* ● *Mid-price* ● *AAD* ● *1951*

French piano recital
There's a really generous French piano music recital disc by the Korean Kun Woo Paik devoted to the music of Debussy, Poulenc and Satie; it has eleven little Poulenc gems (including 'Homages' to Schubert and to Edith Piaf), Debussy's 'Clair de Lune' and his Suite *Pour le Piano*, and all the Satie you could ever want (including the 'Gymnopédies').
● *Virgo VJ7 91465-2* ● *1 CD* ● *Bargain price*
● *DDD* ● *1990* ✪

THE SECOND VIENNESE SCHOOL: EVERYTHING CHAMBER-SIZED

ARNOLD SCHOENBERG

As the Second Viennese School of Musicians, headed by Schoenberg, Berg and Webern, believed that one of the things which had got out of hand in music was size – size of orchestras and length of pieces – they were naturally drawn towards chamber music. All three wrote works for small, sometimes eclectically chosen, groups of instruments; the pieces, too, would be short, some movements being 'blink and you miss them' in their time-scale.

Schoenberg's first two string quartets both belonged to the 'bad old days'; they're both richly harmonic pieces which have actually been ascribed home keys (D minor and F sharp minor). In one sense the 1st Quartet does look forward; it has four sections, but is a one-movement piece. The 2nd was hailed by Schoenberg himself as signalling that the era of 'expanded forms' (which he traced back to Beethoven's C Sharp Minor Quartet) was on its way out; although all four of Schoenberg's quartets are surprisingly long by the standards of much of the Viennese School's music. The 3rd and 4th Quartets are both twelve-tone works, so considerations such as conventional melody fly out of the window, but there is a great deal here for the listener to respond to, not least in the use of rhythmic variation and in the subtle play of dynamics.

One of the seminal pieces of Schoenberg's 'old style' was *Verklärte Nacht* (*Transfigured Night*), inspired by a poem by Richard Dehmel; although best-known now as an orchestral work it was originally a chamber piece, and with its dripping, drenching harmonies it does show why Schoenberg felt he had to change the system. *Verklärte Nacht's* natural successor can be found in the early(ish) 1st Chamber Symphony, which carries on this style, but moves towards the Expressionist mode where emotional expression is more important than any idea of 'beauty'. The 1st Chamber Symphony forms a fascinating counterpart to the 2nd, written in the 1930s after Schoenberg had emigrated to America; here stands the new composer with a style so austere as to be almost Classical. Schoenberg's first wholly atonal music is reckoned to be his Opus 11 Three Piano Pieces (1911), and he wrote a small but significant catalogue of music for the piano. Like much Schoenberg it can seem bleak, but then this composer expected the listener to do as much work as he had. But once it grabs you . . .

ALBAN BERG

Berg is, as I've said, probably the most immediately accessible of the Viennese School. A pupil of Schoenberg, his declared Opus 1 was a piano sonata (written in 1908–9) which, whilst it concluded inside formal tonality, clearly looked beyond those bounds. Berg was in many ways the Romantic among these composers, though some of his earliest works within the strictures of tone-row writing can seem austere; the Four Pieces for Clarinet and Piano were inspired by a set of Schoenberg piano pieces, and emulate their style. However, Berg was not an arid man who could refine personality out of his music, and the Chamber Concerto, for piano, violin and thirteen wind instruments, contains many coded references to himself and his friends. His Lyric Suite for String Quartet is, if you have any grasp at all of this musical language, a truly moving and beautiful piece, deeply Romantic beneath its surface austerity.

ANTON WEBERN (1883–1945)

Webern is the most forbidding of these composers. His life ended tragically and stupidly when an occupying American soldier mistook him for a Viennese black-marketeer and shot him. Webern shrank everything down to bare essentials, spreading his tone-row patterns over the whole force at his disposal, rather than presenting a row on a single instrument or group of instruments, and many of his single movements or single pieces are only between 20 and 30 seconds long. His six Bagatelles for String Quartet clearly show the hard labour necessary to achieve such fleeting 'trifles', whilst his Opus 28 String Quartet (there is a very early quartet in one highly complex movement, as well) is positively expansive, lasting about eight minutes. In some senses everything Webern wrote was chamber music; austere, crystalline, and very hard to penetrate, but underneath all this rather emotional.

DISCOGRAPHY
Second Viennese School: Schoenberg, Berg and Webern
There is a fine four-disc set comprising much of the music by these three composers specifically for string quartet. The musicians are the Lasalle Quartet, who have a long-term commitment to this kind of music and who make it purposeful, thrusting and pointed (it's a little easy for Viennese School music to seem diffuse). Borrow it from a library if you can.
● *Deutsche Grammophon 419 994-2* ● *4 CDs*
● *Full price* ● *ADD* ● *1968–70* ○

Schoenberg's piano music is brilliantly done by Maurizio Pollini, who really understands it, believing that it is some of the most important art of the century.
● *Deutsche Grammophon 423 249-2* ● *1 CD*
● *Mid-price* ● *ADD* ● *1974*

As an introduction to Berg, a disc offering the Chamber Concerto, the Four Pieces for Clarinet and Piano, and the Piano Sonata is excellent value; musicians involved include Pierre Boulez and his Ensemble Intercontemporain, Antony Pay and Daniel Barenboim.
● *Deutsche Grammophon 423 237-2* ● *1 CD*
● *Mid price* ● *ADD* ● *1977*

The Italian Quartet, normally thought of as masters of Beethoven, have also given Webern their finest attention; a beautiful and eloquent performance which might make some see exactly why Webern is so highly regarded.
● *Philips 420 796-2* ● *1 CD* ● *Full price*
● *ADD* ● *1970*

━━━ ━━━ ━━━ ━━━

THE LATENT BRITISH TRADITION: BRITTEN, TIPPETT, SIMPSON

The sad fact must be faced that there is a negligible British tradition in both chamber and instrumental music. Despite some charming minor ensemble pieces by composers like Charles Stanford (1852–1924) and Hubert Parry (1848–1918) around the beginning of this century, the chamber tradition here comes down to three men: Benjamin Britten, Michael Tippett, and, arguably a greater writer for string quartet than either, Robert Simpson. Britten's four quartets span most of his career, although confusingly the first, written in 1931, doesn't have a number, so No. 1 is dated 1941; the 2nd and 3rd are

especially fine, the 2nd having a commemorative chaconne as a finale, written to celebrate the 250th anniversary of Henry Purcell's death. The 3rd, written in 1975, the year before Britten died, is a surprisingly spare work, disguising a huge amount of emotional feeling under an apparently Modernist waywardness.

Michael Tippett has written five quartets to date; opinions are very divided about his 5th Quartet, which appeared in the 1990s, and especially as to whether it is anything more than a rewrite of late Beethoven. But then, Beethoven has been the dominant influence on Tippett as a chamber musician, and the first three quartets, written in the 1930s and 1940s (and so fairly early works), try to combine Beethoven's sound with the kind of music – English traditional and the blues – which has also occupied Tippett's magpie-like musical mind. The 4th Quartet, from the mid-1970s, mirrors his 4th Symphony in describing the passage from birth to death, and is quite abrasive at its core (although still respectful to the language of Beethoven). Tippett's piano sonatas, formidable show pieces all, form the only significant core of serious solo instrumental music in twentieth-century Britain; these are dense, elaborate (almost Romantically so) pieces.

Robert Simpson has written over a dozen quartets, very much sibling works to his symphonies, and a handful of other chamber pieces. Simpson has remained close to tonality even at a time when the lack of fashion for such music might have driven him to despair. His is a careful, subtly crafted vocabulary; he can forge whole works out of simple relationships like the interval of a fourth, stretching these around patterns which are both melodic and intellectual. He too recognises Beethoven as an important influence, but his faith in and commitment to the string quartet as a musical medium are so great that the results of his homages are perhaps more fascinating. At last being recognised as an important composer, Simpson is well worth getting to know.

DISCOGRAPHY
British chamber music
Just to sample the minor ensemble pieces of Parry and Stanford at their most delicious, try the combination of a Nonet by each composer, delightfully played by Capricorn.
● *Hyperion CDA66291* ● *1 CD* ● *Full price*
● *DDD* ● *1989*

Britten and Tippett
Britten's first two quartets have been well done by the Alberni Quartet, and No. 2 comes together with No. 3.
● *CRD CRD 3395* ● *1 CD* ● *Full price*
● *DDD* ● *1989*

However, there's a better buy, Britten's No. 3 coupled with Tippett's 4th Quartet; a fascinating comparison, as the works were composed contemporaneously, and the Tippett here is played by the ensemble for whom it was written, the Lindsay Quartet.
● *ASV CD DCA 608* ● *1 CD* ● *Full price*
● *DDD* ● *1987*

The Lindsays made an admirable job of the earlier Tippett works – so admirable that he decided to write the 4th and 5th Quartets for them.
● *Decca 425 645-2* ● *1 CD* ● *Mid-price*
● *ADD* ● *1975*

Tippett's four piano sonatas are also available, played by modern music expert Paul Crossley.
● *CRD CRD34301* ● *1 CD* ● *Full price* ● *DDD*

Robert Simpson
If you want to try out Robert Simpson, then either of the following would prove useful entrées to his quartets. The 3rd and 6th Quartets have some 20 years between their composition, and the latter is one of Simpson's works most closely related to Beethoven; on the first of these recordings you get a string trio as an interesting filler, all played by the Delmé Quartet.
● *Hyperion CDA66376* ● *1 CD* ● *Full price*
● *DDD* ● *1989* ❂

It's also worth trying the 7th, 8th and 9th Quartets, three admirably diverse works which contain references to insects, astronomy and Haydn.
● *Nos. 7 and 8: Hyperion CDA66117* ● *1 CD*
● *Full price* ● *ADD* ● *1977/78*
● *No. 9: Hyperion CDA66127* ● *1 CD* ● *Full price* ● *ADD* ● *1982*

THE GREATEST
QUARTETS OF THE
TWENTIETH CENTURY:
DMITRI SHOSTAKOVICH
Shostakovich's fifteen string quartets, written between 1938 and 1975, are great music when considered either in the abstract or in some a-historical vacuum; set against the background of Shostakovich's fortunes under the Soviet regime, however, they also become remarkable personal documents, perhaps the supreme example of the quartet as an expression of inner feeling, and the counterpart to the 'public statement' of the symphony. Of course, technically there was no such thing as 'private music' in the Soviet Union of the time, and so often Shostakovich was making his musical constructions do double service. Sometimes the personal reminiscence is allusive, hidden behind musical history; the 3rd Quartet starts with a Haydn-esque tune and circles, through five movements, back to its beginning, apparently positive and upbeat. Sometimes Shostakovich hides behind lyricism or humour, as in the 5th or 7th Quartets, although often the humour is quite bleak, a sort of whistling in the dark. But perhaps the key Shostakovich quartet is the 8th, a work publicly dedicated, for his Soviet masters' benefit, 'To the Memory of the Victims of Fascism' when it first appeared in 1960. In fact, Shostakovich intended the quartet as a suicide note; the strain of continually having to conform to the regime had driven him to the edge (the final straw was being 'admitted' to the Communist Party). The 8th Quartet is an elaborate weave of codes, including a musical representation of Shostakovich's own name and quotations from a number of his works. The great miracle here, though, is that for all the codes, the

music still works independently for the new, first-time listener; even the daring (perhaps despairing, but officially 'elegiac') touch of making both the last two movements slow largos doesn't strain the listener in any way, but adds to the dramatic force of a piece which has some claim to be the greatest single quartet of the century.

The one thing which remains remarkable through all Shostakovich's chamber music, and above all his quartets, is the constant variety of style, the fiery rhythmic music (officially designed to 'celebrate' the people of Soviet Russia, although sometimes flirting dangerously with sections of the people not currently in favour), the sudden haunting melodies. Classical forms are interwoven with folk forms (the G Minor Quintet for piano and conventional quartet line-up, winner of the 1940 Stalin Prize, is particularly noteworthy in this respect).

DISCOGRAPHY
Shostakovich's quartets have become more and more popular with recording companies during the recent 'quartet boom'. For my money, though, the best available are still those by the Borodin Quartet (who once managed to impress Shostakovich so much with their performance of the 8th that he burst into tears). They are Russian performers who have, to some extent, lived through the music, in a way that even very fine musicians like the Brodsky Quartet and the Kronos Quartet haven't. The Borodin Quartet have recorded the 8th three times, always very well, and the most recent version comes with Nos. 3 and 7, making for interesting contrasts.
● *Virgin Classics VC7 91437-2* ● *1 CD* ● *Full price* ● *DDD* ● *1990* ❍

Follow this up with an earlier Borodin Quartet disc, offering Nos. 4, 6 and 11 (lyrical, cryptic and relaxed, respectively).
● *EMI CDC7 49268 2* ● *1 CD* ● *Full price* ● *ADD* ● *1981*

Or try the combination of the same quartet's earlier version of the 8th, again with No. 7, but also with the great Sviatoslav Richter in a mesmerising performance of the G Minor Quintet.
EMI CDC7 47507-2 ● *1 CD* ● *Full price* ● *ADD* ● *1985*

A UNIQUE MASTERPIECE: *QUARTET FOR THE END OF TIME* BY OLIVIER MESSIAEN (1908–1992)

The one twentieth-century chamber work which will undoubtedly stand with Shostakovich's greatest pieces is Messiaen's *Quatuor pour la Fin du Temps*. It is an ambitious eight-movement work for the unusual combination of violin, cello, piano and clarinet, a combination dictated by the instruments available, for Messiaen wrote the piece in a German prisoner-of-war camp in 1941. The quartet perfectly exemplifies its composer's twin inspirations, birdsong and religion, and its high-spot is, in some ways, the enormous, nine-minute movement for solo clarinet, which shows Messiaen's gift for free-flowing, liquid melody. Messiaen is probably the most important French composer of the century after Debussy, and while his work isn't always easy to approach, this piece is an ideal starting-point, and one of the essential compositions of the last 60 years.

DISCOGRAPHY
There is a delightfully profound version of this marvellous piece, featuring French musicians, which actually carries the composer's imprimatur. Although the recording was made 30 years ago, it doesn't show its age. It also includes a fascinating vocal piece by Messiaen.
● *Erato 2292-45505-2* ● *1 CD* ● *Mid-price* ● *AAD* ● *1963* ❍

THE FUTURE OF CHAMBER MUSIC AND THE QUARTET BOOM

Recent years have seen a sudden rise in the formation of a host of 'trendy' quartets peopled by younger musicians who, naturally, don't wear suits all the time or, understandably, don't want to give the impression that they live in white tie and tails. The market-leaders, in every sense, have been the Kronos Quartet, four Americans who have actually been together for the best part of twenty years, and who have not only championed modern music but served as a focal point and channelling source for the inspiration of new compositions. They have played their part in popularising Shostakovich's 8th by including it on their *Black Angels* release, a diverse collection headlined by an extraordinary work for string quartet and a whole host of electronic effects by the American composer George Crumb (1929–), whose reaction to his experiences in Vietnam is contained in this frightening piece. The Kronos Quartet, as determined supporters of modern music, have not only gone in for delightful *jeux d'esprits*, such as an arrangement of Jimi Hendrix's 'Purple Haze' (which makes a fine, sturdy, rhythmic, quartet piece), but were also amongst the first to lift the name of Henryk Górecki into the popular consciousness. Górecki's quartets (both recent works) use something of the same static chordal technique as his celebrated Symphony No. 3, but obviously the textures in a quartet are much sparer, giving an edgier, more keening sound than the plush symphony, with its angelic voice overtopping the orchestra. The quartets are less immediate than the Symphony, perhaps, but still packed with an emotion which belies the label 'Minimalism' that Górecki sometimes attracts. (It is fairer to say that, in searching for a language different from the 'Modern' music approved by Communist-backed regimes, Górecki, whose formative years were spent under Soviet domination in a satellite country, lit upon a deceptively simple style in order to pack an emotional and visceral punch.)

Another Polish composer whom the Kronos Quartet have eagerly publicised is Witold Lutoslawski (1913–), a formally more adventurous and challenging composer than Górecki, but deeply refined and polished. Recently, though, the Kronos have turned their attention to non-European music, in their collaboration with African composers *Pieces of Africa*.

Is the search outside the European tradition the way forward? Clearly Robert Simpson wouldn't agree; and the quartet (and other similar-sized chamber music) has remained resilient, above all as an intimate and personal forum for composers. Solo instrumental music is perhaps not at its highest peak right now (it's hard to think of any major sonatas or anything sonata-like of recent vintage), but it is one form of music that's bound to remain in the composer's vocabulary; after all, it is on instrumental music that most composers usually cut their teeth.

DISCOGRAPHY

Modern quartet recordings: a selection
The Kronos Quartet's two Górecki recordings have been released on one disc, and it's hard to imagine more persuasive performances.
● *Elektra-Nonesuch 79319-2* ● *1 CD* ● *Full price* ● *DDD* ● *1990/92* ✪

Other Kronos discs worth hearing (at least) are *Black Angels*,
● *Elektra-Nonesuch 7559-79242-2* ● *1 CD* ● *Full price* ● *DDD* ● *1989*

Pieces of Africa,
● *Elektra-Nonesuch 7559-79275-2* ● *1 CD* ● *Full price* ● *DDD* ● *1991*

and the mildly more formal *Contemporary Works for String Quartet* (although this is where you'll find the Jimi Hendrix arrangement).
● *Elektra-Nonesuch 7559-79111-2* ● *1 CD* ● *Full price* ● *DDD* ● *1987*

If you want to investigate Lutoslawski, there's an excellent recording by the Polish Varsovia Quartet, which combines his Quartet with two intriguing quartets by Karol Szymanowski (1882–1937) and a slightly less substantial work by Krzysztof Penderecki (1933–).
● *Olympia OCD328* ● *1 CD* ● *Mid-price*
● *AAD* ● *1985*

You may also care to try out Alfred Schnittke, not a personal favourite, but very much in fashion; the Tale Quartet's recordings of his first three quartets exhibit his development as both composer and human being very well.
● *BIS CD467* ● *1 CD* ● *Full price* ● *DDD*
● *1989*

VI

Choral

& OTHER
NON-OPERATIC
VOCAL MUSIC

INTRODUCTION

Choral music is by no means exclusively religious, although the assumption that it is sometimes puts people off a bit. In fact, some of the most convinced atheists I know are capable of revelling in choral masterpieces like Monteverdi's *Vespers*, Bach's Mass in B Minor, Beethoven's *Missa Solemnis* or Brahms's *A German Requiem*. And the smaller vocal, non-operatic music, which is mainly secular, contains some of the greatest music in the entire catalogue; it's amazing to think that the whole tradition of the 'art-song', usually known by its German term, 'Lied', was only 40 or 50 years ago completely neglected, until between them Dietrich Fischer-Dieskau and his accompanist (the king of accompanists, especially in Schubert), Gerald Moore, along with Peter Pears and Benjamin Britten (and a few other great artists like the ultimate Wagnerian, Hans Hotter), resuscitated the form.

Again, in this chapter I shall be following something of a 'great tradition' approach, although I hope to cast the occasional glance down some fascinating byways, and with the odd recommendation here and there.

Baroque Magnificence: Monteverdi

Choral music is also, I think, the greatest glory of the baroque, right from the inception of the baroque ideals in Italy at the beginning of the seventeenth century. This is due in no small measure to the presence and influence of Claudio Monteverdi (1567–1643), whose 1610 set of *Vespers for the Blessed Virgin Mary* stands as one of the great musical achievements of all time; so much so that they have frequently been divorced from their proper liturgical context and performed as purely concert pieces. Vespers, with its set liturgy, is, of course, one of the daily church offices, although the Monteverdi set was written for a special feast day with lots of trimmings, possibly the feast of the Annunciation (25 March). It's equally possible, however, that what we think of as a single set is in fact compounded from various settings. Monteverdi's *Vespers* set various scriptural texts, including a number of psalms, and throughout each different element the composer has always cunningly included (in good old Renaissance style) a plainchant melody around which the rest of his various vocal groupings weave their own melodic magic. He also uses small instrumental ensembles, with plenty of trumpets for magnificence and pomp. There are settings in which soloists echo each other (although always with a liturgical and spiritual purpose), that echo effect being created by subtle dynamics and musical scoring. The longest single item is the Magnificat (Mary's hymn of praise to the Lord, used at Church of England evensong every day) – quite natural in a set of Vespers for the Virgin – which is followed by a dazzling 'sonata' in which a solo soprano sings the words 'Sancta Maria, ora pro nobis' ('Holy Mary, pray for us') over and over again for almost ten minutes, while strings, brass and keyboard weave beautiful patterns around this central line.

Monteverdi wrote a vast amount of vocal music, both sacred and secular, including many books of secular madrigals. He sought to cultivate an ornately beautiful style, but one which always remained within the bounds of sense, not becoming dazzling for its own sake, and thus obscuring the meaning of the words. One of the great things about 'authentic' period performance is that it has rescued a lot of Monteverdi from highly peculiar performances, sharpened it up, made it more immediate, and in doing so has made artists more inclined to perform more of it. He's one of those composers, like Bach or Haydn, in whose work one can continue making exciting new discoveries through the whole of one's musical life.

DISCOGRAPHY

The supreme recording of the Monteverdi *Vespers* is by Andrew Parrott and his Taverner Consort, Taverner Choir and Taverner Players. Parrott did a lot of scholarly work on the proper liturgical context of the *Vespers*, which meant rearranging the order of the pieces from that familiar in the concert hall, and inserting various pieces of pure plainchant to give the background against which Monteverdi was writing. But the triumph of this set isn't academic, it's musical; this is a truly magnificent recording, brilliantly sung (the gorgeous soprano voice of Emma Kirkby, Tessa Bonner's chillingly clear tone in the Sonata, Nigel Rogers's sensitive tenor; in fact everyone singing on the recording is a star), and played with the right blend of verve and spiritual observance. Parrott cut back on the number of instrumentalists used – quite rightly, too. A desert island disc.
● *EMI CDS7 47078 8* ● *2 CDs* ● *Full price*
● *DDD* ● *1983–4* ❂

If you don't want the liturgical context, there's an excellent version by Philip Pickett and the new London Concert, which plays quite a few of the same soloists (including Tessa Bonner) and the marvellous Catherine Bott.
● *L'Oiseau-Lyre 425 832-2* ● *2 CDs* ● *Full price* ● *DDD* ● *1990*

For a fine example of Monteverdi madrigals, try Andrew Parrott and his Taverner Consort and Players in a selection from Book VIII, the *Madrigali guerrieri et amorosi* (*Warlike and amorous madrigals*) of 1638.
● *EMI CDC7 54333 2* ● *1 CD* ● *Full price* ● *DDD* ● *1991*

THE BAROQUE CANTATA: MONTÉCLAIR, CLÉRAMBAULT, CALDARA

There's an assumption, based largely on the fact that the most famous cantatas, J. S. Bach's, were all religious, that the cantata is an exclusively religious musical form. In fact, some of the most glorious cantatas (the word simply means 'sung') are secular, semi-dramatic pieces; composers as famous as Handel and Vivaldi wrote lovely secular cantatas, and among some of my favourite pieces of French Baroque music are the cantatas for solo voice by people like Michel Pignolet de Montéclair (1667–1737) and Louis-Nicolas Clérambault (1676–1749). These pieces are often internalised monodramas, depicting either a mythological or a Classical figure. Medea was quite a favourite; Clérambault and the Italian hot-house chromaticist Antonio Caldara (1670–1736) both used her as the subject for deeply involved cantatas. The Baroque solo cantata moves through several sections, employing different styles as it goes, almost like a sonata or concerto for voice, and each section is usually linked by brief passages of recitative. Such works were, of course, first and foremost designed as vocal showcases, although the role of the supporting instrumental ensemble is vital in helping underpin the mood and – especially in the music of someone like Caldara, who produces all kinds of amazing harmonic twists and turns – brings out the composer's full dramatic intention. Apart from Caldara's 'Medea in Corinth' and Clérambault's 'Medea', other cantatas worth investigating are Montéclair's 'La Bergère' (a lovely miniature of some psychological subtlety) and 'La Mort de Didon', Handel's 'Tra le fiamme' ('In the flames' – an astonishing emotional tour de force for quite large instrumental forces, and with an elusive and complex text), and Vivaldi's 'All' ombra di sospetto' ('In the shadow of doubt').

RELIGIOUS ITALIAN BAROQUE: PERGOLESI, STRADELLA

Amidst the plethora of Italian Baroque religious vocal music, several items stand out as worthy of special attention. Vivaldi's *Gloria*, with its distinctive opening motif of a repeated octave, is an extremely enjoyable, easily accessible choral work, a Gloria on a grand and exuberant scale. The dates of the composer Giovanni-Battista Pergolesi (1710–1736) show just how

brief his life was, and his most famous work, the *Stabat Mater* (a traditional hymn for Good Friday centring on the feelings of the Virgin Mary as she stood at the foot of the cross), is a superbly evocative and expressive work for soprano and contralto and orchestra; its popularity was immediate (J. S. Bach made use of it), and has remained high to the present day. Although inevitably of a basically lenten and sombre cast, Pergolesi's work is full of delightful contrasts, dramatic expression, and some melodic writing of great beauty.

These two late Baroque works are well-established, popular pieces. One earlier work which is currently less well known but which may, I suspect, be about to enjoy a huge revival is the Oratorio (sacred choral work) *San Giovanni Battista* (*St John the Baptist*) by Alessandro Stradella (1644–1682). This piece covers much of the same ground as *Salome*; oddly enough, comparison with Richard Strauss's opera isn't at all inappropriate, for Stradella's musical characterisation of the protagonists in the demise of the Baptist is extreme, at times violent, always highly colourful. One or two recent recordings have been of such high calibre as to pluck this work out of obscurity, and it's an extremely enjoyable, impressive experience.

DISCOGRAPHY
French Baroque cantatas
For French Baroque cantatas, I heartily recommend the crystal-pure voice of American soprano Julianne Baird. *French Cantatas of the Eighteenth Century* is an ideal and happy introduction to the form, with works by Montéclair and Clérambault.
● *Koch International Classics 3-7096-2 H1*
● *1 CD* ● *Full price* ● *DDD* ● *1991* ○

Handel, Vivaldi, Caldara
Julianne Baird turns her attention to Handel and Vivaldi with equally delightful results.
● *Dorian DOR-90147* ● *1 CD* ● *Full price*
● *DDD* ● *1990* ○
For the Vivaldi *Gloria*, see also below under Bach.

Caldara is well served by counter-tenor Gérard Lesne in an exciting collection that includes the wonderful 'Medea in Corinto'.
● *Virgin Classics VC7 91479-2* ● *1 CD* ● *Full price* ● *DDD* ● *1990*

Italian Baroque
Gérard Lesne and Catherine Bott appear together on an excellent new version of Stradella's *San Giovanni Battista*, full of passion and extremity, with forces superbly directed by Marc Minkowski.
● *Erato 2292-45739-2* ● *1 CD* ● *Full price* ● *DDD* ● *1991* ○

A slightly idiosyncratic, but entirely absorbing, devotional Pergolesi *Stabat Mater* is directed by Edwin Loehrer with soloists Lucia Ticinelli-Fattori and Maria Minetto; also included are Pergolesi's *Salve Regina* and a cantata by Alessandro Scarlatti. Good value.
● *Erato Bonsai Collection* ● *1 CD* ● *Bargain price* ● *ADD* ● *1970/3*

There's also a sumptuous new version featuring Cecilia Bartoli.
● *Decca 436 209-2* ● *1 CD* ● *Full price* ● *DDD* ● *1992*

GERMAN VARIATIONS: HEINRICH SCHÜTZ (1585–1672)

The dominant figure in German vocal music, especially religious vocal music, before J. S. Bach was undoubtedly Heinrich Schütz who, although he spent 57 years of his life as Kapellmeister to the court of Dresden, had travelled widely and imbibed the influences of Venice's Giovanni Gabrieli (1557–1612). This meant that he married Protestant forms and approaches with the Italianate Catholic musical styles, and his vocal writing is full of rich, diverse styles. Most of the forms for which Bach is famous were also used before him by Schütz; Schütz wrote his own *Christmas Story*, and an Easter Oratorio (*Die Aufesterstehung unsres Herren Jesu Christi*), and a *St John Passion* (these Passion settings were common amongst German composers up to

Bach, although his versions dwarfed all which had preceded them, so much so that some ultra-Protestants held them in suspicion as being almost 'popish'). Schütz's reputation also revolves around his two great collections *Cantiones Sacrae* (1625) and *Geistliche Chormusik* (1648), enormous collections of religious music for various vocal combinations, some unaccompanied, some with instrumental accompaniment. The stylistic variation in these works is vast, as they offer something for every occasion in the Christian calendar, from the quasi-pastoral celebratory style associated with Christmas through the sombre Lent and Passion season and the triumphal music of Easter.

DISCOGRAPHY
A good cheap introduction to Schütz comes from Pro Cantione Antiqua, with a selection of ten motets done with a good deal of expression.
● *ASV Quicksilva CD QS 6105* ● *1 CD* ● *Bargain price* ● *ADD* ● *1979* ○

For further exploration, I strongly recommend the Knabenchor Hannover's exquisite, crystalline performance of the 1648 *Geistliche Chormusik*.
● *Harmonia Mundi GD 77171* ● *2 CDs* ● *Mid-price* ● *DDD* ● *1981/2/4*

CUT OFF FROM THE MAINLAND: BRITISH MUSIC

Elements of the Renaissance lingered a little longer, perhaps, in England, cut off by both geography and European politics from mainland (primarily Catholic) developments. English music also suffered something of a blow from the Civil War of 1642–1648 between the King and Parliament and the subsequent temporary supremacy of the Puritan faction; as you might expect from a politico-religious grouping which outlawed statuary and decoration in churches and banned Christmas festivities, encouraging music wasn't high on the social agenda.

PARANOIA TO EROTICISM: HENRY PURCELL

In fact, the life of the Puritan leader Oliver Cromwell (who died in 1658) didn't overlap with the greatest British composer of that century (or many centuries to come), Henry Purcell, who was born the year after Cromwell died. Much of Purcell's output was written for voices, prodigious numbers of works of both religious and secular persuasion. His settings of the Anglican liturgy are high points of English church music, and many of his anthems, which set both English and Latin texts, are masterpieces; from the brooding near paranoia of *Jehovah, Quam Multi Sunt Hostes Mei* ('Jehovah, How many are my enemies?') to the lyrical, almost erotic setting of part of the Song of Solomon, 'My Beloved Spake'. His *Funeral Music for Queen Mary*, written only a few months before his own death, contains the short anthem 'Thou Knowest, Lord', which is a concentrated, small-scale piece of genius – hushed, reverent and awe-inspiring. Purcell's use of tonal harmonies and inventive modulations, allied to a great grasp of drama and melody, is always remarkable, and always a treat for the ear.

JOHN BLOW (1649–1708)

The vocal and choral music of Purcell's contemporary, John Blow, is also good; some of the anthems have a distinctive use of close, almost stifling harmony in the Italian style. His *Salvator Mundi* ('Saviour of the World'), a Lenten anthem, is particularly effective in this technique, with a claustrophobic opening half

balanced by a more open, fresher section providing a more optimistic conclusion. Blow and Purcell also wrote fine non-religious vocal music in a variety of styles; recently, some light has begun to fall on the 'rude' songs and those depicting extreme states of mind (usually labelled the 'Mad' songs). Without wishing to seem unduly jingoistic, all of Purcell's music and much of Blow's is the best of its kind of both its time, and all time.

DISCOGRAPHY
Purcell's service settings and anthems are being recorded in full by Robert King and his King's Consort (Hyperion). Any volume of this enterprising project will give you an ideal flavour of Purcell's genius. For 'Mad' songs by Purcell, Blow, their contemporary John Eccles, and others, try Catherine Bott's lovely and generous recital ● *L'Oiseau-Lyre 433 187-2* ● *1 CD* ● *Full price* ● *DDD* ● *1992* ✪

THE CHORAL GENIUS: J. S. BACH

The Cantatas

Johann Sebastian Bach's output of choral works would be remarkable for its sheer volume if for no other reason. The 222 cantatas by themselves make a staggering statistic, even when one allows for the fact that a handful are mere fragments and quite a few are adaptations of other works (Bach, a hard-pressed professional living before the Romantic ideal of 'creativity as hard-won struggle', was never averse to such economic methods as using one part of his work somewhere else if he thought it would be effective). Eleven of the cantatas are secular, the best-known of which are the so-called 'Coffee' Cantata, the Peasant Cantata (which preaches the merits of, amongst other things, a good roll in the hay), and the Wedding Cantata. Sacred or secular, all employ broadly similar musical approaches; a soloist or group of soloists and, usually, a full choir and instrumental ensemble (although this being Bach, the instrumental parts transpose very well to the organ) sing and play music, very often rooted in an old Protestant chorale tune, set to a text appropriate for a particular Sunday or feast day in the church calendar. The range of effects goes from the pomp of full chorus and orchestra, to a more intimate chamber sound with a single soloist and a select ensemble. When choral tunes are used, they are subject to all manner of decoration through each section of the cantata, but always allowed (often at the end) a straightforward hymn-like presentation, although with the supporting parts cast in the famous Bach harmonies. Obviously Bach didn't write all 222 pieces in one fell swoop (at least 25 years separate some), but a surprisingly high percentage of them date from the years around 1723–4.

St John Passion, St Matthew Passion
The year 1724 also saw the first of Bach's great Passions, the *St John*. The Passion was, as I've said, a part of the Germanic Protestant tradition, designed to bring the Scriptures in the German vernacular to the people. Bach rooted both his Passion settings, like many of his cantatas, in the chorale; short one or two-versed hymns designed as commentaries on the action and possibly intended to be sung by the congregation as a whole punctuate the action, and Bach is cunningly economical with his tunes, creating an impression of thematic unity rather than parsimony. The *St John* is less ambitious than the *St Matthew*, which followed in 1727; written for single choir, it employs less

- extrapolated matter. In each of Bach's
- Passions, the music follows the biblical
- text, adding to it not just the chorales
- but a whole range of arias, duets and
- arias with choruses, designed to
- comment on the theology of Passion
- and atonement. Clearly, Bach had
- smaller forces at his disposal in 1724
- than in 1727; either that or he had
- evolved the confidence to write a more
- ambitious work when he came to set
- St Matthew's text. As I've said earlier,
- Bach's Passions (especially the *St*
- *Matthew*) raised eyebrows for their
- sheer drama and their aesthetic
- achievement, as though this somehow
- detracted from their spiritual content.
- In fact, as settings of the Passion story
- it's hard to imagine – whatever one's
- denomination, or lack of it – more
- compelling versions which could serve
- the text any better. The use of the
- chorus is especially clever; apparently
- intellectual figures like the fugue are
- employed in choruses in the *St John* to
- create an impression of gathering
- crowd discontent; in the *St Matthew*,
- the doubled choir effect can be
- terrifying, as in the 4-second choral
- shriek of 'Barabbam!'. And the melodic
- beauty of almost all the arias is
- staggering. If you don't know either of
- these works, you're missing something
- very special, which doesn't require
- religious faith for its appreciation.
-
- **Mass in B Minor**
- That they can be appreciated
- regardless of one's feelings for religion
- is actually true of all Bach's great
- choral works; not only the Passions,
- but the Christmas and Easter Oratorios
- (written in 1734 and 1725 respectively)
- and, above all, the work which many
- feel is Bach's masterpiece and one of
- the greatest of all pieces of religious
- music, the Mass in B Minor. This was
- the product of the later years of Bach's

life, although in places it reworks material conceived much earlier. It seems unique amongst his great choral music in not having been designed for some specific occasion. Bach may have intended, as indeed he may have with his cantatas, that the work should be sung by small-scale forces (as small as one singer per part); this is a matter of little consequence (unless you're an 'authentic' fiend), as what really counts is the way that the music – rich, dramatic, yet entirely contemplative – bears testimony to Bach's own religious faith. There are surprising touches; Bach's mastery of dance music can be seen lurking behind the rhythmic pulse of the Sanctus (especially in some of the more recent, lighter interpretations) and, as always in Bach's music, the mathematical precision and cunning of some of the structure is awesome, but without ever threatening to swamp the musical effect. Bach sometimes attracts labels like 'austere'; well, his music may not be humorous, but his choral music in particular is luxurious and beautiful.

DISCOGRAPHY
The pioneering complete series of Bach cantatas by Nikolaus Harnoncourt and Gustav Leonhardt is well worth trying; two of the most famous are on a single disc (directed by Harnoncourt) – *Wachet auf* (*Sleepers Awake*) and *Herz und Mund und Tat und Leben* (*Heart and Mouth and Deed and Life*), which includes the music known in English as 'Jesu, Joy of Man's Desiring'.
● *Teldec 2292-43109-2* ● *1 CD* ● *Full price*
● *ADD* ✪

I am also a great advocate of Harnoncourt's all-male versions of the two Passions; they were trail-blazers in their day and to my ears they still sound as fresh and exciting and passionate (in the right sense) as any.
St John: ● *Teldec 2292-42492-2* ● *2 CDs*
● *Mid-price* ● *AAD* ● *1970*
St Matthew: ● *Teldec 2292-42509-2* ● *3 CDs*
● *Mid-price* ● *AAD* ● *1970*

John Eliot Gardiner's more modern version of the *St Matthew Passion* is also highly rhythmically crisp and dramatic.

● *Deutsche Grammophon Archiv 427 648-2*
● *3 CDs* ● *Full price* ● *DDD* ● *1988*

A good example of how it used to be done is the slow, marvellously luxuriant, Otto Klemperer version; no one would record the *St Matthew* with these resources any more, but Klemperer makes it work brilliantly.
● *EMI CMS7 63058-2* ● *3 CDs* ● *Mid-price*
● *ADD* ● *1964*

An alternative newer version of the *St John* is Frans Bruggen's; the voices are perhaps mixed a little backward, but Bruggen is always an interesting conductor.
● *Philips 434 905-2* ● *2 CDs* ● *Full price*
● *DDD* ● *1992*

For the Christmas Oratorio, try John Eliot Gardiner.
● *Deutsche Grammophon Archiv 423 232-2*
● *2 CDs* ● *Full price* ● *DDD* ● *1986*

Andrew Parrott's version of the Mass in B Minor opts for minimal forces, but is quite the most impressive currently available; controlled power, clarity and superb musicianship are the hallmarks of this excellent set.
● *EMI CDS7 47293 8* ● *2 CDs* ● *Full price*
● *DDD* ● *1984* ✪

The Bach *Magnificat* is often coupled with the Vivaldi *Gloria*. One especially lively set containing both is directed by Michel Corboz.
● *Erato Bonsai Collection 2292-45923-2* ● *1 CD*
● *Bargain price* ● *ADD* ● *1974/9* ✪

● ● ● ●

GREATNESS FROM ADVERSITY: HANDEL'S *MESSIAH*

In referring briefly, almost in passing, to Handel as a composer of solo cantatas, I might have seemed to be smitten with amnesia; but it was slightly later, in his English years (technically in an Irish month), that Handel produced a vast number of oratorios (as well as quite a few anthems), the crowning glory of which in the popular mind is undoubtedly *Messiah*, first performed in 1742. Handel was at something of a low ebb when he wrote this epic depiction, told by allusive scriptural texts, of the life of Christ; his reputation in London had waned over the 1730s, his health was failing, his operas were out of fashion. So he accepted an invitation to Dublin and announced that he intended to present, while there, a new oratorio called *Messiah* (the proceeds of the first performance to be given to charity). It's quite well known that Handel wrote the whole thing (more or less; he may have roughed some of it out before he went to Dublin) in just over three weeks; there is not a sign, though, of anything rushed, in the whole work, simply a high level of melodic and harmonic invention which has led to this oratorio becoming one of the most popular in English-speaking countries and elsewhere (although it should, correctly, be sung in English, as it was English texts which Handel set). Items such as 'I Know that my Redeemer Liveth' and the 'Hallelujah' Chorus belong to that common repository of musical knowledge which extends way beyond devotees of classical or religious music.

DISCOGRAPHY
There's an all-new, bargain-price *Messiah* which is amongst the best you can find; a beautiful sound with small forces and authentic instruments – another Naxos triumph.
● *Naxos 8.550667/8* ● *2 CDs* ● *Bargain price* ●*DDD* ● *1992* ✪

If you must pay more, try Nicholas McGegan's equally authentic version.
● *Harmonia Mundi HMU90 7050.2* ● *3 CDs* ● *Special price* ● *DDD* ● *1990*

Reflecting the Times: Haydn's Masses

As long as composing was a court- or church-appointed job, the writing of choral music tended to be a major component of the composer's task. Haydn and Mozart (in the first stage of his career) both wrote their fair share of masses and assorted other religious works. Many of Haydn's masses are exciting, ambitious, relatively large-scale works, although cleverly written so as not to be too daunting to performers below the top rank. These fourteen masses range in

date of composition from the 1740s to 1802 (more or less the whole of his creative career) and several reflect the temperament of Europe at the time of their composition, not least the *Mass in Time of War* and the *Mass in Time of Difficulties* (also known as the 'Nelson' Mass, in celebration of Nelson's defeat of the Napoleonic fleet at the Battle of the Nile in 1798, during the time when Haydn was writing the work). Haydn's masses are generally rather expansive (as opposed to Mozart's completed works in this form), with a subdued kind of entirely decorous drama designed not to occlude the liturgy's spirituality; as always with Haydn, deceptively simple melodies and harmonic constructs can lead all over the place. However, the composer would clearly have felt that the kind of drama he used in his Oratorio *Die Schöpfung* (*The Creation*) and his semi-secular cantata *Die Jahreszeiten* (*The Seasons*) wasn't entirely in keeping with music intended as part of a church service.

Haydn's *Creation, The Seasons*

These two huge choral works are in some senses complementary. The first is a dramatisation of the origins of the earth, based entirely on the Genesis story (but conveniently ignoring the Fall of Man), with characterised parts for angels and Adam and Eve. The whole starts with an orchestral picture of Chaos and the Void – ordered by our standards, really, but quite remarkable for all that. In some ways *The Creation* (written between 1796 and 1798) is a vast extension of all those picture portraits which conferred names on Haydn's symphonies and quartets, and it also offers an opportunity for some quite brilliant (though in no way tiresomely virtuosic) singing. Its subject-matter can make it seem slightly heavy-going in the wrong hands these days, but in the right hands, it's still an inspiring experience. *The Seasons*, on the other hand, is less overtly religious (although gratitude to the Deity runs through every word and note), and is based on translations of the work of the English poet James Thomson (who also wrote the words to 'Rule, Britannia!'). It's a comforting, middle-class picture of country life through all the seasons, idealised peasantry carrying on an idealised peasant life. It was the last big choral piece Haydn wrote (1799–1801) and he claimed it exhausted him; personally I feel that it isn't quite his most inventive work, and it's much easier to admire than to love (and easier still to be bored by). It has at one point a sort of choral fugue which seems to borrow a figure from Mozart's *Requiem*; whether this is conscious or not is open to debate.

DISCOGRAPHY
Trevor Pinnock's version of the 'Nelson' Mass (coupled with Haydn's setting of the great hymn of praise, the Te Deum) won a *The Gramophone* Award in 1988; deservedly so, too, for its clarity and spectacularly controlled use of power
● *Deutsche Grammophon Archiv 423 097-2* ● *1 CD* ● *Full price* ● *DDD* ● *1986* ❂

On a non-authentic tack, Leonard Bernstein was a very fine Haydn conductor and his 1960s/1970s performances of the 'Nelson' and the *Mass in Time of War* both have a spectacular grandeur.
● *Sony Classical SM2K 47563* ● *2 CDs* ● *Mid-price* ● *ADD* ● *1969/73*

The best version of *The Creation* remains Nikolaus Harnoncourt's, which boasts the exquisite soprano voice of Edita Gruberová.
● *Teldec 2292-42682-2* ● *2 CDs* ● *Full price* ● *DDD* ● *1986*

Meanwhile, Herbert von Karajan's deeply felt account of *The Seasons* also has the radiant inward artistry of the great Gundula Janowitz.
● *EMI CMS7 69224-2* ● *2 CDs* ● *Mid-price* ● *ADD* ● *1972*

INFLATED REPUTATIONS AND COMPACT DRAMA: MOZART

Mozart's reputation as a choral composer often seems to depend exclusively on the *Requiem*; as this is (famously) an unfinished work, it seems an unextremely unfair state of events. The *Requiem* does contain some very exciting, dramatic music (above all the ground-trembling Dies Irae, describing the day of judgement), but it also tails off rapidly when Mozart's pupil Franz Süssmayr (1766–1803) takes over and starts trying to crib his master's touch. Perhaps the romantic legend of the 'Man in Grey' which hangs around the piece has inflated its reputation, though the idea that this was some harbinger of Death has long been discredited; the 'Man in Grey' was merely a messenger of the notorious commissioning patron and plagiarist Count Walsegg, whose usual practice was to commission a work, and then copy it out in his own handwriting prior to passing it off as his own work.

Most of Mozart's choral work was written, in fact, during his early career when still in the service of the Cardinal Archbishop of Salzburg. Only the last mass (or penultimate if one includes the *Requiem*), the so-called 'Great' C Minor, was written after Mozart's arrival in Vienna; curiously enough, this work of 1782 also remained incomplete – perhaps Mozart's heart wasn't in religious music by this stage. Of the preceding seventeen masses, the 'Coronation' Mass of 1779 is the most famous and outgoing, but I have a great deal of affection for many of the less overtly flashy works like No. 17 in C Major, which is a tightly organised dramatic mass setting taking only slightly longer than fifteen minutes in total; the compact Credo is a small masterpiece.

Mozart's Lieder

Obviously, no piece by Mozart is entirely without merit (although it would be hard to argue that his choral work was the surest foundation for his status as a composer), so it's well worth browsing through this section of his *oeuvre* if time allows. Mozart also composed a whole series of songs which are some of the first to attract the label 'lied' (always understanding the prefix 'kunst', meaning 'art'); the kind of song which sets a short(ish) self-contained poem, with an accompaniment which seeks to draw out the poem's inner meanings. As the form developed in the nineteenth century, lieder with orchestral accompaniment also appeared, although the vast majority of lieder are simply for voice and piano (which made them ideal 'home music'). Mozart's lieder are fairly simply, straightforward affairs, not as emotionally or psychologically complex as Schubert's; but such pieces as 'The Violet' (delicate and simple, with certain colour overtones), 'When Louise burnt her faithless lover's letters' (a short, quite disturbing monodrama), or 'Thoughts at eventide to Laura' (discreetly and touchingly sentimental) all give a strong indication of the form's potential. Had he lived another 30 years (or lived 30 years later), Mozart might well have done what Schubert did with the lied – and let's not forget that Schubert learnt a good deal of his basic skill from Salieri.

DISCOGRAPHY
Nikolaus Harnoncourt is currently engaged on recording all Mozart's religious choral works and two of the releases to data are especially good; the *Missa Solemnis* (K337) is given a superbly dramatic reading and happily coupled with the *Litaniae de Venerabili Altaris Sacramento* and *Regina Coeli*.
● *Teldec das Alte Werk 4509-90494-2* ● *1 CD*
● *Full price* ● *DDD* ● *1992* ❂

The C Major Mass (K257) is equally well performed by the same forces, with the compact drama of the piece brought out to advantage.
● *Teldec das Alte Werk 4509-72304-2* ● *1 CD*
● *Full price* ● *DDD* ● *1992*

Sir Georg Solti's performance of the *Requiem* was staged on the exact 200th anniversary of Mozart's death, and actually incudes the full Requiem liturgy in Mozart's honour. It's a dramatic, exciting performance with a star cast, including Arleen Auger and Cecilia Bartoli.
● *Decca 433 688-2* ● *1 CD* ● *Full price*
● *DDD* ● *1991*

There's an excellent bargain version, one of the best in the catalogue, directed by Richard Hickox; it's quite hard to find these days, but well worth snapping-up when you do.
● *Virgo VJ7 91460-2* ● *1 CD* ● *Bargain price*
● *DDD* ● *1991*

There are two recordings of Mozart's lieder I'd particularly commend; both cover much the same ground, but with different voices. If you prefer a female voice, then the lovely soprano of Barbara Bonney, sensitively accompanied by Geoffrey Parsons, is ideal.
● *Teldec 2292-46334-2* ● *1 CD* ● *Full price*
● *DDD* ● *1990*

One of the most felicitous lieder combinations in recent years has been veteran tenor Peter Schreier and pianist András Schiff; their Mozart disc is a lovely, simple thing, and includes the meaty Masonic Cantata.
● *Decca 430 514-2* ● *1 CD* ● *Full price*
● *DDD* ● *1990*

A Cry for Peace: Beethoven's *Missa Solemnis*

For all the great success of his Choral Symphony, Beethoven wasn't particularly at ease with the human voice as a musical resource. Some have seen his minimal output of religious music (only two masses) as an indication that he was a post-Enlightenment agnostic tending to the atheist; as his greatest choral work, the *Missa Solemnis* in D Major, Opus 123 (which he wrote between 1818 and 1823) makes clear, however, his religious faith was profound, if scarcely conventional. This enormous mass, of which each movement is of exceptional length, is very much a summation of Beethoven's own personal feelings and experiences, its whole driving impetus contained in the repeated pleas in various parts of the mass (particularly the Gloria and the Agnus Dei) for peace. Beethoven's manuscript was littered with references to 'inner and outer peace' (that is, civil peace – he had, after all, spent a good part of his life watching Europe getting torn to shreds by the military – and spiritual peace). The music of the *Missa Solemnis* can be like a ride on a violent roller-coaster; lots of extraordinary extremes of dynamic, choruses asked to sing at the top of their ranges and voices for long periods, strange hushed passages, and, in the middle of the Agnus Dei, traditionally the quietest section of the Mass, a great blaring military outburst. Some have found all this, allied to the fact that Beethoven went deaf, to be proof of an essential doubt, which the music attempts to grope through. Dramatic, frenetic and sometimes downright weird as the music is, though, it's all shot through with spiritual values, and – if you were in any doubt the manuscript bears the inscription (in the composer's handwriting and in German, obviously) 'God above all – God never abandoned me'. For a long time the work has been regarded as a bizarre curiosity, nearly unperformable because of its scale and because of its jagged extremes; recent years suggest that it might at last be coming into its own.

Beethoven's Lieder

Beethoven also wrote a handful of lieder, the most significant of which are in the song cycle *An die ferne Geliebte* (*To the Distant Beloved*), an 1816 setting of six love poems by the same poet (the not especially celebrated Aloys Jeitteles). This is,

arguably the first of the great song cycles, in which both vocal line and piano accompanist share the burden of expressing the psychological state of mind of the lover at the centre of the poems.

DISCOGRAPHY
The most solid recording of Beethoven's *Missa Solemnis*, packed with old-fashioned virtues and some radiantly spiritual singing, is conducted by Otto Klemperer, and in many ways it's as good an introduction to the work as you could hope for.
● *EMI CMS7 69538-2* ● *2 CDs* ● *Mid-price*
● *ADD* ● *1966* ❍

There are two recent versions, both recorded live, which offer a great deal; James Levine's starry version (the cast includes Jessye Norman, Cheryl Studer, Placido Domingo) with the Vienna Philharmonic packs enormous power and is every bit the sum of its parts (these multi-stellar recordings sometimes aren't). Although spread over two discs, it comes at a special(ish) price of just over £20 for the set.
● *Deutsche Grammophon 435 770-2* ● *2 CDs*
● *Special price* ● *DDD* ● *1991*

Levine's recording was made at the 1991 Salzburg Festival; from the same occasion a year later comes Nikolaus Harnoncourt's roller-coaster account, which for my money is the fullest realisation yet of this extraordinary work's dimensions, its jagged contrasts, its full spiritual impact. Harnoncourt's soloists are distinguished, but this is very much an ensemble triumph, using (like his celebrated Beethoven symphonic cycle) the Chamber Orchestra of Europe. Another special-price deal, two discs for around £15.
● *Teldec 9031-74884-2* ● *2 CDs* ● *Special price*
● *DDD* ● *1992*

The most celebrated recent recording is John Eliot Gardiner's much-garlanded, *The Gramophone* Recording of the Year-winner, which does have the advantage of getting the whole work onto a single disc. I find this a flat and tedious account, completely lacking the work's spiritual dimension, but I'm in a minority here.
● *Deutsche Grammophon Archiv 429 779-2*
● *1 CD* ● *Full price* ● *DDD* ● *1990*

There's a good selection of Beethoven's lieder (including *An die ferne Geliebte*) from the prince of lieder, Dietrich Fischer-Dieskau, with sensitive accompaniment from Jörg Demus. There's also a good smattering of Brahms thrown in for good measure. These are 1950s and 1960s recordings, but for all that they probably show Fischer-Dieskau at his most accomplished, before mannerism and technique had taken him over.
● *Deutsche Grammophon 415 189-2* ● *1 CD*
● *Full price* ● *ADD* ● *1959/67*

THE MASTER OF THE LIED: SCHUBERT

Schubert's contribution to music for the solo voice is quite awesome, on the same scale as Bach's for choral forces. Schubert composed over 600 songs of varying lengths, kinds and seriousness. Some, in common with other Schubert works, are fragments; on several occasions he had more than one go at the same set of words. The subject matter ranges across practically everything; life, death, love, Scotland, Italy, spinning, winter, birds, beasts, fish . . . the list is endless. Pianist Graham Johnson, a great Schubert accompanist, is currently engaged on recording every single lied on 36 different releases, each with a different singer (at the time of writing they have reached No. 18; the whole project to be finished by 1997, the 200th anniversary of Schubert's birth). He has found subject matter, chronology (to some extent) and authorship of texts the easiest ways of dividing songs into groups for his purposes; for, apart from the two great song cycles (*Die Schöne Müllerin – The Beautiful Milleress* – and *Winterreise – Winter Journey*) and the last songs, always collected together as *Schwanengesang (Swan Song)* but probably never intended as a cycle, the matter and manner of these songs is prodigious and omnivorous. Each is a little drama; sometimes an internal drama, sometimes a story involving more than one character, sometimes a simple observation of everyday life, sometimes a memorable evocation of forces beyond the human understanding. 'The Erl King', for example, is a three-sided tale of a father driving hard to get his son home through a dark and wintry forest; the son is ailing, and in his

fever he hears the spirit of Death – the Erl King – calling him, trying to seduce him into becoming one of his minions. All three personae are characterised in this four-minute epic; the lulling calls of the Erl King, the reassuring (but anxious) father, the extreme cries of the boy (who is eventually lost), and around them the accompaniment depicts the weather, the night, the Erl King's false promises. Schubert's art is perhaps seens on its grandest scale in the two song cycles, above all in *Winterreise*, one of his last great works, settings of 24 poems by the poet Wilhelm Müller about a rejected lover who sets out on a journey through a petrified winter landscape and, through his journey, his mind is gradually changed, even driven mad. The only other human figure in this landscape turns up at the cycle's end; the abandoned figure of a hurdy-gurdy man, against whose spare, broken music Schubert sets a strange enigmatic ending to this tale of love deferred. It makes for a contrast with the more sociable world of *Die Schöne Müllerin* (which is also by Müller).

Schubert's lieder really are worth dipping into almost anywhere; every listener will discover personal favourites (obviously old standards like 'The Trout' and 'Death and the Maiden' make easy and useful starting points; as perhaps does 'The Shepherd on the Rock', a lovely, slightly longer lied for singer, piano and clarinet), and there are plenty of undiscovered gems yet to emerge into the light. Schubert's choral music is also worth a dabble; his compact, yet exquisitely brilliant, Mass in G is a radiantly sunny piece of writing, full of easy melody and yet completely in keeping with the liturgy. It makes a rather interesting contrast with

Rossini's *Messa di Gloria* (a mass with only a Kyrie and a Gloria, the first two sections), which is brimful of melodic vitality but has more or less no spiritual dimension whatsoever.

DISCOGRAPHY
There are lots of ways of approaching Schubert's lieder; you can start with a good solid Fischer-Dieskau compilation (with Gerald Moore as accompanist) from the 1960s and early 1970s, which contains all the classics like 'The Erl-King' and 'The Trout'.
● *Deutsche Grammophon 431 085-2* ● *1 CD*
● *Full price* ● *ADD* ● *1969–72* ○

Or you can dip at random into the Hyperion Schubert Edition, Graham Johnson's wonderfully imaginative project (seventeen volumes currently available). My particular favourite is Volume 11, cheerful songs about death (actually not as gloomy or morbid as it might seem) with the soloist Brigitte Fassbaender, the greatest mezzo-soprano currently singing. Fassbaender is one of the most expressive of Schubert singers and she sometimes lives dangerously, but she always brings something new to the songs (which is what great artistry is all about).
● *Hyperion CDJ33011* ● *1 CD* ● *Full price*
● *DDD* ● *1990* ○

For some reason all my favourite releases to date in the Hyperion Edition feature female singers: Volume 1, with Dame Janet Baker, makes an excellent introduction.
● *Hyperion CDJ33001* ● *1988*

Volume 7 with the beautiful Dutch soprano Elly Ameling concentrates on Schubert in 1815, the year in which he discovered much of his talent for the lied.
● *Hyperion CDJ33007* ● *1989*

In Volume 9, Arleen Auger's exquisitely pure tones go through a variety of lieder connected with the theatre.
● *Hyperion CDJ33009* ● *1989*

Volume 17, with the radiantly lovely voice of Lucia Popp, concentrates on the year 1816.
● *Hyperion CDJ33017* ● *1992*

All volumes are extremely generous in the amount of music they offer (somewhere in the 70-minute-average region); and really, any one of them is worth dipping into.

Of course, another approach to Schubert is through the great cycles *Winterreise, Die Schöne Müllerin* and the collection known as *Schwanengesang*. The latter two have both been recently recorded by the excellent partnership of Peter Schreier (in many ways, the greatest of

modern lieder tenors) and András Schiff, and both received *The Gramophone* Awards in successive years.
Schöne Müllerin: ● *Decca 430 414-2* ● *1 CD*
● *Full price* ● *DDD* ● *1990;*
Schwanengesang: ● *Decca 425 612-2* ● *1 CD*
● *Full price* ● *DDD* ● *1989*

One of the most exciting recordings of *Winterreise* for many years was by Brigitte Fassbaender, tackling in her unique way songs which have hitherto been very much regarded as the near-exclusive property of men. Her account of this journey into madness takes some dramatic liberties, but is one of the great recorded experiences of the last few years, an indispensable desert island disc. Superb accompaniment from the composer Aribert Reimann, too.
● *EMI CDC7 49846 2* ● *1 CD* ● *Full price*
● *DDD* ● *1988*

To hear an entirely different, cool but magisterial account of the same cycle, Hans Hotter's 1942 recording has just been reissued; the recording quality is quite superb, and this is artistry of a different but equally high order.
● *Deutsche Grammophon 437 351-2* ● *1 CD*
● *Mid-price* ● *ADD* ● *1942*

And one shouldn't forget the classic version by Peter Pears and Benjamin Britten; Pears's tonal range is quite marvellous, and this most famous of partnerships brings all its musicianship to bear.
● *Decca 417 473-2* ● *1 CD* ● *Mid-price*
● *ADD* ● *1963*

Fassbaender and Reimann have also tackled (with great success) the *Schwanengesang* collection, another heart-stopping performance, of great artistry, and a winner of a *The Gramophone* Award.
● *Deutsche Grammophon 429 766-2* ● *1 CD*
● *Full price* ● *DDD* ● *1989/91*

For Schubert's choral music, try a live recording which includes both the Mass in G and Schumann's puzzling *Requiem for Mignon* (as well as two smaller Schubert choral works). The singers include Barbara Bonney and Andreas Schmidt, and Claudio Abbado conducts proceedings with all his talent for Schubert.
● *Deutsche Grammophon 435 486-2* ● *1 CD*
● *Full price* ● *DDD* ● *1990*

Armin Jordan's account of the E Flat Major Mass is quite compelling, too.
● *Erato Emeraude 2292-45300-2* ● *1 CD*
● *Mid-price* ● *DDD* ● *1987*

Rossini
For Rossini's exuberant *Messa di Gloria*, there's an excellent new version (with a starry cast including Sumi Jo and Ann Murray) conducted by Sir Neville Marriner.
● *Philips 434 132-2* ● *1 CD* ● *Full price*
● *DDD* ● *1992* ○

MARITAL BLISS AND GREAT POETRY: SCHUMANN

Although Schumann wrote some choral music, it is his lieder which merit attention here. One of Schumann's choral works, though, the *Requiem for Mignon*, is fascinatingly baffling; a setting of part of a novel by Goethe, its tone is always a problem for performers. Is it a parody? Is it serious? It was his new-found marital domestic bliss in 1840 which provoked Schumann into an outpouring of lyrical love songs – the 'Dichterliebe' ('Words of love'), 'Frauenliebe und Leben' ('Womanly/wifely love and life'), poems from 'Liebesfrühling' ('Love's Spring') and the two collections of *Liederkreis*. Schumann was almost always concerned to set poems by important poets, as he believed that in a lied the words should be as distinguished as the music.

FORESHADOWING WAGNER: LISZT

Liszt was perhaps more casual about the quality of the poems he set, putting the music first by some head. It's only recently that his lieder have begun to attract attention again; quite rightly, as many were extremely influential upon (amongst others) Richard Wagner; one, 'Ich möchte hingehn' ('I would depart') contains the whole musical crux of *Tristan und Isolde*. Liszt's lieder probably go further than any others, up to that point in musical history, in their demands on the human voice. It's almost operatic at times; lieder, essentially a private form, reaching back to the more public arena.

DISCOGRAPHY
A good Schumann selection comprising 'Dichterliebe' and the *Liederkreis* Opus 39, is sung by the expressive and ardent baritone Olaf Bär.
● EMI CDC7 47397 2 ● 1 CD ● Full price
● DDD ● 1985 ❂

But at the risk of seeming like a man obsessed, I would once more turn to Brigitte Fassbaender for both Schumann and Liszt. Her recording of 'Frauenliebe und Leben,' *Liederkreis* Opus 24, and several other lieder by Schumann has great distinction.
● *Deutsche Grammophon 415 519 2* ● 1 CD ● Full price ● DDD ● 1984

For Schumann's *Requiem for Mignon*, see above under Schubert.

Meanwhile Fassbaender's recent disc of Liszt lieder was something of a revelation and may very well help to establish Liszt at the forefront of lieder once more.
● *Decca 430 512-2* ● 1 CD ● Full price ● DDD ● 1990 ❂

HIGH SERIOUSNESS: BRAHMS

Lieder and *A German Requiem*
Naturally, Brahms approached both choral and also vocal music with great seriousness; his solo vocal writing was often deeply beautiful and one of its highlights is the collection of so-called 'Serious' Songs, scriptural settings of some profundity. These, written in 1896, the year before he died, are mainly sombre, although the final song, based on St Paul's famous passage 'Though I speak with the tongues of men and of angels' (1 Corinthians 13), is designed as a counterweight to its three more doom-laden predecessors. Brahms's view of religion as a comfort is apparent in every religious work he wrote, nowhere more so, perhaps, than in the famous *A German Requiem*, an altogether more youthful work inspired in 1865 by the devastating grief Brahms felt on the death of his mother. Rather than writing a formal requiem mass, Brahms wanted something which would speak to people, including himself, in a living language, and so he set passages from the text of the Lutheran Bible rather than the formal Roman liturgy famous

from Mozart's work and others. The composer deliberately set himself a work which was designed to comfort; gone was all the Dies Irae thunder and lightning, fire and brimstone. Deeply mournful music is the work's hallmark some of the time; at other times it is light, melodic, almost pastoral, using its chorus, orchestra and two soloists for lush, beautiful effects.

A Contrasting Requiem: Berlioz

A German Requiem contrasts strongly with Hector Berlioz's *Grande Messe des Morts* (written in 1837); this setting of the formal Roman liturgy aims for every possible theatrical extreme, becoming at times almost lurid in its picture-painting. It is one of Berlioz's greatest works, bearing more than a passing resemblance in manner to Beethoven's *Missa Solemnis* (the same extremes of dynamics) yet on an even more impressive scale. Brahms's *German Requiem* and Berlioz's *Grande Messe* are undoubtedly two of the great pieces of nineteenth-century religious choral music, even though they are diametrically opposed. This opposition comes down to a basic disagreement about religion – Berlioz clearly had nothing like the bedrock of comfort which Brahms could draw upon.

Choral Faith: Brahms's Other Choral Works

In another of his vocal masterpieces, the Alto Rhapsody for female alto, chorus and orchestra, Brahms showed again, in a setting of a poetic fragment by Goethe, how religion seemed to him. After two verses of tonal and melodic uncertainty (very beautiful though it is) by soloist and orchestra, the arrival of the chorus in an almost chorale-like setting restores order and harmony, bringing the lost traveller

refreshment in the form of a prayer for God to find 'in his Psalter' something to ease the traveller's plight. This choral work was written in 1869, the same decade as Wagner's *Tristan*, and something of that off-centred approach to tonality also informs the first part of the Rhapsody; a deeply beautiful piece. Other Brahms choral works such as the 'Schicksalslied' ('Song of Fate') and 'Nänie' also have great merit and beauty, and this area of the composer's work is coming more to the fore these days; in Brahms's close-textured, male-dominated choruses it's possible to hear back to Bach and to the chorale tradition which produced and inspired him.

DISCOGRAPHY
Berlioz
Berlioz's *Grande Messe des Morts* has been given its most convincing interpretation on record by Leonard Bernstein, who really gets to the heart of the drama and terror of this epic work, complemented by an interesting account of the same composer's Te Deum under the control of Daniel Barenboim.
● *Sony M2YK 46461*   ● *2 CDs*   ● *Mid-price*
● *ADD*   ● *1975* ✪

Brahms
Although there's been a recent glut of new Brahms *Requiems* (including, God help us, an 'authentic' version at beltingly fast speeds by Roger Norrington), the best is still a distinguished, venerable entry in the recording catalogue; Otto Klemperer's 1961 recording still outweighs all others for humanity, sympathy, warmth, and sheer beauty of performance. Elisabeth Schwarzkopf and Fischer-Dieskau are at their best in this remarkable benchmark recording, which still hasn't been equalled. It's a performance, too, which gives the lie to the idea that all Klemperer's recordings were deathly slow.
● *EMI CDC7 47238 2*   ● *1 CD*   ● *Full price*
● *ADD*   ● *1961* ✪

There's an excellent collection of Brahms's choral works by Sir Colin Davis and the Bavarian Radio Symphony Orchestra and Chorus, featuring that rare thing, a true contralto (Nathalie Stutzmann) in the Alto Rhapsody. A lovely disc, beautiful, warm, the right amount of drama.
● *RCA Victor Red Seal 09026 61201 2*   ● *1 CD*
● *Full price*   ● *DDD*   ● *1992* ✪

For Brahms's lieder, there's the selection (with some of Beethoven's lieder) sung by Fischer-Dieskau mentioned above (see p. 259); also,

Andreas Schmidt has recorded the four Serious Songs with Wolf's Michelangelo poems and Mahler's Rückert lieder; a great and marvellous disc, superbly sung, if slightly too harrowing for some moods, but strongly recommended as a way of covering all three of these remarkable lieder composers.
● *Deutsche Grammophon 431 649-2* ● *1 CD*
● *Full price* ● *DDD* ● *1989*

And one of the greatest altos who ever drew breath, Kathleen Ferrier (1912–1953), recorded Brahms's Alto Rhapsody, the Sacred Lullaby, the four Serious Songs and three of Mahler's Rückert lieder, all now available on one disc; Ferrier's voice is a thing of remarkable beauty (Bruno Walter once said that the two greatest musical encounters of his life were with Ferrier and Mahler, in that order of importance and talent), and this disc, for all its slight surface noises, shouldn't be missed.
● *Decca Kathleen Ferrier Edition Volume 10*
● *433 477-2* ● *1 CD* ● *Mid-price* ● *ADD*
● *1947–52*

GENIUS AT THE EDGE: HUGO WOLF (1860–1903)

The year after Brahms produced his four Serious Songs (the year of his death, in fact), one of the greatest of all lieder writers produced a masterpiece which quite complements Brahms's work. Hugo Wolf was not the first or last composer to set poetry by the great Renaissance artist Michelangelo; however, the effort turned out to be the last nail in the coffin of his sanity. Concentrating on the brooding, doom-laden accompaniment and melody for a song such as 'Alles endet, was enstehet' ('Everything ends, which exists') turned out to be too much.

Wolf was, in fact, the most versatile lieder writer since Schubert, and it's in his lieder that his entire reputation truly lies. He very much saw his singers as specific personae (the Michelangelo songs were set as though sung directly by the artist himself, protesting against the cruelty of art and time), and some of his wittiest turns came in the *Italian* and *Spanish*

Songbooks; enormous collections of short anonymous poems in these languages translated into German, and turned by Wolf into a dual-perspective dialogue imbued with obliquity and irony by the use of two voices, one male, one female, who take groups of songs each. Many of these songs are extremely brief (in this Wolf looks forward to the trend of the first decade or two of the next century) and melodically elliptical (which is a polite way of saying that the tunes aren't always conventional). All Wolf's songs are really worth trying; their drama and sense of mystery, where appropriate (as in the setting of Goethe's 'Kennst du das Land?' – 'Do you know that land?'), is remarkable, and they all show quite how subtle a reader of poetry Wolf must have been; which is what finished him off in the end.

DISCOGRAPHY
For further encounters with Wolf, I'd recommend the *Italian Songbook*, recorded with great wit and sublety by Ruth Ziesak and Andreas Schmidt.
● *RCA Victor Red Seal RD 60857* ● *1 CD*
● *Full price* ● *DDD* ● *1990* ✪

And Brigitte Fassbaender has recently released a quite superb recital of Wolf's setting of poems by Eduard Mörike.
● *Decca 440 208-2* ● *1 CD* ● *Full price*
● *DDD* ● *1992*

A REQUIEM OR TWO: VERDI, GABRIEL FAURÉ (1845–1924)

Several of the most popular settings of the Requiem date from the latter part of the nineteenth century. Supreme among these is Verdi's, which is, as you'd expect from the master of Italian opera, a huge, graphic, dramatic work, full of exciting colours and fierce characterisation of the liturgy. Gabriel

Fauré's *Requiem* was written and revised during the last decade of the nineteenth century, and is a work most easily (if allusively) characterised as 'French'; delicate, subtle, gentle, and deeply Romantic, it has enjoyed great popularity in our time probably because it is so melodically easy on the ear (Fauré's songs are also undemandingly enjoyable).

DISCOGRAPHY
Verdi
The most convincing account of Verdi's *Requiem* currently around is probably the *The Gramophone* Award-winner conducted by Robert Shaw (who worked with Toscanini in the 1940s and 1950s); good strong singing, especially from soprano Susan Dunn and tenor Jerry Hadley.
● *Telarc CD80152* ● *2 CDs* ● *Full price*
● *DDD* ● *1986* ✪

Fauré
The most authentic Fauré *Requiem* (there were several rogue editions of the piece) is probably Philip Herreweghe's, which makes much use of boy (and boy-like) sopranos and does the piece the greatest, most beautiful justice.
● *Harmonia Mundi HMC90 1292* ● *1 CD*
● *Full price* ● *DDD* ● *1988* ✪

'THE END OF MUSIC': GERMAN LIEDER
Song plays an important role in the career of the great Germanic composers who stand at the end of the Romantic tradition and the beginnings of what we think of as 'Modern' music.

A LIFE OF SONG: RICHARD STRAUSS
Richard Strauss wrote lieder through his whole career (the very last piece he was working on was a song), and being married for much of his long life to a singer, he never ignored the human voice as an instrument. His songs are mainly melodic, written with both piano and orchestral accompaniment (many of the orchestral songs are sumptuous miniatures, arguably the most cunningly orchestrated songs in the repertoire); although it is in the lied that we see Strauss's one serious essay in atonal, amelodic music, his 'Three Songs for Ophelia', settings of the broken texts sung by the mad Ophelia in the fourth act of Shakespeare's *Hamlet* (but translated into German, obviously). In these piano songs Strauss's decision to venture into a more jagged, less Romantic realm is perfectly justified, as it is a mode ideal for the character and nature of the songs. His most famous lieder, though, are undoubtedly his 'Four Last Songs', published after his death; four orchestral songs which more properly constitute a set of three (with words by Herman Hesse) and a fourth describing twilight (words by Josef von Eichendorff) which somehow, although longer, sits perfectly with the rueful, reminiscent style of the three Hesse settings. These songs are part of Strauss's great outburst of creativity at the end of the Second World War, probably provoked by his realisation of the truth about the regime he had served – and ignored – for thirteen years; their 'autumnal' feeling, both melodic and yet with an undertow of melancholy, is very much in keeping with parts of the Oboe Concerto and the dizzying orchestral pieces *Metamorphosen*. Strauss may very well have been the last great lieder writer; the 'Four Last Songs' certainly have some claim on the title of last great lieder, although the superb Michelangelo settings of Dmitri Shostakovich (1974) in their thrilling orchestral form have, perhaps, some claim to this title too.

DISCOGRAPHY
Richard Strauss
Lieder
There are various collections of Richard Strauss's lieder; Felicity Lott, with conductor Neeme Järvi, is currently engaged on a series of orchestra songs. Volume 1 included a very distinguished account of the 'Four Last Songs', but it's really for the other pieces that I'd recommend both volumes that have been issued to date; Lott has a superbly clear voice which remains expressive without being overbearing, and is thus ideal for Strauss.
Volume 1: ● *Chandos CHAN 9054* ● *1 CD*
● *Full price* ● *DDD* ● *1986-88*
Volume 2: ● *Chandos CHAN 9159*

Another marvellous Strauss collection features the soprano Gundula Janowitz, possibly the greatest post-war interpreter of Strauss. Again, clarity, coolness, radiant inwardness, are all in evidence: Janowitz has a voice of great beauty which, though sadly underrated, is possibly one of the greatest of the second half of this century. The disc also include a titanic performance of *Metamorphosen*, dizzingly conducted by Richard Stamp.
● *Virgin Classics VC7 90794-2* ● *1 CD* ● *Full price* ● *DDD* ● *1988/9* ❂

For a selection of piano-accompanied songs, try the superb combination of Margaret Price and Wolfgang Sawallisch.
● *EMI CDC7 47948 2* ● *1 CD* ● *Full price*
● *DDD* ● *1986*

'Four Last Songs'
The 'Four Last Songs' come in all shapes and sizes. For my money the best version is undoubtedly that by Gundula Janowitz, whose voice (captured in the early 1970s) is ideal for these translucent works, and Herbert von Karajan's accompaniment is more or less ideal. This disc, which also offers the Oboe Concerto and *Metamorphosen*, is a generous bargain.
● *Deutsche Grammophon 423 888-2* ● *1 CD*
● *Mid-price* ● *ADD* ● *1973* ❂

The most vaunted and publicised version is probably Schwarzkopf's with George Szell. I actually find her voice a touch dull (heresy of heresies), and this 'classic' has never quite worked its much-acclaimed magic on me, but Schwarzkopf fans swear by it.
● *EMI CDC7 47276 2* ● *1 CD* ● *Full price*
● *ADD* ● *1966*

I'd advise you to steer clear of Jessye Norman's version; her voice is far too creamily statuesque for these songs. The two other versions I'd actually commend are the historic 1950s version by Lisa della Casa, with some extraordinarily quick tempos from Karl Böhm; this disc also offers some lovely selections from Strauss's operas *Arabella, Capriccio* and *Ariadne auf Naxos*.
● *Decca 425 959-2* ● *1 CD* ● *Mid-price*
● *ADD* ● *1953–4*

The best modern digital account comes from Lucia Popp and Klaus Tennstedt; possibly the best orchestral interpretation, and Popp's voice is quite lovely.
● *EMI CDD7 64290 2* ● *1 CD* ● *Mid-price*
● *DDD* ● *1982*

Early twentieth-century German lieder
Lucia Popp has also produced probably the best version of Strauss's 'Ophelia' Songs, on a selection of songs from the turn of the century entitled *Jugendstil [Art-Nouveau] Lieder*. This beautiful disc also offers early songs by Berg and Schoenberg, with Pfitzner and Schreker thrown in for good measure, and is an ideal introduction to the lieder of that epoch.
● *RCA Victor Red Seal RD 60950* ● *1 CD*
● *Full price* ● *DDD* ● *1991* ❂

Shostakovich: Michelangelo Verses
For Shostakovich's Michelangelo Verses, try the outstanding new version by Dietrich Fischer-Dieskau (a titanic performance, brilliantly using the resources of his voice) and Vladimir Ashkenazy (one of his most impressive forays as a conductor). This is vivid, exciting stuff.
● *Decca 433 319-2* ● *1 CD* ● *Full price*
● *DDD* ● *1991* ❂

NATURE AND DEATH: MAHLER

I've already noted the role which song played in Gustav Mahler's career as a composer, its importance in forming his creative imagination, and the part which his songs subsequently played in his symphonies. Apart from the settings of the nature poems *Des Knaben Wunderhorn* (*The Magic Horn of Youth*) and poems by Friedrich Rückert (one of which, 'Ich bin der Welt abhanden gekommen' – 'I am become lost to the world' – is the basis for the celebrated Adagietto of the 5th Symphony) earlier in his career, Mahler also, in his maturity, wrote a series called *Kindertotenlieder* (*Songs of Dead Children*), again based on words by Rückert. These coincided with the early days of his marriage, and his preoccupation with such a morbid subject (although the songs are beautifully set) may have caused some strain within the marriage.

Actually, the first characteristic Mahlerian work, written when he was merely twenty, was a choral work, a cantata based on a folk song, 'Das Klagende Lied' ('The Complaining Song'). Despite its title, this is a highly characterful setting of a folk legend complete with murder, ghostly minstrels and celebrations; although parts of it are clearly pastiche Wagner, parts are equally mature Mahler, sprung fully grown from the creator's forehead, as it were. Probably Mahler's greatest achievement using the human voice was the quasi-symphony *Das Lied von der Erde* (*The Song of the Earth*), for orchestra and two soloists (tenor and mezzo-soprano), setting German translations of Chinese poetry, for which there was a great vogue at the beginning of the twentieth century. Mahler created something of a new musical sound, with just a hint of fake Eastern-ness about it, for this piece; its delicacy is something special in the whole of his *oeuvre*, and there are many who otherwise find Mahler hard to take who draw great joy from *Das Lied von der Erde*.

DISCOGRAPHY
Riccardo Chailly's recent recording of Mahler's 'Das Klagende Lied' captures all the essential qualities of the piece, with some marvellous singing by Brigitte Fassbaender (among others) and a chillingly impressive boy alto (Markus Baur).
● *Decca 425 719-2* ● *1 CD* ● *Full price*
● *DDD* ● *1990* ✪

For a lieder selection which includes *Kindertotenlieder*, I'd strongly recommend Dame Janet Baker's transcendental recording with Sir John Barbirolli; this has a real sense of Mahler's inwardness.
● *EMI CDC7 47793 2* ● *1 CD* ● *Full price*
● *ADD* ● *1967-8*

Elisabeth Schwarzkopf is very much at her best in a 1960s recording, with Dietrich Fischer-Dieskau and George Szell, of *Des Knaben Wunderhorn*.
● *EMI CDC7 47277 2* ● *1 CD* ● *Full price*
● *ADD* ● *1968*

The fullest expression of *Das Lied von der Erde* is to be found in Otto Klemperer's deeply moving reading, featuring Christa Ludwig and Fritz Wunderlich as singers.
● *EMI CDC7 47231 2* ● *1 CD* ● *Full price*
● *ADD* ● *1966* ✪

It's worth trying this piece too in its piano (rather than orchestral) version; a different qualitative experience, but no less impressive, especially with Brigitte Fassbaender singing the mezzo parts.
● *Teldec 2292-46276-2* ● *1 CD* ● *Full price*
● *DDD* ● *1989*

SUMPTUOUS ROMANTICISM: SCHOENBERG

The last great Romantic choral work is Arnold Schoenberg's *Gurrelieder*. Schoenberg actually took ten years, on and off, writing this work, and his style changed from the drippingly chromatic late Romantic to the abrasively Modernist. This is only noticeable in the orchestration of *Gurrelieder* – the last of the three pieces is much more percussive and also has a whole vast section to be spoken at pitch rather than sung, a common preoccupation of Schoenberg the Modernist. Generally, though, *Gurrelieder*, a setting of German translations of Danish poetry about love, death, and ghostly carryings-on on the island of Gurra, is very much in the post-*Tristan* style of Wagner, with some magnificent natural description, some sumptuous love lyrics, a genuinely effective comic interlude (the complaint of a ghostly jester at the company he finds himself forced to haunt in); while the orchestration is subtle and extravagant by turns and the writing for the voice magnificent. *Gurrelieder* was the last 'Romantic' work which Schoenberg allowed himself to conduct, and it is a masterpiece of a very high order indeed.

FORGETTING ROMANTICISM: SCHOENBERG, BERG, WEBERN

Turning one's back on Romanticism, though, didn't mean turning one's back on the human voice, and all the Modernists found their way to a distinctive idiom at least partly through lieder. Schoenberg wrote distinctive settings of allusive Symbolist poetry early in his career; Alban Berg, too, although he didn't write much lieder, wrote some highly descriptive short pieces (which weren't ascribed an official opus number). Webern concentrated a proportion of his early career on the voice, too, bringing his concentrated, highly wrought approach to bear on the relation between the human voice and music. The pieces for voice and various instrumental combinations demand, like all Webern, hard work from the listener, but for many they can prove a useful way into his music.

DISCOGRAPHY
Schoenberg
The best recording yet of Schoenberg's
Gurrelieder again comes from Riccardo Chailly
with the RSO Berlin; not only is Siegfried
Jerusalem a superbly ardent lover, Susan Dunn
makes a fine foil for him, and Brigitte
Fassbaender (again) gives a highly individual
reading of a big ten-minute solo. With Hans Hotter
as the speaker, one is assured of a high level of
artistry at every point. Sumptuous sound, an
irresistible experience.
● *Decca 430 321-2* ● *2 CDs* ● *Full price*
● *DDD* ● *1985* ○

Webern
Anyone truly interested in getting into Webern
would be well advised to splash out on the
collection of his complete works masterminded by
Pierre Boulez; it's something of a bargain, with
much of the vocal work falling to the excellent
soprano interpreter of modern music, Heather
Harper.
● *Sony SM3K 45845* ● *3 CDs* ● *Mid-price*
● *ADD* ● *1969–72* ○

THE GREAT BRITISH TRADITION: ELGAR, BRITTEN, TIPPETT

Although British music produced no single great figure between Purcell at the end of the seventeenth century and Elgar at the end of the nineteenth, the body of English choral writing remains a solid achievement, dominated (like English hymn-writing) by members of the Wesley family – Samuel (1766–1837) and his son Samuel Sebastian (1810–1876) in particular. Figures like Stanford and Parry also made their mark on the choral tradition, and in the twentieth century a composer like Herbert Howells (1892–1983) provided church music by the yard in a distinctive English idiom (somewhat after the pastoral style of Vaughan Williams).

ELGAR

Elgar wrote several great choral masterpieces, including three great oratorios, all produced in a ten-year period around the turn of the century. *The Dream of Gerontius* (1900) is the first and probably greatest of the three; Cardinal Newman's ruminating on the fate of the soul at death seems to provide subject-matter which Elgar's combination of pomp and spirituality fits very well. There is, too, a dramatic edge to *Gerontius* which probably isn't quite as fully achieved in *The Kingdom* (1901–6) and *The Apostles* (1902–3), two works based directly on biblical texts, which have a slightly cosier, more complacent, edge and can be fitted more easily into the late-Victorian mainstream (along with the classic, mawkish, Good Friday British work, *The Crucifixion* – 1887 – by Sir John Stainer; 1840–1901). Elgar also wrote 'public' choral music, a Coronation Ode (used in both 1902 and 1911 for Edward VII and George V respectively) and a wartime piece called *The Spirit of England* (1916). In both cases, Elgar does the drearily imperialistic words more than justice, redeeming them from their own banality by music of some distinction.

BRITTEN

The two great British composers of the later part of this century, Benjamin Britten and Sir Michael Tippett, have both written distinguished works for the human voice. Britten's choral works have tended to be on a smaller scale; religious settings, folk-song arrangements, one or two oddities in the 1930s. The culminating glory of Britten's writing for voices was unquestionably his *War Requiem* (1961), written for the re-dedication of Coventry Cathedral, which had itself been a casualty of war. Britten hit on the ingenious idea of mixing the words of the Requiem liturgy with texts by the Great War poet Wilfred Owen (killed a week before that war ended in 1918); the result is a huge, emotionally devastating indictment of war which uses its vast forces cunningly to a whole variety of effects (especially memorable are the bugles). Britten's *War Requiem* is far and away his most important choral contribution, and it is a titanic one.

TIPPETT

Large choral works have played a vital role in Tippett's development as a composer; it was with a choral work, *A Child of Our Time* (1939–41), that he first made his mark. In this depiction of the events leading up to Kristallnacht ('Crystal Night' – a night of murder, arson and looting by Nazis, so-called from the masses of broken window-glass left after the plundering of – mainly Jewish – shops and businesses) in Berlin on 9/10

November 1938, Tippett blended the influences of Bach, Handel and the negro spiritual with some success, using the structure of an oratorio to make the subject-matter transcend the merely topical. Several decades later he wrote the massive *Mask of Time* (1972–84), about the fate of man, a ten-section piece deploying huge resources. It teeters on the edge of pretension, yet never quite falls in owing to the magnificence of the effects, the occasionally breathtaking nature of the melodies Tippett uses, and the overall magnificence of the piece. Tippett also wrote a short song cycle of some distinction, *The Heart's Assurance*, and one of his most recent works is a setting of part of W. B. Yeat's poem 'Byzantium' for soprano and orchestra (1991), which shows that the grand old man has lost none of his innate sympathy for the splendours of vocal performance.

DISCOGRAPHY
Elgar
The Dream of Gerontius has received two distinguished recordings from two great British conductors. The purer version is Sir Adrian Boult's, a fervid orchestral performance a bit let down by Nicolai Gedda (not an ideal Gerontius).
● *EMI CDS7 47208 8* ● *2 CDs* ● *Full price*
● *ADD* ● *1975* ○

Sir John Barbirolli's is a bit more flawed in its sound, and the orchestra isn't quite as passionate, but Dame Janet Baker and the chorus are especially good.
● *EMI CMS7 63185 2* ● *2 CDs* ● *Mid-price*
● *ADD* ● *1965*

If you want to try *The Kingdom*, Leonard Slatkin's recording is very vivid, much more so than I imagined the work was capable of being.
● *RCA Victor Red Seal RD87862* ● *2 CDs*
● *Full price* ● *DDD* ● *1988*

There's a lovely, spirited disc bringing together the Coronation Ode and *The Spirit of England* with (ironically) the Scottish National Orchestra and Chorus under Sir Alexander Gibson bringing the whole thing off triumphantly without a hint of tongue-in-cheek, and lovely singing from soprano Teresa Cahill.
● *Chandos CHAN 6574* ● *1 CD* ● *Mid-price*
● *ADD* ●.*1977*

Britten
Benjamin Britten's own recording of his *War Requiem* has for long been regarded as definitive, and it is a memorable experience.
● *Decca 414 383-2* ● *2 CDs* ● *Full price*
● *ADD* ● *1963* ○

But recently Richard Hickox made a version which combines great sympathy for the score, brilliant orchestral playing, superb choral singing, excellent soloists, with quite breathtaking engineering work, which has taken the piece to new levels. Hickox's recording won *The Gramophone* Awards both as a musical experience and as a piece of engineering; and quite rightly, too.
● *Chandos CHAN 8983/4* ● *2 CDs* ● *Full price*
● *DDD* ● *1991*

Tippett
Hickox and the same engineering team brought the same marvellous expertise to Tippett's *A Child of Our Time*, using a cast including Willard White, the gorgeous-voiced Cynthia Haymon, and (slightly controversially) Damon Evans, best known to many for performance in *Porgy and Bess*. Personally I find Evans utterly convincing, a refreshing change from Peter Pears sound-alikes, but there are those who prefer a nasal English tone. Still, Hickox's pacing is quite brilliant, and the sound is glorious.
● *Chandos CHAN 9123* ● *1 CD* ● *Full price*
● *1992* ○

If this isn't to your taste, I'd recommend *not* Tippett's own version (he's not the world's greatest conductor, even of his own work), but Sir Colin Davis's.
● *Philips 420 075-2* ● *1 CD* ● *Full price*
● *ADD* ● *1975*

Andrew Davis's recording of *Mask of Time* is a hugely controlled tour de force, with some beautiful individual singing and a sure grasp of this enormous piece's structure.
● *EMI CDS7 47705 8* ● *2 CDs* ● *Full price*
● *DDD* ● *1986*

Sadly *The Heart's Assurance* isn't currently available on CD, but 'Byzantium' has just been issued, together with the première recording of the 4th Symphony, and very lovely it is. All the original forces involved are here; Sir Georg Solti (who has a great gift for Tippett's music) and Fay Robinson, the soprano who leapt in triumphantly when Jessye Norman got nervous about the whole thing.
● *Decca 433 668-2* ● *1 CD* ● *Full price*
● *DDD* ● *1991*

MINIMAL CHORUSES: ARVO PÄRT

In what is largely agreed to be a secular age, one composer who has achieved a degree of commercial success writing sacred choral works is the Estonian Arvo Pärt. Pärt's music belongs, broadly, to that style known as Minimalist, but like the Pole Henryk Górecki, Pärt arrived at this mode of expression not as some intellectual exercise à la Glass or Adams, but as a way through certain political constraints, a way of appealing to something other than the secular, (then Soviet) state-run intellect. Pärt's music is designed to have a visceral impact, every bit as much as Górecki's, and his interest in styles other than that associated with him is clear from one of his short, early international successes, the 'Cantus in Memory of Benjamin Britten' (1976), which uses a simple descending scale, built up intensely through the orchestra, and a bell to create an atmosphere of loss.

This, however, isn't a choral work; it is in pieces like his 'Passio' and 'Miserere' that Pärt has achieved perhaps the fullest expression of his religious aesthetic. As always with this kind of music, intellectual analysis rather misses the point; either the music hits you or it doesn't. Pärt doesn't just use density to make his effects; he's also aware of the subtlety of almost chamber-sized forces. Perhaps no one else does this sort of thing quite as well; certainly, given that new Arvo Pärt releases appear alongside those from Guns 'N' Roses in record shops in the Netherlands and elsewhere in Europe, no one does it quite as successfully.

DISCOGRAPHY
Bridging the centuries (and proving my point that much modern music echoes the Middle Ages), the great Arvo Pärt choral specialists are the Hilliard Ensemble. Any of their excellent recordings may convert you to this composer; the 'Passio' is perhaps the more profound.
● *ECM New Series 837 109-2* ● *1 CD* ● *Full price* ● *DDD* ● *2988* ○

'Miserere', backed up by the mesmerising orchestral piece 'Festina Lente', might equally do the trick.
● *ECM New Series 1430 847 539-2* ● *1 CD*
● *Full price* ● *DDD* ● *1990*

VII

Non-Symphonic Orchestral Music

INTRODUCTION

It is hard to find a narrative thread for this 'tidying-up' chapter, encompassing as it does all the orchestral music not covered under headings such as 'symphony' and 'concerto'. There are two stories which emerge; the symphonic tone-poem of the mid-nineteenth century, and the development, through dance music, of the Modernism of Igor Stravinsky. Dance is, indeed, a recurrent theme here, with the emergence of what we understand as ballet (although a good choreographer can work on music never remotely conceived of as belonging to the province of dance) primarily exemplified in the music of Tchaikovsky in the late nineteenth century; of course, much of the development of the ballet has been touched on lightly in the history of opera.

This chapter also encompasses those small pieces like Pachelbel's Canon and Albinoni's Adagio, two great Baroque favourites which it's hard to categorise. Perhaps to describe these works as orchestral is to over-egg the cake; both were doubtless intended for small ensembles (Albinoni's Adagio is something of a difficult piece, anyway, as it certainly isn't by Albinoni; it's actually an arrangement based on Albinoni by a man called Giazotto). Both have found an easy route to popularity with the modern public by virtue of their simplicity and their easily remembered melodies. A canon is quite simply a tune which recurs; it starts in one voice (or instrumental line) and is then picked up, at a short distance, by another (this was a favourite tactic in hymn tunes by British figures such as Orlando Gibbons – 1583–1625 – and Thomas Tallis), while other voices or instrumental lines weave decoration around the simple 'canon'. Pachelbel's piece revolves around some very basic, easily grasped, harmonic relationships (which explains why it made such an admirable pop song when adapted by The Farm in 1990 for their Top 5 Christmas hit 'All Together Now'). The 'Albinoni' piece operates around a 'ground' bass; a simple bass line which repeats itself constantly and carries within it all the harmonic implications and shifts which are then elaborated on top. Giazotto's cunning arrangement is highly appealing for its melancholic streak, which has led to the Adagio's being used endlessly in films and TV shows as a signifier of sadness and grief.

DISCOGRAPHY
Pachelbel and Albinoni
There are so many versions of Albinoni's Adagio and Pachelbel's Canon around that selecting one or more is all a bit hit and miss. There's a good version of the latter, surrounded by a whole load of other Baroque lollipops, on *Baroque Classics* by Andrew Parrott and the Taverner Players.
● *EMI CDM7 69853-2* ● *1 CD* ● *Mid-price*
● *DDD* ● *1988* ❂

A bit less 'authentic', but definitely rather sumptuous and splendid, are the versions of both pieces (and a few lollies besides) by Karl Munchinger and his Stuttgart Orchestra.
● *Decca 417 712-2* ● *1 CD* ● *Mid-price* ● *ADD*

Bach's Dance Music: The Orchestral Suites

Falling into this catch-all chapter also are Bach's four orchestral suites, organised collections of dance movements. The second and third suites are especially famous; the 2nd in B Minor is probably the most graciously and cunningly organised of the four, with the different tempos of the movements and the tonal relationships being most carefully arranged, culminating in the delightfully throwaway (yet very memorable and highly famous) 'Badinerie' (literally 'gossip' or 'badinage'), with its virtuoso flute melodies. The 3rd in D Major is famous for its slow movement entitled 'Air', better known as the 'Air on a G String', another cunning arrangement around a bass line. The orchestral suites show Bach at his most sophisticatedly playful; they are also, being dance-based, distant ancestors of the ballet suite.

DISCOGRAPHY
Out of a heap of Bach orchestral suites on disc, Ton Koopman's with the Amsterdam Baroque Orchestra have a special zip and polish (hence a 1990 *The Gramophone* Award).
● *Harmonia Mundi RD77864* ● *2 CDs* ● *Full price* ● *DDD* ● *1989* ❂

Perhaps slightly more staid, but still pretty good and excellent value for money, are Sir Neville Marriner's performances with the Academy of St Martin-in-the-Fields.
● *Decca 430 378-2* ● *1 CD* ● *Mid-price*
● *ADD* ● *1970*

Handel: Water Music, Music for the Royal Fireworks

Some of Handel's most famous music was written to be a background to social court events. The Royal Fireworks Music of 1749 is fairly self-explanatory; the much earlier suites of Water Music were written in 1717 to provide diversion on a river trip made by George I and his court. These suites are fairly similar in lay-out to Bach's orchestral suites, being basically collections of dance or dance-based music; the most famous piece is the suitably aquatic Hornpipe.

DISCOGRAPHY
John Eliot Gardiner's new version of Handel's Water Music (complete with alternative movements) really has a musical edge on the competition; fresh, lively, exciting, spirited.
● *Philips 434 122-2* ● *1 CD* ● *Full price*
● *DDD* ● *1991* ❂

A nice, non-'authentic' version comes from Robert Haydon Clark's Consort of London.
● *Collins Classics 10152* ● *1 CD* ● *Full price*
● *DDD* ● *1989*

Trevor Pinnock does a nifty Fireworks, as lively as you might expect from that Baroque specialist.
● *Deutsche Grammophon Archiv 415 129-2* ● *1 CD* ● *Full price* ● *DDD* ● *1984*

Mozart: Serenades, Cassations, *A Musical Joke*

Mozart churned out a great deal of ensemble music which is hard to categorise, especially in his early years when he was expected, as a good court composer in Salzburg, to produce music designed as a backdrop for social occasions. One popular form of social composition was the cassation, an instrumental piece usually designed for performance at an outdoor event, a collection of light, civilised movements with charm and wit and no great intellectual content, all gathered together for the greater amusement of the public. Many of Mozart's cassations were written when the composer was extremely young; as such they don't bear the kind of intense study that *Figaro* repays, but they make delightful soothing listening at the end of a hard day, or a superb backdrtop to a civilised drinks party. The serenades (which we've already touched on in chamber music) belong at least partly to this category, too, although the most famous of them – *Eine Kleine Nachtmusik* (K525) – was written late enough (1787) to be clearly a more thoughtful work, and the fact that its every movement has become an instantly recognisable part of the 'public domain' of music speaks volumes for the subtlety of the piece. This serenade was written at the same time as Mozart's *A Musical Joke* (K522), one of whose movements has become indelibly connected in the British TV watching public's mind with show-jumping and the coverage of The 'Horse of the Year' Show; the joke about this particular movement is that the composer seems to have got stuck in this endlessly circular theme and can't escape. Other movements parody bad musicianship and bad composition, and as a joke the piece is delightfully civilised, a little wicked, and doubtless the kind of thing which didn't endear Mozart to the less talented contemporaries whom he was in some measure belittling.

One exquisitely beautiful work by Mozart which seems to have found no other haven in this book is his Sinfonia Concertante for violin, viola and orchestra (K364, 1779). This piece is possessed above all of a slow movement of staggering sweetness; it's one of those works which shows how rapidly the young Mozart grew to maturity and how, at times, he seemed to have a positively Romantic soul. The use of the two solo instruments' resources is quite beautiful, and this is possibly more of an exploration of virtuosity than any of the five violin concertos.

DISCOGRAPHY
There's a really generous, spirited selection of cassations by the thirteen-year-old Mozart from the Salzburg Chamber Orchestra under Harald Narat on the ever-excellent Naxos label.
● *Naxos 8.550609* ● *1 CD* ● *Bargain price*
● *DDD* ● *1992* ❍

The *Musical Joke* and a selection of other Mozart orchestral pieces are very well presented by the Orpheus Chamber Orchestra.
● *Deutsche Grammophon 429 783-2* ● *1 CD*
● *Full price* ● *DDD* ● *1990*

Alternatively, and with *Eine Kleine Nachtmusik* also, a slightly more old-fashioned version (in the best sense of the phrase 'old-fashioned' – solid, spirited musicianship) comes from Viennese concert-master/conductor Willi Boskovsky.
● *Decca 430 259-2* ● *1 CD* ● *Mid-price*
● *ADD* ● *1968–9*

My favourite version of the E Flat Sinfonia Concertante comes from Iona Brown, Josef Suk and the Academy of St Martin-in-the-Fields, directed by Sir Neville Marriner. The tone which all the musicians achieve (especially in the gorgeous slow movement) is sumptuous and well worth wallowing in. Now available at mid-price in the Mozart Almanac series.
● *Decca 430 118-2* ● *1 CD* ● *Mid-price*
● *ADD* ● *1978*

LISZT AND THE TONE-POEM

Beethoven and Schubert both wrote a handful of overtures for stage plays, which are often to be found as fillers on various recordings of the symphonies; Beethoven also wrote a ballet score (*The Creatures of Prometheus*; 1800). These works are very highly regarded; and in at least one of Schubert's overtures (the Overture in the Italian Style) it's possible to hear an amusing and interesting critique of the prevailing music fashions which the composer saw around him at the time. However, both Beethoven and Schubert found that the symphony provided the main outlet for what they wished to do through orchestral music. It was really Franz Liszt, however, who found that the symphony didn't quite offer the vehicle for the kind of dramatic story-telling he wished to accomplish in his orchestral pieces. His works carry on in the tradition of Berlioz's *Symphonie Fantastique*, although usually concentrating the story into one intense, varied movement. *Les Préludes* (1848, revised in 1853), *Tasso* (1849, revised 1850–1) and *Orpheus* (1853–4) all set out to cover programmatic narrations which move rapidly from mood to mood, narrations often taken from a well-known piece of literature (*Tasso* was based on a poem by Byron; there was also *Mazeppa* – 1851 – after Victor Hugo). Perhaps the most ambitious work was a piece for tenor, chorus and orchestra called the 'Faust' Symphony (1854–7), an attempt to take the symphonic poem into the realms of actual narration. In fact, the most successful narratives are the purely orchestral ones; and it was to these pieces that Richard Strauss looked for models when he wanted

some way of expressing his equally exuberant personality at the end of the century.

DISCOGRAPHY

Liszt's symphonic tone-poems often tend to get tacked onto other works. For the 'Faust' Symphony, you could try Bernstein's pulsating version.
● *Deutsche Grammophon 431 470-2* ● *1 CD*
● *Mid-price* ● *ADD* ● *1976* ○

There's also the earlier, classic account by Sir Thomas Beecham.
● *EMI CDM7 63371 2* ● *1 CD* ● *Mid-price*
● *ADD* ● *1959*

Haitink's recordings of Liszt are usually sound, if a little tame sometimes; the disc including *Mazeppa*, *Les Préludes*, and *Tasso* is well worth sampling.
● *Philips 426 636-2* ● *1 CD* ● *Mid-price*
● *ADD* ● *1969*

Beecham's superbly recorded 1950s version of *Orpheus* (one of the most fascinating of these pieces) comes along with an excellent performance of Richard Strauss's *Ein Heldenleben* (Beecham was a great champion of Strauss).
● *EMI CDM7 63299 2* ● *1 CD* ● *Mid-price*
● *ADD* ● *1958*

RICHARD STRAUSS AND THE TONE-POEM

The conventional symphony never held any attraction for Richard Strauss; he wanted his orchestral works to be altogether more vivid and better grounded in something concrete than the more abstract symphonic form would allow. He looked to marry literature and music together, always infused with his own unique (rather boastful) personality. It was with a succession of symphonic tone-poems that Strauss established his reputation. There was a symphonic fantasy about Italy, *Aus Italien* (1886), a response to a holiday trip, in which Strauss immortalised Luigi Denza's hymn to the Neapolitan funicular railway, 'Funiculì, Funiculà', under the mistaken impression that it was a traditional Italian folk song; this was followed with the rip-roaringly successful *Don Juan* (1888), a twenty-minute *jeux d'esprit* which belts along (although ends with the darker tones befitting a story whose hero ends up in hell). Strauss often found the tone-poem a useful outlet for stories which he thought had operatic potential yet which he couldn't cast in operatic form. Such a piece was *Till Eulenspiegel* (1894–5), which has proved one of his most attractive and popular pieces, with even the section on the gallows proving exuberant and humorous. *Till Eulenspiegel* is typical of the way these pieces work, in that it symbolises the main character in a theme and then puts this theme through a series of variations depicting the adventures of Till (a lovable rogue from a fifteenth-century German folk tale). The most sophisticated working-out of this form probably came in *Don Quixote* (1896–7), described as 'fantastic variations for cello and orchestra', in which both the Don and Sancho Panza, as well as various other facets of the story, have their own themes which are all collided together. Strauss also uses a determinedly 'Modernist' excursion into atonalism to describe the sheep which Quixote attacks; the nearest he gets elsewhere to trying such techniques is in the sneering tones given to the critics who beset the 'Hero' (Strauss himself) of *Ein Heldenleben* (*A Hero's Life*; 1897–8). Strauss's tone-poems always managed to court a bit of outrageous controversy; not merely in the self-obsession of *Heldenleben*, but in the extraordinary choice of a subject from Nietzsche in *Also Sprach Zarathustra* (1896), whose opening chords have become famous to recent generations from their use in the film

2001: A Space Odyssey. Zarathustra depicts the emergence of humanity in Nietzschean terms, and it's possibly in his identification with Nietzschean concepts, and especially that of the '*Ubermensch*', the 'superman', that Strauss laid himself open, later, to charges of Nazi sympathies.

Two slightly later tone-poems are also worthy of note; there are those who find *Eine Alpensinfonie* (1911–15) merely the work of a composer marking time, but its musical description of daybreak on the mountain is quite spectacular; if this is marking time, would that a few other composers did so in this way. And I've already referred to *Metamorphosen for 23 Strings*, written in 1945 in the wake of the ruin of Germany. The *Metamorphosen* is a vertiginous piece, dizzyingly moving around a tonality into which it never quite settles, gathering intensity more and more until the effect is almost sickening. It's almost like a portrayal of destruction which never loses sight of melody and which is half in love with the musical element that is its own chromatic undoing. Almost, one might suggest, a picture of Germany's relationship with the Nazis.

DISCOGRAPHY
Strauss's early works *Don Juan* and *Aus Italien* get a riproaring outing from Vladimir Ashkenazy and the Cleveland Orchestra, deliciously recorded and with plenty of spirit (as well as a full realisation of the darker side of the Don).
● *Decca 425 941-2* ● *1 CD* ● *Full price*
● *DDD* ● *1990* ✪

A superbly dramatic pairing of *Till Eulenspiegel* and *Don Quixote* comes from Kurt Masur and the Leipzig Gewandhaus; many conductors play these works entirely for laughs, but Masur has an expansive, double-edged approach which sees tragedy lurking beneath the humour, especially in *Don Quixote*.
● *Philips 426 262-2* ● *1 CD* ● *Full price*
● *DDD* ● *1990*

Libor Pesek's version of *Ein Heldenleben* is one of the best around; bold, resolute, dramatic, funny, all

the qualities for this piece to work and not seem over burdened with self-importance.
● *Virgin Classics VC7 91171-2* ● *1 CD* ● *Full price* ● *DDD* ● *1990*

Herbert von Karajan's late 1950s/early 1960s accounts of various Strauss tone-poems are all very powerful; the disc combining *Also Sprach Zarathustra* with *Death and Transfiguration* (as well as a classic *Don Juan*) is excellent value for money, well recorded, and in no way displaying its age.
● *Decca 417 720-2* ● *1 CD* ● *Mid-price* ● *ADD* ● *1959/61*

I've already referred to the best *Metamorphosen* (Richard Stamp's with the Academy of London); the best *Alpensinfonie* comes from Herbert Blomstedt and his San Francisco Symphony Orchestra, full of atmosphere and drama.
● *Decca 421 815-2* ● *1 CD* ● *Full price* ● *DDD* ● *1989*

━━━ ━━━ ━━━ ━━━

DESCRIBING FINLAND: SIBELIUS

Another great exponent of the tone-poem at the turn of the century was undoubtedly Jean Sibelius, who used the form to promote a sense of Finnish nationalism through music. His most famous tone-poem is, of course, *Finlandia* (1899, revised 1900), a deeply political work of music aimed against the Russian occupier. The tone-poem remained an object of interest to Sibelius through pieces such as *En Saga* (1892, revised 1902), the symphonic fantasia *Pohjola's Daughter* (1906), *The Oceanides* (1914) and *Tapiola* (1926). Sibelius also wrote descriptive orchestral suites designed to depict various aspects of the Finnish character; *Legends* (the *Lemminkanen* Suite) (1898), which includes *The Swan of Tuonela* and the *Karelia* Suite (1893), descriptive of the folk of Southern Finland.

DISCOGRAPHY
Two of the best Sibelius orchestral selections come from great British conductors. Barbirolli's programme with the Hallé is full of fire, including a magnificent *Karelia* Suite and a dynamic *Finlandia* (*Pohjola's Daughter* is done pretty well, too).
● *EMI CDM7 69205-2* ● *1 CD* ● *Mid-price* ● *ADD* ● *1965* ✪

Beecham's excellent disc also includes *Karelia* and *Finlandia*, as well as incidental music to *The Tempest* which Beecham plays like no one else. It's a slightly odd *Finlandia*, but worth the money for the other items.
● *EMI CDM7 63397-2* ● *1 CD* ● *Mid-price* ● *ADD* ● *1938*

━━━ ━━━ ━━━ ━━━

MORE DANCING: JOHANN STRAUSS II

One of the most famous and successful composers who ever wrote devoted himself almost exclusively to the composition of dance music; the music of Johann Strauss II is the most characteristic and popular music which Imperial Vienna produced in the latter part of the nineteenth century. Strauss's music was almost all designed for the dance, for public dancing; the waltz (new and dangerous), the polka, and other dances, were all going through a vogue, and Strauss took their rhythms and played with them subtly, creating waltzes like the 'Blue Danube', 'Frühlingsstimmen' ('Voices of the Spring') and 'Künstlerleben' ('The Artist's Life') which are small symphonies of the dance. Strauss's may not be deeply intellectual music, but it is deeply joyful, often designed as an antidote to the political difficulties of Imperial Vienna (a city of which it was once said that the situation was 'desperate, but not serious').

DISCOGRAPHY
The best recordings of Johann Strauss's music are those taken from the Vienna New Year's Day concerts. My favourite current conductor of these is the great Carlos Kleiber, who made both the 1989 and the 1992 concerts something special.
● *1989: Sony SK 45938* ● *1 CD* ● *Full price* ● *DDD* ● *1989* ✪
● *1992: Sony CD48376* ● *1 CD* ● *Full price* ● *DDD* ● *1992*

TCHAIKOVSKY'S BALLET MUSIC

It wasn't until the 1870s that composers started trying to make ballet scores work as symphonic wholes; the first was probably Léo Delibes and his still popular *Coppélia* (1870). Oddly enough, although Tchaikovsky admired Delibes he had no knowledge of *Coppelia* when he set to work on his first major ballet, *Swan Lake*, in 1875. Ballet in Russia was at this time newly imported from France (which had been the guardian of the sacred flame of the art), and Tchaikovsky's first work of this type took little account of the entrenched dominance, then, of leading dancers, or of dancers' physical capabilities. In any case, *Swan Lake* (first produced in 1876) was, for all its musical excellence, a failure, and it was only after the success of *Sleeping Beauty* and *The Nutcracker* (first produced in 1890 and 1892 respectively) that it was reappraised. *Swan Lake* is thematically organised (especially around a 'swan-theme' played on the oboe), but is full of diversions like the dances from different countries in the third act. *Sleeping Beauty* (1889–90) is probably the most polished of the Tchaikovsky ballets; but for many it's the fantasy world of *The Nutcracker* (1891), where domestic objects and toys come to life, which most specially typifies the sound-world of Tchaikovsky's ballet scores, possessed as the piece is of a special timbre, with notable prominence given to the woodwind and percussive instruments.

DISCOGRAPHY
If you want an extracts disc to cover Tchaikovsky's ballets, there's an excellent one to be had made up from various André Previn recordings; lavish, rhythmic, sumptuous.
● *EMI CDM7 64332 2* ● *1 CD* ● *Mid-price* ● *DDD* ✪

There's a very good *Nutcracker* by Sir Charles Mackerras (a fine ballet conductor with some experience of arranging music for dance) which really gets to grips with the sound timbres.
● *Telarc CD80137* ● *2 CDs* ● *Full price* ● *DDD* ● *1986*

And why not spoil yourself with the bargain (but in no way cheap-sounding) Naxos *Sleeping Beauty*?
● *Naxos 8.550490–2* ● *3 CDs* ● *Bargain price* ● *DDD* ● *1991*

BALLET'S GREAT MOMENT: STRAVINSKY'S *RITE OF SPRING*

In 1913 ballet made a breakthrough, in terms of modern music, with Igor Stravinsky's *The Rite of Spring*. The sheer energy and rhythmic primitivism of this score came as a shock to the audiences which first heard it (Vaslav Nijinsky's dancing to Sergei Diaghilev's choreography enhanced the effect of near-obscenity), and music was more or less turned on its head, though in a very different way from the ultra-intellectual approach of the Second Viennese School. This was a truly visceral step away from Romanticism and decadent tonality, something which amazed and confounded its audience by its primary concern for rhythm and rhythmic colour-painting. Stravinsky had already surprised with the extravagance and general lack of concern for issues of tonality in *The Firebird* (1910); his music had a vividness which made even experiments then going on in French music look pallid and restrained, and hide-bound by convention. In fact, as Stravinsky's next works were to show, this was a composer who had a great deal of respect for convention in the right places; from *Pulcinella* (1920) a new streak of neo-Classicism – often characterised by the phrase 'back to Bach' – imbued Stravinsky's work, and respect for old Baroque and Classical forms became his basic principle. Through the 1920s and 1930s Stravinsky felt himself very much the leading opponent of the Second Viennese School, and his brand of neo-Classicism (very different from that to be found in Schoenberg) was one way of striking a blow for his own particular values.

DISCOGRAPHY
Perhaps one wouldn't expect the near-ideal *Rite of Spring* to come from an Israeli orchestra, but it's the Israel Philharmonic under Leonard Bernstein which has produced a tour-de-force performance of this key piece; the rhythms are vivid, the drama is awesome, and the whole thing builds up in a manner perhaps possible only in a live performance. This is one of Bernstein's finest moments.
● *Deutsche Grammophon 431 045-2* ● *1 CD*
● *Mid-price* ● *DDD* ● *1982* ✪

For a good Stravinsky compilation from the ballets, two separately available discs conducted by the composer himself offer a fine selection from *The Rite of Spring, Firebird* and *Petrushka*. Stravinsky's own interpretations of his own pieces have a unique sense of the works' phrasing.
Firebird etc.: ● *Sony CD42432* ● *1 CD* ● *Full price* ● *ADD* ● *1962* ✪
Petrushka, Rite: ● *Sony CD42433* ● *1 CD*
● *Full price* ● *ADD* ● *1961*

A complete *Firebird* which is truly full of fire and passion is Antál Dorati's with the London Symphony Orchestra.
● *Mercury Living Presence 432 012-2* ● *1 CD*
● *Mid-price* ● *ADD* ● *1960*

The music from *Pulcinella* gets a good outing in the early days of Sir Neville Marriner and the Academy of St Martin-in-the-Fields.
● *Decca 417 734-2* ● *1 CD* ● *Mid-price* ● *ADD*

● ● ● ●

TONE-POEMS AND TEXTURE: SCHOENBERG

Non-classifiable orchestral music actually played a huge role in Schoenberg's output. In his 'decadent Romantic' days, he wrote two extraordinary tone-poems, very much in the style of his lush *Gurrelieder*, *Verklärte Nacht* (1899, originally a chamber work) and *Pelleas und Melisande* (1902–3), a musical realisation of the Maeterlinck drama which Debussy so successfully

transformed into an opera. These pieces wallow in highly chromatic, 'hot-house' harmony; a far cry from the later Five Orchestral Pieces (1909), key works in Schoenberg's transformation of music, explorations of the orchestral textural possibilities of atonal music, and the Variations for Orchestra (1926–8). This 'variations' form was also used by Webern and his 1940 work in this style is often regarded as the 'ultimate' piece of Webern; compact, precise, subtle, it uses the orchestra's full resources in a series of metamorphoses on a very bare theme to create something rather rich and strange.

DISCOGRAPHY
To contrast the early with the later Schoenberg, Herbert von Karajan's 1970s recordings of *Verklärte Nacht* and the Variations for Orchestra make a superbly balanced programme on a single disc.
● *Deutsche Grammophon 415 326-2* ● *1 CD*
● *Full price* ● *ADD* ● *1974/5* ✪

But if you really want to get to grips with the Second Viennese School, these two performances are available on a specially priced three-disc set which also includes the gorgeous *Pelleas und Melisande* as well as orchestral works by Berg and Webern. This is an ideal programme for beginners with this repertoire, as you can always just wallow among the late Romanticism if you're not in the mood for the more stringent stuff – although the silky touch of Karajan makes an ideal introduction.
● *Deutsche Grammophon 427 424-2* ● *3 CDs*
● *Special price* ● *ADD* ● *1970*

● ● ● ●

COLOUR IN MUSIC: DEBUSSY

Most French composers had never felt particularly warm towards the symphony, and the main concern of much nineteenth-century French music seems to be 'colour' in some form. Claude Debussy sought from the very outset of his career to find new ways to use orchestral and instrumental groupings as sources of 'colour', and he very often thought about the resources at his disposal as the colours on an artist's palate. His great orchestral pieces like *La Mer* (1905) and *Images* (1909) all try to depict visual images and to appeal not only to hearing but also to the other senses (part of 'Iberia', the centre of *Images*, is called 'Les Parfums de la Nuit'). Debussy uses blocks of rhythms, blocks of instruments, to portray certain elements in his overall grand picture; although his work is largely tonal, tonality is only a secondary concern, either made or broken by the combination of elements necessary to create the kind of colour he is after. Although each separate 'colour' has its own unit of sound, as it were, these are all carefully calculated to overlap and run into one another (rather in the way that colours operate in Impressionist painting); Debussy, however, abhorred too much academic analysis. Above all, his great desire in his music is to give pleasure, to create a hedonistic sound-bath in which the listener can wallow. His three-part *Nocturnes* (1899) is especially interesting, particularly the final part, 'Sirènes' (when done properly, complete with sibilant female chorus). *Prélude à l'après-midi d'un faune* (1894) is another Debussyan piece of great repute which works entirely by the atmosphere it creates.

FRENCH ORCHESTRAL MUSIC: DUKAS, CHABRIER, RAVEL, SAINT-SAËNS

Other French composers who specialised in non-symphonic orchestral work include Paul Dukas (1865–1935), best known for his musical realisation of *The Sorceror's Apprentice* (1897); Emmanuel Chabrier (1841–1894), whose *España* was one of the most popular works of the French vogue for fake

Iberianism; and, above all, Maurice Ravel, whose ballet music *Daphnis et Chloë* (1912) includes some subtleties of orchestration which are worthy of Debussy himself, and whose *La Valse* (1920) is a vivid, brutal picture of a world crashing to destruction. Ravel's single most famous orchestral work, though, is *Bolero* (1928), which was actually written more or less as a rhythmically hypnotic exercise in orchestration. It's said that at an early performance a woman cried out that the composer must be mad, evoking from Ravel the response, 'Ah! she understands'. On another occasion Ravel remarked that the work had 'no music in it'. Whatever, the turn-ticketa-turn rhythm which nags through the fifteen minutes or so of *Bolero* has proved a hypnotic success. Ravel's most melodically satisfying short orchestral piece, though, isn't *Bolero*, but the lyrical *Pavanne pour une Infante Défunte* (*Pavane for a Dead Infanta*; 1899), a stately, lovely miniature.

One French composer of a slightly older generation who wrote a famous orchestral work, and one which will probably be eternally popular (though its charm is a little lost on me), is Camille Saint-Saëns. His 'zoological fantasy', *The Carnival of the Animals*, is full of vivid characterisation and portrait-painting in music, and seems to find favour through successive generations; it is, too, a work of bravura orchestration, with a certain degree of wit and charm.

DISCOGRAPHY
Debussy, Ravel, Chabrier, Dukas, Saint-Saëns
For all these French composers, I would strongly recommend the classic recordings made by Ernest Ansermet and the Orchestre de la Suisse Romande. Ansermet knew Debussy, Ravel and many of these other composers, and his performances are informed by both a sense of discipline and a sense of the music's lyricism. Some of the sound quality is a bit doubtful, but

by and large these are great recordings and excellent ways of becoming acquainted with this music. Especially good is the combination of Debussy's *La Mer* and *L'Après-midi d'un faune*.
● *Decca 433 711-2* ● *1 CD* ● *Mid-price*
● *ADD* ● *1957* ☉

Images, Nocturnes and *Printemps* also make a formidable programme; Ansermet was actually involved in the orchestration of *Images*.
● *Decca 433 712-2* ● *1 CD* ● *Mid-price*
● *ADD* ● *1959–61*

Ansermet's two Ravel compilations are also both highly atmospheric, witty and rhythmically charged, especially the disc combining *Bolero*, *Rapsodie Espagnole*, the *Pavane pour une Infante Défunte* and a few others.
● *Decca 433 716-2* ● *1 CD* ● *Mid-price*
● *ADD* ● *1958–63*

There's a wonderful version of *Daphnis et Chloë*, beautifully recorded with wonderful orchestral timbres by Simon Rattle and the City of Birmingham Symphony Orchestra.
● *EMI CDC7 54303-2* ● *1 CD* ● *Full price*
● *DDD*

One of the best programmes of French 'lollipops', including Chabrier's *España*, Dukas's *Sorceror's Apprentice*, and a few others comes from Charles Dutoit and the Montreal Symphony Orchestra (a fantastic bunch, with lots of rhythmic snap) under the title *Fête à la Francaise*.
● *Decca 421 527-2* ● *1 CD* ● *Full price*
● *DDD* ● *1988*

Rather a good combination of Saint-Saëns's orchestral works, including *Carnival of the Animals*, features a whole host of stars like Yo-Yo Ma and Yan-Pascal Tortelier; the sound is a bit dry, but it's such a generous programme (about 75 minutes) that few could complain.
● *Sony SBY 47655* ● *1 CD* ● *Mid-price*
● *ADD* ● *1978*

BRITISH MUSIC: THE PASTORAL TOUCH

ELGAR

Through the twentieth century, several British composers have written excellent orchestral works which aren't too easily classified. Elgar's Introduction and Allegro, Opus 47, written between 1904 and 1905, combined the forces of a string quartet and a string orchestra, almost in the style of the old concerto grosso; the result is one of his most beautiful

orchestral pieces, perhaps more immediately accessible than the slightly more monolithic, formally constructed symphonies. And Elgar's most famous orchestral work also belongs here; the *Enigma Variations*, written in 1898/9, is a series of variations on an original theme, designed to offer a musical portrait of Elgar, his wife, and twelve of his friends (the most famous section, 'Nimrod', is a 'description' of a man who was very keen on hunting; hence the title). The 'enigma' lies in Elgar's 'larger' theme which, in his own words, runs 'through and over the whole set'; many have claimed to be able to solve the riddle of what the tune is and where Elgar found it, but with a series of 'solutions' including part of Mozart's 'Prague' Symphony and 'Auld Lang Syne', the composer's mystery remains intact.

Holst's *Planets*

The Planets Suite (1916) by Gustav Holst (1874–1934) is its composer's single most famous work; a collection of seven interlinked symphonic tone-poems, provoked partly by an interest in astronomy and astrology, and partly as a response to the strife – the Great War – in the world outside, the pieces seek to characterise each of the seven (then) known planets apart from the earth. Holst's talents for both drama and a good stirring tune are well evidenced by such elements as the disturbing 'Mars' and the grand 'Jupiter', with its great main theme (subsequently to become a patriotic hymn, 'I Vow to Thee, My Country').

VAUGHAN WILLIAMS, BRITTEN

The single most famous piece by Ralph Vaughan Williams, the *Fantasia on a Theme by Thomas Tallis*, also belongs in this unclassifiable category;

with its dense string-writing and lush close harmonies, this work is, for many people, the epitome of what 'English' music is all about. It's a work which often finds a natural soulmate in Benjamin Britten's *Variations on a Theme by Frank Bridge* (1937); whilst Bridge's music isn't much played on its own account these days, Britten's work keeps his friend and teacher's name alive (Bridge lived from 1879–1941) with the vitality and wit of the variations.

Another famous set of Britten variations is, of course, that based around the theme from Purcell's Rondeau for the seventeenth-century drama *Abdelazar* and better known as *The Young Person's Guide to the Orchestra* (1945). This work sometimes has a commentary attached to it, explaining which parts of the orchestra are being demonstrated, but it works just as well without the words, and Britten's talent in creating variations for percussion instruments as well as for the more melodic sections is highly witty.

TIPPETT

Sir Michael Tippett is often regarded as something of a vanguard of the new; yet his *Fantasia Concertante on a Theme of Corelli* in many ways out-Vaughan-Williamses Vaughan Williams. Although using an entirely Italian theme, Tippett's use of dense, close harmonic writing is such that this superbly lyrical string work discovers a very 'English' feel; while the structure is so cunningly interwoven that the music becomes one dizzying, thrilling series of climaxes, each one more satisfying than the one before. If you never listen to another work by Tippett, then you should try this; it is one of the most affecting, stirring pieces of orchestral music of the second half of the twentieth century.

DISCOGRAPHY
British music
There's a marvellous English compilation disc, offering Elgar's E Minor Serenade for Strings, Britten's *Variations on a Theme by Frank Bridge*, Vaughan Williams's *Tallis Fantasia* and Tippett's *Corelli Fantasia*, all on one disc, beautifully and lushly performed by the Royal Philharmonic and Sir Charles Groves, a real specialist in this fare. A bargain of enormous proportions.
● *RPO Impact CDRPO 5005*   ● *1 CD*   ● *Bargain price*   ● *DDD*   ● *1989* ○

Elgar
The Introduction and Allegro by Elgar, with several other delightful small pieces, is very well done by the English Chamber Orchestra under Yehudi Menihin.
● *Arabesque Z6563*   ● *1 CD*   ● *Full price*   ● *DDD*   ● *1986* ○

And one shouldn't forget the famous set of variations based on Elgar, his wife and friends, the *Enigma Variations*. Sir John Barbirolli's classic recording is available on CD along with his equally distinguished reading of Elgar's symphonic study of the career of Shakespeare's Falstaff.
● *EMI CDM7 69185 2*   ● *1 CD*   ● *Mid-price*   ● *ADD*   ● *1963–4*

Holst
Two versions of Holst's *Planets* stands out from the crowd; Charles Dutoit's achieves its effects entirely by musical control, drive and rhythmic push by the excellent Montreal Symphony Orchestra, this version won a *The Gramophone* Award.
● *Decca 417 553-2*   ● *1 CD*   ● *Full price*   ● *DDD*   ● *1986* ○

Of course, the playing of the Berlin Philharmonic under Karajan is remarkable (that goes without saying); but the recording engineering that goes with the disc (which has now been enhanced even further) is quite phenomenal. Perhaps this isn't entirely musical excellence, but it's an amazing recording.
● *Deutsche Grammophon 439 011-2*   ● *1 CD*   ● *Full price*   ● *DDD*   ● *1987*

Britten
Apart from the *Frank Bridge Variations* on the Groves disc mentioned above, there are two Britten compilations of great merit. Sir Alexander Gibson's with the English Chamber Orchestra unites the *Variations* with two light-hearted suites, the *Matinées Musicales* and the *Soirées Musicales*; high-voltage performances.
● *EMI Classics for Pleasure CD-CFP 4598*   ● *1 CD*   ● *Bargain price*   ● *DDD*   ● *1983* ○

Neeme Järvi's recordings of *The Young Person's Guide*, the four *Sea Interludes* and the

uncategorisable Cello Symphony are all quite superb, and now available cheap from Woolworths.
- *Woolworth Classics 7041* ● 1 CD ● *Mid-price*
- *DDD* ● *1988*

Tippett
Apart from the version of Tippett's *Corelli Fantasia* on Groves's *English Celebration* (see above), there is also an outstanding performance of this highly infectious piece (along with the Concerto for Double String Orchestra) conducted by the composer himself.
- *Virgin Classics VC7 90701-2* ● 1 CD ● *Full price* ● *DDD* ● *1987* ○

MODERN MUSIC IN MODERN IDIOMS: STEVE REICH, MICHAEL TORKE

My brief survey of contemporary orchestral works begins with Steve Reich (1936–), a Minimalist composer who specialises not only in this modern idiom but in writing for modern instruments. Some might argue that his works for string quartet and electronic instruments or pre-prepared electronic tape belong as much under the heading 'chamber' as here, but the fascination of this style of composition is at least partly that it defies categorisation (as much good music does). Pieces like *Four Sections*, *Different Trains*, and *Electric Counterpoint* may well appeal beyond the boundaries of Minimalism for their sheer imagination; and a natural follow-up might be the work of another American, Michael Torke (1961–), whose *Yellow Pages* and *Adjustable Wrench* have both attracted a great deal of interest.

DISCOGRAPHY
Steve Reich's *Different Trains* and *Electric Counterpoint* receive highly convincing performances from the Kronos Quartet and jazz musician Pat Metheny.
- *Elektra Nonesuch 7559-79176-2* ● 1 CD ● *Full price* ● *DDD* ● *1988* ○

Four Sections has been recorded by Michael Tilson Thomas (a highly dynamic and electrifying

conductor) with the London Symphony Orchestra.
- *Elektra Nonesuch 7559-79220-2* ● 1 CD
- *Full price* ● *DDD* ● *1990*

If you want to explore Michael Torke, all the key works are available on a single disc.
- *Argo 430 209-2* ● 1 CD ● *Full price*
- *DDD* ● *1990*

BRITISH CANDIDATES: TAVENER, BIRTWISTLE, TURNAGE, MACMILLAN

One British piece which has enjoyed a fair degree of success is *The Protecting Veil* by John Tavener (1944–). This piece for cello and orchestra could be described as a quasi-concerto, but really its use of the solo instrument is similar to the use of the human voice in Górecki's 3rd Symphony. Tavener goes in for a similar static, mainly rich, orchestral style, with the cello used to bring a keen, religious edge to the music (Tavener is a devout Greek Orthodox convert, and the imagery in the work's title comes from the Orthodox iconography). It's very heady stuff, although perhaps open to criticism for its lack of formal intellectual content, and what its future status may be is very open to question; it has, though, done very well in 1992. However, I feel that there may be more future in three other British composers. Sir Harrison Birtwistle has already crossed these pages before. His orchestral work *Earth Dances* (1986), now available on a very generous CD single, is much less easy on first hearing than anything by Reich or Torke, yet once its dense structure begins to unfold, the listener is mesmerised. As so often with Birtwistle, the music has a celebratory dimension, and the passage of time is a key concern. Mark Antony Turnage (1960–) modelled his *Three Screaming Popes*

on Francis Bacon's macabre painting;
Turnage's realisation of the artwork is
an exuberant, lively affair which
crosses very serious Classical
influences with Duke Ellington's music
and even the occasional TV theme.
James Macmillan (1959–) is a very
Scottish composer, and his *Confession
of Isobel Gowdie* is based on the story
of a young woman forced into a false
confession of witchcraft at the height
of the Scottish Reformation and of the
witch-hunting hysteria of that time.
Macmillan's music has some affinities
with the dense minimalism of Pärt and
Górecki, yet it moves more freely than
much of their writing does, and seeks
to encompass a larger number of
mood-swings.

All these three works have, I think,
a fair chance of going on for a
generation of two; but making such
predictions is always a bit of a lottery.
Ultimately my advice is to follow your

own musical nose; and always
remember that listening to music must
be first and foremost something to
enjoy, something from which you
derive pleasure, rather than a duty.

DISCOGRAPHY
John Tavener
John Tavener's *Protecting Veil* was written for and
has been very sell served by cellist Steven Isserlis.
● *Virgin Classics VC7 91474-2* ● *1 CD* ● *Full
price* ● *DDD* ● *1991* ✪

Birtwistle, Turnage, Macmillan
Harrison Birtwistle's *Earth Dances*, wonderfully
played by the BBC Symphony Orchestra, is a steal
at CD single price.
● *Collins Classics Coll2001-2* ● *1 CD* ● *Single
price* ● *DDD* ● *1991* ✪

It's the same deal, too, for Simon Rattle's highly
exciting account of Turnage's *Three Screaming
Popes*.
● *EMI TSP 2 04681 2* ● *1 CD* ● *Single price*
● *DDD* ● *1992*

James Macmillan's *Isobel Gowdie* comes coupled
with the same composer's *Tryst*, a chamber
orchestra piece, all sympathetically done by Jerzy
Maksymiuk and the BBC Scottish Symphony.
● *Koch Schwann 3-1050-2* ● *1 CD* ● *Full price*
● *DDD* ● *1992*

YOUR IDEAL STARTER
KIT IN 100 CD PURCHASES

The following 100 CDs should form the core of a reputable collection. They aren't all necessarily 'top' choices for each item, although all the performances are first-rate; but they all represent excellent value for money, and in several cases offer interesting combinations of a composer's work on a single disc. The last five are compilations which I think offer a fine range of compositions. The order of the first 95 is determined solely by the year of birth of the composer.

1 HILDEGARD OF BINGEN: *A Feather on the Breath of God: Sequences and Hymns*. Gothic Voices directed by Christopher Page. Hyperion CDA66039. Full price.

2 PÉROTIN: *Viderunt Omnes* and others. The Hilliard Ensemble directed by Paul Hillier. ECM New Series 1385 837 751-2. Full price.

3 JOSQUIN DES PREZ: *Missa Pange Lingua, Missa La Sol Fa Re Mi*. The Tallis Scholars directed by Peter Phillips. Gimell CDGIM 009. Full price.

4 TALLIS: *Spem in alium* and others. The Tallis Scholars directed by Peter Phillips. Gimell CDGIM 006. Full price.

5 PALESTRINA. *Missa Assumpta est Maria, Missa Sicut Lilium*. The Tallis Scholars directed by Peter Phillips. Gimell CDGIM 020. Full price.

6 BYRD: Mass for Four Voices, Mass for Five Voices, *Infelix ego*. Oxford Camerata conducted by Jeremy Summerly. Naxos 8.550574. Bargain price.

7 GESUALDO: *Tenebrae Responses*. The Hilliard Ensemble directed by Paul Hillier. ECM New Series 1422/23 843 867-2 (2 CDs). Full price.

8 MONTEVERDI: *La Favola d'Orfeo*. Soloists include Anthony Rolfe Johnson, English Baroque Soloists conducted by John Eliot Gardiner. Deutsche Grammophon Archiv 419 250-2 (2 CDs). Full price.

9 MONTEVERDI: *Vespers for the Blessed Virgin*. Taverner Choir and Consort conducted by Andrew Parrott. EMI CDS7 47078 8 (2 CDs). Full price.

10 PURCELL: *Dido and Aeneas*. Soloists include Guillemette Laurens, Les Arts Florissants directed by William Christie. Harmonia Mundi HMC 905173. Full price.

11 VIVALDI: *The Four Seasons* and other concertos. Piero Toso, I Solisti Veneti conducted by Claudio Scimone. Erato Bonsai Collection 2292-45945-2. Bargain price.

12 VIVALDI: *Gloria*. J. S. BACH: *Magnificat*. Soloists, Choir and Orchestra of Lausanne conducted by Michel Corboz. Erato Bonsai Collection 2292-45923-2. Bargain price.

13 J. S. BACH: Brandenburg Concertos Nos. 1–6. Concentus Musicus Wien conducted by Nikolaus Harnoncourt. Teldec 9031-77611-2 (2 CDs). Mid-price.

14 J. S. BACH: *St Matthew Passion*. Soloists, Choir of King's College Cambridge, Concentus Musicus Wien conducted by Nikolaus Harnoncourt. Teldec 2292-42509-2 (3 CDs). Mid-price.

15 J. S. BACH: Mass in B Minor. Soloists, Taverner Consort and Taverner Players conducted by Andrew Parrott. EMI CDS7 47293 8 (2 CDs). Full price.

16 HANDEL: *Messiah*. The Scholars Baroque Ensemble. Naxos 8.550667/8 (2 CDs). Bargain price.

17 HANDEL: Water Music. English Baroque Soloists directed by John Eliot Gardiner. Philips 434 122-2. Full price.

18 GLUCK: *Orfeo ed Euridice*. Soloists include Janet Baker, Glyndebourne Chorus, London Philharmonic Orchestra conducted by Raymond Leppard. Erato 2292-45864-2 (2 CDs). Mid-price.

19 C. P. E. BACH: Six symphonics. English Chamber Orchestra conducted by Raymond Leppard. Philips 426 081-2. Mid-price.

20 HAYDN: Symphonies Nos. 45 ('Farewell') and 48 ('Maria Theresia'). L'Estro Armonico conducted by Derek Solomons. CBS/Sony Masterworks MDK 46507. Mid-price.

21 HAYDN: String Quartets Opus 76, Nos. 1–6. The Kodaly Quartet. Naxos 8.550314/5 (2 CDs). Bargain price.

22 MOZART: Symphonies Nos. 40 and 41 ('Jupiter'). Prague Chamber Orchestra conducted by Sir Charles Mackerras. Telarc CD80139. Full price.

23 MOZART: Piano Concertos Nos. 20, 21, 26 and 27. Geza Anda, Camerata Academica des Salzburger Mozarteums. Deutsche Grammophon 413 427-2 (2 CDs). Bargain price.

24 MOZART: Sinfonia Concertante in E Flat Major (K364). Iona Brown, Josef Suk, Academy of St Martin-in-the-Fields. Decca 430 118-2. Also includes: Mass in C Major ('Coronation Mass'), Symphony No. 32. Mid-price.

25 MOZART: *Le Nozze di Figaro*. Soloists, Vienna State Opera Chorus, Vienna Philharmonic Orchestra conducted by Erich Kleiber. Decca 417 315-2 (3 CDs). Mid-price.

26 MOZART: *Don Giovanni*. Soloists include Kiri te Kanawa, Chorus and Orchestra of the Royal Opera House conducted by Sir Colin Davis. Philips 422 541-2 (Complete Mozart Edition Volume 41). Mid-price.

27 BEETHOVEN: Symphonies Nos. 1–9. Chamber Orchestra of Europe conducted by Nikolaus Harnoncourt. Teldec 2292-46452-2 (5 CDs). Full price.

28 BEETHOVEN: Violin Concerto. Herman Krebbers, Royal Concertgebouw Amsterdam Orchestra conducted by Bernard Haitink. Philips 422 971-4. Bargain price.

29 BEETHOVEN: Piano Concertos Nos. 4 and 5 ('Emperor'). Maurizio Pollini, Vienna Philharmonic conducted by Karl Böhm. Deutsche Grammophon 435 098-2. Mid-price.

30 BEETHOVEN: String Quartets Nos. 12–16 and Grosse Fuge in B Flat. Quartetto Italiano. Philips 426 050-2 (4 CDs). Mid-price.

31 BEETHOVEN: Piano Sonatas Nos. 8 ('Pathétique'), 12, 14 ('Moonlight'), 27, 31 and 32. Bernard Roberts. Nimbus 5059/60 (2 CDs). Special price.

32 BEETHOVEN: *Missa Solemnis*. Soloists, Arnold Schoenberg Choir, Chamber Orchestra of Europe conducted by Nikolaus Harnoncourt. Teldec 9031-74884-2 (2 CDs). Full price.

33 ROSSINI: *L'Italiana in Algeri*. Soloists include Marilyn Horne, Prague Philharmonic Chorus, I Solisti Veneti conducted by Claudio Scimone. Erato 2292-45404-2 (2 CDs). Mid-price.

34 ROSSINI: *Il Barbiere di Siviglia*. Soloists include Victoria de los Angeles, Glyndebourne Festival Chorus, Royal Philharmonic Orchestra conducted by Vittorio Gui. EMI CMS7 64162 2 (2 CDs). Mid price.

35 SCHUBERT: Symphony Nos. 3 and 8 ('Unfinished'). Vienna Philharmonic Orchestra conducted by Carlos Kleiber. Deutsche Grammophon 415 601-2. Full price.

36 SCHUBERT: Symphony No. 9 ('Great' C Major). Orchestra of the Age of Enlightenment conducted by Sir Charles Mackerras. Virgin Classics VC7 90708-2. Full price.

37 SCHUBERT: String Quartets Nos. 12–15. The Juilliard String Quartet. CBS/Sony Maestro M2YK 45617 (2 CDs). Mid-price.

38 SCHUBERT: Piano Sonata No. 21 and *Wanderer* Fantasy. Alfred Brendel. Philips 420 644-2. Full price.

39 SCHUBERT: Lieder (various). Dietrich Fischer-Dieskau, Gerald Moore. Deutsche Grammophon 431 085-2. Full price.

40 SCHUBERT: *Winterreise*. Brigitte Fassbaender, Aribert Reimann. EMI CDC7 49846 2. Full price.

41 DONIZETTI: Various tenor arias. Luciano Pavarotti, various choruses, orchestras and conductors. Decca 417 638-2. Full price.

42 BERLIOZ: *Symphonie Fantastique*. Vienna Philharmonic Orchestra conducted by Sir Colin Davis. Philips 432 151-2. Full price.

43 MENDELSSOHN: Symphonies Nos. 4 ('Italian') and 5 ('Reformation'). English Chamber Orchestra conducted by Raymond Leppard. Erato Bonsai Collection 2292-45932-2. Bargain price.

44 MENDELSSOHN: Violin Concerto. BRUCH: Violin Concerto No. 1. Jaime Laredo, Scottish Chamber Orchestra. Pickwick PCD 829. Bargain price.

45 MENDELSSOHN: Octet, String Quintet No. 2. Academy of St Martin-in-the-Fields Chamber Ensemble. Philips 420 400-2. Full price.

46 SCHUMANN: Piano Concerto. GRIEG: Piano Concerto. Stephen (Bishop) Kovacevich, BBC Symphony Orchestra conducted by Sir Colin Davis. Philips 412 923-2. Full price.

47 SCHUMANN: Fantasia, Fantasiestücke. Alfred Brendel. Philips 411 049-2. Full price.

48 CHOPIN: Preludes, Barcarolle in F Sharp Major, Polonaise in A Flat Major. Martha Argerich. Deutsche Grammophon 415 836-2. Full price.

49 LISZT: Piano Concertos Nos. 1 and 2, *Totentanz*. Alfred Brendel, London Philharmonic Orchestra conducted by Bernard Haitink. Philips 426 637-2. Mid-price.

50 LISZT: *Hungarian Rhapsody*, various piano works. Kun Woo Paik. Virgo VJ7 91458-2. Bargain price.

51 LISZT: Piano Sonata and other works. Alfred Brendel. Philips 410 040-2. Full price.

52 WAGNER: *Die Walküre*. Soloists, Vienna Philharmonic Orchestra conducted by Wilhelm Furtwängler. EMI CHS7 63045 2 (3 CDs). Mid-price.

53 WAGNER: *Tristan und Isolde*. Soloists include Birgit Nilsson, Bayreuth ✓Festival Chorus and Orchestra conducted by Karl Böhm. Philips 434 425-2 (3 CDs). Mid-price.

54 VERDI: *Rigoletto*. Soloists include Maria Callas, Chorus and Orchestra of La ✓Scala Opera House conducted by Tullio Serafin. EMI CDS7 47469 8 (2 CDs). Full price.

55 VERDI: *Otello*. Soloists include Placido Domingo, Ambrosian Opera Chorus, ✓National Philharmonic Orchestra conducted by James Levine. RCA Victor Gold Seal GK82951 (2 CDs). Mid-price.

56 BRUCKNER: Symphony No. 7. Philharmonia Orchestra conducted by Otto Klemperer. EMI CDM7 69126-2. Mid-price.

57 JOHANN STRAUSS II: Various (including 'Blue Danube' Waltz and Overture to *Die Fledermaus*). Vienna Philharmonic Orchestra conducted by Carlos Kleiber. Sony SK 45 938 (also includes works by Johann Strauss I and Josef Strauss). Full price.

58 BRAHMS: Symphony No. 4. Boston Symphony Orchestra conducted by Charles Munch. RCA Victor Silver Seal 09026 61206-2. Bargain price.

59 BRAHMS: Piano Concertos Nos. 1 and 2. Emil Gilels, Berlin Philharmonic Orchestra conducted by Eugen Jochum. Deutsche Grammophon 431 595-2/435 588-2 (2 CDs). Mid-price.

60 BRAHMS: Violin Concerto. Herman Krebbers, Royal Concertgebouw Amsterdam Orchestra conducted by Bernard Haitink. Philips 422 972-2. Bargain price.

61 BRAHMS: Piano Sonata No. 3, Six Piano Pieces, Opus 118. Helen Grimaud. Denon CO-79782. Full price.

62 BRAHMS: Piano Quintet, Clarinet Quintet. James Campbell, Rian de Waal, Allegri String Quartet. CALA CACD 1009. Full price.

63 BRAHMS: Clarinet Sonatas Nos. 1 and 2. WEBER: Grand Duo Concertant for Clarinet and Piano. Michael Collins, Mikhail Pletnev. Virgin Classics VC7 91076-2. Full price.

64 BIZET: *Carmen*. Soloists include Leontyne Price, Vienna State Opera Chorus, Vienna Philharmonic Orchestra conducted by Herbert von Karajan. RCA Victor Gold Seal GD 86199 (3 CDs). Mid-price.

65 TCHAIKOVSKY: Symphonies Nos. 4, 5 and 6. Leningrad Philharmonic Orchestra conducted by Eugene Mravinsky. Deutsche Grammophon 419 745-2 (2 CDs). Full price.

66 TCHAIKOVSKY: Violin Concerto. Xue-Wei, Philharmonia Orchestra conducted by Salvatore Accardo. ASV CD DCA 713. Full price.

67 DVOŘÁK: Symphony No. 8. WAGNER: Prelude and Good Friday music from *Parsifal*. Columbia Symphony Orchestra conducted by Bruno Walter. CBS/Sony Maestro MYK 44872. Mid-price.

68 DVOŘÁK: Symphony No. 9 ('From the New World'), Symphonic Variations. London Philharmonic Orchestra conducted by Zdenek Macal. Classics for Pleasure CD-CFP 9006. Bargain price.

69 JANÁČEK: String Quartets Nos. 1 and 2. Hagen Quartet. Deutsche Grammophon 427 669-2. Full price.

70 ELGAR: Cello Concerto. Jacqueline du Pré, London Symphony Orchestra conducted by Sir John Barbirolli. EMI CDC7 47329 2. Full price.

71 PUCCINI: *La Bohème*. Soloists include Luciano Pavarotti, Berlin Opera Chorus, Berlin Philharmonic Orchestra conducted by Herbert von Karajan. Decca 421 049-2 (2 CDs). Full price.

72 PUCCINI: Tosca. Soloists include Maria Callas, Chorus and Orchestra of La Scala Opera House conducted by Victor de Sabata. EMI CDS7 47175 8 (2 CDs). Full price.

73 WOLF: *Mörike Lieder*. Brigitte Fassbaender, Jean-Yves Thibaudet. Decca 440 208-2. Full price.

74 MAHLER: Symphony No. 5. London Philharmonic Orchestra conducted by Klaus Tennstedt. EMI CDC7 49888 2. Full price.

75 MAHLER: Symphony No. 9, Adagio from Symphony No. 10. Royal Liverpool Philharmonic Orchestra, Czech Philharmonic Orchestra conducted by Libor Pesek. Virgin Classics VCDS7 91219-2 (2 CDs). Special price.

76 ARENSKY: Piano Trio. TCHAIKOVSKY: Piano Trio. Ashkenazy Piano Trio. Naxos 8.550467. Bargain price.

77 DEBUSSY: Orchestral works including *La Mer, Prélude à l'après-midi d'un faune, Jeux*. L'Orchestre de la Suisse Romande conducted by Ernest Ansermet. Mid-price.

78 DEBUSSY: Twelve Études for Piano. Mitsuko Uchida. Philips 422 412-2. Full price.

79 RICHARD STRAUSS: *Salome*. Soloists include Cheryl Studer, Orchestra of the German Opera House, Berlin conducted by Giuseppe Sinopoli. Deutsche Grammophon 431 810-2 (2 CDs). Full price.

80 RICHARD STRAUSS: *Four Last Songs*, Oboe Concerto, *Metamorphosen*. Gundula Janowitz, Ludwig Koch, Berlin Philharmonic Orchestra conducted by Herbert von Karajan. Deutsche Grammophon 423 888-2. Mid-price.

81 SIBELIUS: Symphonies Nos. 1–7. Royal Scottish National Orchestra conducted by Sir Alexander Gibson. Chandos CHAN 6555-7 (3 CDs). Mid-price.

82 VAUGHAN WILLIAMS: Symphony No. 6, *Fantasia on a Theme by Thomas Tallis, The Lark Ascending*. Tasmin Little, BBC Symphony Orchestra conducted by Andrew Davis. Teldec 9031-73127-2. Full price.

83 RACHMANINOV: Piano Concertos Nos. 2 and 3. Earl Wild, Royal Philharmonic Orchestra conducted by Jascha Horenstein. Chandos Collect CHAN 6507. Mid-price.

84 SCHOENBERG: *Verklärte Nacht*, Variations for Orchestra. Berlin Philharmonic Orchestra conducted by Herbert von Karajan. Deutsche Grammophon 415 326-2. Full price.

85 RAVEL: Piano music including *Le Tombeau de Couperin*. Robert Casadesus. CBS/Sony CD46733 (2 CDs). Mid-price.

86 RAVEL: Orchestral music including *Bolero*, *Rapsodie Espagnole* and *Pavane pour une Infante Défunte*. L'Orchestre de la Suisse Romande conducted by Ernest Ansermet. Decca 433 716-2. Mid-price.

87 BARTÓK: Concerto for Orchestra, Music for Strings, Percussion and Celesta. Montreal Symphony Orchestra conducted by Charles Dutoit. Decca 421 443-2. Full price.

88 STRAVINSKY: *The Rite of Spring*, *The Firebird* Suite. Israel Philharmonic Orchestra conducted by Leonard Bernstein. Deutsche Grammophon 431 045-2. Mid-price.

89 BERG: Violin Concerto. Anne-Sophie Mutter, Chicago Symphony Orchestra conducted by James Levine. Deutsche Grammophon 437 093-2 (also includes Wolfgang RIHM's *Time Chant*). Full price.

90 TIPPETT: *A Child of our Time*. Soloists include Willard White, London Symphony Chorus and Orchestra conducted by Richard Hickox. Chandos CHAN 9123. Full price.

91 SHOSTAKOVICH: String Quartets Nos. 3, 7 and 8. Borodin String Quartet. Virgin Classics VC7 91437-2. Full price.

92 SHOSTAKOVICH: Symphony No. 10. Berlin Philharmonic Orchestra conducted by Herbert von Karajan. Deutsche Grammophon 429 716-2. Mid-price.

93 MESSIAEN: *Quatuor pour la Fin du Temps*. Huguette Fernandez, Guy Deplus, Jacques Neilz, Marie-Madeleine Petit. Erato 2292-45505-2 (also includes *Cinq Rechants*). Mid-price.

94 BRITTEN: *Peter Grimes*. Soloists include Jon Vickers, Chorus and Orchestra of the Royal Opera House conducted by Sir Colin Davis. Philips 432 578-2 (2 CDs). Mid-price.

95 BRITTEN: *War Requiem*. Soloists include Philip Langridge, London Symphony Chorus and Orchestra conducted by Richard Hickox. Chandos CHAN 8983/4 (2 CDs). Full price.

COMPILATIONS

96 ROSSINI, BELLINI, DONIZETTI. Various arias. Marilyn Horne, various orchestras, various conductors. Decca 421 891-2. Mid-price.

97 BEETHOVEN, SCHUMANN, LISZT, RACHMANINOV. Various piano works. Murray Perahia. Sony SK 46 437 (disc entitled: *The Aldeburgh Recital*). Full price.

98 BRAHMS: *Four Serious Songs*. WOLF: *Three Poems of Michelangelo*. MAHLER: Songs based on poems by Friedrich Rückert. Andreas Schmidt, Cord Garben. Deutsche Grammophon 431 649-2. Full price.

99 BERG, SCHOENBERG, PFITZNER, SCHREKER, RICHARD STRAUSS: Lieder. Lucia Popp, Irwin Gage. RCA Victor Red Seal RD 60950 (disc entitled: *Jugendstil-Lieder*). Full price.

100 ELGAR: *Serenade for Strings*. BRITTEN: *Variations on a Theme by Frank Bridge*. VAUGHAN WILLIAMS: *Fantasia on a Theme by Thomas Tallis*. TIPPETT: *Fantasia Concertante on a Theme of Corelli*. Royal Philharmonic Orchestra conducted by Sir Charles Groves. RPO Impact Records CDRPO 5005 (disc entitled: *An English Celebration*). Bargain price.

GLOSSARY

ACCELERANDO (speed marking) Gradually getting faster

ADAGIO (speed marking) Slow; genuinely rather than moderately slow

ALLEGRO (speed marking) Fast; the usual speed for the first movements of symphonies

ANDANTE (speed marking) At a walking pace; often interpreted as 'slow', but should be a bit quicker than **ADAGIO**

ARIA Big solo in an opera

ATONAL, ATONALITY Music which rejects the conventional harmonic system on which most classical music is based

AUTHENTIC, AUTHENTICITY The practice of playing music on instruments of the period in which the music was written (or replicas of those instruments), and using the playing styles of that period

BARITONE (voice pitch) A male voice with a range between bass and tenor

BASS (voice pitch) The lowest male voice

BEL CANTO Operatic style of first half of nineteenth century which lays great stress on beauty and melodic vocal line, with lots of opportunity for display of top notes

CANON Also known as a 'round', a melody which is picked up one voice after another, like 'Frère Jacques'. The simplest form of musical imitation

CHORD A group of notes played all together. A **KEY CHORD** (e.g. C major chord) plays the basic harmonic elements of that particular key's scale (do-mi-so-do) together, to produce that key's defining harmonic sound

CHROMATIC (literally 'coloured'), **CHROMATICISM** The chromatic scale uses all the notes (as opposed to the familiar diatonic scale, the do-re-mi-fa-so-la-ti-do scale) including the semitones between do and re and so on, which the other scale leaves out. 'Chromatic' music, therefore, is music which slips and slides around the semitones, disturbing your sense of being settled in a key based around the conventional system. **ATONAL** music makes great use of chromaticism

CODA (literally 'tail') Short section at the end of a movement or piece of music

COLORATURA Ornamental, florid soprano (or mezzo-soprano) singing at the top of the voice's range

CONTRALTO (voice pitch) Also known as 'alto'. The lowest female voice

COUNTERPOINT The device of contrasting one melody with a complementary, but different and independent, melody at a different pitch or on a different instrument

COUNTER-TENOR (voice pitch) A male falsetto voice with a range similar to that of the female contralto

CRESCENDO (dynamic marking) Gradually getting louder

DIATONIC The system of major and minor scales on which **TONALITY** is based; the diatonic scale is the counterpart of the chromatic scale

DIMINUENDO (dynamic marking) Gradually getting softer

FORTE (dynamic marking) Loud

FORTISSIMO (dynamic marking) Very loud

FUGUE A form which employs complex imitation in different melodic lines, or on different instruments, usually at different pitches; e.g. the first, original statement of the fugue's theme (or object) is played in the 'home' key, then the imitation appears in a 'related' key. Fugue is a complex development of **CANON**

HELDENTENOR (literally 'hero-tenor') A particular kind of heroic tenor voice. both strong and melodic (and with a lot of stamina), required in the operas of Richard Wagner

HOMOPHONY, HOMOPHONIC Music whose progress is dictated by harmony; music (especially late Renaissance music) in which all the musical lines move in step, with regard to what each other is doing (the opposite of **POLYPHONY, POLYPHONIC**)

KEY, KEY SIGNATURE The diatonic system rests on a series of musical keys, which a piece of music is said to be 'in'. The easiest way to approach this is through the piano keyboard, where the simplest key is C major, because the scale of C uses only the white notes. Pianists only use black notes when the music instructs them to do so; a key signature denotes which black notes are part of the scale of the music's home key. Keys divide into major and minor keys (each note can be the tonic – 'do' – of a major or minor scale); major keys generally sound more positive, whilst minor keys carry an air of angst or mournfulness about them

LÄNDLER An Austrian country dance popular in the eighteenth and nineteenth centuries, much used by Mahler as a basis for movements in symphonies

LARGO (speed marking, literally meaning 'broad') Slow, somewhere between **ADAGIO** and **ANDANTE**

LIBRETTO The text of an opera

LIED (plural **LIEDER**; abrreviation of *Kunst-Lied*, 'art-song') German word for 'song' and used to refer to a specific, usually quite short, type of German song (whose specialists include Schubert) in which singer and accompaniment (usually piano) are both important, and in which the music is designed so as to pay particular attention to the words

LENTO (speed marking) Slow; as slow as, sometimes slower than, **ADAGIO**

MEZZOFORTE (dynamic marking) Moderately loud

MEZZOPIANO (dynamic marking) Moderately soft

MEZZO-SOPRANO (voice pitch) Female voice with range between contralto and soprano; the second highest pitch of female voice, not quite equipped with pure beauty on the very top notes of the soprano register

MODULATE, MODULATION Music modulates when it moves from one **KEY** to another

NATURAL (of brass instruments, e.g. horns, trumpets, trombones) 'Natural' brass instruments, unlike modern brass instruments, didn't use valves; the tone they produced was therefore purer, but the range of the instruments was more limited (they also tended to go out of tune more quickly). Modern valve instruments are more versatile, but don't make quite as thrilling a noise

PIANO (dynamic marking) Soft

PIANISSIMO (dynamic marking) Very soft

PLAINCHANT, PLAINSONG Earliest known Western musical system, consisting of a single vocal line

POLYPHONY, POLYPHONIC The opposite of **HOMOPHONY**: music (especially Renaissance music) in which each line has its own melody whose progress isn't dictated by the chordal progress of all the parts together

PROGRAMME MUSIC Music written to follow a specific narrative (e.g. Berlioz's *Symphonie Fantastique*)

RALLENTANDO (speed marking) Gradually slowing down

RECITATIVE Sung passage in which the music mirrors the speech over the simplest accompaniment (very often just keyboard); usually a passage of dialogue or narrative, not intended to be primarily melodic

RELATIVE MAJOR, RELATIVE MINOR Each key in the diatonic tonal system has its relative key; every major key has its relative minor and vice versa. The relative key uses the same key signature; generally the relative minor key of any major key is the one whose tonic ('do') is two notes lower; so the relative minor of C major, the all-white-note scale on the piano, is A minor; that of D major is B minor, and so on

SCHERZO (literally 'joke') Title given to movement of a symphony, concerto etc.; always a fast, rhythmic movement, quite often (although not always) the lightest of the work

SEMITONE The smallest interval between two notes in Western music; the **CHROMATIC** scale moves up semitone by semitone

SONATA FORM A musical form evolved in the eighteenth century commonly used for opening movements of symphonies, concertos, sonatas (see pp. 28–9)

SOPRANO The highest female (or boy's) voice, purer and lighter than a **MEZZO-SOPRANO** with greater freedom and ease of movement at the very top of the register

TENOR (voice pitch) The highest natural (non-falsetto) male voice pitch

TERNARY FORM A simple structure, often used in movements of musical works, in which there are three sections, the third of which is a reprise of the first, with a contrasting mood being struck by the central section; a sort of A-B-A shape

TONALITY The basis of Western music since the Renaissance; the system of major and minor keys using the do-re-mi scale whose basic aim is to sound euphonious and instantly pleasing to the ear

TONE A tone is the distance between most notes in the conventional do-re-mi scale; it consists of two semitones

TONIC First note of the scale (i.e. 'do') in the major- and minor-key system

TREBLE (voice pitch) Term used for a boy soprano

TWELVE-TONE, TWELVE-NOTE The name often given to the system employed by figures like Arnold Schoenberg, who abandoned the traditional **DIATONIC** system of keys in favour of a chromatically-based **ATONALISM**. In the twelve-tone/note system, each note is of equal value; there is no do-re-mi, no 'home' key, and in a 'tone-row' each note of the chromatic scale must be used once (at whatever pitch pleases the composer)

UNISON Two or more voices singing the same melodic line

VIRTUOSO, VIRTUOSIC A player of exceptional skill; a piece of music designed to show off a player's virtuosity

INDEX

Page numbers in italics indicate references to recordings listed in the discographies.

Abdelazar (Purcell) 140
Adam de la Halle
  (c. 1245–c. 1288) *7*
Adams, John (b. 1947)
  89, 210
Aida (Verdi) 166, *168–9*
'Air on a G String' (J. S.
  Bach) 274, *274*
Akhnaten (Glass) 210,
  211
Albert Herring (Britten)
  206
Albinoni, Tomaso
  (1671–1751)
  concertos 93, 94, *94*
'Albinoni's Adagio'
  (Giazotto) 273–4,
  274
Alcina (Handel) 142,
  142–3
Alfano, Franco
  (1876–1954) 190
Allegre, Gregorio
  (1582–1652)
  Miserere *16–17*
Alpensinfonie, Eine (R.
  Strauss) 277, *278*
Also Sprach Zarathustra
  (R. Strauss) 277,
  278
American opera 209–11
Andrea Chenier
  (Giordano) 187
Anna Bolena (Donizetti)
  155
'Appassionata' Sonata
  (Beethoven) 224,
  226
Arabella (R. Strauss) *266*
'Archduke' Trio
  (Beethoven) 225,
  227
Arensky, Anton
  Stepanovich
  (1861–1906)
  Piano Trio 236, *236*

String Quartet 236,
  236
Ariadne auf Naxos (R.
  Strauss) 195–6,
  197, 266
Armide (Lully) 139, *139*
Arne, Thomas (1710–78)
  215
Arnold, Malcom (b. 1921)
  symphonies 88, *88*
Aroldo (Verdi) 163
Art of Fugue, The (J. S.
  Bach) 96, 216,
  218
Attila (Verdi) 167
Atys (Lully) 139, *139*
Aus Italien (R. Strauss)
  276–7, *277*

'Babi Yar' (Symphony
  no. 13,
  Shostakovich) 86
Bach, Carl Philipp
  Emanuel (1714–88)
  biography 31
  cello concertos *99*
  oboe concertos 100,
  100
  Oboe Sonata *100*
  symphonies 28, 30–32,
  32
Bach, Johann Sebastian
  (1685–1750) 94
  The Art of Fugue 96,
  216, *218*
  biography 97
  Brandenburg
  Concertos 96–8, *99*
  cantatas 58, 253–4,
  255
  Goldberg Variations
  217, *218*
  harpsichord concertos
  98, *99*
  keyboard works
  215–17, *217–18*

Mass in B Minor
  254–5, *255*
  oboe concertos 98, *99*
  Orchestral Suites 274,
  274
  organ works 217, *218*
  oratorios 254, *255*
  St John Passion 254,
  255
  St Matthew Passion
  93, 254, *255*
  sonatas 215, *217–18*
  violin concertos 98, *99*
  *The Well-Tempered
  Clavier* 96, 216, *218*
Bairstow, Sir Edward
  (1874–1946) 16
Balakirev, Mily
  (1837–1910) 64
  ballet music 44, 64, *273,*
  279–80, 281
  in opera 139, 143, 145
Ballo in Maschera, Un
  (Verdi) 160–61, 165,
  168, 169
Barber of Seville, The
  (Paisiello) 144
Barber of Seville, The
  (Rossini) 153, *154–5*
  baroque chamber music
  213
  baroque concertos 92–3
  baroque instruments
  91–2
  baroque vocal music
  249–51
Bartered Bride, The
  (Smetana) 201
Bartók, Béla (1881–1945)
  biography 128
  Concerto for Orchestra
  128, 129, *129*
  *Duke Bluebeard's
  Castle* 201–2, *202*
  Mikrokosmos 128, 237,
  237

Music for Strings,
Percussion and
Celesta 128, *129*
piano concertos 127,
128, *129*
piano works 237, *237*
string quartets 237,
237
Viola Concerto 129,
129
violin concertos
128–9, *129*
violin rhapsodies *129*
bassoon concertos 101,
127
Bayreuth 170, 172, 173
'Bear, The' (Symphony
no. 82, Haydn) 35,
36
Béatrice et Bénédict
(Berlioz) 177, *177*
Beaumarchais, Pierre
Augustin Caron de
(1732–99) 151
Beethoven, Ludwig van
(1770–1827)
biography 42
'Diabelli' Variations
225, *227*
Fidelio 149–150, *150*
lieder 259, *259*
Missa Solemnis 258–9,
259
piano concertos 107,
108, *108–9*
piano trios 225, *227*
piano works 224–6,
226–7, 236
'Rasumovsky'
Quartets 223, *226*
string quartets 222–4,
226
Symphony no. 1 41,
43, *49–51*
Symphony no. 2 43,
49–51
Symphony no.3
('Eroica') 43–4,
49–51
Symphony no. 4 44–5,
49–51
Symphony no.5 29,
45–6, *49–51*
Symphony no.6
('Pastoral') 46–7,
49–51

Symphony no. 7 47,
49–51
Symphony no. 8 47,
49–51
Symphony no. 9
('Choral') 48–9,
49–51
'Tenth' Symphony 49,
50, 110
Triple Concerto 107,
108, *109–10*
Violin Concerto 107,
109, 110
violin sonatas 225, *226*
Wellington's Victory 47
bel canto 151, 155, 162,
208, 295
Bellini, Vincenzo
(1801–35) 155
operas 156–7, *158*
Bennett, Sir William
Sterndale (1816–75)
82
Berg, Alban (1885–1935)
biography 130
Chamber Concerto
130, 241, *242*
chamber works 241,
242
lieder *266*, 268
Lulu 130–31, 198, *198*
orchestral works *280*
Violin Concerto
130–31, *131*
Wozzeck 197–8, *198*
Berlioz, Hector (1803–69)
143
*Grande Messe des
Morts* 263, *263*
operas 177, *177*
*Symphonie
Fantastique* 54–6,
56
Bernstein, Leonard
(1918–90) 73, 74,
209
Biber, Heinrich
(1664–1704) 15
Billy Budd (Britten) 206
Binchois, Gilles
(c. 1400–60) *8*, 9
Birtwistle, Sir Harrison
(b. 1934) 200, 208
English Dances 284, *285*
Bizet, Georges (1838–75)
181–2

Blitzstein, Marc
(1905–64) 209
Blondel de Nesle
(fl.c. 1200) *8*
Blow, John (1649–1708)
140
vocal works 253, *253*
'Blue Danube' Waltz (J.
Strauss II) 278, *278*
Bohème, La
(Leoncavallo) 187
Bohème, La (Puccini)
187, *191*
Boito, Arrigo
(1842–1918) 165,
166
Bolero (Ravel) 281, *282*
Boris Godunov
(Mussorgsky) 184,
185, *185*
Borodin, Alexander
(1833–87)
chamber works 235,
236
symphonies 64
Brahms, Johannes
(1833–97)
biography 62
choral works 262–3,
263–4
clarinet works 234,
235
Double Concerto 116,
117
A German Requiem
262–3, *263*
lieder *259*, 262, *263–4*
piano concertos 61,
114–15, 115–16,
116–17
piano works 234, *234*,
235
string works *230*, 234,
234–5
symphonies 61–3, *63*
Violin Concerto 115,
116, *117*
Brandenburg Concertos
(J. S. Bach) 96–8, *99*
Brecht, Bertholt
(1898–1956) 199
Brian, Havergal
(1876–1972)
symphonies 88, *88*
British music, early
11–18

British opera 139–42,
180–1, 205–8
Britten, Benjamin
(1913–76)
choral works 269, *270*
concertos 132
operas 205–6, *207*
orchestral works 283,
283–4
Browne, John
(c. 1426–98) *12*
Bruch, Max (1838–1920)
Kol Nidrei 120
Scottish Fantasy
120–21, *121*
violin concertos 113,
113, 120, *121*
Bruckner, Anton
(1824–96) 74
biography 70
symphonies 30, 69–72,
72–3
Brumel, Antoine
(c. 1460–c. 1520) 20,
20–21
Burgundian music *8*, 9,
11, 21
Busoni, Ferruccio
(1866–1924) 192
Byrd, William
(1543–1623) 11, 16
biography 18
instrumental works
17, *19*
vocal works 17, *18–19*

cadenzas 96, 101
Caldara, Antonio
(1670–1736)
cantatas 251, *251–2*
canons 9, 273, 295
cantatas 58, 250–51,
253–4, 257, 267
Capriccio (R. Strauss)
196, *197, 266*
Cardoso, Frei Manuel
(c. 1566–1650) 24,
24
Carmen (Bizet) 181–2, 182
Carmina Burana (Orff) 8
Carnival of the Animals
(Saint-Saëns) 281,
282
Carver, Robert
(c. 1485–c. 1568) 14,
14

Casken, John (b. 1949) 208
cassations 275
Castor et Pollux
(Rameau) 139, *139*
Catalani, Alfredo
(1854–93) 185
cataloguing of music 31,
37
Cavalleria Rusticana
(Mascagni) 185–6,
186
Cavalli, Francesco
(1602–76) 138
cello concertos 82, 99,
100, 121, 123, 132
cello sonatas 239
cello works, solo 215
Cenerentola, La (Rossini)
153, *154–5*
Cerha, Friedrich
(b. 1926) 198
Chabrier, Emmanuel
(1841–94)
España 281, *282*
chamber music, defined
213–14
Charpentier, Gustave
(1860–1956) 183
Chausson, Ernest
(1855–99)
Symphony 84, *84*
Child of our Time, A
(Tippett) 269, *270*
Children's Corner
(Debussy) 239
Chopin, Frédéric
(1810–49) 111
piano concertos 112,
112
piano works 231–2,
233
'Choral' Symphony
(no. 9, Beethoven)
48–9, *49–51*
choral works 249–50,
251, 252, 253, 263,
268, 270
see also cantatas,
masses, oratorios,
passion settings,
requiems, Stabat
Mater
choruses in opera 150,
162
chromaticism 23, 24,
173, 295

Cilea, Francesco
(1865–1950) 187, 188
Cimarosa, Domenico
(1749–1801) 144, 145
'Claire de Lune'
(Debussy) 239, *239,
240*
clarinet concertos 102, 132
clarinet quintets 221, 234
clarinet sonatas 234, 242
'Classical' Symphony
(no. 1, Prokofiev)
85, *85*
Clemens non Popa
(c. 1510–56) 20, *20*
Clemenza di Tito, La
(Mozart) 147
Clérambault,
Louis-Nicolas
(1676–1749)
cantatas 250–51, *251*
commedia dell'arte 156,
186, 195
concert, definition of 91
concerto form,
development of
by baroque composers
91–3
by Bach 96, 98, 99–100
by Mozart 101, 104
by Beethoven 106–7
as symphonic form
114
in twentieth century
119, 127
concerto grosso 93, 96,
98, 131–2
Corelli, Archangelo
(1653–1713)
concertos 92, *93*
Cornysh, William
(c. 1468–1523) *12*
Cosi Fan Tutte (Mozart)
146–7, *149*
counterpoint 216, 295
Creation, The (Haydn)
256–7, *257*
Creatures of Prometheus
(Beethoven) 44
Cristoforo Colombo
(Franchetti) 186–7
Crumb, George (b. 1929)
245
*Cunning Little Vixen,
The* (Janáček) 201,
201

Czech Opera 201
Czerny, Carl (1791–1857)
    45–6

da Ponte, Lorenzo
    (1749–1838) 145, 146
Dafne (Peri) 135
Dallapiccola, Luigi
    (1904–75) 192–3
Damnation de Faust, La
    (Berlioz) 177, *177*
dance music 92, 273,
    274, 278
    see also ballet music
Daphnis et Chloe (Ravel)
    281, *282*
Davy, Richard
    (c. 1467–c. 1516)
    12–13
'Death and the Maiden'
    (quartet, Schubert)
    228, *229*
'Death and the Maiden'
    (song, Schubert)
    260, *261*
*Death and
    Transfiguration* (R.
    Strauss) *278*
Death in Venice (Britten)
    206, *207*
*Death of Klinghoffer,
    The* (Adams) 210,
    211
Debussy, Claude
    (1862–1918)
    chamber works 238–9,
    239
    orchestral works
    280–81, *281–2*
    Pelléas et Mélisande
    183–4, *184*
    piano works 239, *239*,
    240
Delibes, Léo (1836–91)
    178
    Coppélia 279
Delius, Frederick
    (1862–1934)
    Cello Concerto 132,
    132
    Double Concerto 132,
    132
    *A Village Romeo and
    Juliet* 205, *207*
    Violin Concerto 132,
    132

'Diabelli' Variations
    (Beethoven) 225,
    227
Dialogues des Carmélites
    (Poulenc) 202, *203*
diatonic system,
    development of 14,
    16, 19–20, 24, 296
Dido and Aeneas
    (Purcell) 140–41,
    141, 274
'Dissonance' Quartet
    (Mozart) 221, *222*
'Distratto, Il' (Symphony
    no. 60, Haydn) 34,
    35
Doktor Faust (Busoni)
    192, *193*
Don Carlos (Verdi) 161,
    162, 165–6, *168*,
    169
Don Giovanni (Mozart)
    146, *148–9*
Don Juan (R. Strauss)
    277, *277*
Don Pasquale (Donizetti)
    156, *158*
Don Quixote (R. Strauss)
    277, *277*
Donizetti, Gaetano
    (1797–1848) 155–6
    operas 155–6, *157–8*
double concertos 116,
    132
Dowland, John
    (c. 1563–1626)
    17–18, *19*
dramma giocoso 146
*Dream of Gerontius,
    The* (Elgar) 268,
    269
Dreigroschenoper, Die
    (Weill) 199–200
Due Foscari, I (Verdi)
    169
Dufay, Guillaume
    (c. 1400–74) *8*, 9
Dukas, Paul (1865–1935)
    *The Sorceror's
    Apprentice* 281, *282*
Duke Bluebeard's Castle
    (Bartók) 201–2, *202*
Dunstable, John
    (c. 1390–1453) *8*, 9
Dvoràk, Antonin
    (1841–1904)

biography 68
Cello Concerto 121,
    121–2
operas 201, *201*
Piano Concerto 121,
    121
string quartets 236–7,
    237
Symphonic Variations
    69
symphonies 67–8,
    68–9
Violin Concerto 121,
    121

early music
    defined 3
    written down 6–7, 20
Eine Kleine Nachtmusik
    (Mozart) 275, *275*
Elektra (R. Strauss) 125,
    194, *196–7*
Elgar, Sir Edward
    (1857–1934) 123
    Cello Concerto 82, 123,
    124
    choral works 268–9,
    269
    orchestral works 123,
    124, 282, *283*
    symphonies 82–3, *83*
    Violin Concerto 123,
    124
Elisir d'Amore, L'
    (Donizetti) 156, *158*
'Emperor' Concerto
    (Piano Concerto
    no. 5, Beethoven)
    107, *108–9*
*Enfant et les Sortilèges,
    L'* (Ravel) 202, *203*
Enigma Variations
    (Elgar) 123, *124*,
    282, *283*
*Entführung aus dem
    Serail, Die (Mozart)*
    144–5, *148*
'Eroica' Symphony
    (no. 3, Beethoven)
    43–4, *49–51*
Erwartung (Schoenberg)
    198, 199
Estro Armonico, L'
    (Vivaldi) 96
Eton Choirbook 11–12,
    12

Eugene Onegin
(Tchaikovsky) 185,
185
Euridice (Peri) 135–6
Euryanthe (Weber) 159

Falstaff (Verdi) 166, *169*
Fanciulla del West, La
(Puccini) 190, *192*
'Fantasia' (Schumann)
230–1, *233*
*Fantasia Concertante on
a Theme of Correlli*
(Tippett) 283, *284*
*Fantasia on a Theme of
Thomas Tallis*
(Vaughan Williams)
83, *83*, 282–3, *283*
'Fantasiestücke'
(Brahms) 234
'Fantasiestücke'
(Schumann) *233*
'Farewell' Symphony
(no. 45, Haydn) 32,
34, 35, *36*
Fauré, Gabriel
(1845–1924)
Requiem 265, *265*
Faust (Gounod) 177, *178*
'Faust' Symphony
(Liszt) 276, *276*
Favola d' Orfeo, La
(Monteverdi) 136,
137, *138*
Favorita, La (Donizetti)
156
Fidelio (Beethoven)
149 150, *150*
Fierrabras (Schubert)
159, *160*
Fille du Régiment, La
(Donizetti) 156, *158*
Finlandia (Sibelius) 78,
278, *278*
'Fire' Symphony (no.59,
Haydn) 35, *36*
Firebird, The
(Stravinsky) 279,
280
Fireworks, Music for the
Royal (Handel) 274,
274
'Five, The' 64
Fledermaus, Die (J.
Strauss II) 176,
179–80, *180*

Fliegende Holländer, Der
(Wagner) 169–71,
174
Flotow, Friedrich von
(1812–83) 176
flute concertos 93, 98,
101
flute sonatas 215
flute works, solo 239
Flying Dutchman, The
(Wagner) 169–71,
174
Fontaine, Pierre
(c. 1390–c. 1450) 8
Force of Destiny, The
(Verdi) 162, 165,
168, 169
fortepiano 102
Forza del Destino, La
(Verdi) 162, 165,
168, 169
'Four Last Songs' (R.
Strauss) 265, *266*
Four Seasons, The
(Vivaldi) 34, 93, 95,
96
'Four Temperaments,
The' (Symphony
no. 2, Nielsen) 81,
82, *82*
Franchetti, Alberto
(1860–1942) 186–7,
188
Franck, César (1822–90)
Symphony 84, *84*
Franco-Flemish early
music 19–20
Frau Ohne Schatten, Die
(R. Strauss) 196, *197*
Freischütz, Der (Weber)
159, *160*
French baroque opera
138–9
French music, early 7–8,
9–10
French opera 138–9,
177–9, 181–4, 202–3
Freud, Sigmund 75
'Funeral' Symphony
(no. 44, Haydn) 35,
36

Gabrieli, Andrea
(c. 1510–86) 23
Gabrieli, Giovanni
(1557–1612) *19,* 252

Gawain (Birtwistle) 208
Gay, John (1685–1732)
140, 142
German opera 143–50,
158–60, 169–76,
179–80, 193–201
German Requiem, A
(Brahms) 262–3,
263
Gesamtkunstwerk 170
Gesualdo, Don Carlo
(1560–1613) 24–5,
25
Gianni Schicchi (Puccini)
156, 190, *192*
Giazotto, Remo (b. 1910)
273
Gibbons, Orlando
(1583–1625) *19,* 273
Gilbert and Sullivan
operettas 180–81, *181*
Giordano, Umberto
(1867–1948) 187
Giorno di Regno, Un
(Verdi) 162, *167*
Giulio Cesare in Egitto
(Handel) *142–3*
Glass, Philip (b. 1937) 89
operas 210, *211*
Glinka, Mikhail
(1804–57) 184–5
Gloria (Vivaldi) 251,
251, 255
Gluck, Christoph
Willibald (1714–87)
arias *144*
operas 136, 143–4, *144*
Goldberg Variations
(J S Bach) 217, *218*
Golem (Casken) 208, *209*
'Golliwog's Cakewalk'
(Debussy) 239
Górecki, Henryk (b. 1933)
string quartets 245,
245
symphonies 89, *89*
gothic era, music from 7
Götterdämmerung
(Wagner) 171–2,
173, *174–5*
Gounod, Charles
(1818–93)
operas 177, *178*
Grand Duo (Schubert) *53*
Grand Duo Concertant
(Weber) *235*

grand opera 151, 154
Grande Messe des Morts
(Berlioz) 263, *263*
'Great' Symphony (no.
9, Schubert) 53,
53–4
Gregorian Chant 4, *5*, 5
Grieg, Edvard
(1843–1907)
Piano Concerto 114,
114, 120, *120*
'Grosse Fugue'
(Beethoven) 223
ground bass 273–4
guitar concertos 93
Gurrelieder (Schoenberg)
199, 267, *268*
'Gymnopédies' (Satie)
240, *240*

'Haffner' Symphony
(no. 35, Mozart) 39,
40, *41*
Halévy, Jacques
Fromental
(1799–1862) 183
Hamburg Symphonies
(C. P. E. Bach)
31–2, *32*
Hamlet (Thomas) 177,
178
'Hammerklavier' Sonata
(Beethoven) 224–5,
226
Handel, George
Frederick
(1685–1759)
biography 142
Messiah 255–6, *256*
Music for the Royal
Fireworks 274, *274*
operas 27, 141–2,
142–3
organ concertos 100,
100
Water Music 274, *274*
Hansel and Gretel
(Humperdinck) 193,
193
Hanslick, Eduard
(1825–1904) 62, 118,
173
harpsichord concertos 98
harpsichord works, solo
see keyboard
works, solo

Haydn, Franz Joseph
(1732–1809)
biography 33
cello concertos 100,
100
choral works 256–7,
257
Clarinet Quintet 221,
222
The Creation 256–7,
257
'Nelson' Mass 256, *257*
nicknamed quartets
219
nicknamed
symphonies 35
operas 144
piano trios 219–20, *220*
The Seasons 257, *257*
string quartets
218–19, *220*
symphonies 28, 32–5,
35–7
Trumpet Concerto
100, *100*
violin concertos *100*
wind serenades 221,
222
Haydn, Michael
(1737–1806) 39, *40*
'Heiligenstadt
Testament' 42, 43
Heldenleben, Ein (R.
Strauss) *276*, 277,
277–8
heldentenor 174, 296
'Hen, The' (Symphony
no. 83, Haydn) 35,
36
Henze, Hans Werner
(b. 1926) 200–201
Heure Espagnole, L'
(Ravel) 202, *203*
Hildegard of Bingen
(1098–1179)
biography 4
vocal music 4, *4–5*
Hindemith, Paul
(1895–1963) 199
hocket 9
Hoffmann, Ernst
Theodor Amadeus
(1776–1822) 45,
158–9, 178, 231
Holst, Gustav
(1874–1934)

The Planets 282, *283*
'Homme Armé, L' ' *11*,
21, *21–2*
horn concertos 102, 125
'Horn Signal'
(Symphony no.31,
Haydn) 34, 35
Howells, Herbert
(1892–1983) 268
Hummel, Johann
(1778–1837)
piano concertos 132,
132
Humperdinck, Engelbert
(1854–1921) 193
Hungarian opera 201–2
Hungarian Rhapsodies
(Liszt) 232, *233*, *236*
'Hunt, The' (Symphony
no. 73, Haydn) 34,
35

Ice Break, The (Tippett)
207–8, *208*
Idomeneo (Mozart) 144,
148
Images (Debussy) 281,
282
'Imperial' Symphony
(no. 53, Haydn) 35,
36
*Incoronazione di Poppea,
L'* (Monteverdi)
137–8, *138*
Inextinguishable, The
(Symphony no. 4,
Nielsen) 81, *82*
Intermezzo (R. Strauss)
196, *197*
'Introduction and
Allegro' (Elgar)
282, *283*
Iphigénie en Tauride
(Gluck) 143–4
Isaac, Heinrich
(c. 1450–1517) 10,
11, 20
Italian music, early 10,
21–3, 24–5
Italian opera 135–8,
151–7, 160–67,
185–193
'Italian' Symphony
(no. 4,
Mendelssohn) 57–8,
58–9

Italiana in Algeri, L'
(Rossini) 144,
151–3, *154*

Janácek, Leos
(1854–1928)
operas 201, *201*
piano works 238, *238*
string quartets 237–8,
238
Jenůfa (Janácek) 201,
201
'Jeunehomme' (Piano
Concerto no. 9,
Mozart) 102, 103,
104 5
Joachim, Joseph
(1831–1907) 62, 63,
107, 115, 234
Jones, Robert (fl. 1597–
1615) 18, *19*
Josquin Des Prèz
(c. 1440–1521) 9–10,
10–11, 15, 20
'Jupiter' Symphony
(no. 41, Mozart) 39,
39, 40

kapellmeister tradition 97
Katerina Ismailova
(Shostakovich) 87
keyboard works, solo
17, 214–15, 216–17,
220
see also piano works,
solo
Kindertotenlieder
(Mahler) 266 7, *267*
King Priam (Tippett)
207, *208*
Kingdom, The (Elgar)
268, *269*
'Klagende Lied, Das'
(Mahler) 267, *267*
*Knaben Wunderhorn,
Des* (Mahler) 73,
266, *267*
Knot Garden, The
(Tippett) 207
Knussen, Oliver
(b. 1952) 208
Köchel catalogue 37
Kol Nidrei (Bruch) 120
'Kreisleriana'
(Schumann) 231,
233

'Kreutzer' Sonata
(Beethoven) 225,
226
'Kreutzer' Sonata
(Janácek) 238, *238*

*Lady Macbeth of the
Mtsensk District*
(Shostakovich) 87,
204, *205*
Lakmé (Delibes) 178
Lalo, Edouard (1823–92)
Symphonie Espagnole
118–19
'Lamentatione'
(Symphony no.26,
Haydn) 35, *36*
*Lamentations of
Jeremiah* (Tallis)
15–16, *16*
Landini, Francesco
(c. 1325–97) 9
ländlers 28, 73, 198, 229,
296
Lark Ascending, The
(Vaughan
Williams) *83*
Lassus, Orlando
(c. 1530–94) *17*, 19,
19, 20, 22–3, *23*
Lehár, Franz
(1870–1948) 180
leitmotif 159, 172, 184, 197
'Leningrad' Symphony
(no. 7,
Shostakovich) 86,
87
Leoncavallo, Ruggiero
(1858–1919) 187
I Pagliacci 186, *186*
Léonin (fl.c. 1163–1190)
6, *7*
'Letter V' (Symphony
no. 88, Haydn) 35,
36
Lied von der Erde, Das
(Mahler) 74–5, 267,
267
lieder 249, 258, 259, 260,
262, 264, 265,
266–8, 269, 297
Life with an Idiot
(Schnittke) 204–5,
205
'Linz' Symphony (no. 36,
Mozart) 39, *40, 41*

Liszt, Franz (1811–86)
170
biography 111
'Faust' Symphony
276, *276*
lieder 262, *262*
piano concertos 110,
110
Piano Sonata 110, 232,
233
piano works 232, *233*,
234, *236*
tone-poems 276, *276*
Totentanz 55, *110–11*
'Little Russian'
Symphony (no. 2,
Tchaikovsky) 64, *66*
Lloyd, George (b. 1913)
symphonies 88, *88*
'Lobgesang' (Symphony
no. 2, Mendelssohn)
57, *58*
Lôbo, Duarte (c. 1565–
1646) 24, *24*
Lohengrin (Wagner) 171,
174
'London' Symphony
(no. 104, Haydn)
34, 35, *36, 37*
Louise (Charpentier) 183
*Love of Three Oranges,
The* (Prokofiev)
204, *205*
Lucia di Lammermoor
(Donizetti) 155,
157– 8
Luisa Miller (Verdi) 163,
167, 169
Lully, Jean-Baptiste
(1632–87)
operas 139, *139*
Lulu (Berg) 130–31, 198,
198
Lustige Witwe, Die
(Lehár) 180, *180*
Luther, Martin
(1483–1546) 9, 58
Lutoslawski, Witold
(b. 1913)
string quartets 245,
246

Macbeth (Verdi) 163,
167, 169
Machaut, Guillaume
(1300–77) *7, 8*

Macmillan, James
(b. 1959)
orchestral works 285,
285
Madam Butterfly
(Puccini) 189, *191*
madrigals 25, 250
Maelzel, Johann
(1772–1838) 47
Magic Flute, The
(Mozart) 147, *149*
Mahler, Gustav
(1860–1911)
biography 74
lieder *264*, 266–7, *267*
symphonies 30, 44,
73–6, *76–8*, 266
Manon (Massenet) 183,
187
Manon Lescaut (Puccini)
187, *190–91*
Marais, Marin
(1656–1728) 139
Marcello, Alessandro
(1684–1750)
oboe concertos *100*
Maria Stuarda
(Donizetti) 155–6,
158
'Maria Theresa'
(Symphony no.48,
Haydn) 35, *36*
Marriage of Figaro, The
(Mozart) 139,
145–6, *148*, 151
Marschner, Heinrich
(1795–1861) 176
Martland, Steve 9
Mascagni, Pietro
(1863–1945) 188
Cavalleria Rusticana
185–6, *186*
Mask of Orpheus, The
(Birtwistle) 208
Masked Ball, A (Verdi)
160–61, 165, *168*,
169
Massenet, Jules
(1842–1912) 183, 187
masses 8, 9, 10, 11, 13,
14, 15, 17, 20, 21,
22, 23, 24, 254–5,
256, 257, 258–9,
260–61
*Mastersingers of
Nuremberg, The*

(Wagner) 172, 173,
175–6
Mathis de Maler
(Hindemith) 199
Maxwell Davies, Sir
Peter (b. 1934) 208
Meck, Nadezhda von 65
*Meistersinger von
Nürnberg, Die*
(Wagner) 172, 173,
175–6
melisma 5
Mendelssohn(-Bartholdy),
Felix (1809–47) 93
biography 58
Fingal's Cave ('The
Hebrides' Overture)
59
*A Midsummer Night's
Dream 59*
Octet for Strings 58,
230, *230*
piano concertos 112,
113
piano works 230, *230*
String Symphonies 56
string works 230, *230*
symphonies 57–8,
58–9
Violin Concerto
112–13, *113*
Menotti, Carlo (b. 1911)
209
Mephisto Waltzes (Liszt)
232, *233*
Mer, La (Debussy) 281,
281–2
Merry Widow, The
(Lehár) 180, *180*
*Merry Wives of
Windsor, The*
(Nicolai) 176, *176*
Messiaen, Olivier
(1908–92)
*Quatuor pour la Fin
du Temps* 244, *244*
Messiah (Handel) 255–6,
256
Metamorphosen (R.
Strauss) 265, *266*,
277
metronome 47
Meyerbeer, Giacomo
(1791–1864) 169, 177
*Midsummer Marriage,
The* (Tippett) 207

*Midsummer Night's
Dream, A* (Britten)
206, *207*
Mikrokosmos (Bartók)
128, 237, *237*
Milan 157
minimalism 6, 9, 89,
210–11, 245, 270,
284–8
Missa Solemnis
(Beethoven) 258–9,
259
Montéclair, Michel
Pignolet de
(1667–1737)
cantatas 250–51, *251*
Monteverdi, Claudio
(1567–1643)
biography 137
choral works 92,
249–50, *250*
operas 27, 136–8, *138*
'Moonlight' sonata
(Beethoven) 224,
226
Moore, Douglas
(1893–1969) 209
Moran, John 210
Moses und Aron
(Schoenberg) 199,
199
motets 10, 14–15, 17, 21,
22, 23
Mozart, Wolfgang
Amadeus (1756–91)
Bassoon Concerto 101,
106
biography 38
choral works 257, *258*
Clarinet Concerto 102,
105
Clarinet Quintet *105*,
221, *222*
concertos, inventory
of 100
Cosi Fan Tutte 146–7,
149
Don Giovanni 146,
148–9
Flute and Harp
Concerto 101
flute concertos 101, 102
horn concertos 102,
106
keyboard sonatas 220,
222

lieder 258, *258*
nicknamed
  symphonies 38–9
Le Nozze di Figaro
  139, 145–6, *148*, 151
Oboe Concerto 100, *106*
operas 144–7, *148–9*
orchestral works 275,
  275
piano concertos 46,
  101–4, *104–5*
string quartets 219,
  221, *222*
String Trio 221, *222*
symphonies 29, 37–9,
  39–41, 77
violin concertos 102,
  106
violin sonatas 220–21,
  222
wind serenades 221,
  222
Die Zauberflöte 147, *149*
Mundy, John
  (c. 1555–1630) *19*
Musical Joke, A (Mozart)
  275, *275*
musicals, stage 135, 169,
  178, 181, 209
Mussorgsky, Modest
  (1839–81)
  Boris Godunov 184,
  185, *185*

Nabucco (Verdi) 162,
  167, 169
'Nelson' Mass (Haydn)
  256, *257*
'New World' Symphony
  (no. 9, Dvořák)
  67–8, *68–9*
New Year (Tippett) 208
Nicolai, Otto (1810–49)
  176
Nielsen, Carl (1865–1931)
  biography 81
  symphonies 80–82, *82*
  Violin Concerto *125*
Nixon in China (Adams)
  210, *211*
Nocturnes (Debussy)
  281, *282*
Norma (Bellini) 157, *158*
Nozze di Figaro, Le
  (Mozart) 139,
  145–6, *148*, 151

number opera 150, 162,
  171, 182, 203
Nutcracker, The
  (Tchaikovsky) 279,
  279

Oberon (Weber) 160, *160*
oboe concertos 93–4, 98,
  100, 125–6, 265
Ockeghem, Johannes
  (c. 1410–97) 9, 15
octets *see* string octets
Oedipus Rex
  (Stravinsky) 203,
  205
Offenbach, Jacques
  (1819–80) 178
  operas 178–9, *179*
opera, first 135
opera buffa 138, 144,
  145, 146, 151, 177
opera seria 138, 144,
  147, 151, 153, 195
operettas 177–81
oratorios 252, 254,
  255–6, 256–7, 268–9
Orfeo, L' (Monteverdi)
  136, 137, *138*
Orfeo ed Euridice
  (Gluck) 136, 143,
  144
Orff, Carl
  Carmina Burana 8
  organ concertos 100
organ works, solo 217
organum 5–6
*Orpheus in the
  Underworld*
  (Offenbach) 178,
  179
Otello (Verdi) 162, 166,
  169
'Oxford' Symphony
  (no. 92, Haydn) 35,
  37

Pachelbel, Johann
  (1653–1706)
  Canon 273, *274*
Paganini, Niccolò
  (1782–1840)
  violin concertos 113
Pagliacci, I (Leoncavallo)
  186, *186*
Paisiello, Giovanni
  (1740–1816) 144

Palestrina, Giovanni
  Perluigi da
  (c. 1525–94)
  biography 22
  vocal works *17, 19*,
  21, *21*, 22
'Paris' Symphony
  (no. 31, Mozart) 37,
  39, *40*
Parry, Sir Hubert
  (1848–1918) 268
  chamber works 242,
  243
Parsifal (Wagner) 58,
  69, 173–4, *176*, 193
Pärt, Arvo (b. 1935)
  vocal works 270, *270*
  partitas 215
passion settings 12, 252,
  254
'Passione, La'
  (Symphony no. 49,
  Haydn) 35, *36*
'Pastoral' Symphony
  (no. 6, Beethoven)
  46–7, *49–51*
'Pathétique' Sonata
  (Beethoven) 224,
  226
'Pathétique' Symphony
  (no. 6,
  Tchaikovsky) 64,
  65–6, *66*
patrons of composers 10,
  42, 65, 97, 100, 102,
  219
Pearl Fishers, The
  (Bizet) 181, *182*
Pelléas et Mélisande
  (Debussy) 183–4,
  184
Penderecki, Krzysztof
  (b. 1933)
  string quartets *246*
Pergolesi, Giovanni-
  Battista (1710–36)
  choral works 251,
  252
Peri, Jacopo (1561–1633)
  operas 135–6
Pérotin (fl.c. 1200) 6, *7*,
  10
Peter Grimes (Britten)
  205–6, *207*
Petrus de Cruce
  (fl.c. 1290) *7*

Pfitzner, Hans
(1869–1949) 19, 197
lieder 266
Philippe de Vitry
(c. 1291–1361) 7, 7,
8, 9
Philippe the Chancellor
(c. 1160–1236) 7
piano concertos 101–4,
107, 108, 110,
112–13, 113–14,
114–15, 115–16, 118,
119, 120, 121, 122,
127, 128, 131, 132
piano quartets 234
piano quintets 227, 234,
244
piano sonatas see piano
works, solo
piano trios 219–20, 225,
235, 236
piano works, solo 224–6,
228–9, 230–32, 234,
235, 236, 237, 238,
239, 240, 241, 242
see also keyboard
works, solo
Piave, Francesco Maria
(1810–76) 164, 165
Pierrot Lunaire
(Schoenberg) 199
Pique-Dame
(Tchaikovsky) 185,
185
plainchant (plainsong) 4,
5, 22, 297
Planché, James
Robinson
(1796–1880) 159–60
Planets, The (Holst)
282, 283
polyphony 6, 297
Portuguese music, early
24
Potter, Cipriani
(1792–1871) 82
Poulenc, François
(1899–1963)
operas 202–3, 203
piano works 240, 240
Power, Leonel
(c. 1370–1445) 8
Prague 146
'Prague' Symphony
(no. 38, Mozart) 39,
40, 41, 77

Prélude à L'Après-midi
d'un Faune
(Debussy) 281,
281–2
programme music 34,
46, 57, 95, 297
Prokofiev, Sergei
(1891–1953)
biography 85
operas 204, 205
Piano Concerto no. 5
123
symphonies 85, 85
Protecting Veil, The
(Tavener) 6, 284,
285
'Prussian' Quartets
(Mozart) 219
Puccini, Giacomo
(1858–1924)
biography 188
La Bohème 187, 191
La Fanciulla del West
190, 192
Madam Butterfly 189,
191
Manon Lescaut 187,
190–91
Tosca 187–9, 191
Turandot 190, 192
Il Trittico 190, 192
Punch and Judy
(Birtwistle) 208,
208
Purcell, Henry (1659–95)
biography 140
operas 140–41, 141
vocal works 27, 253,
253
Puritani, I (Bellini) 157,
158
Pycard (fl.c. 1410) 8

quartets see piano
quartets, string
quartets
Quatuor pour la Fin du
Temps (Messiaen)
244, 244
Queen of Spades, The
(Tchaikovsky) 185,
185
quintets see piano
quintets, clarinet
quintets, string
quintets

Rachmaninov, Serge
(1873–1943) 122
piano concertos 122,
122–3
piano works 123, 236,
236
Rhapsody on a Theme
of Paganini 122,
122–3
symphonies 84–5, 85
Rake's Progress, The
(Stravinsky) 203–4,
205
Rameau, Jean-Philippe
(1683–1764)
operas 139, 139
Rape of Lucretia, The
(Britten) 206
'Rasumovsky' Quartets
(Beethoven) 223,
226
Ravel, Maurice
(1875–1937)
chamber works
239–40, 240
operas 202, 203
orchestral works
281, 282
piano works 240, 240
recitative 137, 150, 162,
171, 203, 297
recorder concertos 98
'Reformation' Symphony
(no. 5,
Mendelssohn) 58,
58–9
Reich, Steve (b. 1936)
orchestral works 284,
284
Reményi, Eduard
(1830–98) 62
Requiem (Fauré) 265, 265
Requiem (Mozart) 257,
258
Requiem (Verdi) 264,
265
requiems 24, 257, 262,
263–4, 264–5, 269
rescue opera 144, 149
'Resurrection'
Symphony (no. 2,
Mahler) 74, 75, 76–7
'Revolutionary' Study
(Chopin) 231, 233
Rhapsody on a Theme
of Paganini

(Rachmaninov) 122,
122–3
Rheingold, Das (Wagner)
60, 171–2, *174–5*
'Rhenish' Symphony
(no. 3, Schumann)
59, 60, *60–1*
Rienzi (Wagner) 169
Rigoletto (Verdi) 162,
163–4, *167–8*, *169*
Ring Cycle, The
(Wagner) 60, 170,
171–2, *174–5*
Rite of Spring, The
(Stravinsky) 64,
279, *280*
ritornello 93
*Ritorno d'Ulisse in Patria,
Il* (Monteverdi)
136–7, *138*
Rosenkavalier, Der (R.
Strauss) 125, 195,
197
Rossini, Gioacchino
(1792–1868) 53
Il Barbiere di Siviglia
153, *154–5*
biography 152
La Cenerentola 153,
154–5
L'Italiana in Algeri
144, 151–3, *154*
Messa di Gloria 261,
261
operas 151–4, *154–5*
Roussel, Albert
(1869–1937)
symphonies 84, *84*
Rubinstein, Nikolai
(1835–81) 110, 119
'Rückert' Lieder (Mahler)
264, 266
Rusalka (Dvořák) 201,
201
Ruslan and Lyudmila
(Glinka) 184–5
Russian opera 184–5,
203–5

St John Passion (J. S.
Bach) 254, *255*
St Matthew Passion
(J. S. Bach) 93, 254,
255
Saint-Saëns, Camille
(1835–1921)

*Carnival of the
Animals* 281, *282*
Samson et Dalila 182,
183
Violin Concerto no. 3
121
Salieri, Antonio
(1750–1825) 52,
144
Salome (R. Strauss)
193–4, *196*
Samson et Dalila
(Saint-Saëns) 182,
183
Satie, Erik (1866–1925)
piano works 240, *240*
Savoy Operas 180–81,
181
Scarlatti, Alessandro
(1660–1725)
cantatas *252*
concertos 93
Scarlatti, Domenico
(1685–1757)
keyboard sonatas
214–15, *215*
Schikaneder, Emanuel
(1751–1812) 147
Schnittke, Alfred
(b. 1934)
Concerti Grossi 131–2,
132
Life with an Idiot
204–5, *205*
string quartets *246*
Viola Concerto 131–2,
132
Schoenberg, Arnold
(1874–1951) 74, 130
biography 200
chamber works
240–41, *242*
Gurrelieder 199, 267,
268
lieder *266*, 268
operas 199, *199*
orchestral works 280,
280
Piano Concerto *131*
piano works 241, *242*
Violin Concerto *131*
Schöne Müllerin, Die
(Schubert) 260, *261*
'Schoolmaster, The'
(Symphony no. 55,
Haydn) 34, 35

Schreker, Franz
(1878–1934)
lieder *266*
Schubert, Franz
(1797–1828)
biography 52
choral works 260, *261*
impromptus 229, *229*
lieder 260, *261*
opera 159, *160*
orchestral works 276
piano works 227,
228–9, *229*, *233*
string quartets 227–8,
229
String Quintet 228, *229*
symphonies 51–3,
53–4, *61*
'Trout' Quintet 227, *229*
'Wanderer' Fantasy
228, *229*, *233*
Schumann (*née* Wieck),
Clara (1819–96) 60,
61, 62, 114
Schumann, Robert
(1810–56) 59, 107,
112
biography 60
Piano Concerto 60,
105, 113–14, *114*,
117
piano works 230–31,
233, *236*
symphonies 59, 60,
60–61, 78
violin sonatas 231, *233*
vocal works *261*, 262,
262
Schütz, Heinrich
(1585–1672)
choral works 252, *252*
Schwanengesang
(Schubert) 260, *261*
Scottish Fantasy (Bruch)
120–21, *121*
'Scottish' Symphony
(no. 3,
Mendelssohn) 57–8,
58–9
Seasons, The (Haydn)
257, *257*
Second Viennese School
30, 78, 119, 129,
195, 280
chamber works
240–41, *242*

see also Berg,
    Schoenberg, Webern
secular music, medieval
    8
Semiramide (Rossini)
    153–4
sextets see string sextets
Shostakovich, Dmitri
    (1906–75)
  biography 87
  chamber works 243–4,
    244, 245
  Katerina Ismailova 87
  Lady Macbeth of the
    Mtsensk District 87,
    204, 205
  Michelangelo songs
    265, 266
  string quartets 243–4,
    244
  symphonies 86–7, 87
Sibelius, Jean (1865–
    1957)
  biography 79
  orchestral works 78,
    79, 278, 278
  symphonies 78–80, 80
  Violin Concerto 117,
    124–5, 125
Siegfried (Wagner)
    171–2, 174–5
Simon Boccanegra
    (Verdi) 164–5, 168
'Simple' Symphony
    (no. 6, Nielsen) 81,
    82
Simpson, Robert (b. 1921)
  chamber works 242–3,
    243
  symphonies 88, 88
sinfonia, form of 27–8
Sinfonia Concertante
    (Mozart) 275, 275
'Sinfonia Espansiva'
    (Symphony no.3,
    Nielsen) 81, 82
Singspiels 147, 150
Sleeping Beauty
    (Tchaikovsky) 279,
    279
Smetana, Bedrich
    (1824–84) 201
Somnambula, La
    (Bellini) 156–7, 158
sonata form 28–9, 34,
    101, 298

sonatas, unaccompanied
    see under specific
    instruments
Song of the Earth, The
    (Mahler) 74–5, 267,
    267
songs see lieder
'Songs without Words'
    (Mendelssohn) 230,
    230
Sorceror's Apprentice,
    The (Dukas) 281,
    282
'Souvenir of Florence'
    (Tchaikovsky) 235,
    236
Spanish music 23–4, 182
Spem in Alium (Tallis)
    14–15, 16
Spohr, Louis (1784–1859)
  symphonies 56–7, 57
sprechgesang 198, 199
'Spring' Sonata
    (Beethoven) 225,
    226
'Spring' Symphony (no.1,
    Schumann) 60, 60
Stabat Mater (Pergolesi)
    251, 252
Stabat Mater, settings of
    12, 251
Stainer, Sir John
    (1840–1901) 268
Stanford, Sir Charles
    (1852–1924) 268
  chamber works 242,
    243
Stiffelio (Verdi) 162, 163
Stockhausen, Karlheinz
    (b. 1928) 200
Stradella, Alessandro
    (1644–82)
  choral works 251, 252
Strauss II, Johann
    (1825–99)
  dance music 278, 278
  Die Fledermaus 176,
    179–80, 180
Strauss, Richard
    (1864–1949)
  biography 126
  Elektra 125, 194,
    196–7
  horn concertos 125,
    126–7
  lieder 265, 266

Metamorphosen 265,
    266, 277
  Oboe Concerto 106,
    125–6, 126–7, 265,
    266
  operas 193–6, 196–7,
    266
  Der Rosenkavalier 125,
    195, 197
  Salome 193–4, 196
  tone-poems 46, 276–7,
    277–8
  Violin Concerto 125,
    127
Stravinsky, Igor
    (1882–1971)
  ballet music 64,
    279–80, 280
  operas 203–4, 205
  Rite of Spring 64, 279,
    280
  Violin Concerto 131
Striggio, Alessandro
    (c. 1540–92) 14
string octets 230
string quartets 213–14,
    218–19, 221, 222–4,
    227–8, 230, 234,
    235, 236–8, 240–41,
    242, 243–6
string quintets 228, 230
string sextets 234, 235
string trios 221, 242
Sturm und Drang
    30–31, 33, 35
subscription concerts
    102
Suite Bergamasque
    (Debussy) 239, 239
Sullivan, Sir Arthur
    (1842–1900) 180–81
Suor Angelica (Puccini)
    190, 192
Susanna's Secret
    (Wolf-Ferrari) 192
Süssmayr, Franz
    (1766–1803) 257
Swan Lake
    (Tchaikovsky) 279,
    279
Symphonie Espagnole
    (Lalo) 118–19
Symphonie Fantastique
    (Berlioz) 54–6, 56
symphony, origin and
    form 27–30, 34

'Symphony of a
Thousand' (no. 8,
Mahler) 74, 75, *76*,
77–8
Syrinx (Debussy) 239
Szymanowski, Karol
(1882–1937)
string quartets *246*

Tabarro, Il (Puccini)
190, *192*
Tales of Hoffmann, The
(Offenbach) 158,
178–9, *179*
Tallis, Thomas
(c. 1505–85) 11, 273
biography 15
vocal works 14–16,
16–17, 19
Tannhäuser (Wagner)
171, *174*
Tavener, John (b. 1944) 6
The Protecting Veil
284, *285*
Taverner, John (c. 1495–
1545) 13–14, *14*
Tchaikovsky, Peter
Ilyich (1840–93)
ballet music 64, 279,
279
biography 65
chamber works 235,
236
operas 185, *185*
piano concertos *109*,
118, 119, *119*
Piano Trio 235, *236*
symphonies 64–6, *66*
Violin Concerto 118,
119
Telemann, Georg Philipp
(1681–1767) 31
concertos 93, 94, *94*
'Tempora Mutantur'
(Symphony no.64,
Haydn) 33, 35
Tenebrae responses,
settings of 24, 25
Thomas, Ambroise
(1811–96) 177
Thomson, Virgil
(1896–1989) 209
Three Screaming Popes
(Turnage) 284–5, *285*
Threepenny Opera, The
(Weill) 199–200

through-composed opera
144, 165
Till Eulenspiegel (R.
Strauss) 277, *277*
Tippett, Sir Michael
(b. 1905)
chamber works 242,
243
concertos for orchestra
132, 284
operas 207–8, *208*
orchestral works 283,
284
Piano Concerto *132*
symphonies 44, 88,
88, 242, *270*
Triple Concerto 108,
132
vocal works 269, *270*
'Titan' (Symphony no. 1,
Mahler) 75, *76*
*Tombeau de Couperin,
Le* (Ravel) 240, *240*
Tomkins, Thomas
(1572–1656) 18, *19*
tone-poems 276–8, 280
Torelli, Giuseppe
(1658–1709) 93
Torke, Michael (b. 1961)
orchestral works 284,
284
Tosca (Puccini) 187–9,
191
see also Franchetti,
Alberto
Totentanz (Liszt) 55,
110–11
tragédie lyrique 139
Traviata, La (Verdi)
161–2, 164, *168*,
169
*Treal of Harmony and
Invention, The*
(Vivaldi) 95, *96*
trios *see* piano trios,
string trios
triple concertos 107, 108
Tristan und Isolde
(Wagner) 23, 71,
172, 173, *175*, 184,
262
Trittico, Il (Puccini) 190,
192
troubadour songs *8*, 8
'Trout' Quintet
(Schubert) 227, *229*

'Trout, The' (song,
Schubert) 260, *261*
Trovatore, Il (Verdi) 162,
164, *168*, *169*
Troyens, Les (Berlioz)
177, *177*
trumpet concertos 93–4,
100
Turandot (Puccini) 190,
192
Turkish music 144
Turn of the Screw, The
(Britten) 206, *207*
Turnage, Mark Antony
(b. 1960) 208
*Three Screaming
Popes* 284–5, *285*
twelve-note system
129–30, 298
Twilight of the Gods
(Wagner) 171–2,
173, *174–5*

'Unfinished' Symphony
(no. 8, Schubert)
52–3, *53–4, 61*

Valkrie, The (Wagner)
171–2, 174–5
Vaughan Williams,
Ralph (1872–1958)
*Fantasia on a Theme
of Thomas Tallis*
83, *83*, 282–3, *283*
The Lark Ascending 83
stage music 205
symphonies 83, *83–4*
Venice 91, 93–4, 95, 137
Verdi, Giuseppe
(1813–1901)
Aida 166, *168–9*
Un Ballo in Maschera
160–61, 165, *168*,
169
biography 161
Don Carlos 161, 162,
165–6, *168, 169*
Falstaff 166, *169*
La Forza del Destino
162, 165, *168, 169*
Luisa Miller 163, *167*,
169
Macbeth 163, *167, 169*
Nabucco 162, *167, 169*
operas 160–67, *167–9*
Otello 162, 166, *169*

Requiem 264, *265*
Rigoletto 162, 163–4,
  167–8, *169*
Simon Boccanegra
  164–5, *168*
La Traviata 161–2,
  164, *168*, *169*
Il Trovatore 162, 164,
  168, *169*
verismo (realism) in
  opera 183, 185–6,
  187, 190, 204
Verklärte Nacht
  (Schoenberg) 23,
  241, 280, *280*
*Vespers for the Blessed
  Virgin* (Monteverdi)
  92, 249–50, *250*
Vespri Siciliani, I (Verdi)
  167
Viaggio a Reims, Il
  (Rossini) 154, *155*
Victoria, Tomas Luis de
  (c. 1548–1611) *19*,
  19, 23–4, *24*
Vienna 102–3, 143, 149
*Village Romeo and Juliet,
  A* (Delius) 205, *207*
viola concertos 98, 129,
  131–2
violin concertos 94, 98,
  99, 100, 102, 107,
  112–13, 115, 116,
  118, 120, 121, 123,
  124–5, 128–9,
  130–31, 132
violin sonatas 215,
  220–21, 225, 231,
  234, 239, 240
violin works, solo 215
Vitry, Philippe de
  (c. 1291–1361) 7, *7*,
  8, 9
Vivaldi, Antonio
  (1678–1741)
  biography 95
  concertos 93, 94–5, *96*
  L'Estro Armonico 96
  The Four Seasons 34,
  93, 95, *96*
  Gloria 251, *251*, 255
  *The Trial of Harmony
  and Invention* 95, *96*
vocal works
  (non-operatic) *see*
  cantatas, choral

works, lieder,
  madrigals, masses,
  oratorios, passion
  settings, requiems,
  Stabat Mater
Voix Humaine, La
  (Poulenc) 202–3,
  203

Wagner, Richard
  (1813–83) 48, 69,
  143, 152, 159, 160
  biography 170
  *Der Fliegende
  Holländer* 169–71,
  174
  *Die Meistersinger von
  Nürnberg* 172, 173,
  175–6
  operas 169–74, *174–6*
  Parsifal 58, *69*, 173–4,
  176, 193
  Piano Sonata 214
  The Ring Cycle 60,
  170, 171–2, *174–5*
  Tristan und Isolde 23,
  71, 172, 173, *175*,
  184, 262
'Waldstein' Sonata
  (Beethoven) 224,
  226
Walküre, Die (Wagner)
  171–2, *174–5*
Walton, Sir William
  (1902–83)
  Viola Concerto *132*
  Violin Concerto *132*
'Wanderer' Fantasy
  (Schubert) 228, *229*,
  233
War Requiem (Britten)
  269, *270*
Water Music (Handel)
  274, *274*
Weber, Carl Maria von
  (1786–1826) 159
  Bassoon Concerto *127*
  clarinet concertos *132*
  Grand Duo Concertant
  235
  operas 159–60, *160*
Webern, Anton
  (1883–1945), 130
  chamber works 130,
  241, *242*
  lieder 268, *268*

orchestral works 280,
  280
  Symphony 79
Weelkes, Thomas
  (1576–1623) 18, *19*
Weill, Kurt (1900–1950)
  199–200
*Well-Tempered Clavier,
  The* (J. S. Bach) 96,
  216, *218*
Wellington's Victory
  (Beethoven) 47
Werther (Massenet) 183
Wesley, Samuel
  (1766–1837) 268
Wesley, Samuel
  Sebastian (1810–76)
  268
*Where the Wild Things
  Are* (Knussen) 208,
  209
White, Robert
  (c. 1538–74) *17*
Wieck, Friedrich
  (1785–1873) 60
William Tell (Rossini)
  86, 151, 154
wind instruments,
  chamber music for
  221, 241
  see also clarinet
  quintets
Winterreise (Schubert)
  260, *261*
Wolf, Hugo (1860–1903)
  Italian Serenade 238
  lieder 264, *264*
Wolf-Ferrari, Ermanno
  (1876–1948) 192
Wozzeck (Berg) 197–8,
  198
Wylkynson, Robert
  (d.c. 1515) *13*

Xerxes (Handel) 141

*Young Person's Guide to
  the Orchestra*
  (Britten) 283, *283–4*

Zauberflöte, Die (Mozart)
  147, *149*
Zemlinsky, Alexander
  von (1872–1942)
  197